SOPHIA LOREN

SOPHIA LOREN

IN THE CAMERA EYE

PHOTOGRAPHY AND COMMENTARY BY **SAM SHAW**

Exeter Books

NEW YORK

Entire project supervised by Sam Shaw

Cover Design, title page by Jacques Chazaud

Graphic Production by Filmar Graphics, Inc., San Diego, California

Photo Credits
Sam Shaw
Cover, title page, 7, 9-125, 127, 153 , back cover
UPI
128-159

Hy Simon Sunday Features Syndication
151 (top), 160

Printed and bound in the United States of America

CONTENTS

FOREWORD

The following candid photographs and recollections are my homage to Sophia Loren.

My photographs of her date to the early 1950's, when movie tycoon Carlo Ponti, soon to become her husband, took control of her career. The earliest shots of Sophia show her in the apartment bought for her by Carlo; her first sumptuous home (which, characteristically, she opened to her mother, to her younger sister, to her poor cousins).

Afterward, I photographed Sophia often; and over the years, in the course of working together, she and I became friends.

As in the lives of all human beings, the lives of film stars have bright moments and dark ones. My tribute to Sophia reflects happy moments in her life.

The camera falls in love with certain faces. The camera lens (its "eye"), finds the secret, the special magnetism or charisma, in these faces. The camera loves Sophia.

For me, Loren summons up certain lucid, lasting images. In my eyes:

She is off the walls of the House of Mysteries at Pompeii.

She is the goddess of fertility in the Naples museum.

She is the pizza girl in De Sica's "The Gold of Naples."

She is a masked Venetian beauty, painted by Longhi.

She is an Italian peasant, carrying a loaded basket upon her head.

She is earth, poetry, art, life.

She is a movie star . . . and every woman!

SAM SHAW

SOPHIA LOREN: IN THE CAMERA EYE

2

Loren's childhood in wartime Italy was turbulent. She had a difficult time.

She talks about it. She tells us about it. She's written about it.

Not only her, many young Italian women. A lot of them gave themselves for K-rations, silk stockings, cigarettes, chewing gum. These are the ugly facts of war.

Loren's an Italian woman: she has all their qualities.

A tremendous maternal instinct . . . She can be 14, a mother . . . a mother goddess.

Tremendous, undying loves.

Tremendous family ties.

She takes on the burden of her kind: during times of

*stress she will take care of a little brother or little sister as
well and as efficiently as her mother; she will take care
of her cousins as well.*

*Loren probably has it in her book (I haven't read it), but
her great love is her mother. She will protect her mother
from the world, from society, from any ill wind that blows.*

Not only her mother, her sister.

Not only her sister, her cousins . . .

*Before she made "The Pride and the Passion" we made a
little short. I shot her at home — her first luxurious
apartment. There's a photograph of her in that house
with all her cousins living there with her.*

*Her mother was mother to her then; and she was
mother to her mother. She still is mother to her mother.*

An Italian woman . . . all their qualities. . .

KODAK SAFETY FILM ++

19

Sophia's mother (R) and sister Maria (L).

Sophia's first luxurious apartment...

Sophia's sister Maria (l.), and her cousin Patrezia

Sophia told me once, "Posing for the camera is a love affair." And that's true; she falls in love at that moment. The camera loves her and she loves the camera. And the camera can't make a mistake, and she can't make a mistake.

But she's a woman like that in life, too . . . So sure of her beauty that she doesn't ask the right of censorship on pictures, never asks.

For instance: I did a photo-essay; famous personalities and their recipies. She did a thing for me on cooking eggplant. In one shot, a little oil hit her; she blinked and she screwed up her face, looked like a clown. Yet she wouldn't think of censoring that picture. She thought it humorous and had a big laugh.

She's got another self that looks upon herself. She can look at herself from a distance.

"*Posing for the camera is a love affair.*"

Basilio Franchina (c.), whom Sophia calls her closest friend, who's given
important help in her professional life.

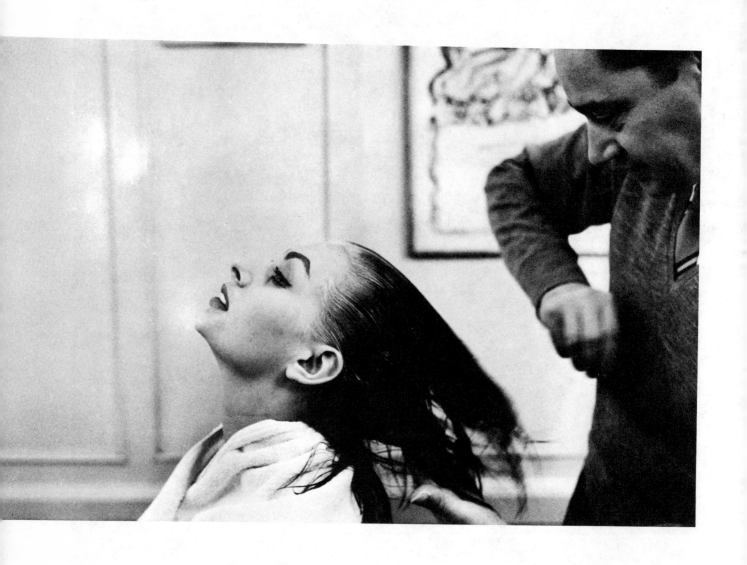

She's a woman like that in life, too. . .

in the background,

me with camera!

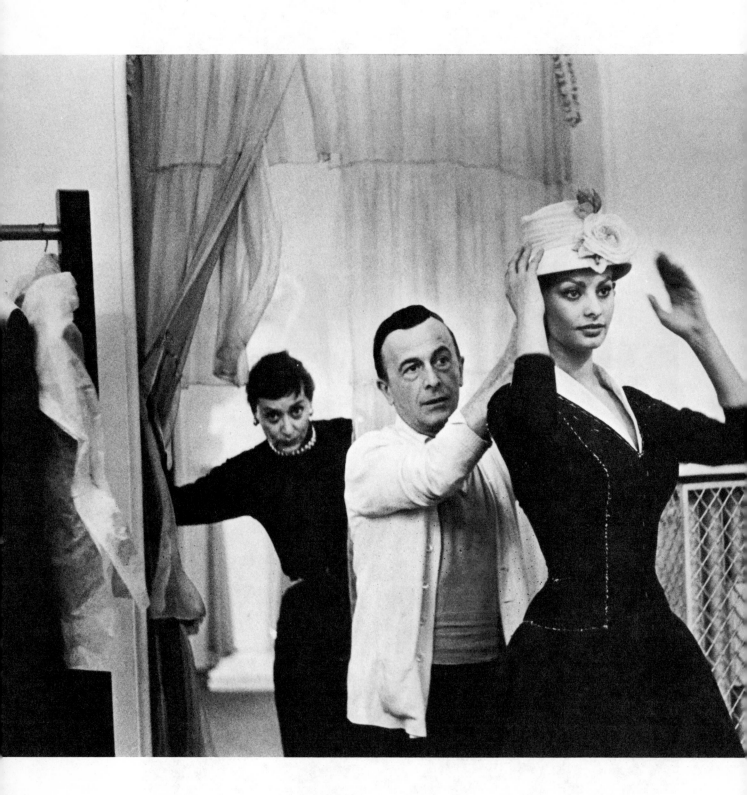

Shubert (c.),
the most popular fashion designer in Rome
at the start of Sophia's career.

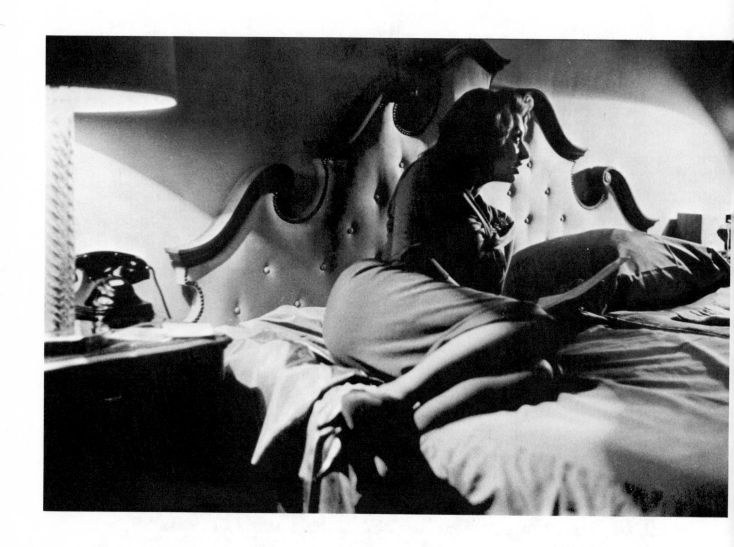

. . .another self that looks upon herself. . .

Sophia's magnificently beautiful. Handsome. Amazonian.

And she continues to grow in beauty with maturity.

She has a lot of self-confidence; she's a beauty who knows she's a beauty.

Sophia accepting her beauty is like Joe DiMaggio accepting his prowess as a ballplayer. Easy grace — you don't have to force it. Joe has that inner confidence; he doesn't have to prove himself . . . Sugar Ray Robinson has it . . . The real great ones don't have to say they're great. Their records stand for them.

I've seen Sophia in a rented house in Beverly Hills, with everything a woman could want. Beauty. Talent. Wealth. Love. Everything except her country; but she herself always was — and is — her country.

Growing in beauty with maturity...

54

. . .a beauty who knows she's a beauty. . .

... in Beverly Hills ...

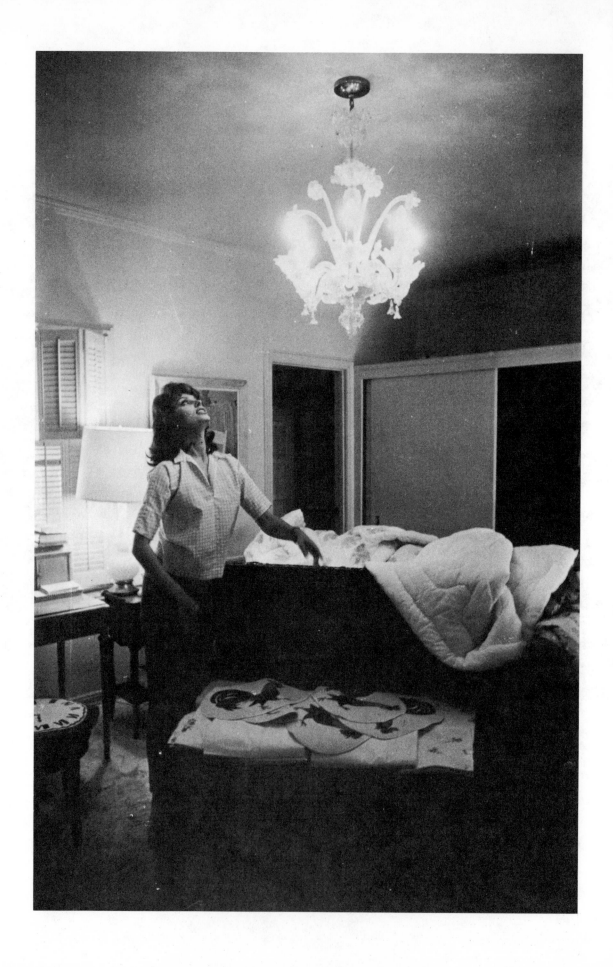

Everything except her country; but she herself always was
— and is — her country...

Leaving normal school at an early age, she knew
Leopardi, D'Annunzio, Manzoni, Cavour, Verdi . . .

Italians are surrounded as kids by Michaelangelo, by
DaVinci, by Roman ruins. Just as Greeks are surrounded
by the ruins of antiquity, the statues, the Parthenon.
That's what they're brought up on; you don't have to
train them to appreciate it, it's part of their lives . . .

I remember being brought up in "Little Italy," Mott
Street. Subway workers, pavement guys, sanitation men,
grocery men, butchers; they knew every opera. They
would stand at the opera in the Met. They were the
balcony in the Met. All you heard in the buildings were
Caruso and Gigli records. You were brought up with that
culture, whether you were in the streets or not . . .

But it wasn't just opera. Many jazz players in the
American jazz renaissance were second generation
Italians . . .

Sophia loves American jazz, loves jazz. It's too
bad Duke died. She was going to make a record with
Duke Ellington. He was itching to write something with
her.

She loves to sing. She could sing blues and jazz. (She did
a movie once, "Aida." But they didn't use her voice. It
was Renata Tibaldi's.)

I think that's Sophia's ambition — to make a blues or
jazz record.

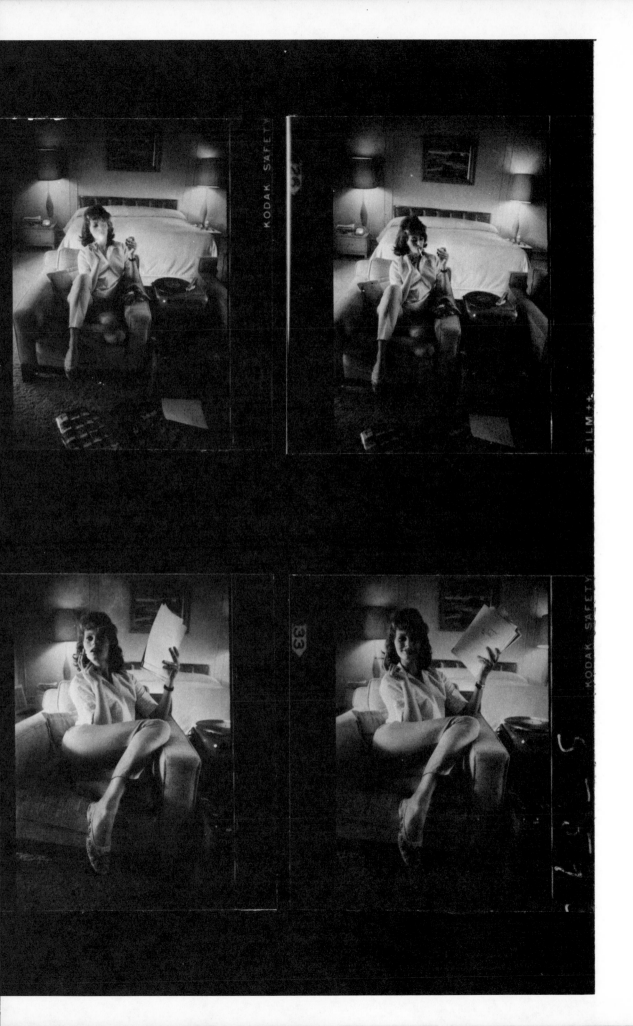

She has a terrific relationship with Carlo.

*I think the origin of the relationship was in the
competition between Carlo Ponti and Dino DeLaurentiis
to create a star. It's a business; you've got to create a
star. How do you create a star and control them? You
marry them. DeLaurentiis took Silvana Mangano, and
Carlo went out to create somebody bigger, better than
Silvana Mangano, and got Sophia . . .*

*Ponti is a well educated man, a very cultured person,
charming. Combination of cultured person, business
person; an international type, an international type in
pictures . . .*

*Pulp literature, the popular woman's magazines,
advertising, Hollywood movies so impress, so brainwash*

the public, the audience, that it's inevitable that Clark
Gable should be with Vivien Leigh. Or a Tyrone Power
and another beautiful dame should be the perfect
combination.

Sophia's such a beautiful woman that on paper the ideal
magazine cover would be her and Cary Grant. Or the
ideal way to sell soap or perfume would be to have a
couple like that. These are romantic notions of what
romance is. Fairy tales . . .

Artists, writers and directors weave through the life
Loren and Ponti lead; Alberto Moravia, Mario Soldati,
Federico Fellini. De Sica, an intimate working relationship.
Basilio Franchina — my God! With Moravia, he wrote the
first story expressly made for Sophia, "Woman of the
River."

Carlo Ponti.

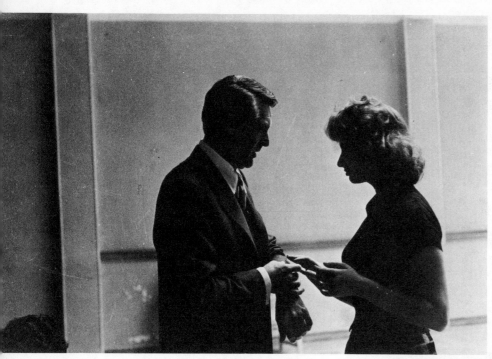

Cary Grant.

Vittorio de Sica.

Loren is an artist. Dead serious, instinctive . . . Learning all the time, giving everything to every role.

Actresses who take their roles seriously are all the same. They all go through the same thing; transposition of character, development of character.

Tony Quinn says, "You put on another skin. When you're through with a role, you shed that skin and take on another one."

Underneath that shedding of the skin, putting off the skin, every actor or actress goes through the same *emotionally traumatic experience . . .*

Actresses have some universal characteristics that their work imposes on them, that their living imposes on them. Acting's a trade, an inherited trade. The very nature of the work brings out traits.

They all have suicide within them . . .

Sophia is a rare exception.

Carlo's protected her all the way.

learning all the time . . .

giving everything to every

role. . .

Every actress goes through the same emotionally traumatic experience. . .

85

Pure motion pictures don't need actors. Luigi Zampa, the great Italian director, told me that.

We were in Naples. Somebody stopped him in the street, started talking, wanted a part.

When he left, Zampa said:

"This guy — I can't use him in a picture. He's in Italian music hall; the professional Italian actor is terrible in motion pictures. But the Italian citizen, the guy off the street, so lacking in personal inhibitions, so very extroverted, he's a terrific motion picture actor. He doesn't have to look at the camera. He's himself; not self-conscious, not bottled up."

Same thing with Sophia . . .

*In the accidental selection of somebody you put in front
of the camera you discover happily that they can sustain
the magic — no matter what occurs.*

Sophia's got a fantastic magic, which few others have.

Sophia's got a fantastic magic. . .

Beyond instinct, Sophia learned a lot from De Sica; and Blasetti, another great Italian director.

De Sica taught her the craft of acting. Secrets of interpretation, restraint. He was a director who knew the craft of acting better than anyone else.

Did you ever see him act? Ever see De Sica on the screen? One of the greatest actors of all time.

It took a director like him to get the talent out of her.

He could get it out of a small kid. He took it out of a man who was a factory worker; "Bicycle Thief," the father — what a performance!

How he got a role and made something out of it!

Then "Umberto D!" The little man who was a professor. What he did with "Umberto D!" Really the portrayal of his own father.

That picture: I took John Cassavettes to see that in the screenings. We both wept like hell! Wept!

De Sica taught her the craft of acting.

De Sica coaching Marcello Mastroianni, Sophia's co-star in many pictures

It took De Sica to get the talent out of her...

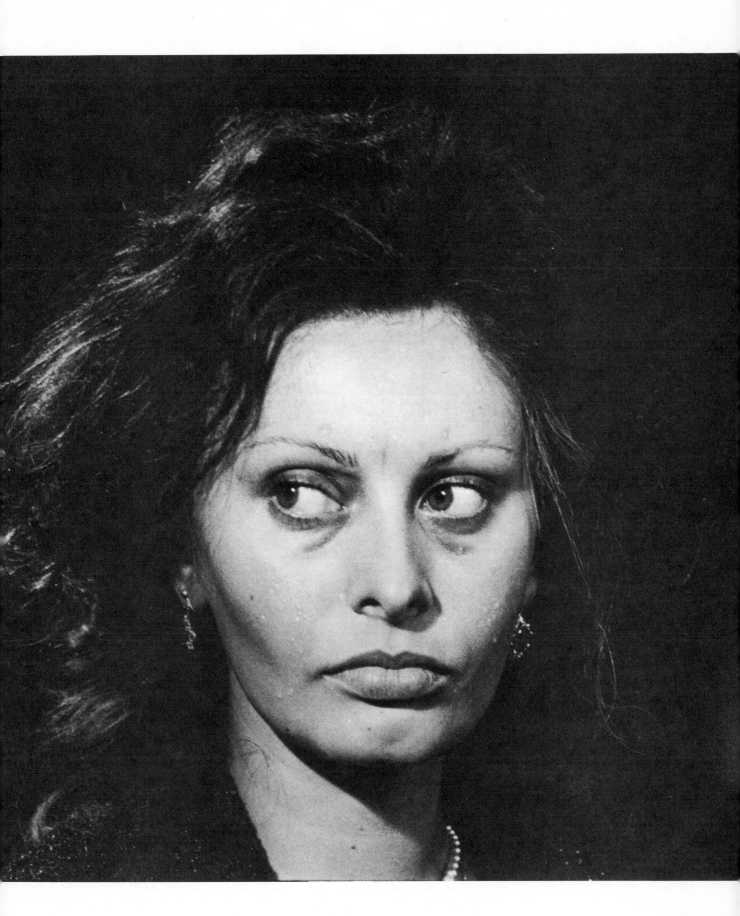

In the beginning, when Sophia knew that as an actress she was going to crack the Hollywood scene, she studied languages. English, French.

She picked up English so quickly you couldn't believe it! With an English coach, reading the poems of T.S. Eliot.

She has a great ear, a great ear . . .

Loren never had a good role until she did "Two Women." Before that she did a lot of commercial pictures. They broke all over the world, but they were never artistic pictures.

Even today she makes pot-boilers, one right after another, and makes a million dollars for each picture. And she's worth it!

These pictures might be disasters in America, but they break box office records everywhere else in the world. "Two Women" was an artistic hit, but it didn't make the millions that other pictures made.

As Quinn did in "La Strada," Sophia in "Two Women" showed the world she could act — in the grand tradition of Magnani . . .

with Stanley Kramer, her first American director

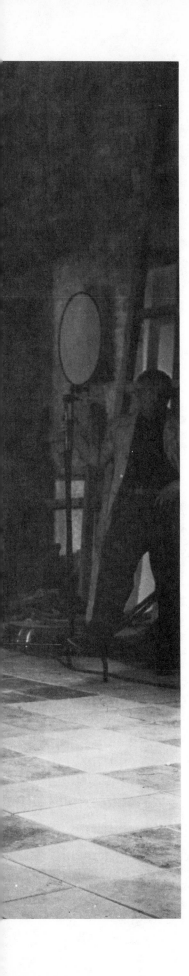

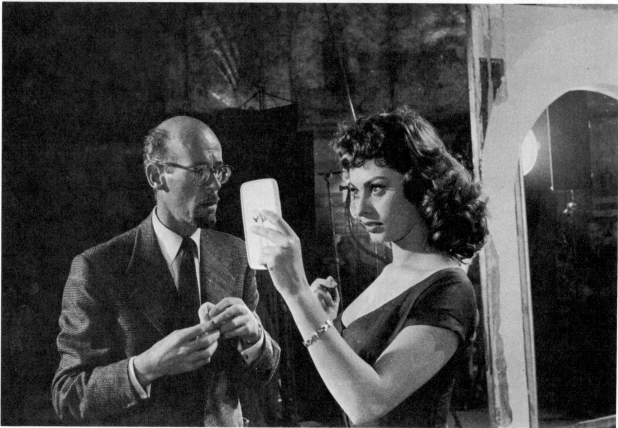

106

As the years go by, Loren grows as an actress and as a woman. She's grown intellectually on a scale equal to that of her beauty. She's developing a tremendous range.

Whatever she does on screen is right. She can do ordinary pictures; and still she remains an international superstar, still she grows as a human being. Actors and actresses don't walk through a role; they do the best that they can.

She doesn't worry. She's sure of herself. She doesn't care whether her back is to the camera. She doesn't fight to steal a scene.

As the years go by, Loren grows as an actress and as a woman. . .

in De Sica's "Marriage Italian Style"

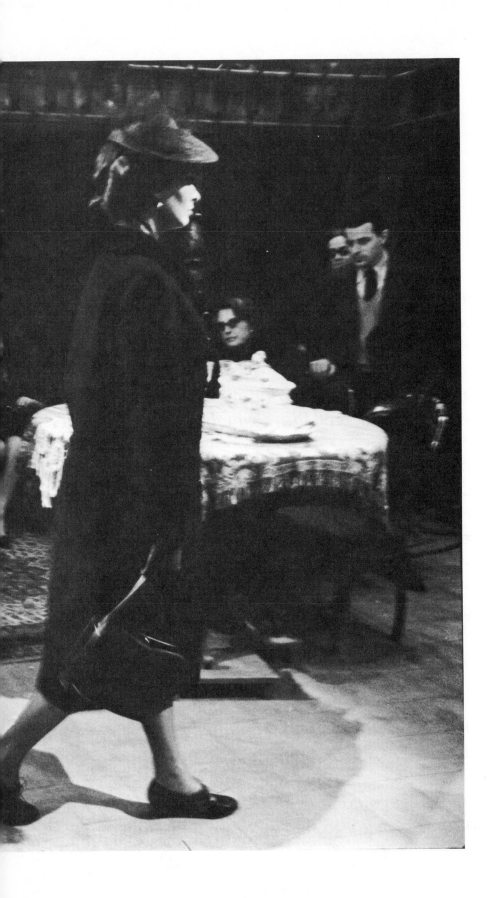

Whatever she does

on screen is right.

In shooting a picture, you sometimes shoot the end in the beginning; sometimes you shoot the beginning at the end. Pictures are often shot out of sequence.

The actors and actresses must remember lines immediately, and feel the development of characters.

Loren's very disciplined. She has intense concentration; wipes everything out.

It's very distracting: lights, electricians, people moving, people gawking . . .

It could be the hottest emotional scene — and a member of the crew will be up in the flies reading a newspaper. He's done his job, done the light, taken care of it.

Nearly every picture I've worked on, I've shot something like that.

You think that couldn't be distracting to an actress who's an artist? You've got to shut all those things out.

She has intense concentration;

wipes everything out...

It's very distracting: lights, electricians, people moving, people gawking...

It could be the hottest emotional scene. . .

SOPHIA LOREN: HER LIFE

3

The Girl Who Won The Prize

In 1932, a contest was held in Italy — to discover an exact double for Greta Garbo. The winner of that contest was Romilda Villani. She won a ticket to Hollywood and a screen test.

For many other girls, this would have been the fulfillment of a dream. But for Romilda, it turned into a nightmare. Her parents refused to let her go to Hollywood. Her ambitions to become an actress were shattered.

A few years later, she had a child — a daughter. The girl was born out of wedlock. Friends and relatives insisted that the child should be given to an orphanage. But Romilda refused. Through years of poverty, disgrace, war, she helped her child to grow and mature.

The mother and child grew strong together, fighting at first for survival. Then for the fame that Romilda was unable to achieve.

Today, Romilda Villani lives in luxury and basks — deservedly — in the fame and success of her daughter . . . Sophia Loren.

The Hungry Years

Sophia Loren was born in a charity hospital in Rome in 1934. While she was an infant, her mother barely made a living giving piano lessons. They survived by the grace of their relatives. Sunday at Grandma's house was the one wholesome meal of the week.

When she went to school, the other girls called Sophia "toothpick." This, and the fact that she did not have a father (everyone knew that her mother had borne her out of wedlock) made school very difficult. She would arrive at the last minute — just before classes began — to avoid the other girls' taunts.

Sophia did not meet her father, Riccardo Scicolone, until she was five. At that time, Romilda Villani phoned him in Rome to tell him that his little girl was terribly sick. Scicolone rushed to where Sophia and her mother lived, only to find out that Sophia was not sick. He was furious.

Though he refused to marry Romilda, he remained in touch with her and the little girl. Three years after Sophia was born, her sister Maria was also born. Again, Scicolone was the father; again, the child was born out of wedlock.

Throughout Sophia's youth, she knew that her mother truly loved Riccardo; she also knew that Riccardo would never become her legal father. Nevertheless, her father gave her his name. (She was also to adopt the name of Lazarro, before finding her screen name, Loren.)

Sophia Loren makes her first Communion.

Sophia checks out the vegetables; a man checks her out, 1954.

During those days of war, Sophia learned of the atrocities of the Germans. She saw German soldiers, first as friends, and then as enemies. She recalls seeing the Germans shooting civilians — almost as sport.

She saw the horrors of war firsthand; the hunger, the brutality. Through it all, she developed a sense of survival that remains with her to this day.

The family lived together in Pozzuoli, a small town outside of Naples. They were poor, very religious. But looking through the torn curtains of her living room, little Sophia would see the sea — blue and beautiful.

In 1940, war came to Pozzuoli. At first, it brought prosperity, then disaster.

A munitions plant stood in the center of town. Night after night, Allied bombs exploded over the entire area — while the townspeople took refuge in a dark tunnel.

Sophia remembers those days with mixed emotions. There was terror, of course, and a sense that death and destruction were everywhere. There was also a sense of unity: huddled together in the dark tunnel, while the bombs blasted overhead, everyone sang and told jokes and laughed to dispel the fear and gloom.

For the first time, little Sophia felt she belonged.

Finally, the bombings became too severe. The whole town was ordered evacuated — north. Sophia and her family went to live near Naples with cousins who hardly knew them.

After her success in "Aida" (1953), Sophia visits GI's in Italy to learn American ways prior to a visit to Hollywood.

Typical cheesecake pose released before "Two Women"

When the Allies conquered Italy, the family was allowed to return to Pozzuoli. Her mother's resourcefulness again came into play. She opened her home to the American soldiers, played the piano for them to make them feel that there — thousands of miles from their real homes — was another home they might enjoy.

The year was 1945. Sophia was eleven. She observed, appreciatively, as her mother did everything that was necessary to keep the family together.

After the war, there were still long periods of cold and hunger; periods when merely surviving took all the power and resourcefulness you could muster.

During this time, Sophia — shy and withdrawn — would spend hours watching films from Hollywood. Here was a totally strange and wonderful world. A world where Fred Astaire and Ginger Rogers danced, where Charlie Chaplin got slapped in the face with a pie and everyone laughed, where fantasy became a wonderful reality.

Meanwhile, Sophia's schoolmates had stopped calling her "toothpick." At the age of 14, she was developing into a magnificently beautiful woman.

Romilda knew that her daughter needed preparation for the career she desired for her. She taught her to play the piano, taught her to walk, taught her all the rules of polite society.

Quo Vadis

In 1948, when Sophia was barely 16, a beauty contest was held near the town of Pozzuoli. First prize was two tickets to Rome. Sophia's mother decided it was time to test her judgement — she entered her daughter in the contest. Sophia won.

But her mother decided to hold the tickets until Sophia was older and had acquired some skill as an actress. She sent Sophia to acting school. Then something unexpected happened.

He mother heard that a huge Hollywood film, "Quo Vadis," was being shot in Rome —

Sophia as local fish seller who nets her man in "Scandal in Sorrento" (1955).

thousands of extras were being hired. She and Sophia immediately packed up and took the train to Rome.

The casting call was total chaos. Even though a "cast of thousands," literally was needed, there were far more people who wanted a job than any studio could hire. The screaming and pushing were intense. When the dust settled, Sophia and her mother had both been hired as extras.

After the filming, Sophia decided to stay on as a model, while her mother returned home. She lived in a small room and made a few friends.

In order to survive, she would take any job that came her way: film extra . . .model . . .clerk.

Sophia was in Rome, determined that she would not leave until she had gained the success she desired. She had inherited her mother's dreams . . . her mother's drive . . . and her mother's beauty.

Charles Boyer is handy when Sophia needs a light in "Lucky to be a Woman" (1955).

Charles Boyer, playing a press agent in "Lucky to be a Woman" (1955), sets Sophia for a publicity shot.

Ponti . . . Always Ponti

Sophia had been in Rome for just a few months. She modeled for the cartoon-like "fumetti" — an Italian version of the soap opera, which appeared regularly in Rome's newspapers. But she barely made a living at it.

One evening, Sophia and several friends decided to splurge. "Let's go to the Colle Oppio," one suggested. "They're holding a beauty contest for Miss Rome . . ."

Sophia agreed. It was the turning point of her life.

She sat at the table, enjoying her plate of pasta. One of the judges came over and asked if she would consider entering the beauty contest. She said no. The man left and sat down.

A few minutes later he returned — and urged her once again to enter the contest. Apparently, one of the other judges thought that she could win. "Which one of the judges?" Sophia asked. The man pointed. Sophia turned her head, and for the first time in her life she smiled at the famous film producer Carlo Ponti.

Ponti returned the smile. Sophia entered the beauty contest — and won second place. She also won a screen test with Ponti.

The screen test took place the following day. It was an utter disaster. Sophia couldn't act, couldn't walk, couldn't do anything right. Carlo had faith in her, however, and insisted that she return in a few weeks for another test . . . with a new cameraman.

The next time, the results were equally bad. Ponti continued to have faith in her. He insisted that she return and take yet another test. It, too, was a disaster.

Nevertheless, Ponti decided to give his young protege bit parts in some pot-boilers. Sophia worked as an extra in "The White Slave Trade" . . . "The Dream of Zorro" . . . "Hearts Upon the Sea" . . . "Bluebeard's Six Wives" and "It's Him, Yes! Yes!" She was a teenager; yet with Ponti's guidance she was learning the film business.

At the age of 18, Sophia landed the first important role of her life: "Aida". Gina Lollobrigida had signed to play the title role in this film version of Verdi's opera. Then she discovered

Wearing native dress, Sophia dances the flamenco after hours during filming of "The Pride and the Passion" (1957).

that she would be doing lip-sync while Renata Tebaldi did the actual singing. Lollobrigida wanted out. The film was ready to roll. Ponti called Sophia to play the part.

She was magnificent! Without uttering a word of her own, she made an unforgettable

In matador's costume for "The Pride and the Passion" (1957).

Exhausted after first encounter with the bull ring.

Between takes Sophia picks up pointers on bullfighting.

Drying off in "Boy on a Dolphin" (1957).

Sophia and director Jean Negulesco chat on the set of "Boy on a Dolphin" (1957).

impact. The film version of "Aida" was distributed throughout the world — and Sophia, overnight, became a sensation. Ponti immediately signed Sophia to a personal contract.

In subsequent films, Sophia (who had now changed her name from Lazarro to Loren) clearly demonstrated that she had the figure and know-how to dominate the screen as a sex goddess. There was hardly a hint, though, that she would evolve into a serious actress until 1953. It was then that she made "The Anatomy of Love" — and the first time she co-starred with Marcello Mastroianni. The cinematic electricity between the two was immediate and explosive.

The team of Loren and Mastroianni returned in "Too Bad She's Bad" — one of her earliest hits. "The Miller's Wife" followed, an artistic as well as box-office triumph.

Carlo decided it was time for his protege to break the image which Italian films had created for Sophia. He wanted her to make her first English language film, and patiently searched for two years before he found a suitable vehicle for Sophia. Finally, in 1957, Ponti found the "right" film, the vehicle destined to catapult Sophia Loren to superstardom; "The Pride and the Passion".

Again, Carlo had made the right decision for Sophia. Throughout their association, she had trusted him totally. And her trust had been amply justified. Each time that her career reached a pivotal point, it was Ponti who decided where she would go and what she would do next. Each time, his judgement was correct.

After "The Pride and the Passion", Ponti felt that Sophia was ready for a truly serious drama. She made "Desire Under the Elms" with Tony Perkins, settling once and for all the question of whether or not Sophia Loren was an actress of the first magnitude.

The Pride and the Passion

In 1957, Stanley Kramer was casting for "The Pride and the Passion". Two male leads were chosen: Cary Grant and Frank Sinatra. Only the female lead remained to be filled.

There were rumors that Ava Gardner would

Waiting for the next take in "Legend of the Lost" (1957).

The marriage was not recognized; instead, Carlo and Sophia were accused of bigamy, a charge that eventually forced the couple to change their legal residence to France.

Legal or not, the marriage between Sophia and Carlo has been one of the strongest in the film world.

One of the things the public finds hard to understand is what Sophia sees in Carlo Ponti, who is twenty years older and several inches shorter than she.

Shortly after their marriage, people raised the question. She replied. "What nobody could understand then and still can't is the extraordinary power of the man. He generates a tremendous excitement for me. He is a sensitive lover, a cultured friend, the understanding father I never had. Every woman's needs are wrapped up inside that man . . . all my needs anyway!"

Gold of Naples

"I think the most important part of my career is when I met my husband," said Sophia, "and then the second man of my life is Vittorio De Sica."

Indeed, it was Ponti who first coached Sophia, transforming her slowly, carefully into star material. He knew that she could do so much

get the role, but Carlo Ponti wanted this to be Sophia's first English-language movie. After a few conversations with Kramer, the announcement was made: Sophia Loren would get the role.

A huge party was held by Kramer, before the filming began. It was the very first time that Sophia met Grant.

Throughout the filming of "The Pride and the Passion", Grant and Loren were often seen together. Grant admitted that he was head over heels in love with Sophia.

Sophia remembered the words that her mother had spoken to her about Carlo Ponti: "He's a married man . . . you will waste your time waiting for him . . . he has a wife and children . . . find someone else."

Pictures of Grant and Loren appeared increasingly in tabloids from Hollywood to Rome, stirring speculation. The pictures were just what Carlo Ponti needed to act. He made up his mind; he would divorce his wife and marry Sophia.

But how? The answer: divorce by proxy and marriage by proxy.

In Catholic Italy, official reaction was swift.

Dealing with rough lovers John Wayne and Rossano Brazzi in "Legend of the Lost" (1957).

Carlo visits Sophia on location in Lybia during the filming of "Legend of the Lost" (1957).

more than pose. Had she been left to others, she may never have realized her potential; she sought to do everything she could to further her talent, but it was Ponti who knew what she had to do, and Ponti who guided her in doing it.

When Ponti had brought Sophia to a certain point, when she was more polished as an actress than she had been when they met, he introduced her to Vittorio De Sica — a man who had distinguished himself through his ability to shape raw talent.

Sophia was then like an uncut gem. De Sica signed her for "Gold of Naples" without even giving her a screen test. Asked to explain what he saw in her that prompted him to take such an unorthodox step, he declared, "A revelation. She was created differently, behaved differently, affected me differently from any woman I have known. I looked at that face, those unbelievable eyes, and I saw it all as a miracle."

As a postscript, De Sica was quick to point out that his feelings about Sophia had always been purely paternal.

"I am not really a director," he said, "just a teacher of elocution. I know how to make people say their lines. And Sophia is clever. She understands this so well with her intuition."

Together she and De Sica became an incomparable team. One writer commented, "it was a performance in itself" when De Sica directed Sophia. She said, "De Sica taught me you can't paint your way into a scene."

Sophia went to Hollywood against De Sica's will. She wanted the glamour, the American fan adoration; De Sica felt this was the worst segment of her career, with the exception of "Desire Under the Elms", which she made with Burl Ives and Anthony Perkins. He summed up her Hollywood foray simply: "She made bad pictures; it was a bad period for her." There are those who would disagree, but for De Sica, Sophia was a Neapolitan, the essential Italian woman. Hollywood, for De Sica, was not fit for comparison with Italy.

When De Sica was ready to film "Two Women", he wired Sophia, who was then in England. The film had originally been planned to star Anna Magnani as the mother and Sophia as the daughter. Although she was only 27-years-old, Sophia had to play the part of a woman nearly 40-years-old who looked and felt older. De Sica asked her to play the part with "no make-up, nothing at all." "Have the courage to become this character," he urged her. "I guarantee that you will give a wonderful interpretation of it."

Sophia's rendition of this role won her the Silver Ribbon (the Italian "Oscar"), The Best Actress Award at Cannes, The New York Film Critics' Award as Best Foreign Actress, and of course, the coveted Oscar from the American Motion Picture Academy.

It was reported that Sophia felt the role so deeply that she broke down in tears several times. She modestly claims that it was one of the easiest roles she has played. "The character was so strong," she said, "nothing could destroy it. Also, I was working within the range of my own experience."

De Sica said, "Though I taught her, directed every move, when the tears came and the anguish in the film, it was her heart, her soul, her own experience that she was drawing on. And when I saw it, I realized that she had come back to Italy. She had come back to me with this vital desire to re-express herself in her own language."

Shaping Up

As a child, Sophia was always considered serious, dedicated, intense. When she launched her career as an actress, these qualities helped her rise above the norm.

Make an appointment with Sophia, and she will always be on time. (She once scolded a reporter for LIFE magazine for being a half-hour late: "You have very bad manners.")

Working on a film, she spends her spare time learning, studying, rehearsing. During takes, she rarely flubs her lines.

Before making her first English-language film, "The Pride and the Passion", she learned English with the aid of the producer's wife by reading the poems of T.S. Eliot.

"When Sophia decided to learn English, she started at the top," quipped one of her co-stars.

A thorough professional, Sophia Loren expects all her co-stars to be professional as well — even if they are only children.

When child actor Paul Peterson kept giggling during a scene (in the movie, "Houseboat") in which he was supposed to cry, Sophia took command of the situation. She went up to Paul, took him aside, shook him gently, and said,

Loren and Carlo return to Los Angeles to continue filming "Houseboat" (1958) after proxy marriage in Mexico.

Knitting to pass time between scenes in "Desire Under the Elms" (1958).

"Listen, Paul! They're giving you a lot of money to do this and if you don't pay attention then they shouldn't pay you. I'm working hard, why don't you?"

Needless to say, this unexpected treatment worked; Paul had no trouble crying during the next take.

Directors, producers, and co-stars, soon realized that Sophia could often be so involved with her work that she took no time to "play."

After filming "The Pride and the Passion" for Stanley Kramer, Sophia flew to Rome — bypassing Kramer's lavish end-of-movie cast party. The filming done, she simply considered her job finished.

In each role, Sophia has become more

Smiling broadly, Sophia and Carlo leave Christian Dior's after buying dresses and shoes. The couple was heading for London, for the premiere of "The Key" (1958).

Sophia at surprise birthday party given for her by three youngsters working with her on "Houseboat" (1958).

fascinated with the business of acting — and more devoted to the art of film.

She has described her favorite roles on screen as "passionate, tragic parts, strong, highly emotional people." But off-screen, it's a different matter. She once told the Italian writer Alberto Moravia: "In life, I'd like to be just the opposite of what I am in art, cool and collected, with a strong inner life."

Those who know her well believe she has achieved both ambitions.

Sophia's Sister

Maria, Sophia's younger sister, was born in 1938. When they were growing up, Sophia's mother tried to treat them equally. Since they lived in a world where actual survival was in question, minor problems and small disagreements between them didn't matter.

An equality is created when children are hungry; when everyone is shivering with cold; when you huddle together as bombs destroy homes and possibly people you know. An equality born out of hardship and war. A shared experience —something Sophia and her sister still remember.

Ironically, that shared memory is today tinged with nostalgia. Sophia recalls a great feeling of unity when she and Maria huddled together in the tunnel in Pozzuoli.

Of course, their lives were in danger. But it was a danger everyone shared. Of course, there was fear and mutual anger. But these were feelings everyone had.

The sense of togetherness that she learned as a child has stood Sophia in good stead as an adult. The humanity she learned in days of war is amply evident in her acting. There is an earthiness about the woman that bespeaks a triumph over hardship.

When Sophia grew rich and famous, she also shared her wealth and fame with all the members of her family.

When Maria's marriage stirred controversy (her wedding to Romano Mussolini, son of the former Italian Fascist dictator, was front page

Embracing Anthony Quinn in "The Black Orchid" (1959).

choirs of ancient Italian cathedrals), a 17-foot fireplace designed by the modern British sculptor Henry Moore, a small cinema room, an antique bed reputed to have once been British Prime Minister Anthony Eden's, and a table made of marble from the villa's catacombs.

To this add antique furnishings of all kinds and an abundance of artwork.

In the midst of so much luxury, Sophia still enjoys simple things most: to lie on the floor and roll around with her two children . . . to tickle them until they laugh with glee . . . to walk barefoot.

And she still recalls that the most delicious food she ever tasted was the glass of goat's milk she enjoyed as a child, when she was hungry.

Thus, in spite of her vast wealth and world-wide fame, Sophia Loren remains the simple, sensitive and direct woman she always was.

Carlo Ponti once said of their lavish villa: "I like to know it exists, that there's a place I can stay."

But Sophia is less comfortable with their grand surroundings. "Even now, with all this, I never feel totally secure. Everything one has, one can lose."

news), Sophia shrugged it off with typical Italian insouciance: her sister was entitled to do anything she wanted — to marry any man she chose to marry.

The Villa Ponti

Few women have ever had their husbands give them a more luxuriously expensive present than Sophia Loren received from Carlo Ponti. It was a Roman villa that Ponti had purchased in the early 1950's.

Later remodeled, added to and decorated, it now contains a four-story guest house built above an old Roman cave, a 135-foot coach-shaped swimming pool, a sauna, a pond with a waterfall and its own little island — and the mansion itself — a 50-room house with fifteen bathrooms, six libraries (some made from the

Two Women

Until 1960, Sophia Loren performed mainly in ordinary movies. Then came the most important film of her life, "Two Women".

Working on this film with Ponti and De Sica, she was forced to recall all the agonies of her childhood . . . and to relive the drama and tragedy of World War II. During many scenes, she was forced to stop the shooting — because of the story's emotional impact on her.

When she was acting the part of a hungry mother, returning to a home that had been bombed, Sophia had merely to recollect her own childhood.

From the very first day of shooting, every-one seemed to realize that "Two Women" was special. There was a reality, an intensity, that occurs only when "acting" ends and true art begins.

The critics agreed. Sophia won awards for

During break in filming of "Black Orchid" (1959) with director Martin Ritt.

Best Actress at Cannes, the New York Film Critics Circle and British Film Academy.

But no foreign language film had ever won an Oscar before. And in 1961 the competition was especially fierce. Audrey Hepburn was the leading contender, as Holly Golightly in "Breakfast at Tiffany's". Geraldine Page was also in the running for "Summer and Smoke" — as was Natalie Wood for "Splendor in the Grass", and Piper Laurie for "The Hustler".

Sophia was so totally convinced that it would be impossible for her to win, that she decided not to travel to Hollywood: besides, it would be a waste of time, for she had begun filming "Boccaccio '70" in Rome.

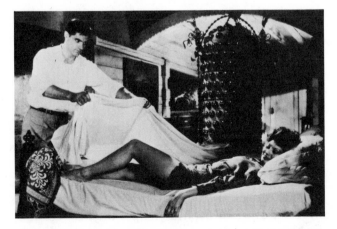
John Gavin tucks in a giddy Sophia in "A Breath of Scandal" (1960).

With Tab Hunter's attention elsewhere, Sophia eases her tired feet in "That Kind of Woman" (1959).

But she did decide to stay up the night of the Academy Awards — and catch the action via wireless.

When the award for Best Actress was announced, Sophia was so overwhelmed that she leaped out of her chair — and ran around kissing everyone in sight. It was an amazing exhibition of youthful exuberance.

The awkward girl from Pozzuoli, whom everybody had once called "toothpick," had earned the highest honor that her peers could bestow!

One Of Us

Few of the world's actresses have the universal appeal that Sophia Loren commands. It is a rare combination of beauty, sensuality, earthiness, sensitivity, warmth and humor.

With equal intensity, she can play mother, wife, mistress and scorned woman. She has played all these roles in real life. She knows them well.

In "Marriage, Italian Style", she revealed her spectacular abilities as a comedienne. Her timing was perfect, her mugging as subtle as Chaplin's, as wildly antic as Groucho Marx's.

In "Two Women", she revealed an intensity of emotion that few people realized till then she possessed. She conveyed the ravages of war, the suffering of humanity, as well as any actor or actress of our time.

In "Arabesque", she created a mood of tension and suspense that an exacting master of suspense, such as Alfred Hitchcock, could applaud.

In "A Perfect Day", she proved that her beauty could survive without make-up. Though the role lacked glamour and romance, her femininity shone through; she evoked a glowing earthiness which few actresses could match.

In "Lady L", she showed her sense of elegance — and contempt for hypocrisy.

In "Boccaccio '70", she revealed a full range of sensuality. Here was a sexiness which left most men limp, while producing in women an equally strong feeling of admiration.

The range of her talents has been truly spectacular.

Whatever role she decides to play —whether it be comedy, drama, social commentary, wild

Fitting costumes for "Heller in Pink Tights" (1960).

Sophia strolls along Manhattan's Seventh Avenue, the fashion district, during a shopping trip, 1959.

sex or suspense — she always brings something very special to the screen: a quality that declares that she is one of us.

From Sex Symbol To Artist

Sophia Loren's range as an actress has grown with each year. She began as a sex goddess, transformed herself into a superb comedienne, then explored the depths of her dramatic talents in some of the most moving portrayals ever seen on the screen. Consider the variety of roles she has played:

In "A Special Day," Loren played an overworked, aging housewife in Mussolini's Rome. It was the first role where she wore no make-up at all.

In "Judith," Loren was the Jewish wife of a Nazi war criminal assigned to train Arab terrorists in Damascus. She is denounced to the Nazis by her husband and subsequently seeks revenge. It was the only part Loren ever played that she felt was "totally unbelievable."

"Quo Vadis" was her first film. She played several bit parts, including a slave girl to Deborah Kerr.

Relaxing during the filming of "A Breath of Scandal" (1960), in which Sophia plays a princess.

Onlookers close in on Sophia and Clark Gable during scene from "It Started in Naples" (1960).

In "A Countess from Hong Kong," she played *Natasha*, an aristocratic refugee of the Russian Revolution who stows away in the cabin of a luxury liner on its way to America. A series of romantic complications and adventures ensue. It was her only film with Marlon Brando, and her first chance to work with Charlie Chaplin.

"Yesterday, Today and Tomorrow" is a trilogy in which Loren plays three different women: *Adelina* is arrested for selling contraband, and keeps herself out of jail by keeping herself pregnant! Wealthy and elegant *Anna* is outrageously concerned with her worldly possessions, and *Mara*, the prostitute, falls in love with a seminary student!

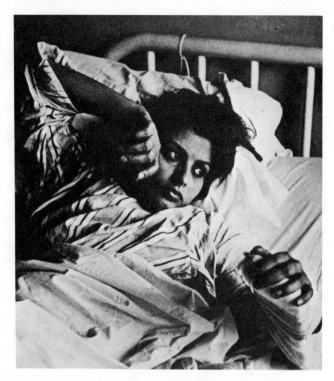

In a pensive mood recovering from a shoulder broken after completion of "El Cid" (1961).

As a sultry laundress in "Madame Sans-Gene" (1961).

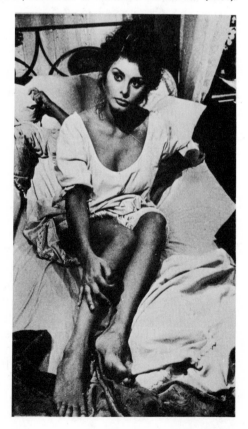

In "Boccaccio '70," she played Zoe, a woman who "raffled herself off" every Saturday night at the fair at her brother-in-law's demand. She's the most popular attraction at the fair, but Zoe gives it all up when she falls in love.

Before shooting "Africa Under the Seas," Loren didn't know how to swim. She learned for the part, though, which required that she spend a good deal of her time under water in her role as Barbara.

Gina Lollobrigida was originally cast, but Loren eventually assumed the title role in "Aida." Though this was one of Loren's first leading roles, her voice was never heard. Renata Tebaldi dubbed the voice of Aida.

In "Two Women," Loren plays Cesira who, along with her 13-year-old daughter, makes a perilous journey through Italy during World War II. In an attempt to reach her native village, Cesira and child encounter extreme danger and many complications in their lives. Loren's moving portrayal of a mother watching her daughter grow up too quickly, too harshly, won her the Oscar.

In "Attila the Hun", Loren plays Honoria, the scheming sister of Emperor Valentinian.

In "Two Nights with Cleopatra," Loren held the title role. Each time she spent the night with an unfortunate member of her guard; he was executed the next morning. But Cesarino's case was different . . .

In "The Miller's Wife," Loren joined together for the first time with Mastroianni and De Sica. This is a light comedy about se-

Sophia "twists" with Mme. Regine, owner of famed Paris discotheque, during filming of "Five Miles to Midnight" (1962).

duction. The governor tries to take advantage of *Carmela* (Loren), but she is too clever a foil for him.

In "Woman of the River," Loren gave a sensual, wide-ranging dramatic performance that would finally establish her as an important actress. In this film, she played an earthy, sultry, working woman — a role that she would return to many times.

Though "Boy on a Dolphin" was far from a highly acclaimed movie, Loren's performance as *Phaedra*, a Greek peasant girl, was lauded by the critics. In one scene Loren appears on a fishing boat. Suddenly, she gets soaked. The picture of her with her wet clothes clinging to her became one of the most famous posters of all time.

In "Legend of the Lost," Loren teamed up with John Wayne, who led her through mile after mile of hot, dry desert on a donkey. She played the role of *Dita*, a lusty slave girl. Filmed on location in the Sahara, the film nearly cost Loren her life when a small heater in her hotel room malfunctioned while she was sleeping.

In "Gold of Naples," Loren portrayed a lusty pizza vendor who gets herself in trouble when she loses her wedding ring in a lovers' tryst. Loren caught pneumonia playing the part of *Sofia* and was confined to a sick bed for a month.

In "The Pride and the Passion," Loren spoke her first English words on film. Set in the milieu of the Spanish Army in 1810, this is a story of war and jealous passion in which Loren plays the object of two men's desire in her role as *Juana*.

In "Desire Under the Elms," Loren played *Anna*, the beautiful young bride of an old time New England farmer in this story involving lust, jealousy and fury in the confines of one family.

In "Heller in Pink Tights," Loren plays *Angelu Rossini*, the star of a renegade theater company always running from the law. Her taste for the finer things in life keeps her constantly in debt and devising schemes to pay her bills.

In "A Breath of Scandal," Sophia plays the elegant but sometimes indiscreet princess *Olympia* who is supposed to marry a Russian prince but instead elopes with a Pittsburgh mining engineer. This was a far cry from her earlier roles as a voluptous Italian peasant girl.

It is hard to imagine a couple more odd than Peter Sellers and Sophia Loren. But that was the starring duo in "The Millionairess" — based on the play by Bernard Shaw. Loren is heiress to an industrial empire and the man she chooses to marry is a poor Indian doctor. Before they marry, they each put the other to a test whose results cause a lot of confusion.

In "Madame," Sophia had the part of *Catherine*, a boisterous, beautiful washerwoman who rises to become the Duchess of Danzig during the Napoleonic Wars. Portraying that astonishing transformation was a challenge even to her maturing skills as an actress. She handled it admirably.

"The Journey," based on a story by Luigi Pirandello, teamed

Richard Burton with Sophia Loren. This was the 30th picture directed by Vittorio De Sica, but even before the filming had begun, two complications set in. Firstly, just prior to the start of the picture, De Sica collapsed with a serious lung illness. Ponti, his lifelong friend, quickly took action. He contacted a surgeon and team of doctors in Switzerland, chartered a plane in Rome and flew De Sica to the doctors. When he was well enough to return to work, Ponti arranged for medical aid to be available on the set.

The second interruption in the filming was that the volatile Mr. and Mrs. Burton broke up in a fury and a frenzy, were apart and separately despondent, (during which time Richard was the house guest of the Ponti's), and re-united.

In the film, Sophia played a peasant Sicilian widow who has a serious heart ailment. Her brother-in-law (Burton) takes her to various specialists whose only advice is to enjoy life to the fullest. She experiences life and love as she has never known it, concluding on the day Archduke Francis Ferdinand is assassinated. They know the world will never again be as innocent.

Supporting Tony Perkins on the set of "Five Miles to Midnight" (1962).

Deglamorized in de Sica's "Yesterday, Today and Tomorrow" (1963).

In "Marriage, Italian Style," her partnership with Marcello Mastroianni truly blossomed. Marcello played a wealthy playboy; Sophia was his beautiful mistress. The movie follows their relationship over a period of years until she finally traps him into marriage.

In "The Priest's Wife," Sophia tries to woo Mastroianni away from the church. It brought howls from the audience and cries of anguish from the pulpit.

In "The White Sister," she was on the other side, becoming *Sister Germana*, the guiding force of a Libyan missionary hospital. Here, Loren, one of the world's most alluring women, was totally convincing as a nun.

"Our Times" is a potpourri of vignettes ranging from the poignant to the comic. Sophia plays an alluring model for a very admiring photographer.

An unsuspecting cab driver is duped time and again by Loren's *Lina* in "Too Bad She's Bad". A routine cab ride reveals that *Lina*

and her family are trying to steal the taxi! After putting up with much conniving and trickery on the part of *Lina* and clan, the driver, (Marcello Mastroianni) hauls them to the police. A lot of fast talk on *Lina's* part gets her out of trouble with the police and married to the driver!

Loren played *Argriese*, an innocently alluring girl who is constantly surrounded by suitors in "The Sign of Venus." Her cousin Cesira, a plainer girl, is more ambitious in her pursuit of a man, but less successful. This was a light role for Loren in which she shared the limelight with Franca Valeri.

Striking an imperial pose with Alec Guinness in "The Fall of the Roman Empire" (1964).

In a harem costume, "Marriage — Italian Style" (1964).

Marcello Mastroianni clowns with Sophia in "Marriage — Italian Style" (1964).

In "Scandal in Sorrento," Loren plays *Donna Sofia*, the local fish vendor who gets what she wants (including a place to live and a man to marry) by using her all-conquering charm.

"Lucky To Be a Woman" is a romantic story in which Loren plays *Antoinette*, a girl who reaches stardom through the efforts of a photographer, who is in love with her. He waits patiently in the wings while she explores her newfound fame. But Antoinette realizes in the end that her love for him is more important than a flashy career.

Loren stars as *Rose Bianco* in "Black Orchid". *Rose* is a widow living in New York and just making ends meet. She is on the threshold of remarrying when her future husband's (Anthony Quinn) daughter steps in and creates problems for them.

After filming "Judith" (1965) in Israel, Sophia tours Jerusalem.

Posing as a widowed countess in "Lady L..." (1965).

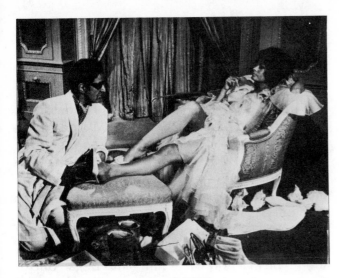
Trying on shoes for "Arabesque" (1966).

In "That Kind of Woman," Loren plays a high class "mistress" named *Kay* who is employed by a millionaire to entertain generals and the like. When a lowly G.I. falls in love with her and pursues her, she has to decide between the life of luxury she's been leading and the young soldier's affections. Love wins after all.

In "It Started in Naples," Loren plays a hot nightclub dancer *Lucia* who's taking care of her orphaned nephew Nando. When Mike (Clark Gable) appears on the scene to settle his late brother's affairs, he discovers that Nando is actually his brother's child. Appalled at the "delinquent" manner in which *Lucia* is bringing up the child, he insists on taking Nando back to America. In the ensuing custody battle, Mike and Lucia fall in love.

"Houseboat" teamed Cary Grant and Sophia who, by a strange turn of affairs, end up setting up housekeeping aboard a rundown houseboat with a trio of kids. This was considered one of Sophia's more "natural" American films.

"Arabesque" brought Gregory Peck and Sophia together in an intriguing and complicated story concerning an American professor at Oxford, an oil magnate, a Middle Eastern premier and an exotic woman. Assassination, death, or the threat of death, by a pair of scissors and a wrecking crane, and decoding of an ancient hieroglyphic code are all worked into the plot.

It is a measure of her abilities that Sophia's sexiness can be submerged — when she must play a role that's totally intellectual. She can play old as well as young, saints as well as sinners, glamorous showgirls as well as dowdy housewives. Perhaps the perfect test of any actress is this: how can she survive aging? Sophia Loren has already passed this test. She is now in her mid-40's, and she continues to play roles of astonishing power, sensitivity, and (when needed) sexiness.

Mama Sophia

In the film, "Yesterday, Today and Tomorrow", Sophia portrayed a pregnant woman. It was a role she had yearned for in real life, and she acted the part with uncanny feeling.

Affectionately hugging Carlo during filming of "The Condemned of Altona" (1962).

147

Soon after her marriage to Carlo Ponti, she realized that her life would never be complete until she had children — his children. (Carlo had children from his first marriage.)

The Pontis first attempts to have children were possibly the most highly publicized miscarriages in history. Millions of people read the papers when Sophia was rushed to the hospital.

The first press releases said she had a toothache; then they told the true story: Sophia had lost her baby.

Her second miscarriage — after four months of pregnancy — evoked a torrent of sympathy from her fans all over the world.

Letters flooded into the Villa Ponti, suggesting all sorts of aids: eat nothing but bananas . . .

A meditative moment on the set of "Countess from Hong Kong" (1966).

take Vitamin E . . . always try to get pregnant on the night of a full moon . . . drink orange juice five times a day . . . check your hormones.

This last piece of advice turned out to be the key. A good friend of Sophia's — who had also lost two babies — suggested a famous Swiss specialist, Dr. Hubert de Watteville. Dr. de Watteville examined Sophia, and advised her that, happily, there was no physical reason that she could not have children. However, once she became pregnant, she would require total rest — total peace.

A few months later, the pregnancy occurred — and Dr. de Watteville decided that Sophia should be in a hotel near him. Thus began one of the great scoop-hunting expeditions in the history of Italian journalism.

As soon as she left, reporters noticed Sophia's absence. They beseiged her family with questions: "Where is she?" . . . "Is she planning a divorce from Ponti?"

Sworn to secrecy, her mother and sister refused to reveal her whereabouts: Sophia was in total seclusion in the Swiss hotel recommended by Dr. de Watteville, lying in bed for all but four hours every day.

Few famous people know what the word "privacy" really means. Sophia Loren was not to be one of them.

For eight months, Sophia remained in her room, simply resting and waiting. No reporters, no stars, no friends visited her. Even her mother and sister waited until just before the baby came before they arrived.

Her only attendants were her secretary, her doctor (who had prescribed this nearly total lying in), and, of course, Carlo Ponti.

Of this unusual experience, Sophia later said, "I think about that period I spent in Geneva with some melancholy, no make it nostalgia. It was more than nice; it was one of the most beautiful times of my life, a beautiful experience. Now, when I think that I spent eight months in a room without ever going out just because I was pregnant, I cannot believe it."

Unfortunately, a maid discovering Sophia's secret sold the information to a local newspaper. The subsequent madness could easily have passed as a scenario for a Marx Brothers' movie.

Playing a peasant girl in "Happily Ever After" (1967).

On Saturday, December 28, 1968, Carlo Ponti, Jr., was born. Actually, his full name was Hubert Leoni Carlo Ponti, Jr. — in honor of the doctor who helped Sophia secure the most important role of her life, the role of mother.

"This boy has a great sense of humor," was Carlo's first comment when he saw his son. Sophia's sister Maria was a bit more effusive. "I hadn't seen Sophia for eight months. That afternoon, when I saw her with the baby, I cried all the more, and so did Sophia."

Carlo Jr. became the most important thing in Sophia's life. For a while, he also became something of an obsession.

Every sound he made was studied. "Is he sick?" "Is he choking?" Every time the phone rang, Sophia was afraid it might be a kidnapper or an extortionist.

Sophia's anxiety was something all her close friends and associates endured. Her personal photographer recalls: "I was there one day when

Sophia and her mother at the premiere of "Happily Ever After" (1967).

Reporters swarmed to Switzerland and tried to gain entry into Sophia's hotel room. Reporters went so far as to try to get jobs as hotel busboys. Or local policemen. Or waitresses. Anything to get an exclusive interview.

Sophia remained in seclusion through it all. Her pregnancy was proceeding on schedule. At one point, she experienced severe pains — and she was afraid that she was going to lose the baby. But Dr. de Watteville quickly administered an injection of estrogen. The pains went away; the baby was safe.

A few months into her pregnancy, Dr. de Watteville brought a high-powered amplifier into her room, along with a stethoscope. He placed the stethoscope against Sophia's stomach. He listened for a few minutes, twisted a few dials and then Sophia heard — faintly but distinctly — the rhythmic sound of her baby's heartbeat. Tears welled up in her eyes as the sound continued.

As Sister Germana in "The White Sister" (1971).

Carlo's crying grew a little faint. Sophia was afraid he was losing his voice. A Swiss nurse, Ruth Bapst, explained that she'd given orange juice to the baby, that the acidity of Vitamin C makes the voice go down. I assured Sophia, 'Yes, it's happened with mine, particularly when the juice is cold. It lasts about two hours.' Sophia looked at me as if I'd saved her life."

One of Sophia's severest frights occured a few months after Carlo, Jr. was born. While winding up a crib toy, Sophia broke part of it — and the broken part landed on little Carlo.

"Naturally, I snatched him up right away. And he cried so much that for awhile he couldn't breathe," Sophia later said of the incident. "It hadn't hurt him much or done him any harm, but I'm sure he reacted because he could feel my own terror."

Sophia's love for her little boy was so strong that it frequently outweighed other obligations. One evening shortly after Carlo was born, she and Carlo Sr. went to a play — and almost left before it was over.

"I began to wonder what I was doing in a theatre when I had a child at home who was all I was thinking about . . . I wanted to leave after the first act, but I had to stay. Everyone knew I was there, and, if I didn't come back, it would have become 'The Play She Walked Out On,' " Sophia later said.

Eventually, as Sophia grew accustomed to motherhood, she took in stride things that alarmed others.

At 3 a.m. one day, a maid woke Sophia with the news that the baby was screaming. A few seconds later, a smiling Sophia said, "Why, he was just practicing his screams. But I think I'll go look at him — and maybe I'll tape-record him."

She spoke of her little son's screaming in greater detail in 1969. "He'd just discovered the sound of his own voice, and he screamed because he wanted to listen to all the noises he could make. He was so happy with them that you knew nothing was the matter. He was busy discovering his own reactions and the day just wasn't long enough."

On January 1, 1973, four years after Carlo Jr. was born, the Pontis had their second child, Eduardo. Life was now complete for Sophia.

Like the devoted mother that she is, Sophia Loren is always concerned that she's not spending enough time with her sons.

En route from Paris, where she's starring in "The Verdict" (1974) to Ankara for Turkish opening of "The Voyage" (1973).

The Pontis.

One day, to see how he would react, she told young Carlo Jr., "I don't want to be an actress anymore."

"You're kidding," young Carlo responded, "It's the most beautiful profession in the world. You should never quit."

That settled the matter.

Sophia Loren has proven that she can play three roles: mother, wife, and actress. And play them all superbly!

After 20 Years

The marriage between Sophia Loren and Carlo Ponti has been one of the most successful in filmdom. What keeps them so totally committed to each other?

The answer lies largely in the temperament of Sophia Loren. When she undertakes a project, she does it with a total dedication that few people understand.

She entered into marriage with the same sense of total dedication.

Sophia is fully aware how much a father her husband is. She understands that her marriage to Carlo is, in many ways, a marriage to the father she never had. She has expressed this many times.

Sophia also respects and accepts Carlo as her mentor. If he decides that she must go from comedienne to serious actress, she never questions his judgement. If he suggests that she read such classics as *Don Quixote* and *The Red and the Black*, she follows his suggestions.

Raised without a father, Sophia observed her mother's yearning for the love and companionship that only a man can bring. When Carlo gave up his wife and children to marry Sophia, she thoroughly comprehended the sacrifice he had made, the total dedication he must have for her to have made it.

Sophia, expressing her strong feelings about Carlo, has remarked: "He is father, husband, lover, big brother, confidant — and, above all, my best friend. I would have to be mad to risk losing him to seek a few moments of pleasure with another man. And I know Carlo is true to me, as I am to him. He found me and helped me to where I am today. He has always been right for me, then and now."

Sophia at 1979 press party for release of her autobiography "Living and Loving."

THE FILMS OF SOPHIA LOREN

4

The Films of Sophia Loren

QUO VADIS 1950 (MGM). The cast included Robert Taylor, Peter Ustinov, Deborah Kerr and Leo Genn. Director was Mervyn LeRoy.

HEARTS UPON THE SEA 1950 (Cine-Albatros). The cast included Doris Dowling, Jacques Sernas, and Milly Vitale. Director was Giorgio Bianchi.

THE VOTE 1950 (ARA). The cast included Georgio de Lullo and Doris Duranti. Director was Mario Bonnard.

BLUEBEARD'S SIX WIVES 1950 (Golden). The cast included Toto, Luigi Parese and Isa Barzizza. Director was Carlo Ludovico.

10 SONO IL CAPATZ 1950 (Jolly). The cast included Silvana Pampanini and Marilyn Buferd. Director was Giorgio Simonelli.

MILANA THE MILLIONAIRESS 1951 (Mambretti). The cast included Toni Scotti and Isa Barzizza. Director was Fictorrio Metz.

ANNA 1951 (Archway). The cast included Silvana Mangano, Raf Vallone and Vittorio Gassman. Director was Alberto Lattuada.

THE MAGICIAN IN SPITE OF HIMSELF 1951 (Amati-Mambretti). The cast included Toni Scotti, Dorian Gray, and Mirella Umberti. Director was Vittorio Metz.

THE DREAM OF ZORRO 1951 (ICS). The cast included Vittorio Gassman, Walter Chiari and Michele Philippe. Director was Mario Soldati.

THE PIANO TUNER HAS ARRIVED 1951 (Itala/Titanus). The cast included Alberto Sordi, Nino Tarranti and Tamara Lees. Director was Duilio Coletti.

IT'S HIM, YES! YES! 1951 (Amati). The cast included Walter Chiari, Silvana Pampanini and Fanfulla. Director was Vittorio Metz.

THE FAVORITE 1952 (MAS). The cast included Gino Sinimberghi, Franca Tamantini and Paolo Silveri. Director was Cesare Barlacchi.

Selling pizza in "Gold of Naples" (1954).

As Cleopatra in "Two Nights With Cleopatra" (1953).

AFRICA UNDER THE SEAS 1952 (Gala). The cast included Steve Barclay and Umberto Malnati. Director was Giovanni Roccardi.

THE WHITE SLAVE TRADE 1952 (Excelsa/Ponti-De Laurentiis). The cast included Vittorio Gassman, Silvana Pampanini, Bruno Rossini and Ettore Manni. Director was Luigi Comencini.

AIDA 1953 (Eagle). The cast included Giulio Neri and Renata Tebaldi. Director was Clemente Fracassi.

GOOD PEOPLE'S SUNDAY 1953 (Trionfalcine). The cast included Maria Fiore, Carlo Romano and Renato Salvatori. Director was Anton Majano.

THE COUNTRY OF BELLS 1953 (Valentina). The cast included Carlo Dapporto and Alda Mangini. Director was Jean Boyer.

A DAY IN COURT 1953 (Excelsa/Documents). The cast included Silvana Pampanini, Alberto Sordi, Walter Chiari and Leopoldo Trieste. Director was Steno.

PILGRIM OF LOVE 1953 (Pisorno). The cast included Alda Mangini, Enrico Viarisio and Charles Rutherford. Director was Andrea Forzano.

NEAPOLITAN CAROUSEL 1953 (Archway). The cast included Vera Nandi, Paolo Stoppa and Leonide Massine. Director was Ettore Giannini.

WE'LL MEET IN THE GALLERY 1953 (Athene-Enic). The cast included Alberto Sordi, Carlo Dapporto and Nilla Pizzi. Director was Mauro Bolognini.

ANATOMY OF LOVE 1953. The cast included Vittorio De Sica and Marcello Mastroianni. Director was Alessandro Blasetti.

TWO NIGHTS WITH CLEOPATRA 1953 (Excelsa-Rosa). The cast included Alberto Sordi, Ettore Manni and Paul Muller. Director was Mario Mattoli.

ATILLA THE HUN 1953 (Archway). The cast included Anthony Quinn, Irene Papas, Henri Vidal and Ettore Manni. Director was Pietro Francisci.

GOLD OF NAPLES 1954 (Gala). The cast included Giacomo Furia, Alberto Farnes and Paolo Stoppa. Director was Vittorio De Sica.

WOMAN OF THE RIVER 1954 (Columbia). The cast included Rik Battaglia, Gerard Oury and Lise Bourdin. Director was Mario Soldati.

Drenched and still gorgeous in "Boy on a Dolphin" (1957).

POVERTY AND NOBILITY 1954 (Excelsa). The cast included Toto, Franca Faldini and Enzo Turco. Director was Mario Mattoli.

TOO BAD SHE'S BAD 1954 (Gala). The cast included Vittorio De Sica, Marcello Mastroianni, and Umberto Malmatti. Director was Alessandro Blasetti.

THE SIGN OF VENUS 1955 (Gala). The cast included Vittorio De Sica, Raf Vallone and Alberto Sordi. Director was Dino Risi.

THE MILLER'S WIFE 1955 (Gala). The cast included Vittorio De Sica, Marcello Mastroianni, Paolo Stoppa and Yvonne Sanson. Director was Mario Camerini.

SCANDAL IN SORRENTO 1955 (Gala). The cast included Vittorio De Sica, Lea Padovani, Antonio Cifariello and Tina Pica. Director was Dino Risi.

LUCKY TO BE A WOMAN 1955 (Intercontinental). The cast included Charles Boyer, Marcello Mastroianni, Nino Besozzi and Titina Di Filippo. Director was Alessandro Blasetti.

THE PRIDE AND THE PASSION 1957 (United Artists). The cast included Cary Grant, Frank Sinatra, Theodore Bikel and Jose Nicto. Director was Stanley Kramer.

BOY ON A DOLPHIN 1957 (20th Century-Fox). The cast included Alan Ladd, Clifton Webb, Alexis Minotis and Jorge Mistral. Director was Jean Negulesco.

LEGEND OF THE LOST 1957 (United Artists). The cast included John Wayne, Rossano Brazzi and Kurt Kaznar. Director was Henry Hathaway.

DESIRE UNDER THE ELMS 1958 (Paramount). The cast included Anthony Perkins, Burl Ives, Frank Overton, Pernell Roberts and Anne Seymour. Director was Delbert Mann.

HOUSEBOAT 1958 (Paramount/Scribe). The cast included Cary Grant, Martha Hyer, Harry Guardino, Paul Peterson and Werner Klemperer. Director was Melville Shavelson.

THE KEY 1958 (Columbia Pictures). The cast included William Holden, Oscar Homolka, Trevor Howard, Kieron Moore and Beatrix Lehman. Director was Carol Reed.

THE BLACK ORCHID 1959 (Paramount). The cast included Anthony Quinn, Ina Balin and Jimmy Baird. Director was Martin Ritt.

THAT KIND OF WOMAN 1959 (Paramount). The cast included Tab Hunter, Jack Warden, George Sanders, Barbara Nichols and Keenan Wynn. Director was Sidney Lumet.

HELLER IN PINK TIGHTS 1960 (Paramount). The cast included Anthony Quinn, Steve Forrest, Eileen Heckart, Margaret O'Brien and Edmund Lowe. Director was George Cukor.

IT STARTED IN NAPLES 1960 (Paramount). The cast included Clark Gable, Vittorio De Sica, Marietto and Paolo Carlini. Director was Melville Shavelson.

A BREATH OF SCANDAL 1960 (Paramount). The cast included John Gavin, Angela Lansbury, Isabel Jeans and Maurice Chevalier. Director was Michael Curtiz.

With Eleanor Brown, who plays her daughter, in "Two Women" (1960).

Sophia uses judo to make Dennis Price behave in "The Millionairess" (1960).

THE MILLIONAIRESS 1960 (20th Century-Fox). The cast included Peter Sellers, Alastair Sim, Vittorio De Sica, Dennis Price and Gary Raymond. Director was Anthony Asquith.

TWO WOMEN 1961 (Gala). The cast included Jean-Paul Belmondo, Eleanor Brown and Raf Vallone. Director was Vittorio De Sica.

EL CID 1961 (Rank). The cast included Charlton Heston, Herbert Lom, John Fraser and Raf Vallone. Director was Anthony Mann.

BOCCACCIO '70 1961 (Embassy Pictures via 20th Century-Fox). The cast included Luigi Giuliani and Alfio Vita. Director was Vittorio De Sica.

MADAME SANS-GENE 1961 (Embassy Pictures via 20th Century-Fox). The cast included Robert Hossein, Julien Bertheau, Marina Berti and Carlo Giuffere. Director was Christian Jacque.

FIVE MILES TO MIDNIGHT 1962 (United Artists). The cast included Jean-Pierre Aumont, Anthony Perkins, Gig Young, Yolande Turner and Mathilde Casdesus. Director was Anatole Litvak.

THE CONDEMNED OF ALTONA 1962 (20th Century-Fox). The cast included Fredric March, Maximilian Schell and Robert Wagner. Director was Vittorio De Sica.

YESTERDAY, TODAY AND TOMORROW 1963 (Embassy Pictures via Paramount). The cast included Marcello Mastroianni, Aldo Giuffre and Agostino Salvietti. Director was Vittorio De Sica.

THE FALL OF THE ROMAN EMPIRE 1964 (Rank). The cast included Alec Guinness, James Mason, Omar Sharif, Christopher Plummer, Stephen Boyd and Anthony Quayle. Director was Anthony Mann.

MARRIAGE, ITALIAN STYLE 1964 (Embassy Pictures via Paramount). The cast included Marcello Mastroianni, Aldo Puglisi and Tecla Scarano. Director was Vittorio De Sica.

JUDITH 1965 (Paramount). The cast included Peter Finch, Jack Hawkins and Hans Verner. Director was Daniel Mann.

OPERATION CROSSBOW 1965 (MGM/Carlo Ponti). The cast included Trevor Howard, George Peppard, Lilli Palmer, Tom Courtenay, John Mills and Paul Henreid. Director was Michael Anderson.

LADY L 1965 (MGM). The cast included Paul Newman, David Niven, Claude Dauphin, Philippe Noiret and Michel Piceli. Director was Peter Ustinov.

ARABESQUE 1966 (Rank/Universal). The cast included Gregory Peck, Alan Badel and Kieron Moore. Director was Stanley Donen.

A COUNTESS FROM HONG KONG 1966 (Rank/Universal). The cast included Marlon Brando, Sydney Chaplin, Tippi Hedren and Michael Medwin. Director was Charles Chaplin.

HAPPILY EVER AFTER 1967. The cast included Omar Sharif. Director was Francesco Rosi.

GHOSTS, ITALIAN STYLE 1967 (MGM). The cast included Vittorio Gassman, Mario Adorf and Margaret Lee. Director was Renato Castellani.

SUNFLOWER 1969 (Avco Embassy). The cast included Marcello Mastroianni, Ludmila Savelyeva and Anna Carena. Director was Vittorio De Sica.

THE PRIEST'S WIFE 1970 (Warner Brothers). The cast included Marcello Mastroianni and Venantino Venantini. Director was Dino Risi.

An affectionate moment with Marcello Mastroianni in "Sunflower" (1969).

LADY LIBERTY 1971 (Warner Brothers). The cast included William Devane, Luigi Proietti and Beeson Carroll. Director was Mario Monicelli.

WHITE SISTER 1971 (Columbia-Warner). The cast included Adriano Celentano, Fernando Rey and Luis Marin. Director was Alberto Lattuada.

MAN OF LA MANCHA 1972 (United Artists). The cast included Peter O'Toole, Ian Richardson and James Coco. Director was Arthur Hiller.

THE VOYAGE 1973 (United Artists). The cast included Richard Burton, Ian Bannen and Paolo Lena. Director was Vittorio De Sica.

VERDICT 1974 (Les Films Concordia/Champion). The cast included Jean Gabin, Henri Garcia and Julien Bertheau. Director was Andre Cayatte.

Well-disguised as a desperate woman, Sophia strides through a poor section of Rome in "Yesterday, Today and Tomorrow" (1963).

The waitress behind the bar? Sophia, in "Angela" (1976).

BRIEF ENCOUNTER 1974. The cast included Richard Burton. Director was Alan Bridges.

GUN MOLL 1974. The cast included Marcello Mastroianni. Director was Giorgio Capitani.

A SPECIAL DAY 1975. The cast included Marcello Mastroianni. Director was Ettore Scola.

CASSANDRA CROSSING 1976. The cast included Richard Harris, Ava Gardner and Burt Lancaster. Director was George Pan Cosmatos.

ANGELA 1976. The cast included John Huston, John Vernon and Steve Railsback. Director was Boris Sagal.

BRASS TARGET 1978. The cast included George Kennedy, Robert Vaughn, Max Von Sydow and John Cassavettes. Director was John Hough.

FIRE POWER 1979. The cast included James Coburn and O.J. Simpson. Director was Michael Winner.

A BLOOD FEUD 1979. The cast included Marcello Mastroianni and Giancarlo Giannini. Director was Lina Wertmuller.

Victor Mature with Sophia in "Fire Power" (1979), shot on Manhattan's East Side.

Contents

Preface

Drug metabolism is a fascinating discipline at the crossroads of numerous sciences such as Chemistry (physical, organic, inorganic, biological, analytical), Biopharmacy (including absorption, distribution, accumulation, excretion, and pharmacokinetics), Pharmacology and Toxicology, Genetics (including genomics, proteomics, and population genetics), and Environmental Sciences (see xenobiotics). As graduates in Pharmaceutical Sciences with a broad education in several of the above fields, we have always tried to combine the broader and the deeper view in our studies and research. But above all, we have it as our objective to convey our fascination to our students. The present Work has emerged from our experience as teachers at the M.Sc. and Ph.D. levels, but it also owes much to our desire to address a wider audience of students and research scientists. Modern computer technology now allows for lively and attractive teaching support, and we have attempted to transpose (and markedly expand) an entire course in *Powerpoint*™ format into a printed format. This was achieved by structuring it into seven Parts consisting mainly of colored figures each with an extensive caption, plus a short introductory text and an extensive bibliography. As a further original feature, the various Parts of the Work are first published as separate review papers before appearing in book form. We hope readers will enjoy these features as much as we enjoyed delivering our lectures and preparing this Work.

When Parts 1, 2, and 3 were published, it was realized that they did fill over 300 pages. With Parts 4 – 7 also estimated at >300 pages, it made sense to publish the Work in two volumes. The first Volume is now in your hand, and we are actively engaged in completing Volume 2.

November 2007

Bernard Testa
Stefanie D. Krämer

Foreword

In the late 1960s, a group of Swedish pharmacologists compared the half-lives of a number of anxiolytic drugs in rats both *in vitro* (microsomal) and *in vivo*, pre- and post-induction of enzymes by phenobarbital. *In vitro* half-lives decreased for all compounds following phenobarbital induction. However, *in vivo*, a significant portion of the anxiolytics showed no obvious change, while the others showed a comparable half-life decrease to that seen *in vitro*. The investigators concluded that *in vitro* studies could not be trusted to predict *in vivo* drug metabolism. In 1983, I spent a sabbatical in the Department of Pharmacology and Toxicology of the University of Tübingen with Professor *Herbert Remer*, a pioneer in cytochrome P450 (CYP) metabolism. Every Friday afternoon, all members of the Institute met for 'tea' – which translates to 'beer' in German. During these Friday afternoon sessions, we discussed philosophical scientific issues related to drugs. However, as I recall, about one half of those sessions in 1983 were devoted to a discussion as to whether there was '*...one CYP or two?*'

The two scenarios about highlight how far we have come in the last three to four decades in our understanding and application of the biochemistry of drug metabolism. *Bernard Testa* and *Stefanie D. Krämer* here document that progress and the major advances in our understanding of drug metabolism in an encyclopedic, but very readable format. The figures in this volume represent a *Powerpoint*™ presentation to simulate a well-organized, comprehensive, and readily understandable series of slides as would be given in an oral presentation. The text provides the reader with the 'sound bites' that the lecturers present to explicate the slides. But as an added bonus, the text contains all the thoroughly referenced citations to the discussion for further examination by the reader. I find the presentation technique to be delightful and expect that other readers will have the same experience.

The two anecdotes above spurred my interest in the development of the principles of intrinsic clearance to explain the *in vivo vs. in vitro* differences, to investigate the multitude of CYP enzymes both in animals and man, and then my recent work to try to explain further discontinuities between *in vitro* and *in vivo* metabolism by examining transporter–enzyme interplay in drug metabolism. I envy today's readers of this volume by *Testa* and *Krämer* since the present work provides an exemplary scientific basis for the biochemistry of drug metabolism upon which both experienced and newly initiated drug-metabolism scientists may depend, as they move the field forward. Understanding the biochemistry of drug metabolism is today one of the most critical aspects of new drug development to assure safe and efficacious medicines of the future. *Testa* and *Krämer*'s contribution to this development is significant.

November 2007

Leslie Z. Benet
University of California San Francisco

4

Stores and Retail Spaces

From the Institute of Store Planners
and the Editors of VM+SD Magazine

MEDIA
GROUP
INTERNATIONAL

CINCINNATI, OHIO

ISBN: 0-944094-40-6

Published by:
ST Books
ST Media Group International Inc.
407 Gilbert Avenue
Cincinnati, Ohio 45202

Tel. 513-421-2050
Fax 513-421-6110

E-mail: books@stmediagroup.com
www.stmediagroup.com

Distributed to the book and art trade in the U.S. and Canada by:
Watson-Guptill Publications
1515 Broadway
New York, NY 10036

Tel. 800-451-1741 (732-363-4511 in NJ, AK, HI)
Fax 732-363-0338

Distributed to the rest of the world by:
HarperCollins International
10 East 53rd Street
New York, NY 10022-5229

Fax 212-207-7654

Book design by Kimberly Pegram

Printed in China

10 9 8 7 6 5 4 3 2 1

Contents

David Jones Ltd.

Rundle Mall, Adelaide, South Australia

Robert Young Associates, Dallas

Department stores aren't dead.

Need proof? Look no further than the new David Jones store design, a brand-new, light and spacious, five-floor, 280,000-square-foot department store in Adelaide's downtown Rundle Mall, balancing top-notch product with an elegant merchandise presentation.

Robert Young Associates (Dallas) gave the store a contemporary attitude that would attract a new generation of shoppers as well as high-profile international (and national) vendors. The redesign was a culmination of several years of planning and research to create a store that would be the best in every measurable category, from customer service to merchandise presentation to store design.

The result is a contemporary, light-infused design with a decidedly down-under feel. A five-floor atrium at the store's center rises to a glass ceiling on level three, flooding the space with natural light and providing open sightlines to the floors below. A primarily creamy, neutral palette unifies all the floors, but materials distinguish them. The ground floor, for example, is paved in polished, cream-colored Italian marble, and furnishings feature hardwood veneers.

But the most dramatic design elements are overhead. A major challenge was dealing with the store's long, narrow footprint, so designers added curves to the ceiling plane to pull traffic through the space. Sweeping soffits and lighting accents provide visual interest and a combination of fluorescent and MR16s add punch.

Client Team:
David Jones Ltd., Sydney, Australia — Peter Wilkinson, ceo; Steven Goddard, operations director; Rob Dickson, general manager, projects; Dieter Poisel, senior store planner; Robert Heaton, general manager, visual merchandising; Linda Millar, buyer representative; John Samartzis, store director; Craig Jones, construction manager

Design Team:
Robert Young Associates, Dallas — Tom Herndon, ceo/principal-in-charge; Mike Wilkins, creative director; John Von Mohr, project designer

Architect:
Hassell Ltd., Adelaide, South Australia

Outside Consultants:
Total Electrical Connection, Sydney, New South Wales, Integrated Lighting Concepts, Los Angeles (lighting); Hansen Juncken, Netley, South Australia (general contractor)

Suppliers:
Arkitex, Sydney, New South Wales, St. James Furnishings, Sydney (fabrics); FMCA, Sydney, Flair, Sydney (fixturing); Commercial Ceramics & Stone, Adelaide, Premium Cork & Timber, Mt. Waverly, Victoria (flooring); Zumtobel Staff Lighting, Sydney (lighting); Paint-Dulux, Clayton, Australia, Spencer Studios, Queensland, Australia (wallcoverings)

Photography:
Tim Griffith, Melbourne, Victoria

New or Completely Renovated Full-Line Department Store First Place / Store of the Year

New or Completely Renovated Full-Line Department Store First Place / Store of the Year

Macy's Roseville

The Galleria at Roseville Mall, Roseville, Calif.

Federated Department Stores, Cincinnati

Macy's Roseville, at The Galleria at Roseville Mall, represents an aesthetic of dramatic contemporary style expressed both inside and out. The store's exterior is a composition of layered planes of color and glass, unified by a bold, horizontal entrance canopy and a two-story glass curtainwall that floods the interior with light.

Inside, a 36-foot-diameter atrium well cut provides unobstructed views of the first floor's fashion accessories departments and the second-floor Home Store. Private-label brand areas are distinguished by a skewed flooring pattern of 24-inch-square Vermont slate with 3-inch mahogany planking. The layering theme continues throughout the store in colors and patterns, ceiling and flooring treatments.

Client Design:
Federated Department Stores, Cincinnati — Rudy Javosky, senior vp, store design and construction; Brian Preussker, senior vp, store design and visual merchandising/San Francisco; Scott Meyer, divisional vp, store planning and design; Steven Bergquist, operational vp and creative director, store design; Jim Kelly, design director; Sharon Masters and Jana Moerlein, colors, products and materials designers; Ken Lay, digital designer

Architect:
Altoon Porter Architects, Los Angeles

Design Consultant:
FRCH Design Worldwide, Cincinnati

Suppliers:
ASC Co., Dallas (audio/video); Armstrong World Industries, Lancaster, Pa., American Acrylic Corp., W. Babylon, N.Y. (ceilings); Continental Store Fixture, Sacramento, Calif., RAP Security, Cudahy, Calif. (fixturing); Atlas Carpet Mills, Los Angeles, Beaulieu Commercial Carpet, Chatsworth, Ga., Mohawk Carpets, Kennesaw, Ga. (carpeting); Classico Tile & Marble, Columbus, Ohio, Hathaway Carpet, Cincinnati, Innovative Marble & Tile, Hauppauge, N.Y. (tile); Buell Hardwood Floors, Dallas (wood flooring); Indy Lighting, Fishers, Ind., Lightron, New Windsor, N.Y., GE Supply, Cincinnati, Litelab, Buffalo, N.Y., Color Kinetics, Boston (lighting); Dooge Veneers, W. Hartford, Conn., Flagg Inc., Fairfield, Ohio, Formica Corp., Cincinnati, M. Bohlke Veneer Corp., Fairfield, Ohio, Nevamar, Odenton, Md., Panolam Industrial Intl., Pionite Division, Auburn, Maine, VenTec Ltd., Chicago (laminates); Art Glass, Cincinnati (decoratives); Cottage Corp., Minneapolis, Federal Sign, Tampa, Fla. (signage)

Photography:
Paul Bielenberg, Bielenberg Associates, Los Angeles

New or Completely Renovated Full-Line Department Store Award of Merit

New or Completely Renovated Full-Line Department Store Award of Merit

Elder Beerman Future Store

Marketplace of Warsaw, Warsaw, Ind.

Horst Design Intl., Cold Spring Harbor, N.Y.

On a limited budget that mandated vinyl flooring, one carpet selection, inexpensive lighting and other cost-cutting measures, the new Elder Beerman prototype at the Marketplace of Warsaw (Indiana) managed to achieve its goal of increasing sales — outpacing existing stores by 20 percent. Its "main street" aisle directs customers to a central core. In the 60-foot-diameter cosmetics department, four custom-designed islands house major vendors. Juniors and young men's are combined into one prominently located shop visually segregated from the rest of the store. And a self-contained, 16,000-square-foot Home Store was designed to compete with both local department store competitors and big-box retailers.

Client Design:
Elder Beerman Department Stores, Dayton, Ohio — Fred Mershad, chairman/ceo; Jim Zamberlan, executive vp of merchandising and stores; Jeff Brown, senior vp of store planning and construction

Design Team:
Horst Design Intl., Cold Spring Harbor, N.Y. — Douglas Horst, president/principal-in-charge; Fidel Miro, planning and design director; Cynthia Davidson, director of colors and materials

Architect:
Omega Architecture, Syracuse, N.Y.

General Contractor:
Robert Henry Construction Co., Warsaw, Ind.

Suppliers:
USG Corp., Chicago (ceilings); Creative Cabinets, Arganum, Ohio (fixturing); J&J Carpeting, New York, Kentile Vinyl Floors, Deer Park, N.Y. (flooring); Lightron, Cornwall, N.Y., Indy Lighting, Fishers, Ind. (lighting); Blumenthal Wallcoverings, Canaan, Conn., Gilford, Jeffersonville, Ind. (wallcoverings)

Photography:
Elliot Fine, New York

New or Completely Renovated Full-Line Department Store Award of Merit

Macy's Home
South Coast Plaza, Costa Mesa, Calif.
Federated Department Stores, Cincinnati

Macy's Home Store in South Coast Plaza (Costa Mesa, Calif.) was originally a 71,617-square-foot I. Magnin store, added to the original Macy's unit there in 1991. (A third building — a 214,000-square-foot former Broadway store — was added to the complex in 1996.)

The renovation reflects a contemporary architectural style developed to brand the building as uniquely Macy's. The goal: To create a cohesive, expanded-service, state-of-the-art shopping environment.

The exterior of the building greets customers with a glass facade/billboard showcasing monumentally scaled graphics, as well as glimpses into the interior selling space. (At night, this elevation serves as a lighted beacon.)

Inside, movable, multi-functional fixtures allow the store to accommodate a variety of trending opportunities. Most of the fixtures are on casters, and all the interior perimeters were designed to allow for maximum vertical merchandise presentation.

A four-story atrium topped by a barrel-vaulted skylight affords a dramatic graphics and video package presentation — both electronic and stationary video elements with navigation and product information that adds to the environment's visual spirit. Circulation aisles of large slab stone guide customers to selling pads of tinted woods, slate and carpeting. Upgraded lighting now meets the federal standard of 45 footcandles. And ceilings feature lighted intersecting drywall planes and an open, stainless-steel, powered grid.

Client Team:
Macy's West, San Francisco — Brian Preussker, senior vp, store design and visual merchandising

Design Team:
Federated Department Stores, Cincinnati — Rudy Javosky, senior vp, store design and construction; Scott Meyer, division vp, store planning and design; Steven Bergquist, operational vp and creative director, store design; Jim Kelly, design director; Sharon Masters and Jana Moerlein, color, products and materials designers; Ken Lay, digital designer

Architect:
BHDP, Cincinnati

General Contractor:
Ron Poulson Associates Inc., Agoura Hills, Calif.

Outside Consultants:
FRCH, Cincinnati (graphics); Madeline Speer Associates, San Francisco (CD production); Francis Krahe & Associates, Laguna Beach, Calif. (lighting design); Sound Visions Consulting, Arlington, Texas (audio/visual consulting)

Suppliers:
MPO Videotronics, Newbury Park, Calif. (audio/video); Armstrong World Industries, Lancaster, Pa. (ceiling); Cowtan & Tout, Cincinnati, Larsen, Cincinnati, Cascade Coil Drapery, Portland, Ore., Designtex, New York, Knoll Textiles, New York, Maharam, Hauppauge, N.Y., Majilite, Dracut, Mass., Scalamandre, Beachwood, Ohio, Sherm Heimburger Associates, Indianapolis, Stroheim & Romann, Long Island City, N.Y. (fabrics); Columbia Showcase, Sun Valley, Calif., Moon Custom Woodwork, Vista Park, Calif., Dillmeier Group, Garden City, N.J., Nomus, Kent, Wash. (fixtures); Atlas Carpet Mills,

Los Angeles, Beaulieu Commercial Carpet, Chatsworth, Ga., Mohawk Carpets, Kennesaw, Ga. (carpets); Architectural Brick & Tile, Indianapolis, Innovative Marble & Tire, Hauppauge, N.Y., London Universal, Monterey, Calif., Kemper Design Center, Cincinnati, Ohio Valley Supply, Cincinnati (tile); Buell Hardwood Floors, Dallas (wood); Arcadia through Gustafson & Co., La Palma, Calif., Barrett Hill, New York, Bernhardt, Lenoir, N.C., Beverly through DeCioccio

Showroom, Cincinnati, Carolina Business Furniture, Cincinnati, Charles Alan, Ft. Worth, Texas, Chelsea Furniture Designs, Syracuse, N.Y., Dakota Jackson through Roth Collection, New York, David Edward, Baltimore, Design Within Reach, San Francisco, Haworth Inc., Holland, Mich., Hickory Business Furniture through Rytell & Associates, Cincinnati, ICF through Dorsey Group, Norwood, N.J., Loewenstein through Dan Binford & Associates, Cincinnati, Steelcase

through Loth/MBI, Cincinnati (furniture); GE Supply, Cincinnati, Indy Lighting, Fishers, Ind., Lightron, New Windsor, N.Y., Litelab, Buffalo, N.Y. (lighting); Formica Corp., Cincinnati, Nevamar, Odenton, Md., Dooge Veneers, W. Hartford, Conn., Flagg, Fairfield, Ohio, Panolam, Auburn, Maine, VenTec Ltd., Chicago (laminates); Cottage Corp., Minneapolis, Federal Sign, Tampa, Fla., Millennium Display, New York (signage); Benjamin Moore Paint Co., Montvale, N.J.,

Design Resources, Beachwood, Ohio, Blackman Designs, E. Bridgewater, Mass., Designtex Fabrics, New York, ICI Paint Stores, Cincinnati, J.M. Lynne Wallcovering, Ronkonkoma, N.Y., Pratt & Lambert, Cleveland, Seibold & Assoc., Perrysburg, Ohio, Surface, Solon, Ohio, Majilite Corp., Dracut, Mass., Trefzger's Inc., Poland, Ohio (wall-coverings)

Photography:
Paul Bielenberg, Los Angeles

New or Completely Renovated Specialty Department Store First Place

New or Completely Renovated Specialty Department Store First Place

Nordstrom

Michigan Avenue, Chicago

Callison Architecture Inc., Seattle

"What's fresh" is the focus of the new 271,000-square-foot Nordstrom store on Chicago's Michigan Avenue. The four-story flagship provides plenty of visual cues to customers, using flexible fixtures and elements such as painted columns, theatrical lighting and draped fabric to signal hot fashions and trends.

The drama starts with a two-story entrance lobby on the Wabash Street side of the complex (at Grand Avenue), which makes shoppers feel like they're entering a display window. Six translucent fabric panels of varying sizes and shapes dominate the main wall. Theatrical lighting, video and sound also contribute to the drama. On the Michigan Avenue level, shoppers saunter along a 250-foot Italian limestone-paved "runway" illuminated by dramatic, changeable overhead lighting.

"Hot shops" located at strategic spots throughout the store are mannequin pads that can be changed seasonally using colors, lighting, video and music. The third floor reflects the chain's new merchandising strategy, which divides women's' apparel into "modern" and "classic" hemispheres. And the ground-level cosmetics department achieves a light, open feeling through light-ash casework, backlit glass panels and decorative-glass accent lighting.

Client Team:
Nordstrom, Seattle — David Lindsey, vp, store planning and architecture; Bob Vauthier, casework coordinator; Clint Kendall, Susan Morton, Nancy Webber, Paige Boggs, Mark MacLachlan, Sonia Parra and Karen Percelle, project team

Design/Architecture:
Callison Architecture Inc., Seattle — Stephen Dwoskin and John Bierly, principals; M.J. Munsell, principal, design direction; Barbara Grubb, interior designer; John Mengedoht, project architect; Matt Billerbeck, project designer; Dave Brown, Tina Negri, Christian Jochman, Chris Beza, Curtis Hughes, Ron Singler, Kelly Earls, Barry Shuman, Annette Hillesland, Ching Chung, department design

Lighting Consultant:
James Aitken, Jucy Lim Productions, New York

General Contractor:
W.E. O'Neil Construction, Chicago

Suppliers:
Innovative Design Technologies, Valencia, Calif., Leibold Communications, Seattle (audio/video); Armstrong World Industries, Lancaster, Pa. (ceilings); Goebel Fixture Co., Hutchinson, Minn., Ontario Store Fixtures, Toronto, Columbia Showcase, Sun Valley, Calif., Fetzers' Inc., Salt Lake City, Pacific Coast Showcase, Puyallup, Wash., Nomus, Kent, Wash., Northwest Building Tech, Seattle, Edron Fixture Corp., Miami, Allied Steel, Redmond, Wash., Universal Showcase, Woodbridge, Ont. (fixturing/casework); Innovative Marble & Tile Inc., Hauppauge, N.Y. (marble flooring); Flaviker, Modena, Italy (ceramic tile); Dodge-Regupol Inc., Lancaster, Pa. (rubber flooring); Kentucky Wood Floors, Louisville, Ky., Hartco, Knoxville, Tenn. (wood flooring); Harris Tarkett, Whitehall, Pa. (wood); Ardex, Caraopolis, Pa. (concrete); Masland Carpets, Mobile, Ala. (carpet); Kaasco Inc., Mukilteo, Wash., The Mercier Group, Los Angeles, GDM, Paramount, Calif. (furniture); Pionite, Auburn, Maine, Nevamar, Odenton, Md., Wilsonart Intl., Temple, Texas, Formica Corp., Cincinnati (laminates); Terzani Inc., Miami Beach, Fla., CX Design Inc., New York, Donghia Furniture, New York, Charles Loomis Inc., Kirkland, Wash. (custom lighting); DK Display, New York, Pucci, New York, M. Goldsmith, Long Island City, N.Y., Patina-V, City of Industry, Calif. (mannequins/forms)

Photography:
Chris Eden, Seattle

DRESSING ROOMS

New or Completely Renovated Specialty Department Store Award of Merit

La Maison Simons

Carrefour De L'Estrie, Sherbrooke, Ont.

The International Design Group Inc., Toronto

For its first foray into a suburban mall setting, La Maison Simons, a Canadian fashion department store, chose to go bold, juxtaposing the rectilinear lines and shapes of the typical "mall box" with curving lines and rounded shapes. Serpentine ceiling lines, concentric flooring patterns, skewed walls and a functional, rectilinear traffic flow create a fluid, open retail space at Carrefour de L'Estrie in Sherbrooke, Ont.

Aisles leading from both the mall and exterior entrances converge at a central elliptical roundabout, reinforced with an elliptical spiral ceiling and capped by a silver-leaf dome. Custom fixtures create a specific vocabulary for each department while allowing for extremely dense merchandising. Custom screen walls in each department maximize merchandising space while allowing transparency.

Design Team:
The International Design Group Inc., Toronto — Ron Harris, president; Donna Lawson, project manager; Andrew Gallici, senior design consultant; G. Eng, J. Janz, J. Nixon, J. McDonald and I. Grant, designers

Architect:
Lemay Michaud Architecture, Quebec City, Que.

Suppliers:
Robert Allen, Toronto, Telio and Cie, Toronto, Betsy Sumner, Toronto, Maharam, Hauppauge, N.Y. (fabrics); Atlas Carpet Mills Inc., Los Angeles, Stonetile Intl. Inc., Toronto, National Ceramic & Granite Ltd., Montreal (flooring); Louis Interiors, Toronto (furniture); Bendheim Architectural Glass, New York, Euroverre, Montreal, Nevamar, Odenton, Md., Formica Corp., Cincinnati, Abet Laminati, Englewood, N.J. (laminates); Eurolite, Toronto, SEG, Montreal, Nelson & Garrett Inc., Toronto (lighting); Moss & Lam, Toronto (paints); Danielle April, Quebec City, Que. (sculpture); Metro Wall Coverings & Fabrics, Toronto, Blumenthal Wallcovering, Canaan, Conn., Crown Wallpaper & Fabrics, Toronto, Maharam, Hauppauge, N.Y., Telio & Cie, Toronto (wallcoverings)

Photography:
Yves Lefebvre Photography, Montreal (exterior); Robert Burley, Design Archive, Toronto (interior)

Bergdorf Goodman Level of Beauty

Fifth Avenue, New York

Yabu Pushelberg, Toronto

The main floor of the Bergdorf Goodman store on New York's Fifth Avenue was getting cluttered, and a leading candidate for relocation was the store's smallish cosmetics department. But taking what is traditionally a retailer's prime merchandise attraction and moving it into the basement flew against all conventional wisdom. Yet that's just what Bergdorf did.

So designers at Yabu Pushelberg (Toronto) aimed to make the new Level of Beauty a destination, a special place worth the trip downstairs, in keeping with the unique Bergdorf Goodman style. Low ceilings and no light added to the challenge. And so did the below-the-ground infrastructure of the classic former Vanderbilt townhouse.

Yabu Pushelberg created a residential "Americanized French" feel, with warm period furniture, custom-finished cabinets, floors that are part terrazzo and part print carpeting, and a 21-foot chandelier.

The light, neutral palette and efficient lighting plan work to keep the space bright, and mirrors throughout the department help disperse illumination. Internally illuminated glass display cabinets have sandblasted exteriors that create a misty, airy look — the secret weapon in the battle to create a sense of light and space, say designers at Neiman Marcus.

Client Team:
Bergdorf Goodman, New York — Ron Frasch, chairman; Peter Rizzo, vice chairman; Muriel Gonzales, senior vp/gmm; Wayne Hussey, senior vp, properties and store development; Mike Eppler, director of construction; Raymond Gearheard Jr., vp, properties/project management; Christine Nakaoka, vp, store planning; Linda Fargo, vp, visual merchandising; Pat Saxby, dimensional merchandising manager

Design Team:
Yabu Pushelberg, Toronto — George Yabu, creative director; Glenn Pushelberg, managing partner; Kevin Storey, project manager; Polly Chan, lead designer; Gary Chan, Mary Mark and Christina Gustavs, design team; Tony Teh, technical leader; Minh Duong, Reg Andrade and Ayako Kawafuchi, technical team

Architect:
Don Lavin, Bridges & Lavin, New York

Construction Manager:
Sweet Construction Co., New York

Lighting Consultant:
Cooley Monato Studio, New York

Suppliers:
Fresco Decorative Painting, New York, Moss & Lam, Toronto (finishes); Sullivan Source, Toronto (wood flooring); Elte Carpets, Toronto (custom carpet); Enmar Natural Stone, Scarborough, Ont. (stone); Blackstock Leather, Aurora, Ont. (leather); Atelier Mecibah, Brasschaat, Belgium, Luminary Tool, Brooklyn, N.Y. (custom lighting fixtures); Pancor Industries Ltd., Mississauga, Ont., Unique Store Fixtures, Concord, Ont. (millwork); Louis Interiors, Toronto (seating); IDMD Design & Mfg., Toronto (tester units)

Photography:
David Joseph, New York

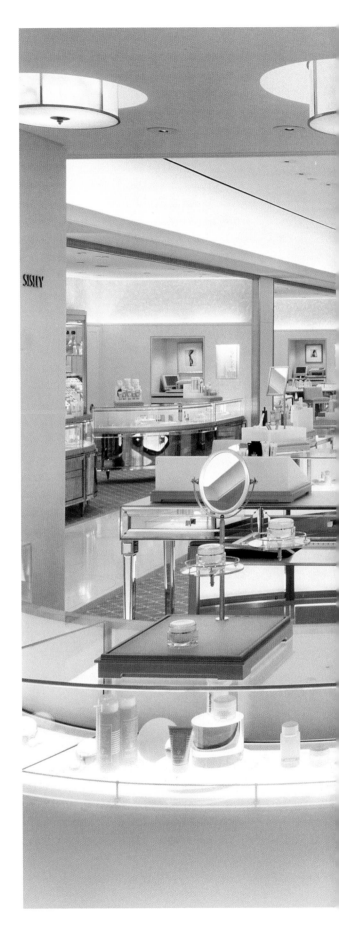

SISLEY

New Shop within an Existing Full-Line or Specialty Department Store First Place

New Shop within an Existing Full-Line or Specialty Department Store First Place

Zondervan Bible Shop

Berean Christian Stores, Cincinnati

Retail Planning Associates, Columbus, Ohio

Believe it or not, nearly 40 percent of shoppers intending to buy a Bible leave the store empty-handed because the Bible selection process is too overwhelming. To make Bible buying easier, Retail Planning Associates (Columbus, Ohio) designed the Zondervan Bible Shop as a relaxing atmosphere that encourages browsing.

The shop is divided into "Lifescape" vignettes such as Aging Parents, Facing Fear, Milestones and Self Image. A major focal point is the NIV translation area, which houses the best-selling Bible translation in print. The area features a 16-foot feature wall with a huge cloud graphic and the NIV brand statement etched in frosted glass.

Client Team:
Zondervan Publishing, Grand Rapids, Mich. — Mark Rice, marketing director; Cris Doornbos, senior vp, sales; Tom Mockabee, senior vp, publisher Bible group; Sueanne Boylan, vp, information systems; Jim Schreiber, cfo

Design Team:
Retail Planning Associates, Columbus, Ohio — Rachel Badin, project director; Vince Notaroberto, senior merchandise planner; Joanne Putka, environmental designer; Deron Husak, visual communications; Mark Holman, lighting; Tonya Schloemer, client service coordinator; Carl Riley and Chris Peterson, retail strategists; Nancy Fritz, research specialist; Russ Finley, production manager

Suppliers:
Accel Group, Wadsworth, Ohio, Cozmyk Enterprises, Columbus, Ohio (fixturing); Production Photo/Graphics, Hawthorne, Calif., The Printing Co., Columbus, Ohio (graphics); Dan Binford & Associates, Cincinnati, Anzea Textiles, Ft. Worth, Texas (furniture); Pionite, Auburn, Maine (laminates)

Photography:
Michael Houghton, StudiOhio, Columbus, Ohio

Nordstrom Halogen In-store Shop

Buford, GA

Callison Architecture Inc., Seattle

Nordstrom wanted a fresh, distinctive setting for its launch of a new private-label women's offering. It needed to reinforce Nordstrom's new fashion-forward attitude and strongly characterize the brand in a boutique-like setting. The solution, by Callison Architecture Inc. (Seattle), was a modular pavilion comprised of translucent panels, rectilinear display units and feature walls. Wall-mounted video monitors and contemporary furnishings keep the space lively, while large blocks of bold color can be changed seasonally to keep it fresh. Modular fixtures and furniture accommodate frequent change while suggesting a modern sensibility, and simple merchandise presentation keeps the space clean.

Client Team:
Nordstrom, Seattle — David Lindsey, vp, store planning and architecture; Bob Vauthier, casework coordinator; Susan Morton, Nancy Webber, Paige Boggs, Clint Kendall and Tim Rausch, project team

Design Team:
Callison Architecture Inc., Seattle – John Bierly, M.J. Munsell, Arthur Teller, Diane Emick, Doug Shaw, Karen Oshiro, Dave Brown, Tina Negri, Christian Jochman, Erin Krohn, Barbara Grubb, Curtis Hughes, Ron Singler, Kelly Earls, Barry Shurman and Annette Hillesland, design team

Outside Consultants:
Candela Lighting, Seattle (lighting consultant); Winter Construction, Newhall, Calif. (general contractor)

Suppliers:
Armstrong World Industries, Lancaster, Pa. (ceiling); ArcCom Fabrics, Orangeburg, N.Y. (fabrics); Innovations, New York, Carolyn Ray, Yonkers, N.Y. (flooring); GMD, Paramount, Calif., Kaasco Inc., Mukilteo, Wash., The Mercier Group, Los Angeles (furniture); Jucy Lime Design, Seattle, Barbizon, Woburn, Mass. (lighting); DK Display, New York, Pucci, New York (mannequins/forms); Pacific Coast Showcase, Puyallup, Wash., Allied Steel, Redmond, Wash., Fetzers' Inc., Salt Lake City (merchandising hardware); Blumenthal Wallcoverings, Canaan, Conn. (wallcoverings)

Photography:
Chris Eden, Seattle

New Shop within an Existing Full-Line or Specialty Department Store Award of Merit

Skechers

Manhattan Beach, Calif.

ME Productions Inc., Marina del Rey, Calif.

Skechers' first freestanding prototype, designed by ME Productions Inc. (Marina del Rey, Calif.), occupies 10,000 square feet at a busy intersection of Manhattan Beach, Calif. Facing the corner, the angled store entrance is highlighted by an illuminated, curved sign and "Skechers Blue" terrazzo flooring. Inlaid in the blue triangle, a stainless-steel logo announces the brand. Once inside, ceiling-suspended lifestyle graphics act as wayfinders, and shoes are lined up in profile along walls of deep and aquamarine blue. The perforated-aluminum ceiling reflects the multiple shades of blue, conveying a technical appeal.

Special merchandise, such as the upscale men's "Collection," is distinguished by signage and materials. The men's line is set apart on a 360-degree display, while branded accessories and T-shirts housed in wooden fixtures and shelving add warmth to the high-tech atmosphere.

Aside from the merchandise, elements intended to keep the youthful customer base running back include a two-player Playstation unit on a 360-degree swivel base, and a circular gumball-machine bench that accepts Skechers tokens and distributes logo-imprinted candy. The sounds of a dance club and a monolithic video wall further emphasize the techno atmosphere.

Client Team:
Skechers USA, Manhattan Beach, Calif. — Tony Fuller, director of construction; Mark Nason, director of retail development

Design Team:
ME Productions Inc., Marina del Rey, Calif. — Michael Eschger, principal-in-charge; Marlene Lento and Emilio Verdugo, project management and design

Architect:
MPA Architects, San Diego

Lighting Consultant:
Lighting Design Alliance, Long Beach, Calif.

General Contractor:
Innerspace Construction, Culver City, Calif.

Suppliers:
Impart, Seattle (video); DMX Music, Lake Forest, Calif. (audio); USG Ceilings, Chicago (ceiling); SCM Store Contract Management, Mississauga, Ont. (fixturing); Floor Covering Consultants Group, Culver City, Calif. (flooring); Pratt, Indianapolis (graphics); Premium Quality Lighting, Simi Valley, Calif. (lighting); Wilsonart Intl., Temple, Texas (laminates); Acme Displays, Los Angeles (mannequins/forms); Promotional Signs, Lake Forest, Calif. (signage)

Photography:
Robert Rooks, Fullerton, Calif.

Specialty Store, Sales Area 501-1500 Sq. Ft. First Place

Guinness World Records Experience

Orlando

Pavlik Design Team, Ft. Lauderdale, Fla.

To continue the fun of the main attraction, this 950-square-foot gift shop in Orlando was conceived as a futuristic research lab and database where Guinness compiles new and exciting world records. Pavlik Design Team (Ft. Lauderdale, Fla.) created a "mission central" video tower visible through store windows that makes for can't-miss street visibility. Guests enter the store through "beam me up Scotty"-style light rings. Inside, 20-foot-high ceilings and an open plan visually enlarge the space. Merchandise is presented on flexible lab carts and tall wall cases. The futuristic theme is continued with flooring, metallic surfaces, special lighting effects and the flash tower, a focal fixture outfitted with lighted glass rings and neon electrical sparks that light up randomly.

Design Team:
Pavlik Design Team, Ft. Lauderdale, Fla. — R.J. Pavlik, president/ceo; Fernando Castillo, senior project director; Christopher Urbanick, project manager

General Contractor:
Nassal Co., Orlando

Suppliers:
Nassal Co., Orlando (fixturing); Amtico Intl. Inc., Atlanta, Creative Edge, Fairfield, Iowa, Builders Specialties, Deerfield Beech, Fla., Quarrella, Toronto (flooring); Wilsonart Intl., Temple, Texas (laminates); Artex Mfg., Culver City, Calif., Lonseal, Carson, Calif., Moz Designs Inc., Oakland, Calif., Stylmark, Minneapolis, Aresys Inc., Palm Beach Gardens, Fla. (laminates)

Photography:
Myro Rosky, Ft. Lauderdale, Fla.

Specialty Store, Sales Area 501-1500 Sq. Ft. Award of Merit

Cadbury-Fox Studio

Fox Studios, Sydney, New South Wales

Synthesis Design and Display Pty. Ltd., Melbourne, Victoria

Who needs a lot of floor space to communicate the sensory delights of chocolate? Certainly not Synthesis Design and Display Pty. Ltd. (Melbourne, Victoria), designers of the tiny Cadbury-Fox Studio store in Melbourne. Piped-in chocolate smells, digital photographic flooring that depicts chocolate bars, and three-dimensional versions of Cadbury products carry the day in the diminutive store. Curved shelving mimics the packaging detail of the Cadbury dairy milk chocolate bar, and giant overhead graphics create added visual impact.

Client:
Cadbury Schweppes Pty. Ltd., Sydney, New South Wales — Dale Rees, display development manager

Design Team:
Synthesis Design and Display Pty. Ltd., Melbourne, Victoria — Jason Laity, design director; Suzy Suzic, designer; Les Laity, chairman

Suppliers:
Synthesis Design and Display Pty. Ltd., Melbourne (fixturing/ceiling/signage); Amtico Intl. Inc., Atlanta (flooring); Cal Graphics, Melbourne (graphics); Zaftech Pty. Ltd., Melbourne (lighting); Designer Laminates, Melbourne (laminates)

Photography:
Gary Lewis Photography, Melbourne

Specialty Store, Sales Area 501-1500 Sq. Ft. Award of Merit

Surefoot

Whistler, B.C.

Chute Gerdeman, Columbus, Ohio

The Surefoot store was designed to tell a big story in a small space. Designers at Chute Gerdeman (Columbus, Ohio) used every inch of real estate, especially walls, to explain how Surefoot's ski boots and orthotics — custom made in the store — can enhance skiers' performance. The graphics-intensive "fit wall" illustrates the three steps in the fitting process, using a high-tech, informational approach to reinforce Surefoot's credibility as experts. Materials such as polished and brushed stainless-steel and cast-aluminum shelving add to the high-tech feel, and an LED board provides continuous updates on weather and slope conditions.

Client Team:
Surefoot, Park City, Utah — Bob Shay, Russell Shay, Inge Alpers

Design Team:
Chute Gerdeman, Columbus, Ohio — Dennis Gerdeman, principal; Lee Peterson, strategy; Margaret Sheldon, program manager; Bob Welty, creative director and designer; Eric Daniel, graphic designer; Steve Andreano, implementation; Tina Burnham and Susan Siewny, production; Carmen Costinescu, materials sourcing

General Contractor:
John Girvan, Whistler, B.C.

Suppliers:
Excell Store Fixtures, Toronto, Robelan, Hempstead, N.Y., McNichols Fixture Manufacturer, Tampa, Fla. (fixturing); Van Dijk Carper, Cartersville, Ga., Lonseal, Carson, Calif., Prince Street Technologies, Cartersville, Ga., Atlas Carpet Mills, Los Angeles (flooring); Allemir Furniture, Lower Darwen, Lancastershire, U.K. (furniture); Andre's Imaging and Graphics, Chicago, Exhibit Pro, Columbus, Ohio (graphics); Juno Lighting, Des Plaines, Ill., Tech Lighting, Chicago, Abolite, Cincinnati (lighting); High Tech Electronic Displays, Clearwater, Fla., Replex Plastics, Mt. Vernon, Ohio (signage); Alaskan Moose, Westerville, Ohio (illustration)

Photography:
Mark Steele Photography, Columbus, Ohio

Specialty Store, Sales Area 501–1500 Sq. Ft. Award of Merit

Atom & Eve
Promenade Mall, Thornhill, Ont.
II By IV Design Associates Inc., Toronto

A children's footwear retailer wanted a refreshing, appealing shopping environment aimed at upscale parents and grandparents. Using Atom & Eve's lighthearted logo and apple icon as a focal point, II By IV Design Associates Inc. (Toronto) created a clean, playful design at the Promenade Mall in Thornhill, Ont.

Vinyl flooring with a gameboard-like pattern fills the extra-wide aisles. The logo repeats itself outside and inside, mounted on a translucent storefront header panel, and acting as departmental identifiers above the merchandising panels.

An iconic shiny red apple stands outside the store line, with a doorway cut through it to create a magical, inviting portal. Inside the store, the apple has been sliced away, revealing its white flesh and seeds. An oversized graphic of green apples accents the wall behind the cashwrap. And in dynamic suspended mobiles, bright green apples appear to fall toward the bowls of real apples on display cubes.

A giant green apple graphic in the back is flanked by backlit lifestyle images of a boy and girl at play. Below that, a large-screen TV plays video movies and cartoons. There are also tiers of benches and dozens of plush animals to keep youngsters occupied while parents shop. Everything is clean and bright: no-fuss epoxied MDF, edge-lit Plexiglas®, cherry-colored plastic laminate and neutral stone surfaces.

A reluctant landlord fought the design as too niche and playful for the upscale mall, especially given the obtrusive apple doorway in such a prime corner location. Positive sales figures, however, have made the store the apple of everybody's eye.

Client:
Ninett Wasserman, Thornhill, Ont.

Design Team:
II BY IV Design Associates Inc., Toronto — Dan Menchions and Keith Rushbrook, partners; Jenny Lee and Nancy Lem, design team

General Contractor:
Straight Line Construction, Toronto

Suppliers:
Bad Dog Graphics, Oakville, Ont. (display application); Convenience Group, Toronto (glass film); Compusign, N. York, Ont. (graphics); McCowan Mfg., Scarborough, Ont. (metal risers, light display above cash desk); Litemore Distributing, Weston, Ont. (lighting); Storewood Industries, Weston, Ont. (millwork); Mobilflex, Mississauga, Ont. (grill door); Elizabeth Bailey, Toronto (murals); Ciot Marble & Granite, Concord, Ont. (stone floor); Betsy Sumner Agencies, Willowdale, Ont. (fabric); Laird Plastics, Mississauga, Ont. (acrylic); The Sullivan Source, Toronto (carpet); Benjamin Moore Paint Co., Montvale, N.J. (paint); Flortech Distributors, Markham, Ont. (vinyl flooring)

Photography:
David Whittaker, Toronto

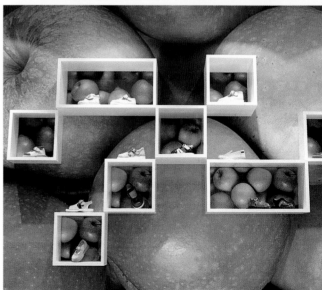

Specialty Store, Sales Area 1501-3000 Sq. Ft. First Place

The Planetarium Shop
at the Rose Center for Earth and Space

The American Museum of Natural History, New York

JGA Inc., Southfield, Mich.

Visitors to the Rose Center for Earth and Space can continue their scientific mission in this space-age-themed gift shop. Highly trafficked because of its location immediately off the visitors' entrance to the museum, the shop's design makes use of every inch of space. Merchandise seems to float on tall pole fixtures that integrate signage, and custom vitrines house higher-end products, such as jewelry and collectibles. A high-tech palette of blue, gray, glass and aluminum furthers the space theme, and a cove-dome ceiling in the center of the store is painted silver and illuminated with blue neon.

Client Team:
The Rose Center for Earth and Space, New York — Paul Murawski, general merchandise manager; David Harvey, vp, exhibitions; Joel Sweimler, exhibition coordinator; Karen Newitts, visual merchandising manager; Jennifer Kowalsky, graphic and production design manager

Design Team:
JGA Inc., Southfield, Mich. — Ken Nisch, chairman; Mike Curtis and Mike Benincasa, creative directors; Arvin Stephenson, project manager; Eva Knutson, designer; Stephanie Gach, color and materials manager; Teresa Brown, senior draftsperson

Architect of Record:
Polshek Partnership Architects LLP, New York

Lighting Consultant:
Illuminating Concepts, Farmington Hills, Mich.

General Contractor:
Morse Diesel Intl., New York

Suppliers:
ALU, New York, Display Intl. Corp., E. Miami Lake, Fla. (fixturing); Innovative Marble & Tile, Hauppauge, N.Y. (flooring); Formica Corp., Cincinnati (laminates); Charles Loomis, Kirkland, Wash., Hess America, Shelby, N.C., Targetti-Tivoli, Santa Ana, Calif., Tech Lighting, Chicago, Nordic Aluminum, Atlanta (lighting); Exhibit Works, New York (millwork); Benjamin Moore Paint Co., Montvale, N.J., ICI Dulux Paints, Cleveland, Ralph Lauren Paints, Cleveland (paints); Citadel Architectural Products, Indianapolis (wallcoverings)

Photography:
Laszlo Regos, Berkley, Mich.

Specialty Store, Sales Area 1501-3000 Sq. Ft. Award of Merit

Skechers USA

Universal City Walk, Universal City, Calif.

ME Productions Inc., Marina del Rey, Calif.

Skechers Universal City Walk store was the prototype representing the retailer's move from an industrial street look to a more high-tech, club-like design. An entertainment venue in itself, the store combines a sleek palette of blues, glass and metal with plenty of high-tech toys for shoppers. Playstation and Internet kiosks are stationed near the lounge area, and video monitors are everywhere — incorporated into displays, lining the store's music wall, and studding a Skechers globe at the cashwrap. Undulating backwalls and perforated-aluminum ceilings draw customers through the space and add to the club atmosphere.

Client Team:
Skechers USA, Manhattan Beach, Calif. — Mark Nason, vp retail development; Tony Fuller, director of construction

Design Team:
ME Productions Inc., Marina del Rey, Calif. — Michael Eschger, president; Marlene Lento and Emilio Verdugo, design team

Architect:
MPA Architects, San Diego

Lighting Consultant:
Lighting Design Alliance, Los Angeles

General Contractor:
Innerspace Construction, Los Angeles

Suppliers:
Impart, Seattle (audio/video); USG Interiors, Chicago (ceiling); Premier Displays, Cypress, Calif. (fixturing); Floorcoverings Consultants Group, Culver City, Calif. (flooring); Pratt, Indianapolis (graphics); Premium Quality Lighting, Simi Valley, Calif. (lighting); Wilsonart Intl., Temple, Texas (laminates); Promotional Signs, Lake Forest, Calif. (signage)

Photography:
Robert Rooks, Fullerton, Calif.

Specialty Store, Sales Area 1501-3000 Sq. Ft. Award of Merit

Carolina Herrera

Madison Avenue, New York

Yabu Pushelberg, Toronto

Carolina Herrera wanted her first North American flagship store to represent the style and fashion of its New York neighborhood. This was especially important because the three-level, 3000-square-foot store is housed in the landmark Hubert de Givenchy building on Madison Avenue. At the same time, the store — devoted to Herrera's New York and bridal collections — was to be in keeping with the Herrera aesthetic: a place that epitomized the fashion doyenne's timeless design infused with sophisticated modernity.

Yabu Pushelberg (Toronto) achieved this specific intent by creating an interior concept based on what it called "a return to traditional materials updated in true modern fashion." And it based its design on the personal qualities and tastes of the designer herself, someone who exemplifies the rarified New York shopper.

According to the designer, "The environment has been conceived as the antithesis of the 'big box' trend to a more discreet shopping environment that espouses a return to the traditional salon rather than a brash commercial aesthetic for a true sense of luxurious modernity." To that end, design details — including custom fixtures and furnishings — were pared back to set the stage for the clothing. Signature one-of-a-kind furniture (chairs, stools, sofa day beds) were covered in striped silk. In the true salon tradition, the couture collection is organized sparingly throughout the store.

Client Team:
Carolina Herrera, New York — Carolina Herrera, owner; Claudia Thomas, president/ceo; Yuta Powell, managing partner; David Spector, project manager

Design Team:
Yabu Pushelberg, Toronto — Glenn Pushelberg, managing partner; George Yabu, creative director; Gary Chain, Andrew Kimber and Fabienne Moureaux, design lead and team; Cirilo Fonacier, Shane Park, Catherine Chan, Sunny Leung, Alex Edward and Wilson Lau, technical team; Kevin Storey, project manager

General Contractor:
IDI Construction Ltd., New York

Suppliers:
Perfection Rugs, Toronto (carpet); Primavera, Toronto, Telio & Cie, Toronto (fabrics); Louis Interiors, Toronto (furniture); Sullivan Source, Toronto (wood flooring); Erik Cabinets, Hamilton, Ont. (millwork and fixture contractor); TPL Marketing Inc., Toronto (lighting); Kai Leather Product Design, Toronto (leather); Moss & Lam, Toronto (special wall finish); Big Apple Sign Corp., New York (signage)

Photography:
David Joseph, New York

Specialty Store, Sales Area 3001-5000 Sq. Ft. First Place

Specialty Store, Sales Area 3001-5000 Sq. Ft. First Place

Polo Sport SoHo

New York

BAR Architects, San Francisco, and Timothy Morgan Associates, New York

Unique in its ability to encompass a very broad product range appealing to a wide demographic, Polo Ralph Lauren chose to highlight one segment of this broad audience in the "Sportsman" style store in SoHo. Subtly minimal yet still comfortable in the Ralph Lauren style, the store is a contemporary backdrop to a wide mix of merchandise. Floor fixtures echo a classical yet contemporary feel without being trendy, and more rustic elements such as reclaimed pine flooring contrast elegantly with the detailed steel storefront and fixtures.

Client:
Polo Ralph Lauren Store Development, New York —
Michelle Kirschtein, store development

Design Team:
BAR Architects, San Francisco — Richard Beard, principal-in-charge; Michael Gilmore and Laura Brezel, design team

Architect of Record:
Timothy Morgan Associates, New York

Outside Consultants:
Precision Glass & Metal, Maspeth, N.Y., Mark Albrecht Designs, Long Island City, N.Y., Face Design, New York, Lindfors Tubebending, Plymouth, Minn.

General Contractor:
Richter+Ratner Contracting Corp., Maspeth, N.Y.

Suppliers:
Proco Wood Products, Osseo, Minn. (millwork)

Photography:
Doug Dun, San Francisco

Specialty Store, Sales Area 3001-5000 Sq. Ft. Award of Merit

Specialty Store, Sales Area 3001–5000 Sq. Ft. Award of Merit

Takashimaya Bath & Beauty

New York

M.R. Architecture + Decor, New York

Originally located in the back on the ground floor of Takashimaya (New York), the Bath & Beauty department became so successful it needed more space. So the retailer moved it to the sixth floor, convinced that loyal customers would find their way there. Designers at M.R. Architecture + Décor (New York) fashioned the space in true Takashimaya style, with nature and luxury reigning supreme at the new department.

Features include concrete flooring textured to resemble a Japanese sand garden, a bronzed "thicket" complete with real birds' nests and butterflies, planting wells and a tiered ceiling designed to resemble stone-tossed ripples in a pond. Product is displayed on glass shelving, some semi-covered with aluminum-leaf sliding panels. Custom bronze and glass carts each contain different product lines.

Client Team:
Tadahiko Hatano, New York — Corliss Tyler, Ellen DeCresie

Design Team:
M.R. Architecture + Décor, New York — David Mann, William Clukies, Sophie Brouzes, design team

Lighting Consultant:
Cooley Monato Lighting, New York

Suppliers:
J. Robert Scott, New York (fabrics); Studio Source, New York (fixturing); Stone Source, New York (flooring); Modernature, New York (furniture)

Photography:
Formula Z/S, New York

Specialty Store, Sales Area 3001–5000 Sq. Ft. Award of Merit

the Levi's® store

Seattle

Bergmeyer Associates Inc., Boston/Checkland Kindleysides, Leicester, U.K.

Levi Strauss & Co. (San Francisco) tapped designers from two continents — Checkland Kindleysides (Leicester, England) and Bergmeyer Associates (Boston) — for the design of its specialty flagship in Seattle — the Levi's® store.

Charged with repositioning the Levi's brand to connect with youthful shoppers, designers chose to break the "denim wall" mold by hanging or resting product on flexible shelves, allowing the fabrics' individual characteristics to speak for themselves. Wall systems display splashes of product, with unfolded merchandise strapped down for flair.

A simple matrix of movable poles and wall sockets serves as the basic merchandising system, but because it allows for minimal storage, stock can be found behind translucent doors, available to customers and staff.

The store's contemporary look is carried out through the use of uniquely integrated graphics and digital projections of art and film from local artists. Instead of traditional material, wide, translucent Simplex PVC strips serve as video projection screens.

Client Team:
Levi Strauss & Co., San Francisco — Paul Loux, associate director of store design; Theresa Kent, senior project manager, store design; Chad Hinson, visual merchandising manager; David Bobrow, digital media content manager

Design Team:
Bergmeyer Associates Inc., Boston

Checkland Kindleysides, Leicester, U.K. — Jeff Kindleysides, co-founder; Jason West, director of design; David Wright, design director; Carl Murch and Geoff Bogacki, senior designers; Russell Ashdown, designer

Architect:
Bergmeyer Associates Inc., Boston — David Tubridy, AIA, president; Joseph Nevin, Jr., principal-in-charge; Claudette Lavoie L'Huillier, associate-in-charge; John Weglarz, project manager; Andy Estabrooks, job captain; Joseph Fiorello, Jr. and John Turner, designers; Jamie Roark, junior designer

Lighting Consultant:
The Lighting Design Group, Allston, Mass.

General Contractor:
Richter+Ratner, Maspeth, N.Y.

Suppliers:
Edwards Technologies Inc., El Segundo, Calif. (audio/video); Garcy Corp., Clifton, N.J. (furniture); Andre's Imaging and Graphics, Chicago (graphics); Standard Electric, Wilmington, Mass. (lighting); Priority Sign Co., Birmingham, Ala. (signage)

Photography:
Chun Y Lai, New York

Specialty Store, Sales Area 5001-10,000 Sq. Ft. First Place

Specialty Store, Sales Area 5001-10,000 Sq. Ft. First Place

The Disney Store

Maihama, Tokyo

Disney Store Inc., Glendale, Calif.

To establish Disney's signature presence in a new 11,500-square-foot flagship in Tokyo, Disney Stores' Design Development Group appealed to their audience's love of all things Hollywood. In the multi-level entertainment-themed mall where the store is located, design criteria required a "theater marquee" themed storefront. So Disney created an homage to "The Golden Age of Hollywood."

The store's exterior features a 49-foot-high skylit entrance tower atrium with a custom-faceted spiral panel design, bas-relief panels, metal character finials and a synchronized light and sound show. Inside, a central icon that can be changed seasonally features a circular coffered ceiling with soffit lighting and a timed light, motion and sound show. Spinning mechanics make two-dimensional characters "dance." Specialty floor fixtures reflect the thematic art deco design and provide innovative ways of displaying hard and softline products. Wall bays have repositionable pilasters to easily change merchandise presentations.

Design Team:
The Disney Store Inc., Design and Property Development Group, Glendale, Calif./Tokyo — Jeff SooHoo, manager, design development; Stan Dodd, design team director

Architect:
Linane/Drews Architects, Burbank, Calif.

General Contractor:
Zeniya Co. Ltd., Tokyo

Suppliers:
Semba Corp., Tokyo (fixtures and furniture); Zeniya Co. Ltd., Tokyo (ceiling); Tajima Inc., Tokyo (flooring); Photobition, New York (graphics); Ruzika Lighting, Irvine, Calif. (lighting); Imagine That, Valencia, Calif. (mannequins/forms); Global Entertainment, N. Hollywood, Calif. (props/decoratives); Artech Intl. Inc., Tokyo (signage)

Photography:
Noriake Kosuge, Tokyo

Specialty Store, Sales Area 5001-10,000 Sq. Ft. Award of Merit

Data Info

Helsinki, Finland

Retail Planning Associates, Columbus, Ohio

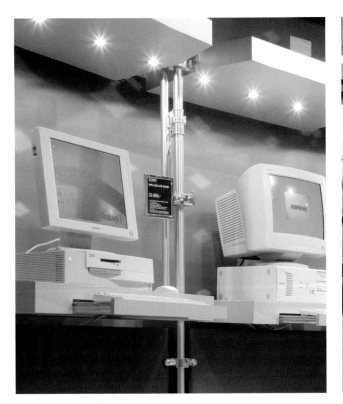

High-tech products and services often don't seem tangible to the average customer, so marketing this sort of "vaporware" is a huge challenge, especially for those charged with designing store environments around it.

But Data Info, a new store in Helsinki, Finland, gives substance and clarity to three high-tech brands brought under one roof. The store provides turnkey communications solutions by integrating the offerings of an information technology company, a cell-phone operator and a wireless communications expert.

Retail Planning Associates (Columbus, Ohio) handled the task by creating three separate "worlds" that converge in the store's nucleus. Each world is color-coded and distinguished by wood flooring, curved ceiling elements, special lighting and shield-like sign posts that lead customers to graphic panels and monitors introducing the three brands. Minimalist fixtures disappear within the environment so that graphics and products can take center stage. Vivid colors draw shoppers in and bold informational graphics guide them through the space.

Client:
Sonera, Helsinki, Finland

Design Team:
Retail Planning Associates, Columbus, Ohio — Doug Cheesman, ceo; Peter McIlroy, account executive; Jeff McCall, project director/strategist; Paul Hamilton, environmental designer; David Denniston, graphic designer; Perry Kotick, lighting designer

Suppliers:
ALU, New York (fixturing); Oksasen Rakenne, ja Kalustetyo, Helsinki, Finland (custom fixturing and cabinetry)

Photography:
Juha Salminen, Sorvi, Helsinki, Finland

Specialty Store, Sales Area 5001-10,000 Sq. Ft. Award of Merit

Sephora

Showcase at MGM Grand, Las Vegas

Sephora AAP, San Francisco

For its second Las Vegas store, Sephora maintained its signature red, black and white look while adding a few twists that make it seem right at home on the Strip. Above the store's clear glass front, an 8-foot-high Sephora sign continuously changes colors and patterns. Adding to the storefront appeal, Sephora makeup artists can be seen at work in the upper-level windows. To entice shoppers from the lower level (which houses fragrances and private-label products) to the upper level (where color and treatment products are located), the escalator well is finished in black handpainted glass featuring Sephora's familiar perfume bottles accented with fiberoptics.

Design Team:
Sephora AAP, San Francisco — Barbara Emerson and Ramona Escano, design and planning; David Rohloff, manager of animations/visual; Pamela Quinn, project manager/construction

Architect:
Thomas Bond & Associates, Irvine, Calif.

General Contractor:
Fisher Development, San Francisco

Suppliers:
AEI, Seattle (audio/video); RTC Industries, Schaumburg, Ill. (fixtures); Corniche Carpet, Oakland, Calif. (carpet); Innovative Tile & Marble, Hauppauge, N.Y. (tile); Chroma Copy, San Francisco (graphics); Weidenbach Brown, San Francisco (lighting); Sephora Animations, San Francisco (props/decoratives); Chandler Signs, Oceanside, Calif. (exterior sign); Sephora Animations, San Francisco (interior signage)

Photography:
Ronald Modre & Associates, Tustin, Calif.

RECEIVERS

Specialty Store, Sales Area Over 10,000 Sq. Ft. First Place

The Wiz

New York

Retail Planning Associates, Columbus, Ohio

The Wiz prides itself on being more than just an electronics store. So the goal of the design was to raise awareness, interest and understanding of technology by encompassing all the elements of entertainment — music, movies, events, cable, Internet, phone service and hardware — under one roof.

Designers at Retail Planning Associates (Columbus, Ohio) segmented products by zones to create visual accessibility in the blue-saturated store. A tower of monitors provides a screen view from any perspective and showcases cable services and Internet access from The Wiz's parent company, Cablevision.

Communicating the store's dedication to customer interaction with technology, "Find Your Muze" panels in the music/movie zone feature sunken monitors highlighting product selections. The music department and Ticketmaster are tucked in the rear of the store to draw people in. (The Wiz holds a reputation for selling CDs at a lower price than its competition.) Flex zones act as promotional vehicles, displaying seasonal graphics and announcing the product offering.

The overall look of the store is high-tech, but inviting. Unlike typical electronics stores, wires and cables are hidden behind large panel graphics, there are no visible cardboard-boxed stock and even the open-grid ceiling plays a role in the interior design.

Client Team:
The Wiz, New York — Tosso Koken, executive vp, sales and marketing; Ed Pettersen, vp, design and construction; Charlie Better, project director; Marcel Lamberti, director of facilities services; Frank Riggio, design director; Ralph Bernardo, visual merchandise director; Steve Marciano, design manager

Design Team:
Retail Planning Associates, Columbus, Ohio — Doug Cheesman, ceo; Diane Perduk Rambo, executive vp and director of creative and studio operations; Paul Hamilton, senior environmental designer; Perry Kotick, senior lighting designer; Jim Penn, senior planner; Dave Spurbeck, documentation specialist; Beth Mulick, project coordinator; Steve Sukokics, implementation specialist; Scott Hagely, project director

Suppliers:
Atlas Carpet Mills, Los Angeles (carpet); Gerbert Ltd., Lancaster, Pa. (flooring); Sherwin-Williams, Cleveland, Benjamin Moore Paint Co., Montvale, N.J. (paint); Wilsonart Intl., Temple, Texas, Nevamar, Odenton, Md., Formica Corp., Cincinnati (plastic laminate); Morton Powder Coatings, Reading, Pa. (special finish); Armstrong World Industries, Lancaster, Pa. (wallbase); PermaGrain Products, Newtown Square, Pa. (wood flooring); Dan Binford & Associates, Cincinnati, Knoll, E. Greenville, Pa., Haworth, Holland, Mich. (furniture); Action Group, Columbus, Ohio (TV towers); J&S Construction, Woodhaven, N.Y. (perimeter wall units and gondolas); P&S Professional, St. Petersburg, Fla. (music browsers); Neriani, Windsor, Conn. (millwork)

Photography:
Michael Houghton, StudiOhio, Columbus, Ohio

Specialty Store, Sales Area 5001-10,000 Sq. Ft. Award of Merit

Johnny Morris,
Bass Pro Shops Outdoor World

Opry Mills Mall, Nashville, Tenn.

Bass Pro Shops Inc., Springfield, Mo.

To create a destination that would delight and inspire lovers of the great outdoors, the Bass Pro Shops in-house team conceived an Adirondack-style lodge theme customized to the regional fishing and hunting heritage. A 22,000-gallon aquarium houses indigenous species and is sometimes used for casting demonstrations. The store also includes an indoor putting green and archery range.

The materials palette incorporates natural logs, heavy timber and local stone. And in keeping with corporate philosophy, principles of sustainable design were used in the project. Use of natural light, roof monitors, reclaimed materials and responsible construction methods make for a strong environmental statement.

Design Team:
Bass Pro Shops Inc., Springfield, Mo. — Tom Jowett, vp, design and development; Tom Reiss, vp, retail; Tom Gammon, director of construction; Mark Tuttle, director of architecture; Steve Slaten, project manager, construction; Jason Hairline, project designer; Bonnie Boldt, interior project manager; Russ Halley, project interiors; Mardi Roberts, taxidermy; Will Clark, marine; Joe Sunseri, food and beverage; Ray Fitzgerald, store planning manager; Steve Kuhn, loss prevention

Architect of Record:
The Wischmeyer Architects, Springfield, Mo.

General Contractor:
Centex Rooney Construction Co. Inc., Kansas City, Mo.

Outside Consultants:
Butler, Rosenbury & Partners, Springfield, Mo. (signage and visual); Randy Burkett Lighting Design Inc., St. Louis (lighting); Spaid Associates, St. Louis (landscape architect)

Suppliers:
Oklahoma Fixture Co., Tulsa (fixturing); Sunbelt Scenic Studios Inc., Tempe, Ariz., Branson Sign & Neon Inc., Branson, Mo., Garage Graphics, Springfield, Mo. (signage); Concept Fiberglass Specialties, Springfield, Mo. (fiberglass tree wraps); Design 101, Atlanta (murals); Dream Themes, Tampa, Fla. (arcade targets)

Photography:
John Stillman Photography, Hollywood, Fla.

Specialty Store, Sales Area Over 10,000 Sq. Ft. Award of Merit

Specialty Store, Sales Area Over 10,000 Sq. Ft. Award of Merit

REI Denver Flagship Class Store

Denver

Mithun, Seattle

Basing its store design on the corporate mission of environmental preservation, recreation and education, REI also preserved a Denver landmark when it opened its Flagship Class Store. The former site of a coal-fired electric powerhouse for Denver's trolley system, the 95,000-square-foot store was designed using the building's existing wood, brick and steel features where possible.

Designers at Mithun (Seattle) organized the store into specialty shops and included an auditorium, café, gallery, repair shops and a play area. The store also features REI's customary, specially designed features, such as water-filter and stove-test stations, a test mountain-bike trail and a mammoth climbing pinnacle, which encourage customers to test-drive the merchandise. Emphasizing limited use of new materials, designers employed concrete, engineered wood, reclaimed wood decking, exposed structures and systems, low-VOC products, recycled countertop materials and salvaged steel and masonry.

The location also takes advantage of the city's major bike path routes and the Platte River whitewater kayak course — two forms of recreation that bring REI's target customers right to the door.

Client Team:
Recreational Equipment Inc., Kent, Wash. — Jerry Chevassus, vp, retail development; Laura Rose, retail design coordinator; Elaine Jorgenson, merchandise presentation; Peter Emsky, retail construction coordinator

Design Team:
Mithun, Seattle — Bert Gregory, principal-in-charge; Rob Deering, project manager; Ken Boyd, project architect; Uwe Bergk, interior designer; Jim Brown, Chris Butler, Masumi Saito, Lynn Robbins, Clement King, Craig Brooks and Craig Synnesvedt, project team

General Contractor:
Hensel Phelps Construction Co., Greeley, Colo.

Outside Consultants:
J. Miller & Associates, Seattle (lighting); Trademark Sign and Display Corp., Seattle (signage)

Suppliers:
Electromedia, Denver, Sound Products, Eden Prairie, Minn., Bose Corp., Framingham, Mass. (audio/visual); Armstrong World Industries, Lancaster, Pa. (ceiling); REI Construction Shop, Kent, Wash., M. Lavine Design Workshop, Cold Spring, Minn. (fixturing); Masland Carpets, Mobile, Ala. (carpet); Daltile, Dallas, Pratt & Larsen, Portland, Ore. (flooring); Chuckanut Design, Bellingham, Wash. (furniture); Photobition, Denver (graphics); ETC Source Four, Middleton, Wis., Kolbe & Kolbe, Wasau, Wis., Altman Stage Lighting, Yonkers, N.Y., Pauluhn, Pearland, Texas, Amerlux, Fairfield, N.J., Thomas Daybrite, Tupelo, Miss., Litelab, Buffalo, N.Y. (lighting); Fusion Specialties Inc., Broomfield, Colo. (mannequins/forms); McNichols Co., Tampa, Fla. (metal mesh); Timber Creek, Ketchum, Idaho (reclaimed timbers); Trademark Sign & Display Corp., Seattle, National Sign Network, Carlsbad, Calif. (signage); Designtex, New York (wallcoverings)

Photography:
Robert Pisano, Seattle

Specialty Store, Sales Area Over 10,000 Sq. Ft. Award of Merit

88

Specialty Store, Sales Area Over 10,000 Sq. Ft. Award of Merit

Liquor Control Board of Ontario (LCBO) Kiosk

Sherway Gardens, Etobicoke, Ont.

The International Design Group, Toronto

The LCBO Millennium Program, entitled "Celebrate 2000," brought select products to various Ontario shopping centers that lacked permanent Liquor Control Board of Ontario (LCBO) stores. The modular kiosks were intended for temporary display, but because of the success of the Sherway Gardens kiosk, it has retained a lasting place on the mall floor.

A rectangle of showcases comprises the island's perimeter, and two interior display units, capped in a wooden arch, form a bridge, emblazoned with the LCBO logo. Clear signage, ample lighting and light-colored birch wood speak the signature characteristics of the permanent stores. Neutral materials allow the jewel-toned bottles to be the focus, and corner blocks feature a still-life representation of a wine bottle and bouquets of complementary-colored flowers.

Internally illuminated display "beds" house a variety of liquors and wines, and because the 10-by-20-foot space is self-contained, the displays serve double-duty as storage, housing stock inside (and can be locked at closing time).

Client:
LCBO, Toronto — Jacqueline Bonic, director of store development

Design Team:
The International Design Group, Toronto — Ron Maclachlan, managing director; David Newman, design director; Ron Mazereeuw, senior designer

General Contractor:
Salwood General Contractors, Mississauga, Ont.

Suppliers:
Salwood General Contractors, Mississauga, Ont. (birch wood); Dramex Metals, Toronto (decorative mesh); Rohm & Haas Canada, Toronto (opaque white Plexiglas); Octolam, Toronto (brushed aluminum); Juno Lighting, Toronto (incandescent/fluorescent lighting); Forbo Industries Inc., Hazleton, Pa. (Marmoleum)

Photography:
Richard Johnson, Interior Images, Toronto

Clearnet Kiosk

Richmond, B.C.
burdifilek, Toronto

To extend the reach of its flagship stores and promote dual branding for its Clearnet PCS and Mike products, Clearnet launched a kiosk program in mall locations across Canada. Working within a 10-by-15-foot space, burdifilek (Toronto) designed two L-shaped display counters (one for Clearnet and one for Mike). Separately, they articulate the two brands; together, they form a harmonious rectangle.

The clean, crisp design features bright white Corian counters to bounce light from the surrounding mall and colored fluorescent light — green for Clearnet and blue for Mike. The kiosk's longer sides showcase products, and custom counter displays on each side are interactive so that customers can browse with or without assistance.

Client:
Clearnet, Scarborough, Ont.

Design:
burdifilek, Toronto — Diego Burdi, design director; Paul Filek, managing partner; Anna Jurkieqicz, designer

General Contractor:
Pancor Industries, Mississauga, Ont.

Suppliers:
Woodland Industries, Mississauga, Ont. (fixturing); Taxi Advertising & Design, Toronto (graphics); Eurolite, Toronto (lighting); Dupont Corian, Wilmington, Del. (solid surfacing); Cyro Industries, Rockaway, N.J. (laminates); Daytech Mfg., Toronto (lightboxes)

Photography:
Ben Rahn, Metropoli Pictures, Brooklyn, N.Y.

Shopping Center Kiosk Award of Merit

Fox Sports Skybox

Sky Harbor International Airport, Phoenix

Fitch/AAD, Scottsdale, Ariz.

The objective was as clear and crisp as a Sunday afternoon in autumn: to create an 1800-square-foot sports bar in the Phoenix Sky Harbor International Airport that mirrors the visual elements and icons featured on the Fox Sports Television Network.

On first down, Fitch/AAD (Scottsdale, Ariz.) recreated the feel of the "live from the Fox Sports Studio" set. The bar, for example, resembles the anchor desk featured on the network's "Fox NFL Sunday" broadcast.

On second down, the designers established a high-tech environment through the use of state-of-the-art materials, fiberoptic lighting and audio/visual equipment (such as a central ring of TV monitors, with 22 live satellite feeds continuously downloading up-to-the-minute sports information).

On third down, AAD displayed authentic artifacts from local professional sports teams and signature items from the show's on-air talent (JB, Terry, Howie and Chris). Menu items are named after Fox Sports personalities. (Could the Terry Bradshaw be camera-hogging chili?)

Touchdown!

Client Team:
HMS Host, Bethesda, Md. — Stan Novack, vp, concept development; Larry Jones, executive vp, Fox Sports

Design Team:
Fitch/AAD, Scottsdale, Ariz. — Carl Schaffer, principal-in-charge; Nicolas Sherman, studio director; Colette Post Imayr, design director; Keith Heinemann, Ann Laber, Steve Rains and Brett Martin, development team

General Contractor:
Wolfe Construction, Phoenix

Suppliers:
MPO Videotronics, Newbury Park, Calif. (audio/visual); National Mallfront, Peoria, Ariz. (fixturing/signage); Associated Imports, Seattle (flooring); Fox Sports, Los Angeles (graphics); Juno Lighting, Des Plaines, Ill. (lighting); Chemetal, Easthampton, Mass., Cyro Industries, Rockaway, N.J. (laminates); Fox Sports, Los Angeles (props and decoratives); Blumenthal, Canaan, Conn. (wallcoverings)

Photography:
Norton Photography, Phoenix

√ı

Flatiron Crossing Food Court

Flatiron Crossing Shopping Center, Broomfield, Colo.

Callison Architecture Inc., Seattle

Taking advantage of the region's 300 sunny days per year, the Flatiron Crossing Food Court was designed to blur the lines between indoors and out. Clerestories and expansive glass "garage" doors bathe the food court in sunlight and let in fresh breezes; natural materials such as wood, steel and stone abound. To create the relaxed ambience of an elegant picnic, designers used strings of white lights, assorted sizes and shapes of metal and wood tables and chairs, and a large-scale, open-fire pit surrounded by a sandstone hearth. Leather lounge chairs, floor lamps with handcrafted shades and throw rugs surround the hearth to create a homey feel.

Client Team:
Westcor Partners, Phoenix — Gilbert Chester, Bob Williams, Fred Collins, David Scholl, Darrell Beach, Mike Treadwell, Lynn Lovell, Ron Kuhn and Jim Harrison

Design and Architecture:
Callison Architecture Inc., Seattle — Bob Tindall, Doug Stelling, Dennis Rogers, Judd Eddy, Scott Brown, Jennifer Carlisle, Joan Insel, Mike Riggs, John Ginn, Esther Foerderer, Fernand Ricard and Josephine Wong, design team

Outside Consultants:
Candela, Seattle (lighting); Murase Associates, Seattle (landscape architect)

General Contractor:
Roche Constructors, Greeley, Colo.

Suppliers:
Pacific Wood Systems, Eugene, Ore. (ceiling); Vintage Lumber Co., Denver, PIR Intl., Seattle (flooring); Cascade Furniture Co., Seattle, Shelby Williams Industries, Portland, Ore., Emeco USA, Seattle, Falcon, Seattle, Allied Steel Fabricators, Redmond, Wash., KAASCO, Seattle, Thomasville Contract, Seattle (furniture); Callison Architecture Inc., Seattle (graphics); Natural Selections, Seattle (lighting shades)

Photography:
Chris Eden, Seattle

Specialty Food Court or Counter-Service Restaurant Award of Merit

Atrium-Le 1000 De La Gaughetiére

Montreal

Ædifica, Montreal

Designed around an ice skating rink inside a Montreal office building, the Atrium food court reflects the surrounding urban landscape. Designers at Ædifica (Montreal) used a leaf motif of mahogany wood ceiling panels, slate tiles and an earthy color palette to create a relaxing tone, while "Slinky" lighting mimics the skaters' movements. Decorative glass panels and overhead awnings delineate zones, improve acoustics and recreate the feeling of a public square.

Client:
Le 1000 de la Gaughetiére, Montreal — Sonia Trudel, general director

Design Team:
Ædifica, Montreal — Michel Dubuc, president, partner-in-charge; Fabien Nadeau, senior designer, architect; Jean-Luc Vadeboncoeur, architect, director of construction

General Contractor:
JCB General Contractors, Montreal

Suppliers:
Heritage Ebenisterie Architectural Inc., Brossard, Que. (millwork); Telio & Cie, Montreal (fabrics); Les Importations Ciot Ltee, Montreal (slate, quartz tile flooring); Montreal Parquetry Floors Inc., Montreal (hardwood); SEG System d'Eclairage, Montreal (lighting); CAB Deco Import Export, Montreal, Triede, Montreal (furniture)

Photography:
Michel Tremblay, Montreal

Taberna de Tequila

Sky Harbor International Airport, Phoenix

Fitch/AAD, Scottsdale, Ariz.

The Taberna de Tequila manages to embrace both the fun and tradition inherent in this intoxicating elixir. The 2800-square-foot bar and restaurant is divided into two distinct sections: the fun bar area and the traditional dining area. The bar boasts bright colors and whimsical graphic elements, such as multicolored chairs with zigzag backs. Custom-designed tabletops sport sayings like, "Did I hear someone say Congo line?" and "Lick, shoot, suck." Customers belly up to two lizard-shaped standup counters where Mexican tin starlights hang overhead, and a video wall behind offers tequila facts and trivia.

The Blue Burrito Grill's more traditional atmosphere features faux-chiseled stone tables surrounded by chairs with wooden bottoms and rounded, waxed leather backs. The ceiling features the traditional Mexican "Latilla and Viga," constructed from the actual skeletons of the saguaro cactus and wooden crossbeams. A handpainted mural depicts the angel symbol of the Gran Centario Jose brand. Additionally, a working fireplace is decorated with spurs, keys, brands and other ornamental iron. And the focal point of the Agavero Room is a wall clad with a sun mask and backlit rays of sun, above a depiction of the "Stairs to Nowhere" — a Mexican tradition that symbolizes the ascent to heaven.

Client Team:
HMS Host, Bethesda, Md. — Perry Brush, director of design and construction; Terry Ell, developer and general manager

Design and Architecture:
Fitch/AAD, Scottsdale, Ariz. — Carl Schaffer, principal-in-charge; Keith Sullivan, studio director; Jennifer Reynolds, design director; Tom Higgins, Rodney Jakes, Stacy Molnar, Sudeep Dey, development team

General Contractor:
Wolfe Construction, Phoenix

Suppliers:
MPO Videotronics, Newbury Park, Calif. (audio/visual); National Mallfront, Peoria, Ariz. (ceiling/fixturing/resin tabletops/graphics/signage); Pindler & Pindler, Scottsdale, Ariz., Commercial Custom Seating, Santa Ana, Calif. (fabrics); Tile West, Phoenix (flooring); Shaffer Seating, Denver (chairs and barstools); Casa Talamantes, Albuquerque (leather chairs); Innovative Surfaces, Phoenix (stone tabletops); J&J Industries, Santa Ana, Calif. (table bases); National Mallfront, Peoria, Ariz., Juno Lighting, Des Plaines, Ill., Lumature, Scottsdale, Ariz. (lighting); Interiors for Architecture, Scottsdale, Ariz. (props/decoratives); J.M. Lynne, Ronkonkoma, N.Y., Xquest Wall Surfaces, Hackensack, N.J. (signage/wallcoverings)

Photography:
Norton Photography, Phoenix

Specialty Food Court or Counter-Service Restaurant Award of Merit

WB Stage 16

The Venetian Hotel, Las Vegas

Fitch, Columbus, Ohio

Everyone comes to Rick's place. Only Rick's place was moved from Casablanca to Las Vegas, along with Gotham City, Danny Ocean's favorite Vegas lounge and the stage where Busby Berkeley's Gold Diggers of 1933 danced their hearts out (and got them broken).

The design intent of the WB Stage 16 restaurant in the new Venetian Hotel was to provide the real look and feel of old Hollywood film sets. Fitch (Columbus, Ohio) studied actual film footage and old Warner Brothers storyboards for authenticity, and they vetoed the idea of one enormous sound stage in favor of six different dining areas, encouraging exploration.

Ceilings were brought down for intimacy, and the overall venue is surprisingly (for Las Vegas) restrained. It's lush and detailed, to be sure, but less in-your-face than so many Las Vegas attractions because it can be. Who's not familiar with the world of Bruce Wayne?

Perhaps the most thematic stretch came for the Gold Diggers of 1933 room, though the "We're In the Money" musical number from the movie is a perfect Las Vegas fit. But the gala dance routines required high ceilings and a bigger interior, so vertical lines were used to draw the eye upwards, and a 35-foot-high mirror emphasizes the depth of the space. Busby Berkeley's grand staircase becomes a staircase fragment blending into a *trompe l'oeil* mural of a staircase. The mural took 10 men a month to complete.

Client Team:
WB Stage 16 Restaurant, Orlando — Gerard O'Riordan, president; Mark McClenney, vp, development; John Baydale, vp, operations; Patrick Harnett, vp, merchandising

Design Team:
Fitch, Columbus, Ohio — Bill Faust, ceo; Mark Artus, principal-in-charge; Lynn Rosenbaum, project manager; Todd Rowland, senior environments designer; Michele Hofer, environments designer; Brandy Shearer, communications designer; Steve Pottschmidt, senior implementation designer; Allison Tuller, implementation designer; Tim Baker, architectural designer

Architect:
Fitch, Columbus, Ohio

General Contractor:
Mark Schaefer, Sedona, Ariz.

Design Consultants:
Karl Sjodahl, Metuchen, N.J. (audio/visual content); Paul Haney, Los Angeles (set fabrication and construction); Tom Martin, N. Hollywood, Calif. (audio/visual design and installation); Intech Engineering Group, Phoenix (mechanical, electrical engineers); Caruso, Turley, Scott, Phoenix (structural engineers); Lighting Management Inc., New York (lighting design and supply); MSLD&C, New York (set lighting design)

Suppliers:
Brass and Stainless, Dallas (kitchen design and bar fabrication); Einsohn Group, Dallas (banquette seating fabrications); Showbiz Enterprises, Van Nuys, Calif. (drapery fabrication); Sunburst Construction Co., Las Vegas (millwork); DaNite Sign Co., Columbus, Ohio (mallfront sign fabrication); Studio Busters, Dallas (custom lighting fixtures); Plessi, Plessiville, Que. (retail apparel fixtures); Mike Connor, Los Angeles (props and decoratives); Shafer Commercial Seating, Denver, Sandler Seating, Atlanta, Rattan Interiors, Burbank, Calif., Keilhauer, Scarborough, Ont. (dining furnishings, general seating and bar seating); Durkan, Greenville, Miss. (carpeting supply)

Photography:
Mark Steele, Columbus, Ohio

Sit-Down Restaurant First Place

Stars on Huntington

Boston

Fitch, Columbus, Ohio

The Eat Well Restaurant Group wanted to create something different than Boston's traditional, wood-paneled dining-room fare. So Stars — a restaurant that mixes sleek modernism with funky boutique/hotel appointments — was born.

Designers at Fitch (Columbus, Ohio) used a circle as the restaurant's main motif. In the entry vestibule, an interior wall suspended four inches away from a supporting wall has circular cutouts lit by fluorescent tubes that cause them to glow. Portholes on exterior windows allow diners to see outside without feeling like they're eating in a fishbowl. A marble-topped community-seating table glows with embedded fiberoptics. And funky elements like Philippe Starck "Dr. No" stools, fabric-covered backlit ceiling rafts and high-definition projectors beaming art images add to the hip quotient.

Client Team:
Eat Well Restaurant Group, Hingham, Mass. — Ed Kane, president; Greg Acerra, president; George O'Malley, project manager

Design Team:
Fitch, Columbus, Ohio — Mark Artus, principal-in-charge; Christian Davies, project manager; Pam Dull, creative director, on-site project manager; Alicia Taylor, senior graphic designer; Christie Landry, implementation

Architect:
BKA, Brockton, Mass.

Lighting Consultant:
Lighting Management, New City, N.Y.

General Contractor:
Cafco Construction, Boston

Suppliers:
Xibitz, Grand Rapids, Mich. (ceiling); DesignWeave Commercial Carpets, Santa Fe Springs, Calif. (carpet); Carlisle Restoration Lumber, Stoddard, Mass. (wood flooring); Crossville Ceramics, Crossville, Tenn. (tile flooring); Furniture Concepts, Malden, Mass. (banquette seating); Magis, Motta di Livenza, Italy (bar stools); Maderniea, Los Angeles (bar stools); Sandler Seating, Atlanta (dining room tables); Windham Wood Interiors Corp., Woburn, Mass. (millwork)

Photography:
Mark Steele, Columbus, Ohio

108

Upstream Restaurant

Phillip's Place Shopping Center, Charlotte, N.C.

Wagner Murray Architects, Charlotte, N.C.

Wagner Murray Architects (Charlotte, N.C.) looked to nature for inspiration when designing Upstream, a new restaurant at Phillip's Place Shopping Center in Charlotte. The venue is designed with a sensual mix of textures, materials and colors. Patterns on a textured ceiling treatment, combined with fabric-covered leaf forms, recall autumn leaves floating on a mountain stream. Ceramic shades molded in bright, freeform compositions are used with raw stainless-steel panels to create distinctive lighting fixtures. And structural columns wrapped in an arrangement of fired-ceramic frits create the illusion of birch bark. The palette is filled out with cleft-cut natural sandstone, polished stainless steel, woven fabric and mahogany.

Client:
Harper's Inc., Charlotte, N.C.

Design/Architecture:
Wagner Murray Architects, Charlotte, N.C. — David Wagner, project architect/designer; Lisa Arendas, art installations

General Contractor:
Tyler II Construction, Charlotte, N.C.

Suppliers:
Cottonwood Interiors, Kannapolis, N.C. (ceiling); Donghia Textiles, New York, Stratford Hall, Ft. Worth, Texas, Maharam, Hauppauge, N.Y. (fabrics); Danka Persing, Red Lion, Pa., Holder Restaurant Furniture, Lenoir, N.C. (furniture); Black Dog, San Anselmo, Calif. (graphics/signage); Electric Lighting, San Rafael, Calif. (lighting); Fireslate, Lewiston, Maine (laminates); Gary Sweeney, San Antonio, Texas (artwork); Paul Freund, Talking Rock, Ga. (hostess stand)

Photography:
Stan Capps, Monroe, N.C.

Sit-Down Restaurant Award of Merit

Sit-Down Restaurant Award of Merit

Cha Tea Bar

Longwood Galleria Food Court, Boston

Connor Architecture, Arlington, Mass.

The Cha Tea Bar strays from the typical food-court tenant, both in terms of appearance and product offering. In a sea of neon and plastic laminate at the Longwood Galleria Food Court in Boston, the natural, calming space — designed by Connor Architecture (Arlington, Mass.) — commands attention. Occupying only 125 square feet, the three-sided bar utilizes every visible element to its benefit.

Teas are displayed in clean, stainless-steel canisters, placed neatly in a wood grid backdrop. The food and the people also play an important part in the overall ambience, providing a theatrical appeal. Natural materials, like the Japanese maple canopy, hand-oiled soapstone bar and maple and black steel stools, reflect the shop's natural teas and gift pottery. Golden-toned, suspended light fixtures illuminate the bar in a soft glow. And interlocking maple shelves house the artful crafts while a clear glass display case presents pastries, muffins and sandwiches.

Client Team:
Cha Tea Bar, Boston — Kim and Mike Lefebvre, owners

Design Architect:
Connor Architecture, Arlington, Mass. — Mark Connor, principal; Lee Connor, interior design; Rob Weir, designer

Design:
Skymedia, Boston — Rich Kendall, owner

General Contractor:
Cafco, Boston

Suppliers:
Windham Wood Interiors, Woburn, Mass. (fixturing); ISA Furniture, Toronto (furniture); Wolfers Lighting, Boston (lighting); Cyr Sign & Banner, Medford, Mass. (signage)

Photography:
Anton Grassl, Boston

Specialty Food Shop First Place

Liquor Control Board of Ontario (LCBO) Flagship Store

Ottawa, Ont.

Fiorino Design Inc., Toronto

The 28,000-square-foot Liquor Control Board of Ontario (LCBO) flagship is the largest of its 600 retail outlets and the first two-level retail space. Well-versed in creating spaces for LCBO, Fiorino Design Inc. (Toronto) used design to convey two shopping options: Customers can purchase from the general product line on street level or head directly to the lower-level vintage fine wine and premium products area, which is more service oriented. Integration of the two levels was crucial, so designers connected them with elevators as well as a dramatic staircase.

The main floor features an oval-shaped power aisle anchored by various feature departments, while a central power aisle acts as a secondary means of traffic flow. High levels of light encourage browsing throughout, and upscale details like custom pearwood fixturing, chandeliers, ironwork and handfinished walls create an environment shoppers want to spend time in.

Client Team:
Liquor Control Board of Ontario, Toronto — Jackie Bonic, vp, store development and real estate; Sylvie Rioux and Nancy Cardinal, visual merchandising

Design Team:
Fiorino Design Inc., Toronto — Nella Fiorino, principal; Vasco Pires and Vilija Gacionis, designers

Design Coordinator:
Dynar Architects Inc., Kanata, Ont.

General Contractor:
Westeinde Construction Ltd., Nepean, Ont.

Suppliers:
David Adolphus, Highland Creek, Ont. (murals); Hutton Bielmann Design Inc., London, Ont. (fixturing); Forbo Industries, Hazleton, Pa., Ciot Marble & Granite Inc., Concord, Ont. (flooring); Nevamar, Odenton, Md., Formica Canada Inc., Etobicoke, Ont. (laminates)

Photography:
David Whittaker, Toronto

Pusateri's Specialty Food Market

Toronto

Gervais Harding Associates, Montreal

Renovated and expanded from 13,000 to 16,000 square feet, Pusateri's Specialty Food Market — a gourmet food icon in Toronto — veers away from the typical grocery store layout and takes its inspiration from restaurant design. Gervais Harding Associates (Montreal) redefined departments and added elements that reflect the international origins of the products.

Naturally, the design pays homage to the food itself. Cheeses spill from a marble-topped showcase, huge copper pots of coffee beans grace the coffee bar area, and olive oil has its own specialty section complete with a testing station. Mahogany and walnut display cases and wrought-iron light fixtures add to the Old World ambience.

Client:
Pusateri's Specialty Food Market, Toronto — Frank Luchetta, owner

Design Team:
Gervais Harding Associates, Montreal — Frank Di Niro, partner; Serge Prud'homme, designer/technician

Architect:
gabor+popper architects, Toronto

General Contractor:
Freed Development Corp., Toronto

Suppliers:
PGM Inc., Woodbridge, Ont. (metalwork); Panigas Group of Companies, Concord, Ont. (millwork); Ciot Tiles, Toronto, Olympia Tiles, Toronto (flooring); Litemor, Montreal (lighting); Aquamarin, Laval, Que. (fountain); Calfolia, Montreal (olive trees)

Photography:
Ron Katz, Kamdar Studios, Toronto

Specialty Food Shop Award of Merit

Sentry Foods

Madison, Wis.

Marco Design Group, Northville, Mich.

Marco Design Group (Northville, Mich.) remodeled and expanded the Sentry Foods supermarket with a design intending to appeal to the diverse customer base in the store's urban market. Unlike most grocery stores, Sentry Foods focuses mainly on merchandise — especially in the produce department — with well-lit foods and no ambient lighting, providing a dramatic effect.

The fresh seafood department features hand-sculpted metal fish swimming in translucent-blue ceiling panels and highlighted with ocean-blue neon lighting and signage. The deli, bakery and gourmet food sections continue the focus on merchandise with minimal decorative and architectural elements and a broad selection of products.

Client:
Sentry Foods, Madison, Wis. — Jay Overholt, project manager

Design Team:
Marco Design Group, Northville, Mich. — Nicholas Giammarco, president; Julie Dugas, senior designer; Sharon Morden, designer

Architect:
Strang Architects, Madison, Wis.

General Contractor:
Bogel Brothers, Madison, Wis.

Suppliers:
Creative Lighting Design, Germantown, Wis. (lighting); Kyle Connolly, Ann Arbor, Mich. (props/decoratives); Tri-Color Photographic, Royal Oak, Mich. (digital imaging); Daltile, Dallas (ceramic tile); Minds Eye Studio, Sterling Heights, Mich. (murals)

Photography:
Laszlo Regos Photography, Berkley, Mich.

Supermarket First Place

Hannaford Bros. Supermarket

Falmouth, Maine

Arrowstreet Inc., Somerville, Mass.

Designers at Arrowstreet Inc. (Somerville, Mass.) brought nature inside this farmer's market. Wood and timber construction and custom stained concrete flooring establish Hannaford Bros. as a market environment. An unusually large atrium space and "outdoor" lighting distinguish the produce department, and designers used large-scale graphics, custom casework and varying finishes to brand individual departments. At the neighborhood deli, artisan tile and metal canopies over the counter convey the feeling of a specialty store and encourage customer/staff interaction.

Client Team:
Hannaford Bros. Co., Scarborough, Maine — Dave Tovey, owner; Fred Conlogue

Design Team:
Arrowstreet Inc., Somerville, Mass. — John Cole, principal-in-charge, design architect; Dennis Carlberg, interior architect

Graphic Consultant:
Arrowstreet Graphic Design, Somerville, Mass.

Suppliers:
Kysor Warren, Conyers, Ga. (fixturing); American Decorative Concrete, Houston (flooring); Amerlux Lighting, Fairfield, N.J. (lighting); Treescapes Intl., Oceanside, Calif. (decorative trees)

Photography:
Anton Grassl, Boston

Supermarket Award of Merit

Sunny Supermarket

Nanokawa, Fukuoka, Japan

CDI Group Inc., New York

CDI Group's (New York) prototype design for the Sunny Super-market chain is based on the Japanese retailer's reputation as "The Food Experts." Graphic elements help convey the fresh-ness message, while individual departments within the store were given distinct identities. Cooking demonstrations and classes are scheduled to engage shoppers. Designers say the overall look aims to create a feeling of reverence for food.

Client Team:
Sunny Co. Ltd., Fukuoka, Japan — Ell Chi Matsumoto, president; Hiroshi Miura, store development manager

Design Team:
CDI Group Inc., New York — Gerry Lewis, chairman; Joseph Bona, president; Kaoru Yamamoto, creative director/designer; Nadia Zadniprianska, graphic designer

Photography:
CDI Group, New York

Twin Cities Travel Mart

Minneapolis-St. Paul International Airport, St. Paul, Minn.

Architectura Planning Architecture Interiors Inc., Vancouver

The Twin Cities Travel Mart in the Minneapolis-St. Paul International Airport offers weary travelers a bright, clean environment — designed by Architectura Planning Architecture Interiors Inc., Vancouver — that incorporates the natural beauty of Minnesota and the architectural nuances of the Twin Cities area.

Reflecting the bridges of Minneapolis-St. Paul, the storefront is fabricated from painted-steel bridge trusses on limestone pillars. The liberal entryway is located below the central truss, and large murals of the Minnesota landscape fill the spaces below the other two trusses. The murals change seasonally, and the two walls of the storefront are connected by an illuminated skyline with a copper bridge that wraps the storefront bulkhead.

The bridge theme continues inside the store with one truss spanning the store end to end, supporting the store's lighting. Polished granite flooring provides a clean look, and honey-maple millwork with stainless-steel accents offer a touch of warmth. Illuminated signage allows customers to find products quickly, and a centrally located cashwrap makes for a speedy checkout, ideal for airport shoppers.

Client Team:
The Paradies Shops, Atlanta — Richard Dickson, president; Gregg Paradies and Lou Bottino, senior vp's; Lynn Bennet, vp, marketing; Alex Malsky, project manager; Jeff Mason, visual director; David Quinn, regional manager

Design Team:
Architectura Planning Architecture Interiors Inc., Vancouver — Stanis Smith, president; Susan Smallenberg, director and principal-in-charge; Orest Klufas, project manager; Glenn Burwell, Carol Curren and Jeffrey Staates, project designers

Architect:
Brantingham Architects, Minneapolis

General Contractor:
NBC General Contractors, Minneapolis

Suppliers:
Intalite-Simplex Ceilings, St. Laurent, Que. (ceiling); Bishop Fixtures, Wyoming, Minn. (fixturing); Focus Inc., Vancouver, Tile & Marble Collection Inc., Atlanta (flooring); Architectura, Vancouver (graphics); Indy Lighting, Fishers, Ind., Eureka, Montreal (lighting); Chemetal, Easthampton, Mass., Wilsonart Intl., Temple, Texas (laminates); Signsations, Minneapolis (signage)

Photography:
Mitch Legget, Minneapolis

Your Northwest Travel Mart

Portland International Airport, Portland, Ore.

The Paradies Shops Inc., Atlanta

The Paradies Shops (an Atlanta-based airport retail group) opened Your Northwest Travel Mart to offer local flavor with fast, convenient service in the Portland (Ore.) International Airport.

The 1100-square-foot store is a joint effort between Paradies and an area retailer of the same name. In addition to locally made specialty food items, it carries the traditional airport fare. And it's designed to grab the attention of the passing traveler. So one of the keys in creating inviting oasis was to create an open, convenient space with easy ingress and egress. Details like a handpainted mural around the store's perimeter, highly reflective granite-flooring and cash register areas, and custom maple fixturing also inspire hurried travelers to slow down and stay awhile.

Design Team:
The Paradies Shops Inc., Atlanta — Jeff Mason, visual merchandising director
Your Northwest Travel Mart, Portland, Ore. — Linda Strand

Architect:
Architectura Planning Architecture Interiors Inc., Vancouver — Carol Curran and Orest Klufas

Suppliers:
Key Mechanical, Kent, Wash., Cecilware, New York (fixturing); Tile & Marble, Atlanta (flooring); Juno Lighting, Des Plaines, Ill. (lighting)

Photography:
Sally Painter, Portland, Ore.

TRAVEL

NEEDS

Marriott News Network

Orlando World Center Marriott, Orlando

FRCH Design Worldwide, Cincinnati

Marriott set out to reinvent the convenience-store concept format when it designed the new Marriott News Network at its largest property in Orlando. Created for an international base of theme park and convention visitors, the 1300-square-foot store is focused on a global theme.

FRCH Design Worldwide (Cincinnati) used a balance of cool and warm colors to allude to global weather conditions and connote "quick, fresh and current." Glass panels incorporate lines of longitude and latitude and map cartography, while merchandise is presented on proprietary fixtures that use graphic communication to transcend language barriers. Video monitors communicating the latest world news and a stock ticker reinforce the concept of a Marriott "newsroom."

But the Florida sun that draws so many international guests posed a lighting problem during construction: It flooded the 12-story atrium outside the shop's entrance, where there is no storefront, and threatened to wash out the merchandise. The design team offset the glare by pushing merchandise farther back in the store. The walls were darkened to deep shades of blue, red and purple to make products stand out in contrast. Also, adjustable cans and low-voltage track heads in the ceiling illuminate merchandise more precisely without over-brightening the space.

Client Team:
Marriott Intl., Washington, D.C. — Roy Muth, director of design and construction; Anna Mancebo, director of retail services; Susan Miller, national merchandise manager; Debra Schneider, senior buyer; Tammy Viney, director of retail, Marriott Orlando World Center

Design Team:
FRCH Design Worldwide, Cincinnati — Kyle Kieper, principal interior designer; Karen Pelletier, project architect and project manager; Michael Chaney, interior architect and production coordinator; Jeff Waggoner, graphic design director; Jenny Kerr, graphic design; James Frederick, visual merchandising director; Larrissa Thayer, visual merchandising

General Contractor:
Centex Rooney, Orlando

Local Architect:
HLM Design, Orlando

Suppliers:
FixDesign Fabricators Inc., Denver, ALU, New York (fixturing); Armstrong World Industries, Lancaster, Pa. (vinyl tile flooring); Gordan Intl./Hampton Products, Cincinnati (furniture); Design Communications, Denver (graphics); Wilsonart Intl., Temple, Texas (laminates); Lightolier, Fall River, Mass. (lighting); Benjamin Moore Paint Co., Montvale, N.J., Sherwin Williams, Cleveland (paint)

Photography:
Dan Forer Photography, Miami

Convenience Store Award of Merit

Illusionz

Issaquah, Wash.

Callison Architecture Inc., Seattle

Illusionz is an entertainment environment that incorporates the wonder and the-atrics of magic in an atmosphere that entices the whole family. Once a 39,000-square-foot big-box hardware store, the space allowed for multiple activities, but designers at Callison Architecture Inc. (Seattle) were challenged to avoid visual clutter and barriers.

A glowing "jewel" at the center of the spiraling lobby floor draws visitors' eyes to lighted curtains and a 16-foot-high, corrugated, perforated curved wall, which offers a veiled view of the main arcade. Two 19-foot-high cones, or wizard hats, create a portal through which visitors pass into a hallway lined with lithographs of famous magicians.

The 100-game arcade is distinguished by celestial chandeliers and separated from the children's Magicastle "disappearing" play area by a glowing green wall emblazoned with giant letters spelling "POOF." The WackyPutt miniature golf area and batting cages are splashed with graphic floor and wall patterns, and 16-foot clouds are suspended overhead. The two live performance theaters and Magicafe eating area feature custom light fixtures, bold colors and shapes and an abstract backwall mural. A suspended green wall with oval cutouts delineates the café entrance.

Client Team:
Games Unlimited, Issaquah, Wash. — Michael Dobias, president; Michael Hartzell, general manager

Design Team:
Callison Architecture Inc., Seattle — Steve Epple, principal-in-charge; Ryan Phelps, project manager; Rod Bannon, project architect; Alex Shapleigh and Ron Singler, project designers

Outside Consultants:
PNTA, Seattle, Pacific Studios, Seattle (theater); AEI Music, Seattle (sound); Pacific Restaurant Design, Seattle (restaurant); A Touch of Magic, Seattle (illusion); Signtech, Seattle (signage)

General Contractor:
RAS Builders, Issaquah, Wash.

Suppliers:
PNTA, Seattle (audio/video); Pierre Desjardins, St. Jerome, Que., Athletic Training Equipment Co., Sparks, Nev., Jack Durban, Seattle, Primeplay Systems Inc., Sparks, Nev., Darklight, Dursley, U.K. (props/decoratives); DillonWorks, Seattle (signage)

Photography:
Chris Eden, Seattle

Entertainment Facility First Place

Muvico Tampa Palms

Tampa, Fla.

Development Design Group Inc., Baltimore

Inspired by the 1950s American diner, the Muvico Starlight 20 Theater in Tampa, Fla., treats moviegoers to a highly themed environment and amenities like a children's play room and a lobby video arcade. To reach the box office — which Development Design Group (Baltimore) created as a giant 1950s-era radio — patrons walk across pavement with a green-and-rose checkered tablecloth pattern. Kiosks flanking the box office resemble diner jukeboxes, and seats behind it integrate the tail fins of 1950s autos. A second-story mock highway overpass winds along the walls through the interior. The centerpiece concession area, called the Hot Diner, is set against a night-sky backdrop and bounded by imitation gas pumps.

Client Team:
Muvico Theaters, Ft. Lauderdale, Fla. — Hamid Hashemi, president; Jeff Davis, project manager

Design Team:
Design Development Group Inc., Baltimore — Jim Andreone, Janey Gregory, Val Knauff, Debbie Bennett, Curtiss Taylor and Jose Morales, design team

Suppliers:
EAW, Whitinsville, Mass. (audio/video); Decoustics, Eto-bicoke, Ont. (ceiling); deBall, New York, Dur-a-Flex, Miami (fabrics); Masland Contract, Mobile, Ala. (flooring); L&B Empire, Valley Cottage, N.Y. (furniture); Development Design Group, Baltimore (graphics/signage); Formica Corp., Cincinnati (laminates); Penwal Industries, Rancho Cucamonga, Calif. (props/decoratives)

Photography:
Muvico Theaters, Ft. Lauderdale, Fla.

Entertainment Facility Award of Merit

Famous Players Paramount Theatre

Festival Hall, Toronto

The International Design Group Inc., Toronto

The Paramount Theatre is Famous Players' first entry into a city's downtown core. To make the debut memorable for movie-goers, The International Design Group (Toronto) used the metaphor of a light- and movement-filled journey that starts on the sidewalk outside the theater. A passage into the complex takes patrons from a visually stimulating ticket lobby to one of Canada's longest escalator rides, around a corner into the puls-ing "Vivid Lounge," through a media-packed food court, and into an almost surreal "Decompression Chamber" — complete with glowing floors and color-morphing lights. The ride culminates with the individual theater destinations. Static low-voltage light, chasing neon, pulsing and projecting theatrical lighting, end-point fiberoptics, new "spectrum morphing" light technology and blacklights add to the dynamic journey.

Client:
Famous Players Inc., Toronto — Ron Rivet, executive director

Design Team:
The International Design Group Inc., Toronto — Ron Harris, president; Andrew Gallici, project manager; Constantza Carsten, Paulic Ciskevicius, John MacDonald and Henriette Shenderey, designers

Architect:
Kirkland Partnership Inc., Toronto

General Contractor:
Ellis Don Construction, Mississauga, Ont.

Audio/Visual Consultant:
Novita, Toronto

Suppliers:
CGC, Toronto (ceiling); Moss and Lam, Toronto (faux finishes); Edwood Fixtures Inc., Toronto (fixturing); Domcor, Toronto (vinyl flooring); Gordon T. Sands, Toronto (custom carpet); Olympia Tile, Toronto (tile); Louis Interiors, Toronto (custom banquettes); ULA Intl. Corp., Toronto (tables and chairs); LK Trading, Toronto (vinyl upholstery); Chemetal, Easthampton, Mass., Octolam, Toronto, Formica Corp., Cincinnati (laminates); Eureka, Toronto, Artemide, Farmingdale, N.Y., Eurolite, Toronto, Christie Lights, Toronto (lighting); Wallis and Latinovich, Toronto (custom mirror balls); Feature Factory, Toronto (spherical TV surrounds); Para Paints, Toronto, Surface Solutions, Toronto, Sico Acrythane, Toronto (paint)

Photography:
Richard Johnson, Toronto (interior); Patrick Kennedy Photography, Etobicoke, Ont. (exterior)

Entertainment Facility Award of Merit

Dickson CyberExpress

Kowloon Station, Hong Kong

JGA Inc., Southfield, Mich.

Calling itself the world's first "clicks-and-mortar cybermall," Dickson CyberExpress is located within Kowloon Station, where 2.2 million people go each day to use Hong Kong's transit railway. In the shop, customers can explore six worlds: "Entertainment World" for books, CDs and DVDs; "E-World" for high-tech electronics; "Kiddy World" for games and toys; "Fashion World" for men's, women's and children's apparel and accessories; "iCosmetics World" for hair, skin and health products; and "Sports World" for gear, activewear and fitness products. The edited merchandise is made unlimited by 85 in-store Internet stations and multimedia interactive kiosks.

Making visual reference to the borderless nature of cyberspace, designers at JGA Inc. (Southfield, Mich.) blurred the boundaries of the physical space using sound systems, projected images and theatrical lighting that creates a constantly changing color palette. Signature global icons reinforce the "Dickson Connects the World" theme, and virtually all fixtures and finishes are glass or metal to adhere to strict flammability guidelines within the station.

Client Team:
The Dickson Group of Companies, Kowloon, Hong Kong — Dickson Poon and Mei Ho

Design Team:
JGA Inc., Southfield, Mich. — Ken Nisch, chairman; Gordon Eason, creative director; Eva Knutson, designer; Stephanie Gach, materials and finishes manager

Architect:
Gensler Intl. (HK) Ltd., Hong Kong

Outside Consultants:
Illuminating Concepts, Farmington Hills, Mich. (concept for media and lighting); Light Directions Ltd., Hong Kong (lighting); Di:5, Ferndale, Mich., View Studio, Royal Oak, Mich. (design); Media Projects Intl., London (media experience design); Electrosonic, Hong Kong (media technology systems developer

Photography:
Laszlo Regos, Berkley, Mich.

Entertainment Facility Award of Merit

Entertainment Facility Award of Merit

Bell World

Eaton Centre, Toronto

HOK Canada, Toronto

The Bell World prototype isn't just a showcase for new communications technologies. Established as a test site for product and service demonstration, the design — by HOK Canada (Toronto), was intended to enhance the customer experience with engaging visuals and interactivity. In a nod to the high-tech product and services offering, video, satellite and interactive media are used throughout the store. Ceiling-hung video terminals are positioned near p-o-p areas, and Internet cafes and satellite-fed TVs allow customers to explore and shop a variety of available telecommunications products and services.

A 6-foot drop midway through the store posed a design challenge, which eventually became a store focal point. An open-framed, stainless-steel, conical tower envelopes the gently curved staircase, which leads to the customer-service area, a children's play area and a second Internet café. Custom metal pole fixtures with clear-acrylic shelves and chrome accents display the most innovative products and provide flexible merchandising opportunities. The spiraling drywall ceiling and swirling custom carpet patterns add a whimsical appeal, and programmable color-changing LED lighting illuminates bulkheads and graphics to create visual excitement.

Client:
Bell Distribution Inc., Toronto — Bruce McLaws, design manager

Design Team:
HOK Canada, Toronto — Joseph Pettipas, vp, design manager; Cindy Bierworth and Cristina Antunes, intermediate designers; Tiera Robinson, junior designer/CAD

General Contractor:
Century Group Inc., Toronto

Suppliers:
Ken Lewis Group Inc., Markham, Ont. (video); DMX Music, Toronto (audio); L.K. Trading Co. Ltd., Richmond Hill, Ont. (vinyl bench fabric); Provincial Store Fixtures, Toronto, Mallet Millwork Inc., Toronto (fixtures); Milliken Carpet, Toronto (custom carpet); Mannington Commercial Carpet, Calhoun, Ga. (laminate flooring); Photo Imaging Techniques, Markham, Ont. (graphics); Juno Lighting Inc., Des Plaines, Ill., Eureka Lighting Ltd., Mississauga, Ont., Color Kinetics, Boston (lighting); Wilsonart Intl., Temple, Texas, Nevamar-International Paper, Odenton, Md., Formica Canada Inc., St. Jean sur Richelieu, Que., Octopus Products Ltd., Toronto (laminates); Zip Signs, Burlington, Ont. (signage); Sico Paints, Longueuil, Que., Sherwin-Williams Co., Cleveland (wallcoverings); Concord Elevator, Brampton, Ont. (barrier free lift)

Photography:
Ronald Ng Photography, Thornhill, Ont.

Lunn Poly

Fosse Park Shopping Centre, Leicester, U.K.

Checkland Kindleysides, Leicester, U.K.

The Lunn Poly "Holiday Superstore," so lovingly coined by its British developers, was intended to revolutionize travel retailing by making vacation booking a stress-free, pleasurable experience. Designers at Checkland Kindleysides (Leicester, U.K.) created a concept aimed at bringing consumers closer to vacation spots, at least figuratively, while planning their trips.

The store combines sights, sounds and smells appropriate to holiday destinations. For instance, the entrance features the smell of coconut, the sound of ocean waves and a canopy of either rippling water or palm tree fronds, depending on the projection chosen for that moment.

The beach setting is only one of the store's five specialized vacation zones, each delineated by color and larger-than-life graphics. Curved shelving in each area displays brochures covered by large parasols and accompanied by vacation-themed sounds and smells. All materials were chosen based on their relevance to vacation atmospheres. Shells, sand and pebbles form the paradise beach, teak flooring mimics a boardwalk and mosaic tiles recall sunny destinations.

Client Team:
Lunn Poly, Leamington Spa, U.K. — Nigel David, managing director; Vince Gunn, retail operations director; John Moody, project leader, customer innovations; Peter Povey, customer inovations director; Doug Glenwright, customer innovations manager; Jackie Edkins, operations

Design Team:
Checkland Kindleysides, Leicester, U.K. — Jeff Kindleysides, partner; Adam Devey Smith, sales and marketing director; John Churton and Tony Bell, senior project managers; Des Curran, director of architecture; Sally Smith, project manager, graphics; Richard Collier, senior designer, 3-D interiors; Vejay Vyas and Matt Fawell, senior designers, 2-D graphics; Louise Almond, designer, 2-D graphics

General Contractor:
J Quinn Ltd., Rochdale, U.K.

Suppliers:
Satvision Plc, Manchester, U.K. (audio/video); Benchline Projects Ltd., Ossett, U.K. (fixturing); Amtico, Coventry, U.K., Esco Desso Ltd., Abingdon, U.K. (flooring); Into Lighting Design, London (lighting); Sygnet Signs, Leicester, U.K. (signage)

Photography:
Courtesy of Checkland Kindleysides, Leicester, U.K.

Alexander Keith's Nova Scotia Brewery

Brewery Market, Halifax, Nova Scotia

Shikatani Lacroix, Toronto

Founded in 1820, Alexander Keith's is one of Canada's oldest breweries. To celebrate its rich heritage and build sales of its branded products, management decided to add an interactive tour and working brewery in keeping with the traditions of its founder. Working within the challenges imposed by two historic buildings and the original tunnel connecting the two, Shikatani Lacroix (Toronto) designed an experience that winds visitors through a recreation of Keith's dining room, then through the brewhouse and into the Stag's head pub to sample beer. Icons such as a stag's head, barrels, a draught wagon, the color green and images of Alexander Keith are repeated throughout the tour and in the site's two retail spaces, one at each end of the tour. Custom fixtures share similar distressed wood finishes and accessories are interchangeable.

Client Team:
Oland Brewery, Halifax, Nova Scotia — Nigel Miller, director of public relations; Aidan Tracy, director of marketing; Mike Bannister and Bill Scollard, project managers

Design Team:
Shikatani Lacroix, Toronto — Jean-Pierre Lacroix, president; Ed Shikatani, design director; Beverly Wells and Eric Boulden, retail designers; Jason Hemsworth, Emo Greco, Sheryl Keller, Lisa Olay and Jerry Alfieri, graphic designers

Architect:
Connor Architects & Planners, Halifax, Nova Scotia

Outside Consultants:
Victor Superek, Halifax, Nova Scotia (visual merchandising and design); CCL, Halifax, Nova Scotia (video presentation)

Suppliers:
DDC, Cambridge, Mass. (audio/video); Custom Millwork Atlantic Inc., Halifax, Nova Scotia (fixturing); Woodcraft Custom Interiors, Halifax, Nova Scotia (furniture); Crane Signs Ltd., Halifax, Nova Scotia (graphics/signage); Juno Lighting, Des Plaines, Ill. (lighting)

Photography:
David Whittaker, Toronto

Service Retailer Award of Merit

SunLife Financial

Toronto

HOK Canada, Toronto

To support its new corporate identity and IPO, SunLife Financial asked HOK Canada (Toronto) to design its storefront space in downtown Toronto's financial district. A stainless-steel canopy and five jewel-like, illuminated, recessed display boxes establish SunLife's identity and reinforce the brand. Inside the store, the "museum" or story room employs a showcase system that allows display of objects and artifacts, as well as a hanging system that includes a movable wood overlap wall to support graphics and artwork.

The opposite wing is a multipurpose space with a recessed theater set-up and a branding and image display wall. Three 9-foot-high laminate, wood and glass graphic panels can be moved on a ceiling-mounted track to open the space, and a concealed wood partition allows SunLife to divide the center into several spaces.

Client Team:
SunLife Financial, Toronto — Robert Pattillo Sr., vp, public and corporate affairs; Barbara Buchanan, manager, corporate presentations and publications; James Anderson, property manager

Design Team:
HOK Canada, Toronto — Joseph Pettipas, vp, design manager; Janet Jones, Annie Bergeron and Laura Jones, senior designers

Outside Consultants:
Ove Design, Toronto (graphics); First Vision Audio and Visual Systems, Toronto (audio/visual)

General Contractor:
Govan Brown and Associates, Toronto

Suppliers:
Woeller Contract Inc., Kitchener, Ont. (fabrics); Enmar Natural Stone Inc., Toronto (flooring); Vecta, Toronto, CCI Custom Furnishings Inc., Toronto (furniture); Folia Industries Inc., Huntingdon, Que. (laminates); Eurolite, Toronto (lighting); AMJ Perguson, Toronto (metalwork); Svend Nielsen Ltd., Toronto (millwork); Moderco Inc./Patry Products, Toronto (movable partition); ALU, New York, Photo Imaging Techniques Inc., Toronto, Wallis and Latinovich Design Build Inc., Toronto, Ove Design, Toronto, King Products Inc., Toronto (signage/graphics/displays)

Photography:
David Whittaker, Toronto, and Vincenzo Pietro-Paulo, Toronto

Service Retailer Award of Merit

Steelcase at NeoCon 2000

Merchandise Mart, Chicago

Lee Stout Inc., New York

The Steelcase showroom at Chicago's Merchandise Mart was renovated in preparation for NeoCon 2000. The two-level space had previously been designed with display areas on both floors, intermixed with work settings. The new plan, designed by Lee Stout Inc. (New York), separates the private sales office, upstairs, from the public showroom, below, making for a less-congested, less-confusing environment.

New products and paradigm presentations are intended to illustrate Steelcase's objective: "transforming the ways people work." Settings are meant to exemplify teamwork situations, including high-performance teams and leadership communities. Large photo murals reinforce changing work patterns worldwide, while adding visual interest.

Two areas are devoted to new office-style seating. The front windows house groups of new styles, and a corridor, mirrored at both ends, displays new designs with changeable upholstery. A selection of fabrics is organized in 12 color families, and sample blankets of the different weaves are hung from a grid of ceiling hooks, showcased in an all-white portion of the showroom.

Client Team:
Steelcase Inc., Grand Rapids, Mich. — David Gresham, vp, industrial design; Sue Warmels, administration; Renee Fici, Patricia Kammer and Heather Barton, designers

Design Team:
Lee Stout Inc., New York — Lee Stout, creative director; Cam Lorendo, senior designer; David Williams and Lynn Campbell, designers

Architect:
McBride & Kelley, Chicago

Outside Consultants:
Jim Conte, Brooklyn, N.Y. (lighting); Williams Marketing, Grand Rapids, Mich. (graphics)

General Contractor:
Pepper Construction, Chicago

Suppliers:
Wooden & Gooden, Grand Rapids, Mich., Steelcase, Grand Rapids, Mich. (audio/video); Armstrong World Industries, Lancaster, Pa. (ceiling); Designtex, New York, Steelcase, Grand Rapids, Mich. (fabrics and wallcoverings); Tate, Red Lion, Pa., Milliken, La Grange, Ga. (flooring); Steelcase, Grand Rapids, Mich., Brayton, High Point, N.C., Metro, Burlingame, Calif., Turnstone, Grand Rapids, Mich., Vecta, Grand Prairie, Texas (furniture); Xibitz, Grand Rapids, Mich. (graphics and signage); Interlume, Grand Rapids, Mich., Flos, Huntington Station, N.Y., LiteLab, Buffalo, N.Y., Artemide, Farmingdale, N.Y. (lighting); Wilsonart Intl., Temple, Texas (laminates); Details, Grand Rapids, Mich., Nava, Milan, Italy (props/decoratives)

Photography:
Tom Wedell, Canton, Mass.

Manufacturer's Showroom to the Public or Trades First Place

Designtex Chicago Showroom

Merchandise Mart, Chicago

Lee Stout Inc., New York

In a departure from traditional fabric showroom design, Designtex's new showroom at the Merchandise Mart makes no effort to merchandise the company's more than 400 textile selections. Instead, it presents a highly stylized "snapshot" of the company's most recent introductions.

The all-white space with a flexible ceiling grid is more gallery than showroom, designed by Lee Stout Inc. (New York) to change frequently in response to the changing Designtex collection. Only two permanent elements anchor the space: an entrance sign and a reception station. The entrance sign is a fabric banner blown vertically by a high-powered fan. The cone-shaped reception station is a standing-height counter with a lower work surface tethered to the floor with utility connections. Wheeled work tables and library cabinets provide maximum flexibility, and one long wall supports a ladder-like structure on which large fabric samples are hung in a spectrum procession.

Client Team:
Designtex Inc., New York — Tom Hamilton, president; Sue Lyons, vp, design; Kathryn Gabriel, director of marketing

Design Team:
Lee Stout Inc., New York — Lee Stout, president, creative director; Cam Lorendo, senior designer

General Contractor:
Thorne Associates, Chicago

Suppliers:
Duxbury, New York, USG Interiors, Chicago (ceiling); Designtex, New York (fabrics); Creative Edge, Fairfield, Iowa (fixturing/graphics); Yemm & Hart, Marquand, Mo. (flooring); Vecta, Grand Prairie, Texas (furniture); Halo Lighting, Elk Grove Village, Ill., Flos, Huntington Station, N.Y., Artemide, Farmingdale, N.Y., Lightolier, Fall River, Mass. (lighting); Wilsonart Intl., Temple, Texas (laminates); Rathe Productions, New York (signage); Designtex, New York (wallcoverings)

Photography:
Christopher Barrett, Hedrich Blessing, Chicago

New Dream Home Studio

Tempe, Ariz.

The Retail Group, Seattle

Kaufman & Broad contracted The Retail Group (Seattle) to consult and develop a unique manufacturer's showroom and service facility that would position Kaufman & Broad as a turnkey home ownership solution. The Retail Group designed an entry sequence followed by a well-defined path that leads customers through the home-buying decision process. A centrally located service hub acts as a base of operations as they experience each department. Strategically placed graphics guide and inform customers throughout the process, and each department is organized into "Good-Better-Best" room vignettes. Based on the success of the Tempe prototype, a nationwide rollout is underway.

Client Team:
Kaufman & Broad, Tempe, Ariz. — Lisa Kalbach, senior vp; Janet Smith, corporate showroom marketing and merchandising manager; Kelley Robbins, showroom manager; Bill Harrill, operations manager

Design Team:
The Retail Group, Seattle — J'Amy Owens, president; Cristopher Gunter, managing principal; Paul Biondolillo, senior store planner; DJ Baker, senior graphic designer; John Liberato, store planner; Greg Arhart and Ashley Bogel, creative directors; Tracy Lorelli, project manager

General Contractor:
Custom Realities, Scottsdale, Ariz.

Suppliers:
USG, Chicago (ceiling); Kaufman & Broad, Tempe, Ariz. (fixturing/flooring); Color Kinetics, Boston, Aerolite, Glendale, Calif. (lighting); Wilsonart Intl., Temple, Texas (laminates); Aerolite, Glendale, Calif. (exterior signage); Sign Tech, Seattle (interior signage)

Photography:
John Liberato, Seattle

Manufacturer's Showroom to the Public or Trades Award of Merit

Burdines

Florida Mall, Orlando

The Lighting Practice, Philadelphia

Burdines has always communicated its image as "the Florida store" through the individualistic design of its stores. For its new store in Orlando's Florida Mall, it cast lighting to play a key role in creating that image. Specifically, it wanted to highlight the architecture and decorative elements of the building to attract both residents and tourists.

By day, the store is an impressive white building. By evening, the lighting scheme — conceived of by lighting designers Alfred Borden, Michael Barber and William Kader of Philadelphia-based The Lighting Practice — accents the concrete texture of the front facade and dramatizes the 11 two-story-high palm tree structures that flank the main entrances and corners of the building.

Because the tall and narrow spaces were difficult to access for maintenance, the designers specified low-energy, long-life metal halide lamps rated at 10,000 hours, so that relamping would be necessary only once every 20 months or so.

Client Team:
Federated Department Stores, Cincinnati — Bruce Quisno, vp, construction; Paul Reeder, project manager; Ken Capra, construction coordinator

Lighting Design:
The Lighting Practice, Philadelphia — Alfred Borden, principal designer; Michael Barber and William Kader, lighting designers

Architect:
Cooper Carry & Associates, Atlanta — Gar Muse, project principal

General Contractor:
Whiting Turner, Orlando

Suppliers:
Altman Stage Lighting, c/o Katie Group Inc., Long Beach, Calif. (fixtures for illumination of palm tree sculptures); Hydrel, Sylmar, Calif. (fixtures for landscape and facade illumination); Philips Lighting Co., Somerset, N.J. (lighting supplier); Simtec, Salt Lake City (palm tree sculptures)

Photography:
Gabriel Benzur, Atlanta

Special Award: Lighting

The Zone

Glendale Galleria, Glendale, Calif.
WalkerGroup/CNI, New York

The Zone, a unique area in the Glendale (Calif.) Galleria, was the product of 146 Gen Y'ers (10 to 24 years old) communicating their opinions, reactions and needs. It was critical to designers from Walker-Group/CNI (New York) to create a retail neighborhood where this youthful market segment would feel comfortable. Members of the Y generation are 55 million strong who spent nearly $100 billion in 1999. Image is an important aspect of their lifestyle, and they interpret it in their culture and fashion-consciousness.

The result of all this research is an urban-destination shopping street (much like Melrose Avenue in Hollywood, Calif.), abounding with colorful storefronts and crowded, noisy restaurants and cafes.

Because The Zone's focus group indicated that moving water was a popular theme, a terrazzo tile floor appears to flow through the area like a blue and green eddy. For the stores lining the Zone's circulation area, the design team recommended an open format that encourages browsing and interaction.

The designers were also involved in the creation of interactive kiosks and sales outposts, as well as the Z Station, The Zone's visual and audio media entertainment center. Live broadcasts from KIIS-FM in Los Angeles, and its Internet counterpart KIIS Fmi, emanate from the station. There's also an on-site TV network, Channel Z and a zone_online.com web site, which will promote the retailers located in The Zone.

Client:
Donahue Schriber, Glendale, Calif.

Design Team:
WalkerGroup/CNI, New York — Mark Pucci, chairman/ceo; Douglas Fowler, regional vp/project manager; David Glover, designer

General Contractor:
Centre Builders, Santa Ana, Calif.

Production Architect:
Deenihan Design Group, Glendale, Calif.

Suppliers:
CraneVeyor Corp., S. El Monte, Calif. (fixturing); Corradini Corp., Los Angeles (flooring); Joe Kaplan Architectural Lighting, Los Angeles (lighting); John Richards, Mira Loma, Calif. (signage)

Photography:
Weldon Brewster, La Crescenta, Calif.

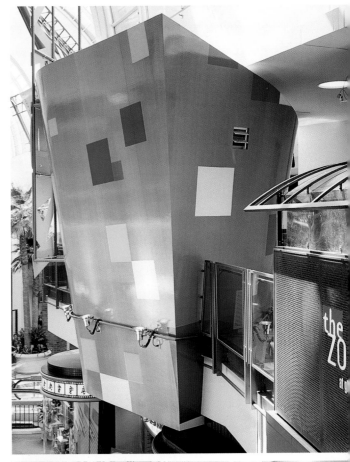

Index of Design Firms

For more information on visual merchandising and store design, subscribe to:

Books on visual merchandising and store design available from ST Media Group International:

Budget Guide to Retail Store Planning & Design
In-Store Signage & Graphics: Connecting With Your Customer
Retail Store Planning & Design Manual, 2nd Ed.
Stores and Retail Spaces 1,2 & 3
Visual Merchandising 2
Visual Merchandising and Store Design Workbook

To subscribe, order books or to request a complete catalog of related books and magazines, please contact:

ST Media Group International Inc.
407 Gilbert Avenue
Cincinnati, Ohio 45202

Telephone 1.800.421.1321 or 513.421.2050
Fax 513.421.5144 or 513.421.6110
Email: books@stmediagroup.com
Web sites: visualstore (www.visualstore.com) and www.stmediagroup.com

Part 1

Principles and Overview

Drug metabolism as a multidisciplinary science was born in the first half of the 19th century, when hippuric acid (the glycine conjugate of benzoic acid) was discovered in horse urine (hence its name). In 1841, it was discovered in the urine of a human after ingestion of 2 g of benzoic acid, an experiment that marked the beginning of human drug-metabolism studies [1][2]. Subsequent progress was impressive, but it remained restricted to a narrow circle of biochemists. It was only in the 1950s that drug metabolism really took off due to a convergence of factors including *a*) the progressive awareness among pharmaceutical scientists of the variety and significance of metabolic reactions, and the involvement of metabolites in unwanted drug effects; *b*) the groundbreaking studies of distinguished pioneers; *c*) the explosive development of analytic instrumentation; and *d*) the acknowledged scientific and didactic impact of a few books [3–6].

Since then, many books have appeared, most of them being edited ones offering expertly written reviews; some such books are listed in the *References* [7–20]. Other books were written by one or two authors, their import and tone being more unitarian and didactic (*e.g.*, [21–28]).

Before embarking on a systematic review of biotransformation reactions and their enzymes (*Parts 2–4*), of their pharmacological and toxicological consequences (*Part 5*) and of the factors affecting drug metabolism (*Parts 6* and *7*), it seems appropriate, if not necessary, to take a bird's-eye view and look at the extent and diversity of this multifaceted discipline. In doing so, a number of concepts will come to light and be explained. This will allow the readers to create a mental scaffold allowing the organization and classification of the many data and mechanisms to be presented in *Parts 2–7*.

The Biochemistry of Drug Metabolism –
An Introduction

Part 1 Principles and Overview

Part 2 Redox Reactions and Their Enzymes

Part 3 Reactions of Hydrolysis and Their Enzymes

Part 4 Conjugation Reactions and Their Enzymes

Part 5 Metabolism and Bioactivity

Part 6 Inter-Individual Factors Affecting Drug Metabolism

Part 7 Intra-Individual Factors Affecting Drug Metabolism

Fig. 1.1. The *Figure* presents the seven Parts of the work. These are being published first as seven separate reviews, and then together as a textbook. The construction of the entire work and the sequence of its Parts obeys a logic we found best adapted to our didactic mission and objectives. *Part 1* brings an overview and explains some basic principles. The core of drug metabolism, *i.e.*, its actors (the enzymes) and their actions (the metabolic reactions), are presented in *Parts 2, 3*, and *4*. This is done by considering first oxidoreductases and their redox reactions (oxidations and reductions; *Part 2*), then hydrolases and reactions of hydrolysis (*Part 3*), and finally the vast diversity of conjugating enzymes (transferases) and their reactions of conjugation (*Part 4*). The pharmacological and toxicological consequences of drug and xenobiotic metabolism are explained in *Part 5*. The work ends with *Parts 6* and *7* which present in systematic form the many biological factors that influence (modulate) the metabolism of foreign compounds, namely inter-individual factors (which are 'written' in the genome of the organism; *Part 6*) and intra-individual factors (which change over time in a given organism; *Part 7*).

Part 1 Principles and Overview

1.1. Drugs and Xenobiotics

1.2. What Are Drug Disposition and Metabolism?

1.3. Where Does Drug Metabolism Occur?

1.4. Consequences of Drug Metabolism – An Overview

1.5. Drug Metabolism and Drug Discovery

Fig. 1.2. The content of *Part 1* is summarized in this *Figure. Chapt. 1.1* defines xenobiotics and shows that drugs are but one class thereof. In other words, toxicological issues resulting from biotransformation (toxification) are a problem that goes well beyond medicinal compounds to encompass all foreign compounds our organism is exposed to. *Chapt. 1.2* examines the components of drug disposition, thus placing metabolism (= biotransformation) in the broader context of a drug's fate in the organism. We then take a brief look at where metabolism does occur in the body (*Chapt. 1.3*). This is followed (*Chapt. 1.4*) by a systematic overview of the consequences of biotransformation in terms of bioactivity (pharmacological and toxicological effects), pharmacokinetic-toxicokinetic behavior [29], and clinical effects. Finally, *Chapt. 1.5* takes a look at drug research, showing how and why drug metabolism has become so important in discovery and development. This Chapter also summarizes the *in vitro* biological methods and *in silico* tools used to assess or predict biotransformation.

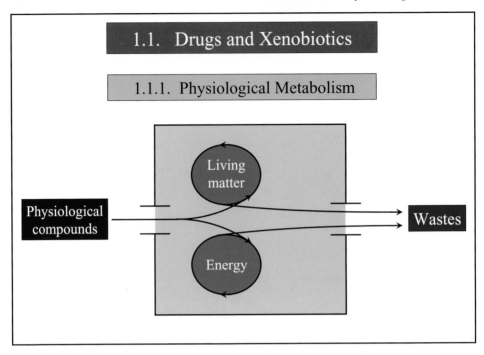

Fig. 1.3. This *Figure* opens *Chapt. 1.1*, whose aim is to define xenobiotics [21–23][25][26][30–32]. The definition is best approached by beginning with the *physiological metabolism*. Indeed, all organisms are open systems, *i.e.*, complex adaptive systems which maintain their low entropy content by extracting energy and 'building material' from a permanent flux of matter that enters them as physiological compounds, and exits as wastes and heat (plants obtain their energy directly from photons). After entering the organism, these physiological compounds (see *Fig. 1.4*) undergo catabolic and/or anabolic reactions. *Catabolic (degradation) reactions* liberate part of the energy content of these compounds and/or break them down to small building blocks (*e.g.*, amino acids). *Anabolic (synthetic) reactions* incorporate physiological compounds or some smaller components into living matter. The waste products resulting from physiological metabolism have a higher entropy content than the entering physiological compounds; they are, thus, of low or no value to the organism and are excreted mainly in the urine and feces.

Physiological compounds

Chemical compounds having essential biological functions:

• **Air** (oxygen) and **water**
• **Nutrients**
  – Protides (amino acids, peptides, and proteins)
  – Carbohydrates
  – Lipids (glycerides, fatty acids, …)
• **Minerals** (*e.g.*, sodium, calcium, chloride, phosphate, …)
• **Trace elements** ('oligos', *e.g.*, zinc, manganese, boron, …)
• **Vitamins**
• **Natural antioxidants** (*e.g.*, flavonoids, carotinoids, …)
• **Cellulose**, …

Fig. 1.4. The *Figure* defines *physiological compounds* as chemicals having essential biological functions, namely, which are indispensable to the survival of our body. Most of these compounds are listed here, beginning with the air we breathe and the water we take in. Note that differences exist between species, since oxygen, for example, is toxic to anaerobic microorganisms. Nutrients are conveniently classified into protides, carbohydrates, and lipids, but again some prokaryotes may not need them all. The list continues with the 'micronutrients', namely, inorganic compounds needed in modest (minerals) or trace amounts (oligo-elements). The list also contains compounds whose vital role was uncovered rather recently. These include those natural antioxidants which are not included among vitamins, *e.g.*, flavonoids and lycopene. It may well be that some of them are not indispensable individually, but representatives from different chemical classes are necessary, *i.e.*, acting by different mechanisms and differing in their hydro- and liposolubility. And finally, 'inert' compounds such as cellulose are now recognized to be vitally important in the long term.

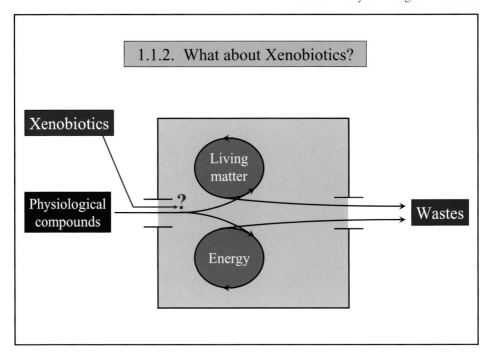

Fig. 1.5. This *Figure* completes *Fig. 1.3* by including xenobiotics and raising the question of their fate in the body. The word '*xenobiotic*' was coined in the early 1970s to indicate compounds that enter the body but have no physiological function and must, therefore, be eliminated [22]. This definition is correct but not complete, since there is also a tendency to view as xenobiotics endogenously produced compounds (endo-biotics [32]) administered at relatively high doses, be it for medical or non-medical reasons. A proposed definition and a list of xenobiotics will be given in *Fig. 1.6.* To answer the question mark in the present *Figure* is the objective of the entire Work.

What are xenobiotics?

Foreign compounds that enter the body but are not normally present in it and have no physiological role, or are present at unphysiologically high concentrations after uptake from an external source:

- **Drugs** (therapeutic and diagnostic agents)
- **Food constituents** devoid of physiological function
- **Food additives** (preservatives, flavors, coloring agents, …)
- **Cosmetics**
- **Doping agents** (EPO, anabolic steroids, growth hormone, …)
- **Hallucinogens** (ecstasy, LSD, THC, cocaine, …)
- So-called **'social stimulants'** (nicotine, alcohol, caffeine, …)
- **Natural toxins** (animal venoms, plants, and bacterial toxins)
- Innumerable **technical and industrial compounds** (agrochemicals such as insecticides, herbicides, and fertilizers, plasticizers, fire-retardants, …)
- Environmental **natural pollutants** produced by volcanos, fire, *etc.* (*e.g.*, radon, sulfur dioxide, and hydrocarbons)
- Environmental **synthetic pollutants** (heavy metals, insecticides, …)

Fig. 1.6. Our proposed definition is shown here, although it may not satisfy everybody. As a result, the best way to grasp the meaning of the concept is to list all classes of chemicals viewed as xenobiotics [25]. The first, and for us central, class is obviously that of *drugs*, with the reminder that drugs are chemicals administered for preventive, therapeutic (treatment), or diagnostic purposes, and the further note that some endobiotics administered to patients (*e.g.*, L-DOPA, hormones such as insulin) are also drugs. Two further groups are the *innumerable chemicals present in our foods*, and *articles for personal hygiene*, be they natural compounds or synthetic additives. For example, it is recognized that a cup of coffee contains several hundreds of compounds many of which contribute to its characteristic flavor and odor. There are then the damaging compounds that are usually taken deliberately, *e.g.*, *doping agents* (including endobiotics such as testosterone), *hallucinogens*, and so-called *'social stimulants'* (nicotine and ethanol are certainly toxic, but caffeine in reasonable amounts should not be considered as damaging). The last groups are the more or less *toxic chemicals to which we are exposed involuntarily*, *e.g.*, natural toxins, industrial compounds, and pollutants of various origins. Most classes of xenobiotics listed here contain synthetic compounds, but natural compounds are almost everywhere in the list.

How does the body protect itself against xenobiotics?

*1) By preventing xenobiotics from entering into the bloodstream
or organs* (**prevented absorption or distribution**):
– The xenobiotic passes along the intestine but *i*) cannot cross the
intestinal mucosa, or *ii*) is expelled by efflux transporters.
– The xenobiotic cannot cross the skin or the pulmonary mucosa.
– The xenobiotic cannot penetrate into some organs (*e.g.*, the brain).

2) By physical elimination (**excretion**):
– *via* the kidneys (urinary excretion)
– *via* the bile and the intestine (intestinal excretion)
– in the saliva
– *via* the skin (perspiration)
– *via* the lungs (expiration)
– in the milk, eggs, sperm, …

3) By chemical elimination (**metabolism = biotransformation**):
The xenobiotic is transformed in the body into products
(metabolites) which are usually more water-soluble and
easier to excrete.

Fig. 1.7. Given that the endless accumulation of even nontoxic xenobiotics is incompatible with survival, natural selection led to the evolution of protective strategies of which metabolism (= biotransformation) is but one [33][34]. Indeed, we owe our current biological protection against xenobiotics to the innumerable natural xenobiotics in existence before the appearance of humankind [35–37]. Schematically, *three protective strategies* have emerged. Taken in a toxicokinetically relevant order, the first strategy is *inhibited entry* into the organism or a given organ. This prevention can be passive, relying on membranes acting as barriers, or active by transporter-mediated efflux. The second strategy is by *excretion* (*physical elimination*), which can be either passive (*e.g.*, urinary excretion) or active (transporter-mediated excretion, *e.g.*, into the bile). Note that a given compound can be barred entry or excreted by passive and active mechanisms acting simultaneously. The third strategy is the focus of this Work, namely *chemical elimination*, better known as '*metabolism*' as synonymous with '*biotransformation*'. Another meaning of the word 'metabolism' is that of 'disposition', namely the sum of the processes affecting the fate of a chemical in the body [29]; this meaning will not be used in this Work. The biotransformation strategy has evolved to increase the hydrophilicity of lipophilic xenobiotics, and hence facilitate their renal and biliary excretion. However, as will be illustrated repeatedly in this Work (mainly in *Part 5*), this strategy fails in a number of cases when biotransformation yields reactive or more lipophilic metabolites [38][39].

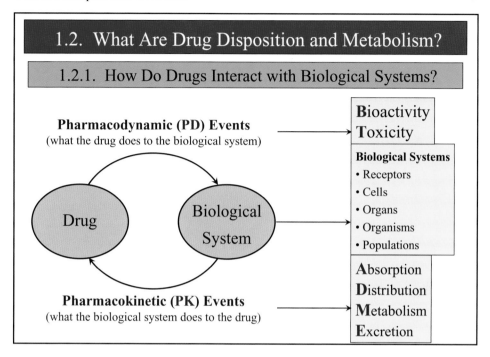

Fig. 1.8. *Chapt. 1.2* takes a closer look at drug metabolism and disposition by presenting definitions and placing these processes in a broader biological context. This *Figure* illustrates in schematic form the two aspects of the interactions between a xenobiotic and a biological system. Note that '*biological system*' is defined here very broadly and includes functional proteins (*e.g.*, receptors), monocellular organisms and cells isolated from multicellular organisms, isolated tissues and organs, multicellular organisms, and even populations of individuals, be they uni- or multicellular. As for the interactions between a drug (or any xenobiotic) and a biological system, they may be simplified to 'what the compound does to the biosystem' and 'what the biosystem does to the compound'. In pharmacology, one speaks of '*pharmacodynamic effects*' to indicate what a drug does to the body, and '*pharmacokinetic effects*' to indicate what the body does to the drug. But one must appreciate that these two aspects of the behavior of xenobiotics are inextricably interdependent. Absorption, distribution, and elimination will obviously have a decisive influence on the intensity and duration of pharmacodynamic effects, whereas biotransformation will generate metabolites which may have distinct pharmacodynamic effects of their own. Conversely, by its own pharmacodynamic effects, a compound may affect the state of the organism (*e.g.*, hemodynamic changes, enzyme activities, *etc.*) and hence its capacity to handle xenobiotics [40]. Only a systemic approach as used in pharmacokinetic/pharmacodynamic (PKPD) modeling and in clinical pharmacology is capable of appreciating the global nature of this interdependence.

1.2.2. The Main Phases of Drug Disposition and Action

Phase	Processes	Research objectives
Pharmaceutical phase	• Disaggregation of pharmaceutical form • Liberation and dissolution of drug	Drug available for absorption (optimization of pharmaceutical availability)
Pharmacokinetic phase	• Absorption, Distribution (incl. binding & storage) • Metabolism (biotransformation) • Excretion	Drug available for action (optimization of biological availability)
Pharmacodynamic phase	Interaction of drug (and metabolites) with: • targets (sites) of therapeutic Activity (receptors, *etc.*) • sites of Toxic effects	Therapeutic effects (optimization of wanted effects, and minimization of unwanted effects)

Fig. 1.9. The pharmacokinetic (PK) processes of absorption, distribution, metabolism, and excretion, and the pharmacodynamic (PD) phenomena of bioactivity and toxicity, are now placed in a broader medicinal perspective by considering the three phases of a drug's action. The (chronologically) first phase, which was not mentioned up to this point, is the *pharmaceutical phase* during which the drug is liberated from the pharmaceutical form (and is dissolved in case of a solid form). In the schematic presentation of this *Figure*, the *pharmacokinetic* and *pharmacodynamic phases* are taken to be consecutive, which is misleading and in apparent contradiction with *Fig. 1.8*. Indeed, it is obvious that the PK and PD phases occur simultaneously, their separation in this *Figure* serving to draw a parallel with the main objectives of drug research. In other words, the three phases of drug disposition and action correspond quite logically to the three research objectives of pharmaceutical, biological, and therapeutic optimization.

L iberation

A bsorption

D istribution

M etabolism

E xcretion

T oxicity

Fig. 1.10. This *Figure* offers an eye-catching reminder of the *LADMET* concept as the counterpart of '*Bioactivity*' in drug discovery and development (drug D&D). Since a number of decades, the pharmacy curriculum has extended the original pharmacokinetic core (ADME) to pharmaceutics and biopharmacy by including '*Liberation*'. More recently, drug researchers have come to realize that '*Toxicity*' could not be separated from the ADME core as a criterion of '*drugability*' and a major challenge in the optimization of '*drug-like*' properties [41].

1.2.3. Processes of Drug Disposition and Metabolism

• *Weak* (reversible) *interactions*

(**ABSORPTION, DISTRIBUTION** incl. **STORAGE,**

and **EXCRETION**)

– Membrane permeation

– Reversible binding to macromolecules and transporters

– Accumulation in adipose tissues and in some organelles

• *Covalent reactions*

(**METABOLISM = BIOTRANSFORMATION**)

– Redox reactions ⌐   ⌐ Possibility of covalent binding

– Hydrations   ├───→ { to proteins, nucleic acids, or

– Conjugations ──────┘   └ membrane lipids

Fig. 1.11. The previous *Figures* have placed metabolism in the broader context of ADME, LADME, and ADMET. The message in the present *Figure* is to demonstrate that absorption, distribution (including storage), metabolism, and excretion can be examined in a common *physicochemical* context. Indeed, these pharmacokinetic phenomena show a bimodal distribution when arranged according to the energy levels involved. *Reversible interactions* such as membrane crossing, reversible binding to soluble proteins and transporters, and accumulation in adipose tissues and organelles involve weak energies in the approximate range of 10 to 60 kJ mol^{-1}. In contrast, metabolic reactions are irreversible in the sense that the formation of metabolites involves the cleavage and formation of (high-energy) *covalent bonds*, and occurs in the approximate range of 200 to 400 kJ mol^{-1}. Note also that redox and conjugation reactions sometimes generate *reactive metabolites* which will react spontaneously with proteins, nucleic acids, or membranes to form *adducts*. Such reactions caused by reactive metabolites are termed '*post-enzymatic*' and are of great toxicological significance [25], as discussed mainly in *Part 5*.

Classification of reactions of drug metabolism		
Chemical entities being transferred to or from the substrates		
Functionalizations (Phase I)		**Conjugations** (Phase II)
Redox reactions	Hydrolyses	
O	H_2O	Methyl group
O_2	HO^-	Sulfate and phosphate moieties
e^-		Glucuronic acid and some sugars
$2 e^-$		Acetyl and other acyl groups
H^- (hydride)		Glycine and other amino acids
		Diglycerides
	Following conjugation with Coenzyme A	Cholesterol and other sterols
		Unidirectional chiral inversion
		β-Oxidation
		Chain elongation by two-carbon units
		Glutathione
	Acetaldehyde, pyruvic acid, other carbonyl compounds	
	CO_2	

Fig. 1.12. Having moved one step closer to metabolism proper and to its chemical aspects, we can now enter the biochemistry of xenobiotic metabolism. A first classification is between 'phase I' and 'phase II'. While the classification is relevant and useful, the terminology is misleading and outdated, since 'phase II' reactions can occur without or before 'phase I'. We prefer to label 'phase I' as reactions of *functionalization*, and 'phase II' as reactions of *conjugation* [25][28][30][42][43]. The term 'functionalization' may be a source of confusion, since it means different things to different experts; in our mind, it implies the creation of a functional group or the modification of an existing one, and it includes the all important redox reactions (*Part 2*) and hydrolyses/hydrations (*Part 3*). The second major class is that of conjugations, which, as shown, involves a large variety of moieties which can be transferred to the substrate. The term 'conjugation' is used universally and without problem, and it will be defined in *Part 4* according to clear criteria. In the present *Figure*, reactions marked in red are those which, in a few well-defined cases, can occur *nonenzymatically* (*e.g.*, oxidation of polyphenols, hydrolyses of labile esters, glutathione conjugation of strong electrophiles) [44]. Unidirectional chiral inversion (*e.g.*, of profens) and β-oxidation (of fatty acid analogs) are written in italics since they are not conjugations *stricto sensu*, but deserve to be so classified, since a coenzyme A conjugate is the indispensable intermediate.

| Example: The metabolism of dimethyl sulfoxide |

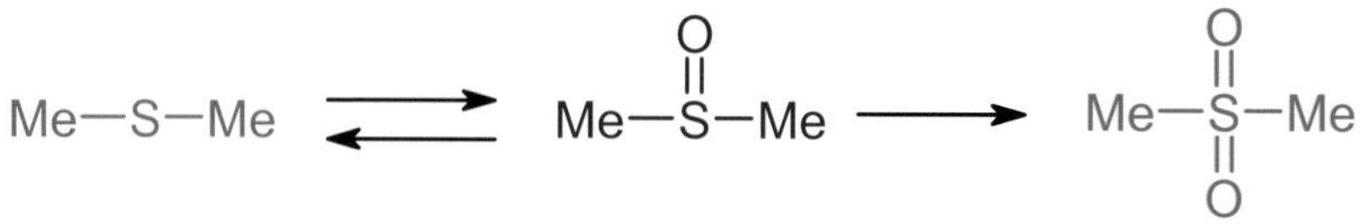

$$\text{Me}-\text{S}-\text{Me} \rightleftarrows \text{Me}-\overset{\displaystyle O}{\underset{\displaystyle \|}{\text{S}}}-\text{Me} \longrightarrow \text{Me}-\overset{\displaystyle O}{\underset{\displaystyle \|}{\overset{\displaystyle \|}{\text{S}}}}-\text{Me}$$

1) **Dimethyl sulfoxide** (DMSO) is a solvent, an excipient and a former drug.

2) It enters the body through the skin.

3) At high percutaneous doses, it acts as an analgesic in muscles and joints.

4) One part of the dose is excreted in urine.

5) The other part is metabolized in the liver
   to **dimethyl sulfide** (by loss of one oxygen atom)
   and **dimethyl sulfone** (by gain of one oxygen atom).

6) **Dimethyl sulfone** is excreted in urine.

7) **Dimethyl sulfide** is volatile, has a garlic smell, and is excreted *via* the lungs
   in the expired air.

Fig. 1.13. A concrete and simple case is presented here to help readers get a feeling of some aspects of drug metabolism and its consequences. The example shown is that of dimethyl sulfoxide (DMSO). This highly polar liquid has exceptional solvent properties and is practically inert chemically and biologically, making it an (almost) ideal solvent in drug research. The compound was used in the 1960s as an analgesic in case of arthritis and arthrosis, being applied externally in undiluted form. This therapeutic use was soon discontinued due to the discovery of potential ocular toxicity in dogs, but it continues to be used at low percent concentrations as an excipient in gels and oitments due to its good pharmaceutical properties. The metabolism of DMSO is comparatively simple, consisting of irreversible oxidation to dimethyl sulfone, and reversible reduction to dimethyl sulfide. Whereas DMSO and dimethyl sulfone are excreted in urine, dimethyl sulfide is excreted partly *via* the lungs due to its volatility. This creates an esthetic problem given the pungent garlic smell of the sulfide (see [5]).

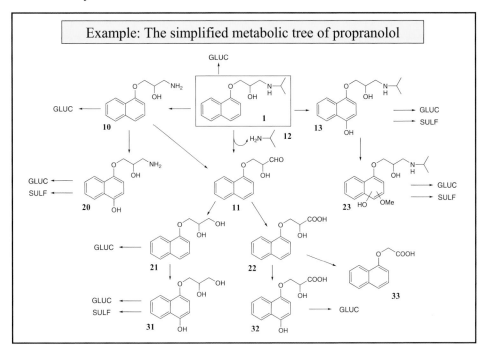

Example: The simplified metabolic tree of propranolol

Fig. 1.14. Propranolol (**1**), the first β-blocking drug, is extensively metabolized in humans (> 90% of an oral dose) [45]. Its major human metabolites are presented here to illustrate the concept and potential complexity of a *metabolic tree*. The primary metabolites of propranolol (**1**) are its *O*-glucuronide, the primary amine **10** resulting from oxidative *O*-dealkylation, the aldehyde **11** formed by a reaction of oxidative deamination which also liberates isopropylamine (**12**), and the phenol 4-hydroxypropranolol (**13**); minor positional isomers of **13** have also been characterized in humans. Note that the aldehyde **11** is also a secondary metabolite formed from the primary amine **10**. All the oxidative reactions so far are catalyzed by cytochromes P450 (CYPs, see *Part 2*). Secondary metabolites are the primary alcohol **21** and the carboxylic acid **22** formed from the aldehyde **11** by alcohol dehydrogenases and aldehyde dehydrogenases, respectively (see *Part 2*). Other secondary metabolites are the phenol **20** and isomeric phenols **23**. Tertiary metabolites include the two phenols **31** and **32**, and the minor α-naphthoxyacetic acid metabolite formed by oxidative chain-shortening. Many of these metabolites are also excreted as the *O*-glucuronide and the *O*-sulfate (see *Part 4*).

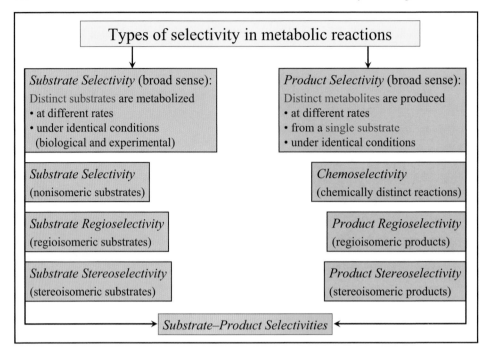

Fig. 1.15. In this work, the specificity of an enzyme will be taken to mean an ensemble of properties, the description of which makes it possible to specify the enzyme's behavior. In contrast, the present Work will apply the term selectivity to metabolic processes, indicating that a given metabolic reaction or pathway is able to select some substrates or metabolites from a larger set. In other words, the *selectivity of a metabolic reaction* is the expression of the *specificity of an enzyme*. Having clarified these definitions, we turn our attention to the various types of selectivities a metabolic reaction can show. When two or more substrates are metabolized at different rates under identical conditions, *substrate selectivity* is observed (left side of the *Figure*). Substrate selectivity is distinct from *product selectivity* (right side of the *Figure*), which is observed when two or more metabolites are formed at different rates from a single substrate under identical conditions. In other words, substrate-selective reactions discriminate between different compounds, while product-selective reactions discriminate between different groups or positions in a given compound. The *substrates being metabolized* at different rates may share various types of relationships. They may be chemically very or slightly different (*e.g.*, analogs, resulting in *substrate selectivity in a narrow sense*). Alternatively, the substrates may be isomers such as positional isomers (regioisomers, resulting in *substrate regioselectivity*), stereoisomers (diastereoisomers or enantiomers, resulting in *substrate stereoselectivity*, substrate diastereoselectivity (seldom used) or *substrate enantioselectivity*). Products formed at different rates in product-selective reactions may also share various types of relationships. Thus, they may be analogs (*product selectivity in a narrow sense*), regioisomers (*product regioselectivity*), or stereoisomers (*i.e.*, diastereoisomers or enantiomers, resulting in *product stereoselectivity*, product diastereoselectivity (seldom used) or *product*

enantioselectivity). And since Nature is never as simple as we would like it, the product selectivity displayed by two distinct substrates in a given metabolic reaction may be different, implying that product selectivity itself may be substrate-selective. The term *substrate–product selectivity* is used to describe such complex cases, which have been reported mainly for stereoselectivity. As presented here, these concepts are quite abstract and not straightforward to grasp. But their repeated application in *Parts 2 to 4* will reveal their usefulness [25][46].

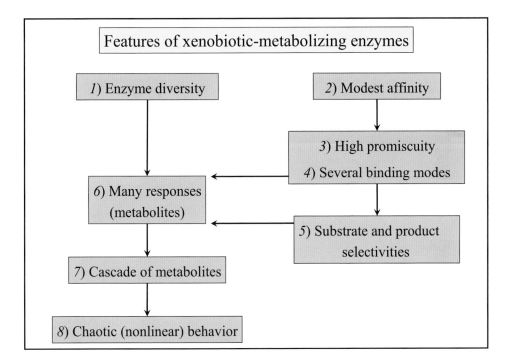

Fig. 1.16. Having introduced metabolic reactions in previous *Figures*, we now take our first look at the agents of these reactions, namely the *enzymes*. Six main classes of enzymes are recognized based on the reactions being catalyzed [47], namely *Oxidoreductases* (EC 1) which catalyze oxidoreduction reactions; *Transferases* (EC 2) which transfer a group from a donor to an acceptor; *Hydrolases* (EC 3), which catalyze the hydrolytic cleavage of C–O, C–N, C–C, and some other bonds; *Lyases* (EC 4) which cleave C–C, C–O, C–N, C–S, and other bonds by elimination, leaving double bonds or rings, or conversely add groups to double bonds; *Isomerases* (EC 5) which catalyze geometric or structural changes within one molecule; *Ligases* (EC 6) which catalyze the joining together of two molecules coupled with the hydrolysis of a pyrophosphate bond in ATP. The vast majority of enzymes known to act on xenobiotics belong to oxidoreductases (*Part 2*), hydrolases (*Part 3*), and transferases (*Part 4*). As exemplified in *Fig. 1.14* with propranolol (**1**), a single substrate

usually yields several (often many) metabolites which are produced '*parallel-wise and series-wise*'. Such a cascade of metabolites allows for *nonlinear responses* (chaotic behavior) in the sense that small causes can have large effects, and large cause can have small effects (see Caption to *Fig. 1.42*). As for the production of many metabolites from a given substrate, this is caused by two factors, namely *a*) the variety and diversity of enzymes that act on a given substrate, and *b*) the product selectivity of a given reaction. In turn, these two factors can be explained as a consequence of the low affinity and the promiscuity (*i.e.*, the capacity to recognize and metabolize a large structural variety of substrates) of xenobiotic-metabolizing enzymes toward their substrates. However, the core factor is the property of promiscuity shown by xenobiotic-metabolizing enzymes. Indeed, this property has been favored by Evolution, since it broadens the chemical space of potential substrates; but promiscuity comes at a cost, the trade-off being reduced turnover.

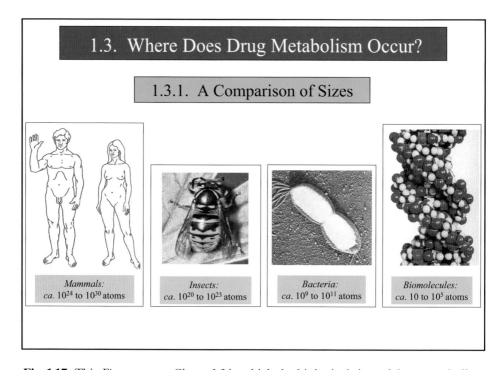

Fig. 1.17. This *Figure* opens *Chapt. 1.3* in which the biological sites of drug metabolism will be summarized. Here, and in the spirit of *Adrian Albert* [21], our readers are offered a comparison of sizes as a reminder of the huge differences in scale and complexity between human subjects and biomolecules. Our voyage from the macro-world to the microworld begins with the moving image of a human couple as carried into interstellar space by the NASA spacecraft Pioneer 10 launched March 3, 1972. While the linear dimensions of an insect are *ca.* 2–3 order of magnitude smaller than human ones, their volume/weight/number of atoms is smaller by *ca.* 8 orders of

magnitude. About 10–15 orders of magnitude are lost when comparing the volume of insects and bacteria. And biomolecules (micro- as well as macromolecules) are 5–19 orders of magnitude lighter than bacteria. The point we want to make here is that biological phenomena at the macroscopic-medical level are often explainable (if only in part) by underlying biochemical processes at the microlevel, but cannot be deduced from them with acceptable certainty. Given the biochemical focus of the Work, caution is urged when trying to infer macroscopic consequences.

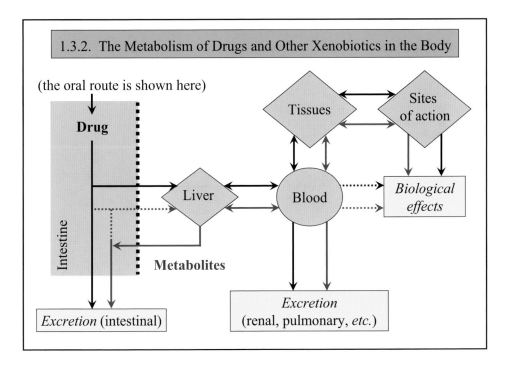

1.3.2. The Metabolism of Drugs and Other Xenobiotics in the Body

Fig. 1.18. Where does drug metabolism occur? This *Figure* does not answer the question, but it brings us one step closer to it by schematizing the fate of a drug in the body. The *black arrows* represent the drug itself (*i.e.*, the parent compound), whereas the *red arrows* represent its metabolites. Assuming oral administration, part or all of the dose is *absorbed* intestinally, arrives in the liver from where it will be *distributed* by the blood into the tissues and its sites of action. *Reversible binding* to blood and tissue constituents is an important component of a drug's fate [48]. As shown, *metabolite formation* can occur in the intestine and in the liver. However, metabolism in the blood and in peripheral tissues is also a possibility (see *Fig. 1.19*). In most cases, *excretion* of a large fraction of a dose is from the blood *via* the kidneys, minor fractions possibly being excreted *via* the lungs (volatile compounds), skin, saliva, milk [49], *etc.* Excretion of the unabsorbed fraction is intestinal; biliary excretion of some metabolites (mainly large anions) can also result in fecal excretion of part of the dose [50]. The phenomenon of *enterohepatic cycling* is worth a mention. Glucuronides of sufficient molecular weight (in humans, $> ca.\ 500$) undergo biliary excretion. When hydrolysis by the intestinal bacteria is possible (this is the case for *O*-glucuronides; see *Part 4*), the phenol or alcohol so liberated can be re-absorbed, reach the liver and circulate again.

Organs and tissues that metabolize drugs and other xenobiotics		
Adipose tissues	**Intestinal microflora**	**Placenta**
Adrenal glands	Intestine (large)	Prostate
Aorta	**Intestine (small)**	Salivary glands
Blood cells	**Kidneys**	Seminal vesicle
Blood serum	Larynx	**Skin**
Blood vessels	**LIVER**	Spleen
Bone marrow	**Lungs**	Stomach
Brain	Lymph nodes	Testes
Breasts	Muscles	Thymus
Bronchi	Nasal mucosa	Thyroid gland
Cheeks	Oesophagus	Tongue
Endometrium	Ovaries	Trachea
Eyes	Pancreas	Urinary bladder
Heart	Pineal gland	Vagina
	Pituitary gland	

Fig. 1.19. The *liver* has been called the 'chemical factory of the body', and indeed it is an organ whose function is to breakdown and synthetize compounds, xenobiotics included. Most drug-metabolizing enzymes are expressed in the liver, and at comparatively high levels. When introducing drug-metabolizing organs of secondary or tertiary importance, it becomes important to consider these two criteria namely *a*) the variety of enzymes expressed, and *b*) the levels of expression. To visualize the two criteria, one can just think of a histogram with each enzyme being a bin. In the liver, most bins are occupied, and at relatively high levels. The *organs and tissues of secondary importance* (bold in the *Figure*) either express most xenobiotic-metabolizing enzymes at comparatively lower levels (*e.g.*, the brain), or express a limited number of enzymes at relatively high levels (*e.g.*, blood and the kidneys). *Tissues and organs of tertiary importance* express low or very low levels of xenobiotic-metabolizing enzymes. However, their significance should not be underestimated, since they may be involved in the bioactivation or toxification of a few specific substrates. Taken globally, the list in this *Figure* includes almost all organs, a notable exception being the ossified organs (bones and teeth) whose xenobiotic-metabolizing activity appears all but impossible to investigate.

1.3.3. Microscopic Location of Drug Metabolism

Drug-metabolizing enzymes are found:

• *Extracellularly*, *e.g.*, in blood plasma (cholinesterase).

• *Intracellularly*,

> • in the membrane of the *smooth endoplasmic reticulum, e.g.*, cytochromes P450, some carboxylesterases, glutathione S-transferases, *etc.*;

> • in other intracellular membranes, *e.g.*, *mitochondria* (monoamine oxidases);

> • in other organelles, *e.g.*, *lysosomes* (some pepdidases);

> • in the *cytoplasm* (soluble enzymes, *e.g.*, dehydrogenases).

Fig. 1.20. This *Figure* is the continuation of the former one by considering the cellular location of xenobiotic-metabolizing enzymes. Indeed, blood plasma is an important and easily accessible *extracellular fluid* which contains high levels of hydrolases such as cholinesterase (EC 3.1.1.8) and paraoxonase (EC 3.1.8.1), and, for example, a copper-containing amine oxidase (EC 1.4.3.6). However, the vast majority of xenobiotic-metabolizing enzymes are found *intracellularly* (see the previous *Figure* for a list of organs). The *endoplasmic reticulum* (ER) is the location of the most important xenobiotic-metabolizing enzymes such as cytochromes P450 (CYPs, EC 1.14.14.1), glutathione transferases (EC 2.5.1.18), and glucuronyltransferases (EC 2.4.1.17) [51]. How the ER is transformed into microsomes is explained in *Fig. 1.22*. Some enzymes are located in *other organelles* (*e.g.*, mitochrondria and lysosomes). Soluble enzymes (*e.g.*, alcohol dehydrogenase, EC 1.1.1.1) are found in the *cytoplasm*.

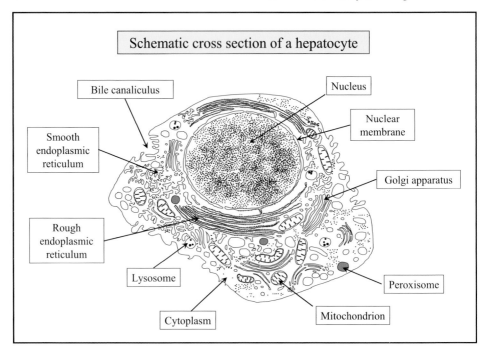

Fig. 1.21. The cellular components mentioned in the previous *Figure* are shown in this schematic representation of a hepatocyte. In addition to the *ER*, *mitochondria*, *lysosomes*, and *cytoplasm* mentioned above, one notes that some weak CYP activities have also been found in the *nuclear membrane*. Taken as a whole, this *Figure* makes it clear that a cell is an entity densely packed with strongly interacting components.

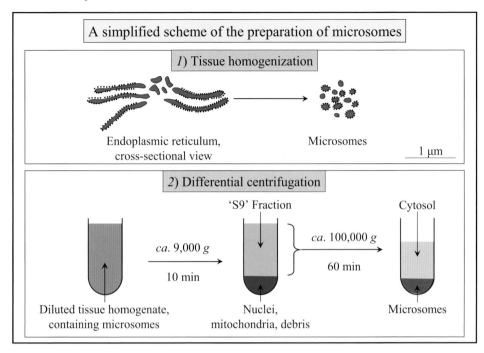

A simplified scheme of the preparation of microsomes

1) Tissue homogenization

Endoplasmic reticulum,   Microsomes
cross-sectional view   1 μm

2) Differential centrifugation

'S9' Fraction   Cytosol

ca. 9,000 g   *ca.* 100,000 g

10 min   60 min

Diluted tissue homogenate,   Nuclei,   Microsomes
containing microsomes   mitochondria, debris

Fig. 1.22. *In vitro investigations* are an essential aspect of drug metabolism studies [52]. The models used are, in decreasing order of biological complexity, isolated organs, liver slices, cell cultures (mainly hepatocytes), subcellular preparations, and isolated enzymes. Among these, subcellular preparations offer an excellent compromise between information yield on the one hand, and, on the other hand, ease of use, low material consumption and throughput. This *Figure* offers a schematic presentation of the preparation of metabolically relevant subcellular fractions [20]. The tissue to be used (fragments of liver or other organs, hepatocytes, *etc.*) is first *homogenized*. This breaks up the endoplasmic reticulum into small spheres visible under the microscope and called *microsomes*. A first centrifugation removes debris, nuclei, and mitochondria, which can be further separated and isolated. The supernatant is called '*S9*' (an abbreviation of *9,000*-g *supernatant*) and is of particular interest, since it is made of microsomes and *cytoplasm*, and hence contains most of the xenobiotic-metabolizing enzymes present in the tissue. Ultracentrifugation then separates the cytoplasm (now called *cytosol*) and the microsomes. The entire procedure is carried out at low temperature (*ca.* 4 °C). The microsomal pellet can now be resuspended in a buffer, supplemented with the necessary cofactors, and incubated with the substrate.

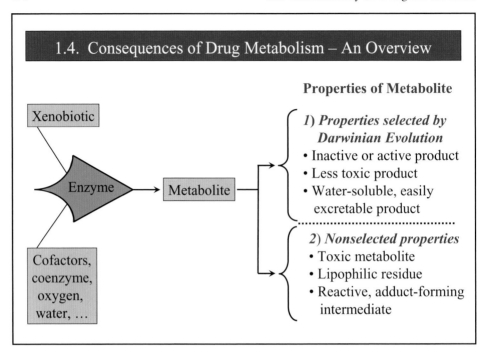

Fig. 1.23. *Chapt. 1.4* is dedicated to a short overview of the consequences of drug and xenobiotic metabolism. As discussed in *Fig. 1.7*, xenobiotic-metabolizing enzymes are believed to have arisen by *co-evolutionary arm race* between *herbivores* and *plants*, with plants evolving chemical defences (alkaloids, terpenoids, *etc.*), which decreased (however slightly) their probability of being consumed, and herbivores evolving counter-strategies to detoxify and excrete these chemicals [35]. Protection against *natural environmental toxins* (*e.g.*, heavy metals, sulfur dioxide, aliphatic and aromatic hydrocarbons, see *Fig. 1.6*) must also have provided a selective advantage not only to herbivores, but to any monocellular or multicellular organism. In other words, Evolution has favored the appearance and fine-tuning by random mutations of enzymes able to recognize and detoxify potentially detrimental xenobiotics of huge chemical diversity. As shown here, *beneficial effects* to the organism included the inactivation–detoxification of toxins and the facilitated excretion of useless compounds. But as we shall see, *exceptions* do exist in the sense that some metabolites can be reactive, more toxic, or more lipophilic than the parent xenobiotic. As a result, innumerable examples now exist of the beneficial or detrimental consequences of drug metabolism in pharmacology, toxicology, and pharmacokinetics.

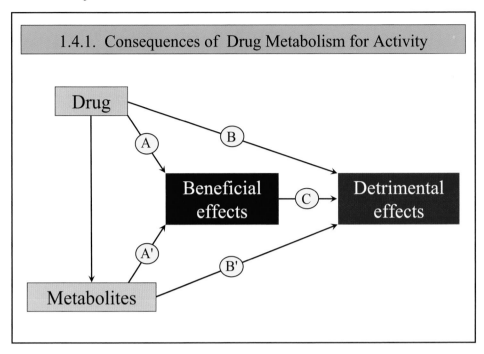

Fig. 1.24. We begin with the consequences of drug metabolism on global activity. As schematized here, a drug is expected to have *beneficial effects* (it would not be a drug otherwise) which can be caused by the parent compound (the drug itself) and/or one or more metabolites (arrows *A* and *A'*). But drug and/or metabolite(s) can also have *detrimental effects*. Interestingly, it is not always realized that such detrimental effects can be of two origins. One possibility (arrows *B* and *B'*) is for the drug and/or metabolite(s) to have side-effects resulting from interaction with biological targets different from the site of wanted action. A highly relevant example is that of several lipophilic drugs belonging to various pharmacological classes which cause cardiotoxicity (QT prolongation) by blocking at therapeutic doses the human ERG potassium channel [53]. Another and more subtle example is provided by antifungal azoles, which work by inhibiting a fungal cytochrome P450 (CYP51), thereby interfering with ergosterol biosynthesis. However, some of these drugs also inhibit human cytochromes P450 (CYP2C9, also 2D6 and 3A4) involved in drug metabolism, thereby causing potentially severe drug–drug interactions [54][55] (as discussed in *Part 7*). The other cause of detrimental effects is shown by arrow *C*, which, in plain language, means 'too much of a good thing is a bad thing'. For example, administering a β-blocker can be very useful to reduce hypertension, but overdosing will 'overshoot' and result in orthostatic hypotension.

Pharmacological aspects

- Only *inactive metabolites* are produced, as exemplified by oxazepam.

- One or more *active metabolites* are produced which contribute to the therapeutic effects of the drug.

- The drug is inactive *per se* (*prodrug*) but is transformed into an active metabolite responsible for the therapeutic effects.

- Whether active and/or inactive metabolites are formed, the rate of metabolism affects the *duration and intensity of action* of the drug.

Fig. 1.25. The pharmacological aspects of drug metabolism can be quite varied and have a major impact in therapy. Numerous drugs have *active metabolites* [56][57] whose activity needs to be evaluated by two criteria. These criteria are *a*) does the metabolite have the same mechanism of action as the parent drug, and *b*) if yes, how does it compare quantitatively? Another case is that of drugs having *no pharmacologically active metabolite*. Interestingly, this situation is far rarer than assumed, a clear example being that of oxazepam whose metabolites are all inactive. At the other extreme, we find the 'drugs' that are inactive *per se* but are rapidly transformed into a bioactive metabolite; the name 'produgs' is used to label such therapeutic agents [28][58][59] (see *Part 5*).

Toxicological aspects

- An intrinsically toxic drug (*e.g.*, an antitumor agent) is *detoxified* (*i.e.*, inactivated) by metabolism.

- A *reactive, adduct-forming metabolite* is generated, as exemplified by paracetamol and numerous carcinogenic xenobiotics.

- A metabolite is formed which *interacts with a site of toxicity* on which the drug itself does not act. One example among many different ones is the accumulation of an endogenous waste product due to the inhibition of its detoxifying enzyme, *e.g.*, a phenolic metabolite that would compete with the glucuronidation of bilirubin.

Fig.1. 26. The toxicological aspects of drug metabolism are even more important than pharmacological ones. Note, in particular, that the previous *Figure* is specifically addressed to drugs, whereas toxicology concerns all xenobiotics and not drugs exclusively. As we shall see in detail in *Part 5* and as summarized in this *Figure*, a number of toxicological consequences of xenobiotic metabolism are known. First, a xenobiotic (or a drug such as some antitumor agents) may be highly reactive and undergo *detoxification* by metabolism. The opposite is also true and unfortunately quite frequent, with some drugs and numerous chemicals undergoing *toxification* (arrow *B'* in *Fig. 1.24*). A first case is when the metabolite is chemically reactive and able to *bind covalently to biotargets* such as membrane lipids, proteins, or nucleic acids [60][61]. Many other cases of toxification do not involve adduct-forming metabolites, but simply metabolites whose structure allows them to *interact with a site of toxicity* on which the drug itself does not act. A number of such cases are known, but we believe that many more remain to be understood at the biomolecular level.

1.4.2. Pharmacokinetic Aspects of Drug Metabolism

Pharmacokinetic scenarios		
Drugs and other xenobiotics	Biotransformation	Excretion unchanged
Hydrophilic	minor	major
Lipophilic	major	minor
Very lipophilic	very minor	very minor

Fig. 1.27. A number of scenarios and consequences emerge when examining the pharmacokinetic aspects of drug metabolism. *Metabolic scenarios* can be simplified as shown here, with hydrophilic xenobiotics undergoing limited biotransformation but direct excretion, and lipophilic ones being extensively metabolized but poorly excreted as such. These four schematic scenarios are entirely in line with a *Darwinian Evolution* toward enzymes acting preferentially on poorly excretable, lipophilic xenobiotics to produce more hydrophilic, easily excretable metabolites (see *Fig. 1.23*). But it is humankind's misfortune that Evolution could not prepare us for our own creations, namely, synthetic xenobiotics of such high lipophilicity that our body is not equipped to excrete or metabolize them in any significant amount (see the next *Figure*).

Insecticides and other Persistent Organic Pollutants (POPs)

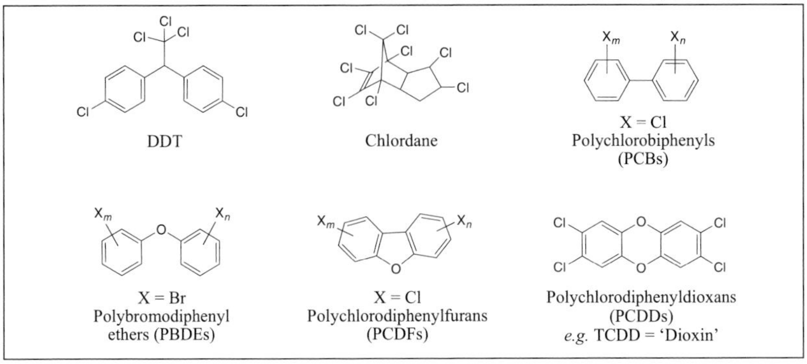

DDT

Chlordane

X = Cl
Polychlorobiphenyls
(PCBs)

X = Br
Polybromodiphenyl
ethers (PBDEs)

X = Cl
Polychlorodiphenylfurans
(PCDFs)

Polychlorodiphenyldioxans
(PCDDs)
e.g. TCDD = 'Dioxin'

- Many *insecticides* and *other pollutants* are highly lipophilic.
- They are *very resistant to metabolism*, and therefore are *not* transformed to water-soluble, easily excretable products.
- They have a *high affinity for lipid-rich tissues* (*e.g.*, adipose tissues, the CNS).
- As a result of the above, *they remain in the body for decades or even for life.*

Fig. 1.28. The highly lipophilic compounds alluded to in the previous *Figure* are eliminated very slowly from the body [62]. A small fraction may be metabolized over years and excreted *via* the bile. Mammalian females may also excrete a fraction of their body load with their milk, thus putting their progeny at risk. But a majority of the load will tend to remain as residue in the adipose tissues and nervous system, often for life [37]. The vast majority of such compounds are environmental xenobiotics known as *POPs* (persistent organic pollutants) [63]. They include a number of insecticides such as DDT ('dichloro-diphenyl-trichloroethane') and many industrial pollutants such as polyhalogenated biphenyls, diphenyl ethers, diphenylfurans, and diphenyldioxanes. The use of a number of such POPs is now prohibited or severely restricted, at least in environmentally mindful countries, but the ecosphere is already badly polluted and will remain so for centuries.

Pharmacokinetic consequences

• The drug induces one or more enzymes mediating its
  metabolism (*auto-induction*), resulting in a therapeutic
  response that changes over days or weeks.

• A metabolite acts as *inhibitor* of one of the metabolic
  pathways, resulting in complex kinetics.

• One or more metabolites have *physicochemical properties*
  vastly different from those of the parent drug, *e.g.*, a high
  polarity resulting in fast urinary excretion, or a very high
  lipophilicity resulting in accumulation and retention in
  tissues.

Fig. 1.29. An important consequence of drug metabolism is its pharmacokinetic
impact. By this, we mean two aspects. First, a drug may affect its own disposition by
inducing an enzyme involved in its metabolism. This is well illustrated with the
antiepileptic carbamazepine, which induces its own CYP3A4-catalyzed oxidation such
that its half-life in humans is reduced about two- to threefold or even more after
repeated administration [64]. A different case is seen when a metabolite *inhibits* one of
the metabolic pathways of the drug. This will result in a complex kinetics and render
dose adjustment more difficult. Some phenolic metabolites, for example, may inhibit
cytochromes P450, but this type of situation does not appear to be well documented.
The last scenario summarized in the *Figure* concerns metabolites whose *physicochemical properties* differ greatly from those of the parent compound, resulting in a vastly
different disposition, be it distribution, storage and/or excretion. The case of highly
lipophilic residues is of particular interest and will be exemplified in *Part 4*.

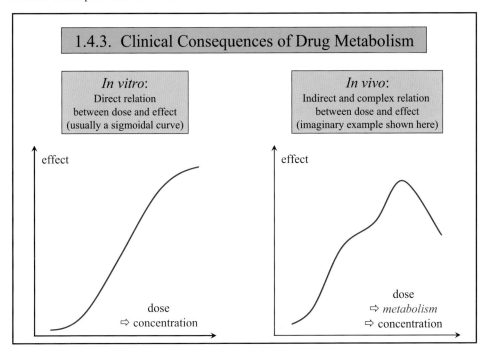

Fig. 1.30. The message in this *Figure* is a simple one, that dose–effect relations may differ greatly between *in vitro* and *in vivo* investigations due to metabolism being an interfering factor. In *in vitro* assays, there is a simple relation between the dose and the concentration, resulting in a direct relation (usually sigmoidal as shown) between concentration and effect. In *in vivo* situations, metabolism may blur the picture, rendering the dose–effect relation an indirect and complex one (an imaginary example is shown here). This is particularly true in clinical settings involving highly heterogeneous populations of patients, hence, the need for therapeutic drug monitoring and medical experience.

| Clinico-toxicological evidence |

In the USA between 1966 and 1996:

6.7% of all hospitalized patients suffered **serious detrimental effects** to drugs, and *ca.* **0.32%** (**106,000** in 1994) **died** because of them.

Some causes of adverse drug reactions:

• Drug–drug interactions (*e.g.*, metabolic inhibition, competition for storage binding sites) resulting in *pharmacological potentiation*;

• Drug–drug interactions (*e.g.*, metabolic induction) resulting in *decreased clinical response*;

• Low tolerance of *genetic origin* (*e.g.*, low metabolic capacity);

• Immunological intolerance.

Fig. 1.31. The upper part of this *Figure* shows some sobering data on drug toxicity [65]. The incidence of detrimental effects due to inadequate pharmacotherapy is appaling, as is the number of deaths. Major questions are the predictability and avoidability of such damaging effects, and whether they are iatrogenic (caused by the medical persons). In the lower part of the *Figure*, we list the major causes of *adverse drug reactions* (ADRs) related to metabolism. *Drug–drug interactions* come first, resulting either in *pharmacological potentiation* (apparent overdosing) or *decreased clinical response* (apparent underdosing). Both situations can obviously be life-threatening, especially with narrow-margin drugs. Drug–drug interactions should be avoidable, at least when well documented and in patients receiving a very limited number of medicines. The same is no longer true in most clinical situations with patients receiving five, ten, or more different drugs each day. Low tolerance due to *genetic causes* is a main justification for pharmacogenomic studies [66]. Here, again, some level of predictability is possible by phenotyping or genotyping patients, and by the systematic use of therapeutic drug monitoring. The truly unpredictable metabolism-related toxicity is immunological intolerance, *e.g.*, an allergic reaction to an antigenic hapten–protein conjugate (a hapten being an adduct-forming reactive metabolite). The mechanisms of *immunotoxicity* begin to be understood [67]. An example of trans-acylation potentially leading to allergic reactions will be discussed in *Part 4*.

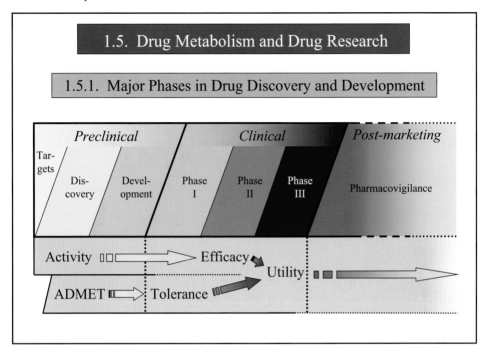

Fig. 1.32. *Chapt. 1.5* is dedicated to the significance of drug metabolism in drug discovery and development [68]. Not so long ago, the metabolism, disposition, and toxicology of selected candidates were studied mainly during preclinical and clinical development. In those days, the mission of medicinal chemistry was to discover and supply very potent compounds, with less interest being given to their behavior in the body. However, the research and development (R&D) paradigm in the pharmaceutical industry has undergone dramatic changes since the 1970s and particularly since the mid-1990s. Rigorous analyses of the root *causes of attrition* during development revealed that lack of efficacy, toxicity, as well as inappropriate absorption, distribution, metabolism, and excretion are among the major determinants of the failure of candidates [69]. A schematic picturing of current drug discovery, development, and clinical assessment is shown in the *Figure. Pharmacodynamics (i.e.,* bioactivity) is obviously the first object of study, but the new paradigm of drug R&D now has it that ADMET screening must be initiated rapidly. Bioactivity and *ADMET* screening and evaluation thus run in parallel throughout the preclinical phases, and this is when medicinal chemists find themselves in close collaboration with pharmacologists, pharmacists, biologists, biochemists, bioanalysts, physicochemists, computer scientists, and other experts. Assessment of efficacy and tolerance, to merge into utility assessment, then become the objectives of clinical trials.

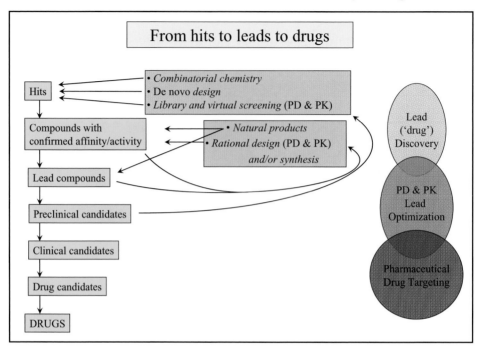

Fig. 1.33. A more detailed picture of the hits-to-leads-to-drugs is presented here. To improve the efficiency of discovery, medicinal chemists have developed new synthetic strategies such as combinatorial chemistry and parallel synthesis. Specialized biotech companies as well as universities also began offering compound collections and focused libraries. As a result, much attention is currently being paid to the design and/or purchase criteria of lead- and drug-like compounds. Increasingly, this includes considerations on ADME-related *physicochemical properties* as well as on the *ADME properties* themselves [70][71]. The concept of *property-based design*, in addition to structure-based design where target structures are available, is now commonly used to address ADME issues as early as possible. High-throughput biological assays were developed which have enabled large series of compounds to be screened, including considerations on ADME properties (see *Fig. 1.38*). In addition, it became reasonable and even essential to develop *in silico* tools (see *Figs. 1.39* to *1.42*) to predict and simulate various physicochemical and ADME properties, and to balance these in decision making processes together with combined *in vivo* and *in vitro* approaches. As shown in *Fig. 1.36*, metabolism-related questions continue to arise throughout the drug development stages.

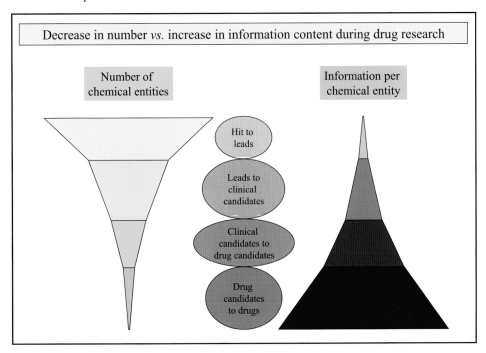

Fig. 1.34. This *Figure* draws a parallel between the number of chemical compounds produced and/or examined at the various stages of drug discovery and development, and how the information available per compound evolves during these stages. A clear if schematic trend is apparent, such that the smaller the number of compounds remaining in the pipeline, the *more information per compound* is needed to advance to further stages. Information on biotransformation is but one facet in the multidisciplinary profiling of candidates. The following *Figures* will show why and how this information is obtained during the discovery and early development stages.

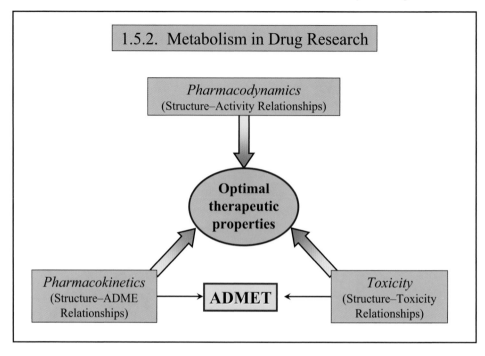

Fig. 1.35. For many years, *structure–activity relationships* (*SARs*) were the dominating paradigm in drug research. This changed when the importance of ADMET properties in developing well-behaved candidates was fully realized. At this point, it was a comparatively simple move to replace the 'activity' component in SARs with a global concept including all drug-like properties to be optimized. And, indeed, *structure– toxicity relationships* and *structure–ADME relationships* could grow in efficiency by using the same *in vitro* techniques (high-, intermediate-, and low-throughput assays) and *in silico* tools (quantitative SARs (QSARs), 3D-QSARs, molecular mechanics, molecular modeling, *etc.*) as used in SARs [72–75]. The ultimate objective now is to optimize all drug-like properties during the preclinical phases so as to minimize attrition during clinical trials. This challenge rests critically on the extrapolation of *in silico*, *in vitro*, and *in vivo* results to humans.

Metabolism-related questions to be answered in …

A) …lead discovery and optimization
- *Susceptibility* to metabolism? Expected *rate* of metabolism?
- Nature of *initial and major metabolites*?
- *Enzymes/isozymes* involved?
- Potential for enzyme *inhibition* and *induction*?

B) …the preclinical and clinical phases
- Nature and relative formation of *major and minor metabolites*?
- *Enzymes/isozymes and tissues* involved?
- *Distribution and elimination* of metabolites?
- *Activity and toxicity* of metabolites?
- Activity as *inducer*, autoinducer, and/or *inhibitor*?
  ⇒ **Potential for and occurrence of drug–drug interactions?**
- Influence of *genetic and other biological factors*?
  ⇒ **Potential for and occurrence of *genetic polymorphism*?**

Fig. 1.36. What are the metabolism-related issues to be answered during drug discovery and development? In the *early phases*, susceptibility to metabolism and a first estimate of metabolic stability in humans are required [71][76][77]. The nature of major metabolites and the enzymes involved are investigated. Assessing the potential for metabolic drug–drug interactions has also become of significance [78]. This includes enzyme induction and inhibition [79–81]. In *later phases*, more detailed answers to the above aspects are required. And new queries come to the front and must be answered, such as the activity and toxicity of metabolites [57][82], their distribution and excretion, and the influence of genetic and other biological factors [66][83][84].

Further aspects of drug metabolism of interest in drug research

- The *mechanism* and biochemistry of metabolic reactions;

- A *rationalization* of such reactions in terms of activation and inactivation, toxification and detoxification;

- Active metabolites as *new leads*;

- *Prodrug* and *soft-drug* design;

- *Changes in physicochemical properties* (pK_a, lipophilicity, *etc.*) resulting from biotransformation;

- *Predictions* of drug metabolism based on quantitative structure–metabolism relationships, expert systems, and molecular modeling of enzymatic sites.

Fig. 1.37. The previous *Figure* is specifically oriented toward drug discovery and development, and it does not cover all metabolism-related aspects of drug research. Further aspects of interest in drug research are listed here. Some of these aspects are also of high interest in drug discovery, *e.g.*, active metabolites as lead compounds [57], prodrug and soft-drug design [28][30][58][59][85], and *in silico* predictions of drug metabolism [15][86][87]. Other aspects are of a more fundamental nature in drug research, *e.g.*, the mechanisms and biochemistry of metabolic reactions [13][25][28][88][89], a rationalization of such reactions in terms of bioactivity and toxicity [60][61], and the changes in physicochemical properties resulting from biotransformation (*e.g.*, [90]).

1.5.3. *In vitro* and *in silico* Tools to Study Drug Metabolism in Drug Discovery and Early Development

Some common and less common *in vitro* tools

Enzymes
- Isolated enzymes;
- Specific human enzymes expressed in microorganisms or other cells;

Subcellular preparations
- Liver microsomes (rat, human, *etc.*);
- Other hepatic subcellular preparations (*e.g.*, cytosol, mitochondria);
- Liver S9 preparations (rat, human, *etc.*);
- Extrahepatic subcellular preparations (*e.g.*, skin, lung, kidney, *etc.*);

Cell cultures, *e.g.*, hepatocytes (rat, human, *etc.*);

Liver slices

Perfused organs, *e.g.*, rat liver.

(Analysis by HPLC-MS, MS/MS, high-resolution NMR, *etc.*)

Fig. 1.38. The tools used to study drug metabolism during drug discovery and early development must ensure good throughput and be as relevant as possible to metabolism in human subjects [91]. *In vitro* tools are listed here in a classification that goes from the simplest to more complex ones [20][75]. The simplest systems are isolated *enzymes* or human enzymes expressed in genetically engineered micro-organisms or multicellular organisms (insects, plants, ...). At a higher level of biological complexity, we find the *subcellular preparations* obtained by homogenization and centrifugation of cells or tissues (see *Fig. 1.22*). More than often, such subcellular preparations are hepatic ones obtained from hepatocytes. Human microsomes and hepatocytes, despite their cost, are of particular interest given their relevance. In some special cases, other tissues are used, *e.g.*, lung or skin. *Liver slices*, particularly of human origin, are also of value. *Cell cultures*, mainly primary cultures of *hepatocytes*, afford a level of information unequaled by subcellular preparations [92][93]. First, the integrity of the cellular organization preserves the functional interactions between enzymes. Second, the viability and functionality of intact cells is maintained over longer durations (several hours), allowing longer experiments to be carried out. And finally, there is a permeation component in cell experiments which better reflects the *in vivo* situation where substrates must cross a membrane before reaching intracellular enzymes. *Perfused organs* are labor-intensive and difficult to carry out. They are often performed *in situ*, namely, with the animal alive under deep anesthesia, and are, therefore, *in vivo* investigations which will not be discussed here.

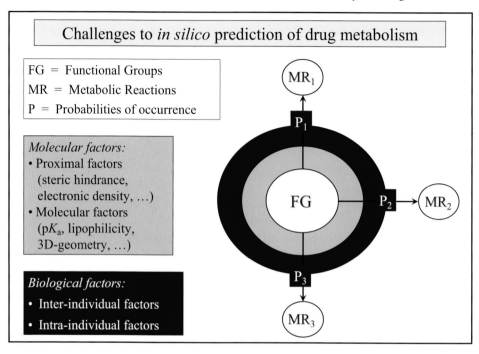

Fig. 1.39. Metabolic prediction in itself is a fuzzy and broad concept which calls for definition and clarification [30][86][94]. Schematically, a number of *objectives* toward predicting the metabolism of a given compound can be listed, namely, *a*) a list of all reasonable phase I and phase II metabolites, taking molecular factors into account; *b*) the metabolites organized in a metabolic tree; *c*) a warning for reactive/adduct-forming metabolites; *d*) a prioritization of pathways depending on biological conditions. What is explicit in this list of objectives are the factors that influence the transformation of a substrate into metabolites [95][96], as schematized in the *Figure*. A given functional group in the substrate (FG_i, also labeled a target site) will enter a given metabolic reaction (MR_i) with a probability of occurrence P_i, which depends on a number of factors conveniently subdivided into molecular and biological ones. *Proximal molecular factors* are features near the target site which will influence the catalytic reaction, for example, steric hindrance and electronic properties (densities, delocalizations, *etc.*). *Global molecular factors* (ionization, lipophilicity, 3D geometry) influence the penetration of the substrate into the enzyme compartment, the recognition of the substrate by the enzyme, and the catalytically productive binding mode of the substrate in the catalytic pocket. The *biological factors* are so many, so varied, and of such immense importance that they will need two Parts to be discussed in this Work, namely *Parts 6* and *7*. Suffice it to say here that they represent at present an apparently unsurmountable challenge to entirely successful predictions of drug metabolism.

Specific ('local') in silico *predictive methods,*

i.e., methods applicable to simple biological systems
(single enzyme, *etc.*) and/or to series with limited chemical diversity

- *Quantitative Structure–Activity Relationships* = QSARs (linear,
  multilinear, multivariate, *etc.*):
  → affinities, relative rates, *etc.*;
- *Quantum-mechanical* (MO) methods (*ab initio*, semi-empirical):
  → regioselectivity, mechanisms, relative rates, *etc.*;
- *3D-QSARs* (*CoMFA™, Catalyst™, GRID/GOLPE™, etc.*):
  → substrate behavior, relative rates, inhibitor behavior, *etc.*;
- *Molecular modeling and docking:*
  → ligand yes or no (substrate? inhibitor?), regioselectivity, *etc.*;
- *Expert systems combining docking, 3D-QSARs, and MO*
  (*MetaSite™, etc.*).

Fig. 1.40. In a simplified manner, one can distinguish between two types of algorithms to predict drug and xenobiotic metabolism, namely, specific ('local') systems and comprehensive ('global') systems. *Specific systems* apply to simple biological (*e.g.*, single enzymes) and/or to single metabolic reactions, and they may or may not be restricted to rather narrow chemical series. Such systems include *quantitative structure– metabolism relationships* (QSMRs) based on structural and physicochemical properties [96][97]. *Quantum mechanical calculations* may also shed light on SMRs and generate parameters to be used as independent variables in QSMRs, revealing, for example, correlations between rates of metabolic oxidation and energy barrier in H-atom abstraction [98][99]. *Three-dimensional QSMRs* (3D-QSMRs) methods yield a partial view of the binding/catalytic site of a given enzyme as derived from the 3D-molecular fields of a series of substrates or inhibitors (the training set). In other words, they yield a 'photographic negative' of such sites, and will allow a quantitative prediction for novel compounds structurally related to the training set [100][101]. The *molecular modeling* of xenobiotic-metabolizing enzymes affords another approach to rationalize and predict drug–enzyme interactions [102][103]. Its application to drug metabolism was made possible by the crystallization and X-ray structural determination of cytochromes P450, first bacterial, and now human ones. While such pharmacophoric models cannot yet give highly accurate quantitative affinity predictions, they nevertheless afford fairly reliable answers as to the relative accessibility of target sites in the substrate molecules. The 3D models of a large number of mammalian and mostly human CYPs are now available, as well as other xenobiotic-metabolizing enzymes such as DT-diaphorase and various transferases. The last approaches mentioned in this *Figure* are *expert systems* combining several methods, for example, pharmacophore models (obtained by 3D-QSAR), protein models (obtained by molecular modeling), and docking [104][105]. Another powerful combination are *a*) 3D models obtained by molecular modeling, and *b*) sophisticated QSAR approaches based on multivariate analyses of parameters obtained from molecular interaction fields (MIFs), as found in the *MetaSite* algorithm [106]. *MetaSite* is a specific system in the sense that it is currently restricted to the major human cytochromes P450. At the end of the procedure, the atoms of the substrate are ranked according to their accessibility and reactivity. In other words, *Metasite* takes the 3D stereoelectronic structure of both the enzyme and the ligand into account to prioritize the potential target sites in the molecule.

Comprehensive ('global') in silico *predictive methods,*

i.e., methods applicable to versatile biological systems
(many enzymes and many reactions, …)

- *'Meta'-systems combining* A) *docking, 3D-QSAR, MO,*
  and B) *a number of enzymes and other functional proteins*
       (*MetaDrug™, etc.*);
            → nature of major and minor metabolites, metabolic trees,
               reactive/adduct-forming metabolites,
               induction, inhibition, transport, *etc.*
- *Databases* (*Metabolite™, Metabolism™*)
            → nature of major and minor metabolites,
               reactive/adduct-forming metabolites, *etc.*;
- *Rule-based expert systems* (and their databases)
       (*MetabolExpert™, META™, METEOR™*)
            → nature of major and minor metabolites, metabolic trees,
               reactive/adduct-forming metabolites, *etc.*

Fig. 1.41. Comprehensive expert systems are, in principle, applicable to versatile biological systems (*i.e.*, to any enzyme and reaction) and to any chemical compound. As shown in the *Figure*, this is the final goal of *'meta'-systems* combining docking, 3D-QSAR, and MO method not for a single enzyme, but for a number of them (ultimately, all!). The inclusion of other functional proteins such as transporters can also be envisaged. Combining several specific models to form a meta-model is a most appealing if ambitious strategy, and much work remains before such approaches can be seen as genuinely comprehensive. To the best of our knowledge, the release of *MetaDrug* is currently the most significant and promising step in this direction [107]. As reviewed by *Hawkins* [87], one approach to global prediction of metabolism is to use *databases* in the form of either knowledge-based systems or predictive, rule-based systems [15]. Existing *knowledge-based systems* include the *MDL Metabolite Database* [108] and the *Accelrys Metabolism* database [109] originally established using data compiled in the book series *Biotransformations* [110]. These databases can be searched to retrieve information on the known metabolism of compounds with similar structures or containing specific moieties. *Predictive, rule-based systems* attempt to portray the metabolites of a compound based on knowledge rules, defining the most likely products [111]. Existing systems of this type are *MetabolExpert* [112], *META* [113], and *METEOR* [114].

The systems view of xenobiotic metabolism challenges *in silico* predictions

- Organisms not only *react* to drugs like a machine to a switch; they also *respond proactively and adaptively* to eliminate xenobiotics by metabolism and excretion.
- Many *endogenous and exogenous factors* (many known, but others still unknown) influence such biological responses either:
  - directly, or
  - indirectly (by modulating each other's influence).
- The resulting interplay of actions, reactions and modulations results in *nonlinear behavior* (small causes can have large effects, while large causes can have small effects).
- This behavior is characteristic of *complex adaptive systems*.
- This renders *in silico* predictions difficult.

Fig. 1.42. This *Figure* concludes *Part 1* and brings some forward-looking words about metabolism predictions in particular, and the complexity of xenobiotic metabolism in general. First, biological systems are not machines; they respond to xenobiotic invasion by an array of defensive strategies (*Fig. 1.7*) such as prevented absorption, facilitated excretion, and chemical breakdown reactions (*Parts 2–4*). Rather than being rigidly fixed, such responses are adaptable and can be adjusted within limits to the nature and magnitude of the invasion. Many endogenous factors are involved in these adjustements and are themselves influenced by exogenous factors. While many factors influencing xenobiotic metabolism have now been uncovered (*Parts 6* and *7*), their interdependcharacter of the responses, such that small causes can have small or large effects, and large causes can have large or small effects. This chaotic behavior is the characteristic of complex adaptive systems; it is also the source of the apparently unsurmountable difficulty of making close-to-perfect *in silico* predictions, and above all it is the source of the endless satisfactions one obtains when studying drug metabolism.

REFERENCES

[1] A. Conti, M. H. Bickel, 'History of drug metabolism: discoveries of the major pathways in the 19th century', *Drug Metab. Rev.* **1977**, *6*, 1–50; C. Bachmann, M. H. Bickel, 'History of drug metabolism: the first half of the 20th century', *Drug Metab. Rev.* **1986**, *16*, 185–253.

[2] International Society for the Study of Xenobiotics, www.issx.org.

[3] R. T. Williams, 'Detoxication Mechanisms', Chapman & Hall, London, 1947.

[4] R. T. Williams, 'Detoxication Mechanisms', 2nd edn., Chapman & Hall, London, 1959.

[5] B. Testa, P. Jenner, 'Drug Metabolism: Chemical and Biochemical Aspects', Dekker, New York, 1976.

[6] B. Testa, P. Jenner, 'The coming of age of drug metabolism', *Curr. Contents Life Sci.* **1990**, *33*, 17.

[7] 'Concepts in Drug Metabolism', Eds. P. Jenner, B. Testa, Dekker, New York, 1980 and 1981, Part A and Part B.

[8] 'Drug Metabolism – from Molecules to Man', Eds. D. J. Benford, J. W. Bridges, G. G. Gibson, Taylor & Francis, London, 1987.

[9] 'Conjugation Reactions in Drug Metabolism', Ed. G. J. Mulder, Taylor & Francis, London, 1990.

[10] 'Pharmacokinetics of Drugs', Eds. P. G. Welling, L. P. Balant, Springer, Heidelberg, 1994.

[11] 'Conjugation-Deconjugation Reactions in Drug Metabolism and Toxicity', Ed. F. C. Kauffman, Springer Verlag, Berlin, 1994.

[12] 'Conjugation-Dependent Carcinogenicity and Toxicity of Foreign Compounds', Eds. M. W. Anders, W. Dekant, Academic Press, San Diego, 1994.

[13] 'Cytochrome P450. Structure, Mechanism, and Biochemistry', 2nd edn., Ed. P. R. Ortiz de Montellano, Plenum Press, New York, 1995.

[14] 'Handbook of Drug Metabolism', Ed. T. F. Woolf, Dekker, New York, 1999.

[15] 'Drug Metabolism: Databases and High-Throughput Testing during Drug Design and Development', Ed. P. W. Erhardt, International Union of Pure and Applied Chemistry and Blackwell Science, London, 1999.

[16] 'Enzyme Systems that Metabolise Drugs and Other Xenobiotics', Ed. C. Ioannides, John Wiley & Sons, Chichester, 2002.

[17] 'Drug-Drug Interactions', Ed. A. D. Rodrigues, Dekker, New York, 2002.

[18] 'Handbook of Drug-Nutrient Interactions', Eds. J. Boullata, V. T. Armenti, Humana Press, Totowa, 2004.

[19] 'Drug Metabolism and Transport', Ed. L. H. Lash, Humana Press, Totowa, 2005.

[20] 'Cytochrome P450 Protocols', Eds. I. R. Phillips, E. A. Shephard, Humana Press, Totowa, 2006.

[21] A. Albert, 'Selective Toxicity', Chapman & Hall, London, 1985; A. Albert, 'Xenobiosis', Chapman & Hall, London, 1987.

[22] J. A. Timbrell, 'Principles of Biochemical Toxicology', 2nd edn., Taylor & Francis, London, 1991.

[23] R. B. Silverman, 'The Organic Chemistry of Drug Design and Drug Action', Academic Press, San Diego, 1992.

[24] B. Testa, 'The Metabolism of Drugs and Other Xenobiotics – Biochemistry of Redox Reactions', Academic Press, London, 1995.

[25] W. N. Aldridge, 'Mechanisms and Concepts in Toxicology', Taylor & Francis, London, 1996.

[26] G. G. Gibson, P. Skett, 'Introduction to Drug Metabolism', 3rd edn., Nelson Thornes, Cheltenham UK, 2001.

[27] B. Testa, J. M. Mayer, 'Hydrolysis in Drug and Prodrug Metabolism – Chemistry, Biochemistry, and Enzymology', Verlag Helvetica Chimica Acta, Zurich, and Wiley-VCH, Weinheim, 2003.

[28] J. P. Uetrecht, W. F. Trager, 'Drug Metabolism – Chemical and Enzymatic Aspects', Informa, New York, 2007.

[29] F. J. Di Carlo, 'Metabolism, pharmacokinetics, and toxicokinetics defined', *Drug Metab. Rev.* **1982**, *13*, 1–4.

[30] B. Testa, W. Soine, 'Principles of drug metabolism', in 'Burger's Medicinal Chemistry and Drug Discovery', 6th edn., Vol. 2, Ed. D. J. Abraham, Wiley-Interscience, Hoboken, 2003, p. 431–498.

[31] A. Albert, 'The behaviour of foreign substances in the human body', *Trends Pharmacol. Sci.* **1987**, *8*, 258–261.

[32] P. Jenner, B. Testa, F. J. Di Carlo, 'Xenobiotic and endobiotic metabolizing enzymes: an overstretched discrimination?', *Trends Pharmacol. Sci.* **1981**, *2*, 135–137.

[33] W. B. Jakoby, D. M. Ziegler, 'The enzymes of detoxication', *J. Biol. Chem.* **1990**, *265*, 20715–20718.

[34] D. W. Nebert, 'Proposed role of drug-metabolizing enzymes: Regulation of steady state levels of the ligands that effect growth, homeostasis, differentiation, and neuroendocrine functions', *Mol. Endocrinol.* **1991**, *5*, 1203–1214.

[35] F. J. Gonzalez, D. W. Nebert, 'Evolution of the P450 gene superfamily: animal-plant 'warfare', molecular drive and human genetic differences in drug oxidation', *Trends Genet.* **1990**, *6*, 182–186.

[36] B. N. Ames, M. Profet, 'Nature's pesticides', *Nat. Toxins* **1992**, *1*, 2–3.

[37] W. R. Jondorf, 'Drug metabolism and drug toxicity: Some evolutionary considerations', in 'Concepts in Drug Metabolism', Part B, Eds. P. Jenner, B. Testa, Dekker, New York, 1981, p. 305–376.

[38] J. R. Gillette, 'The use of theoretical pharmacokinetic concepts in studies of the mechanisms of formation of chemically reactive metabolites in vitro and in vivo', *Drug Metab. Rev.* **1983**, *14*, 9–33.

[39] T. J. Monks, S. S. Lau, 'Reactive intermediates and their toxicological significance', *Toxicology* **1988**, *52*, 1–54.

[40] B. Testa, 'Pharmacokinetic and pharmacodynamic events: can they always be distinguished?', *Trends Pharmacol. Sci.* **1987**, *8*, 381–383.

[41] 'ADME-Tox: The Fate of Drugs in the Body', Eds. B. Testa, H. van de Waterbeemd, Vol. 5 in 'Comprehensive Medicinal Chemistry', 2nd edn., Eds. J. B. Taylor, D. J. Triggle, Elsevier, Oxford, 2007.

[42] B. Testa, P. Jenner, 'Novel metabolites produced by functionalization reactions: Chemistry and toxicology', *Drug Metab. Rev.* **1978**, *7*, 325–369.

[43] J. Caldwell, 'Conjugation reactions in foreign-compound metabolism: definition, consequences, and species variations', *Drug Metab. Rev.* **1982**, *13*, 745–777.

[44] B. Testa, 'Nonenzymatic contributions to xenobiotic metabolism', *Drug Metab. Rev.* **1982**, *13*, 25–50.

[45] T. Walle, U. K. Walle, L. S. Olanoff, 'Quantitative account of propranolol metabolism in urine of normal man', *Drug Metab. Dispos.* **1985**, *13*, 204–209.

[46] B. Testa, P. Jenner, 'The concept of regioselectivity in drug metabolism', *J. Pharm. Pharmacol.* **1976**, *28*, 731–744.

[47] 'Enzyme Nomenclature', Nomenclature Committee of the International Union of Biochemistry and Molecular Biology (IUBMB), www.chem.qmul.ac.uk/iubmb/enzyme.

[48] T. Rodgers, D. Leahy, M. Rowland, 'Tissue distribution of basic drugs: Accounting for enantiomeric, compound and regional differences amongst β-blocking drugs in rat', *J. Pharm. Sci.* **2005**, *94*, 1237–1248; L. Z. Benet, B. Y. T. Perotti, L. Hardy, 'Drug absorption, distribution, and elimination', in 'Burger's Medicinal Chemistry and Drug Discovery', 6th edn., Vol. 2, Ed. D. J. Abraham, Wiley-Interscience, Hoboken, 2003, p. 633–647; B. Fichtl, A. von Nieciecki, K. Walter, 'Tissue binding versus plasma binding of drugs: General principles and pharmacokinetic consequences', in 'Advances in Drug Research', Vol. 20, Ed. B. Testa, Academic Press, London, 1991, p. 117–166.

[49] P. J. McNamara, M. Abbassi, 'Neonatal exposure to drugs in breast milk', *Pharm. Res.* **2004**, *21*, 555–566.

[50] I. Mahmood, 'Interspecies scaling of biliary excreted drugs: A comparison of several methods', *J. Pharm. Sci.* **2005**, *94*, 883–892.

[51] A. E. Cribb, M. Peyrou, S. Muruganandan, 'The endoplasmic reticulum in xenobiotic toxicity', *Drug Metab. Rev.* **2005**, *37*, 405–442.

[52] S. A. Robert, 'High-throughput screening approaches for investigating drug metabolism and pharmacokinetics', *Xenobiotics* **2001**, *31*, 557–589.

[53] M. Recanatini, E. Poluzzi, M. Masetti, A. Cavalli, F. De Ponti, 'QT prolongation through hERG K$^+$ channel blockade: Current knowledge and strategies for the early prediction during drug development', *Med. Res. Rev.* **2005**, *25*, 133–166.

[54] W. J. Watkins, T. E. Renau, 'Antifungal agents', in 'Burger's Medicinal Chemistry and Drug Discovery', 6th edn., Vol. 5, Ed. D. J. Abraham, Wiley-Interscience, Hoboken, 2003, p. 881–918.

[55] M. Strolin Benedetti, M. Bani, 'Metabolism-based drug interactions involving oral azole antifungals in humans', *Drug Metab. Rev.* **1999**, *31*, 665–717.

[56] D. E. Drayer, 'Pharmacologically active metabolites of drugs and other foreign compounds. Clinical, pharmacological, therapeutic and toxicological considerations', *Drugs* **1982**, *24*, 519–542.

[57] A. Fura, Y. Z. Shu, M. Zhu, R. L. Hanson, V. Roongta, W. G. Humphreys, 'Discovering drugs though biological transformation: Role of pharmacologically active metabolites in drug discovery', *J. Med. Chem.* **2004**, *47*, 4339–4351.

[58] P. Ettmayer, G. Amidon, B. Clement, B. Testa, 'Lessons learned from marketed and investigational prodrugs', *J. Med. Chem.* **2004**, *47*, 2393–2404.

[59] B. Testa, 'Prodrug research: Futile or fertile?', *Biochem. Pharmacol.* **2004**, *68*, 2097–2106.

[60] D. P. Williams, D. J. Naisbitt, 'Toxicophores: Groups and metabolic routes associated with increased safety risk', *Curr. Opin. Drug Discov. Dev.* **2002**, *5*, 104–115.

[61] A. S. Kalgutkar, I. Gardner, R. S. Obach, C. L. Schaffer, E. Callegari, K. R. Henne, A. E. Mutlib, D. K. Dalvie, J. S. Lee, Y. Nakai, J. P. O'Donnell, J. Boer, S. P. Harriman, 'A comprehensive listing of bioactivation pathways of organic functional groups', *Curr. Drug Metab.* **2005**, *6*, 161–225.

[62] M. H. Bickel, 'Factors affecting the storage of drugs and other xenobiotics in adipose tissue', in 'Advances in Drug Research', Vol. 25, Eds. B. Testa, U. A. Meyer, Academic Press, London, 1994, p. 56–86.

[63] E. Stokstad, 'Pollution gets personal', *Science* **2004**, *304*, 1892–1894; P. Webster, 'Exposure to flame retardants on the rise', *Science* **2004**, *304*, 1730.

[64] K. R. Scott, 'Anticonvulsants', in 'Burger's Medicinal Chemistry and Drug Discovery', 6th edn., Vol. 6, Ed. D. J. Abraham, Wiley-Interscience, Hoboken, 2003, p. 263–328.

[65] J. Lazarou, B. H. Pomeranz, P. N. Corey, 'Incidence of adverse drug reactions in hospitalized patients: a meta-analysis of prospective studies', *J. Am. Med. Assoc.* **1998**, *279*, 1200–1205.

[66] R. Bullingham, 'Pharmacogenomics: how gene variants can ruin good drugs', *Curr. Drug Discov.* **2001** (March), 17–20.

[67] C. Esser, 'Immunotoxicology', in 'ADME-Tox: The Fate of Drugs in the Body', Eds. B. Testa, H. van de Waterbeemd, Vol. 5 in 'Comprehensive Medicinal Chemistry', 2nd edn., Eds. J. B. Taylor, D. J. Triggle, Elsevier, Oxford, 2007, p. 215–229.

[68] H. van de Waterbeemd, B. Testa, 'The Why and How of ADMET Research', in 'ADME-Tox: The Fate of Drugs in the Body', Eds. B. Testa, H. van de Waterbeemd, Vol. 5 in 'Comprehensive Medicinal Chemistry', 2nd edn., Eds. J. B. Taylor, D. J. Triggle, Elsevier, Oxford, 2007, p. 1–9; 'Pharmacokinetic Optimization in Drug Research: Biological, Physicochemical, and Computational Strategies', Eds. B. Testa, H. van de Waterbeemd, G. Folkers, R. Guy, Verlag Helvetica Chimica Acta, Zurich, and Wiley-VCH, Weinheim, 2001; 'Pharmacokinetic Profiling in Drug Research: Biological, Physicochemical, and Computational Strategies', Eds. B. Testa, S. Krämer, H. Wunderli-Allenspach, G. Folkers, Verlag Helvetica Chimica Acta, Zurich, and Wiley-VCH, Weinheim, 2006; L. G. Yengi, L. Leung, J. Kao, 'The evolving role of drug metabolism in drug discovery and development', *Pharm. Res.* **2007**, *24*, 842–858.

[69] D. A. Smith, E. F. Schmid, 'Drug withdrawals and the lessons within', *Curr. Opin. Drug Discov. Dev.* **2006**, *9*, 38–46.

[70] D. A. Smith, E. F. Schmid, B. Jones, 'Do drug metabolism and pharmacokinetic departments make any contribution to drug discovery?', *Clin. Pharmacokin.* **2002**, *41*, 1005–1019.

[71] T. N. Thompson, 'Optimization of metabolic stability as a goal of modern drug design', *Med. Res. Rev.* **2001**, *21*, 412–449.

[72] C. Helma, 'In silico predictive toxicology: The state-of-the-art and strategies to predict human health effects', *Curr. Opin. Drug Discov. Dev.* **2005**, *8*, 27–31.

[73] N. Greene, 'Computational models to predict toxicity', in 'ADME-Tox: The Fate of Drugs in the Body', Eds. B. Testa, H. van de Waterbeemd, Vol. 5 in 'Comprehensive Medicinal Chemistry', 2nd edn., Eds. J. B. Taylor, D. J. Triggle, Elsevier, Oxford, 2007, p. 909–932.

[74] M. Cronin, M. Hewitt, 'In silico models to predict passage through the skin and other biological barriers', in 'ADME-Tox: The Fate of Drugs in the Body', Eds. B. Testa, H. van de Waterbeemd, Vol. 5 in 'Comprehensive Medicinal Chemistry', 2nd edn., Eds. J. B. Taylor, D. J. Triggle, Elsevier, Oxford, 2007, p. 725–744.

[75] Y. Parmentier, M. J. Bossant, M. Bertrand, B. Walther, 'In vitro studies of drug metabolism', in 'ADME-Tox: The Fate of Drugs in the Body', Eds. B. Testa, H. van de Waterbeemd, Vol. 5 in 'Comprehensive Medicinal Chemistry', 2nd edn., Eds. J. B. Taylor, D. J. Triggle, Elsevier, Oxford, 2007, p. 231–257; Y. Chen, M. Monshouwer, W. L. Fitch, 'Analytical tools and approaches for metabolite identification in early drug discovery', *Pharm. Res.* **2007**, *24*, 248–257.

[76] I. A. M. De Graaf, C. E. Van Meijeren, F. Pektas, H. J. Koster, 'Comparison of in vitro preparations for semi-quantitative prediction of in vivo drug metabolism', *Drug Metab. Dispos.* **2002**, *30*, 1129–1136.

[77] H. C. Rawden, D. J. Carlile, A. Tindall, D. Hallifax, A. Galetin, K. Ito, J. B. Houston, 'Microsomal prediction of in vivo clearance and associated interindividual variability of six benzodiazepines in humans', *Xenobiotica* **2005**, *35*, 603–625.

[78] R. J. Weaver, 'Assessment of drug-drug interactions: concepts and approaches', *Xenobiotica* **2001**, *31*, 499–538.

[79] D. C. Evans, D. P. Hartley, R. Evers, 'Chapter 31. Enzyme Induction – Mechanisms, Assays, and Relevance to Drug Discovery and Development', *Annu. Rep. Med. Chem.* **2003**, *38*, 315–331.

[80] D. A. Smith, 'Induction and drug development', *Eur. J. Pharm. Sci.* **2000**, *11*, 185–189.

[81] C. Yao, R. H. Levy, 'Inhibition-based metabolic drug-drug interactions: predictions from in vitro data', *J. Pharm. Sci.* **2002**, *91*, 1923–1935.

[82] B. Oesch-Bartlomowicz, F. Oesch, 'Mechanisms of toxification and detoxification which challenge drug candidates and drugs', in 'ADME-Tox: The Fate of Drugs in the Body', Eds. B. Testa, H. van de Waterbeemd, Vol. 5 in 'Comprehensive Medicinal Chemistry', 2nd edn., Eds. J. B. Taylor, D. J. Triggle, Elsevier, Oxford, 2007, p. 193–214.

[83] M. Ingelman-Sundberg, 'Implications of polymorphic cytochrome P450-dependent drug metabolism for drug development', *Drug Metab. Dispos.* **2001**, *29*, 570–573.

[84] H. Reiser, 'Pharmacogenetics and drug development', *Annu. Rep. Med. Chem.* **2005**, *40*, 414–427.

[85] B. Testa, 'Prodrug objectives and design', in 'ADME-Tox: The Fate of Drugs in the Body', Eds. B. Testa, H. van de Waterbeemd, Vol. 5 in 'Comprehensive Medicinal Chemistry', 2nd edn., Eds. J. B. Taylor, D. J. Triggle, Elsevier, Oxford, 2007, p. 1009–1042.

[86] B. Testa, A.-L. Balmat, A. Long, 'Predicting drug metabolism – Concepts and challenges', *Pure Appl. Chem.* **2004**, *76*, 907–914.

[87] D. R. Hawkins, 'Comprehensive expert systems to predict drug metabolism', in 'ADME-Tox: The Fate of Drugs in the Body', Eds. B. Testa, H. van de Waterbeemd, Vol. 5 in 'Comprehensive Medicinal Chemistry', 2nd edn., Eds. J. B. Taylor, D. J. Triggle, Elsevier, Oxford, 2007, p. 795–807.

[88] W. F. Trager, 'Principles of drug metabolism 1: Redox reactions', in 'ADME-Tox: The Fate of Drugs in the Body', Eds. B. Testa, H. van de Waterbeemd, Vol. 5 in 'Comprehensive Medicinal Chemistry', 2nd edn., Eds. J. B. Taylor, D. J. Triggle, Elsevier, Oxford, 2007, p. 87–131.

[89] B. Testa, 'Principles of drug metabolism 2: Hydrolysis and conjugation reactions', in 'ADME-Tox: The Fate of Drugs in the Body', Eds. B. Testa, H. van de Waterbeemd, Vol. 5 in 'Comprehensive Medicinal Chemistry', 2nd edn., Eds. J. B. Taylor, D. J. Triggle, Elsevier, Oxford, 2007, p. 133–166.

[90] Y. Giroud, P. A. Carrupt, A. Pagliara, B. Testa, R. G. Dickinson, 'Intrinsic and intramolecular lipophilicity effects in O-glucuronides', *Helv. Chim. Acta* **1998**, *81*, 330–341.

[91] R. DeWitte, 'Overcoming the quantity-quality trade-off in preclinical profiling', *DrugPlus Intern.* **2006** (April/May), 16–19.

[92] K. P. Persson, S. Ekehed, C. Otter, E. S. M. Lutz, J. McPheat, C. M. Masimirembwa, T. B. Andersson, 'Evaluation of human liver slices and reporter gene assays as systems for predicting the cytochrome P450 induction potential of drugs in vivo in humans', *Pharm. Res.* **2006**, *23*, 56–69.

[93] D. M. Cross, M. K. Bayliss, 'A commentary on the use of hepatocytes in drug metabolism studies during drug discovery and development', *Drug Metab. Rev.* **2000**, *32*, 219–240.

[94] D. S. Wishart, 'Bioinformatics in drug development and assessment', *Drug Metab. Rev.* **2005**, *37*, 279–310; L. Afzelius, C. Hasselgren Arnby, A. Broo, L. Carlsson, C. Isaksson, U. Jurva, B. Kjellander, K. Kolmodin, K. Nilsson, F. Raubacher, L. Weidolf, 'State-of-the-art tools for computational site of metabolism predictions: comparative analysis, mechanistic insights, and future applications', *Drug Metab. Rev.* **2007**, *39*, 61 – 86; L. J. Jolivette, S. Ekins, 'Methods for predicting human drug metabolism', *Adv. Clin. Chem.* **2007**, *43*, 131–176.

[95] B. Testa, G. Cruciani, 'Structure-metabolism relations, and the challenge of predicting biotransformation', in 'Pharmacokinetic Optimization in Drug Research: Biological, Physicochemical, and Computational Strategies', Eds. B. Testa, H. van de Waterbeemd, G. Folkers, R. Guy, Verlag Helvetica Chimica Acta, Zurich, and Wiley-VCH, Weinheim, 2001, p. 65–84.

[96] B. Testa, P. Crivori, M. Reist, P. A. Carrupt, 'The influence of lipophilicity on the pharmacokinetic behavior of drugs: Concepts and examples', *Perspect. Drug Discov. Des.* **2000**, *19*, 179–211.

[97] C. Hansch, S. B. Mekapati, A. Kurup, R. P. Verma, 'QSAR of cytochrome P450', *Drug Metab. Rev.* **2004**, *36*, 105–156; R. P. Sheridan, K. R. Korzekwa, R. A. Torres, M. J. Walker, 'Empirical regioselectivity models for human cytochromes P450 3A4, 2D6, and 2C9', *J. Med. Chem.* **2007**, *50*, 3173 – 3184.

[98] J. P. Jones, M. Mysinger, K. R. Korzekwa, 'Computational models for cytochrome P450: A predictive electronic model for aromatic oxidation and hydrogen atom abstraction', *Drug Metab. Dispos.* **2002**, *30*, 7–12.

[99] D. L. Harris, '*In silico* predictive metabolism: A structural/electronic filter method', *Curr. Opin. Drug Discov. Dev.* **2004**, *7*, 43–48.

[100] L. E. Korhonen, M. Rahnasto, N. J. Mähönen, C. Wittekindt, A. Poso, R. O. Juvonen, H. Raunio, 'Predictive three-dimensional quantitative structure-activity relationship of cytochrome P450 1A2 inhibitors', *J. Med. Chem.* **2005**, *48*, 3808–3815.

[101] M. J. Sorich, J. O. Miners, R. A. McKinnon, P. A. Smith, 'Multiple pharmacophores for the investigation of human UDP-glucuronosyltransferase isoform substrate selectivity', *Mol. Pharmacol.* **2004**, *65*, 301–308.

[102] D. F. V. Lewis, 'Molecular modeling of human cytochrome P450-substrate interactions', *Drug Metab. Rev.* **2002**, *34*, 55–67; D. F. V. Lewis, ' Homology modelling of human CYP2 family enzymes based on the CYP2C5 crystal structure', *Xenobiotica* **2002**, *32*, 305–323.

[103] A. D. Costache, D. Trawick, D. Bohl, D. S. Sem, 'AmineDB: large scale docking of amines with CYP2D6 and scoring for druglike properties – towards defining the scope of the chemical defense against foreign amines in humans', *Xenobiotica* **2007**, *37*, 221–245.

[104] M. J. de Groot, A. A. Alex, B. C. Jones, 'Development of a combined protein and pharmacophore model for cytochrome P450 2C9', *J. Med. Chem.* **2002**, *45*, 1983–1993.

[105] C. de Graaf, N. P. E. Vermeulen, K. A. Feenstra, 'Cytochrome P450 in silico: An integrative modeling approach', *J. Med. Chem.* **2005**, *48*, 2725–2755.

[106] L. Afzelius, I. Zamora, C. M. Misimirembwa, A. Karlén, T. B. Andersson, S. Mecucci, M. Baroni, G. Cruciani, 'Conformer- and alignment-independent model for predicting structurally diverse competitive CYP2C9 inhibitors', *J. Med. Chem* **2004**, *47*, 907–914; G. Cruciani, E. Carosati, B. De Boeck, K. Ethirajulu, C. Mackie, T. Howe, R. Vianello, 'MetaSite: Understanding Metabolism in Human Cytochromes from the Perspective of the Chemist', *J. Med. Chem.* **2005**, *48*, 6970–6979; www.moldiscovery.com; D. Zhou, L. Afzelius, S. W. Grimm, T. B. Andersson, R. J. Zauhar, I. Zamora, 'Comparison of methods for the prediction of the metabolic sites for CYP3A4-mediated metabolic reactions', *Drug Metab. Dispos.* **2006**, *34*, 976–983.

[107] S. Ekins, S. Andreyev, A. Ryabov, E. Kirillov, E. A. Rakhmatulin, A. Bugrim, T. Nikolskaya, 'Computational prediction of human drug metabolism', *Exp. Opin. Drug Metab. Toxicol.* **2005**, *1*, 303–324; www.geneco.com.

[108] *MDL Information Systems Inc.*, www.mdl.com.

[109] *Accelyrs Ltd.*, www.accelrys.com.

[110] 'Biotransformations: A Survey of the Biotransformations of Drugs and Chemicals in Animals', Vols. 1–7, Ed. D. R. Hawkins, Royal Society of Chemistry, Cambridge, UK, 1988–1996.

[111] S. A. Kulkarni, J. Zhu, S. Blechinger, 'In silico techniques for the study and prediction of xenobiotic metabolism: A review', *Xenobiotica* **2005**, *35*, 955–973; S. Boyer, C. Hasselgren Arnby, L. Carlsson, J. Smith, V. Stein, R. C. Glen, 'Reaction site mapping of xenobiotic biotransformation', *J. Chem. Inf. Model.* **2007**, *47*, 583 – 590.

[112] P. Darvas, S. Marokházi, P. Kormos, G. Kulkarni, H. Kalász, A. Papp, 'MetabolExpert: Its use in metabolism research and in combinatorial chemistry', in 'Drug Metabolism: Databases and High-Throughput Testing During Drug Design and Development', Ed. P. W. Erhardt, International Union of Pure and Applied Chemistry and Blackwell Science, London, 1999, p. 237–270; www.compu-drug.com.

[113] G. Klopman, M. Tu, 'META: A program for the prediction of the products of mammal metabolism of xenobiotics', in 'Drug Metabolism: Databases and High-Throughput Testing During Drug Design and Development', Ed. P. W. Erhardt, International Union of Pure and Applied Chemistry and Blackwell Science, London, 1999, p. 271–276; www.multicase.com.

[114] J. J. Langowski, A. Long, 'Computer systems for the prediction of xenobiotic metabolism', *Adv. Drug Delivery Rev.* **2002**, *54*, 407–415; B. Testa, A. L. Balmat, A. Long, P. Judson, 'Predicting drug metabolism – An evaluation of the expert system METEOR', *Chem. Biodiv.* **2005**, *2*, 872–885; www.lhasalimited.org.

Part 2

Redox Reactions and Their Enzymes

This *Part 2* of our biochemical introduction to drug metabolism [1a] presents the redox reactions (oxidations and reductions) and their enzymes. As stated in *Part 1* (also published as a review [1b]), these reactions are clearly the most important ones in drug and xenobiotic metabolism. There are at least three reasons for this state of affairs. First, the biotransformation of a xenobiotic often *begins with redox reactions*, and particularly reactions catalyzed by cytochromes P450 (abbreviated as CYPs). Second, a *vast majority of drugs* (and of other xenobiotics, as far as this information is available) are substrates of CYPs [2–10]. Although any attempt to quantify the total number of marketed drugs, drug candidates, and preclinical candidates that are substrates of human CYPs is but a 'guess-estimate', a figure of *ca.* 90% is generally accepted. This percentage is certainly higher when all drug-metabolizing oxidoreductases are taken into account.

The third reason for the predominance of redox reactions in drug metabolism is the *large diversity of metabolites* that may be produced from a single substrate. This diversity involves differences in the chemical nature of the resulting functional groups (*chemoselectivity, e.g.,* a phenolic OH *vs.* an *N*-oxido group), as well as positional or stereochemical differences in the creation of a single type of functional group (*regioselectivity, e.g.,* an *ortho- vs.* a *para*-phenolic OH, or *stereoselectivity, e.g.,* a *cis- vs. trans*-alcoholic OH; see Fig. 1.15 in *Part 1*). As a first glance of what will be summarized in *Part 2*, we note here that the metabolites resulting from redox reactions are *alcohols, phenols, aldehydes, ketones, carboxylic acids, primary* and *secondary amines, hydroxyl-amines, N-oxides, sulfides, sulfoxides* or *sulfones,* to name the major ones. Many of these types of metabolites can be produced by CYP-catalyzed oxidations or reductions. None the less, the contribution of other oxidoreductases should not be underestimated.

Some of the reactions catalyzed by CYPs are also carried out (often in parallel on the same substrate) by the flavin-containing monooxygenases (FMOs), another important class of xenobiotic-metabolizing enzymes which will be presented in parallel with the CYPs. Indeed and as we shall see, *numerous further oxidoreductases* are involved in drug and xenobiotic metabolism [4][7][9]. Like CYPs, they can act directly on a foreign substrate or on a metabolite thereof, but none of these oxidoreductases metabolizes as many substrates as CYPs. Still, some of these enzyme systems metabolize a *marked number of compounds* (*e.g.,* alcohol dehydrogenases) and are thus considered as being of secondary importance in drug metabolism. Others have a *limited number of known foreign substrates* (*e.g.,* aldehyde oxidase and xanthine oxidase); however, their significance should not be underestimated given their potential involvement in molecular toxicology and the ever present possibility of new chemical series being characterized as substrates. A perfect example of this situation is provided by the recognition around 1980 that monoamine oxidase is able to oxidize some heterocyclic tertiary amines to highly neurotoxic metabolites, as will be discussed. As a result of the above, most of *Part 2* is dedicated to the CYPs.

As a general rule, the reaction products of the oxidoreductases are less lipophilic than the parent compounds, and are, therefore, easier to excrete in the urine. Alternatively, many products are good substrates for conjugation reactions as shall be seen in *Part 4*. Conjugation usually renders the compound even more hydrophilic and may also lead to active (transporter-mediated) excretion into the bile or urine. The net result is an accelerated removal of the xenobiotic and its metabolites from the body. However, redox reactions can also lead to reactive and sometimes toxic metabolites. Some examples are shown in this *Part*. Some of the consequences will be discussed in more detail in *Part 5*.

Part 2 Redox Reactions and Their Enzymes

2.1. Cytochromes P450 (CYPs) and Flavin-Containing Monooxygenases (FMOs)

2.2. CYP-Catalyzed sp^3-C-Oxidations

2.3. CYP-Catalyzed sp^2-C- and sp-C-Oxidations

2.4. Oxidations of N- and S-Atoms Catalyzed by CYPs and/or FMOs

2.5. Other Reactions Catalyzed by CYPs

2.6. Other Oxidoreductases and Their Reactions

Fig. 2.1. The table of content of *Part 2* is shown here. Given the overwhelming predominance of *cytochromes P450* (*CYPs*) in the metabolism of drugs and other xenobiotics, most of our attention will be dedicated to their structure, multiplicity, catalytic mechanisms, and the vast diversity of reactions they mediate (*Chapt. 2.1–2.5*). Because *flavin-containing monooxygenases* (FMOs) catalyze some of the reactions mediated by CYPs and do so in parallel, we will also present these enzymes in *Chapt. 2.1* and *2.4*. To close this *Part*, a number of *other oxidoreductases* (including dehydrogenases) and their reactions will be introduced in *Chapt. 2.6*.

> ## Oxidoreductases (EC 1) playing a major or secondary role in xenobiotic metabolism
>
> - **Alcohol dehydrogenases** (EC 1.1.1.1, *ADH*; EC 1.1.1.2, *AKR1A1*)
> - **Aldehyde dehydrogenases** (EC 1.2.1.3, 1.2.1.5, *ALDH*)
> - Aldehyde oxidase (EC 1.2.3.1, *AOX1*)
> - **Aldo-keto reductases** (EC 1.1.1.50, *etc.*, *AKR1*)
> - Copper-containing amine oxidases (EC 1.4.3.6, *AOC*)
> - **CYTOCHROMES P450** (EC 1.14.13 and 1.14.14.1, *CYP*)
> - Dihydrodiol dehydrogenases (EC 1.3.1.20, *DHDH*; *AKR1C*)
> - Dopamine β-monooxygenase (EC 1.14.17.1, *DBH*)
> - **Flavin-containing monooxygenases** (EC 1.14.13.8, *FMO*)
> - Monoamine oxidases (EC 1.4.3.4, *MAO*)
> - Myeloperoxidases (EC 1.11.1.7, *MPO*) and other peroxidases (EC 1.11.1)
> - Prostaglandin-endoperoxide synthase (EC 1.14.99.1, *PTGS*)
> - Quinone oxidoreductases (EC 1.6.5.2, 1.10.99.2, *NQO*)
> - Xanthine dehydrogenase/oxidase (EC 1.17.1.4, -3.2, *XOR*)

Fig. 2.2. To give the reader a better grasp of the variety of oxidoreductases known to be involved in xenobiotic metabolism, we give here an alphabetical list which aims at comprehensiveness but not exhaustiveness. Enzyme classes are shown with their EC number (or major EC numbers) [11], and with their major gene label(s). The primordial significance of *CYPs* translates into the fact that this superfamily of enzymes is shown in red, uppercase characters. Note that the EC numbers listed here for CYPs are those of the xenobiotic-metabolizing ones. *Enzymes of secondary importance* (bold in the *Fig.*) have fewer substrates and carry out a markedly narrower range of reactions than the CYPs. *Enzymes of tertiary importance* have even less known xenobiotic substrates, although we recognize that our classification is subjective and might change due to new findings. Furthermore, this classification says nothing about the potential toxicological consequences of the reactions. For example, myeloperoxidases are responsible for the ultimate toxification of some phenolic metabolites of benzene, and, as such, account in part for the carcinogenicity of benzene and the numerous cases of leukemia it is believed to cause. As a final word of caution, we repeat that this list of enzymes is not complete; for example, *oxyhemoglobin* is also known to oxidize some xenobiotics, particularly hydrazines and hydroxylamines, thereby being oxidized to methemoglobin and producing potentially toxic metabolites [4].

2.1. The Biochemistry of Cytochromes P450 (CYPs) and Flavin Monooxygenases (FMOs)

2.1.1. The Structure of CYPs

- The ancestral gene may date back *ca.* 3.5 billions years.

- *Ca.* 6000 *CYP* genes are currently known (> 60 in humans, excluding pseudogenes).

- *CYP* genes are present and expressed (as their products, CYPs) in all organisms except when lost through regressive mutations.

- Cytochromes P450 metabolize a vast majority of drugs and drug candidates (perhaps as much as 90% or even more).

- Beside drugs, many other xenobiotics are also known CYP substrates, sometimes with major toxicological consequences.

- Monooxygenation is by far their most frequent enzymatic mechanism, but CYPs may also act as reductases, oxidases, and hydroperoxidases.

Fig. 2.3. This *Figure* opens *Chapt. 2.1* by highlighting some key features of CYPs. These include their great (one may even say extreme) *evolutionary age* [12], implying that they appeared shortly after the emergence of life and well before an oxygen-containing atmosphere. The *number of sequenced and named* CYP *genes* keeps increasing (it is > 6000 at the time of writing), and scientists can keep abreast thanks to the '*Cytochrome P450 Homepage*' [13][14] and other public Web-based databases [15][16]. Interestingly, CYP enzymes are present in most organisms including prokaryotes and plants, but there are exceptions such as helminths due to regressive mutations [17][18]. Whereas the vast majority of drugs and drug candidates are known substrates of CYPs as already mentioned, the percentage of other xenobiotics being substrates is not well-known due to lack of evidence but can be estimated to be comparable. This *Figure* also highlights another significant fact, that CYPs can act not only as *monooxygenases*, but also as *reductases, oxidases,* and *hydroperoxidases*. The reductase activity of CYPs will receive due attention in this *Part*.

Enzyme ID Card: Cytochrome P450	
EC Numbers	CYP2C9, CYP2C19, CYP3A4 in EC 1.14.13 Other xenobiotic-metabolizing CYPs in EC 1.14.14.1
Enzyme subclass and sub-subclasses	*EC 1.14*: Oxidoreductases acting on paired donors, with incorporation or reduction of molecular oxygen // *EC 1.14.13*: With NADH or NADPH as one donor, and incorporation of one atom of oxygen // *EC 1.14.14*: With reduced flavin or flavoprotein as one donor, and incorporation of one atom of oxygen
Systematic name	Substrate, reduced-flavoprotein:oxygen oxidoreductase (RH-hydroxylating or -epoxidizing)
Gene root, isoforms	*CYP*, many isoforms
Prosthetic group	Protoporphyrin IX
Cofactors	NADPH, NADH
Subcellular localization	Membrane of smooth endoplasmic reticulum, also mitochondria
Organs (highest levels)	Liver, small intestine, lungs
Exogenous substrates	Innumerable drugs and other xenobiotics belonging to a huge variety of chemical classes
Endogenous substrates	Sterols and steroids, fatty acids, prostaglandins, *etc.*
Miscellaneous	Induction and inhibition relevant to drug and other xenobiotic metabolism

Fig. 2.4. Some significant characteristics of CYPs are shown in this '*Enzyme ID Card*'. With respect to xenobiotic-metabolizing CYPs, the *Nomenclature Committee of the IUBMB* has assigned specific numbers only to CYP2C9, 2C19, and 3A4 (EC 1.14.13...). All other xenobiotic-metabolizing CYPs are gathered under EC 1.14.14.1 'unspecific monooxygenase' [11][16]. Other CYPs which are not involved in xenobiotic metabolism are assigned other numbers [15]. CYPs are expressed to high levels in the *liver*, with significant activities also in the *small intestine wall*. However, marked activity also exists for example in the *lungs*, and smaller activities for example in the brain and skin [19]. CYPs are *membrane-bound* enzymes (excepting the soluble forms in bacteria); their highest concentration is in the smooth endoplasmic reticulum membrane [20]. A number of steroid-metabolizing CYPs are found in mitochondria [21]. The *reducing equivalents* (two single-electron steps as we shall see in *Fig. 2.23*) are supplied by NADPH, with the second electron sometimes being provided by NADH. These reducing equivalents are transferred to cytochrome P450 by two distinct *electron transfer systems* (see *Fig. 2.23*). The reactions carried out by CYPs and their substrates will receive due attention in many of the following *Figures*, whereas the clinically important phenomena of induction and inhibition will be covered in *Part 7*.

Structurally, CYPs are hemoproteins composed of a constant coenzyme (protoporphyrin IX) and a variable protein of *ca.* 50 kDa.

Protoporphyrin IX

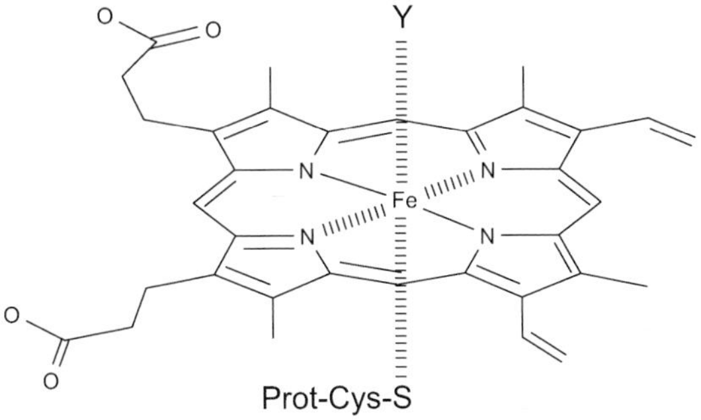

In their main function, they are monooxygenases since they cleave O_2 and insert one O-atom into the substrate XH or X:

$$O_2 + XH + 2\,e^- + 2\,H^+ \;\rightarrow\; XOH + H_2O$$

or

$$O_2 + X + 2\,e^- + 2\,H^+ \;\rightarrow\; XO + H_2O$$

Fig. 2.5. As a hemoprotein, cytochrome P450 consists of an *apoprotein* and a heme moiety as prosthetic group, namely *iron-protoporphyrin IX*. This porphyrin is common to all CYP enzymes as well as to other hemoproteins and enzymes such as hemoglobin, myoglobin, catalase, and most peroxidases. In contrast to the constant porphyrin, the protein part of the enzyme varies markedly from one enzyme/isozyme to the other and accounts for the differences in their properties, *e.g.*, molecular weight (approximate range 45 to 60 kDa), and substrate and product specificities. The *iron cation* in the prosthetic heme is coordinated to the four pyrrole N-atoms. Two additional non-porphyrin ligands exist in axial positions, the *thiolate ligand* (donated by an essential cysteine residue) and the *ligand Y*. The Fe−S bond is an unusually strong one which transfers considerable electron density to the Fe-atom. These electronic features are indispensable for the catalytic activity of cytochrome P450 (*cf. Figs. 2.22* and *2.23*); the formation of the inactive cytochrome P420, as induced for example by denaturation of the protein, involves displacement of the thiolate ligand (Fe−S cleavage). The sixth ligand (*Y* in the *Fig.*) is a weaker one, namely a OH group from an adjacent amino acid (*e.g.*, Tyr) or a H_2O molecule. The foremost activity of CYPs is as monooxygenases, whereby one molecule of oxygen (O_2) is taken up, reduced, and cleaved, with one O-atom leaving the enzyme as a H_2O molecule and the second O-atom being transferred to the substrate (see *Fig. 2.23*) [4–7].

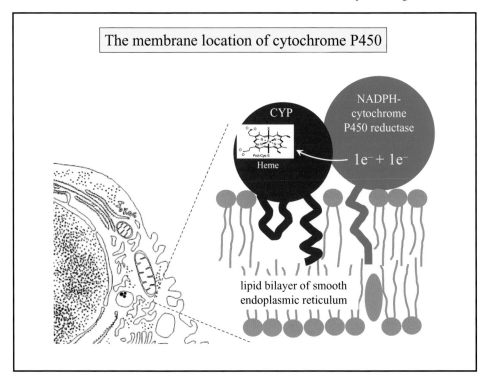

Fig. 2.6. CYPs are peripheral membrane proteins and are located mainly in the endoplasmic reticulum, with some forms being found in mitochondria. This *Figure* depicts their topology and organization in the endoplasmic reticulum [22–24]. As shown, these enzymes are anchored to the membrane bilayer by one or two N-terminal segments. The remainder of the protein up to the C-terminus is exposed to the cytosolic compartment, from which its catalytic center is accessible. The *Figure* also indicates how NADPH-cytochrome P450 reductase (see *Fig. 2.23*) is similarly located and is organized relative to the CYP. The same is true for the other components of the electron-transfer systems, namely NADH-cytochrome b_5 reductase and cytochrome b_5 [25]. Thus, NADPH-cytochrome P450 reductase contains an intramembrane segment with high hydrophobicity and two flanking hydrophilic segments located in the cytoplasm, one of which contains the FAD and FMN cofactors [24]. The CYPs and reductases of the monooxygenase system thus appear to 'float' on the membrane to which they are attached by intramembrane segments.

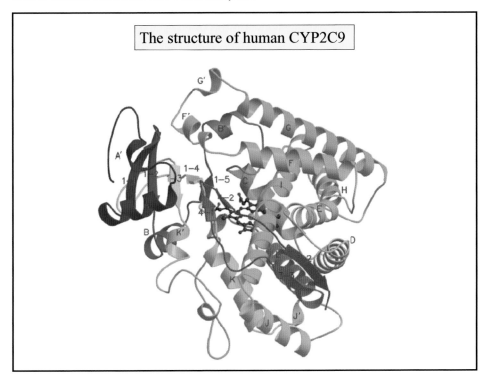

The structure of human CYP2C9

Fig. 2.7–2.9. These milestone *Figures* represent the first successful crystallization and direct structural elucidation of a human cytochrome P450, namely CYP2C9 [26a]. The crystal structure of CYP3A4 was reported one year later [26b]. *Fig. 2.7* presents the *hemoprotein* of CYP2C9 minus the membrane anchor, with color evolving from blue at the N-terminus to red at the C-terminus. Protoporphyrin IX is shown as a ball-and-stick model. The channel to the catalytic site is acknowledged to involve the loops between helices B and C, and helices F and G. *Fig. 2.8* zooms in on *protoporphyrin IX*, showing how it is held in place by what appear to be reinforced H-bonds (hybrids of hydrogen and ionic bonds) between Arg97 and the two propionate side chains of heme. Backbone carbonyls (Val113 and Pro367) maintain Arg97 in position and hence contribute indirectly to anchoring the heme. *Fig. 2.9* brings complementary information on the heme (here in side view) by showing how the iron cation is bound to the Cys435 thiolate group. Furthermore, this *Figure* is of direct relevance to drug metabolism as it shows the large *substrate binding site* of CYP2C9 (violet cavity). One molecule of (*S*)-warfarin is seen in the binding site, which, however, appears large enough to accomodate substrates larger than warfarin, or perhaps more than one molecule of warfarin's size. (Reproduced by permission from *Macmillan Publishers Ltd.: Nature* **2003**, *424*, 464–468 [26a].)

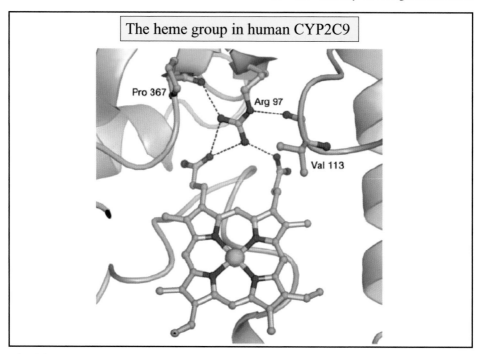

The heme group in human CYP2C9

Fig. 2.8.

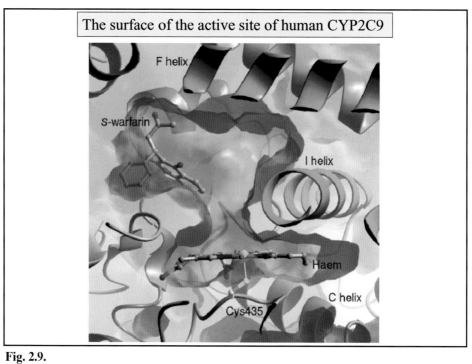

The surface of the active site of human CYP2C9

Fig. 2.9.

2.1.2. The Multiplicity of CYPs

The nomenclature of genes

CYP (root)

  1 (family)

    A (sub-family)

      1 (individual gene)

The nomenclature of proteins

CYP (root)

  1 (family)

    A (sub-family)

      1 (individual protein)

Example: The human *CYP3A4* gene codes for the human cytochrome P450 3A4 (= CYP3A4)

Distribution of *CYP* gene families:

Animals incl. humans: *CYP* 1-49, 51, 301-353-

Plants: *CYP* 51, 71-99, 701-766-

Lower eukaryotes: *CYP* 51-69, 97, 501-699, 5001-5121-

Bacteria: *CYP* 51, 101-281-

Fig. 2.10. Having presented the structure of cytochrome P450 and repeatedly alluded to its many forms, the time is now ripe to focus explicitly on the multiplicity of CYPs and its significance. Since the 1970s and 1980s, various lines of evidence (*e.g.*, physical separation and characterization of many forms, differences due to biological factors) demonstrated the multiplicity of CYPs [2–5]. In more recent years, the explosive growth of molecular biology has revealed protein and gene sequences in huge numbers. A universal and univocal *nomenclature system* rapidly became indispensable. In this system, the root is written first; genes and gene products are then classified in families and subfamilies based on criteria of homology. Individual genes and their products are then numbered in the order of discovery, or sometimes according to their function (*e.g.*, CYP17A1 is a steroid 17α-hydroxylase). Genes are written in italics and proteins in Roman script, with a number of additional conventions for mouse genes (only first letter capitalized, *e.g.*, Cyp3a), some organelles, *etc.* [13][14b]. Pseudogenes (*i.e.*, noncoding degenerate genes) end with the uppercase letter 'P'. This nomenclature system is increasingly being used also for other xenobiotic-metabolizing enzymes [16]. As for the CYPs, serial numbers of families are being attributed to high taxa of organisms as shown, with CYP51 being present in almost all organisms [14][15]. The hyphen added at the end of some series means that the series continues to grow. And note that the multiplicity and nomenclature of *CYP* genes and proteins goes exponentially beyond what we present in *Figs. 2.10–2.14* to take *alleles* into account (see *Part 6*) [27].

The human *CYP* gene superfamily and its products		
Families	Subfamilies	Representative gene products
CYP 1 Family (Aryl hydrocarbon hydroxylases. Substrates: xenobiotics and some endobiotics. Inducible by polycyclic aromatic hydrocarbons)		
	CYP 1A Subfamily	CYP1A1, **CYP1A2**
	CYP 1B Subfamily	CYP1B1
CYP 2 Family (Substrates: xenobiotics and steroids. Constitutive and xenobiotic-inducible)		
	CYP 2A Subfamily	**CYP2A6**, CYP2A7, CYP2A13
	CYP 2B Subfamily (Includes phenobarbital-inducible forms)	
		CYP2B6
	CYP 2C Subfamily (Constitutive forms. Includes sex-specific forms)	
		CYP2C8, **CYP2C9**, CYP2C18, **CYP2C19**
	CYP 2D Subfamily	**CYP2D6**
	CYP 2E Subfamily (Ethanol-inducible)	
		CYP2E1
	CYP 2F Subfamily	CYP2F1
	CYP 2J Subfamily	CYP2J2
	CYP 2R Subfamily	CYP2R1

Fig. 2.11–2.14. The four *Figs. 2.11* to *2.14* present a single *Table* of the human families and subfamilies of CYP enzymes [2–5][13–16]. It appears that enzymes in the *Families 1–3* have evolved to metabolize mainly *xenobiotics*. Indeed, the CYP1 family contains the enzymes that metabolize, and are induced by, polycyclic aromatic hydrocarbons such as 3-methylcholanthrene. In the large CYP2 family, we find the constitutive and inducible enzymes that metabolize steroids and a large variety of drugs. The CYP3 family also contains members that are highly active toward steroids and many different drugs. In humans, a number of CYPs are of particular significance in the metabolism of drugs and other xenobiotics, *i.e.*, 1A1, 1A2, 2B6, 2C9, 2C19, 2D6, 2E1, and 3A4. Essential physiological functions are fulfilled by members of the *Families 4–51*, which are mainly involved in the anabolism (biosynthesis) and catabolism (degradation) of *highly lipophilic endogenous substrates*. Thus, enzymes of the CYP4 family are involved in the oxidation of fatty acids and of a few drugs, and those of the CYP7, CYP11, CYP27, CYP39, and CYP46 families in the metabolism of cholesterol. The biosynthesis of prostaglandin derivatives is catalyzed by enzymes in the CYP5 and CYP8 families. Members of the CYP11, CYP17, and CYP19 and CYP21 families are involved in the metabolism of steroid hormones. Lipophilic vitamins such as vitamin D and retinoic acid are metabolized by enzymes in the CYP24, CYP26, and CYP27 families. CYPs with known polymorphisms relevant for drug therapy are in red (see *Part 6*); major human xenobiotic-metabolizing CYPs are indicated in bold [28–31].

Families	Subfamilies	Representative gene products
	CYP 2S Subfamily	CYP2S1
	CYP 2U Subfamily	CYP2U1
	CYP 2W Subfamily	CYP2W1
CYP 3 Family (Substrates: xenobiotics and steroids. Inducible by xenobiotics and steroids)		
	CYP 3A Subfamily	**CYP3A4**, CYP3A5, CYP3A7 (fetal CYP enzyme), CYP3A43
CYP 4 Family (Peroxisome proliferator-inducible)		
	CYP 4A Subfamily	CYP4A11 (Fatty acid ω- and $(\omega-1)$-hydroxylases), CYP4A22
	CYP 4B Subfamily	CYP4B1
	CYP 4F Subfamily	CYP4F2, CYP4F3, CYP4F8, CYP4F11, CYP4F12, CYP4F22
	CYP 4U Subfamily	CYP4U2
	CYP 4X Subfamily	CYP4X1
	CYP 4Z Subfamily	CYP4Z1
CYP 5 Family		
	CYP 5A Subfamily	CYP5A1 (TXA synthase)
CYP 7 Family		
	CYP 7A Subfamily	CYP7A1 (Biliary acids synthesis, Steroid 7-hydroxylase)
	CYP 7B Subfamily	CYP7B1 (Brain steroid 7-hydroxylase)

Fig. 2.12.

Families	Subfamilies	Representative gene products
CYP 8 Family		
	CYP 8A Subfamily	CYP8A1 (Prostacyclin synthase)
	CYP 8B Subfamily	CYP8B1
CYP 11 Family (Mitochondrial steroid hydroxylases)		
	CYP 11A Subfamily	CYP11A1 (Cholesterol side-chain cleavage)
	CYP 11B Subfamily	CYP11B1, CYP11B2 (Aldosterone synthase)
CYP 17 Family		
	CYP 17A Subfamily	CYP17A1 (Steroid 17α-hydroxylase)
CYP 19 Family		
	CYP 19A Subfamily	CYP19A1 (Steroid aromatase)
CYP 20 Family		
	CYP 20A Subfamily	CYP20A1
CYP 21 Family		
	CYP 21A Subfamily	CYP21A2 (Steroid 21-hydroxylase)
CYP 24 Family		
	CYP 24A Subfamily	CYP24A1 (25-Hydroxyvitamin D 24-hydroxylase)

Fig. 2.13.

Families	Subfamilies	Representative gene products
CYP 26 Family		
	CYP 26A Subfamily	CYP26A1 (Retinoic acid hydroxylase)
	CYP 26B Subfamily	CYP26B1
	CYP 26C Subfamily	CYP26C1
CYP 27 Family (Mitochondrial steroid hydroxylases)		
	CYP 27A Subfamily	CYP27A1 (Biliary acids synthesis, steroid 27-hydroxylase)
	CYP 27B Subfamily	CYP27B1 (Vitamin D 1α-hydroxylase)
	CYP 27C Subfamily	CYP27C1
CYP 39 Family		
	CYP 39A Subfamily	CYP39A1 (24-Hydroxycholesterol 7α-hydroxylase)
CYP 46 Family		
	CYP 46A Subfamily	CYP46A1 (Cholesterol 24-hydroxylase)
CYP 51 Family		
	CYP 51A Subfamily	CYP51A1 (Lanosterol 14α-demethylase, present in most organisms)

Fig. 2.14.

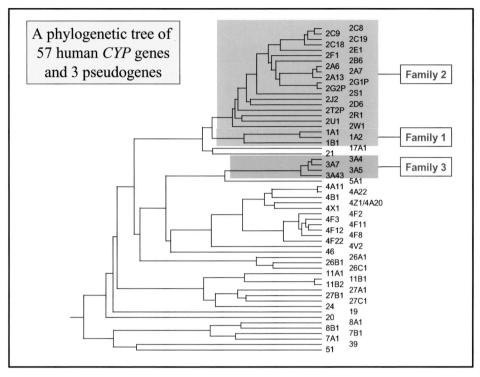

Fig. 2.15. This *Figure* shows the phylogenetic tree of the 57 human genes that code for the CYP enzymes listed in *Figs. 2.11–2.14* above. Three human pseudogenes *2G1P*, *2G2P*, and *2T2P* are also included. This tree was simplified from a larger tree also comprizing 55 *CYP* sequences from fish species [14e]. The enzymes in each major family are closely related and have a common ancestor gene, as highlighted for CYP1, CYP2, and CYP3. *Families 1* and *2* share a common ancestor gene, and together they are closely related to *Families 17* and *21*. *Family 3* shares a common ancestor with *Families 4*, *5*, and *46*. As for the remaining families, their relation to the xenobiotic-metabolizing *Families 1*, *2*, and *3* are more distant (*i.e.*, more ancient).

The substrate specificity of major human drug-metabolizing CYP450 enzymes		
CYP1A2	Common features of substrates	Planar polyaromatic/heterocyclic amines and amides, neutral or basic, lipophilic, with one putative H-bond donor site
	Model substrates	Caffeine (N(3)-demethylation), 7-ethoxyresorufin (O-deethylation), phenacetin (O-deethylation), (R)-warfarin (C(6)-hydroxylation)
	Substrates	Acetanilide, aminopyrine, antipyrine, aromatic amines, chlorzoxazone, clozapine, 17β-estradiol, flutamide, imipramine, lidocaine, (S)- and (R)-mianserin, (S)- and (R)-naproxen, paracetamol, phenacetin, propafenone, tacrine, tamoxifen, theophylline, trimethadone, verapamil, (R)-warfarin, zolpidem

Fig. 2.16–2.21. These six *Figures* summarize the substrate specificity of major human drug-metabolizing CYPs [2][4][5][9][32–36]. Whereas the content of these *Figures* appears explicit enough, some words of clarification may be useful regarding *qualitative vs. quantitative descriptions* of substrate specificity. Indeed, rationalizations as shown here are purely *qualitative* and aim at presenting the broad chemical space of known substrates of a given enzyme. Molecular modeling and X-ray crystallography of enzymes allow a *graphical and semiquantitative* grasp of their substrate specificity. As for the various methods in quantitative structure–activity relationships (QSARs), *e.g.*, 3D-QSARs (see *Part 1*, Fig. 1.40), their rationalizations are *quantitative* by definition. However, such QSARs results being based on limited chemical series can never include the full diversity of substrates recognized by a given enzyme, not to mention the fact that the databases used as training sets may use affinity data rather than catalytic values, and hence do not always discriminate between substrates and competitive inhibitors. The final warning concerns all rationalizations, be they qualitative or quantitative, since these seldom take the flexibility and adaptability of binding sites into account. The unexpected experimental results, shown in *Fig. 2.9*, that CYP2C9 has room to accommodate two molecules of warfarin is proof of the difficulty of rationalizing substrate specificities.

CYP2A6	Common features of substrates	Nonplanar molecules of relatively low MW, including ketones and nitrosamines, with usually two H-bond acceptors 2 – 3 Å apart and 5 – 7 Å from the site of metabolism
	Model substrate	Coumarin (C(7)-hydroxylation)
	Substrates	Cyclophosphamide, buta-1,3-diene, N,N-dimethylnitrosamine, halothane, paraxanthine, phenothiazines, valproic acid, zidovudine
CYP2B6	Common features of substrates	Nonplanar molecules, many with V-shaped structure, neutral or weakly basic, fairly lipophilic, one or two H-bond acceptors
	Model substrate	7-Benzyloxyresorufin (O-dealkylation)
	Substrates	Atrazine, bupropion, cyclophosphamide, dextromethorphan, diazepam, dibenzo[a,h]anthracene, halothane, lidocaine, (S)-mephenytoin, (S)- and (R)-mianserin, nicotine, testosterone

Fig. 2.17.

CYP2C9	Common features of substrates	Neutral or acidic molecules with lipophilic site of oxidation at 5 – 8 Å from one or two H-bond donor/acceptors
	Model substrates	Diclofenac (C(4')-hydroxylation), tolbutamide (para-methyl-hydroxylation)
	Substrates	Benzo[a]pyrene, clozapine, dapsone, fluoxetine, hexobarbital, ibuprofen, lauric acid, losartan, N-nitrosodimethylamine, ondansetron, paracetamol, piroxicam, sulfamethoxazole, tetrahydrocannabinol, trimethoprim, (S)-warfarin, zidovudine
CYP2C19	Common features of substrates	Neutral or weakly basic, moderately lipophilic, with two or three H-bond donors/acceptors 4 – 5 Å apart and 5 – 8 Å from the site of metabolism.
	Model substrates	(S)-Mephenytoin (C(4')-hydroxylation), omeprazole (C(5)-hydroxylation)
	Substrates	Amitriptyline, barbiturates, chlorproguanil, citalopram, clomipramine, cyclophosphamide, diazepam, hexobarbital, imipramine, pentamidine, phenobarbital, phenytoin, propranolol, quinine, (S)- and (R)-warfarin, zidovudine

Fig. 2.18.

CYP2D6	Common features of substrates	A basic nitrogen 5 – 7 Å from the lipophilic site of metabolism, generally located on or near an aromatic system
	Model substrates	Bufurolol ($C(1')$-hydroxylation), debrisoquine ($C(4)$-hydroxylation), dextromethorphan (O-demethylation), sparteine (C-oxidations)
	Substrates	Ajmaline, alprenolol, amiflamine, amphetamine, aprindine, captopril, chlorpheniramine, cinnarizine, citalopram, clomipramine, clozapine, codeine, desipramine, dolasetron, encainide, flecainide, fluoxetine, fluphenazine, haloperidol, hydrocordone, imipramine, loratidine, methoxyphenamine, 3,4-(methylenedioxy)methamphetamine, metoprolol, mexiletine, (S)- and (R)-mianserin, nifedipine, olanzapine, omeprazole, oxycodone, perhexiline, phenformin, propafenone, propranolol, remoxipride, ritonavir, saquinavir, selegiline, tamsulosin, timolol, tomoxetine, tramadol, trifluperidol, zolpidem

Fig. 2.19.

CYP2E1	Common features of substrates	Neutral, small, hydrophilic, relatively planar, structurally diverse, may have one or two H-bond donors/acceptors at 4 – 6 Å from the site of metabolism
	Model substrates	Aniline (*para*-hydroxylation), chlorzoxazone ($C(6)$-hydroxylation), *para*-nitrophenol (aromatic hydroxylation)
	Substrates	Aliphatic alcohols, benzene, buta-1,3-diene, caffeine, clozapine, dapsone, *N,N*-dimethylnitrosamine, enflurane, ethanol, felbamate, fluoxetine, halothane, halogenated alkanes, isoflurane, methylformamide, nitrosamines, ondansetron, paracetamol, phenobarbital, sulfadiazine, styrene, theophylline, toluene

Fig. 2.20.

CYP3A4	Common features of substrates	Large to very large lipophilic molecules, structurally diverse, with position of metabolism determined by chemical reactivity
	Model substrates	Lidocaine (N-deethylation), erythromycin (N-demethylation), midazolam ($C(1')$-hydroxylation), testosterone ($C(6\beta)$-hydroxylation)
	Substrates	Aldrin, alfentanil, amiodarone, aminopyrine, amitriptyline, androstenedione, antipyrine, astemizole, benzphetamine, budesonide, caffeine, carbamazepine, celecoxib, chlorzoxazone, cisapride, clarithromycin, clozapine, cocaine, codeine, cortisol, cyclosporin, delavirdine, dextromethorphan, digitoxin, diltiazem, diazepam, estradiol, etoposide, ketoconazole, loratidine, losartan, lovastatin, methadone, mianserin, miconazole, mifepristone, nevirapine, nicardipine, ondansetron, omeprazole, proguanil, quinine, rapamycin, retinoic acid, ritonavir, saquinavir, selegiline, tacrolimus, tamoxifen, taxol, terfenadine, tetrahydrocannabinol, triazolam, trimethoprim, verapamil, zolpidem

Fig. 2.21.

2.1.3. The Catalytic Mechanism of CYPs

The spin states of cytochrome P450

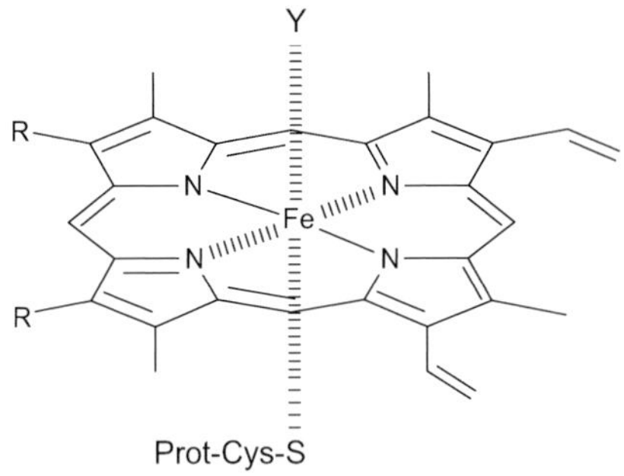

- Low-spin form (S = 1/2)
- Hexacoordinated
- Reduction potential *ca.* –360 to –300 mV (high-energy reduction)
- Resting state (Y = hydroxy group or H_2O)
- Inhibition (Y = xenobiotic hydroxy or amino)

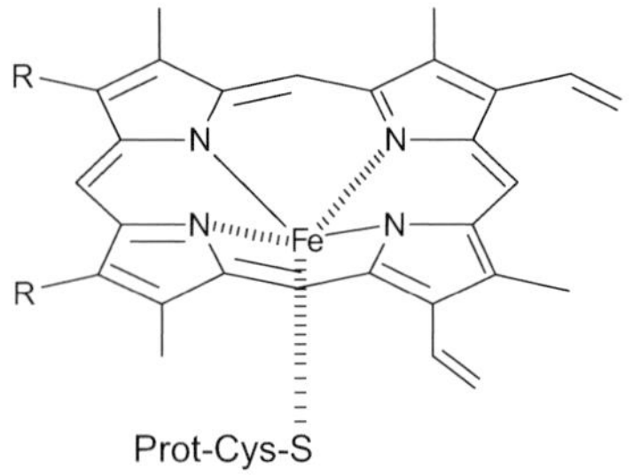

- High-spin form (S = 5/2)
- Pentacoordinated
- Reduction potential *ca.* –175 mV (low-energy reduction)
- Active (reducible) state

Fig. 2.22. Before embarking on a presentation of the many types of reactions catalyzed by CYPs, it is essential to discuss their general catalytic mechanism. This begins with the electronic state of the prosthetic heme moiety and, more accurately, of its iron cation. The latter can exist in its ferric (Fe^{3+}, also written Fe^{III}) and ferrous (Fe^{2+}, also written Fe^{II}) states, although higher oxidation states also play a role in oxygen activation (see *Fig. 2.23*). The *Figure* shows the heme as it exists before beginning of the catalytic cycle, namely with the iron cation in its ferric state and in equilibrium between two discrete electronic states, which are responsible for many of the properties of cytochrome P450, most significantly for ligand binding and oxygen activation. In the low spin form (S = 1/2, abbreviated 'ls'), Fe^{III} is hexacoordinated, with the Fe-atom coplanar with the four pyrrole N-atoms, and the six ligands occupying the vertices of an octahedron (left part of the *Figure*). In its high spin state (S = 5/2, abbreviated 'hs'), Fe^{III} is too large in diameter to be coplanar with the porphyrin ring and is, therefore, pentacoordinated (loss of ligand Y; right part of the *Figure*). A significant information in this *Figure* is the fact that reduction of the low-spin form is energetically much more difficult than that of the high-spin form. The former is, therefore, the 'resting' (inactive) state of CYPs, the equilibrium between the two forms being controlled by the cellular environment and by ligand binding [4][37][38].

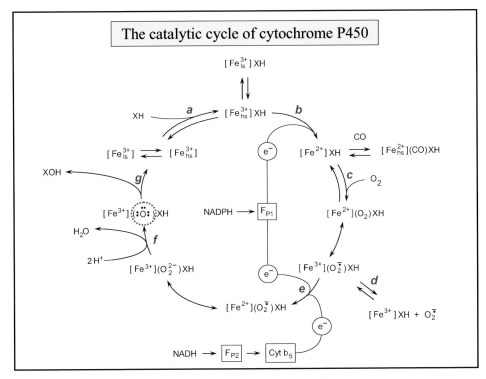

Fig. 2.23. Basically, the catalytic cycle of CYP-mediated monooxygenation involves the reduction of molecular oxygen (O_2, the first substrate) [4][39–41] by two electrons carried by two electron transfer chains [42–46]. The catalytic cycle of cytochrome P450 in its monooxygenase function comprizes a number of steps which are summarized in this *Figure* [4][5][9][27][47–54]. Following binding of the substrate, there is a shift of the hemoprotein to its high-spin form (*Step a*). This allows the first reduction step to occur, the electron being transferred to microsomal CYPs from NADPH (redox potential -320 mV) by the flavoprotein *NADPH-cytochrome P450 reductase* (redox potential -270 mV; symbolized as F_{Pl} in the *Figure*) to form the ferrous form of the CYP–substrate complex (*Step b*). This reductase (NADPH:hemoprotein reductase; NADPH-cytochrome c reductase; EC 1.6.2.4) is a flavoprotein containing both FAD (flavin-adenine dinucleotide) and FMN (riboflavin 5′-phosphate). As all other hemoproteins in their reduced state, the reduced cytochrome P450 has a high affinity for diatomic gases; carbon monoxide binding strongly inhibits the reaction, whereas the binding of molecular oxygen (*Step c*) allows the cycle to continue. The resulting CYP(O_2)substrate ternary complex rearranges by resonance due to the strong electronegativity of O_2 to a formal ferriheme(superoxide)substrate complex. This *ferric-superoxide complex* represents a branching point in the catalytic cycle of cytochrome P450. For the monooxygenation reaction to occur, the second electron must be delivered rapidly, otherwise the complex dissociates with release of the superoxide radical anion (*Parasitic reaction d*). Release of this activated dioxygen species from CYPs is commonly observed in *in vitro* metabolic studies and is

considered an autoxidative decomposition of the oxygenated enzyme. This is an *oxidase function* of cytochrome P450, and it is favored by a number of factors, in particular, the absence of substrate or the binding of poor substrates (*e.g.*, some barbiturates) or pseudo-substrates such as perfluoroalkanes. Such compounds bind with good affinity to the substrate binding site, but the ternary CYP(dioxygen)substrate complex is destabilized to some extent, and substrate oxygenation becomes uncoupled from electron transfer.

Returning to the catalytic cycle, CYPs in the endoplasmic reticulum receive their second electron either from NADPH or from NADH (redox potential $-320\,mV$). In the former case, the electron transfer is again mediated by NADPH-cytochrome P450 reductase. When the reducing equivalent comes from NADH, it first serves to reduce another flavoprotein, *NADH-cytochrome b_5 reductase* (EC 1.6.2.2; NADH-ferricyto-chrome b_5 oxidoreductase; symbolized as F_{P2}; redox potential $-290\,mV$), before being transferred to *cytochrome b_5* (redox potential $+30\,mV$) which, in turn, reduces the cytochrome P450 (*Step e*). The origin of the second reduction equivalent, either NADPH-cytochrome P450 reductase or cytochrome b_5, depends in part on the CYP involved. The doubly reduced CYP(oxygen)substrate complex can have several possible resonance structures and particularly the two shown here, namely the ferro-superoxide and the ferri-peroxide states. The reactivity of this complex is partly explained by the second resonance structure, *i.e.*, the ferric form with bound peroxide dianion.

A monooxygenase reaction implies the transfer to the substrate of an activated O-atom, a reaction that necessitates splitting of the reduced dioxygen (*Step f*). It is likely that the splitting of molecular oxygen is catalyzed by acylation of the Fe-bound peroxide, the acyl moiety presumably being a free carboxy group from a neighboring amino acid. Following acylation, *irreversible heterolytic cleavage of the peroxide O—O bond* occurs, with the thiolate ligand also playing a determining role in increasing the electron density on the two O-atoms, in particular, the distal one. Upon cleavage, the two electrons depart with the distal O-atom which protonates to yield a H_2O molecule. The remaining oxygen in the CYP(monooxygen)-substrate complex is known as an oxene, a neutral, electrophilic atom with only six electrons in its outer layer. It is this oxene which is transferred to the substrate molecule (*Step g*) as exemplified in *Chapt. 2.2–2.4.*

Reactions catalyzed by cytochrome P450

1. *Reactions of monooxygenation*

   Oxidations of sp^3-C, sp^2-C, and sp-C

   N-Oxidations

   S-Oxidations

   O-Oxidations

   Oxidations of Si, P, As, *etc.*

2. *Oxidase reaction*

   Liberation of superoxide (O_2^-)

3. *Hydroperoxidase reactions*

4. *Reactions of reduction*

Fig. 2.24. The metabolic versatility of CYPs is seen not only in the broad chemical space of their substrates, but also in the variety of reactions they catalyze. Thus, reactions of *monooxygenation* result in the oxidation of sp^3-hybridized (aliphatic) C-atoms, sp^2-hybridized (aromatic and olefinic) C-atoms, sp-hybridized (acetylenic) C-atoms, amino and amido N-atoms, S-atoms in various S-containing groups, O-atoms in phenolic groups, as well as other atoms such as Si-, P-, and As-atoms. The *oxidase activity* liberates a reduced dioxygen species, generally the superoxide radical anion as briefly mentioned in the caption of *Fig. 2.23*. This has toxicological significance in that it may lead to lipid peroxidation. The *hydroperoxidase* and *reductase activities* of CYPs are metabolically significant and will be presented in *Chapt. 2.5*.

2.1.4. Flavin-Containing Monooxygenases (FMOs)

Enzyme ID Card: Flavin-Containing Monooxygenase

EC Number	EC 1.14.13.8
Enzyme subclass and sub-subclass	*EC 1.14*: Oxidoreductases acting on paired donors, with incorporation or reduction of molecular oxygen // *EC 1.14.13*: With NADH or NADPH as one donor, and incorporation of one O-atom
Systematic name	*N,N*-Dimethylaniline,NADPH:oxygen oxidoreductase (*N*-oxide-forming)
Gene root, isoforms	*FMO*, five functional human enzymes (FMO1 to FMO5)
Prosthetic group	Flavin-adenine dinucleotide (FAD)
Cofactor	NADPH
Subcellular localization	Membrane of smooth endoplasmic reticulum
Organs (highest levels)	Liver, lungs, kidneys
Substrates	See next *Figure*
Miscellaneous	No known induction or marked inhibition

Fig. 2.25. As explained earlier, some of the metabolic reactions carried out by CYPs and flavin-containing monooxygenases yield the same metabolites (*e.g.*, *N*-oxides and sulfoxides), so much so that they may metabolize the same substrate in parallel and render their relative contributions difficult to assess. We have, therefore, included here the characteristics of FMOs in order to be able, in *Chapt. 2.4*, to discuss together the CYP- and FMO-catalyzed reactions of N- and S-oxidation. Some significant characteristics of FMOs are shown in this '*Enzyme ID Card*' [55–65]. Thus, the *Nomenclature Committee of the IUBMB* assigned EC 1.14.13.8, with the common (yet seldom used) name '*dimethylaniline monooxygenase (*N*-oxide-forming)*' [11]. *Five functional enzymes* are known, with a number of them showing genetic polymorphism in humans. Their apparent molecular weight is in the range 52 to 64 kDa. A sixth gene (*FMO6*) has been sequenced, but its transcripts appear incapable of encoding a functional protein. FMOs are expressed to high levels in the *liver*, but there are also noteworthy activities in the *lungs*, *kidneys*, and *small intestine* [31]. FMOs are *membrane-bound* enzymes in the endoplasmic reticulum. In contrast to CYPs, they receive their reducing equivalents directly from their cofactor NADPH without an electron-transfer chain. Another major difference with CYPs is that they are not induced or readily inhibited, resulting in a low potential for drug–drug interactions at their level (see *Part 7*).

Some characteristics of FMO	
Isoforms most relevant for drug metabolism	• FMO1 (fetal human liver, adult kidney, intestine, liver of nonhuman mammals) • FMO2 (lung) • FMO3 (adult liver)
Substrate characteristics	• Soft nucleophiles (basic amines, sulfides, Se- or P-containing compounds) • Favorable: neutral or with single positive charge • Unfavorable: zwitterions, anions, dications
Typical reactions	• Formation of *N*-oxides (aliphatic, heterocyclic amines), *S*-oxides, *Se*-oxides, phosphine oxides • No direct dealkylations or deaminations by *C*-hydroxylation as with CYPs
Typical drug substrates	Albendazole, benzydamine, chlorpheniramine, cimetidine, clindamycin, fenbendazole, itopride, olopatadine, pargyline, ranitidine, sulindac sulfide, thioridazine, xanomeline, zimeldine
Endogenous substrates	Cysteamine, cysteine conjugates, lipoic acid, methionine, trimethylamine (FMO3)

Fig. 2.26. A number of characteristics of FMOs are presented here to complement the Enzyme ID Card in the previous *Figure*. As we shall see in *Chapt. 2.4*, FMO substrates are *soft nucleophiles* with an electron lone pair available to form a polar, coordinate covalent bond. This includes various S-containing groups (*e.g.*, *sulfides*) and *basic amines*, the metabolites being for example *S*-oxides and *N*-oxides. The reason why FMOs effectively catalyze the *N*-oxygenation of protonated amines is not due to the positive charge *per se* but to basicity being directly related to lone pair availability [4][9]. *C-Atom hydroxylation* appears beyond the catalytic capacity of FMOs, despite a few reports postulating the contrary. The endogenous substrates and physiological functions of FMOs remain to be better understood. For example, the failure to efficiently *N*-oxygenate trimethylamine leads to the genetic diasease known as trimethylamineuria (fish-odor syndrome) [64].

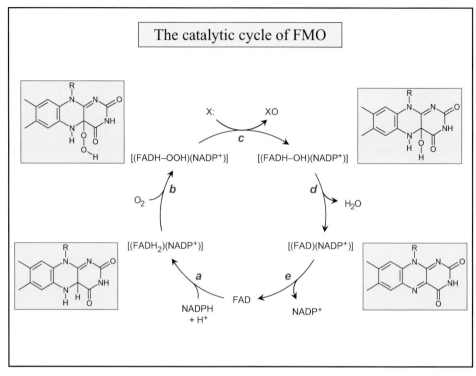

Fig. 2.27. This *Figure* shows the catalytic cycle of FMO together with the redox state of the FDA prosthetic group in the corresponding rectangles. The cycle begins with the binding of NADPH to the oxidized (FAD) state of the enzyme and reduction of the flavin to $FADH_2$ (*Step a*). Although NADH can replace NADPH, its affinity is markedly smaller. Molecular oxygen then binds to the complex and is reduced to a hydroperoxide form (*Step b*). Both steps are fast. The resulting FADH–OOH complex is the 4a-hydroperoxyflavin; this is a stable intermediate in the absence of a substrate, and it is thought to be the predominant form of FAD in FMO within the cell. However, the bound $NADP^+$ is required for the stability of the 4a-hydroperoxyflavin. Furthermore, this stability is not complete, since the release of superoxide and H_2O_2 (reactions not shown) is documented and may be involved in the control of the redox state of the cell and in the expression of H_2O_2-controlled genes. In the presence of a nucleophilic substrate (X:), attack occurs on the distal O-atom. The latter is thus transferred to the substrate to yield the oxygenated product (*Step c*). After substrate oxygenation, the flavin product is the 4a-hydroxyflavin. The latter compound breaks down with release of water (*Step d*), seemingly the rate-limiting step in the catalytic cycle of FMO. $NADP^+$ is not released until the end of the cycle (*Step e*) due to the low dissociation constant of the $FMO(NADP^+)$ complex [4][55][56][59][61][64–66].

2.2. CYP-Catalyzed sp³-C-Oxidations

2.2.1. The Oxygen Rebound Mechanism

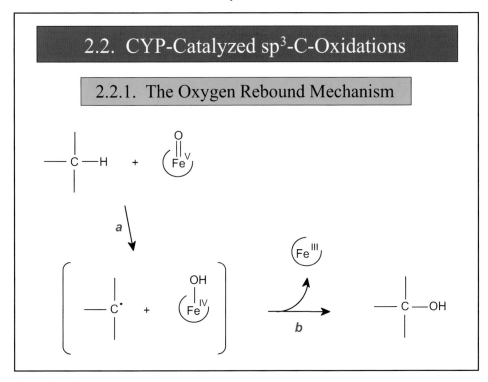

Fig. 2.28. Here, we take a closer look at the substrate oxygenation reaction summarized as *Step g* of the CYP catalytic cycle in *Fig. 2.23*. The reaction begins with hydrogen radical abstraction and involves what is known as the *oxygen rebound mechanism* [4–6][9][40][41][47][48][54][67–70]. The perferric-oxygen intermediate (with the iron shown here in the formal 5+ oxidation state) is postulated to mediate the homolytic cleavage of the C–H bond. This transforms the substrate into a C-centered free radical, while the enzyme becomes an iron hydroxide intermediate in which the hydroxyl radical can be bound more or less tightly. Collapse of this complex to form the hydroxylated product is presumably a cage reaction with a low-energy barrier; its velocity is so high that racemization of the C-centered free radical remains low [4][47][54][71], as will be exemplified in later *Figures*. The reaction leaves the enzyme in its ferric state ready to enter a further catalytic cycle. As shown, the product of the oxygen rebound mechanism is an alcohol. However, another metabolite is possible in a few cases, which is formed by the rare reaction of *CYP-catalyzed sp³-C-desaturation* to be presented in *Fig. 2.57.*

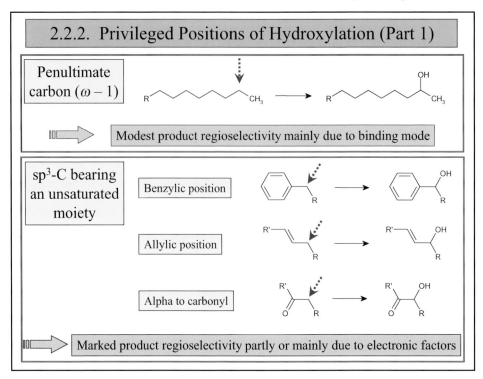

2.2.2. Privileged Positions of Hydroxylation (Part 1)

Penultimate carbon ($\omega - 1$)

Modest product regioselectivity mainly due to binding mode

sp³-C bearing an unsaturated moiety

Benzylic position

Allylic position

Alpha to carbonyl

Marked product regioselectivity partly or mainly due to electronic factors

Fig. 2.29. CYP-Catalyzed sp³-C-hydroxylations can conveniently be described and partly rationalized in terms of their product regioselectivity (*i.e.*, the privileged positions of hydroxylation), and sometimes also in terms of product stereoselectivity when the target carbon is a prochiral CH_2 group (see *Part 1*, Fig. 1.15). This *Figure* presents the first two rationalizations we will examine and exemplify in this *Chapter*, namely the case of relatively long *n*-alkyl chains and positions α to an unsaturated region. *Relatively long* n-*alkyl chains* (No. of C-atoms ≥ 3) are found in a number of xenobiotic alkanes to which humans are exposed, in some natural products (*e.g.*, cannabinoids) and in some drugs. Here, there is no activating functionality and regioselectivity is quite variable, resulting mostly from proteins constraints and the binding mode they impose [72]. In contrast, an *unsaturated function in the α-position* acts as an activating factor for electronic (*i.e.*, mechanistic) reasons and facilitates oxidative attack [4][52][72]. In other words, the regioselectivity caused by the presence of a vicinal activating group results in a regioselectivity which will be more or less independent of the specific CYP involved. Other activating groups will be considered in *Fig. 2.33*. *Figs. 2.30–2.32* will exemplify the various reactions shown here.

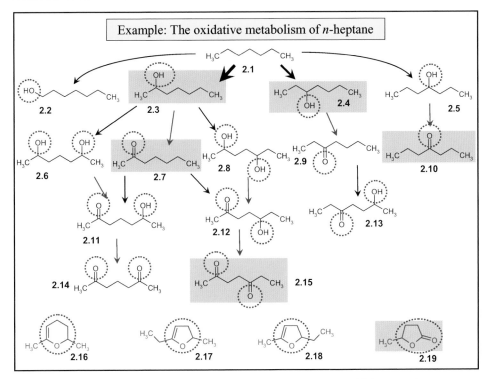

Fig. 2.30. n-*Heptane* (**2.1**) is a simple xenobiotic *n*-alkane to which many humans are exposed daily, since it is a component found in fuel and industrial solvents. Here, we use this compound to offer a first illustration of regioselectivity and the complexity of intertwined metabolic oxidations. The careful and comprehensive study we present here was conducted in rats exposed to ambient *n*-heptane under controlled conditions, and in a number of factory workers known to be exposed to the solvent [73]. The oxidative metabolic pathways of *n*-heptane as found in this and previous studies is schematized in the *Figure*, with the compounds detected in human urine being placed in *blue boxes*. Heptan-2-ol (**2.3**) was the major metabolite, with heptan-3-ol (**2.4**) second in importance; heptan-1-ol (**2.2**) and heptan-4-ol (**2.5**) were minor metabolites or were not detected directly. These *first-generation metabolites* exemplify the *regioselectivity* outlined in *Fig. 2.29*. Although reactions of dehydrogenations will not be discussed specifically before *Chapt. 2.6*, we have represented these reactions with blue arrows when they lead to known *second-generation* (*i.e.*, **2.6** to **2.10**), *third-generation*, and *fourth-generation metabolites* (*i.e.*, **2.11** to **2.15**). *Cyclic metabolites*, **2.16–2.19**, formed by incompletely understood sequences or possibly as analytical artefacts are shown in blue. An artefactual formation is certainly excluded for γ-valerolactone (**2.19**), an important urinary metabolite of *n*-heptane and *n*-hexane in humans and rats.

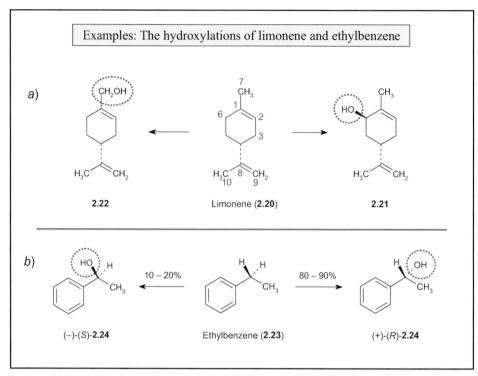

Fig. 2.31. In this *Figure*, we begin with examples where sp³-*C*-hydroxylation is directed by activating moieties, which facilitate attack and homolytic cleavage of the C−H bond by the oxene atom [4][52][54]. Our first example is the preferred hydroxylation of *allylic positions*, namely a C−H target carrying a −CH=CH− substituent. *(+)-(R)-Limonene* (*a*; **2.20**) and its (−)-(*S*)-enantiomer show five such positions, namely C(3), C(4), C(6), C(7), and C(10). Incubation of these two substrates in rat liver microsomes showed that allylic hydroxylation occurred at two positions only, namely C(6) to yield *trans*-carveol (**2.21**) and C(7) to yield perillyl alcohol (**2.22**) [74][75]. Epoxidation of the two C=C bonds is also known but is not relevant here. The next example illustrates regioselectivity at a *benzylic position* induced by an aromatic moiety. *Ethylbenzene* (*b*; **2.23**) is a case in point, as it is the simplest molecule for this purpose, and an important xenobiotic found for example in unleaded fuel. In rat-liver preparations, this compound was hydroxylated with high regioselectivity at the benzylic position to afford 1-phenylethanol (**2.24**) [76]. *In vivo* studies in humans and rats confirmed these results but indicated that hydroxylation of the CH₃ group also occurs, most likely as a second metabolic step to afford phenylethylene glycol [77]. What the *Figure* also shows is that the reaction yields predominantly (+)-(*R*)-1-phenylethanol. This high *product stereoselectivity* cannot be due to electronic factors but results from the binding mode of the substrate and the extremely short existence of the radical intermediate (see caption to *Fig. 2.28*).

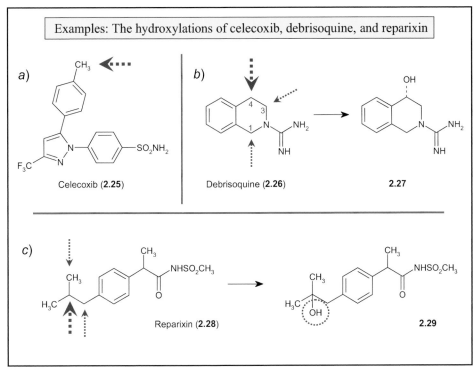

Examples: The hydroxylations of celecoxib, debrisoquine, and reparixin

a) Celecoxib (**2.25**)

b) Debrisoquine (**2.26**)   **2.27**

c) Reparixin (**2.28**)   **2.29**

Fig. 2.32. Here, we use three medicinal compounds to exemplify the preferred (but not necessarily unique) hydroxylation at a benzylic position. Our first example is that of *celecoxib* (*a*; **2.25**), an inhibitor of cyclooxygenase 2 (COX2) which features a *p*-CH_3 group (thick red arrow) as a good target for CYP oxidation. And, indeed, this drug is extensively metabolized in humans and rats, the practically sole pathway being methyl hydroxylation, rapidly followed by dehydrogenation to the carboxylic acid (which accounts for *ca.* 75% of a dose in humans) [78][79]. *Debrisoquine* (*b*; **2.26**) is a well-known substrate of CYP2D6 which is extensively metabolized (and inactivated) by 4-hydroxylation to (+)-(*S*)-4-hydroxydebrisoquine (**2.27**). Yet other sp^3-C sites of metabolic oxidation are also known, *i.e.*, 1- and 3-hydroxylation leading to ring-opened products (oxidation of a C-atom α to N; see later) [80]. Large genetically based variations in the metabolic inactivation of debrisoquine led to its withdrawal several years ago (see *Part 6*). Our last case here is that of *reparixin* (*c*; **2.28**), an inhibitor of the chemokine CXCL8 and a sobering metabolic example. Indeed and contrary to what could be expected based on the previous examples, the benzylic position was a minor site of oxidation, as were each of the enantiotopic CH_3 groups in the isobutyl chain [81]. Remarkably, the major site of CYP attack was the methine (C–H) group.

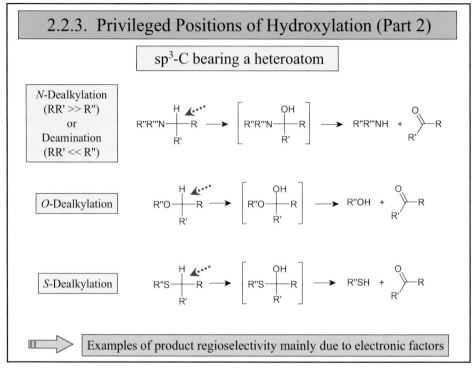

2.2.3. Privileged Positions of Hydroxylation (Part 2)

sp³-C bearing a heteroatom

Fig. 2.33. This *Figure* contains important CYP-catalyzed hydroxylations involving sp³-C-atoms bearing an N-, O-, or S-heteroatom, and which result in reactions of *N*-dealkylation, deamination, *O*-dealkylation, or *S*-dealkylations. As for allylic and benzylic positions, the electronic influence of *the heteroatom adjacent to the target sp³-C-atom* accounts for the regioselectivity of these reactions by facilitating oxene attack and homolytic cleavage of the C–H bond. The reactions in this *Figure* have also in common the noteworthy fact that the primary metabolite (*i.e.*, the hydroxylated product) is an *unstable intermediate*, which can seldom be observed. Indeed, these hydroxylated intermediates break down or hydrolyze spontaneously (see also *Fig. 2.124*), a reaction that cleaves the C–heteroatom bond, as schematized without mechanistic details. Reactions at N-bearing C-atoms (*N-dealkylations and deaminations*) are special not only for their quantitative and qualitative importance, but also for the fact that, in some cases, they may proceed by an alternative mechanism, namely initial N-oxidation (one-electron abstraction) [4][52]. A further peculiarity exists in that the intermediate (here called a 'carbinolamine') may be stable enough to be observed when the N-atom is an amido one. The following *Figures* will exemplify the various reactions shown here.

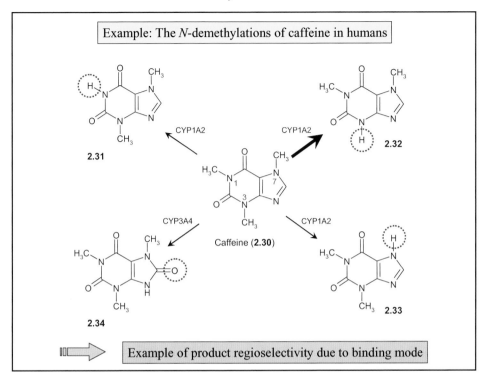

Example: The *N*-demethylations of caffeine in humans

Example of product regioselectivity due to binding mode

Fig. 2.34. We begin with reactions of dealkylation, a well-known example being provided by *caffeine* (**2.30**) and the three *N*-CH$_3$ substituents it bears. Indeed, three reactions of *N*-demethylation occur, all of which are catalyzed by CYP1A2 in humans at realistic levels of the substrate. However, the regioselectivity among these reactions was unexpected, since *N(3)*-demethylation leading to *paraxanthine* (**2.32**) contributes to *ca.* 80% to caffeine clearance in humans, whereas *N(1)*-demethylation to *theobromine* (**2.31**) and *N(7)*-demethylation to *theophylline* (**2.33**) contribute to *ca.* 11 and 4%, respectively [82–85]. Electronic factors cannot explain these differences, since, for example, the pK_a values of the three dimethylxanthines are comparable (9.9, 8.5, and 8.7 for **2.31**, **2.32**, and **2.33**, resp.). The fourth reaction shown is *C(8)*-hydroxylation leading to *1,3,7-trimethyluric acid* (**2.34**), which probably derives from an intermediate also leading to N(7)–C(8) bond scission (see *Fig. 2.36*).

Example: The *N*-dealkylations and *O*-demethylations of gallopamil

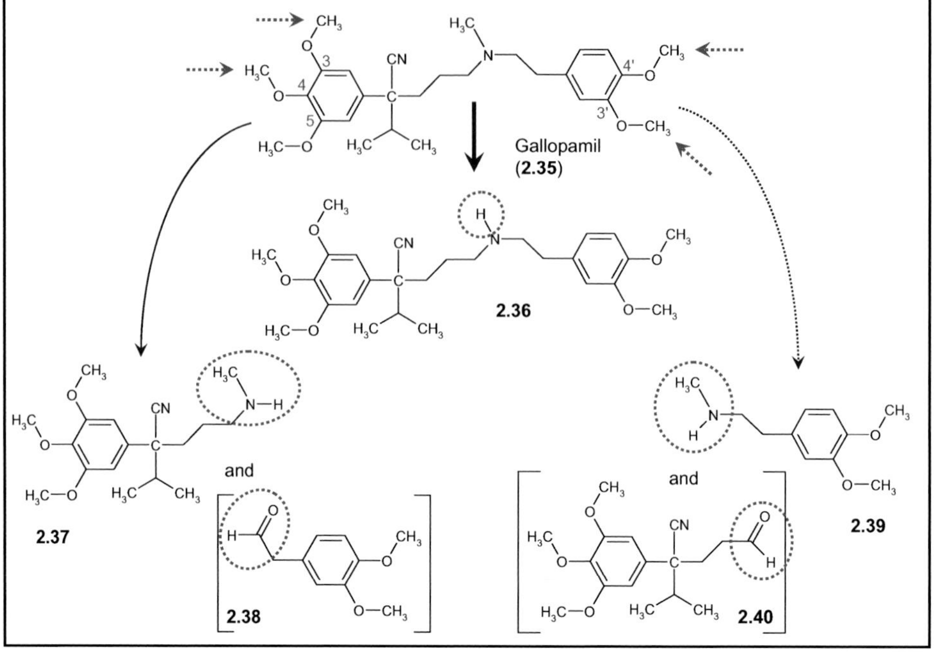

Fig. 2.35. *Gallopamil* (**2.35**) is a calcium channel-blocking drug whose complex biotransformation can serve to illustrate several metabolic reactions of interest. This molecule features sp^3-C-atoms adjacent to N- and O-atoms, which makes them potential target sites for competitive and sequential reactions of *N*- and *O*-dealkylation. N-*Demethylation* to norgallopamil (**2.36**) was the predominant reaction in human and rat liver microsomes [86]. Secondary in importance was N-*dealkylation* to **2.37**, with loss of the *N*-(2-phenylethyl) substituent. The last reaction of N–C oxidative cleavage was minor (a few percents) and led to the secondary amine **2.39**; it is a subjective matter whether one calls this reaction an *N*-dealkylation or a *deamination*. Note that the two non-nitrogenated moieties **2.38** and **2.40** are shown here as the direct products of N–C bond cleavage, namely as the aldehydes which were not identified as such but as the respective alcohol and carboxylic acid. The metabolic fate of aldehydes will be discussed in *Chapt. 2.6*. In addition to reactions of N–C bond cleavage, the five CH_3O groups of gallopamil are also potential targets of *O*-demethylation. Because the 3- and 5-CH_3O groups are equivalent, gallopamil can only yield four *O*-monodemethylated products. All four reactions were observed in human and rat liver microsomes, the relative rates being $4' \geq 4 \geq 3 > 3'$ [87]. However, *N*-dealkylations to **2.36** and **2.37** were markedly faster than the *O*-demethylations. Please note that these relative rates cannot be generalized, since, for example, the same reactions had different relative rates in the analogue *verapamil* (**2.35** with no CH_3O group at C(5)) [88][89].

2.2.4. Privileged Positions of Hydroxylation (Part 3)

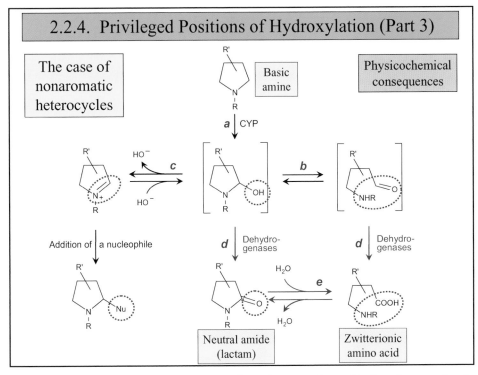

| The case of nonaromatic heterocycles | Basic amine | Physicochemical consequences |

Neutral amide (lactam)

Zwitterionic amino acid

Fig. 2.36. In *saturated* (or *partly saturated*) *azaheterocycles*, oxidative ring opening is analogous to *N*-dealkylation/deamination, but the cyclic nature of the substrate gives rise to additional metabolites [4][90]. This type of reaction has indeed been detected in numerous cases of medicinal or toxicological relevance. As shown here, the α-hydroxylated intermediate (*i.e.*, the cyclic carbinolamine produced by the CYP-catalyzed *Reaction a*) can undergo N–C bond cleavage (*Reaction b*) as in the case of non-cyclic substrates. However, the reaction is a reversible one, more precisely a *ring–chain tautomeric equilibrium*, and both tautomers are substrates of dehydrogenases (*Reactions d*) to yield a *lactam* and a *zwitterionic amino acid*, respectively, as stable metabolites. The arrows leading to these two second-generation metabolites are shown in blue to indicate that the enzymes and reactions that form them will be discussed later (see *Chapt. 2.6*). The possibility exists of a lactam ⇌ amino acid equilibrium due to hydration/dehydration (*Reaction e*). The formation of an *iminium species* (*Reaction c*) has repeatedly been detected by trapping it with a nucleophile such as the cyanide anion. Note that an iminium species can also be formed from linear carbinolamines, but the case is not mentioned in *Fig. 2.33*. A point of significance in an ADME perspective (*Part 1*) is the difference in physicochemical properties between the substrate (a basic amine) and its two major metabolites, the neutral lactam and the zwitterionic amino acid.

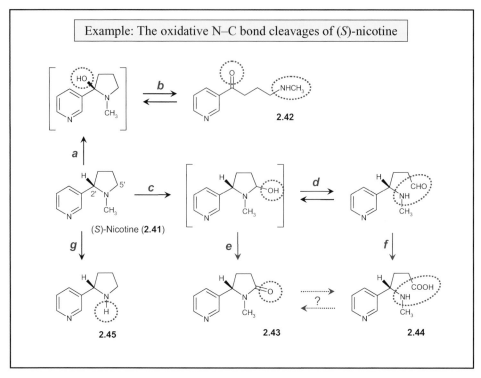

Fig. 2.37. The natural *(−)-(S)-nicotine* (**2.41**) is a widely consumed xenobiotic whose metabolism has been investigated extensively in humans and animals, revealing the formation of a large number of metabolites [4][91][92]. The first route shown here (*Reaction a*) is C(2′)-hydroxylation (*ca.* 10% in humans) which leads to a whole range of 3-substituted pyridine derivatives *via Reaction b* and the amino ketone **2.42**. The most important metabolic route of (*S*)-nicotine (*ca.* 70–80% in humans) is C(5′)-hydroxylation (*Reaction c*) leading to ring opening by C(5′)-N bond cleavage. The 5′-*carbinolamine* exists in a ring ⇌ chain tautomeric equilibrium with an aldehyde (*Reaction d*). Neither tautomer is stable metabolically, being both substrates for oxidases and/or dehydrogenases to yield the lactam **2.43** (*Reaction e*) and the amino acid **2.44** (*Reaction f*), respectively. The arrows leading to these two second-generation metabolites are shown in blue to indicate that the relevant enzymes and reactions will be discussed later in this *Part*. *Reaction e* in particular is catalyzed by aldehyde oxidase (*Chapt. 2.6*); the lactam thus produced is *cotinine* (**2.43**), by far the major human metabolite of nicotine. The third reaction around the basic N-atom is *N*-demethylation (*Reaction g*) to nornicotine (**2.45**), a minor route (<1% in humans).

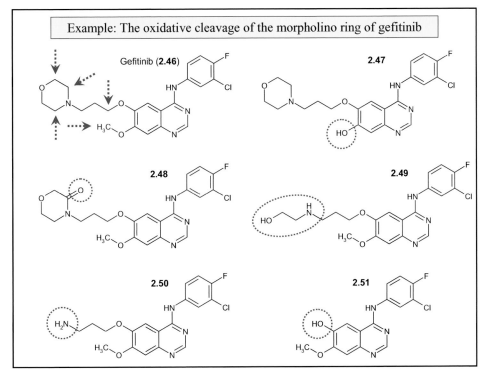

Fig. 2.38. A pyrrolidin-2-yl ring as in nicotine is of course not the only type of saturated ring to undergo metabolic oxidation and ring opening [4]. Here, we use a morpholino ring to illustrate its potential for CYP attack and the nature of some metabolites. *Gefitinib* (**2.46**) is an antitumor drug which inhibits the tyrosine kinase that acts on the epidermal growth factor receptor. Investigations in human liver microsomes have shown that its major pathways involve morpholino ring opening to yield metabolites **2.48**, **2.49**, and **2.50**. The occurrence of *O*-demethylation and *O*-dealkylation is illustrated by metabolites **2.47** and **2.51**, respectively [93][94].

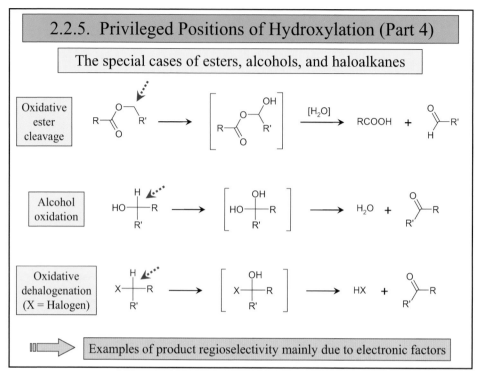

Fig. 2.39. This *Figure* continues the various types of CYP-catalyzed sp³-*C*-hydroxylations (see *Figs. 2.29, 2.33,* and *2.36*) by listing oxidative ester cleavage, alcohol oxidation, and oxidative haloalkane dehalogenation. Here again, the electronic influence of *the adjacent O- or halogen atom* accounts for the greater reactivity of the target sp³-*C*-position. Two of the CYP reactions listed here are noteworthy, since they yield metabolites which can also be formed by other enzymes with an entirely different catalytic mechanism. Thus, *oxidative ester cleavage* is a minor reaction compared to hydrolysis catalyzed by hydrolases (*Part 3*), and is irrefutably documented only for a limited number of substrates. Similarly, the *in vivo* toxicological significance of *CYP-catalyzed alcohol oxidation* to an aldehyde or ketone is difficult to assess given that the same reaction is mediated with high efficiency by alcohol dehydrogenases (*Chapt. 2.6*). As for *oxidative dehalogenation* (*Chapt. 2.5*), it is in competition with reductive dehalogenation carried out by the same or different CYPs, but here the two mechanisms can be clearly distinguished given that they yield different metabolites.

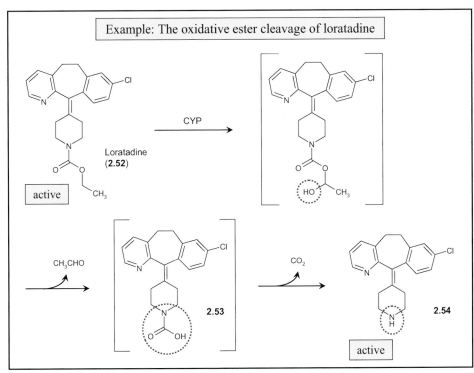

Fig. 2.40. There is unambiguous *in vitro* evidence that a number of carboxylic acid esters can undergo CYP-catalyzed oxidative cleavage in addition to hydrolysis catalyzed by hydrolases (*Part 3*) [4][52][95]. This is the case for several model compounds (*e.g.*, methyl and ethyl alkanoates) as well as a few medicinal compounds, *e.g.*, *loratadine* (**2.52**). This is a well-known and potent antihistaminic drug with low sedative side-effects. The compound is metabolized to de(ethoxycarbonyl)loratadine (also known as *desloratadine* (**2.54**)), itself a potent H_1-receptor antagonist whose production probably accounts for the long duration of action of the drug. Although enzymatic hydrolysis, followed by spontaneous decarboxylation, is a likely mechanism leading to desloratadine formation in patients, there is evidence that, in human liver microsomes, its formation is catalyzed by cytochrome P450, primarily CYP3A4 and CYP2D6 [96]. The reaction generates the unstable hydroxylated intermediate which loses acetaldehyde as expected to yield the '*carbamic acid*' **2.53**. The latter is again unstable and undergoes decarboxylation spontaneously to desloratadine (**2.54**). The relative contributions of CYPs and carboxylesterases in the *in vivo* production of desloratidine appear difficult to investigate even in animals and remains unassessed [97].

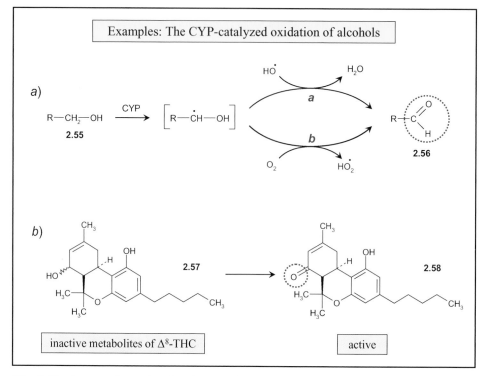

Examples: The CYP-catalyzed oxidation of alcohols

inactive metabolites of Δ^8-THC   active

Fig. 2.41. As stated previously, the usual oxidative route of primary and secondary alcohols is dehydrogenation by alcohol dehydrogenases (*Chapt. 2.6*) to aldehydes and ketones, respectively. However, a number of CYPs are able under proper conditions to produce the same metabolites from the same substrates, but by a mechanism of oxidation (*i.e.*, oxygenation or electron withdrawal) rather than dehydrogenation [4][98–101]. Proofs of the reaction come from *in vitro* (*e.g.*, type of subcellular preparations, cofactors, oxygen, inhibitors, and inducers) and *in vivo* (*e.g.*, effect of inducers) studies. Thus, *primary alcohols* of low molecular weight such as methanol, ethanol, propan-1-ol, and butan-1-ol (*a*; **2.55**; R=H, methyl, ethyl, propyl, resp.) are oxidized by CYP2E1 to the corresponding aldehyde. There is still some uncertainty about the detailed mechanism(s) involved [4][52]. The oxygen rebound mechanism generates the C-centered radical which reacts with the Fe-bound hydroxyl radical to form a geminal diol (not shown here) which breaks down to the aldehyde **2.56** (*Mechanism a*). Another postulated mechanism involves homolytic cleavage of the C–H bond by a hydroxyl radical produced in the catalytic site and loosely bound therein; molecular oxygen then reacts with the C-centered radical to dehydrogenate it and become a superoxide radical ($O_2^{\cdot-}$) in protonated form (*Mechanism b*). Some secondary alcohols of comparatively large molecular weight can also be oxidized by CYP. Indeed, *7α- and 7β-hydroxy-Δ^8-tetrahydrocannabinol* (*b*; **2.57**), which are inactive metabolites of Δ^8-tetrahydrocannabinol, were oxidized to the active 7-oxo metabolite **2.58** when incubated with mouse liver microsomes [100]. Evidence was provided for the involvement of CYP3A11.

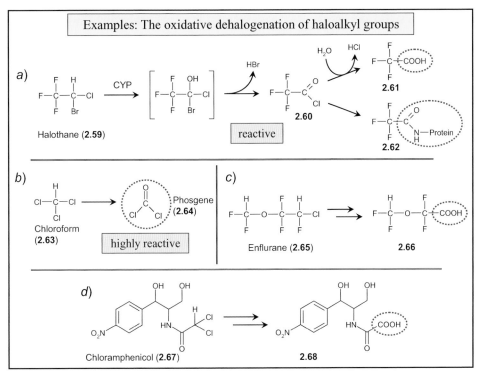

Fig. 2.42. CYP-Catalyzed *oxidative dehalogenation* is simplified here for the general anesthetic *halothane* (*a*; **2.59**) [4][102]. The reaction is often catalyzed by CYP2E1 and involves hydroxylation of a C-atom bearing one, two, or three halogen atoms and at least one H-atom. The hydroxylated metabolite is unstable and loses an HX molecule to form an acyl halide (here *trifluoroacetyl chloride* (**2.60**)). This is a highly reactive, electrophilic metabolite which reacts with H_2O to form the carboxylic acid (*i.e.*, *trifluoroacetic acid* (**2.61**)) or may react with endogenous molecules and proteins. Trifluoroacetylated liver proteins (**2.62**) serve as antigens and are associated with (sometimes fatal) idiosyncratic hepatitis [103]. Other aspects of the toxicity of halothane such as jaundice or hepatitis appear to be associated mainly with its CYP-catalyzed *reductive metabolism* (*Chapt. 2.5*). *Chloroform* (*b*; **2.63**) undergoes the same metabolic route [4], the acyl halide formed being the highly reactive and toxic *phosgene* (**2.64**). There is regioselectivity in oxidative dehalogenation in that the order of preference is $CHClBr = CHCl_2 \gg CHFCl > CHF_2$. Thus, *enflurane* (*c*; **2.65**) has two potential target sites for oxidative dehalogenation, namely the CHClF and CHF_2 groups [104]. The former group is indeed the preferred (and in fact practically unique) site of dehalogenation to form the acid **2.66** as a rat liver microsomal and human urinary metabolite [4]. Our last example is the antibiotic *chloramphenicol* (*d*; **2.67**) whose *N*-dichloroacetyl moiety is dechlorinated to an oxamyl chloride (COCOCl) which can hydrolyze to the oxamic acid derivative **2.68** or acylate proteins [105].

2.3. CYP-Catalyzed sp²-C- and sp-C-Oxidations

2.3.1. The Oxygenation of Aldehydes to Carboxylic Acids

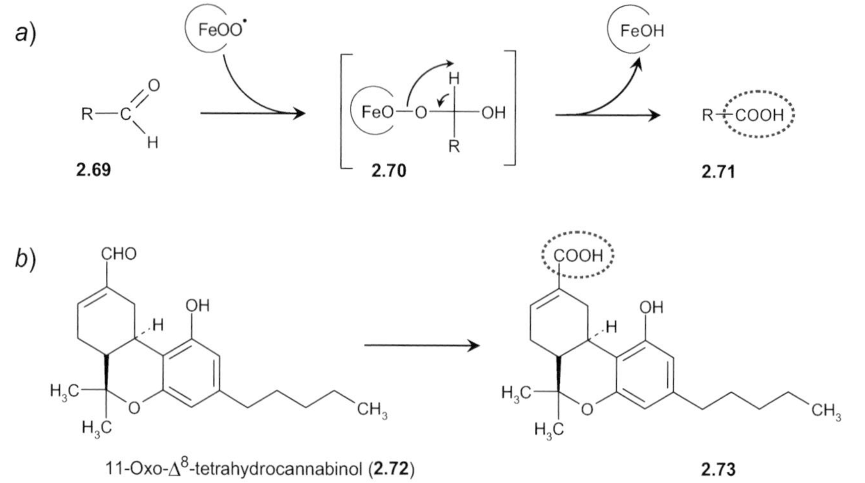

11-Oxo-Δ^8-tetrahydrocannabinol (**2.72**)   **2.73**

Fig. 2.43. The CYP-catalyzed oxidation of sp²-hybridized C-atoms again demonstrates the versatility of these enzymes in terms of functional groups being modified and reactions being carried out. The most frequent cases of sp²-C-oxidations in xenobiotic metabolism occur clearly in aromatic rings. Before discussing these reactions, we briefly examine two other cases of lower quantitative importance. The literature contains a limited number of examples of *aldehydes* (*a*; **2.69**) being oxidized by CYPs to carboxylic acids (**2.71**). The O-atom inserted into the substrate comes from molecular oxygen, and a plausible mechanism is summarized here [52][106][107]. The oxygenating species is postulated to be a peroxyferryl state of the enzyme symbolized here, presumably the *ferric-superoxide complex* formed in *Step c* of *Fig. 2.23*. Nucleophilic attack of the carbonyl C-atom leads to the covalent complex **2.70**. Cleavage of the O–O bond in the complex transfers the distal O-atom to the substrate. A number of xenobiotic aldehydes are proved substrates of the reaction [106]. In the case of *acetaldehyde* (**2.69**; R=CH₃) incubated with human liver microsomes, the highest activity was shown by CYP2E1, followed by 1A2, 2C18, and 3A4. In rat liver microsomes, the highest activity was also shown by 2E1, followed by 1A2 and 4A2 [101]. A more complex substrate is *11-oxo-Δ^8-tetrahydrocannabinol* (*b*; **2.72**), which is oxidized *in vitro* to Δ^8-*tetrahydrocannabinol-11-oic acid* (**2.73**) [107].

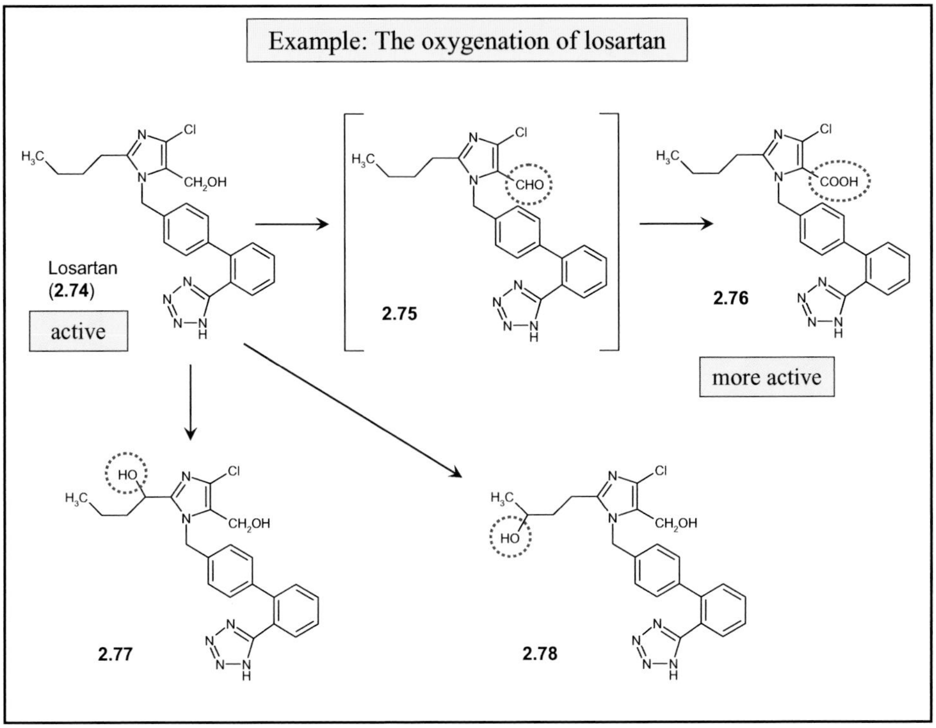

Fig. 2.44. *Losartan* (**2.74**) is an orally active angiotensin II receptor antagonist used as an antihypertensive agent. Its metabolism is of particular interest in our context given its fast oxidation to the *carboxylic acid* **2.76**, a metabolite which is more active and has a much slower plasma clearance than the parent drug. Studies using human liver microsomes have demonstrated that the primary alcoholic group of losartan is oxidized to the *aldehyde* **2.75** and then to the carboxylic acid **2.76** by CYP2C9 and 3A4 [108]. The aldehyde was not observed during the oxygenation of losartan to the carboxylic acid (hence its presentation in square brackets), but incubation of the aldehyde rapidly led to its oxygenation to the acid. Interestingly, the *butyl side chain* of losartan is also a target of CYPs, being hydroxylated in the benzyl and penultimate positions to yield the secondary alcohols **2.77** and **2.78**, respectively.

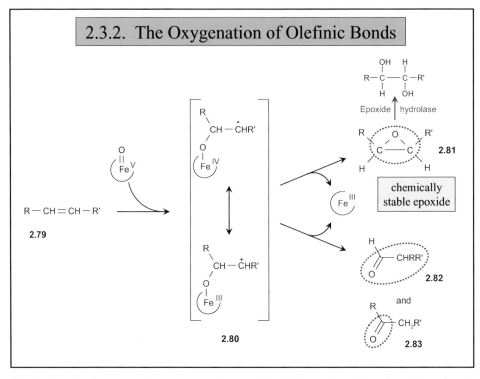

Fig. 2.45. The CYP-catalyzed oxygenation of C=C bonds in *alkenyl moieties* (**2.79**; R, R′ = H, alkyl or aryl) yields primarily epoxides **2.81**. The mechanism of the reaction is fairly well-understood, but some ambiguities remain [4][52]. As shown, the reaction involves two distinct formations of C−O bonds. Following the formation of the first C−O bond, at least two transient and interconverting intermediates, **2.80**, have been postulated. In a first step, the O-atom in the CYP−oxene complex binds covalently to one of the two target C-atoms to form the intermediates **2.80**. Formation of the second C−O bond generates the *epoxide* **2.81** and liberates the ferric cytochrome P450, a rearrangement that occurs without group migration. The epoxide is often the predominant or sole product characterized, and, under physiological conditions of pH and temperature, olefinic epoxides are chemically stable as a rule [109]. However, olefinic epoxides are seldom isolated as such in metabolic studies given their high sensitivity to *epoxide hydrolase* (*Part 3*) which converts them to *diols* (reaction shown in blue). The CYP−intermediate complex **2.80** may also undergo another rearrangement pathway which leads to *carbonyl metabolites* **2.82** and **2.83**. This pathway may (*i.e.*, **2.82**) or may not (*i.e.*, **2.83**) be accompanied by a *shift* (*i.e., migration*) *of the R substituent* (*e.g.*, D, Cl). Furthermore, the CYP−intermediate complex **2.80** may also alkylate the heme moiety of the enzyme and irreversibly inactivate the latter, a process of *enzyme inhibition* known as *mechanism-based inactivation* (see *Part 7*).

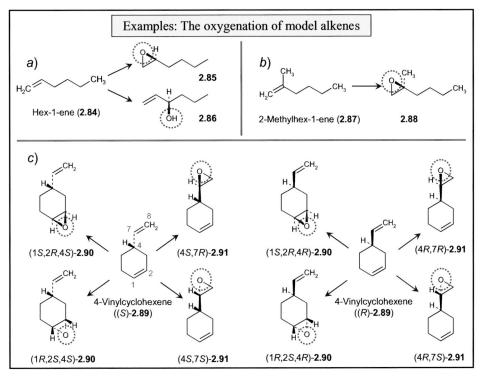

Fig. 2.46. A significant number of olefinic groups (conjugated or not) have been shown to undergo CYP-catalyzed epoxidation, rapidly followed by epoxide hydrolase-catalyzed hydration to a diol. Two simple examples are hex-1-ene and 2-methylhex-1-ene [110]. Incubation with rat and human liver microsomes showed *hex-1-ene* (*a*; **2.84**) to be oxygenated to the epoxide by rat CYP2B1 and human CYP2A6 and 2C9, with some *product enantioselectivity* for the (*S*)-enantiomer **2.85** [110]. Allylic hydroxylation was also observed, with a modest product enantioselectivity for the (*R*)-enantiomer **2.86**. *2-Methylhex-1-ene* (*b*; **2.87**) was epoxidated even faster than hex-1-ene, but it was not hydroxylated; the (*S*)-epoxide **2.88** was again produced selectively. A much more complicated example is provided by *4-vinylcyclohexene* (*c*; **2.89**). Indeed, this compound is chiral, and it exhibits two target sites for epoxidation. When incubated with rat liver microsomes, both the *1,2-epoxide* **2.90** (resulting from oxygenation of the endocyclic C=C bond) and the *7,8-epoxide* **2.91** (resulting from the oxygenation of the exocyclic C=C bond) were produced [111]. Due to the occurrence of chirality and two target sites in the substrate, the reaction of epoxidation showed *substrate stereoselectivity* and *product regioselectivity*. However, this is not the whole story, since epoxidation generated new stereogenic centers in the metabolites (*product stereoselectivity*). In summary, each enantiomer of 4-vinylcyclohexene was metabolized to four metabolites, namely two pairs of diastereoisomers as shown. The details of these selectivities depended on gender and conditions of induction and need not be discussed.

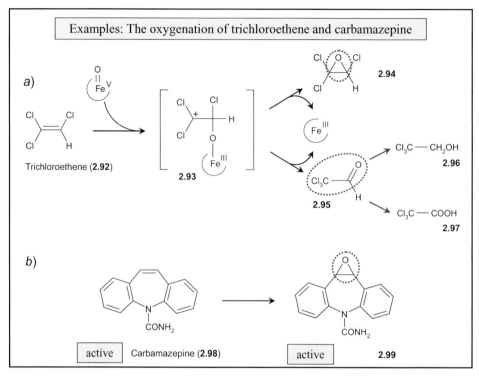

Fig. 2.47. *Halogenated alkenes* are also monooxygenated by cytochrome P450, and some of them may lead to metabolic intermediates of high reactivity and toxicological significance [28]. Thus, genotoxicity and mechanism-based CYP inhibition are documented for some haloalkenes. The mechanism of the CYP oxidation of haloalkenes can be summarized as shown here using *1,1,2-trichloroethene* as an example (*a*; **2.92**). The transition state is rationalized to be a carbocation **2.93**, which either collapses to the *epoxide* **2.94** or undergoes Cl migration to *chloral* (**2.95**), the major *in vitro* metabolite [112]. *In vivo*, chloral is a substrate of dehydrogenases (*Chapt. 2.6*), being reduced to 2,2,2-trichloroethanol (**2.96**) and dehydrogenated to 2,2,2-trichloroacetic acid (**2.97**). As for the epoxide **2.94**, it is a substrate of epoxide hydrolase (*Part 3*), or it can be further transformed upon release of Cl⁻ anions to such metabolites as glyoxylic acid, formic acid, and carbon monoxide [4][52]. Turning our attention to medicinal cases, we find that a number of drugs or metabolites form olefinic epoxides which can be stable or rearrange intramolecularly. In humans, the antiepileptic drug *carbamazepine* (*b*; **2.98**) yields over 30 metabolites, among which the 10,11-epoxide **2.99** is a predominant and pharmacologically active one [113–115]. In fact, epoxidation, followed by enzymatic hydration, is a major pathway in the human metabolism of tricyclic drugs of this type.

2.3.3. The Oxygenation of Aromatic Rings

A simplified mechanism of aryl oxidation

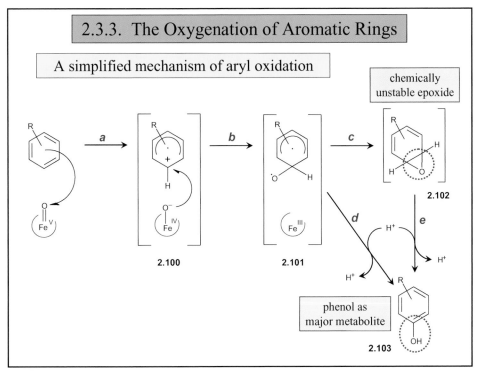

Fig. 2.48. The mechanism of CYP-catalyzed ring oxygenation involves loss of aromaticity due to the formation of tetrahedral transition states, and it is only in metabolites like phenols that aromaticity is restored [4][52][54]. The first step (*Reaction a*) is believed to be a one-electron oxidation by the activated cytochrome P450 O-atom. Substituents containing an electron lone pair (*e.g.*, a halogen) are known to accelerate ring oxidation, presumably because they facilitate this first step (see *Fig. 2.53*). The product is a radical cation **2.100**, which binds the activated O-atom (*Reaction b*) and becomes an oxygenated diradical **2.101**. At least two products can be formed by rearrangement of this diradical **2.101**, namely an *epoxide* **2.102** (*Reaction c*) and a *phenol* **2.103** (*Reactions d* and/or *e*). An interesting feature is that some of these rearrangement reactions involve migration of the geminal H-atom as observed when this is a deuterium or tritium. This displacement, which can also affect the lower halogens and perhaps other small substituents, is known as the *NIH shift* (named after the *US National Institutes of Health* where it was first observed). Arene oxides are usually unstable and undergo ring opening by a mechanism of general acid catalysis (*Reaction e*), ultimately leading to phenols. As examples of arene oxide instability, the metabolite naphthalene 1,2-oxide has a half-life of less than 3 min in H_2O at neutral pH, whereas that of bromobenzene 3,4-oxide in blood at 37° is *ca.* 13 s. Polycyclic aromatic hydrocarbons form more stable epoxides (see, however, *Part 5*).

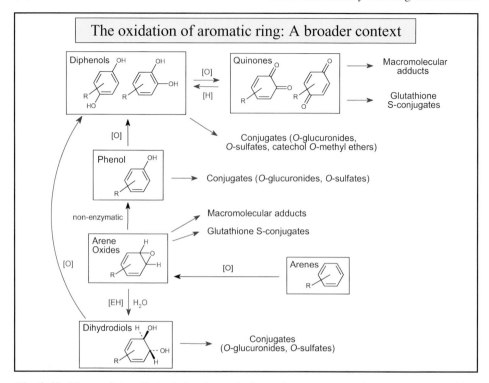

Fig. 2.49. The variety of intertwined metabolic pathways centered around arene oxides is not always easy to grasp. Nevertheless, the general scheme presented here should contribute some clarity and facilitate connections with the reactions (shown in blue) to be presented in further *Chapters* and *Parts* in this Work. Indeed, the epoxides generated by the CYP-catalyzed oxygenation of arenes are a crossroads to a number of metabolic routes [4][54][116][117]. The chemical reactivity and further fate of arene oxides depends heavily on their chemical structure and properties. Of foremost relevance in the present context is their proton-catalyzed *isomerization to phenols* presented in *Fig. 2.48*. Phenols are the most stable and the most frequently excreted products of CYP-catalyzed aromatic ring oxidation. However, they may undergo further CYP-catalyzed *oxidation to benzene-diols* (*i.e.*, diphenols), possibly followed by peroxidase-catalyzed *oxidation to quinones* to be presented in *Chapt. 2.6*. An alternative and significant metabolic route of epoxides is their *hydration to* trans-*dihydrodiols* catalyzed by epoxide hydrolases (*Part 3*). These diols are also chemically stable metabolites, and they can be *oxidized to catechols* by dihydrodiol dehydrogenase (*Chapt. 2.6*). The chemically stable hydroxylated metabolites (phenols and diols) may undergo *conjugation with glucuronic or sulfuric acid*, and catechols may be *mono*-O-*methylated* (*Part 4*). In contrast, the reactive metabolites (quinones and sometimes epoxides) form *glutathione conjugates* (*Part 4*), a reaction of detoxification which prevents within limits such reactive metabolites from *binding covalently to nucleophilic macromolecules* such as proteins and nucleic acids (*Part 5*).

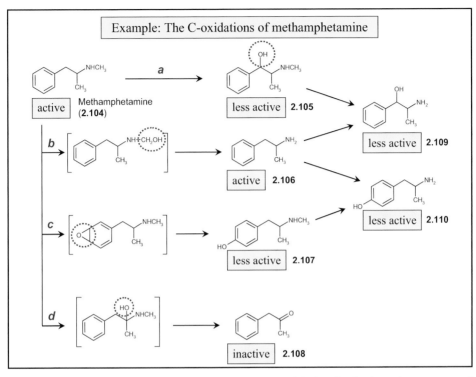

Fig. 2.50. This example is meant to illustrate aryl oxidation in the broader context of CYP-catalyzed oxidation of C-atoms and some possible consequences. *Methamphetamine* (**2.104**) is a proscribed, highly active central stimulant and a neurotoxin. The results presented here are a qualitative summary of innumerable investigations carried out *in vivo* and *in vitro* in a number of species, with no consideration being given to stereochemical aspects. As shown, four C-atom positions are major sites of oxidative attack. In three cases (*Reactions a, b,* and *d*), a sp³-C-atom is hydroxylated, whereas *Reaction c* is one of aryl oxidation. *Reaction a* is a benzylic hydroxylation yielding *ephedrine* (**2.105**), a weaker stimulant of the nervous system. *Reactions b* and *d* are *N*-demethylation and deamination, respectively. They have in common that the hydroxylated intermediates are unstable and break down by N−C bond cleavage, but with vastly different physicochemical and pharmacological consequences. Indeed, the product of N-*demethylation* is *amphetamine* (**2.106**), which retains the basicity of methamphetamine and its activity. In contrast, the product of *deamination* (*phenylacetone* (**2.108**)) is neutral and devoid of activity. Aromatic oxidation (*Reaction c*) yields *para*-hydroxymethamphetamine (**2.107**). Metabolites **2.105** to **2.108** are metabolized further by CYPs (and other enzymes), as illustrated by two second-generation metabolites, namely norephedrine (**2.109**) and *para*-hydroxyamphetamine (**2.110**), both remain active, albeit considerably less than the parent compound.

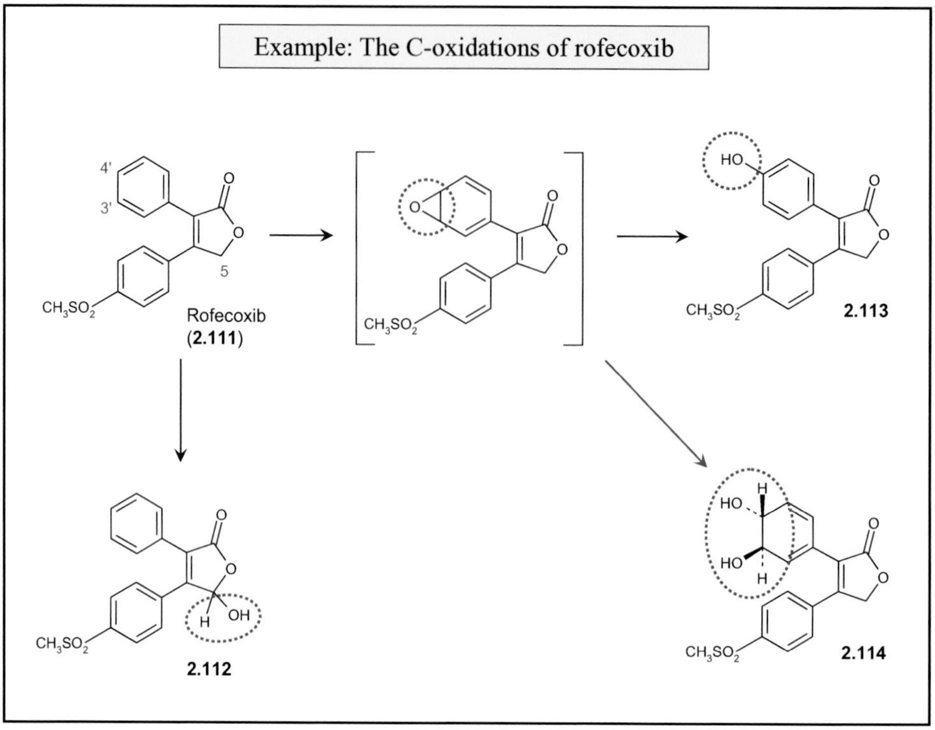

Fig. 2.51. *Rofecoxib* (**2.111**), a potent and selective COX-2 inhibitor (see also *Fig. 2.32*), offers another informative example of C-oxidation. The drug was extensively metabolized in human subjects, yielding 5-hydroxyrofecoxib (**2.112**) as a main metabolite [118]. However, aryl oxidation was also important, yielding the 4'-phenolic metabolite (4'-hydroxyrofecoxib (**2.113**)) and *trans*-dihydrorofecoxib-3',4'-diol (**2.114**) resulting from epoxide hydration catalyzed by epoxide hydrolase (*Part 3*). This is one of the limited number of examples where both a phenol and a dihydrodiol were characterized *in vivo*.

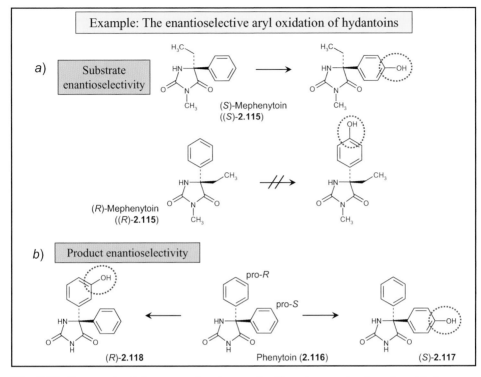

Fig. 2.52. Stereoselectivity can also be a significant aspect of aryl oxidation, as illustrated here with a compilation of data on the metabolism of some hydantoins [4]. These are antiepileptic agents oxidized mainly by CYP2C enzymes. *Substrate enantioselectivity* in aromatic hydroxylation is observed with a number of drugs, *mephenytoin* (**2.115**) being a case in point. One or more CYPs in the 2C subfamily catalyze the *para*-hydroxylation of (*S*)-mephenytoin with high efficacy and a marked substrate selectivity. Indeed, the *para*-hydroxylation of (*R*)-mephenytoin is slow compared to that of its enantiomer. *Product enantioselectivity* in aryl oxidation is aptly illustrated with *phenytoin* (**2.116**). This drug is prochiral, having a center of prochirality to which two enantiotopic phenyl rings are attached, the *pro-R* and the *pro-S* phenyl groups. Phenyl hydroxylation in humans is again mediated by a CYP2C enzyme, preferentially on the *pro-S* ring and almost exclusively in the *para*-position, yielding the phenol (*S*)-**2.117**. Modest oxidation of the *pro-R* ring does occur, the (*S*)/(*R*) ratio of the two enantiomeric metabolites being *ca.* 10:1. In contrast, the *meta*-phenol is formed preferentially in dogs and is the pure (*R*)-enantiomer (**2.118**). There is evidence that the *meta*- and *para*-phenols are both formed from the respective 3,4-oxide.

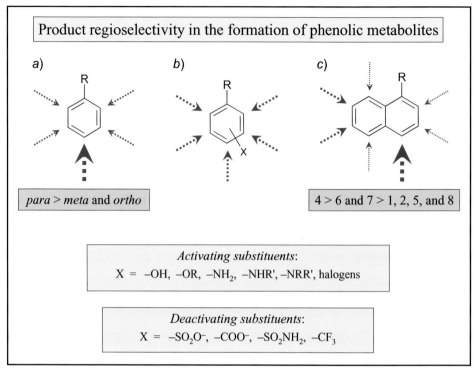

Fig. 2.53. Here, we summarize some *global trends* observed in the CYP-catalyzed oxidation of aryl moieties, as deduced from innumerable observations. However, substrate selectivity and product regioselectivity in ring oxidations is influenced not only by the structural and physicochemical properties of the substrate molecule, but also by biological factors such as animal species, nature of the isozyme(s) involved, and supply of cofactors (see *Parts 6* and *7*). In other words, the trends shown here are not without exceptions, but they can prove quite useful if applied reasonably. The first case shown (*a*) is that of an *unsubstituted phenyl moiety*, where CYP oxidation results mainly in 3,4-epoxidation and *para*-hydroxylation (*i.e.*, 4-hydroxylation; see *Fig. 2.52*). While markedly less frequent, *meta*-hydroxylation (see *Fig. 2.52*) and *ortho*-hydroxylation can occur. The second case considered (*b*) is that of a *substituted phenyl moiety* where the X substituent may favor (activating substituents) or hinder (partly or completely; deactivating substituents) ring oxidation. In case *b*, the position(s) of oxidative attack will depend on the steric and electronic effects of the substituent. A particular case is that of ipso-*substitution* to be exemplified in *Figs. 2.54* and *2.55*. The third case shown (*c*) is that of a *naphthyl ring* system; here, hydroxylation occurs preferentially in the 4-position, but other sites can also be observed (see propranolol in *Fig. 2.56*). More complex aryl ring systems and aromatic heterocycles represent special cases [4][52][54][119][120].

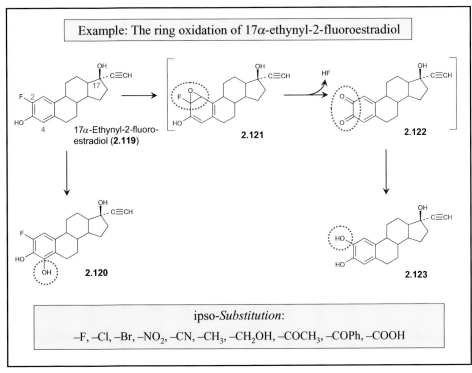

Example: The ring oxidation of 17α-ethynyl-2-fluoroestradiol

17α-Ethynyl-2-fluoro-estradiol (**2.119**)   **2.121**   **2.122**

2.120   **2.123**

ipso-*Substitution*:

–F, –Cl, –Br, –NO₂, –CN, –CH₃, –CH₂OH, –COCH₃, –COPh, –COOH

Fig. 2.54. The example shown here is a rather complex one which aims at illustrating regioselective ring hydroxylation and dehalogenation. Metabolic investigations of *17α-ethynyl-2-fluoroestradiol* (**2.119**) in female rats revealed two pathways of hydroxylation [121]. 4-Hydroxylation **2.120** (*i.e.*, *ortho* to the 3-OH group) leading to the 3,4-catecholestrogen and then to 4-*O*-methylation (*Part 4*) accounted for 10–12% of a dose. This pathway of *catecholestrogen* formation is known to be a minor one for natural and synthetic estrogens. The major pathway of aryl hydroxylation in estrogens is at the 2-position, a reaction *a priori* impossible for compound **2.119**. Unexpectedly, 2-hydroxylation with defluorination accounted for 20–25% of a dose. This is, in fact, a reaction of ipso-*substitution* whose mechanism has been postulated to involve ipso-*attack*, possibly leading to an epoxide (here **2.121**) and convincingly to an intermediate quinone (here the *ortho*-quinone **2.122**) [52][121]. Reduction of the quinone then leads to the 2,3-catecholestrogen **2.123**, itself a substrate for 2-*O*-methylation (*Part 4*). It is interesting to note that reactions of ipso-*substitution* are receiving a marked attention, CYP-catalyzed *substituent elimination and replacement by a OH group* (*i.e.*, producing a *para*-benzenediol) having been observed for a number of *para*-substituted phenols as shown in the *Figure* [122].

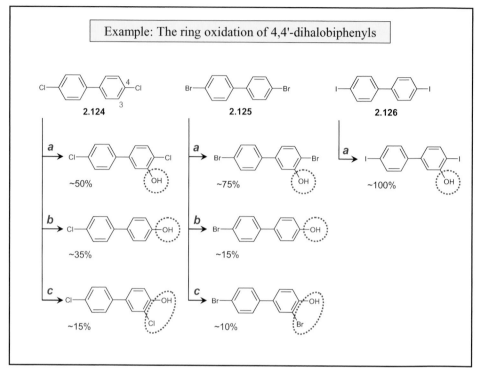

Fig. 2.55. Reactions of substituent elimination and substituent migration (the *NIH shift*; see *Fig. 2.48*) share a number of mechanistic similarities, and they may occur in parallel as seen for example with a deuterium, tritium, CH₃, F, Cl, or Br substituent. This fact is clearly significant as far as drugs are concerned, yet relevant examples are few. An informative case involving model compounds is that of *4,4'-dihalo-1,1'-biphenyls* (**2.124**, **2.125**, and **2.126**) [123]. When administered to rabbits, the three substrates yielded the 3-OH derivative (*Reaction a*) as the main metabolite, a typical example of ortho-*hydroxylation*. However, the Cl and Br analogs were oxidized to two additional metabolites. *Reaction b* was the second in importance and generated the [1,1'-biphenyl]-4-ol with *loss of the 4-halo substituent*. *Reaction c* was the less important quantitatively and led to the 3-halo-4-hydroxy analog with the *shift of the 4-halo substituent*. *Reactions b* and *c* did not occur for the di-iodo analog, indicating absence of an *NIH* shift for this bulky substituent. And indeed, elimination and shift of the halo substituent decreased in the order Cl, Br, I [123].

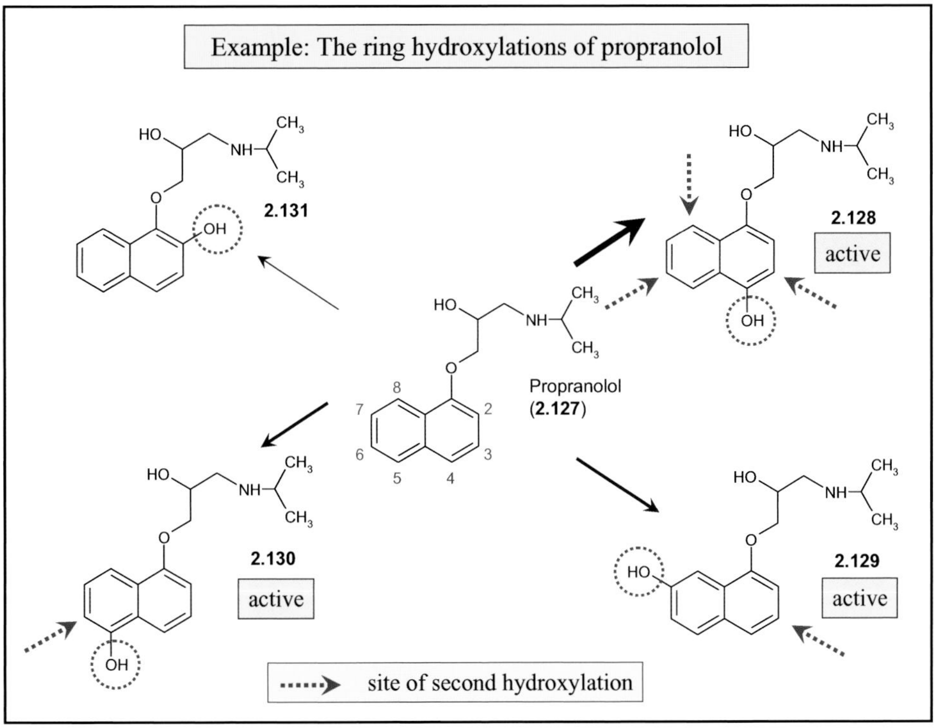

Example: The ring hydroxylations of propranolol

....➤ site of second hydroxylation

Fig. 2.56. *Propranolol* (**2.127**) is a highly informative example of product regioselective aryl hydroxylation. *Fig. 1.14 (Part 1)* showed a simplified metabolic tree of propranolol where 4-hydroxylation was the only reaction involving the aromatic ring. Here, we examine in greater detail the various ring hydroxylations undergone by this traditional β-blocker [124–128]. Four ring *monophenols* have been characterized as first-generation metabolites in humans and rats. *4-Hydroxypropranolol* (**2.128**) is by far the predominant phenol formed; in humans, the reaction is catalyzed by CYP2D6 and is markedly selectivite for (+)-(*R*)-propranolol, whereas it is only slightly selective for the (−)-(*S*)-enantiomer in rats. *7-Hydroxypropranolol* (**2.129**) is second in importance in rats, its formation being highly selective for (+)-(*R*)-propranolol. *5-Hydroxypropranolol* (**2.130**) is second in importance in humans, whereas *2-hydroxypropranolol* (**2.131**) is a minor metabolite in both species. It is noteworthy that these monohydroxylated metabolites have significant β-adrenoceptor antagonist activity. While these metabolites are excreted predominantly as glucuronide and sulfate conjugates (*Part 4*), they also undergo further ring hydroxylation to *second-generation diphenols*. Thus, the metabolite 4-hydroxypropranolol (**2.128**) is known to undergo 3-, 6- and 8-hydroxylation in humans and rats. In addition, 3-hydroxylation of 7-hydroxypropranolol (**2.129**) and 6-hydroxylation of 5-hydroxypropranolol (**2.130**) is also documented in rats. These sites of second hydroxylation are in line with the activating properties of the first OH group. In humans, the relative importance of these diols appears to be 4,8- $\approx$3,4->4,6-diol. In rats, the relative importance was 4,6->3,4->4,8-$\approx$3,7->5,6-diol.

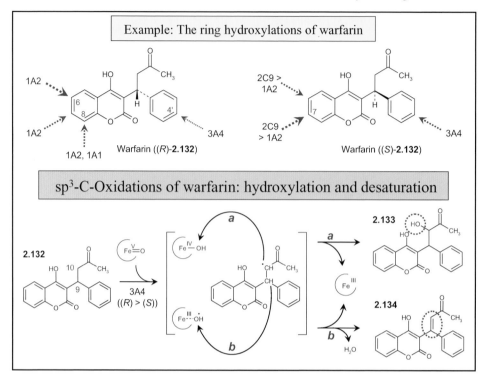

Fig. 2.57. The example of *warfarin* (**2.132**) offers additional information [129–133]. Indeed, the two enantiomers of warfarin are oxidized with different product regioselectivities and partly by different CYPs. In humans, the more active (−)-(*S*)-warfarin is metabolized faster than its (+)-(*R*)-enantiomer. And as shown in the upper part of the *Figure*, the favored sites of *ring hydroxylation* in (*R*)- and (*S*)-warfarin are the 6- and 7-positions, respectively. The ring hydroxylation of (*R*)-warfarin is catalyzed mainly by CYP1A2, and that of (*S*)-warfarin by 2C9 and 3A4. Furthermore, and as shown in the lower part of the *Figure*, *oxidation of the alkyl chain* occurs in parallel with aryl hydroxylation. The enzyme involved is mainly 3A4, and substrate enantioselectivity favors (*R*)-warfarin. An important fact here is that two metabolites result from alkyl oxidation, namely *10-hydroxywarfarin* (**2.133**) and *9,10-dehydrowarfarin* (**2.134**). The former is a major metabolite in humans. The second is produced by a reaction mechanism we just alluded to in the caption of *Fig. 2.28* but have not illustrated yet, namely *CYP-catalyzed sp³-C-desaturation*. In this reaction, the first homolytic C–H bond cleavage is followed by a second one to yield what is usually a markedly delocalized C=C bond. Note that dehydrowarfarin can conceivably also result from initial C(9)-oxidation.

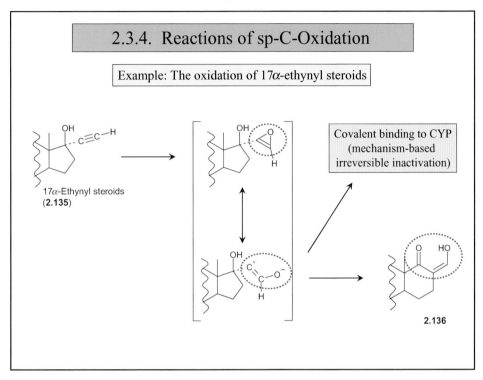

2.3.4. Reactions of sp-C-Oxidation

Example: The oxidation of 17α-ethynyl steroids

Fig. 2.58. C≡C Bonds as found in *alkynes*, far from being metabolically inert as believed earlier, undergo CYP-catalyzed oxidation. In particular, a variety of *acetylenic* (=*ethynyl*) *derivatives*, be they drugs or other xenobiotics, share with chemicals belonging to many other classes the property of being mechanism-based, irreversible inactivators of cytochrome P450 [134]. As shown in simplified form here for *17α-ethynyl steroids* (**2.135**), monooxygenation of the acetylenic (*i.e.*, ethynyl) moiety yields an intermediate existing in at least two resonance forms. The intermediate is so reactive that it generally reacts within the catalytic site. This can occur *intramolecularly* in a reaction of D-*homoannulation* which yields D-*homosteroids* (steroids with a six-membered *D*-ring; **2.136**) [135]. However, the intermediate can also react with the catalytic site, leading to heme alkylation and irreversible inactivation (*i.e.*, destruction) of the enzyme [4][52].

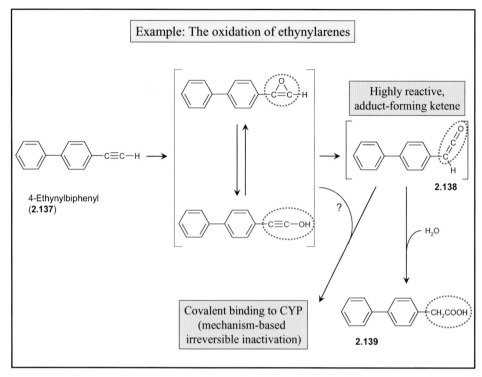

Fig. 2.59. *Ethynylarenes* (*e.g.*, *4-ethynyl-1,1'-biphenyl*; **2.137**) may also be mechanism-based inactivators of, *e.g.*, CYP1A2, 2B1 and 2E1 depending on the size of the aromatic ring and the position of the ethynyl group [136]. Here, rearrangement of the oxirene moiety leads to a *ketene* **2.138** by a H-shift from C(2) to C(1). This is an electrophilic and highly reactive molecule which may or may not be the heme-alkylating species, but it is stable enough to leave the enzyme and cause major cellular damage by binding covalently to nucleophilic sites in proteins and even nucleic acids (see *Part 5*). Besides adduct formation, the ketene molecule also reacts with H_2O to form an *arylacetic acid* metabolite **2.139** [137][138]. Thus, a dose of 4-ethynyl-1,1'-biphenyl (**2.137**) administered to rats and rabbits was accounted for predominantly as [1,1'-biphenyl]-4-ylacetic acid (**2.139**) and 4'-hydroxy[1,1'-biphenyl]-4-acetic acid. In this context, we note that a terminal ethynyl group in an *alkyne* (Alkyl$-$C$\equiv$C$-$H) or an *alkynyl aryl ether* (Aryl$-$O$-$CH$_2$$-C\equiv$C$-$H) can also be activated to a CYP-inhibitory species [139][140]. Among positional isomers, a C$\equiv$C bond in a *propynyl* group (R$-$C$\equiv$C$-$CH$_3$) appears as reactive as a terminal ethynyl group in beeing activated to an inhibitory species. This seems to occur by C(2) $\rightarrow$ C(1) migration of the CH$_3$ group in analogy with the C(2) $\rightarrow$ C(1) H-migration in the ethynyl group. A medicinal example is provided by the antiprogestin mifepristone, a 17α-propynyl steroid and a selective inactivator of CYP3A4 [141]. C$\equiv$C Bonds in more central positions appear less or unreactive.

2.4. Oxidations of N- and S-Atoms Catalyzed by CYPs and/or FMOs

Selected types of substrates undergoing N- or S-oxidation

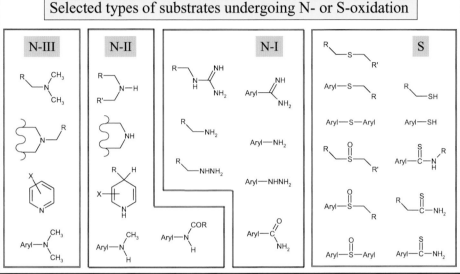

Fig. 2.60. We now move to reactions of oxidation of N- or S-containing functional groups. As we shall see, most of these reactions are in fact oxygenations in the sense that an O-atom is transferred to the substrate. This *Figure* opens the *Chapter* by presenting a *selection of substrate types*, as classified into tertiary amines (N-III), secondary amines and amides (N-II), primary amines and amides (N-I), and S-containing xenobiotics (S). Please note also that, in each of the first three *Boxes* (N-III, N-II, and N-I), the compounds are ranked according to their *basicity*, with the more basic compounds on top and the lesser or nonbasic compounds in the lower part. Such a classification is metabolically meaningful given the rule of thumb that *basic amines tend to be FMO substrates whereas nonbasic compounds are oxidized by CYPs*, with the degree of *N*-substitution also playing a distinct role [4][59–62][64][65][142]. Thus, tertiary amines are preferably FMO substrates in contrast to primary amines which are better CYP substrates; secondary amines are less clear-cut. The classification of the S-containing substrates (*Box S*) follows a simple structural logic, the compounds being grouped according to their functional moiety (thioethers, thiols, sulfoxides, and thioamides).

2.4.1. *N*-Oxygenation of Basic or Weakly Basic Tertiary Amines

Basic amines tend to be *N*-oxygenated by FMOs and weakly basic amines by CYPs

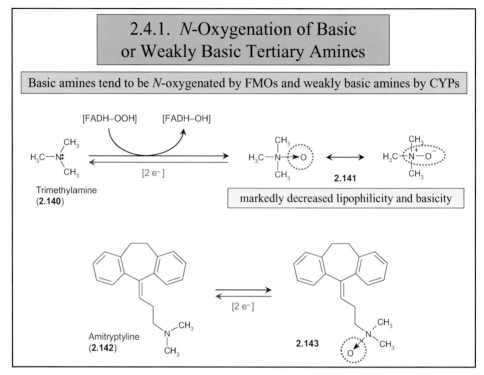

markedly decreased lipophilicity and basicity

Fig. 2.61. We begin our presentation of N-oxidations with tertiary amines, the simplest of which is *trimethylamine* (**2.140**; TMA). This compound is derived *in vivo* from dietary sources such as choline, and it is characterized by a strong fish-like odor. In humans, it is *N*-oxygenated with great efficiency by *FMO3* to the odorless *TMA N-oxide* (**2.141**), with less than 5% of a dose being excreted as TMA [143]. TMA (**2.140**) is a basic amine, and its oxidation by FMO is thus in line with the trend of *basic amines being FMO substrates*. The deficiency of FMO3 in some individuals produces the so-called 'fish-odor syndrome'. Independently of *N*-oxygenation being catalyzed by FMOs or CYPs, N-*oxides* (also called *amine oxides*) have *physicochemical properties* markedly different from those of their parent compound, most notably a strongly *increased hydrophilicity* and a much *decreased basicity* [144]. Indeed, the N−O bond in the *N*-oxide functionality is highly polarized, since its two electrons originate from the N-atom; in graphical terms, the N−O bond is represented by either of its two resonance forms, namely by an arrow or with formal charge separation, *i.e.*, **2.141**. Note also that TMA *N*-oxide can be reduced back to TMA in the human gut and likely also in the liver, probably a general feature of *N*-oxides [145]. Thus, *amitryptyline* (**2.142**) and numerous analogous tricyclic antidepressants and neuroleptics form the *N*-oxide (*e.g.*, **2.143**) in humans, but their *back reduction* in the gut and possibly the liver renders the *in vivo* importance of this reaction difficult to assess [146].

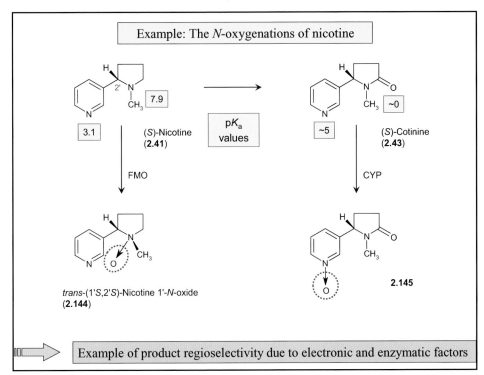

Fig. 2.62. Our first encounter with the metabolism of nicotine was in *Fig. 2.37.* Here, we return to the natural *(−)-(S)-nicotine* (**2.41**) and its *N*-oxygenation. Indeed, there are two tertiary amino groups as potential sites of *N*-oxygenation in nicotine, namely its more basic pyrollidine N-atom (pK_a 7.9), and the lesser basic pyridine N-atom (having here a pK_a value of 3.1) [4]. *N*-Oxygenation occurs only *at the more basic center* and hence is *product-regioselective*. It is also *product-stereoselective* since only trans-*(1'S,2'S)-nicotine N-oxide* (**2.144**) is formed and excreted in humans, the reaction being catalyzed primarily by *FMO3* [64][91][147]. In contrast, pig liver *FMO1* also produces *cis-(1'R,2'S)*-nicotine *N*-oxide. *Cotinine* (**2.43**), the major metabolite of nicotine in humans, also undergoes *N*-oxygenation. However, the pyrollidine N-atom is not oxygenated by FMOs probably due to its lack of basicity as an amide N-atom. Interestingly, the more basic center is now the pyridine N-atom (pK_a *ca.* 5), and, indeed, it yields the *N*-oxide **2.145** as a minor nicotine metabolite [64]. The mono-oxygenation of pyridine-type N-atoms atoms appears to be preferentially mediated by *CYPs*, as documented for cotinine [64].

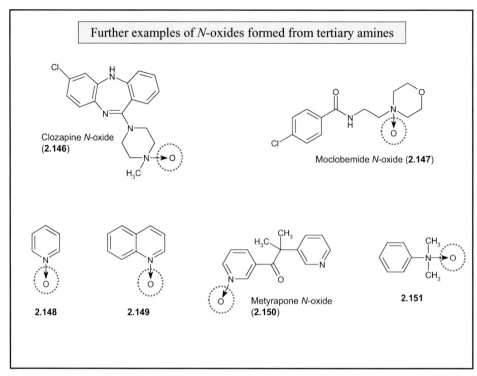

Fig. 2.63. A few further examples of *N*-oxides formed from tertiary amines are shown in this *Figure*. Note the absence of N,N-*disubstituted amides*, since, to the best of our knowledge, none has been reported to undergo *N*-oxygenation. *Clozapine* offers a relevant example of a saturated azaheterocycle yielding an *N*-oxide **2.146**. In humans, the reaction is efficiently catalyzed by *FMO3* [60]. Another example is provided by *moclobemide* N-*oxide* (**2.147**), a metabolite of the MAO inhibitor *moclobemide* in various animal species, and a major metabolite in human plasma [148]. As for a pyridine N-atom, we find that *pyridine* itself is detoxified by *N*-oxygenation to *pyridine* N-*oxide* (**2.148**), an important metabolite accounting for a marked or significant proportion of a dose in a number of species [4]. In rabbit liver for example, two CYPs are mainly responsible for the *N*-oxygenation of pyridine, namely *CYP2E1* as a high-affinity enzyme playing the major role at low substrate concentrations, and *CYP4B* as low-affinity enzyme playing the major role at high substrate concentrations. An analogous substrate is quinoline which yields *quinoline* N-*oxide* (**2.149**). A few interesting cases of *regioselective N*-oxygenation have been reported for compounds containing two pyridine rings. In *metyrapone* for example, the pyridine ring adjacent to the carbonyl group was predominantly *N*-oxygenated in rats *in vivo* and in rat liver microsomes to yield the *N*-oxide **2.150**. In contrast to pyridine-type substrates and despite the similarities in basicity, FMO is the main system responsible for the formation of N,N-*dimethylaniline* N-*oxide* (**2.151**) from N,N-dimethylaniline in human tissues [4].

2.4.2. N-Oxidation of Secondary and Primary Amines

Aliphatic (basic) amines

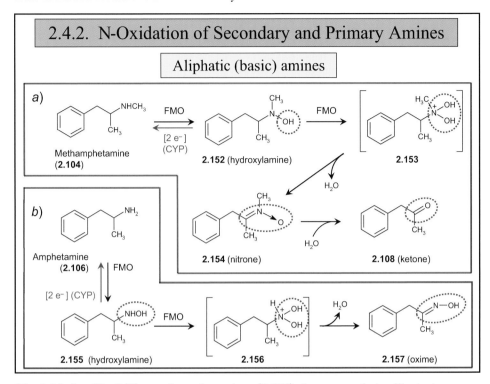

Fig. 2.64. In *Fig. 2.50*, *methamphetamine* (**2.104**) has served to illustrate some important reactions of C-oxidation. Here, the same neurotoxin and its metabolite *amphetamine* (**2.106**) are used again to exemplify typical reactions of *N*-oxygenation undergone respectively by basic (*i.e.*, aliphatic) secondary and primary amines [149–151]. A first observation is that the oxygenation of such amines is more complex than that of basic tertiary amines. Indeed, *basic secondary amines* are *N*-oxygenated by FMO to form a *hydroxylamine* **2.152**. In a second oxygenation step, a dihydroxylated intermediate, **2.153**, is formed which rearranges to a *nitrone* **2.152** by loss of H_2O. Both oxidative steps are catalyzed by FMO3 in humans. A subsequent postenzymatic step occurs slowly, namely the spontaneous hydrolysis of the nitrone to a *ketone* (here phenylacetone (**2.108**)). This is in effect an alternative route of deamination (see *Fig. 2.50*). As far as *primary basic amines* are concerned, and as exemplified with *amphetamine* (**2.106**), a hydroxylamine, **2.155**, and a dihydroxylated intermediate, **2.156**, are also formed. The latter rearranges to an *oxime* **2.157** with loss of a molecule of H_2O. FMO3 is again the main human enzyme involved. Note that like *N*-oxides (see *Fig. 2.61*) and various other *N*-oxygenated metabolites, hydroxylamines can be *retroreduced* to the parent amine by a variety of enzymatic systems. These include poorly characterized gut flora reductases, CYPs, NADPH-cytochrome P450 reductase, the NADH-cytochrome b_5/cytochrome b_5 system, xanthine oxidase, aldehyde oxidase, and other systems (see *Chapt. 2.5* and *2.6*) [152]. The same reactions of reduction can occur for xenobiotics containing an *N*-oxygenated moiety (*e.g.*, nitro-arenes, see *Figs. 2.87* and *2.88*).

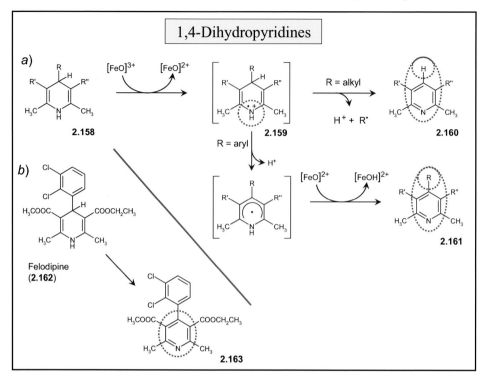

Fig. 2.65. *1,4-Dihydropyridines* of general structure **2.158** are special for a number of reasons. Pharmacologically, several members of this class are important cardiovascular drugs acting as calcium channel blockers. Enzymatically, they are substrates of CYPs rather than FMOs, in line with their weak basicity. And in terms of reaction pathways, their enzymatic oxidation follows a course largely different from that of other secondary amines. Indeed and as shown in *Part a* of the *Figure*, 1,4-dihydropyridines are *oxidized to pyridines* rather than being *N*-oxygenated [4][47][153][154]. The reaction begins with a CYP-catalyzed, one-electron abstraction which creates a *radical cation* of general structure **2.159**. When the 4-substituent is an alkyl or aralkyl group (*e.g.*, ethyl, propyl, isopropyl, or benzyl), the radical cation breaks down with loss of this substituent in the form of an alkyl free radical. The latter reacts covalently with cytochrome P450; *mechanism-based inactivation* (irreversible inhibition) is thus documented for CYP1A1, 2C11, 3A4, and 4A. In this case, the metabolite formed from the dihydropyridine is the pyridine derivative **2.160**. When the 4-substituent is an aryl group as is the case of medicinal 1,4-dihydropyridines, the radical cation **2.159** loses a proton and undergoes a second oxidation step to yield a *4-arylpyridine* **2.161**. This reaction is documented for a variety of calcium channel blockers, among them *felodipine* (**2.162**) whose oxidation to its 4-arylpyridine metabolite **2.163** is a major reaction.

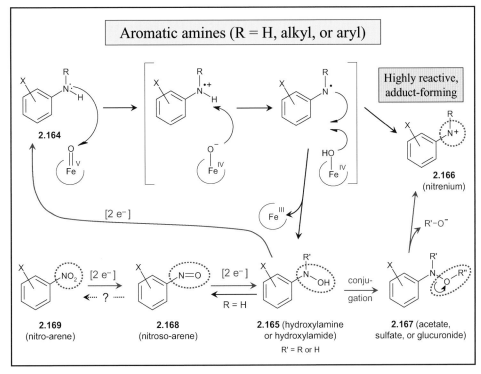

Fig. 2.66. N-*(Hydroxy)arylamines* (**2.165**) are important crossroads in the metabolism of primary and secondary amines. Our first encounter with hydroxylamines was in *Fig. 2.64* (**2.152** and **2.155**) where the oxygenation of basic amines was exemplified. We now turn to *primary* and *secondary arylamines* (**2.164**; R = H, alkyl or aryl), *i.e.*, amines of low basicity (pK_a in the usual range of 2 to 4). At least three types of enzymes can catalyze their N-oxidation, namely CYPs (mainly 1A2), FMOs (seldom), or peroxidases (*Chapt. 2.6*) [4][64]. A simplified mechanism for the CYP-catalyzed reaction is shown here. Following electron and proton abstraction, the hydroxyl anion is transferred to an intermediate radical cation to generate the *hydroxylamine* **2.165** [52][155]. Instead of forming the hydroxylamine, the intermediate radical can also be oxidized by loss of an electron and become a *nitrenium cation* **2.166**. Such nitrenium ions are highly electrophilic, and their capacity to bind covalently to nucleic acids and other nucleophilic biomacromolecules is a major concern in molecular toxicology (see *Part 5*) [155][156]. Nitrenium ions are also formed from hydroxylamines following their O-*sulfonation* or O-*glucuronidation* to a conjugate **2.167** (*Part 4*) and heterolytic cleavage of the N−O bond. N-(Hydroxylaryl)amines are also known to be oxidized to *nitroso-arenes* when R = H (**2.168**), whereas their further oxidation to *nitro-arenes* **2.169** is poorly documented. Importantly, N-hydroxylamines (**2.165**; R = H) also arise as reductive metabolites of nitro-arenes and nitroso-arenes. Primary and secondary N-hydroxylamines in turn can be reduced to the arylamine (**2.164**) (see *Chapt. 2.5*).

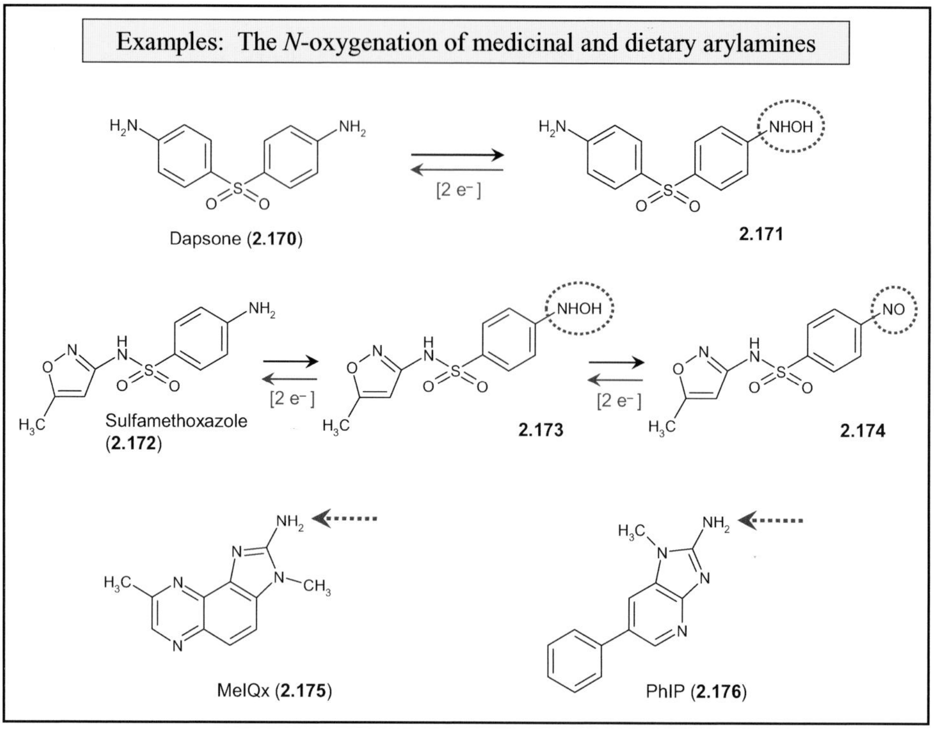

Examples: The *N*-oxygenation of medicinal and dietary arylamines

Fig. 2.67. This *Figure* presents a few examples of primary arylamines known to be *N*-oxygenated and selected here for their medicinal and/or toxicological significance. Thus, the antileprosis drug *dapsone* (**2.170**) produces methemoglobin in some humans and experimental animals. This toxicity toward erythrocytes appears to be related to its *hydroxylamine* metabolite **2.171**, the formation of which is catalyzed by CYP2C9, 2E1, and 3A4 in humans, and 2C11 and 3A1 in rats [157][158]. Interestingly, dapsone hydroxylamine is effectively reduced back to dapsone in microsomal preparations, suggesting a role for cytochrome P450 or CYP-reductase in this *retroreduction* (see also *Chapt. 2.5*). The antibacterial sulfonamide *sulfamethoxazole* (**2.172**) is also oxidized to its *hydroxylamine* **2.173** in humans, a reaction catalyzed by cytochrome P450 and peroxidases (*Chapt. 2.6*). There is also evidence for the further oxidation to a *nitroso* metabolite, **2.174**, formed enzymatically and by *autoxidation*. Both metabolites appear to be related to some adverse effects of the drug, including hypersensitivity reactions [159][160]. The nitroso metabolite was shown to be reduced nonenzymatically by *glutathione* (GSH; see *Part 4*) back to the hydroxylamine, a reaction that can prevent the toxicity of sulfamethoxazole and its hydroxylamine. The last two compounds in the *Figure* are two *aminoazaheterocycles*, namely 2-amino-3,8-dimethylimidazo[4,5-*f*]-quinoxaline (**2.175**; MeIQx) and 2-amino-1-methyl-6-phenylimidazo[4,5-*f*]pyridine (**2.176**; PhIP). Both compounds are dietary mutagens following CYP1A2-catalyzed toxification to the respective hydroxylamine [161].

2.4.3. *N*-Oxygenation of Aromatic Amides

The reactivity of *N*-aryl-*N*-hydroxyamides

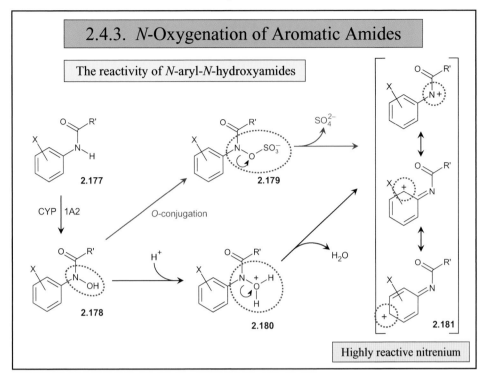

Highly reactive nitrenium

Fig. 2.68. As a rule, *aliphatic amides* are not *N*-hydroxylated, and neither are tertiary aromatic amides. This leaves us with primary and secondary aromatic amides. *Primary aromatic amides* (aryl$-CONH_2$) are of limited interest here, given their prefered metabolism by hydrolysis or conjugation. In contrast, *secondary aromatic amides* (N-arylamides; **2.177**) constitute important substrates of CYP1A; their N-oxidation leads to N-*hydroxyamides* (**2.178**), also known as *hydroxamic acids*. The catalytic mechanism of their formation appears comparable to that of aromatic amines (*Fig. 2.66*), although there is also evidence for a direct H˙ abstraction from NH to form an N-centered radical, followed by radical combination with HO˙ (*i.e.*, *oxygen rebound*) [162]. The formation of *N*-hydroxyamides is documented for a number of compounds, in particular *carcinogenic N-arylamides* [4][163]. Hydroxamic acids are acidic in nature and considerably more stable than *N*-arylhydroxylamines, their autoxidation for example being much slower. Yet hydroxamic acids can yield *nitrenium ions* **2.181** with relative ease due to a resonance stabilization of the positive charge facilitated by electronic conjugation with the carbonyl group. Two mechanisms are known to lead from *N*-hydroxyamides to nitrenium ions. The first is *via conjugation of the OH group* (*O*-sulfonation or *O*-glucuronidation; see **2.179** and *Part 4*), followed by heterolytic cleavage of the N−O bond (see also *Fig. 2.66*). The second mechanism is a *proton-catalyzed dehydroxylation* (*i.e.*, **2.180**) [164]. Once formed, nitrenium ions bind covalently to nucleophilic macromolecules, hence their *mutagenicity* and *carcinogenicity*. They can also react in the *ortho-* or *para-*position with hydroxyl ions to form phenols [4][165].

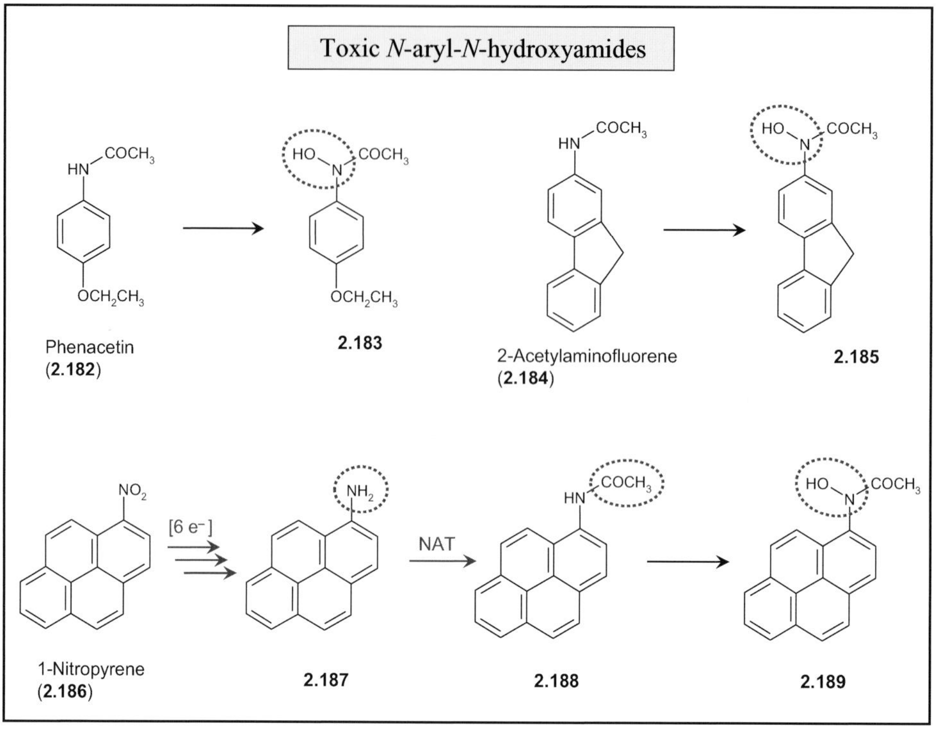

Fig. 2.69. The few arylamides presented here form *N*-hydroxyamides of toxicological significance. A historical example is *phenacetin* (**2.182**), an analgesic drug which decades ago was (ab)used by factory workers to relieve stress-induced headache, resulting in uncounted deaths from *renal failure*. The molecular mechanism of this toxicity involves oxidation to the *N*-hydroxyamide **2.183**, followed by formation of the nitrenium cation (*Fig. 2.68*) under acidic urinary conditions [4][166]. And indeed, phenacetin *N*-hydroxylation has recently been confirmed in human subjects [167]. A nontherapeutic example of *N*-hydroxylation is afforded by *2-(acetylamino)fluorene* (**2.184**), whose *carcinogenicity* is again due to the *N*-hydroxyamide metabolite **2.185** and its breakdown to a nitrenium ion which binds covalently to DNA. A further toxicological concern with this mechanism is the fact that the initial toxin may not be an amide. Thus, many *polycyclic aromatic nitro compounds* (nitro-PAHs) display a marked *genotoxicity* (see *Fig. 2.87*). These compounds are *environmental pollutants* produced by combustion and are found for example in diesel exhaust and urban aerosols. Probably the most studied compound in this class is *1-nitropyrene* (**2.186**), a known mutagen and carcinogen whose binding to DNA follows reduction. 1-Nitropyrene and its congeners are reduced by xanthine oxidase, aldehyde oxidase, cytochrome P450, or the intestinal microflora to yield a *polycyclic arylamine* **2.187** (see *Chapt. 2.5* and *2.6*). Interestingly, the easier their metabolic reduction, the greater their genotoxicity. The last enzymatic steps are *N*-acetylation by *N*-acetyltransferase (*Part 4*) to the amide **2.188** and *N*-hydroxylation to **2.189** [168].

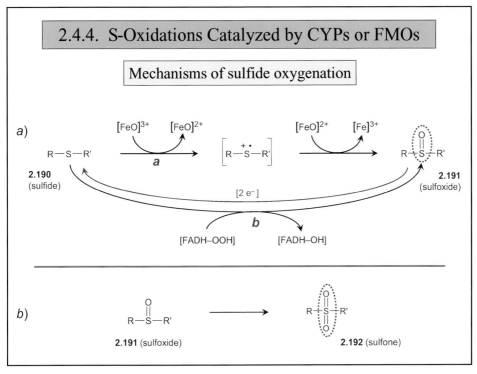

2.4.4. S-Oxidations Catalyzed by CYPs or FMOs

Mechanisms of sulfide oxygenation

Fig. 2.70. Many xenobiotics featuring a thioether group (*i.e.*, sulfides **2.190**) yield sulfoxides (**2.191**) and sulfones (**2.192**) in reactions catalyzed by FMOs and/or CYPs. It also seems that FMOs are more efficient in forming sulfoxides, and CYPs in forming sulfones. Other enzymes can also *S*-oxygenate some sulfides, *e.g.*, some peroxidases and cytosolic cysteine oxidases [4][64][169–171]. The S=O bond in sulfoxides and sulfones is a polarized one and is best understood as a hybrid between a double bond and semipolar bond. The polarized character of the S=O bond explains the high polarity and hydrophilicity of sulfoxides. Interestingly, it is not always realized that sulfones are markedly less hydrophilic and more lipophilic than sulfoxides due to partial cancellation of the two S=O vectors of dipolarity [172]. The *mechanisms of sulfoxidation* are shown here; the reaction catalyzed by CYPs (*Reaction a*) is initiated by a one-electron oxidation of the S-atom, followed by transfer of the activated O-atom (oxygen rebound). Such a mechanism implies that the more readily a substrate can lose an electron, the more effective its cytochrome P450-catalyzed sulfoxidation. A comparable mechanism operates in the CYP-catalyzed oxygenation of sulfoxides to sulfones. In contrast to CYPs, the FMOs form sulfoxides and sulfones by a direct, electrophilic attack, and transfer of the activated oxygen atom (*Reaction b*). As a consequence, the nucleophilicity of the S-atom should be one of the factors controling the rate of sulfoxidation. And, whereas sulfoxides can be reduced to sulfides, sulfones cannot be reduced to sulfoxides.

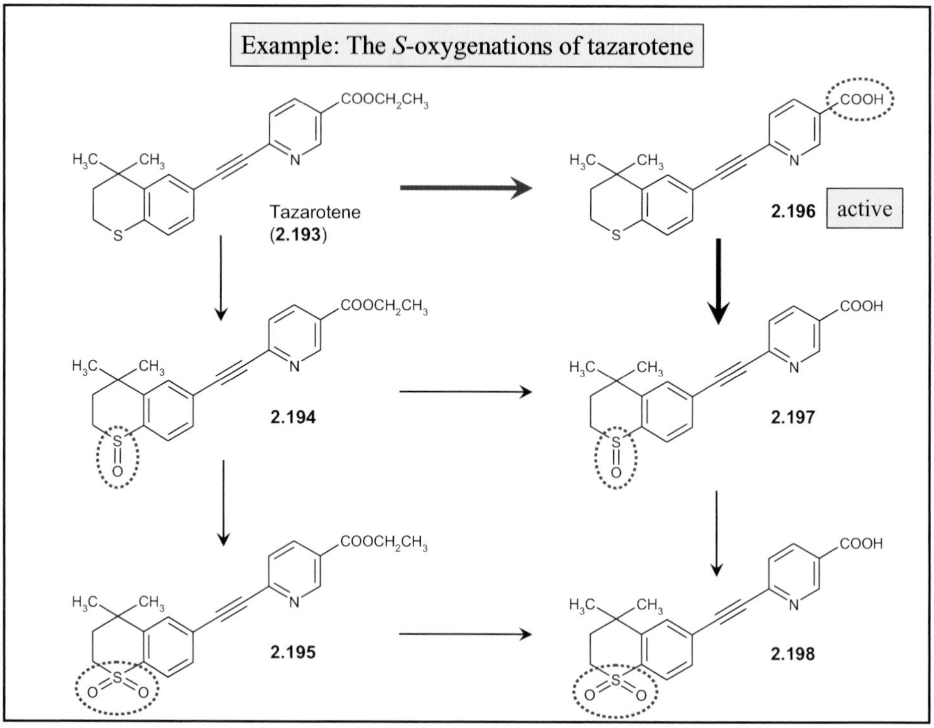

Fig. 2.71. The retinoid *tazarotene* (**2.193**) offers an apt illustration of the fate of sulfides in the human body [173][174]. Following oral administration, the prodrug is rapidly hydrolyzed by esterases (*Part 3*) to the active metabolite *tazarotenic acid* (**2.196**). Tazarotene and tazarotenic acid undergo further metabolism *via* oxidation to the corresponding sulfoxides **2.194** and **2.197**, and sulfones **2.195** and **2.198**. These reactions were shown to be catalyzed by CYP2C8, FMO1, and FMO3. The fastest metabolic reactions are the hydrolysis of tazarotene and the *S*-oxygenation of tazarotenic acid to the inactive sulfoxide **2.197**. The latter was indeed the primary metabolite found in human urine.

Further examples of sulfide *S*-oxygenation

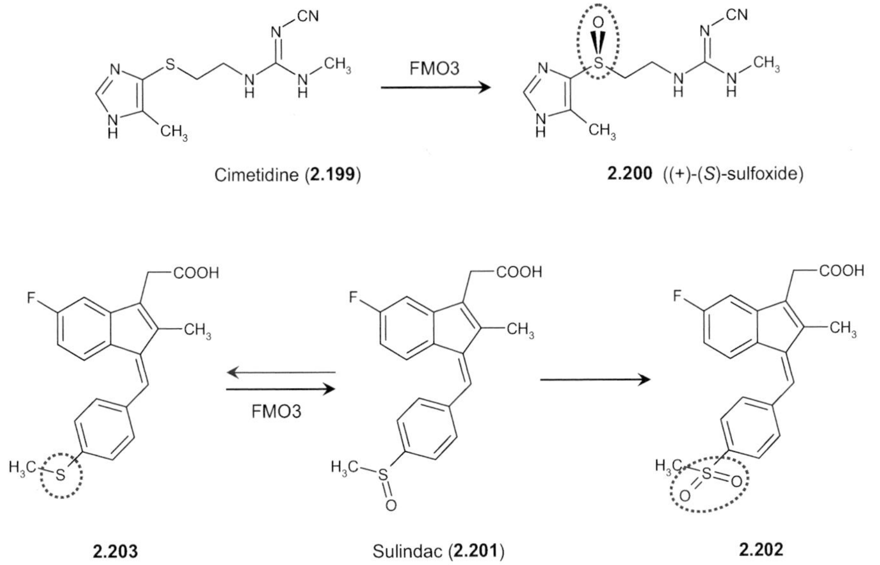

Cimetidine (**2.199**)

2.200 ((+)-(*S*)-sulfoxide)

2.203

Sulindac (**2.201**)

2.202

Fig. 2.72. Two examples of medicinal relevance are presented here the first of which is *cimetidine* (**2.199**), the first H$_2$-histamine receptor antagonist used in pharmacotherapy. The compound contains a sulfide group, and indeed *S*-oxygenation is a major metabolic route in humans and experimental animals [60][147]. This reaction is catalyzed by FMO3 (and seemingly also FMO1) in humans, and FMO1 in pigs. Cytochrome P450 does not contribute significantly to the reaction, since cimetidine is an inhibitory ligand to its catalytic center (*Part 7*). Because sulfoxides are *configurationally stable three-coordinate centers*, sulfoxidation can generate a stereogenic center when the sulfide substrate is prochiral (R ≠ R′) [175][176]. This is the case for cimetidine, and product stereoselectivity is indeed observed. In humans, there is a clear predominance of (+)-(*S*)-cimetidine sulfoxide (**2.200**) being excreted, whereas in the pig the (−)-(*R*)-enantiomer is produced in slight excess. Another compound of great interest is *sulindac* (**2.201**), a racemic sulfoxide used as an anti-inflammatory drug. In humans and experimental animals, the compound is irreversibly oxidized to the inactive *sulindac sulfone* (**2.202**), a major and long-lasting metabolite in plasma and urine [177]. Another important reaction is reduction to *sulindac sulfide* (**2.203**), the active metabolite formed by nonmicrosomal enzymes [178]. The sulfide itself is oxidized back to the sulfoxide, with a marked preference for the (*R*)-enantiomer being shown by pig liver FMO1, rabbit lung FMO2, and human FMO3.

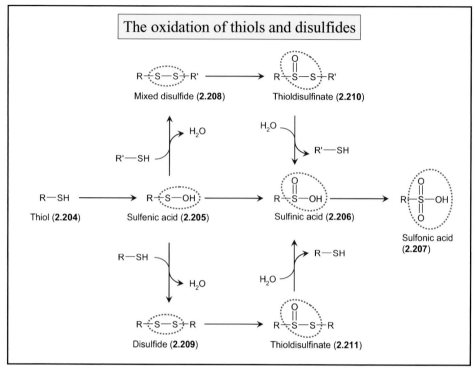

Fig. 2.73. *Thiols* (*mercaptans*) (**2.204**) are good substrates of CYPs and particularly of FMOs, but they can also be oxidized by endogenously generated superoxide [55][61][179]. As a rule, thiols with a negative charge on the S-atom (*e.g.*, dithioacids) are excellent substrates of FMOs [180]; in contrast, the less marked the nucleophilic character of the S-atom, the greater the probability of its oxidation by cytochrome P450. The mechanisms of the monooxygenase-mediated oxidation of thiols are analogous to those shown for sulfides in *Fig. 2.70* [4]. The reaction yields first a *sulfenic acid* (**2.205**), which can be oxidized further to a *sulfinic acid* (**2.206**) and then a *sulfonic acid* (**2.207**). Sulfenic acids are reactive electrophiles whose S-atom can be a center of nucleophilic substitution by a thiol group to yield H_2O and a disulfide. A *mixed disulfide*, **2.208**, is produced when the sulfenic acid reacts with a thiol different from the original substrate, *e.g.*, the tripeptide *glutathione* (see *Part 4*). The reaction of the sulfenic acid with the original thiol yields a *symmetrical disulfide* **2.209**. Note that disulfides can also undergo enzymatic monooxygenation to *thioldisulfinates* **2.210** and **2.211**, and possibly to thiolsulfonates ($R-SO_2-S-R$ or $R-SO_2-S-R'$). And, as exemplified later, thioldisulfinates can hydrolyze nonenzymatically to a sulfinic acid and a thiol.

Example: The *S*-oxygenations of spironolactone

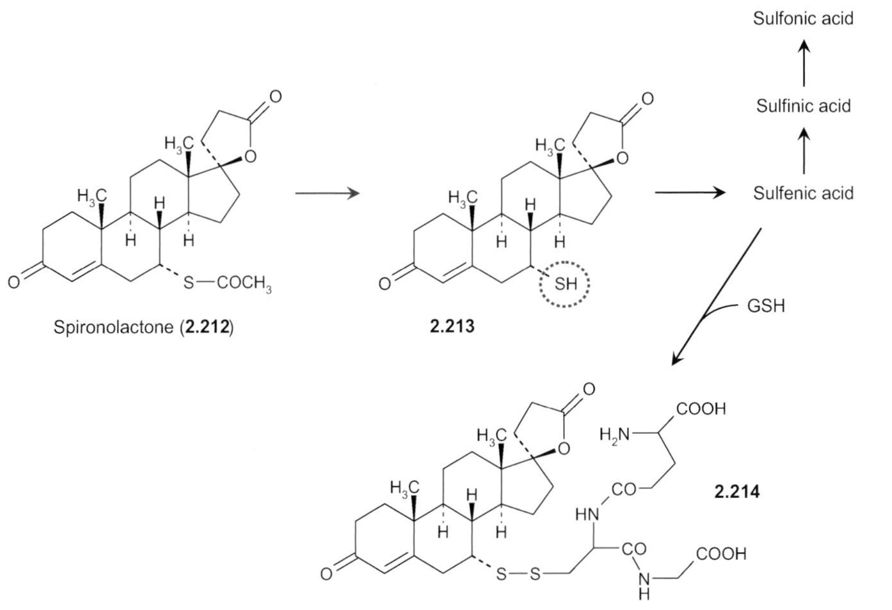

Spironolactone (**2.212**)   **2.213**   Sulfenic acid → Sulfinic acid → Sulfonic acid

GSH

2.214

Fig. 2.74. *Spironolactone* (**2.212**) is a diuretic drug containing an acetylsulfanyl moiety. The major metabolic route of this aldosterone receptor antagonist is deacetylation by hydrolysis to yield the *7α-thiol metabolite* **2.213**. When spironolactone was incubated with rat liver microsomes, *S*-oxygenation by cytochrome P450 yielded the *sulfinic* and *sulfonic acid metabolites*. There was indirect evidence for the initial formation of a sulfanyl radical, followed by oxygen rebound to yield the *sulfenic acid* [181]. This metabolic pathway was accompanied by destruction of cytochrome P450, the key intermediate(s) possibly being the sulfanyl radical and/or the sulfenic acid. In the presence of rat liver microsomes or hog liver FMOs, there was also a reaction of the sulfenic acid with glutathione, an endogenous thiol we will discuss in detail in *Part 4*; this reaction led to the formation of the *glutathionyl-spironolactone mixed disulfide* **2.214** [182]. The latter is in fact a conjugate and as such should be discussed in *Part 4*, but its inclusion here is justified by the oxidative step its formation entails.

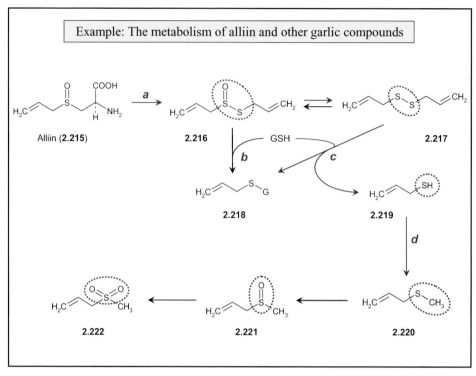

Example: The metabolism of alliin and other garlic compounds

Fig. 2.75. Nature offers some fascinating examples of S-containing compounds and their metabolic reactions. Here, we summarize a few reactions involving *alliin* (*S-allylcysteine sulfoxide*; **2.215**), a compound found in fresh garlic cloves. When such cloves are crushed or cut, the enzyme *alliinase* converts alliin (*Reaction a*) to *diallyl thiosulfinate* (*allicin*; DADSO; **2.216**). This is an unstable compound which breaks down or is transformed enzymatically to numerous organosulfur compounds, among them *diallyl disulfide* (DADS; **2.217**) and the *glutathione conjugate* **2.218** produced by a *nonenzymatic reaction* (*Reaction b*). Diallyl disulfide is a volatile compound and is found in human breath after garlic consumption. Its metabolism in human liver microsomes showed its effective oxygenation to allicin (**2.216**), a reaction catalyzed mainly by CYP2E1 and 2C9, and, to a lesser extent, by other CYPs and by FMOs [183]. Diallyl disulfide was also conjugated *enzymatically* (*Reaction c*) with glutathione (GSH; see *Part 4*). The reason the latter reaction is presented is that its second product is *prop-2-ene-1-thiol* (*allyl mercaptan*; **2.219**), again a compound of relevance here. Prop-2-ene-1-thiol underwent *S*-methylation (*Reaction d*) to *allyl methyl sulfide* (**2.220**), a reaction catalyzed by thiol methyltransferase and/or thiopurine methyltransferase (see *Part 4*). The sequence did not stop here, however, since allyl methyl sulfide was further oxidized to its *sulfoxide* **2.221** and *sulfone* **2.222**, which proved to be important metabolites of diallyl disulfide [184].

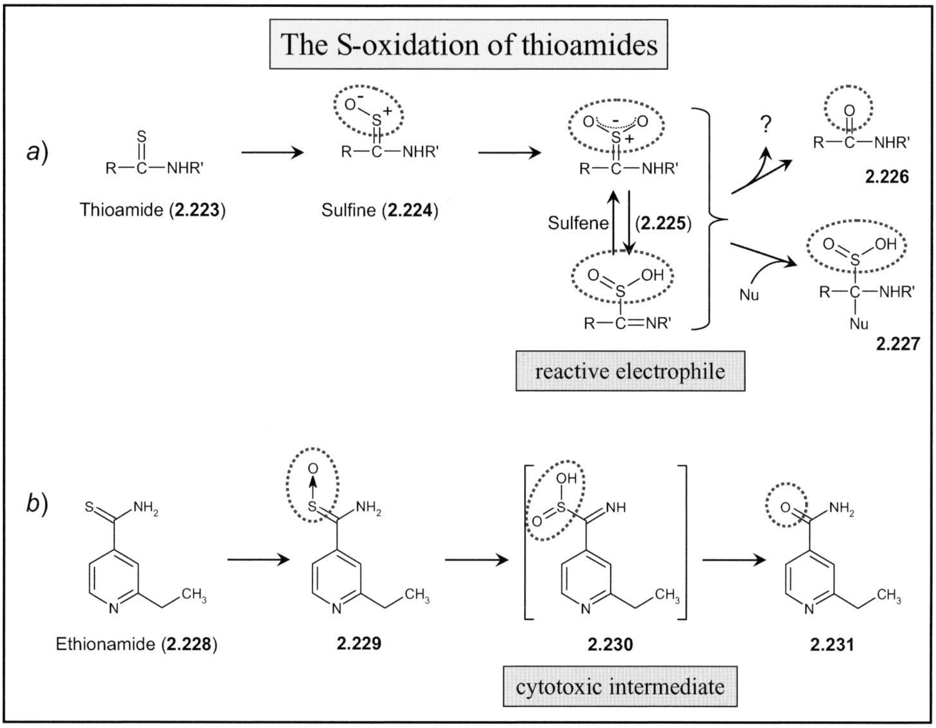

Fig. 2.76. The sulfoxidation of *thioamides* (**2.223**; R = alkyl or aryl) and *carbothioamides* (**2.223**; R = NR″R‴) is of marked interest due to the potential toxicity of some metabolites, in particular their hepatotoxicity and carcinogenicity [4][185][186]. A number of studies have examined the biotransformation of *thioacetamide* (**2.223**; R = methyl, R′ = H) and *thiobenzamide* (**2.223**; R = phenyl, R′ = H), two good substrates of FMOs. However, thioamides are also *S*-oxygenated by cytochrome P450 (*e.g.*, CYP2E1), and the same compound is often found to be oxidized by either or both monooxygenases depending on the biological preparation being used in the study. The *S*-oxygenation of thioamides leads to a *sulfine* (**2.224**) and then to a *sulfene* (**2.225**). The latter can undergo desulfuration to a stable *amide metabolite* **2.226**; such a reaction is known as *oxidative desulfuration*, and it is exemplified for thiobarbiturates. However, some sulfenes are *highly reactive electrophiles* which can form *adducts*, **2.227**, by reacting covalently with nucleophilic groups in endogenous macromolecules such as nucleic acids and proteins, *e.g.*, with the amino group of lysine in albumin. A compound of medicinal relevance is *ethionamide* (**2.228**), a second-line drug in the treatment of multidrug-resistant tuberculosis. In fact, ethionamide (like isoniazid) is a prodrug which must be activated in the bacterial cell. The responsible mycobacterial enzyme has been characterized as a flavoprotein monooxygenase which forms the S-*oxide* **2.229** and then the unstable, doubly oxygenated *sulfinic acid intermediate* **2.230** [187]. The latter is believed to be the final cytotoxic species, and it breaks down by desulfuration to the stable 2-ethylpyridine-4-carboxamide metabolite (**2.231**).

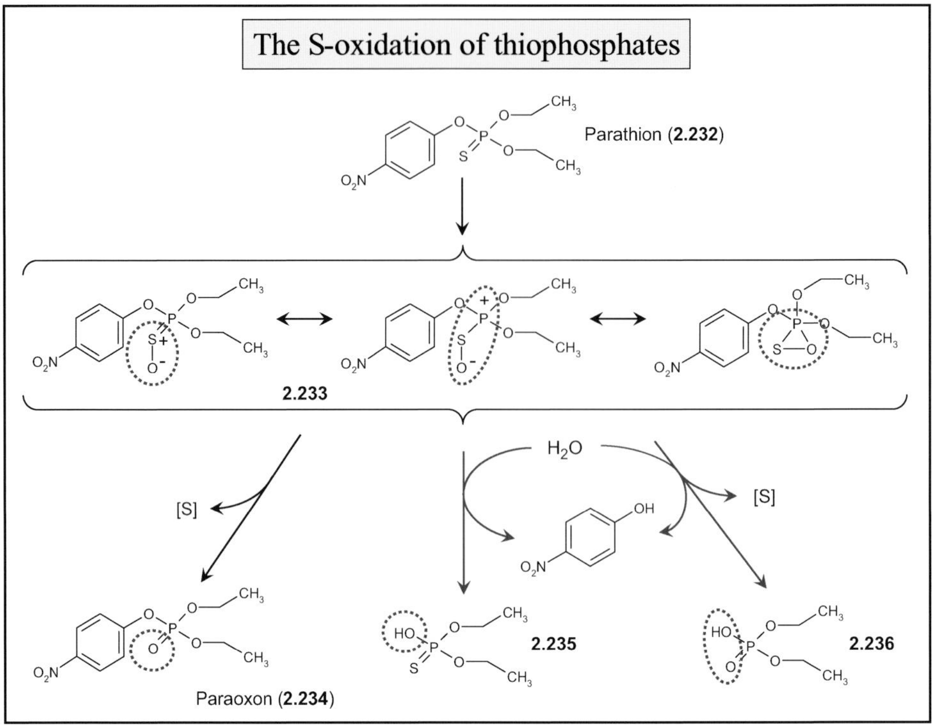

Fig. 2.77. Oxidative desulfuration is also documented for a number of xenobiotics containing a thiono-S-atom bonded to a P-atom, namely *thiophosphates* and *thiophosphonates* [4]. These compounds are insecticides and inhibitors of acetylcholinesterase. Oxidative desulfuration can transform them into their *oxon analog*, a reaction generally accompanied by a marked increase in activity and hence toxicity. This is the case for the insecticide *parathion* (**2.232**). Oxidation by cytochrome P450 leads to an unstable monooxygenated species postulated to be an S-*oxide*, **2.233**, which exists in equilibrium with an *oxathiaphosphirane, i.e.*, a three-membered ring structure analogous to an epoxide. Rearrangement of the latter intermediate can explain the formation of *paraoxon* (**2.234**) with concurrent loss of sulfur. Good evidence indeed exists that sulfur is released in an atomic, activated form that binds covalently to apocytochrome P450 and inhibits the enzyme. Specifically, the activated sulfur binds to the SH group of cysteinyl residues, forming hydrodisulfides (RSSH). In addition, covalent binding to proteins also involves tyrosine and amino acids with branched side chains (isoleucine, leucine, and valine) [188]. Besides forming paraoxon, the monooxygenation of parathion can also be followed by hydrolysis and leads to the formation of *diethyl thiophosphate* (**2.235**) and *diethyl phosphate* (**2.236**). Indeed, the intermediate S-oxide is activated toward nucleophilic attack by H_2O or the hydroxyl anion.

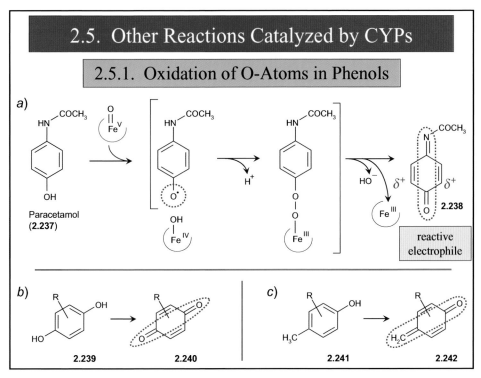

2.5. Other Reactions Catalyzed by CYPs

2.5.1. Oxidation of O-Atoms in Phenols

Fig. 2.78. With this *Figure*, we initiate a survey of additional reactions catalyzed by CYPs, namely oxidation of O-atoms in phenols, peroxidase reactions, and various important reactions of reduction. This *Chapter* thus illustrates the amazing variety of catalytic mechanisms the CYPs have evolved to carry out, and which markedly extend their enzymatic efficiency beyond mono-oxygenation reactions. Beginning with the *oxidation of phenols*, we note that the presence of two oxidizable substituents in a *para*- or *ortho*-relation of aromatic rings allows oxidation to quinone or quinone-like metabolites. Such oxidizable substituents are a OH group, a primary or secondary amino or amido group, and even a methyl or short *n*-alkyl group. Depending on the nature of these groups, oxidation will yield a para- or ortho-*quinone*, a *quinoneimine* or a *quinone methide*. As far as xenobiotic metabolism is concerned, such reactions can be nonenzymatic (oxidation by O_2) or enzymatic [4]. A number of enzymes may catalyze such reactions, in particular *peroxidases* to be discussed in *Chapt. 2.6*. Cytochrome P450 is also known to catalyze the oxidation of some diphenols, aminophenols, amidophenols, and 4-alkylphenols to the corresponding quinone, quinoneimine, or quinone methide, and they can do so by acting either as *monooxygenases* as discussed below, or as *peroxidases* as discussed in *Sect. 2.5.2*. Our understanding of the formation and reactivity of quinone and quinone-like metabolites has gained significantly from studying the metabolic fate of *paracetamol* (*a*; **2.237**; acetaminophen), a well-known analgesic agent. The metabolic oxidation of paracetamol yields two main products, namely the catechol analog (*i.e.*, the 3-hydroxylated metabolite) and N-*acetyl*-para-*quinoneimine* (**2.238**; NAPQI) which is usually characterized as the glutathionyl conjugate (*Part 4*). NAPQI is a highly reactive metabolite able to cause life-threatening hepatotoxicity beyond threshold doses. Paracetamol oxidation displays a marked enzyme selectivity (CYP1A1, 1A2, and 3A4), with 2E1 being particularly active in forming NAPQI [189–191]. Quantum-mechanical calculations and indirect evidence indicate that H abstraction proceeds from the OH group rather than from the amide group, the resulting radical being predominantly O-centered [192]. This first single-electron enzymatic oxidation is followed by a second one as shown, leading to the quinoneimine **2.238**. The enzymology of the oxidation of benzene-diols (*e.g.*, **2.239**) to *quinones* (**2.240**) is quite complex, as a variety of systems have the capacity to catalyze the reaction (*Chapt. 2.6*). Thus, cytochrome P450 itself may play a direct role in some cases, as seen in the oxidation of *naphthalen-1-ol* to naphthalene-1,4- and -1,2-diols, and ultimately to 1,4- and 1,2-naphthoquinone by a reconstituted system [4]. Of further biological and toxicological interest is the oxidation of some *4-alkylphenols* (*e.g.*, **2.241**) to *quinone methides* (**2.242**) [4]. These metabolites are strong alkylating agents which undergo *Michael* additions at the exocyclic methylidene C-atom, thereby binding covalently to soluble and macromolecular nucleophiles [193]. This reaction of oxidation is exemplified by the antioxidant *butylated hydroxytoluene* (BHT; 2,6-di(*tert*-butyl)-4-methylphenol; **2.241** with R = 2,6-di(*tert*-butyl)), which gave the corresponding quinone methide when incubated in the presence of hepatic and pulmonary microsomes from rats and mice [194].

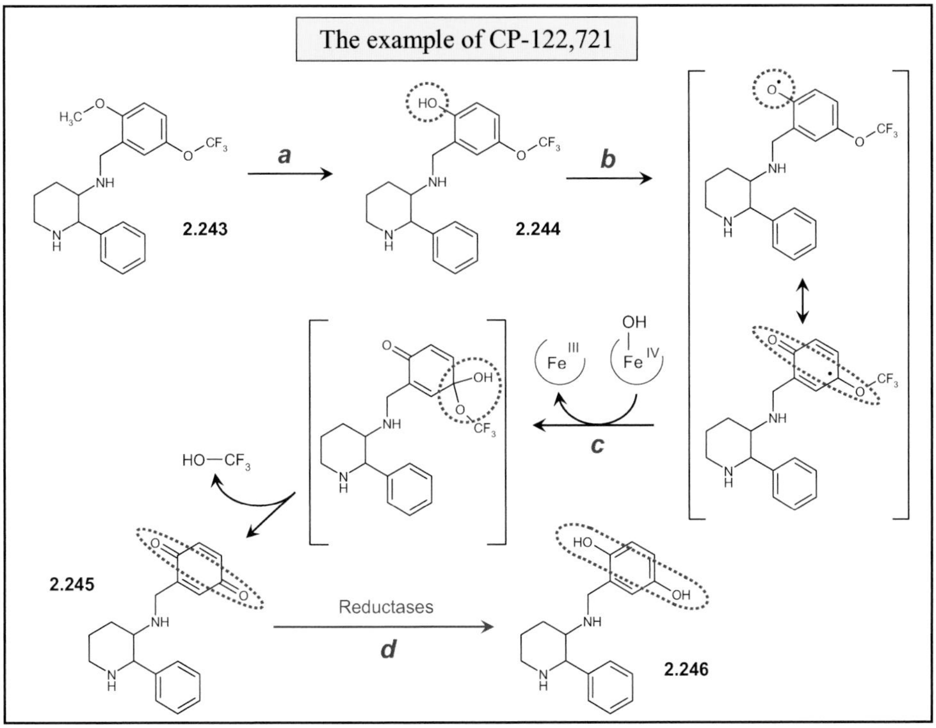

The example of CP-122,721

Fig. 2.79. An interesting metabolic pathway has recently been reported for the developmental compound *CP-122,721* (**2.243**), a potent tachykinin NK1 receptor antagonist [195]. When administered to rats, the compound was extensively metabolized, no unchanged drug being detected *in excreta*. A major route (*Reaction a*) was O-*demethylation* to the phenol **2.244**. Other major routes of oxidation were aliphatic and aromatic hydroxylations (not shown). A quantitatively minor yet qualitatively significant metabolite was the *hydroquinone analogue* **2.246**, which was excreted as the *O*-glucuronide. This metabolite is intriguing, since it must have been generated by a previously unreported pathway, namely O-*dealkylation of an O-trifluoromethyl* (CF$_3$O) *group*. Two CYP-catalyzed mechanisms can be postulated for its formation, namely *a*) *ipso*-substitution (not shown here, but see *Fig. 2.54* for mechanistic details), or *b*) phenol oxidation to yield a radical intermediate (*Reaction b*). Further oxidation of this radical intermediate (*Reaction c*), followed by loss of the CF$_3$O group would yield the para-*quinone* **2.245**. Currently available data do not allow one to consider one mechanism more likely than the other, nor do they tell us whether a peroxidase was also involved. The final phase I reaction (quinone reduction, *Reaction d*) will be presented in *Chapt. 2.6*.

2.5.2. Peroxidase Reactions Catalyzed by CYPs

The peroxidase cycle of cytochrome P450

Global mechanism: R–OOH + [Fe^{3+}] + XH → R–OH + [Fe^{3+}] + XOH

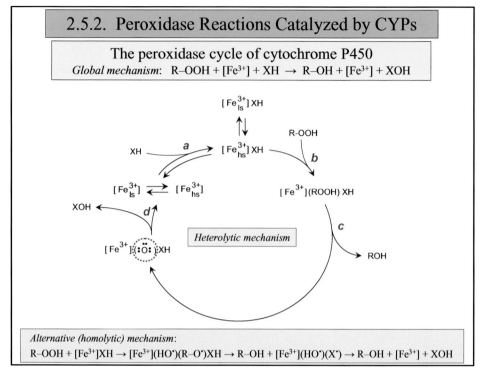

Alternative (homolytic) mechanism:

R–OOH + [Fe^{3+}]XH → [Fe^{3+}](HO$^{•}$)(R–O$^{•}$)XH → R–OH + [Fe^{3+}](HO$^{•}$)(X$^{•}$) → R–OH + [Fe^{3+}] + XOH

Fig. 2.80. It was discovered in the early 1970s that hydroperoxides or H$_2$O$_2$ can support the cytochrome P450-catalyzed hydroxylation of various substrates in a reaction that requires neither NADPH/O$_2$ nor NADPH-cytochrome P450 reductase, and which is not inhibited by carbon monoxide [4][40][52][196–197]. This reaction has physiological significance, since it may contribute to the detoxification of endogenous peroxides such as fatty acid peroxides. The overall mechanism of the reaction is shown in the upper part of the *Figure*. The O-atom transferred to the substrate comes from a hydroperoxide ROOH, where R can be H, alkyl or acyl (*i.e.*, a peracid R′–CO–OOH). As shown, the mechanism of cytochrome P450 peroxygenase activity begins with the formation of a ternary complex (*Reactions a and b*) having the two substrates (*i.e.*, the hydroperoxide and the substrate XH) bound to the oxidized (ferric) form of cytochrome P450. Cleavage of the O–O bond occurs following formation of this complex and usually involves a *heterolytic mechanism* (*Reaction c*), whereby the two O–O bonding electrons remain with the proximal O, and the distal O is transferred as oxene to the iron cation. This is a *two-electron process* in which the hydroperoxide is reduced to an alcohol while the ferric CYP is oxidized to the [FeO]$^{3+}$ state. Another cleavage mechanism has also been characterized, namely a *homolytic mechanism* (bottom of the *Figure*). This is a one-electron process which yields an alkoxyl RO$^{•}$ radical and the [FeOH]$^{3+}$ form of the enzyme. Both the heterolytic and the homolytic mechanism end up abstracting a H-atom from the substrate XH and transferring the HO$^{•}$ radical to the activated substrate X$^{•}$.

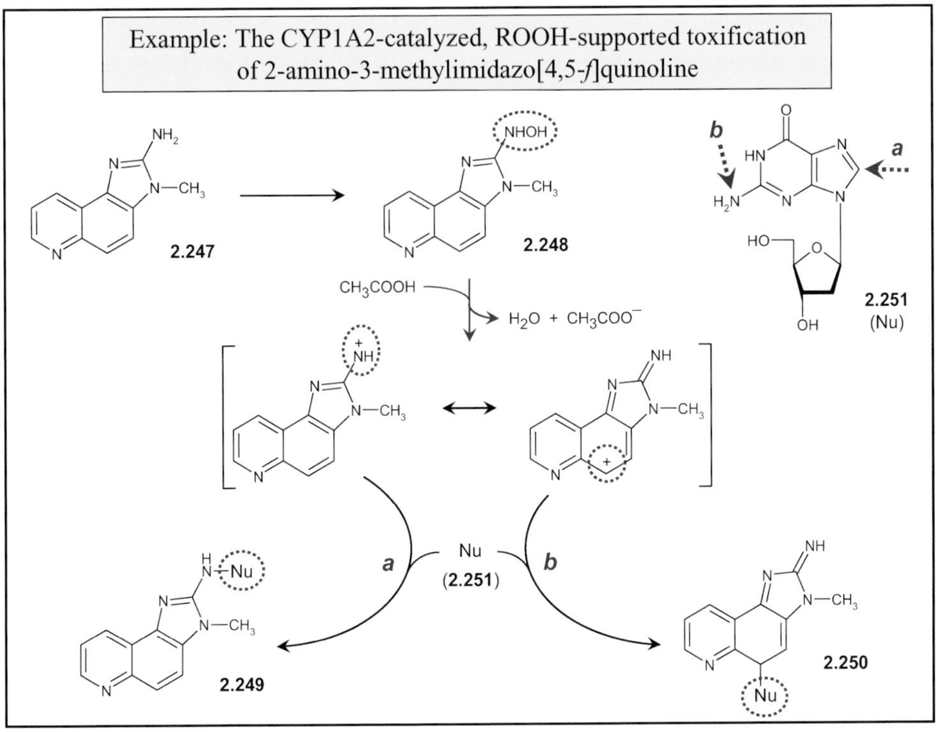

Example: The CYP1A2-catalyzed, ROOH-supported toxification of 2-amino-3-methylimidazo[4,5-*f*]quinoline

Fig. 2.81. A large number of xenobiotics are known to be oxidized *in vitro* by the peroxygenase activity of cytochrome P450. The *in vivo* significance of these reactions remains to be fully understood, *e.g.*, to which extent is the reaction driven by peroxides of membrane lipids, and to which extent by NADH and O_2 present in the respective tissues. Representative *in vitro* reactions of xenobiotic metabolism catalyzed by the peroxygenase activity of CYPs include *aromatic oxidation, aliphatic hydroxylation*, N-*dealkylation, N-oxidation*, O-*dealkylation*, and *O-oxidation* [4]. Here, we illustrate this activity with an example of toxicological significance. *2-Amino-3-methylimidazo[4,5-f]quinoline* (**2.247**) is a heterocyclic aromatic amine formed pyrolytically from proteins during food cooking. As some analogs, it is known to be a potent bacterial mutagen and a rodent carcinogen. Its bioactivation occurs through N-oxidation to the hydroxyl-amine **2.248**. In rat or human liver microsomes, this reaction was shown to be mediated mainly by CYP1A2 and resulted in bacterial mutagenicity when supported either by NADPH/O_2 or by H_2O_2 [198]. The formation of an adduct of structure **2.249** or **2.250** was observed after incubation in the presence of the deoxyribonucleoside *2'-deoxyguanosine* (**2.251**, where the two red arrows *a* and *b* point to the two nucleophilic sites involved in the formation of **2.249** and **2.250**, resp.). Such adduct formation was observed only when the reaction was supported by H_2O_2 or *tert*-butyl hydroperoxide, and not when NADPH/O_2 or linoleic hydroperoxide were the cofactor(s). These findings give evidence for the initial formation of a hydroxylamine, followed by its probable *O*-acetylation (*Part 4*) and subsequent breakdown to a delocalized, highly electrophilic nitrenium cation (see also *Fig. 2.66*).

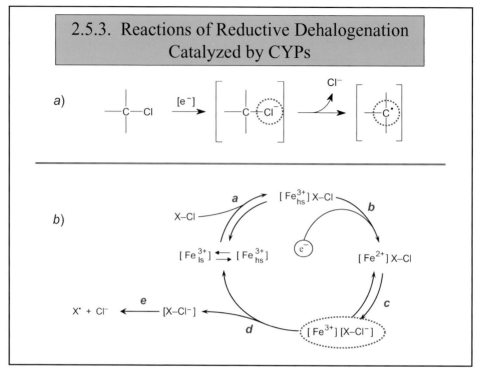

Fig. 2.82. The relative contributions of oxidation and reduction to xenobiotic metabolism are quite different [4][152], since the high positive redox potential of aerobic organisms tends to favor oxidative over reductive reactions. This is in sharp contrast with anaerobic bacteria whose metabolism is largely hydrolytic and reductive. As a result, the gut flora of humans and animals can contribute significantly to the bioreduction of xenobiotics [199]. Systemic xenobiotic reduction does occur in the liver and other major organs of biotransformation, especially for easily reducible substrates, but its *in vivo* contribution remains difficult to assess because *in vitro* investigations may not reflect physiological conditions of oxygen concentrations and redox equilibria of cofactors such as NADPH *vs.* NADP⁺. In *Sect. 2.5.3* and *2.5.4*, we turn our attention to reductive reactions catalyzed by *CYPs* and *NADPH-cytochrome P450 reductase* (see *Figs. 2.6* and *2.23*), which, in contrast to other reductive enzymes such as quinone reductases (*Chapt. 2.6*), involve *single-electron reduction steps*. Reductive dehalogenation is a significant metabolic reaction mediated by CYPs; the reaction is outlined in the upper part of the *Figure* (*a*), whereas its *mechanism* is summarized under *b*. The reaction begins as seen before (*i.e.*, *Steps a* and *b* here and in *Fig. 2.23*). However, a branching occurs after entry of the first electron (*i.e.*, after *Step b* in *Fig. 2.23*), such that the [ferrous-CYP]–substrate complex rearranges to a *[ferric-CYP]–[reduced substrate] complex* (*Step c*) due to *electron-withdrawing by the substrate*. The latter being unstable in the anionic form loses a halide anion to become a *radical* (*Step e*).

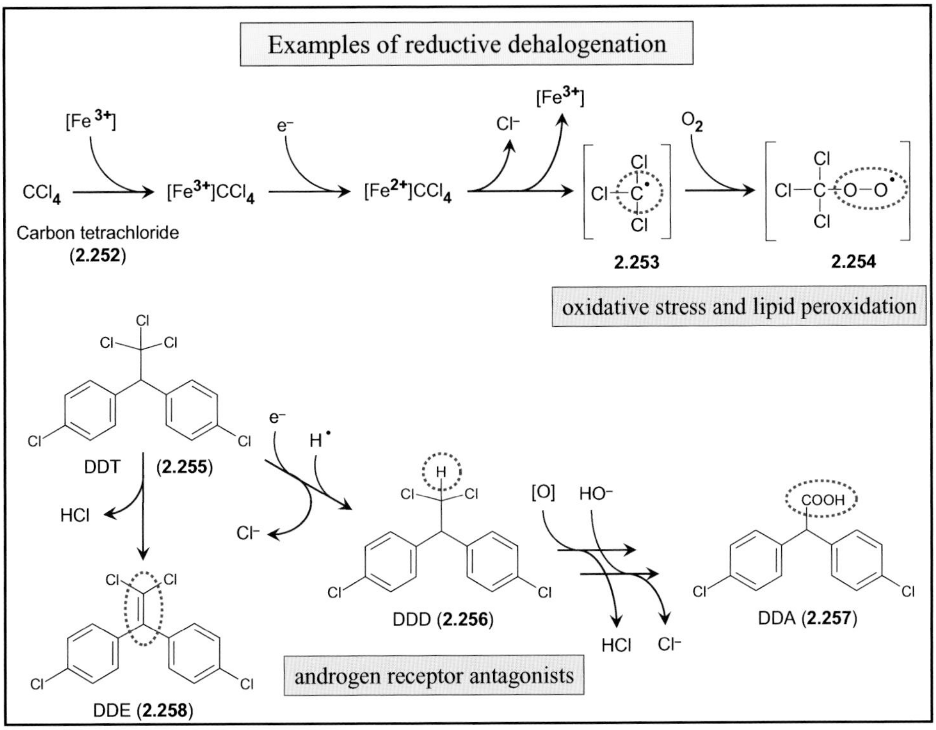

Examples of reductive dehalogenation

$[Fe^{3+}]$

CCl$_4$ $\longrightarrow$ $[Fe^{3+}]CCl_4$ $\xrightarrow{e^-}$ $[Fe^{2+}]CCl_4$ $\xrightarrow{[Fe^{3+}]}_{Cl^-}$ [Cl–C•(Cl)Cl] $\xrightarrow{O_2}$ [Cl–C(Cl)(Cl)–O–O•]

Carbon tetrachloride
(2.252)

2.253   2.254

oxidative stress and lipid peroxidation

DDT (2.255)

DDD (2.256)   [O]   HO⁻   DDA (2.257)   COOH

HCl   Cl⁻

androgen receptor antagonists

DDE (2.258)

Fig. 2.83. Toxicologically relevant reactions of reductive dechlorination are shown here. The case of *carbon tetrachloride* (**2.252**) is particularly revealing, since its metabolic activation accounts for its high hepatotoxicity, which can be acute or chronic depending on amounts ingested or inhaled. Indeed, hepatic CYP2E1 and perhaps other CYPs catalyze CCl$_4$ bioreduction to the *trichloromethyl radical* (**2.253**) [200][201]. This toxic intermediate is able to abstract a hydrogen radical from polyunsaturated fatty acids; but its fastest reaction is with molecular oxygen to yield the highly toxic *(trichloromethyl)peroxyl radical* **2.254**. Further toxic intermediates are phosgene (**2.64** in *Fig. 2.42*), fatty acid peroxyl radicals and hydroperoxides, and a host of other compounds involved in lipid peroxidation, hepatocyte death and liver necrosis [4][54][202]. The case of *DDT* (**2.255**; 'dichloro-diphenyl-trichloroethane', see also *Fig. 1.28* in *Part 1* [1]) is vastly different yet also toxicologically relevant. This persistent organic pollutant ('POP' [1]) is reduced by cytochrome P450 to a similarly hydrophobic metabolite known as *DDD* (**2.256**; 'dichloro-diphenyl-dichloroethane') [4][203]. The latter can be further metabolized by oxidation and hydrolysis to *DDA* (**2.257**; 'dichloro-diphenylacetic acid'), a somewhat less hydrophobic metabolite which is excreted slowly in animals and humans exposed to DDT. Another metabolite is *DDE* (**2.258**; 'dichloro-diphenyl-dichloroethylene') whose overall mechanism of formation involves loss of HCl and retention of the oxidation state. DDT and its two hydrophobic metabolites DDD and DDE bind to the androgen receptor and inhibit testosterone binding, with DDE being a more potent antagonist by at least one order of magnitude [204]. This activity is believed to account for the abnormalities observed in male sex development in wildlife animals exposed to DDT.

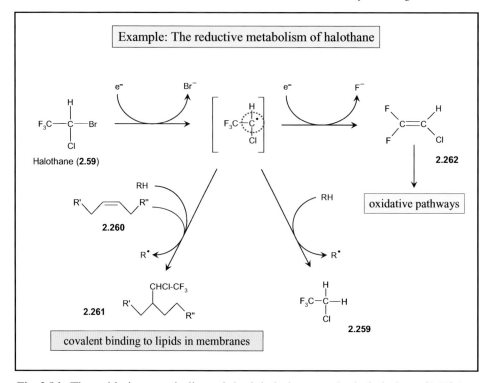

Fig. 2.84. The oxidative metabolism of the inhalation anesthetic *halothane* (**2.59**) has been presented in *Fig. 2.42* where emphasis is given to the toxicological implications of highly reactive metabolites capable of acylating proteins. Here, we examine the mechanism of *reductive dehalogenation* of halothane and its significant toxicological hazards [4][54]. In human liver microsomes, the reductive metabolism of halothane is catalyzed by CYP2A6 and 3A4 [205], and it displays many analogies with that of CCl_4 (*Fig. 2.83*). The main pathway leads to the formation of the *1-chloro-2,2,2-trifluoro-ethyl radical*; this radical intermediate can abstract a H-atom from lipids or other biomolecules, resulting in the formation of *2-chloro-1,1,1-trifluoroethane* (**2.259**), a major metabolite observed *in vitro* under conditions of low oxygen tension. More importantly, the 1-chloro-2,2,2-trifluoroethyl radical can bind covalently to proteins and (mainly) to unsaturated fatty acids in phospholipids **2.260**. The latter reaction first forms transient fatty acyl free radical adducts which pull a H-atom from other lipids to yield *stable adducts* **2.261**. Rather than dissociating from its complex with cytochrome P450, the 1-chloro-2,2,2-trifluoroethyl radical can also undergo *further reduction* to the 1-chloro-2,2,2-trifluoroethyl anion; the latter then loses a fluoride anion and rearranges to *2-chloro-1,1-difluoroethylene* (**2.262**), another major metabolite of halothane. The pathway leading from halothane to 2-chloro-1,1-difluoroethylene is known as *vic-bisdehalogenation*. In addition, and like CCl_4, halothane is able to *inhibit cytochrome P450 irreversibly* and does so by heme destruction following the formation of the chloro(trifluoro)ethyl radical [206].

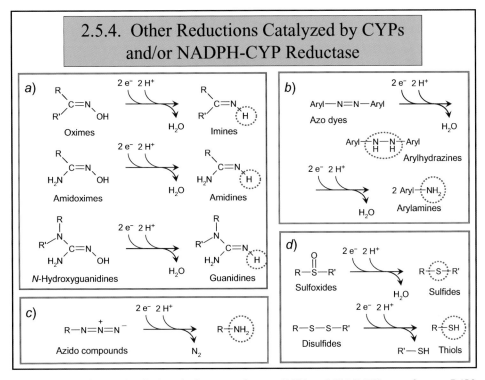

2.5.4. Other Reductions Catalyzed by CYPs and/or NADPH-CYP Reductase

Fig. 2.85. Besides haloalkyl moieties, *cytochrome P450* and *NADPH-cytochrome P450 reductase* are also known to reduce other functional groups and particularly N-containing ones in which reduction to the first stable metabolite necessitates two electrons [4][54][152][201]. Note, however, that the reductions discussed in this *Section* are also catalyzed by *other reductases* (*e.g.*, EC 1.7.1.6, EC 1.7.1.9, EC 1.7.2.3; see also *Chapt. 2.6*). Because *CYP and its reductase act by single-electron reduction steps*, the singly reduced intermediate must remain in the catalytic center until the second electron is transferred. This is in contrast with reductive dehalogenation, which involves departure of the singly reduced substrate [4]. *Box a* shows the three types of *oximes* (oximes, amidoximes, and *N*-hydroxyguanidines) whose reduction by CYP and/or NADPH-CYP reductase leads to an *imino metabolite* (imines, amidines, and guanidines, resp.) [46][207][208]. Attention is currently given to such *N*-hydroxylated imines as potential *bioreductive prodrugs* [209]. *Box b* shows the reduction of *diarylazo dyes* whose coloring capacity has been exploited since more than a century. The first stable metabolite resulting from their reduction is a *1,2-diarylhydrazine*, but the reaction is usually found to continue to yield two aromatic amines (*Fig. 2.86*) [210–212]. Re-oxidation of the latter can lead to genotoxic metabolites such as *nitrenium ions*, as explained in *Fig. 2.66*. *Box c* shows the bioreduction of the *azido group* [4], a rather uncommon moiety in medicinal chemistry and one best illustrated by *zidovudine* (AZT; see *Fig. 2.86*). *Box d* shows the reduction of *sulfoxides* and *disulfides* to *sulfides* and *thiols*, respectively, some examples of which have already been encountered in *Figs. 2.70, 2.72,* and *2.75*. More reactions of reductions are shown in *Fig. 2.87.*

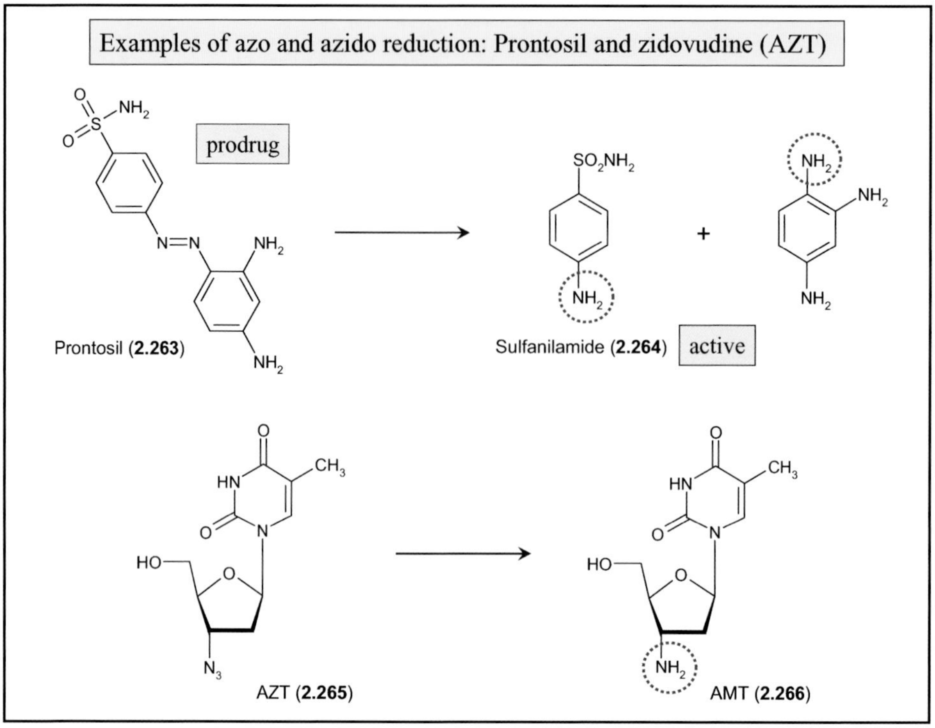

Fig. 2.86. Schematically, *azo dyes* fall into two categories. Some *lipophilic azo dyes* are known or suspected *carcinogens* as a result of their metabolic reduction to arylamines, followed by re-oxidation of the latter to genotoxic metabolites such as a nitrenium ion. In contrast, *hydrophilic azo dyes* bearing sulfonate or other polar groups are extensively reduced *in vivo* to polar, often nontoxic, and readily excretable compounds [4]. This is the case for *prontosil* (**2.263**), an orally active antibacterial of great historical interest. Prontosil was introduced in therapy in the early 1930s following the epoch-making work of *Gerhard Domagk*, and shown in 1935 by *Tréfouël et al.* to be inactive *per se* but to undergo *in vivo* activation by reduction to *sulfanilamide* (**2.264**) [4]. This discovery opened the door to the creation of antibacterial, hypoglycemic, and diuretic sulfonamides. While *azides* have been used extensively as photoaffinity labels for biochemical studies, the azido substituent (N_3) is rather rare in drug design. *3'-Azido-3'-deoxythymidine* (**2.265**; zidovudine, AZT) is a case in point as a major drug in the treatment of HIV infections. This compound undergoes reduction to the primary amine, *i.e.*, *3'-amino-3'-deoxythymidine* (**2.266**; AMT), as demonstrated under aerobic conditions for AZT and a number of 3'-azido analogs using rat or human liver microsomes. The involvement of cytochrome P450, NADPH-cytochrome P450 reductase, and, more recently, *cytochrome b_5* has been demonstrated [213][214]. Of great importance is the fact that AMT proved to be five- to sevenfold more toxic than AZT to human bone marrow cells.

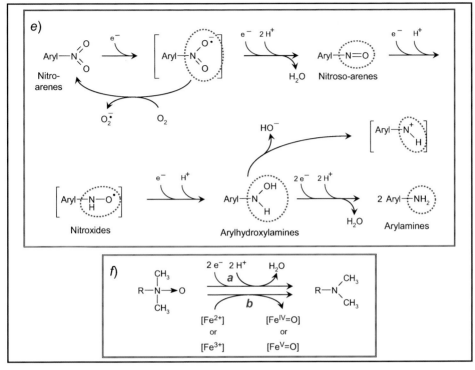

Fig. 2.87. The two boxes here are a continuation of the four ones in *Fig. 2.85. Box e* shows the sequential reduction of *aromatic NO₂ groups* to the corresponding primary amine [4][54][201]. One-electron reduction of a nitro-arene yields a *reactive nitro radical anion*, which can either undergo further reduction or be reoxidized by O_2 to the parent compound (futile cycling). One-electron reduction of the nitro radical anion gives the stable *nitroso metabolite*. Further reductive steps yield an *intermediate nitroxide*, a stable *hydroxylamine*, and the ultimate *primary arylamine*. This direct pathway is not the only one leading from a NO₂ to a primary NH₂ group, since disproportionation of nitro radical anion and other bimolecular reactions may also play a role (reactions not shown). It is also important to note that besides CYPs and NADPH-CYP reductase, *other enzymes* catalyze at least some steps in nitro-arene reduction, namely xanthine oxidase, aldehyde oxidase, and other *cytosolic reductases* (*Chapt. 2.6*), some *mitochondrial reductases*, and *gut microflora enzymes* [215]. As a result, synergism between microsomes and cytosol is sometimes seen in *in vitro* studies. *Box f* shows the *reduction of* N-oxides. Two single-electron reduction steps (*Mechanism a*) characterize the reduction catalyzed by NADPH-CYP reductase, a reaction that may be privileged for aromatic azaheterocyclic *N*-oxides. In contrast, the CYP-catalyzed reduction of *N*-oxides seems to involve direct oxene transfer from the *N*-oxide to either the ferrous or the ferric CYP, which is thus oxidized to the ferryl oxide form [Fe^{IV}=O] or to the perferryl oxide form [Fe^{V}=O], respectively (*Mechanism b*). In the latter form, the enzyme is immediately competent to catalyze *N*-demethylation.

Mechanism b appears privileged for tertiary *N,N*-dimethylated amine oxides.

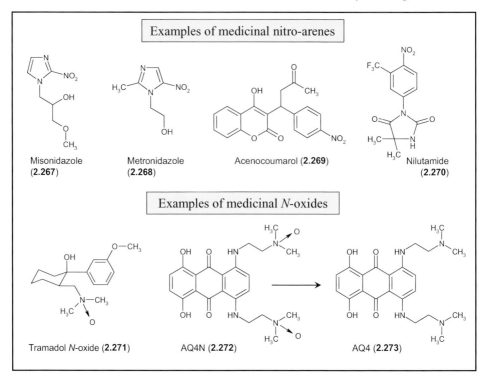

Fig. 2.88. The *reduction of nitro-arenes* and the toxicological hazard of *environmental polycyclic nitro-arenes* have been mentioned in *Figs. 2.66* and *2.69* [216]. As a general rule, the one-electron reduction potential of nitro-arenes is related to their reduction rate by NADPH-CYP reductase [217]. This has been seen with model compounds and drugs such as *nitroheterocyclic antibacterial and antiparasitic agents*. Thus, the reduction of *misonidazole* (**2.267**) in germ-free rats was more extensive than that of *metronidazole* (**2.268**), as expected from their reduction potential [4]. Other drugs whose *in vivo* nitro reduction accounts for a marked proportion of the dose are the anticoagulant *acenocoumarol* (**2.269**) and the nonsteroidal antiandrogen derivative *nilutamide* (**2.270**) [218][219]. The *retroreduction of* N-*oxide metabolites* has been shown in *Fig. 2.61* and is well-illustrated by *tramadol* N-*oxide* (**2.271**), an important metabolite of the analgesic drug tramadol [220][221]. The *in vivo* metabolism of tramadol is qualitatively similar in humans and mice. When tramadol *N*-oxide and tramadol where administered orally to pathogen-free and germ-free mice, the two compounds showed a remarkably similar metabolism indicative of effective reduction of the *N*-oxide in mice cells. N-*Oxide reduction* is also being explored as a tool for *targeted delivery of antitumor agents* to hypoxic cancer cells (see also *Part 5*). This is illustrated by the bioreductive drug candidate *AQ4N* (**2.272**) now in clinical trials. As shown *in vitro* and *in vivo* in rodents, the compound undergoes two successive reductions to AQ4 (**2.273**), a high-affinity DNA-binding agent and topoisomerase II inhibitor [54][222][223]. Bioreduction was dependent on anaerobic conditions; the involvement of CYP2B and 2E was demonstrated.

2.6. Other Oxidoreductases and Their Reactions

2.6.1. Monoamine Oxidase and Other Amine Oxidases

2.6.2. Aldehyde Oxidase and Xanthine Dehydrogenase

2.6.3. Peroxidases and Prostaglandin G/H Synthase

2.6.4. Dehydrogenases/Reductases

Fig. 2.89. *Chapt. 2.6* is dedicated to a survey of *other oxidoreductases besides CYPs and FMOs* which are of significance in xenobiotic metabolism [4][224]. The enzymes presented here were selected because they play an important role either *quantitatively* (*i.e.*, having a relevant number of xenobiotic substrates) or *qualitatively* (*i.e.*, producing active or toxic metabolites) or both. The chapter begins with oxidoreductases which carry out *oxygenation reactions* as do CYPs and FMOs, albeit by essentially different mechanisms. This is the case of *monoamine oxidase* and other amine oxidases (*Sect. 2.6.1*), of *aldehyde oxidase* and *xanthine oxidoreductase* (*Sect. 2.6.2*), and of *peroxidases* including *prostaglandin G/H synthase* (*Sect. 2.6.3*). *Sect. 2.6.4* is dedicated to *dehydrogenases* and *reductases* which catalyze reactions of dehydrogenation and/or hydrogenation. Whereas a huge number and variety of such enzymes exist to carry out physiological functions, we will focus our attention to those dehydrogenases and reductases which play a significant role in xenobiotic metabolism, *e.g.*, alcohol and aldehyde dehydrogenases, aldo-keto reductases, dihydrodiol dehydrogenases, carbonyl reductases, and quinone reductases.

2.6.1. Monoamine Oxidase and Other Amine Oxidases

Enzyme ID Card: Monoamine Oxidase

EC Number	EC 1.4.3.4
Enzyme subclass and sub-subclass	*EC 1.4*: Oxidoreductases acting on the CH–NH$_2$ group of donors// *EC 1.4.3*: With oxygen as acceptor
Systematic name	Amine:oxygen oxidoreductase (deaminating) (flavin-containing)
Human genes and enzymes	*MAOA* $\Rightarrow$ MAO-A; *MAOB* $\Rightarrow$ MAO-B
Bound cofactor (prosthetic group)	Flavin-adenine dinucleotide (FAD)
Subcellular localization	Outer membrane of mitochondria (nerve terminals)
Organs (highest levels)	Liver, brain, heart, blood vessels, kidney
Substrates	Primary amines, also some secondary and tertiary amines; dopamine, MPTP, noradrenaline, phenylethylamine (MAO-B), serotonin (MAO-A), tryptamine, tyramine.
Miscellaneous	Therapeutic indications for MAO-A and MAO-B inhibitors are depression and *Parkinson*'s disease, respectively.

Fig. 2.90. *Monoamine oxidase* (MAO) has for decades interested medicinal chemists as a target for irreversible inhibitors used therapeutically as antidepressants. These agents are now considered obsolete due to side-effects such as the well-known 'cheese effect', *i.e.*, hypertensive crises due to inhibition of the degradation of alimentary tyramine. A more modern approach has been the development of selective, *reversible inhibitors* of MAO [225]. In addition, MAO has gained considerable significance since the 1980s when its capacity to *activate exogenous neurotoxins* was discovered [226]. MAO is an *FAD-containing enzyme* which is widely distributed in most tissues of mammals and other animals [227–232]. The presence of MAO in *brain* is of particular importance as a therapeutic target and an activator of xenobiotics. MAO is a membrane-bound enzyme mainly located in the *mitochondria*, although some activity has also been found in other cellular compartments. Two MAO enzymes are known, MAO-A and MAO-B, whose sequence is coded in the genes *MAOA* and *MAOB*, respectively. The overall structural homology between the two enzymes in a given species is *ca.* 70%, with highly conserved regions. Regarding the structural features of MAO substrates, the endogenous ones are *mainly primary amines*. The same may not be entirely true for xenobiotic substrates (*Fig. 2.94*), among which *some secondary and tertiary amines* are known. An interesting rationalization derived from both endogenous substrates and mechanism-based irreversible inactivators (*Fig. 2.95*) is that MAO-A and MAO-B react with aralkyl amines characterized by a distance of 2–3 atoms and 1–2 atoms between the basic N-atom and the aromatic ring, respectively.

Enzyme ID Card: Copper-Containing Amine Oxidases	
EC Number	EC 1.4.3.6
Enzyme subclass and sub-subclass	*EC 1.4*: Oxidoreductases acting on the CH–NH$_2$ group of donors // *EC 1.4.3*: With oxygen as acceptor
Systematic name	Amine:oxygen oxidoreductase (deaminating) (copper-containing)
Genes and enzymes	*AOC*, two relevant human genes and enzymes: *ABP1 = AOC1 = DAO1* ⇒ DAO (diamine oxidases); *AOC3* ⇒ SSAO (semicarbazide-sensitive amino oxidases)
Bound cofactors	2,4,5-Trihydroxyphenylalanine quinone (topaquinone), plus copper
Subcellular localization	DAO: extracellular space, membrane of endoplasmic reticulum; SSAO: membrane-bound protein
Organs (highest levels)	DAO: kidney, placenta; SSAO: liver, lung, lymph nodes, small intestine; also in blood serum
Substrates	DAO: histamine, diamines; SSAO: monoamines
Miscellaneous	DAO: inhibited by amiloride; SSAO: inhibited by semicarbazide

Fig. 2.91. The broad group of *copper-containing amine oxidases* comprises a variety of activities/enzymes including *diamine oxidase* (DAO) and *semicarbazide-sensitive amine oxidase* (SSAO) [4][227–232]. These enzymes are found in many tissues either as membrane-bound or soluble forms, but, in contrast to MAO, they are not mitochondrial enzymes. One form of SSAO found in blood serum is known as *plasma amine oxidase*. A number of them contain two subunits of molecular mass around 85–90 kDa and are associated with *copper as an inorganic cofactor* (two atoms per dimer). Furthermore, these enzymes contain a covalently bound, organic cofactor which is *2,4,5-trihydroxyphenylalanine (TOPA) quinone*. This cofactor is commonly known as topaquinone, and these enzymes are often referred to as *copper quinoproteins* [232–236]. We will not enter into the details of their catalytic mechanism, but need simply to stress that the substrate reacts with a carbonyl group in topaquinone to form a *quinone-imine* which isomerizes and hydrolyzes to liberate the aldehyde (*i.e.*, the deaminated metabolite). In other words, only *primary amines* (both monoamines and diamines) can be oxidatively deaminated by copper-containing amine oxidases, with large differences observed between tissues and animal species.

The overall mechanism of amine oxidases

$$R{-}CH_2{-}NH_2 + O_2 + H_2O \rightarrow R{-}CHO + NH_3 + H_2O_2$$

The case of monoamine oxidases

First half-reaction (oxidative deamination):

$$[FAD] + R{-}CH_2{-}NH_2 + H_2O \rightarrow [FADH_2] + R{-}CHO + NH_3$$

Second half-reaction (cofactor recycling):

$$[FADH_2] + O_2 \rightarrow [FAD] + H_2O_2$$

The covalently bound FAD (flavin-adenine dinucleotide) cofactor of MAOs

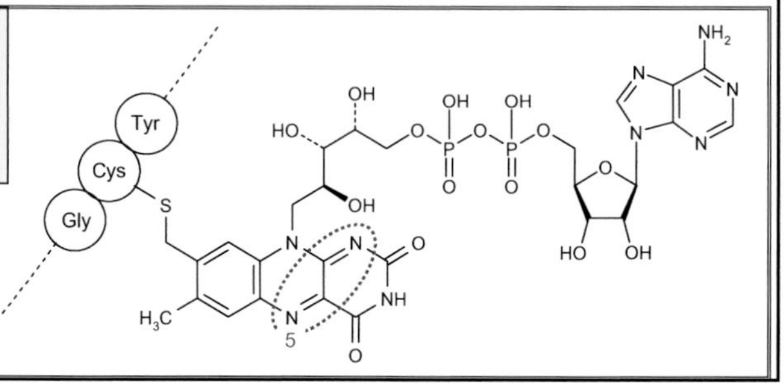

Fig. 2.92. All amine oxidases (including MAO) catalyze the oxidative deamination of amines according to the *overall equation* shown in the upper part of the *Figure*. This reaction is clearly different from the oxidative deamination catalyzed by cytochrome P450 (*Figs. 2.23* and *2.33*). Not only are the mechanisms vastly different (as we shall illustrate in more details for MAO), but one of the products of the amine oxidase-catalyzed reaction is H_2O_2, whereas it is H_2O for the CYP-catalyzed reaction. The H_2O_2 thus released may activate some *neurotoxins* such as 6-hydroxydopamine and 5,7-dihydroxytryptamine, a fact of potential toxicological significance. Most of the *Figure* is dedicated to *monoamine oxidase*, whose covalently bound cofactor (*flavin-adenine dinucleotide*; FAD) is shown in the lower part. This covalent attachement (Cys406 for MAO-A, and Cys397 for MAO-B) is in one of the highly conserved regions near the C-terminus. The critical functionality in FAD is its *N=C−C=N moiety*, whose role in the catalytic mechanism will be illustrated in *Fig. 2.93*. In the present *Figure*, we show how the overall reaction of MAO can be decomposed into two half-reactions. The *first half-reaction* is that of *oxidative deamination*, where the substrate (like in the CYP-catalyzed reaction) is decomposed into an aldehyde and an amine. At the end of this first half-reaction, the cofactor has undergone a two-electon reduction to $FADH_2$. The *second half-reaction* is that of *cofactor recycling*, *i.e.*, O_2-mediated re-oxidation of $FADH_2$ to FAD occurs with production of H_2O_2.

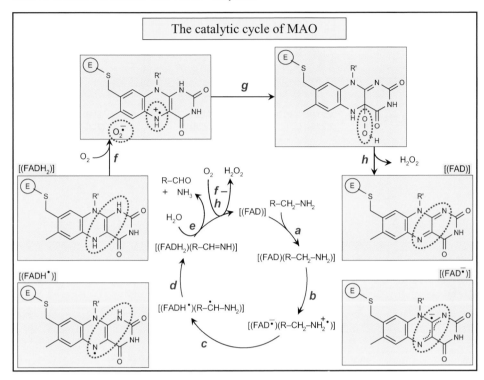

Fig. 2.93. This *Figure* presents the catalytic mechanism of MAO in a somewhat simplified form allowing a better visibility of its essential features [4][227][231][232]. The reaction begins with *binding* of the substrate to the oxidized form of the enzyme, *i.e.*, the FAD state (*Step a*). This is followed by a *single-electron oxidation* of the amino group in the substrate. Simultaneously, the cofactor is reduced to the FAD$^{\cdot-}$ state (*Step b*). This step renders more acidic the α-H-atoms in the amino radical cation and facilitates the next step of H-atom *abstraction* from the substrate with simultaneous protonation of the cofactor (now in the FADH$^{\cdot}$ state, *Step c*) [4][237]. Specifically, the *pro*-R H-atom is removed from the substrate as demonstrated by a variety of examples. This *product stereoselectivity* implies catalysis, presumably by a nucleophilic group in the protein. Following proton abstraction, a second oxidation step occurs to generate an *imine*, while the enzyme reaches its two-electron reduced form FADH$_2$ (*Step d*). The imine then undergoes *hydrolysis* to liberate the corresponding *aldehyde* and *amine* (*Step e*), a reaction of oxidative deamination showing analogies and differences with the CYP-catalyzed reaction. As for the reduced enzyme, it *binds molecular oxygen and undergoes re-oxidation*. This occurs in three steps, the first of which is a *single-electron oxidation* to the FADH$_2$$^{\cdot+}$ state with simultaneous formation of a superoxide anion (*Step f*). A *hydroperoxide* (FADH–OOH) is formed next (*Step g*), followed by *release of H$_2$O$_2$* and return of the cofactor to the FAD state (*Step h*). In summary, *Steps a to e* correspond to the *first half-reaction* in *Fig. 2.92*, whereas *Steps f to h* correspond to the *second half-reaction*.

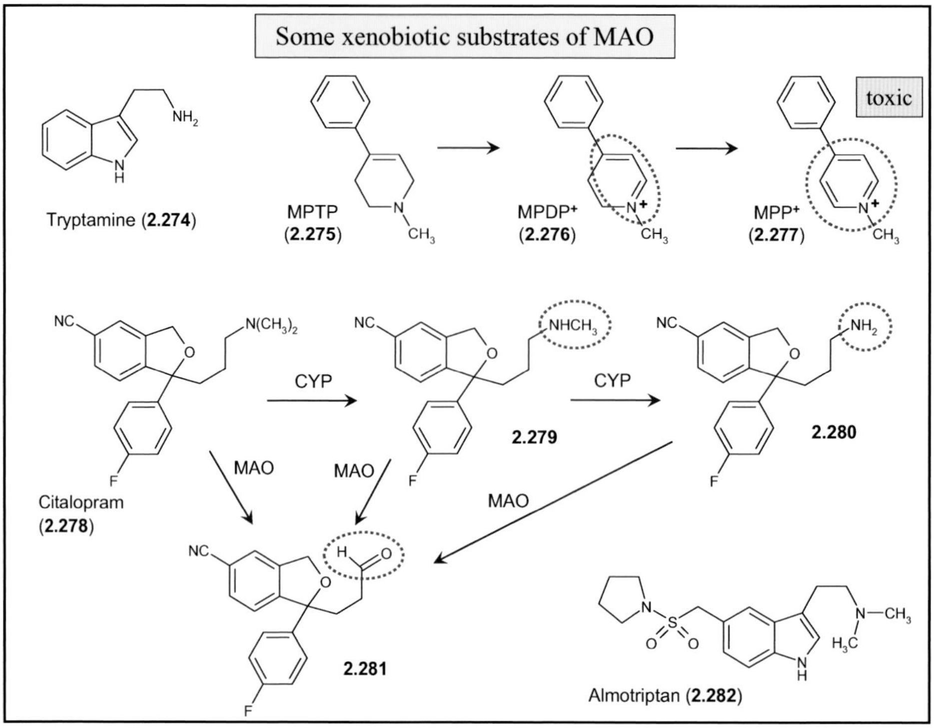

Fig. 2.94. The *physiological substrates* of MAO are predominantly primary amines such as dopamine, noradrenaline, and serotonin [238]. Another example is that of *tryptamine* (**2.274**), a trace amine in the mammalian CNS which is rapidly deaminated by MAO-A but is not a substrate of CYPs; the same is true for 2-phenylethylamine-derived designer 'drugs' [239]. For many years, little was known about the MAO-catalyzed deamination of *exogenous substrates*, particularly secondary and tertiary amines. The discovery that MAO activates *1-methyl-4-phenyl-1,2,3,6-tetrahydropyridine* (MPTP; **2.275**) to a *neurotoxin* causing *Parkinsonism* in humans and monkeys raised a major interest in this enzyme and led to the characterization of many tertiary amines as exogenous substrates [240–242]. The activation of MPTP is mainly due to MAO-B and to a lesser extent to MAO-A. The first steps of the reaction are identical to those outlined in *Fig. 2.93* (*Steps a* to *d*) and lead to the iminium analog MPDP$^+$ (*1-methyl-4-phenyl-2,3-dihydropyridinium* (**2.276**)). But rather than undergoing extensive hydrolysis like imines formed from 'normal' substrates, MPDP$^+$ can be further oxidized by dismutation or by membrane-bound enzymes to MPP$^+$ (*1-methyl-4-phenylpyridinium* (**2.277**)), the ultimate neurotoxin. In recent years, evidence has accumulated that some *basic drugs* are indeed deaminated by MAO [228–230][232]. Thus, the antidepressant *citalopram* (**2.278**) is a tertiary amine whose metabolism involves CYP-catalyzed *N*-demethylation to the secondary (*i.e.*, **2.279**) and primary amines (*i.e.*, **2.280**). All three amines were shown to be deaminated by MAO to the aldehyde metabolite **2.281** in human liver and brain preparations [243][244]. A comparable fate has been observed in the metabolism of the antimigraine drug *almotriptan* (**2.282**), which is *N*-oxygenated by FMO3, *N*-demethylated, and ring-hydroxylated by CYP2D6, 3A4, and others, and deaminated by MAO-A [245].

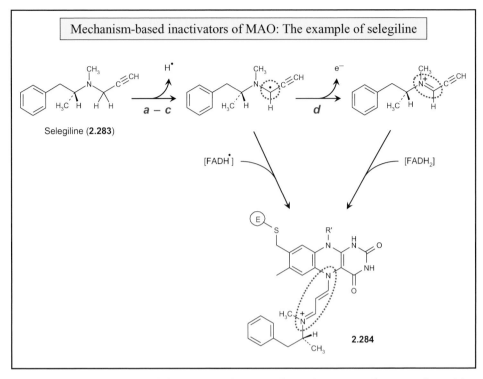

Fig. 2.95. Various N-containing groups in a number of compounds are activated by MAO to reactive intermediates which inactivate the enzyme irreversibly, *e.g.*, hydrazines, propargylamines, and cyclopropylamines [4][237][241][246]. Such compounds are *mechanism-based inactivators*, also (but not quite properly) known as *suicide substrates*. Their therapeutic interest has decreased strongly in the last 2–3 decades, an exception being the MAO-B inhibitor (−)-(*R*)-deprenyl (*selegiline*; **2.283**) which remains of value in the treatment of *Parkinson*'s disease. Selegiline is a *propargylamine* whose mechanism of inactivation is schematized here. The formation of a C-centered radical may occur by the usual pathway (*Steps a* to *c* in *Fig. 2.93*). This C-centered propargyl radical is in resonance with a C-centered allenic radical which *binds covalently to N(5)* of the one-electron reduced cofactor (FAD$^{-•}$ or FADH$^•$). In addition, the radical intermediate may undergo the usual second-electron oxidation to an iminium intermediate (*Step d* in *Fig. 2.93*) which binds covalently to FADH$_2$. Covalent binding to FAD is also the mechanism by which other mechanism-based inactivators such as hydrazines irreversibly inhibit MAO. Other inhibitors are activated to an intermediate which binds to the protein (probably to a cysteinyl residue) in a covalent yet slowly reversible manner. Such *time-dependent, reversible inhibitors* are exemplified by lazabemide and its R−N−C−C−NH$_2$ active moiety [4].

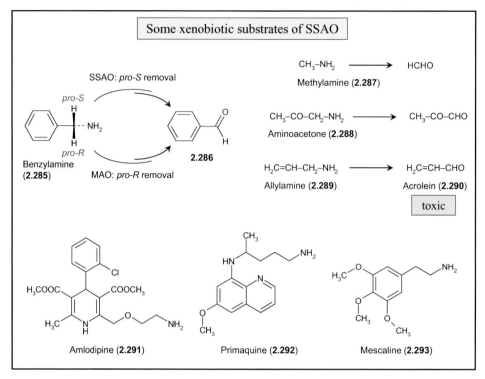

Fig. 2.96. As mentioned earlier, only primary amines can be oxidatively deaminated by *semicarbazide-sensitive amine oxidases* (SSAOs). These enzymes derive their name from the fact that semicarbazide ($H_2N-CO-NH-NH_2$) reacts directly and covalently with a carbonyl group in the active site. As far as monoamine substrates are concerned, *benzylamine* (**2.285**) is a good substrate of some SSAOs and of MAO-B, hence the name 'benzylamine oxidase' sometimes given to plasma SSAO is not appropriate. While we do not consider the mechanistic details of SSAO-catalyzed deamination to benzaldehyde (**2.286**) [4][234], it is interesting to note that MAO acts by removal of the *pro-R* benzylic H-atom, whereas the SSAO reaction involves *pro-S* removal [247][248]. Substrates specific for SSAO include *methylamine* (**2.287**), which is deaminated to formaldehyde, and *aminoacetone* (**2.288**) which is deaminated to methylglyoxal [227–232][249]. The unsaturated primary amine *allylamine* (**2.289**) is a cardiovascular toxin due to its deamination by tissue-specific SSAO to *acrolein* (**2.290**), a reactive aldehyde. Thus, pretreatment of rats with semicarbazide indeed protects animals against allylamine-induced cardiotoxicity. While few drugs with a primary amino group have been investigated for their biotransformation by SSAOs, a number of findings suggest that the phenomenon deserves better attention. Thus, the calcium channel blocker *amlodipine* (**2.291**) is oxidatively deaminated in humans and dogs, but not in rats. This reaction was shown to occur on incubation of the drug in dog plasma but not in rat plasma, and the involvement of plasma amine oxidases was suggested [250]. There is also some evidence to suggest that the antimalarial drug *primaquine* (**2.292**) and the hallucinogenic agent *mescaline* (**2.293**) may be substrates of SSAO [229][232].

2.6.2. Aldehyde Oxidase and Xanthine Oxidoreductase

Enzyme ID Card: Aldehyde Oxidase

EC Number	EC 1.2.3.1
Enzyme subclass and sub-subclass	*EC 1.2*: Oxidoreductases acting on the aldehyde or oxo group of donors // *EC 1.2.3*: With oxygen as acceptor
Systematic name	Aldehyde:oxygen oxidoreductase
Human gene and enzyme	*AOX1* $\Rightarrow$ AO
Bound cofactors	Molybdopterin, [Fe$_2$/S$_2$] clusters, flavin-adenine dinucleotide (FAD)
Subcellular localization	Cytoplasm
Organs (highest levels)	Liver; lower levels in lung, skeletal muscle, pancreas
Substrates	Endogenous and exogenous aldehydes, azaheterocyclic xenobiotics and drugs

Fig. 2.97–2.99. The enzymes discussed here are *molybdo-flavoenzymes* (also known as *molybdenum hydroxylases*); they comprise *aldehyde oxidase* (AO) and *xanthine oxidoreductase* (XOR). Note that *aldehyde dehydrogenase* (*Sect. 2.6.4*) is completely unrelated to AO despite a (misleading) parallel in names. As for XOR, it exists in two interconvertible forms, *xanthine oxidase* (XO) and *xanthine dehydrogenase* (XDH) [251–255]. XDH is the native form in rat liver but is converted to XO during extraction and purification. In contrast, the enzyme exists mostly in the XO form in some other animal tissues. One major difference between the two forms is found in the flavin binding site, which shows the presence of a strong negative charge in XDH but not in XO. AO, XO, and XDH are widely distributed throughout the animal kingdom. They are *cytosolic enzymes* fulfilling roles complementary to those of the monooxygenases in the metabolism of both endogenous and exogenous compounds. They are *homodimers* consisting of identical subunits of approximately 150 kDa. The subunits have a tripartite structure, an N-terminal domain containing two *Fe$_2$/S$_2$ redox clusters*, an *FAD*-containing region, and a C-terminal domain containing a *molybdopterin prosthetic group* and the substrate binding site. This results in a complex *electron flow* from the substrate (which undergoes a two-electron oxidation) to the final acceptor, as shown in *Fig. 2.99*. A prototypic substrate is *xanthine* (**2.294**), whose two-electron oxidation yields *uric acid* (**2.295**; shown here in its two tautomeric forms). As discussed in greater detail in the next *Figure*, the *final electron acceptor* can be either molecular oxygen (*Case a*), NAD$^+$ (*Case b*), or a reducible xenobiotic such as some quinones or nitro-arenes (*Case c*).

Enzyme ID Card: Xanthine Oxidoreductase	
EC Number	EC 1.17.1.4 (dehydrogenase) and 1.17.3.2 (oxidase)
Enzyme subclass and sub-subclass	*EC 1.17*: Oxidoreductases acting on CH or CH$_2$ groups // *EC 1.17.1*: With NAD$^+$ as acceptor (dehydrogenase form); *EC 1.17.3*: With oxygen as acceptor (oxidase form)
Systematic name	Xanthine:NAD$^+$ oxidoreductase; xanthine:oxygen oxidoreductase
Human gene and enzyme	*XOR* $\Rightarrow$ XDH (dehydrogenase form) and XO (oxidase form)
Bound cofactors	Molybdopterin, [Fe$_2$/S$_2$] clusters, flavin-adenine dinucleotide (FAD)
Subcellular localization	Cytoplasm, peroxisome
Organs (highest levels)	Liver, intestine
Substrates	Endogenous purines, azaheterocyclic xenobiotics and drugs
Miscellaneous	Can be converted from the XDH form to the XO form irreversibly by proteolysis or reversibly by the oxidation of sulfhydryl groups

Fig. 2.98.

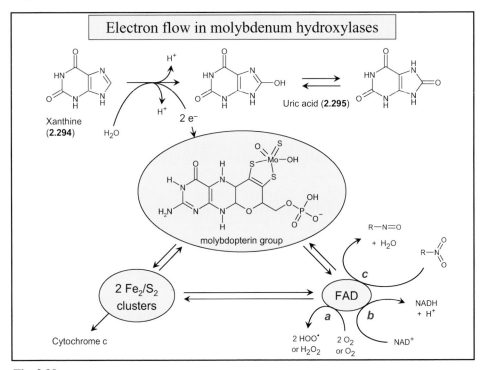

Fig. 2.99.

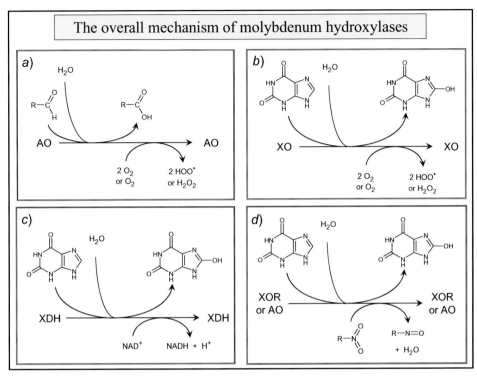

Fig. 2.100. The *global reaction* of molybdenum hydroxylases involves the stripping of two electrons from the O-atom in a H_2O molecule, and insertion of this reactive O-atom into the substrate [4][256][257]. In other words, the O-atom transferred to the substrate comes from a H_2O molecule. The difference between AO, XO, and XDH lies in the *electon acceptor* with which they interact, and which explains their name (*Reminder:* an oxidase transfers electrons to molecular oxygen; a dehydrogenase transfers hydride or electrons plus protons to an acceptor). *Aldehyde oxidase* (shown here oxidizing an aldehyde substrate) also uses molecular oxygen as an electron acceptor (*Box a*), most likely two molecules of O_2 to yield two molecules of superoxide, or perhaps also one molecule of O_2 to yield one molecule of H_2O_2. However, disproportionation of superoxide may account for part or most of H_2O_2 produced [258][259]. The same is true for *xanthine oxidase* (*Box b*). In contrast to XO and AO, *xanthine dehydrogenase* (*Box c*) uses oxidized NAD^+ as the electron acceptor. A more intriguing case is the *reductive capacity* of aldehyde oxidase and xanthine oxidoreductase (*Box d*). Here, these enzymes use a reducible xenobiotic as electron acceptor, as seen *in vitro* under low oxygen tension conditions and in the presence of an electron donor (*i.e.*, an oxidizable substrate).

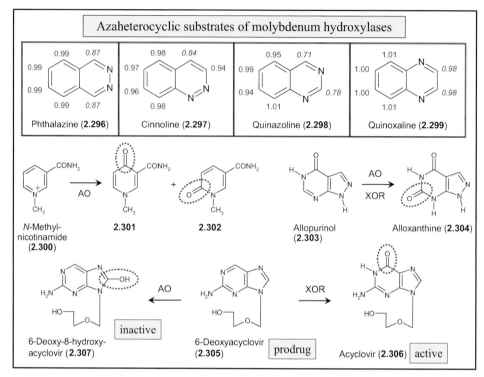

Fig. 2.101. A first and important point is that AO and XOR have *overlapping but not identical substrate specificities and product regiospecificities* [4][260–262]. Also, most medicinally relevant examples published in recent years have pointed to *AO as the major cytosolic hydroxylase*, rather than XOR [263]. The targets of AO and XOR are sp²-hydridized C-atoms rendered electron-deficient by a N- or O-atom to which they are directly linked by a double bond (*i.e.*, CH=X). The hydroxylation of such C-atoms is thus a *nucleophilic oxidation* in contrast to the electrophilic oxidation mediated by monooxygenases. In this *Figure*, we exemplify the case of *aromatic azaheterocycles* (*i.e.*, containing the moiety CH=N) and of *aromatic or nonaromatic charged azaheterocycles* (*i.e.*, containing the moiety CH=N⁺<). The case of aldehydes (*i.e.*, containing the moiety CH=O) is presented in the next *Figure*. Formally, the reaction catalyzed by XO and AO is one of hydroxylation, and indeed aldehydes are oxidized to carboxylic acids. However, hydroxylated aromatic azaheterocycles are seldom isolated as such, since they have a marked tendency to *tautomerize* to the lactam form (see *Fig. 2.99*). The exclusive attack by molybdenum hydroxylases at *electron-deficient C-atoms* is well-illustrated by the regioselective hydroxylation of aromatic azahetero-cycles, and particularly diazaheterocycles, catalyzed by rabbit liver AO [4]. Thus, the electron densities of C-atoms in *phthalazine* (**2.296**), *cinnoline* (**2.297**), *quinazoline* (**2.298**) and *quinoxaline* (**2.299**) are shown here, with the positions of oxidation indicated in italics. And indeed, oxidation occurred at most electron-deficient C-atom(s), even when it was not adjacent to a N-atom (*i.e.*, cinnoline (**2.297**)). The fact that these four compounds are poor substrates of cytochrome P450 is one of the many

examples of the complementary roles of molybdenum hydroxylases and monooxygenases in the biotransformation of xenobiotics. And, indeed, examples have accumulated in recent years for the significant role of XOR and mainly AO as cytosolic alternatives to the membrane-bound CYPs in the oxidation of aromatic azaheterocycles.

Aromatic azaheterocycles rendered cationic by *N*-alkylation are far better substrates of AO than of XOR. Thus, the endogenous N^{1}-*methylnicotinamide* (**2.300**) is a neurotoxin detoxified by oxidation to form the (predominant) pyridin-4-one (**2.301**) and the pyridin-2-one (**2.302**) [264]. Various azaheterocyclic compounds of biological or medicinal interest are substrates of the molybdenum hydroxylases. One such compound is *allopurinol* (**2.303**), which is oxidized by both XO and AO to alloxanthine (**2.304**) [259]. The latter is a tight-binding, potent *in vitro* and *in vivo* inhibitor of XO but is devoid of inhibitory effects on AO [265]. Another interesting compound is *6-deoxyacyclovir* (**2.305**), a 2-aminopurine nucleoside analog that is efficiently converted by XOR to *acyclovir* (**2.306**) [261]. Acyclovir is an antiviral agent with high activity against the herpes group of viruses, and its formation from 6-deoxyacyclovir offers a rare and promising example of XO-mediated prodrug activation. However, a competitive yet minor reaction exists since 6-deoxyacyclovir is oxidized by AO at C(8) to yield the inactive 8-hydroxy metabolite **2.307**. The fact that 6-deoxyacyclovir is a nucleoside analog is not fortuitous, since some nucleosides, but not nucleotides, are known to be substrates of molybdenum hydroxylases.

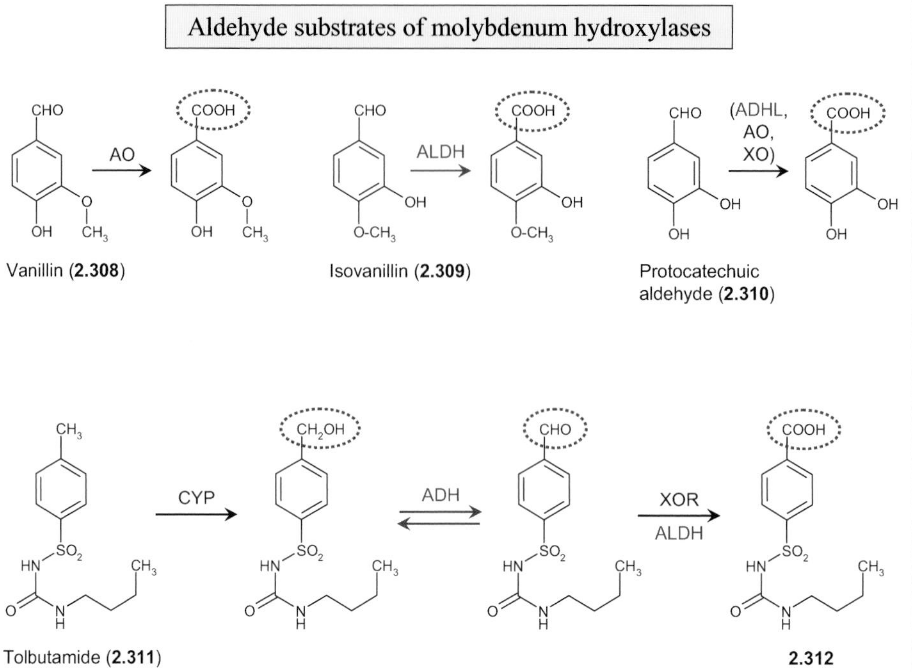

Fig. 2.102. Aldehydes also represent an important group of substrates of AO and XOR, which catalyze their oxidation to the corresponding carboxylic acids. The molybdenum hydroxylases are usually more active toward aromatic and chemically complex endogenous aldehydes than toward aliphatic aldehydes, although comparison is difficult [260][261]. However, their *in vivo* contribution appears usually less important than that of the cytosolic and mitochondrial *aldehyde dehydrogenases* (ALDH; EC 1.2.1.3 and EC 1.2.1.5) to be presented in *Sect. 2.6.4*. An illustration of the activity of the three enzymes is provided by the oxidation of three aromatic aldehydes, namely the natural compound *vanillin* (**2.308**), its regioisomer *isovanillin* (**2.309**), and their *O*-demethyl analog *protocatechuic aldehyde* (**2.310**) [266]. All three aldehydes were oxidized to the corresponding aromatic acid when incubated in the presence of guinea pig liver aldehyde oxidase, bovine milk xanthine oxidase, and guinea pig liver aldehyde dehydrogenase. Vanillin was rapidly oxidized by AO, isovanillin was predominantly metabolized by aldehyde dehydrogenase, whereas protocatechuic aldehyde was slowly oxidized possibly by the three enzymes. A good example of the complexity of the *in vivo* metabolic situation is offered by the hypoglycemic drug *tolbutamide* (**2.311**), whose CH$_3$ group is readily oxidized by cytochrome P450 to the primary alcohol; the latter is dehydrogenated reversibly to the aldehyde by *alcohol dehydrogenase* (ADH; EC 1.1.1.1 and EC 1.1.1.2; see *Sect. 2.6.4*). The fate of the aldehyde metabolite is of relevance here, since its oxidation to *carboxytolbutamide* (**2.312**) has been shown to be catalyzed by both XO and aldehyde dehydrogenase [4][257].

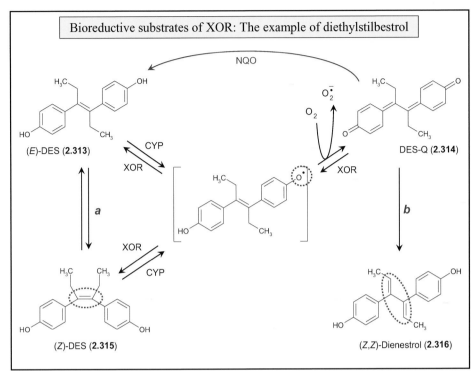

Fig. 2.103. The role of molybdo-flavoenzymes in drug metabolism may be more important than hitherto assumed, given the plethora of xenobiotics and their metabolites that contain potential target functions. This is all the more true considering their involvement in *reductive reactions* [4][152][257][260]. Thus, xanthine oxido-reductase is known to play a role in the reduction of *quinones*, an important issue which we will consider again in *Sect. 2.6.5*. As we shall then see, some enzymes reduce quinones by a single *transfer of two electrons*, *e.g.*, *quinone reductase* (DT-diaphorase; EC 1.6.99.2) and *carbonyl reductase* (1.1.1.84). Other reductases act by two consecutive single-electron transfers, *e.g.*, *CYPs, NADPH-CYP reductase* (see *Sect. 2.5.3* and *2.5.4*) and other *flavoproteins*. As far as xanthine oxidase is concerned, a single-electron mechanism is documented in the reduction of various quinones to their respective semiquinone [267]; this is best observed under aerobic conditions where molecular oxygen re-oxidizes semiquinones to their quinone. For example, the synthetic estrogen *diethylstilbestrol* (**2.313**; (*E*)-DES) undergoes CYP-catalyzed oxidation to its semi-quinone, followed by nonenzymatic oxidation by O_2 or a second CYP oxidation to the *diethylstilbestrol quinone* (**2.314**; DES-Q). Two mechanisms were observed when xanthine oxidase reduced the quinone and the semiquinone back to diethylstilbestrol, namely two enzyme-catalyzed *single-electron transfers* and *indirect reduction by XO-released superoxide* (not shown in the *Figure*) [268]. The picture is rendered more complex by the *spontaneous equilibrium* (*Reaction a*) between (*E*)-DES (**2.313**) and its (*Z*)-DES diastereoisomer (**2.315**), and by the *spontaneous rearrangement* (*Reaction b*) of DES-Q (**2.314**) to its (*Z,Z*)-dienestrol tautomer (**2.316**). As for the blue arrow, it will be considered in *Fig. 2.131*.

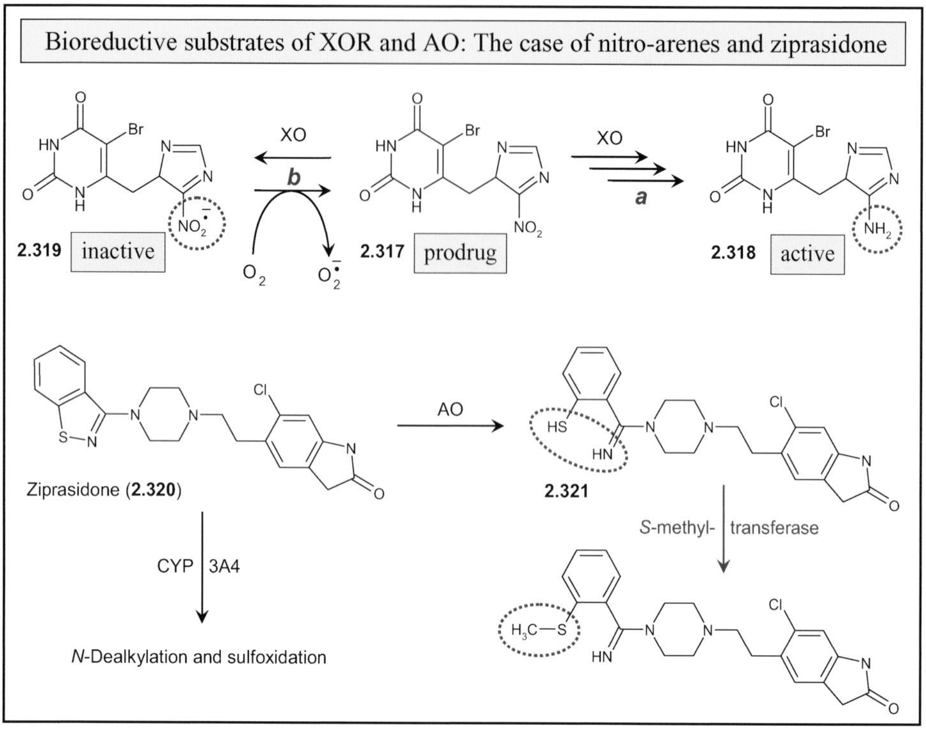

Fig. 2.104. Other chemical classes potentially reduced by XOR and/or AO include *N*-oxides, sulfoxides, nitrosamines, and azo compounds [257], and the cases illustrated. The reduction of nitro-arenes by XOR involves *carcinogenic xenobiotics* such as 2-nitrofluorene [269] and compounds of medicinal interest, particularly *bioreductive antitumor agents* [270]. This concept is aptly illustrated by a recent study on *aminoimidazolyl-methyluracil analogues* as potent inhibitors of thymidine phosphorylase. The nitro analogues were examined as bioreductive prodrugs, *e.g.*, *5-bromo-6-[(5-nitro-4H-imidazol-4-yl)methyl]uracil* (**2.317**), which proved good substrates of XO [271]. Their reduction under anaerobic condition proceeded readily to the *2'-amino metabolite* (*e.g.*, **2.318**), *i.e.*, the active agent. Of significance is the fact that, under aerobic conditions, reduction proceeded only to the *nitro radical anion*, **2.319**, due to back-oxidation to the prodrug by molecular oxygen. In pharmacological terms, this fact implies a *selective activation in hypoxic tumor cells*, but a futile redox cycling without activation in normoxic cells. While there seem to be less published examples of reduction by aldehyde oxidase, compelling evidence for the reaction does exist. Thus, reductive ring opening is known for isoxazole and isothiazole rings, a recent example being that of the antipsychotic agent *ziprasidone* (**2.320**) [272]. This compound is a substrate of CYP3A4, which catalyzes its *N*-dealkylation and *S*-oxygenation. Another metabolite is *dihydroziprasidone* (**2.321**) produced by the AO-catalyzed reductive opening of the isothiazole ring. This is, in fact, the major metabolic pathway in humans, since it accounts for about two thirds the metabolism of ziprasidone. However, dihydroziprasidone is not excreted as such but is rapidly *S*-methylated by an S-methyltransferase (see *Part 4*).

2.6.3. Peroxidases and Prostaglandin G/H Synthase

Enzyme ID Card: Various Peroxidases

EC Numbers	EC 1.11.1.7; EC 1.11.1.8
Enzyme subclass and sub-subclass	*EC 1.11*: Oxidoreductases acting on a peroxide as acceptor // *EC 1.11.1*: Peroxidases
Systematic name	Donor:hydrogen-peroxide oxidoreductase
Human genes and enzymes	*EPO* ⇒ EPO (eosinophil peroxidase) *LPO* ⇒ LPO (lactoperoxidase) *MPO* ⇒ MPO (myeloperoxidase) *TPO* ⇒ TPO (EC 1.11.1.8; thyroid peroxidase)
Bound cofactor	Protoporphyrin IX
Subcellular localization and tissue	EPO: Cytoplasmic granules; eosinophils LPO: Secreted protein; mammary and salivary glands MPO: Lysosomes; polymorphonuclear leukocytes TPO: Membrane-bound; thyroid gland
Xenobiotic substrates	Hydroquinones, amines

Fig. 2.105. Various peroxidases (EC 1.11.1) have a role as xenobiotic-metabolizing enzymes. Our attention is focused on mammalian and especially *human peroxidases* of toxicological significance, but a glance at the literature shows that much relevant information can also be gained from the use of nonmammalian peroxidases such as *horseradish peroxidase* (HRP) and *chloroperoxidase* [4]. The enzymes presented here are *eosinophil peroxidase* (EPO), *lactoperoxidase* (LPO), *myeloperoxidase* (MPO), and *thyroid peroxidase* (TPO; aka iodide peroxidase) [273–275]. Enzymes not considered in this overview include *catalase* (EC 1.11.1.6) and *glutathione peroxidase* (EC 1.11.1.9). *Prostaglandin G/H synthase* is a special case which we will discuss separately. A number of characteristics of EPO, LPO, MPO, and TPO are listed in the '*Enzyme ID Card*' shown here. Like cytochrome P450, they are *hemoproteins* which contain protoporphyrin IX as the prosthetic group. The similarity goes beyond mere structure, since we saw that CYPs can display peroxidase activity (*Figs. 2.80* and *2.81*). However, there are differences in the catalytic mechanism which will soon come to light. An important function of peroxidases is protection against pathogens. They exist in a large variety of tissues and cell types, of which *leukocytes* have received particular attention due to the potential toxicological relevance of some of the reactions of xenobiotic metabolism they catalyze [276]. We remind that leukocytes comprise monocytes, lymphocytes, polymorphonuclear leukocytes (eosinophils and neutrophils), and platelets.

Enzyme ID Card: Prostaglandin G/H Synthase	
EC Number	EC 1.14.99.1
Enzyme subclass and sub-subclass	*EC 1.14*: Oxidoreductases acting on paired donors, with incorporation or reduction of molecular oxygen // *EC 1.14.99*: Miscellaneous
Systematic name	(5Z,8Z,11Z,14Z)-Icosa-5,8,11,14-tetraenoate,hydrogen-donor:oxygen oxidoreductase
Human genes and enzymes	*PTGS (COX)* $\Rightarrow$ PGHS-1 (COX-1) and PGHS-2 (COX-2)
Bound cofactor	Protoporphyrin IX
Subcellular localization	Membrane of endoplasmic reticulum and nucleus
Organs (highest levels)	Many organs (COX-1 constitutive, COX-2 inducible by cytokines and mitogens)
Xenobiotic substrates	Aromatic amines, paracetamol, phenols, polycyclic aromatic hydrocarbons
Miscellaneous	Acts both as a dioxygenase (synthesis of PGG_2) and a peroxidase (synthesis of PGH_2).

Fig. 2.106. *Prostaglandin G/H synthase* is a hemoprotein like other peroxidases, but major differences exist as this '*Enzyme ID Card*' shows [277][278]. Thus, it is expressed in many tissues and organs of the body where the *constitutive enzyme* (PGHS-1) fulfils 'housekeeping' functions. The *inducible PGHS-2* is involved among others in inflammatory processes and its the main target of the nonsteroidal anti-inflammatory drugs (NSAIDs). Prostaglandin G/H synthase is associated with the endoplasmic reticulum and nuclear membrane, and is thus present in microsomal preparations. Its major difference to other peroxidases, and the one that justifies a separate presentation, is the fact that prostaglandin G/H synthase is more than a peroxidase. Indeed, PGHS is a single enzyme which *catalyzes two distinct and consecutive activities*. Its enzymatic role begins with a *cyclooxygenase activity* whereby arachidonic acid is metabolized to PGG_2 (see *Fig. 2.111*), which is both an endoperoxide and a hydroperoxide. A *peroxidase activity* follows which uses the hydroperoxide group of PGG_2 as an oxygen donor group, thereby transforming PGG_2 into PGH_2. A large number and variety of *xenobiotics* have been found to act as cofactors for the peroxidase reaction and are, therefore, called *reducing substrates* [279][280]. However, and as we shall see, some poorly reducible xenobiotics can be oxygenated during the cyclooxygenase step, again highlighting the special character of PGHS among peroxidases.

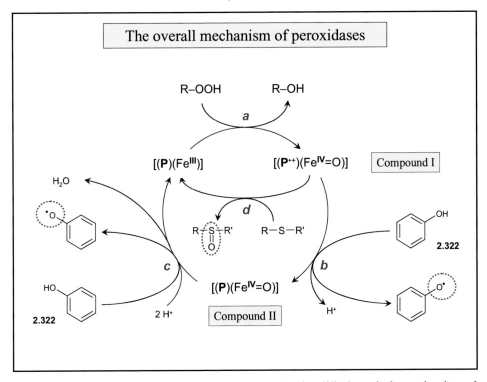

Fig. 2.107. This *Figure* brings us into the core of the simplified catalytic mechanism of peroxidases [4][273–276]. In partial analogy with what we saw for cytochrome P450 (*Fig. 2.23*), the resting enzyme is symbolized by $[(\mathbf{P})(Fe^{III})]$ where the bold '**P**' stands for protoporphyrin IX. Following its binding, the oxygen donor (a hydroperoxide R−OOH or H_2O_2) is cleaved heterolytically to yield R−OH or H_2O, plus an oxygenated form of the enzyme known as *compound I* (*Reaction a*). Compared to the resting enzyme, compound I has undergone a two-electron loss (oxidation) to which protoporphyrin IX contributes with one electron in the resonance form shown here. Similarities exist between this oxidation/oxygenation state of hemoprotein peroxidases and the $[FeO]^{3+}$ state of cytochrome P450. And indeed, compound I can react by direct oxygen transfer (*Reaction d*), *e.g.*, to a sulfide. But depending on the nature of both the substrate and the enzyme itself, the more frequently observed reaction appears to be the one-electron oxidation of a reducing substrate, most notably *phenol* (**2.322**) to form a *phenoxyl radical* (*Reaction b*). During this reaction, compound I undergoes a one-electron reduction to *compound II*. In turn, compound II can oxidize another molecule of the reducing substrate (*Reaction c*); alternatively, the radical produced by *Reaction b* can undergo a *second one-electron oxidation*. In either case, a H_2O molecule is liberated, and the enzyme is returned to its resting state. Xenobiotics oxidized by a single-electron transfer form *radical intermediates* which can react in a number of manners, several of which have toxicological significance (see next *Figure*).

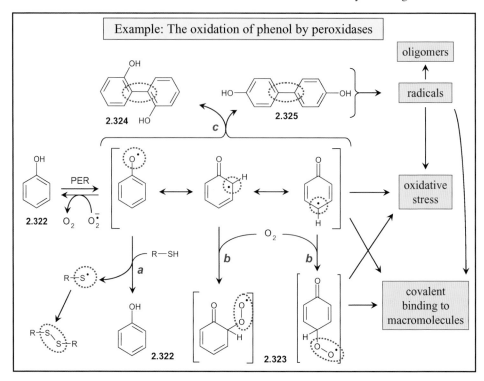

Fig. 2.108. Phenols are good reducing substrates of all peroxidases discussed here. As shown in the previous *Figure*, the reaction is a one-electron oxidation to phenoxyl radicals. These reactive metabolites can react in a number of ways as schematized here for *phenol* (**2.322**) itself [4] [281–283]. The resonance forms of the phenoxyl radical not only stabilize it, they also explain some of the reactive intermediates or stable compounds generated by this radical. First, the phenoxyl radical can be reduced back to phenol by thiols (*Reaction a*); this produces a *sulfanyl radical*, which can react with a second thiyl radical to form a *disulfide*. Second, resonance forms of some phenoxyl radicals can also add O_2 to form highly reactive *peroxyl radicals* (*Reaction b*) which can oxidize a second substrate. A common reactivity of phenoxyl and peroxyl radicals is initiation of *oxidative stress* and *covalent binding* to biomacromolecules such as nucleic acids. In addition, the phenoxyl radical can *dimerize* (*Reaction c*). Thus, human myeloperoxidase was found to oxidize phenol to two stable metabolites, namely *[1,1'-biphenyl]-2,2'-diol* (**2.324**) and *[1,1'-biphenyl]-4,4'-diol* (**2.325**). These metabolites, in turn, can be oxidized to radicals which induce oxidative stress and can lead to oligomers. Diol **2.325** also behaved like hydroquinone (see next *Figure*) and was oxidized to the corresponding quinone. A large variety of monophenols are known to be oxidized by peroxidases to the corresponding phenoxyl radical and other more or less reactive species.

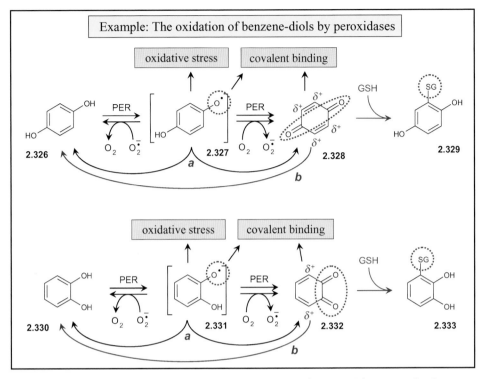

Fig. 2.109. Due to their easy oxidation, benzene-diols (diphenols) are good substrates of peroxidases such as EPO, LPO, and MPO. However, their peroxidase-catalyzed oxidation differs from that of monophenols, as illustrated here by *hydroquinone* (**2.326**) as a typical *para*-benzenediol and *catechol* (**2.330**) as a typical *ortho*-benzenediol [4][284–287]. As with monophenols (*Fig. 2.108*), the first step in the reaction is a one-electron oxidation to a *semiquinone* (**2.327** and **2.331**, resp.), a phenoxyl radical which can react in a number of ways. Like other phenoxyl radicals, it can be reduced back to the phenol by superoxide, but the *in vivo* significance of this reaction is dubious. More importantly and depending on the enzyme, a semiquinone can undergo a second one-electron oxidation to the corresponding quinone, here *1,4-benzoquinone* (**2.328**) and *1,2-benzoquinone* (**2.332**). This second oxidation can be catalyzed by the peroxidase or may be due to *autoxidation* (oxidation by O_2 to yield superoxide). The same quinones can also be formed by a different mechanism, namely *dismutation* of the semiquinone (*Reaction a*). This phenomenon involves a redox reaction between two molecules of semiquinone, one of which is reduced and the other oxidized. Like other phenoxyl radicals, semiquinones can lead to *oxidative stress*. More important from a toxicological viewpoint are the quinones, which can bind covalently to endogenous nucleophiles. Such *covalent binding* was seen in rat and human bone marrow cells under the influence of MPO [286][287], and it may explain the myelotoxicity of benzene. *Protective mechanisms* exist, namely conjugation with *glutathione* (GSH) to the conjugates **2.329** and **2.333** (*Parts 4* and *5*) and reduction by *quinone reductases* (*Reaction b; Fig. 2.131*).

Examples: The oxidation of arylamines and aminophenols by peroxidases

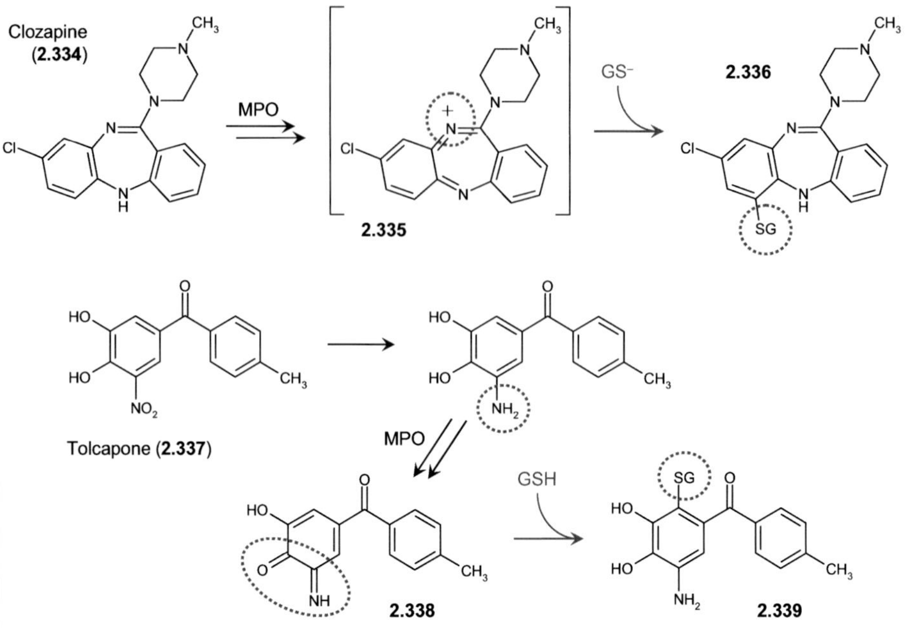

Fig. 2.110. Peroxidases also oxidize other compounds besides phenols, most notably amines as illustrated here and in *Fig. 2.112* [288]. The antipsychotic *clozapine* (**2.334**) is a case in point. This drug is known to induce *agranulocytosis* in some patients, a toxicity which has been attributed to chemically reactive metabolites. Incubations with human neutrophils and bone marrow cells in the presence of glutathione (GSH) led to the identification of two conjugates, the major of which is shown here, *i.e.*, **2.336** [289]. Covalent binding to tissue constituents was also seen. All evidence points to a *diimine cation* (**2.335**) as the reactive species produced by two consecutive single-electron oxidations catalyzed by MPO. The case of the catechol *O*-methyltransferase (COMT, see *Part 4*) inhibitor *tolcapone* (**2.337**) is somewhat different. This drug has been used as an adjuvant to L-DOPA in the treatment of *Parkinson*'s disease, but, in contrast to other drugs in this class, it can elicit hepatotoxicity in some patients. Recent evidence points to metabolic activation in eliciting this toxicity [290]. Nitro reduction to the amino metabolite is the first step in this sequence, followed by MPO oxidation to a reactive ortho-*quinoneimine intermediate* (**2.338**) which can be trapped as a glutathione conjugate (**2.339**). Interestingly, human liver microsomes and CYP2E1 and 1A2 also catalyze the formation of the quinoneimine intermediate. Note that the *N*-acetyl conjugate (*Part 4*) of the amine metabolite was also a substrate of the same toxification reaction.

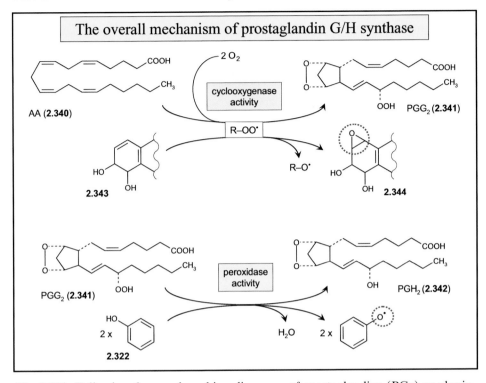

Fig. 2.111. Following the epoch-making discovery of prostaglandins (PGs) as physiologically active metabolites of arachidonic acid and other essential polyunsaturated fatty acids, it was reported more than three decades ago that various xenobiotics are oxidized during PG formation [291]. *Arachidonic acid* (**2.340**; AA) is converted by *prostaglandin G/H synthase* (PGHS; see *Fig. 2.106*) to *prostaglandin G$_2$* (**2.341**; PGG$_2$), which is both an endoperoxide and a hydroperoxide, and then to *prostaglandin H$_2$* (**2.342**; PGH$_2$). A number of enzymes are involved in the formation of subsequent active metabolites such as prostaglandins, prostacyclin, thromboxane, and leukotrienes, but this falls outside the scope of this work. The *cyclooxygenase* and *peroxidase* activities of PGHS catalyze the synthesis of PGG$_2$ and PGH$_2$, respectively (see also text to *Fig. 2.106*). Reducing substrates then restore the resting form of the enzyme, in complete analogy with the catalytic cycle of other peroxidases (*Fig. 2.107*) [277][278]. A large number and variety of xenobiotics have been found to be metabolized by PGHS [4][279][280]. Some are not good reducing cofactors and are oxygenated by a peroxyl radical intermediate of AA (R−OO˙) during the *cyclooxygenase step*. This is the case for some dihydrodiol metabolites of *polycyclic aromatic hydrocarbons* (**2.343**), which will yield an *epoxy diol* **2.344** (commonly known as diol-epoxide). However, the majority of xenobiotics oxidized by prostaglandin G/H synthase are *reducing substrates* which undergo *one or two single-electron transfers* (*Fig. 2.112*). In a few cases, direct oxygen transfer from the oxygenated heme can occur (see *Reaction d, Fig. 2.107*).

Examples: The oxidation of amidophenols, arylamines, and imides by PGHS

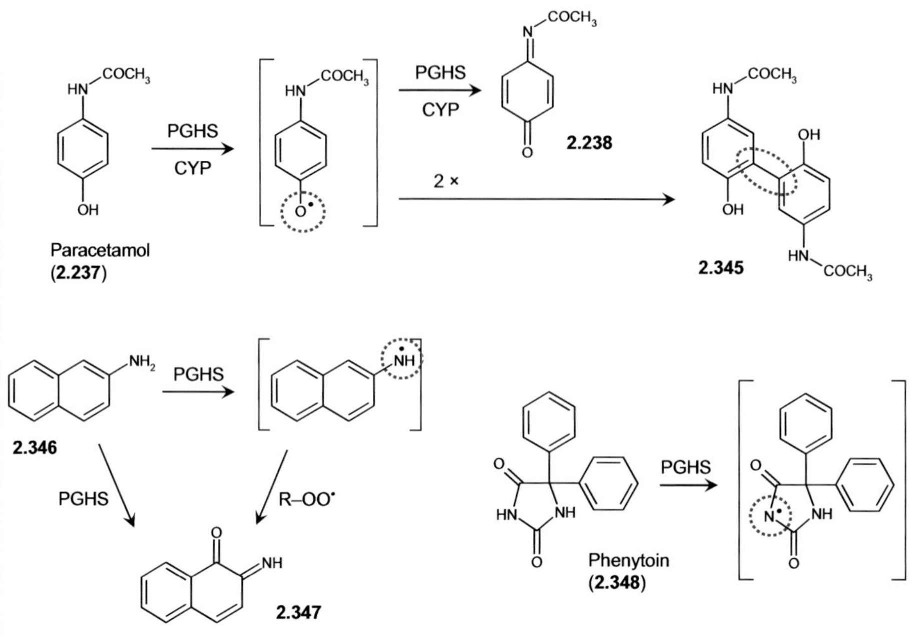

Fig. 2.112. An informative phenol in the present context is *paracetamol* (**2.237**), whose CYP-catalyzed oxidation to *N*-acetyl-*p*-benzoquinoneimine (**2.238**; NAPQI) *via* the semiquinoneimine has been discussed in *Fig. 2.78*. Prostaglandin G/H synthase also catalyzes this reaction. In addition to forming NAPQI, this enzyme also leads to oligomers derived from the semiquinoneimine, as exemplified by the *dimer* **2.345** [4]. The formation of these oligomers does not occur in the NADPH-supported oxidation mediated by cytochrome P450. This indicates that, during the NADPH-supported cycle, the semiquinoneimine is not able to leave the active site of CYP where it immediately undergoes the second oxidation step. In contrast, it is able to do so during the PGHS-catalyzed oxidation. The fact that paracetamol is both an inhibitor and a cosubstrate of PGHS is worth noting. At higher concentrations (>10 mM), the drug indeed inhibits both the formation of PGG_2 and its own oxidation. At lower concentrations (<0.2 mM), however, it stimulated PGHS activity [292]. Compared to phenols, arylamines appear as poorer reducing substrates of prostaglandin G/H synthase, but the possibility of a reaction of *oxygenation* is documented. Thus, *naphthalen-2-amine* (**2.346**) formed the ortho-*quinoneimine* (**2.347**) and a dimer thereof [293]. All available evidence indicated that ring oxygenation occurred both by direct oxygen transfer from the enzyme to the amine, and by the attack of a peroxyl radical on the naphthalen-2-amine radical. Although formation of such a N-centered radical was not directly observed with napthalen-2-amine, it appears to occur readily for cyclic imide such as the antiepileptic *phenytoin* (**2.348**) and the infamous *thalidomide* [294][295]. For both compounds, embryonic PGHS-catalyzed formation of an N-centered radical appears to be involved in their *teratogenicity* (*Part 5*).

2.6.4. Dehydrogenases/Reductases

Enzyme families and activities of importance in drug metabolism

Alcohol dehydrogenases (ADHs)

(mostly belonging to medium-chain dehydrogenases/reductases, MDRs)

Aldehyde dehydrogenases (ALDHs)

Aldo-keto reductases (AKRs) including

• Aldehyde reductases (ALRs)

• Dihydrodiol dehydrogenases (DDs)

• Many Hydroxysteroid dehydrogenases, *e.g.*, 3α- and 17β-HSD

Short-chain dehydrogenases/reductases (SDRs) including

• Carbonyl reductases (CRs)

• 11β-Hydroxysteroid dehydrogenases (11β-HSDs)

Quinone reductases (NQOs)

Fig. 2.113. In this *Section*, we examine a vast variety of enzymes which have two main properties in common [16][224][231][296–298]. First, and, in the perspective of xenobiotic metabolism, the reactions they catalyze center on *carbonyl-containing compounds*, be they aldehydes, ketones or even quinones (*Fig. 2.120*). And second, the enzymes of interest in this *Section* use *nicotinamide adenine dinucleotide* (NAD$^+$, NADH) and/or *nicotinamide adenine dinucleotide phosphate* (NADP$^+$, NADPH) or a similar cofactor to transfer a *hydride anion* (H$^-$) to or from the substrate. In other words and depending on the oxidation state of the cofactor, they can oxidize or reduce a suitable substrate by a reaction of *dehydrogenation* or *hydrogenation*, respectively. Note, however, that the term of hydrogenation is seldom used, in contrast to *reduction*. These enzymes are thus grouped under the generic name of *dehydrogenases/reductases* rather than dehydrogenases/hydrogenases. The relevant superfamilies or families of enzymes are shown here, with more detailed *Enzyme ID Cards* presented in *Figs. 2.114–2.119*.

Enzyme ID Card: Alcohol Dehydrogenases	
EC Number	EC 1.1.1.1
Enzyme subclass and sub-subclass	*EC 1.1*: Oxidoreductases acting on the CHOH group of donors// *EC 1.1.1*: With NAD$^+$ or NADP$^+$ as acceptor
Systematic name	Alcohol:NAD$^+$ oxidoreductase
Gene root, human enzymes	*ADH* ⇒ ADH1A, 1B and 1C (class I), ADH4 (class II), ADH5 (class III), ADH7 (class IV) and ADH6 (class V). The enzymes are homo- or heterodimers of chains of 3 types: alpha, beta, and gamma.
Active site	Zn^{2+}, His, Ser, ...
Cofactor	NAD$^+$
Subcellular localization	Cytoplasm
Organs (highest levels)	Liver, stomach, brain, *etc.*
Substrates	Primary and secondary alcohols (oxidation); aldehydes and ketones (reduction)
Miscellaneous	Higher *ADH1B*1* and *ADH1C*2* allele frequencies were observed in alcoholics than in controls. Gastric ADH activity markedly lower in women than in men.

Fig. 2.114–2.119. The *alcohol dehydrogenases* of importance in xenobiotic metabolism (*Fig. 2.114*) are the only enzymes in the superfamily of medium-chain dehydrogenases/ reductases (MDRs) to be considered here [299–303]. They are cytoplasmic, dimeric, Zn-containing enzymes. They are widely distributed in the body, but their highest activities are found in barriers of entry (*e.g.*, stomach and liver) and in organs which need special protection, *e.g.*, the brain. Alcohol dehydrogenases have a marked preference for the *dehydrogenation of primary alcohols*, but are also able to oxidize secondary alcohols and even some aldehydes, and to reduce aldehydes and ketones. The genetics of some ADHs shows a noteworthy relation with alcoholism (*Part 6*) [304][305]. The *aldehyde dehydrogenases* are an important family of enzymes summarized in *Fig. 2.115* [306–309]. They are widely distributed in the body and occur as cytosolic, microsomal, or mitochondrial enyzmes which are isolated as dimers or tetramers. They are involved in the dehydrogenation of a wide variety of aliphatic and aromatic aldehydes, which can be endogenous compounds as well as xenobiotics or xenobiotic metabolites. Important polymorphisms have been discovered for a number of these enzymes, which influence the risks of alcoholism and ethanol-induced cancers. Moving to the *aldo-keto reductases*, we see that they form a complex superfamily as suggested by the partial list of activities in *Figs. 2.116* and *2.117* [310–313]. A well-known problem with the dehydrogenases/reductases in general, and with the aldo-keto reductases in particular, is that the same protein can have more than one enzymatic activity and hence be listed under several EC numbers [11][16]. This is illustrated by the aldo-keto reductases of the AKR1C subfamily, which are simultaneously classified

as *hydroxysteroid dehydrogenases* (HSDs) and *dihydrodiol dehydrogenases* (DDs). In terms of xenobiotic metabolism and molecular toxicology, the *dihydrodiol dehydrogenases* are the most important enzymes in this superfamily. *Aldehyde reductases* are also of some importance, although fewer studies investigate their specific roles. As for the *aflatoxin B1 aldehyde reductases* (AKR7A), they had not yet received an EC number at the time of this manuscript [11][314]. *Fig. 2.118* summarizes some characteristics of the superfamily of *short-chain dehydrogenases/reductases* (SDRs). The genes of greatest interest in our context are those coding for the *carbonyl reductases*, although 11β-hydroxysteroid dehydrogenases (11β-HSDs) may also be involved in the oxidation or reduction of some xenobiotics [315–318]. Carbonyl reductases are generally monomeric, cytosolic, NADPH-dependent enzymes. They are widely distributed in nature and specifically in human tissues. They catalyze a number of physiological reactions in the metabolism of endogenous compounds such as steroids and prostaglandins. However, they are also able to reduce a range of exogenous carbonyl compounds, especially *aromatic ketones* and *quinones*. The final *Enzyme ID Card* is that of the *quinone reductases* (*Fig. 2.119*) [319–323]. Two enzymes are known in this family. The first (NQO1) resembles all other dehydrogenases/reductases presented here, which use NAD and/or NADP as acceptor. NQO2 is different, since its acceptor is *1-(β-D-ribosyl)-1,4-dihydronicotinamide*, abbreviated as NRH, hence the name NRH:quinone reductase 2. Quinone reductases are cytoplasmic enzymes, and, as their name indicates, they act on quinones. Endogenous substrates of NQO1 are vitamin K quinone and ubiquinone.

Enzyme ID Card: Aldehyde Dehydrogenases	
EC Number	EC 1.2.1.3; EC 1.2.1.5
Enzyme subclass and sub-subclass	*EC 1.2*: Oxidoreductases acting on the aldehyde or oxo group of donors // *EC 1.2.1*: With NAD$^+$ or NADP$^+$ as acceptor
Systematic names	*EC 1.2.1.3*: Aldehyde:NAD$^+$ oxidoreductase; *EC 1.2.1.5*: Aldehyde:NAD(P)$^+$ oxidoreductase
Gene root, human enzymes	*ALDH* (19 humans genes in 11 families and 13 subfamilies) $\Rightarrow$ *e.g.*, ALDH1A1, 1A2, 1A3, 1B1, 2, 3A1, 3A2, 3B1, 3B2, 8A1, and 9A1
Active site	Cys, Glu, Asp
Cofactor	NAD$^+$ (EC 1.2.1.3); NAD$^+$/NADP$^+$ (EC 1.2.1.5)
Subcellular localization	Cytoplasm, mitochondria (ALDH2), membrane of endoplasmic reticulum
Organs (highest levels)	Liver, stomach, pancreas, kidney, muscles, many other tissues
Substrates	Aldehydes (oxidation and reduction)
Miscellaneous	Allele *ALDH2*2* is associated with a high incidence of acute acetaldehyde intoxication following ethanol ingestion in Orientals and South American Indians, as compared to Caucasians.

Fig. 2.115.

Enzyme ID Card: Aldo-Keto Reductases	
EC Numbers	EC 1.1.1.2; EC 1.1.1.21; EC 1.1.1.50; EC 1.1.1.62; EC 1.1.1.149; EC 1.1.1.213; EC 1.3.1.20; *etc.*
Enzyme subclasses and sub-subclasses	*EC 1.1*: Oxidoreductases acting on the CHOH group of donors; *EC 1.3*: Oxidoreductases acting on the CHCH group of donors // *EC 1.1.1*; *EC 1.3.1*: With NAD$^+$ or NADP$^+$ as acceptor
Systematic names and synonyms	*EC 1.1.1.2*: Alcohol:NADP$^+$ oxidoreductase, aldehyde reductase (ALR1); *EC 1.1.1.21*: Alditol:NAD(P)$^+$ 1-oxidoreductase, aldehyde reductase, polyol dehydrogenase (ALR2); *EC 1.1.1.50 and 1.1.1.213*: 3α-Hydroxysteroid:NAD(P)$^+$ oxidoreductase, 3α-hydroxysteroid dehydrogenase (3α-HSD); *EC 1.1.1.62*: 17β-Hydroxysteroid dehydrogenase (17β-HSD); *EC 1.1.1.149*: 20α-Hydroxysteroid:NAD(P)$^+$ oxidoreductase, 20α-hydroxysteroid dehydrogenase (20α-HSD); *EC 1.3.1.20*: *trans*-1,2-Dihydrobenzene-1,2-diol:NADPH$^+$ oxidoreductase, dihydrodiol dehydrogenase (DD)

Fig. 2.116.

Enzyme ID Card: Aldo-Keto Reductases (cont.)	
Gene root, relevant human enzymes	*AKR* $\Rightarrow$ AKR1A1 (ALR1), AKR1B1 (ALR2), AKR1C1 (DD1, 20α-HSD), AKR1C2 (DD2, 3α-HSD type 3), AKR1C3 (DD3, 3α-HSD type 2, 17β-HSD type 5), AKR1C4 (DD4, 3α-HSD type 1), AKR7A2, 7A3 and 7A4 (aflatoxin B1 aldehyde reductases 2, 3 and 4)
Active site	Tyr, Asp, Lys, His, ...
Cofactor	NAD(P)$^+$
Subcellular localization	Cytoplasm
Organs (highest levels)	Liver, mammary gland, brain
Substrates	Alcohols (oxidation); Aldehydes and ketones (reduction)
Miscellaneous	Polymorphism in AKR1C4 with decreased activity

Fig. 2.117.

Enzyme ID Card: Short-Chain Dehydrogenases/Reductases	
EC Number	EC 1.1.1.184 : Carbonyl reductases (CRs) EC 1.1.1.146 : 11β-Hydroxysteroid dehydrogenases (11β-HSDs)
Enzyme subclass and sub-subclass	*EC 1.1*: Oxidoreductases acting on the CHOH group of donors // *EC 1.1.1*: With NAD⁺ or NADP⁺ as acceptor
Systematic names and synonyms	*EC 1.1.1.184*: Secondary-alcohol:NADP⁺ oxidoreductase, aldehyde reductase I, xenobiotic ketone reductase; *EC 1.1.1.146*: 11β-Hydroxysteroid:NADP⁺ 11-oxidoreductase
Human genes and enzymes	*CBR1* ⇒ CR1; *CBR3* ⇒ CR3; *DHRS4* ⇒ CR; *HSD11B1* ⇒ 11β-HSD1
Active site	Tyr, Lys, Ser
Cofactor	NADPH
Subcellular localization	CRs: cytoplasm 11β-HSD: membrane of endoplasmic reticulum
Organs (highest levels)	Ubiquitous
Substrates	Secondary alcohols, ketones, aldehydes, also quinones

Fig. 2.118.

Enzyme ID Card: Quinone Reductases	
EC Number	EC 1.6.5.2; EC 1.10.99.2
Enzyme subclass and sub-subclass	*EC 1.6*: Oxidoreductases acting on NADH or NADPH // *EC 1.6.5*: With a quinone or similar compound as acceptor // *EC 1.10*: Oxidoreductases acting on diphenols and related substances as donors // *EC 1.10.99*: With other acceptors than NAD(P)⁺, cytochrome or oxygen
Systematic names, synonyms	*EC 1.6.5.2*: NAD(P)H:quinone oxidoreductase; DT-diaphorase; *EC 1.10.99.2*: 1-(β-D-ribofuranosyl)-1,4-dihydro-nicotinamide:quinone oxidoreductase, quinone oxidoreductase 2
Gene root and human enzymes	*NQO* ⇒ NQO1 (EC 1.6.5.2) and NQO2 (EC 1.10.99.2). The enzymes are homodimers.
Prosthetic group	Flavin-adenine dinucleotide (FAD)
Cofactor	NQO1: NAD(P)H; NQO2: *N*-Ribosyl-dihydronicotinamide (NRH)
Subcellular localization	Cytoplasm
Organs (highest levels)	Liver, brain, gut
Substrates	Quinones, some nitro-arenes

Fig. 2.119.

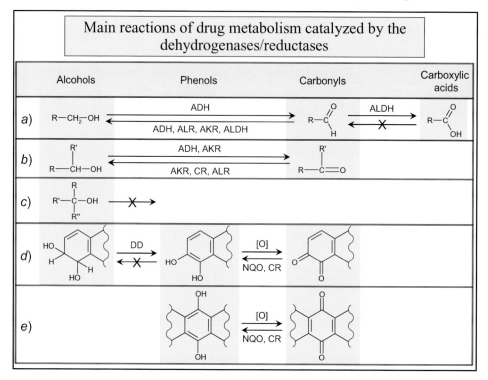

Fig. 2.120. This *Figure* summarizes the various reactions presented in this *Section*, and the major dehydrogenases/reductases which catalyze them. These reactions center on the OH or C=O group as found in alcohols, phenols, aldehydes, ketones, and quinones. The dehydrogenation of *primary alcohols* (*Reactions a*) is catalyzed by alcohol dehydrogenases (*ADHs*) and yields aldehydes. The dehydrogenation of *aldehydes* to carboxylic acids is catalyzed by aldehyde dehydrogenases (*ALDHs*), but ADHs have also been found to catalyze the reaction by acting on hydrated aldehydes [324]. An important difference is that the second step is *irreversible* (at least in vertebrates), whereas the dehydrogenation of alcohol is *reversible*, being catalyzed by *ADHs*, *ALDHs*, aldehyde reductase (*ALR*), and some aldo-keto reductases (*AKRs*). The *Reactions b* concern the oxidation of *secondary alcohols* to ketones, and the reduction of *ketones* to secondary alcohols. The enzymes involved in dehydrogenation are ADHs and AKRs, while ketone reductions are catalyzed mainly by AKRs, carbonyl reductases (*CRs*) and ALR. Note that the *further oxidation of ketones* necessitates cleavage of a C−C bond and is not catalyzed by the oxidoreductases considered here. The same is true for the oxidation of *tertiary alcohols* (*Case c*). *Reactions d* describe the fate of the *dihydrodiol metabolites* formed by the hydration of *arene oxides* (aryl epoxides; see *Figs. 2.48, 2.49,* and *2.51*) catalyzed by epoxide hydrolases (see *Part 3*). These dihydrodiols are substrates of the dihydrodiol dehydrogenases (*DDs*), which oxidize them irreversibly to *catechols* (*ortho*-benzenediols). However, such benzenediols autoxidize readily in the presence of molecular oxygen or superoxide, and are usually recovered as *ortho*-quinones, at least in *in vitro* investigations. The same autoxidation occurs for para-*hydroquinones* (*Reactions e*). Both types of quinones are substrates of the quinone reductases (*NQOs*).

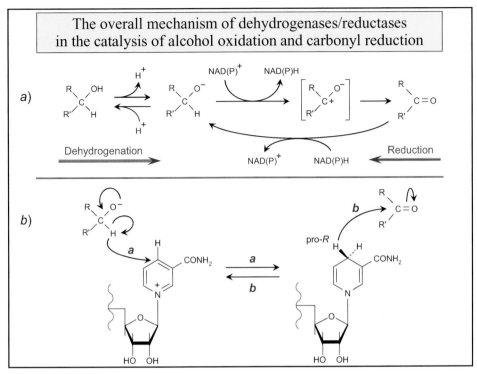

The overall mechanism of dehydrogenases/reductases in the catalysis of alcohol oxidation and carbonyl reduction

Fig. 2.121. This *Figure* summarizes in schematic form the *overall catalytic mechanism of dehydrogenases/reductases in the reversible oxidation of alcohols* (R' = H in primary alcohols or aldehydes; R' = alkyl or aryl in secondary alcohols or ketones) [4]. The dehydrogenation of aldehydes is not shown explicitly but is comparable to that of alcohols. The *upper part* of the *Figure* (*a*) shows that the *dehydrogenation reaction* is driven by $NAD(P)^+$, and involves deprotonation and hydride transfer from the substrate to the cofactor. In contrast, the *reduction reaction* is driven by $NAD(P)H$ and involves hydride transfer from the cofactor to the substrate. Note, however, that this depiction may be misinterpreted as implying sequential steps when the mechanism is in fact a concerted one (see *Fig. 2.122*). Furthermore, the representation is unrealistically simple and neglects the ordered mechanism leading to the obligatory formation of a ternary complex. The *lower part* of the *Figure* (*b*) shows the details of the proton transfer to $NAD(P)^+$ (dehydrogenation) and from $NAD(P)H$ (reduction). Following reduction of the pyridino ring, C(4) in the 1,4-dihydropyridine ring has become *prochiral*, and its two hydrogens are *enantiotopic*. Depending on the enzyme, the hydride transferred to and from the cofactor is either the *pro-R* (as shown here) or the *pro-S* one.

A closer look at the mechanism of dehydrogenation catalyzed by ADH

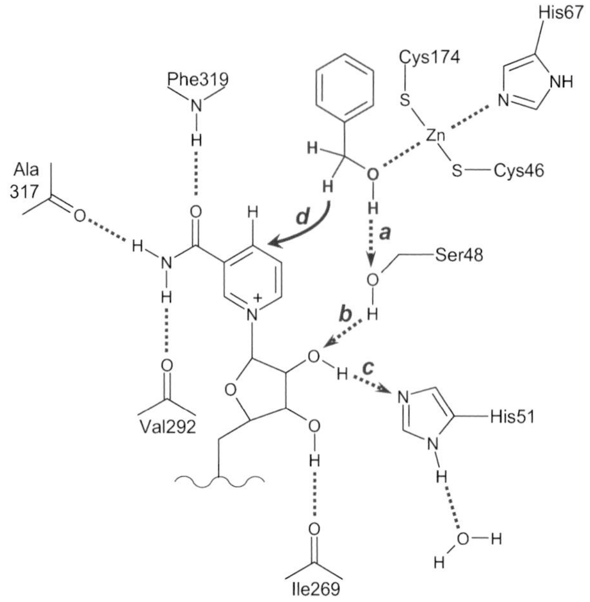

Fig. 2.122. The reaction of alcohol dehydrogenation is rendered possible by a complex mechanism of substrate activation which has been the object of considerable interest. This *Figure* summarizes some of the *intermolecular forces* which allow *formation of the ternary complex* (horse liver alcohol dehydrogenase plus cofactor plus substrate) and *initiation of the catalytic reaction* [4][325–327]. The *cofactor* is bound by a number of ionic and hydrophobic bonds, plus several *H-bonds*. Thus, its ribosyl-nicotinamide moiety forms H-bonds (red dotted lines) with the backbone (Ile269, Val292, Ala317, and Phe319) and two residue side chains (Ser48 and His51). The *substrate* (here benzyl alcohol, drawn in blue) is weakly bound by various hydrophobic bonds. An essential interaction is the *polarization of the alcohol group* by a *Van der Waals* bond (red dotted line) with the zinc cation (itself coordinated to Cys46, Cys174, and His67). The deprotonation of the alcohol group is rendered possible by this polarization, and it further involves a proton relay whose three first components are represented as *Steps a, b* and *c* (red dotted arrows). This proton relay chain allows the *concerted hydride transfer* to the cofactor (*Red arrow d*). Marked differences exist between alcohol dehydrogenases in their substrate specificities, rates of reactions, and sensitivity to inhibitors. This can now be understood as resulting from some amino acids in key positions being replaced by others playing a qualitatively comparable, but quantitatively different, role.

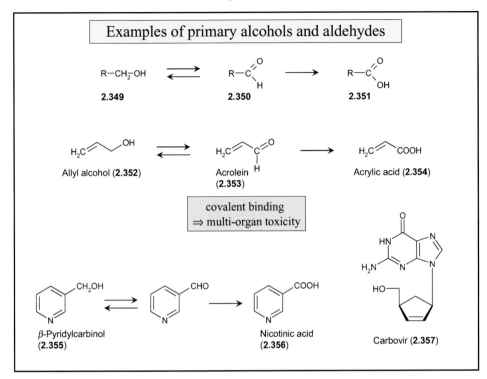

Fig. 2.123. Having presented the dehydrogenases/reductases and summarized their catalytic mechanism, we now turn to representative examples of substrates and reactions. As shown in *Fig. 2.121 (a)*, the *dehydrogenation of alcohols* liberates one proton and this, among other causes, explains why reaction rates and selectivities are markedly *pH-dependent*. *In vitro*, higher pH values will shift the equilibrium toward dehydrogenation of alcohol, whereas lower (neutral) values will favor carbonyl reduction, an informative example of chemospecificity. Mammalian alcohol dehydrogenases are characterized by a *broad substrate specificity* which includes many primary and secondary aliphatic, and aromatic alcohols (*i.e.*, **2.349**); however, bulky secondary alcohols are poor substrates [4]. Similarly, *aldehyde dehydrogenases* have a broad substrate specificity toward aliphatic and aromatic aldehydes (**2.350**) to form carboxylic acids (**2.351**) [328]. An important alcohol is obviously *ethanol* (**2.349**; R = CH$_3$). Its first metabolite (*acetaldehyde* (**2.350**); R = CH$_3$) is relatively toxic, but its concentrations are kept low by fast back-reduction and fast dehydrogenation. In humans, this oxidation is catalyzed by mitochondrial ALDHs [329]. Examples of marked toxification are provided by 2,3-unsaturated alcohols such as *allyl alcohol* (**2.352**) and its C$_4$ counterpart crotyl alcohol [330]. Indeed, the oxidation of allyl alcohol produces *acrolein* (**2.353**), a highly reactive (electrophilic) *α,β*-unsaturated aldehyde (see also *Part 4*) whose further oxidation to acrylic acid (**2.354**) by ALDHs can offer partial protection. *α,β-Unsaturated aldehydes* are environmental pollutants and are also produced endogenously by lipid peroxidation; some of them are known to inhibit their ALDH-catalyzed detoxification [331]. *Primary alcohols of medicinal relevance* include *β-pyridylcarbinol* (**2.355**), a prodrug of *nicotinic acid* (**2.356**), and synthetic antiviral nucleoside analogs such as *carbovir* (**2.357**) [4][332].

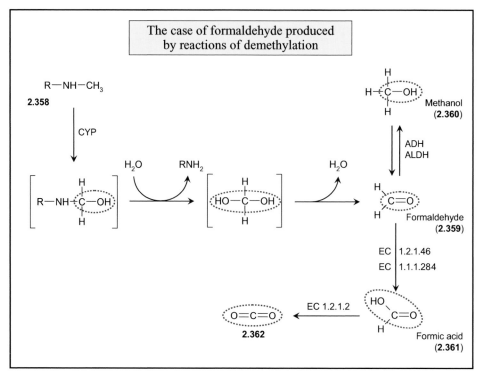

Fig. 2.124. This *Figure* summarizes an important function of alcohol and aldehyde dehydrogenases, namely the further redox metabolism of aldehydes or ketones produced by reactions of *dealkylations* or *deaminations* (see *Sect. 2.2.3* and *2.2.4*, and *Figs. 2.33–2.38*). This is illustrated here with the special case of reactions of demethylation. Using a *generic* N-*methylamine* (**2.358**) as example, we follow its metabolic route from its beginning, namely its CYP-catalyzed monooxygenation to an intermediate carbinolamine. The latter hydrolyzes spontaneously to *formaldehyde* (**2.359**), presumably *via* the intermediate hydrate. Formaldehyde is the branching point in this route. As expected, it is reduced reversibly to *methanol* (**2.360**) by alcohol dehydrogenase and aldehyde dehydrogenase, and is dehydrogenated irreversibly to *formic acid* (**2.361**). When the alkyl moiety is detached as a ketone, reversible reduction to the secondary alcohol will be its only metabolic reaction (see *Fig. 2.120*). When the alkyl moiety is oxidized to an aldehyde, various ALDHs can catalyze its dehydrogenation [306]. The *case of formaldehyde* deserves special attention for two reasons. First, its oxidation to formic acid is mediated by specific enzymes, namely *formaldehyde dehydrogenase* (EC 1.2.1.46; formaldehyde:NAD$^+$ oxidoreductase) and S-*(hydroxymethyl)glutathione dehydrogenase* (EC 1.1.1.284; S-(hydroxymethyl)glutathione:NAD$^+$ oxidoreductase). The second reason is that formic acid, in contrast to all other carboxylic acids, still contains a removable H-atom attached to its carboxylic C-atom. *Formate dehydrogenase* (EC 1.2.1.2; formate:NAD$^+$ oxidoreductase) is the enzyme which dehydrogenates formic acid to *carbon dioxide* (**2.362**). In animal studies, the pulmonary excretion of $^{14}CO_2$ is sometimes taken as a marker of *in vivo* demethylation of a suitably labeled drug.

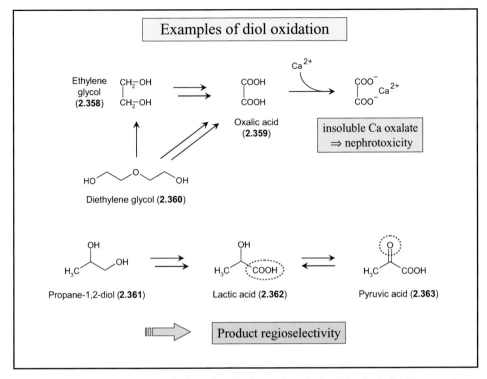

Fig. 2.125. The oxidation of *diols* and *polyols* can be of physiological significance (*e.g.*, glycerol, sugar alcohols), but in other cases it can have marked toxic consequences. In this respect, a comparison between ethylene glycol and propane-1,2-diol (**2.361**) is revealing. Both compounds are substrates of dehydrogenases, and, from a metabolic view point, their fate is comparable. *Ethylene glycol* (**2.358**) is metabolized in part to *oxalic acid* (**2.359**) by multiple oxidations (not shown here) which involve glycolaldehyde, glyoxal, glycolic acid, and glyoxylic acid [333][334]. Oxalic acid is the toxic metabolite of ethylene glycol, its toxicity being due to the low solubility of calcium oxalate which crystallizes in the kidneys. *Diethylene glycol* (**2.360**; human $LD_{30} \approx 1$ mg/ kg) is also toxic given that part of a dose is cleaved by CYPs to ethylene glycol and glycolaldehyde. Human deaths following systemic exposure to diethylene glycol were due to its untested use as a solvent for intravenous sulfanilamide (in the 1930s). Accidents have also been reported following its illegal use in low quality wines. In contrast to ethylene glycol, *propane-1,2-diol* (**2.361**) is oxidized to nontoxic metabolites which are well-known physiological compounds [4]. Dehydrogenation occurs preferentially at the primary alcohol group to yield *lactic acid* (**2.362**), followed by reversible oxidation of the secondary alcohol group to *pyruvic acid* (**2.363**). In other words, propane-1,2-diol also exemplifies a *product regioselectivity* in the oxidation of its primary *vs.* secondary alcohol groups. However, an overall comparison between the reactivity of primary and secondary alcohols is difficult, and may be misleading due to the many factors involved (*e.g.*, competitive reactions, differential affinities for numerous dehydrogenases, and reactivity in the enzyme–substrate complex).

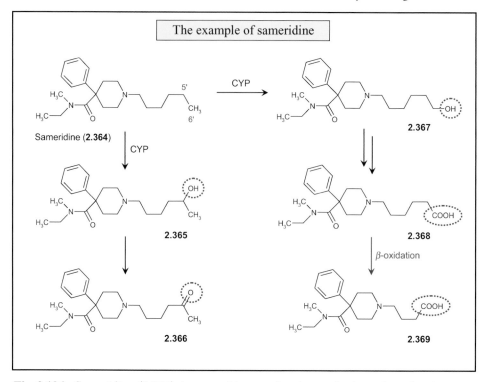

Fig. 2.126. *Sameridine* (**2.364**) is an amide-type local anesthetic and analgesic agent whose metabolism offers relevant examples. When incubated with rat hepatocytes, the compound underwent hydroxylations in its *n*-hexyl side chain seemingly catalyzed by cytochrome P450 4A [335]. The primary metabolites characterized were the secondary alcohol *5′-hydroxysameridine* (**2.365**; produced by ($\omega - 1$)-hydroxylation) and the primary alcohol *6′-hydroxysameridine* (**2.367**) (produced by ω-hydroxylation). The former was dehydrogenated to *5′-ketosameridine* (**2.366**) as a major metabolite. The reversibility of this dehydrogenation was not investigated. As for 6′-hydroxysameridine (**2.367**), it was oxidized to the *6′-oic acid metabolite* (**2.368**) by cytosolic dehydrogenases. This carboxylic acid was then a substrate of peroxisomal β-oxidation to the *4′-oic acid metabolite* **2.369**, a metabolic route centered on Coenzyme A and to be discussed in *Part 4* of this work.

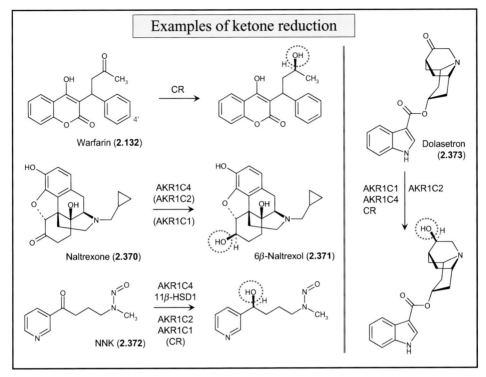

Fig. 2.127. A number of drugs and other xenobiotics contain a ketone group, and numerous data have accumulated on their bioreduction by *carbonyl reductases* and *aldo-keto reductases*, including aldehyde reductases [296][315]. Note that quinones are somewhat special ketones which we will consider later. Four xenobiotics are shown here as examples of keto reduction, namely three drugs and a toxin. The CYP-catalyzed oxidation of *warfarin* (**2.132**) was presented in *Fig. 2.57*. Here, we look at its reduction as mediated by cytoplasmic *carbonyl reductases* [336]. This reaction has the potential to be *product-stereoselective*, since it transforms the prochiral keto group into a stereogenic alcohol center. Indeed, reduction occurs with a marked preference for the (*S*)-alcohol. Furthermore, warfarin itself is chiral and may thus exhibit *substrate enantioselectivity* in its metabolism. This is verified in that (*R*)-warfarin is reduced preferentially. The same is true for the 4′-nitro analog, *i.e.*, the drug *acenocoumarol* (*Fig. 2.88*). The opioid antagonist *naltrexone* (**2.370**) is also reduced stereoselectively in humans to *6β-naltrexol* (**2.371**), a long lasting and active metabolite [337][338]. This is again a product-stereoselective reaction, and it occurs also with a number of other opioids [339]. *4-(Methylnitrosamino)-1-(pyridin-3-yl)butan-1-one* (**2.372**; NNK) is a tobacco-specific carcinogen which is detoxified by product enantioselective keto reduction, followed by glucuronyl conjugation (*Part 4*) [340]. Our last example is again a drug, namely the antiemetic 5-HT₃ receptor antagonist *dolasetron* (**2.373**), which was reduced rapidly, extensively, and stereoselectively to its (*R*)-alcohol metabolite in humans, or when incubated with various of human carbonyl reductases [341]. The metabolite proved to be *ca.* 40 times more active than dolasetron, which can, therefore, be considered as a prodrug.

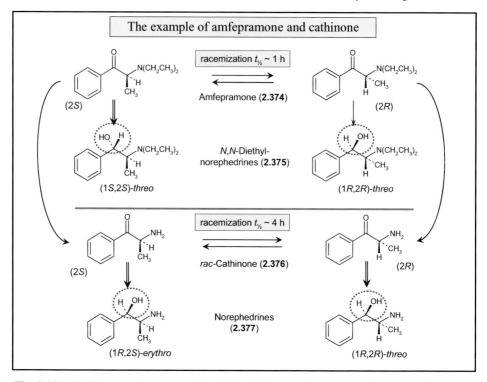

Fig. 2.128. To illustrate in greater detail the difference between substrate and product stereoselectivity, we take a look at the human metabolism of *amfepramone* (**2.374**; also known as *diethylproprion*) [342]. This anorectic drug undergoes reactions of *N*-deethylation to the secondary amine and then to *aminopropiophenone* (**2.376**), its primary amine. The latter is of special interest, since (*S*)-aminopropiophenone is in fact *cathinone*, an alkaloid found in khat leaves whose abusive consumption causes excitement and euphoria. The configurational stability of amfepramone and its two ketone metabolites is low. Thus, the half-lives of racemization of amfepramone and aminopropiophenone under physiological conditions of pH and temperature are *ca.* 1 and 4 hours, respectively. In addition to *N*-dealkylation, amfepramone and its two ketone metabolites undergo fast reduction in the human body to the configurationally stable ephedrine derivatives. As shown, the reduction of (*2S*)-amfepramone is markedly faster than that of (*2R*)-amfepramone (marked substrate enantioselectivity), and each enantiomer yields preferentially one of the two diastereomeric N,N-*diethylnorephedrines* (marked product stereoselectivity). The same is true for *N*-(ethylamino)propiophenone (not shown). For aminopropiophenone (**2.376**), the stereochemical selectivity of reduction is quite different from that of the secondary and tertiary amino ketones. Here, substrate enantioselectivity is low, the two enantiomers being reduced at comparable rates. Product stereoselectivity, on the other hand, is large for both enantiomers. Here, however, the newly formed stereogenic center has the (*1R*)-configuration independently of the (*2S*)-configuration of the substrate.

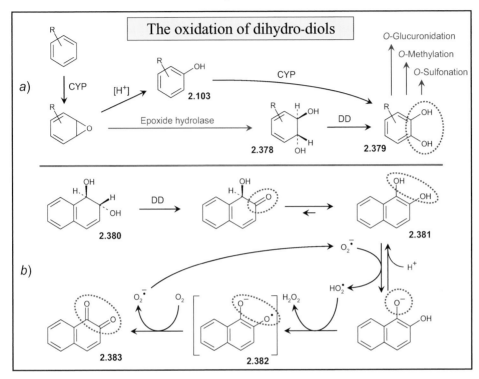

Fig. 2.129. Several aldo-keto reductases show *dihydrodiol dehydrogenase* activity, most notably AKRs of the AKR1C subfamily (*Figs. 2.116* and *2.117*). This is not restrictive, however, since the same is true for AKR1A1 and AKR1B1 [343–346]. In a medicinal perspective, *trans*-dihydrodiols are of interest as metabolites of aromatic rings and most notably of phenyl rings. As discussed in *Sect. 2.3.3* (*Figs. 2.49* and *2.51*) and repeated here (*a*), cytochromes P450 oxidize such rings to *epoxides* which will rearrange to phenols (**2.103**) but can also be hydrated by *epoxide hydrolase* (*Part 3*) to yield trans-*dihydrodiols* (**2.378**). These are then dehydrogenated to *catechols* (**2.379**). However, experimental results may be ambiguous, since catechols can also be formed from phenols by CYPs. Further oxidation of catechols to *ortho*-quinones can occur *in vivo*, but it is decreased by competitive reactions of conjugation and can only be observed indirectly (*Part 4*). A more detailed *metabolic sequence for the oxidative metabolism of dihydrodiols* is shown under *b* taking as example *1,2-dihydronaphtha-lene-1,2-diol* (**2.380**), a well-known metabolite of naphthalene [347][348]. Dihydrodiol dehydrogenases oxidize one of the two secondary alcohol groups to form a keto-alcohol which isomerizes to *naphthalene-1,2-diol* (**2.381**). This diphenol *autoxidizes* relatively easily, a likely mechanism involving superoxide as the initiator of the reaction [344–346]. The intermediates en route to *naphthalene-1,2-quinone* (**2.383**) are a catechol monoanion and an *ortho*-semiquinone radical anion **2.382**. Note that the positions of dehydrogenation, deprotonation, and H$^{\bullet}$ abstraction shown here are arbitrary.

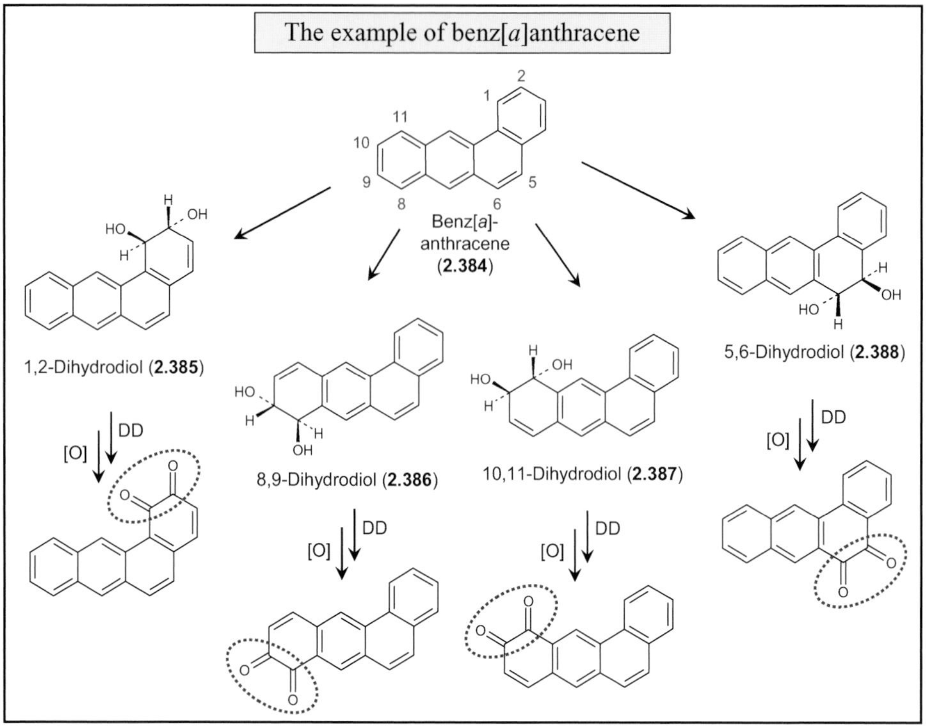

Fig. 2.130. Polycyclic aromatic hydrocarbons (PAHs) and heterocyclic aromatic hydrocarbons are xenobiotics of environmental and toxicological great concern due to their potential for mutagenicity and carcinogenicity. These compounds undergo complex CYP-catalyzed routes of toxification which we will examine in *Part 5*. One such sequence involves the formation of trans-*dihydrodiols* and their *further activation by oxidation*. Many PAHs have been investigated in this respect [343–346][349], with particular attention being paid to the toxicity of the reactive oxygen species and *ortho*-quinones formed in the reaction [350–352]. In an interesting study, four regioisomeric trans-*dihydrodiol* metabolites of *benz[a]anthracene* (**2.384**) were incubated with recombinant DD (AKR1C22) [353]. The endpoints monitored were covalent binding to DNA and DNA damage. The *1,2-dihydro-1,2-diol* **2.385** proved a better substrate toward dihydrodiol dehydrogenase than the other isomers **2.386–2.388**. Furthermore, the AKR1C22-activated *1,2-dihydro-1,2-diol* led to high DNA covalent binding and to the most extensive DNA damage as a result of autoxidation to the corresponding *ortho*-quinone.

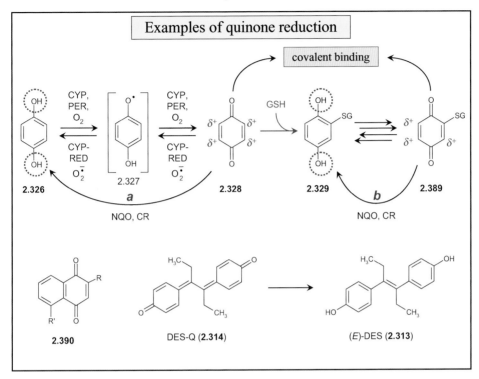

Fig. 2.131. A large number of quinones have been reported to be substrates of carbonyl reductases and/or quinone reductases, thereby being reduced directly to the corresponding diphenol in a single two-electron step [296][315][319–323][354][355]. To put things in a perspective, we summarize in the upper part of the figure the redox metabolism of *hydroquinone* (**2.326**) as discussed previously. Two single-electron steps mediated by CYPs, peroxidases, or autoxidation produce the toxic *benzoquinone* (**2.328**) *via* the intermediate *benzo-semiquinone* (**2.327**). This is an electrophilic, toxic metabolite which can bind covalently to bio(macro)molecules and can be detoxified by *glutathione* (GSH) to form the conjugate **2.329** (see *Part 4*). However, the conjugate retains a hydroquinone motif and can readily be oxidized in turn to a *quinone thioether* **2.389** which is just as toxic as other quinones [356]. One of the major protection mechanisms againt such reactive quinones is reduction by carbonyl and quinone reductases (*Reactions a* and *b*) [357]. The lower part of the *Figure* present a few quinones whose reduction has been given particular attention. Compounds such as *menadione* (**2.390**; vitamin K_3; R = CH$_3$, R' = H) and the natural product *juglone* (**2.390**; R = H, R' = OH) offer examples of the easy reduction and detoxification of *1,4-naphthoquinones* and other polycyclic aromatic hydrocarbon quinones [355][358][359]. As for *diethylstilbestrol* (**2.313**), we presented in *Fig. 2.103* its oxidation to diethylstilbestrol quinone **2.314**, followed by tautomerization to dienestrol (**2.316**). A two-electron retroreduction of *diethylstilbestrol quinone* (**2.314**) to diethylstilbestrol (**2.313**) by quinone reductase does occur in competition with one-electron reductions catalyzed by NADPH-cytochrome P450 reductase, NADH-cytochrome b_5 reductase, or xanthine oxidase [4].

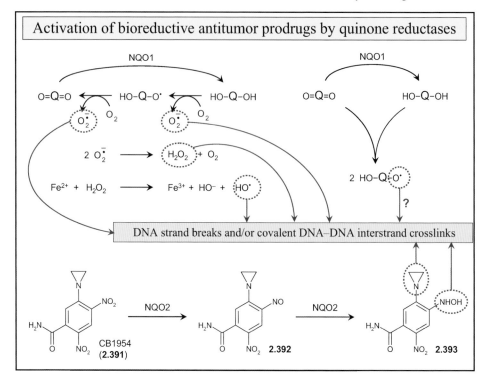

Fig. 2.132. To close *Part 2*, we briefly examine the case of *cytotoxic agents* which are of great interest as *bioreductive antitumor prodrugs* when activated by quinone reductase [270][360]. The *upper part* of the *Figure* shows the simplified mechanism by which cytotoxic quinones are believed to act, as based on extensive studies with the *former candidate EO9* (see the next *Figure*) [361]. The single-step and fast NQO1-catalyzed reduction of the quinone (symbolized here by $O=Q=O$) yields an easily oxidable hydroquinone ($HO-Q-OH$). In the presence of O_2, the hydroquinone will cycle back to the quinone with production of two molecules of superoxide. Other reactive forms of oxygen are formed as secondary products, namely H_2O_2 and mainly the highly reactive hydroxyl radical ($HO^•$) [362]. These metabolites of oxygen cause DNA damage and mostly strand breaks. Under low oxygen concentrations (*i.e.*, in hypoxic cells), another mechanism can operate, namely comproportionation of the quinone with the hydroquinone to form two molecules of the semiquinone radical ($HO-Q-O^•$). Whether this semiquinone radical is directly toxic to DNA, or whether the high activity of such agents in hypoxic cells is still due to reactive oxygen species remains to be fully ascertained. The *lower part* of the *Figure* shows the activation of *CB1954* (**2.391**), an entirely different class of bioreductive prodrugs bearing an *aromatic NO_2 group*. Activation by NQO2 involves two two-electron steps to the nitroso and then to the *hydroxylamino metabolite* **2.392** and **2.393**, respectively. The latter acts as a bifunctional alkylating agent capable of forming DNA–DNA interstrand cross-links *via* the hydroxylamino and aziridin-1-yl groups [363].

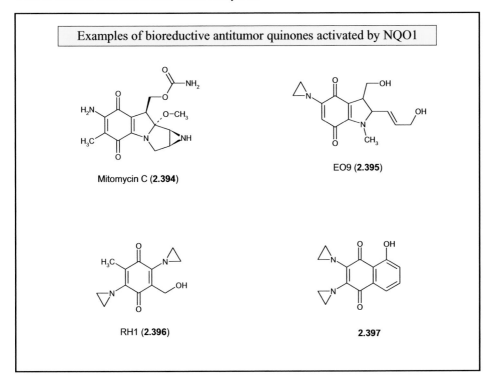

Examples of bioreductive antitumor quinones activated by NQO1

Mitomycin C (**2.394**)

EO9 (**2.395**)

RH1 (**2.396**)

2.397

Fig. 2.133. This *Figure* presents a few examples of *bioreductive antitumor quinones* activated by NQO1-catalyzed reduction. The prototype compound is *mitomycin C* (**2.394**), although its mechanism of action may not be identical to that of other agents in this class [364]. Much attention is being paid to the design and development of prodrugs given their potential to undergo *selective activation in tumor cells* expressing high levels of quinone reductases [365]. The former drug candidate *EO9* (**2.395**) mentioned in the previous *Figure* showed great promise but failed in phase-II clinical trials due to rapid plasma clearance, poor penetration into tumor tissues, and reversible kidney toxicity [361][366]. A chemically simpler yet quite interesting compound is *RH1* (**2.396**), an excellent substrate of quinone reductase with pharmacokinetic properties different from that of EO9 [366]. And finally, we find again *1,4-naphthoquinones* (see also *Fig. 2.131*), a large series of which was extensively investigated for its pharmacological and biological properties [367]. The *diaziridin-1-yl compound* **2.397** emerged as particularly promising, showing good substrate selectivity for NQO1, and cytotoxic selectivity for tumor cells with high expression levels of NQO1, both under normoxic and hypoxic conditions. One important point to note before closing is that these quinone prodrugs all have the *four* ortho-*positions blocked* by substituents, an exception being EO9. In other words, direct toxicity due to adduct formation is excluded for such quinones, in contrast to the high reactivity of un- or partly substituted quinones discussed in *Fig. 2.131*.

REFERENCES

[1] a) B. Testa, S. D. Krämer, 'The Biochemistry of Drug Metabolism – An Introduction. Part 2: Redox Reactions and Their Enzymes', *Chem. Biodiv.* **2007**, *4*, 257–405; b) B. Testa, S. D. Krämer, 'The Biochemistry of Drug Metabolism – An Introduction. Part 1: Principles and Overview', *Chem. Biodiv.* **2006**, *3*, 1053–1101.

[2] S. Rendic, F. J. Di Carlo, 'Human cytochrome P450 enzymes: A status report summarizing their reactions, substrates, inducers, and inhibitors', *Drug Metab. Rev.* **1997**, *29*, 413–580; S. Rendic, 'Summary of information on human CYP enzymes: Human P450 metabolism data', *Drug Metab. Rev.* **2002**, *34*, 83–448.

[3] O. Pelkonen, 'Human CYPs: in vivo and clinical aspects', *Drug Metab. Rev.* **2002**, *34*, 37–46.

[4] B. Testa, 'The Metabolism of Drugs and Other Xenobiotics – Biochemistry of Redox Reactions', Academic Press, London, 1995.

[5] 'Cytochrome P450. Structure, Mechanism, and Biochemistry', 2nd edn., Ed. P. R. Ortiz de Montellano, Plenum Press, New York, 1996.

[6] 'Handbook of Drug Metabolism', Ed. T. F. Woolf, Dekker, New York, 1999.

[7] 'Enzyme Systems that Metabolise Drugs and Other Xenobiotics', Ed. C. Ioannides, Wiley, Chichester, 2002.

[8] 'Drug–Drug Interactions', Ed. A. D. Rodrigues, Dekker, New York, 2002.

[9] B. Testa, W. Soine, 'Principles of drug metabolism', in 'Burger's Medicinal Chemistry and Drug Discovery', 6th edn., Ed. D. J. Abraham, Wiley-Interscience, Hoboken, 2003, Vol. 2, p. 431–498.

[10] 'Cytochrome P450 Protocols', Eds. I. R. Phillips, E. A. Shephard, Humana Press, Totowa, 2006; J. P. Uetrecht, W. F. Trager, 'Drug Metabolism – Chemical and Enzymatic Aspects', Informa, New York, 2007.

[11] Nomenclature Committee of the International Union of Biochemistry and Molecular Biology (IUBMB), 'Enzyme Nomenclature', www.chem.qmul.ac.uk/iubmb/enzyme.

[12] F. J. Gonzalez, 'Molecular genetics of the P-450 superfamily', *Pharmacol. Ther.* **1990**, *45*, 1–38.

[13] D. R. Nelson, D. C. Zeldin, S. M. G. Hoffman, L. J. Maltais, H. M. Wain, D. W. Nebert, 'Comparison of cytochrome P450 (*CYP*) genes from the mouse and human genomes, including nomenclature recommendations for genes, pseudogenes and alternative splice variants', *Pharmacogenetics* **2004**, *14*, 1–18.

[14] a) D. R. Nelson, 'Cytochrome P450 homepage', http://drnelson.utmem.edu/CytochromeP450.html; b) http://drnelson.utmem.edu/Nomenclature.html;   c) http://drnelson.utmem.edu/hum.html; d) http://drnelson.utmem.edu/P450lect.html; e) http://drnelson.utmem.edu/P450trees.html.

[15] 'Directory of P450-containing Systems', http://www.icgeb.org/~p450srv/.

[16] 'Brenda: The Comprehensive Enzyme Information System', www.brenda.uni-koeln.de; 'ExPASy Proteomics Server', www.expasy.org.

[17] T. A. Holton, F. Brugliera, D. R. Lester, Y. Tanaka, C. D. Hyland, J. G. T. Menting, C. Y. Lu, E. Fracy, T. W. Stevenson, E. C. Cornish, 'Cloning and expression of cytochrome P450 genes controlling flower colour', *Nature* **1993**, *366*, 276–279.

[18] W. Y. Precious, J. Barrett, 'Xenobiotic metabolism in helminths', *Parasitol. Today* **1989**, *5*, 156–160.

[19] X. Ding, L. S. Kaminsky, 'Human extrahepatic cytochromes P450: Function in xenobiotic metabolism and tissue-selective chemical toxicity in the respiratory and gastrointestinal tracts', *Annu. Rev. Pharmacol. Toxicol.* **2003**, *43*, 149–173.

[20] A. E. Cribb, M. Peyron, S. Muruganandan, L. Schneider, 'The endoplasmic reticulum in xenobiotic toxicity', *Drug Metab. Rev.* **2005**, *37*, 405–442.

[21] I. Hanukoglu, 'Antioxidant protective mechanisms against reactive oxygen species (ROS) generated by mitochondrial P450 systems in steroidogenic cells', *Drug Metab. Rev.* **2006**, *38*, 171–196.

[22] D. R. Nelson, H. W. Strobel, 'On the membrane topology of vertebrate cytochrome P-450 proteins', *J. Biol. Chem.* **1988**, *263*, 6038–6050.

[23] R. J. Edwards, B. P. Murray, A. M. Singleton, A. R. Boobis, 'Orientation of cytochromes P450 in the endoplasmic reticulum', *Biochemistry* **1991**, *30*, 71–76.

[24] F. Centero, C. Gutiérrez-Merino, 'Location of functional centers in the microsomal cytochrome P450 system', *Biochemistry* **1992**, *31*, 8473–8481.

[25] B. S. Masters, C. C. Marohnic, 'Cytochromes P450 – a family of proteins and scientists – understanding their relationships', *Drug Metab. Rev.* **2006**, *38*, 209–225.

[26] a) P. A. Williams, J. Cosme, A. Ward, H. C. Angove, D. M. Vinkovic, H. Jhoti, 'Crystal structure of human cytochrome P450 2C9 with bound warfarin', *Nature* **2003**, *424*, 464–468; b) P. A. Williams, J. Cosme, D. M. Vinkovic, A. Ward, H. C. Angove, P. J. Day, C. Vonrhein, I. J. Tickle, H. Jhoti, 'Crystal structure of human cytochrome P450 3A4 bound to metarypone and progesterone', *Science* **2004**, *305*, 683–686.

[27] F. J. Gonzalez, D. W. Nebert, 'Evolution of the P450 gene superfamily: animal-plant 'warfare', molecular drive and human genetic differences in drug oxidation', *Trends Genet.* **1990**, *6*, 182–186; A. K. Daly, J. Brockmöller, F. Broly, M. Eichelbaum, W. E. Evans, F. J. Gonzalez, J. D. Huang, J. R. Idle, M. Ingelman-Sundberg, T. Ishizaki, E. Jacqz-Aigrain, U. A. Meyer, D. W. Nebert, V. M. Steen, C. R. Wolf, U. M. Zanger, 'Nomenclature for human *CYP2D6* alleles', *Pharmacogenetics* **1996**, *6*, 193–201; homepage of the Human Cytochrome P450 (CYP) Allele Nomenclature Committee, www.cypalleles.ki.se.

[28] B. Oesch-Bartlomowicz, F. Oesch, 'Mechanisms of toxification and detoxification that challenge drug candidates and drugs', in 'ADME-Tox Approaches', Eds. B. Testa, H. van de Waterbeemd, Vol. 5 in 'Comprehensive Medicinal Chemistry', 2nd edn., Eds. J. B. Taylor, D. J. Triggle, Elsevier, Oxford, 2007, p. 193–214.

[29] M. Ingelman-Sundberg, 'Implications of polymorphic cytochrome P450-dependent drug metabolism for drug development', *Drug Metab. Dispos.* **2001**, *29*, 570–573; H. Reiser, 'Pharmacogenetics and drug development', *Annu. Rep. Med. Chem.* **2005**, *40*, 414–427.

[30] B. R. Bauer, A. E. Rettie, 'CYP4B1: an enigmatic P450 at the interface between xenobiotic and endobiotic metabolism', *Drug Metab. Rev.* **2006**, *38*, 451–476; M. Z. Wang, J. Y. Saulter, E. Usuki, Y.-L. Cheung, M. Hall, A. S. Bridges, G. Loewen, O. T. Parkinson, C. E. Stephens, J. L. Allen, D. C. Zeldin, D. W. Boykin, R. R. Tidwell, A. Parkinson, M. F. Paine, J. E. Hall, 'CYP4F enzymes are the major enzymes in human liver microsomes that catalyze the O-demethylation of the antiparasitic prodrug DB289 [2,5-bis(4-amidinophenyl)furan-bis-O-methylamidoxime]', *Drug Metab. Dispos.* **2006**, *34*, 1985–1994; I. A. Pikuleva, 'Cholesterol-metabolizing cytochromes P450', *Drug Metab. Dispos.* **2006**, *34*, 513–520.

[31] R. A. Totah, A. E. Rettie, 'Principles of drug metabolism 3: Enzymes and tissues', in 'ADME-Tox Approaches', Eds. B. Testa, H. van de Waterbeemd, Vol. 5 in 'Comprehensive Medicinal Chemistry', 2nd edn., Eds. J. B. Taylor, D. J. Triggle, Elsevier, Oxford, 2007, p. 167–191.

[32] D. A. Smith, M. J. Ackland, B. C. Jones, 'Properties of cytochrome P450 isoenzymes and their substrates. Part 1: active site characteristics', *Drug Discov. Today* **1997**, *2*, 406–414; D. A. Smith, M. J. Ackland, B. C. Jones, 'Properties of cytochrome P450 isoenzymes and their substrates. Part 2: properties of cytochrome P450 substrates', *Drug Discov. Today* **1997**, *2*, 479–486.

[33] D. A. Smith, S. M. Abel, R. Hyland, B. C. Jones, 'Human cytochrome P450s: selectivity and measurement in vivo', *Xenobiotica* **1998**, *28*, 1095–1128.

[34] D. F. V. Lewis, M. Dickins, P. J. Eddershaw, M. H. Tarbit, P. S. Goldfarb, 'Cytochrome P450 substrate specificities, substrate structural templates and enzyme active site geometries', *Drug Metab. Drug Interact.* **1999**, *15*, 1–49.

[35] D. F. V. Lewis, 'On the recognition of mammalian microsomal cytochrome P450 substrates and their characteristics', *Biochem. Pharmacol.* **2000**, *60*, 293–306.

[36] S. A. Wrighton, E. G. Schuetz, K. E. Thummel, D. D. Shen, K. R. Korzekwa, P. B. Watkins, 'The human CYP3A subfamily: practical considerations', *Drug Metab. Rev.* **2000**, *32*, 339–361.

[37] W. R. Scheidt, C. A. Reed, 'Spin-state/stereochemical relationships in iron porphyrins: implications for the hemoproteins', *Chem. Rev.* **1981**, *81*, 543–555.

[38] D. F. V. Lewis, 'Physical methods in the study of the active site geometry of cytochromes P-450', *Drug Metab. Rev.* **1986**, *17*, 1–66.

[39] W. F. Trager, 'The postenzymatic chemistry of activated oxygen', *Drug Metab. Rev.* **1982**, *13*, 51–69.

[40] M. J. Coon, A. D. N. Vaz, D. F. McGinnity, H. M. Peng, 'Multiple activated oxygen species in P450 catalysis. Contributions to specificity in drug metabolism', *Drug Metab. Dispos.* **1998**, *26*, 1190–1193.

[41] T. M. Makris, R. Davydov, I. G. Denisov, B. M. Hoffman, S. G. Sligar, 'Mechanistic enzymology of oxygen activation by the cytochromes P450', *Drug Metab. Rev.* **2002**, *34*, 691–708.

[42] A. L. Shen, M. J. Christensen, C. B. Kasper, 'NADPH-Cytochrome P450 oxidoreductase. The role of cysteine 566 in catalysis and cofactor binding', *J. Biol. Chem.* **1991**, *266*, 19976–19980.

[43] K. Shirabe, T. Yubisui, T. Nishino, M. Takeshita, 'Role of cysteine residues in human NADH-cytochrome b5 reductase studied by site-directed mutagenesis', *J. Biol. Chem.* **1991**, *266*, 7531–7536.

[44] D. N. Li, M. P. Pritchard, S. T. Hanlon, B. Burchell, C. R. Wolf, T. Friedberg, 'Competition between cytochrome P-450 isozymes for NADPH-cytochrome P-450 oxidoreductase affects drug metabolism', *J. Pharmacol. Exp. Ther.* **1999**, *289*, 661–667.

[45] C. R. Nishida, G. Knudsen, W. Straub, P. R. Ortiz de Montellano, 'Electron supply and catalytic oxidation of nitrogen by cytochrome P450 and nitric oxide synthase', *Drug Metab. Rev.* **2002**, *34*, 479–501.

[46] J. R. Kurian, S. U. Bajad, J. L. Miller, N. A. Chin, L. A. Trepanier, 'NADH cytochrome b_5 reductase and cytochrome b_5 catalyze the microsomal reduction of xenobiotic hydroxylamines and amidoximes in humans', *J. Pharmacol. Exp. Ther.* **2004**, *311*, 1171–1178.

[47] P. R. Ortiz de Montellano, 'Cytochrome P-450 catalysis: radical intermediates and dehydrogenation reaction', *Trends Pharmacol. Sci.* **1989**, *10*, 354–359.

[48] L. Koymans, G. M. Donné-Op den Kelder, J. M. te Koppele, N. P. E. Vermeulen, 'Cytochromes P450: Their active-site structure and mechanism of oxidation', *Drug Metab. Rev.* **1993**, *25*, 325–387.

[49] J. Everse, 'The structure of heme proteins compounds I and II: some misconceptions', *Free Radical Biol. Med.* **1998**, *24*, 1338–1346.

[50] F. P. Guengerich, 'Cytochrome P450 3A4: Regulation and role in drug metabolism', *Annu. Rev. Pharmacol. Toxicol.* **1999**, *39*, 1–17.

[51] I. Schlichting, J. Berendzen, K. Chu, A. M. Stock, S. A. Maves, D. E. Benson, R. M. Sweet, D. Ringe, G. A. Petsko, S. G. Sligar, 'The catalytic pathway of cytochrome P450 cam at atomic resolution', *Science* **2000**, *287*, 1615–1622.

[52] F. P. Guengerich, 'Common and uncommon cytochrome P450 reactions related to metabolism and chemical toxicity', *Chem. Res. Toxicol.* **2001**, *14*, 611–650.

[53] M. T. Green, J. H. Dawson, H. B. Gray, 'Oxoiron(IV) in chloroperoxidase compound II is basic: Implications for P450 chemistry', *Science* **2004**, *304*, 1653–1656.

[54] W. F. Trager, 'Principles of drug metabolism 1: Redox reactions', in 'ADME-Tox Approaches', Eds. B. Testa, H. van de Waterbeemd, Vol. 5 in 'Comprehensive Medicinal Chemistry', 2nd edn., Eds. J. B. Taylor, D. J. Triggle, Elsevier, Oxford, 2007, p. 87–132.

[55] D. M. Ziegler, 'Flavin-containing monooxygenases: catalytic mechanism and substrate specificities', *Drug Metab. Rev.* **1988**, *19*, 1–32.

[56] J. R. Cashman, 'Structural and catalytic properties of the mammalian flavin-containing monooxygenases', *Chem. Res. Toxicol.* **1995**, *8*, 165–181.

[57] I. R. Phillips, C. T. Dolphin, P. Clair, M. R. Hadley, A. J. Hutt, R. R. McCombie, R. L. Smith, E. A. Shephard, 'The molecular biology of flavin-containing monooxygenases of man', *Chem.-Biol. Interact.* **1995**, *96*, 17–32.

[58] A. A. Elfarra, 'Potential role of the flavin-containing monooxygenases in the metabolism of endogenous compounds', *Chem.-Biol. Interact.* **1995**, *96*, 47–55.

[59] L. L. Poulsen, D. M. Ziegler, 'Multisubstrate flavin-containing monooxygenases: applications of mechanism to specificity', *Chem.-Biol. Interact.* **1995**, *96*, 57–73.

[60] J. R. Cashman, 'Human flavin-containing monooxygenase: substrate specificity and role in drug metabolism', *Curr. Drug Metab.* **2000**, *1*, 181–191.

[61] D. M. Ziegler, 'An overview of the mechanism, substrate specificities, and structure of FMOs', *Drug Metab. Rev.* **2002**, *34*, 503–511.

[62] J. R. Cashman, 'The role of flavin-containing monooxygenases in drug metabolism and development', *Curr. Opin. Drug Discov. Dev.* **2003**, *6*, 486–493.

[63] J. R. Cashman, 'The implications of polymorphisms in mammalian flavin-containing monooxygenases in drug discovery and development', *Drug Discov. Today* **2004**, *9*, 574–581.

[64] S. K. Krueger, D. E. Williams, 'Mammalian flavin-containing monooxygenases: structure/function, genetic polymorphisms and role in drug metabolism', *Pharmacol. Ther.* **2005**, *106*, 357–387.

[65] J. R. Cashman, 'Some distinctions between flavin-containing and cytochrome P450 monooxygenases', *Biochem. Biophys. Res. Commun.* **2005**, *338*, 599–604; J. R. Cashman, J. Zhang, 'Human flavin-containing monooxygenases', *Annu. Rev. Pharmacol. Toxicol.* **2006**, *46*, 65–100.

[66] R. N. Hines, K. A. Hopp, J. Franco, K. Saeian, F. P. Begun, 'Alternative processing of the human *FMO6* gene renders transcripts incapable of encoding a functional flavin-containing monooxygenase', *Mol. Pharmacol.* **2002**, *62*, 320–325.

[67] S. G. Sligar, M. H. Gelb, D. C. Heimbrook, 'Bio-organic chemistry and cytochrome P450-dependent catalysis', *Xenobiotica* **1984**, *14*, 63–86.

[68] F. P. Guengerich, T. L. Macdonald, 'Chemical mechanisms of catalysis by cytochromes P-450: a unified view', *Acc. Chem. Res.* **1984**, *17*, 9–16.

[69] J. T. Groves, 'Key elements of the chemistry of cytochrome P-450. The oxygen rebound mechanism', *J. Chem. Educ.* **1985**, *62*, 928–931.

[70] R. E. White, J. P. Miller, L. V. Favreau, A. Bhattacharyya, 'Stereochemical dynamics of aliphatic hydroxylation by cytochrome P-450', *J. Am. Chem. Soc.* **1986**, *108*, 6024–6031.

[71] J. K. Atkinson, K. U. Ingold, 'Cytochrome P450 hydroxylation of hydrocarbons: variation in the rate of oxygen rebound using cyclopropyl radical clocks including two new ultrafast probes', *Biochemistry* **1993**, *32*, 9209–9214.

[72] R. E. White, M. B. McCarthy, K. D. Egeberg, S. G. Sligar, 'Regioselectivity in the cytochrome P-450: control by protein constraints and by chemical reactivity', *Arch. Biochem. Biophys.* **1984**, *228*, 493–502; L. Olsen, P. Rydberg, T. H. Rod, U. Ryde, 'Prediction of activation energies for hydrogen abstraction by cytochrome P450', *J. Med. Chem.* **2006**, *49*, 6489–6499.

[73] L. Perbellini, F. Brugnone, V. Cocheo, E. De Rosa, G. B. Bartolucci, 'Identification of the n-heptane metabolites in rat and human urine', *Arch. Toxicol.* **1986**, *58*, 229–234.

[74] T. Ishida, 'Biotransformation of terpinoids by mammals, microorganisms, and plant-cultured cells', *Chem. Biodiv.* **2005**, *2*, 569–590.

[75] M. Miyazawa, M. Shinto, T. Shimada, 'Sex differences in the metabolism of (+)- and (−)-limonene enantiomers to carveol and perillyl alcohol derivatives by cytochrome P450 enzymes in rat liver microsomes', *Chem. Res. Toxicol.* **2002**, *15*, 15–20.

[76] R. E. McMahon, H. R. Sullivan, J. C. Craig, W. E. Pereira Jr., 'The microsomal oxygenation of ethylbenzene: isotopic, stereochemical, and induction studies', *Arch. Biochem. Biophys.* **1969**, *132*, 575–577.

[77] L. Drummond, J. Caldwell, H. K. Wilson, 'The metabolism of ethylbenzene and styrene to mandelic acid: stereochemical considerations', *Xenobiotica* **1989**, *19*, 199–207.

[78] S. K. Paulson, J. Y. Zhang, A. P. Breau, J. D. Hribar, N. W. K. Liu, S. M. Jessen, Y. M. Lawal, J. N. Cogburn, C. J. Gresk, C. S. Markos, T. J. Maziasz, G. L. Schoenhard, E. G. Burton, 'Pharmacokinetics, tissue distribution, metabolism, and excretion of celecoxib in rats', *Drug Metab. Dispos.* **2000**, *28*, 514–521.

[79] S. K. Paulson, J. D. Hribar, N. W. K. Liu, E. Hajdu, R. H. Bible Jr., A. Piergies, A. Karim, 'Metabolism and excretion of [14C]celecoxib in healthy male volunteers', *Drug Metab. Dispos.* **2000**, *28*, 308–314.

[80] B. Eiermann, P. O. Edlund, A. Tjernberg, P. Dalén, M. L. Dahl, L. Bertilsson, '1- and 3-hydroxylations, in addition to 4-hydroxylation, of debrisoquine are catalyzed by cytochrome P450 2D6 in humans', *Drug Metab. Dispos.* **1998**, *26*, 1096–1101.

[81] I. Midgley, K. Fitzpatrick, S. J. Wright, B. A. John, A. J. Peard, R. M. Major, J. D. Major, J. D. Holding, A. McBurney, R. Anacardio, R. Novellini, M. P. Ferrari, 'Species differences in the pharmacokinetics and metabolism of reparixin in rat and dog', *Xenobiotica* **2006**, *36*, 419–440.

[82] M. M. Callahan, R. S. Robertson, M. J. Arnaud, A. R. Branfman, M. F. McComish, D. W. Yesair, 'Human metabolism of [1-methyl-14C]- and [2-14C]caffeine after oral administration', *Drug Metab. Dispos.* **1982**, *10*, 417–423.

[83] F. Berthou, B. Guillois, C. Riche, Y. Dreano, E. Jacqz-Aigrain, P. H. Beaune, 'Interspecies variations in caffeine metabolism related to cytochrome P4501A', *Xenobiotica* **1992**, *22*, 671–680.

[84] J. O. Miners, D. J. Birkett, 'The use of caffeine as a metabolic probe for human drug metabolizing enzymes', *Gen. Pharmacol.* **1996**, *27*, 245–249.

[85] G. Ginsberg, D. Hattis, A. Russ, B. Sonawane, 'Physiologically based pharmacokinetic (PBPK) modeling of caffeine and theophylline in neonates and adults: implications for assessing children's risks from environmental agents', *J. Toxicol. Environ. Health A* **2004**, *67*, 297–329.

[86] A. E. Mutlib, W. L. Nelson, 'Pathways of gallopamil metabolism. Regiochemistry and enantioselectivity of the N-dealkylation processes', *Drug Metab. Dispos.* **1990**, *18*, 331–337.

[87] A. E. Mutlib, W. L. Nelson, 'Pathways of gallopamil metabolism. Regiochemistry and enantioselectivity of the O-demethylation processes', *Drug Metab. Dispos.* **1990**, *18*, 309–314.

[88] M. Eichelbaum, M. Ende, G. Remberg, M. Schomerus, H. J. Dengler, 'The metabolism of DL-[14C]verapamil in man', *Drug Metab. Dispos.* **1979**, *7*, 145–148.

[89] L. Shen, J. F. Fitzloff, C. S. Cook, 'Differential enantioselectivity and product-dependent activation and inhibition in metabolism of verapamil by human CYP3As', *Drug Metab. Dispos.* **2004**, *32*, 186–196.

[90] S. Vickers, S. L. Polsky, 'The biotransformation of nitrogen-containing xenobiotics to lactams', *Curr. Drug Metab.* **2000**, *1*, 357–389.

[91] J. Hukkanen, P. Jacob III, N. L. Benowitz, 'Metabolism and disposition of nicotine', *Pharmacol. Rev.* **2005**, *57*, 79–115.

[92] D. Yildiz, 'Nicotine, its metabolism and an overview of its biological effects', *Toxicon* **2004**, *43*, 619–632.

[93] D. McKillop, A. D. McCormick, G. S. Miles, P. J. Phillips, K. J. Pickup, N. Bushby, M. Hutchison, 'In vitro metabolism of gefitinib in human liver microsomes', *Xenobiotica* **2004**, *34*, 983–1000.

[94] D. McKillop, A. D. McCormick, A. Millar, G. S. Miles, P. J. Phillips, M. Hutchison, 'Cytochrome P450-dependent metabolism of gefitinib', *Xenobiotica* **2005**, *35*, 39–50.

[95] H. M. Peng, G. M. Raner, A. D. N. Vaz, M. J. Coon, 'Oxidative cleavage of esters and amides to carbonyl products by cytochrome P450', *Arch. Biochem. Biophys.* **1995**, *318*, 333–339.

[96] N. Yumibe, K. Huie, K. J. Chen, M. Snow, R. P. Clement, M. N. Cayen, 'Identification of human liver cytochrome P450 enzymes that metabolize the nonsedative antihistamine loratadine. Formation of descarboxyethoxyloratadine by CYP3A4 and CYP2D6', *Biochem. Pharmacol.* **1996**, *51*, 165–172.

[97] R. Ramanathan, N. Alvarez, A. D. Su, S. Chowdhury, K. Alton, K. Stauber, J. Patrick, 'Metabolism and excretion of loratadine in male and female mice, rats and monkeys', *Xenobiotica* **2005**, *35*, 155–189.

[98] C. S. Lieber, L. M. DeCarli, 'Hepatic microsomal ethanol-oxidizing system', *J. Biol. Chem.* **1970**, *245*, 2505–2512.

[99] H. Asai, S. Imaoka, T. Kuroki, T. Monna, Y. Funae, 'Microsomal ethanol oxidizing system activity by human hepatic cytochrome P450s', *J. Pharmacol. Exp. Ther.* **1996**, *277*, 1004–1009.

[100] T. Matsunaga, N. Kishi, H. Tanaka, K. Watanabe, H. Yoshimura, I. Yamamoto, 'Major cytochrome P450 enzyme responsible for oxidation of secondary alcohols to the corresponding ketones in mouse hepatic microsomes', *Drug Metab. Dispos.* **1998**, *26*, 1045–1047.

[101] S. Kunitoh, S. Imaoka, T. Hiroi, Y. Yabusaki, T. Monna, Y. Funae, 'Acetaldehyde as well as ethanol is metabolized by human CYP2E1', *J. Pharmacol. Exp. Ther.* **1997**, *280*, 527–532.

[102] D. K. Spracklin, D. C. Hankins, J. M. Fisher, K. E. Thummel, E. D. Kharasch, 'Cytochrome P450 2E1 is the principal catalyst of human oxidative halothane metabolism in vitro', *J. Pharmacol. Exp. Ther.* **1997**, *281*, 400–411.

[103] J. Gut, U. Christen, J. Huwyler, 'Mechanisms of halothane toxicity: novel insights', *Pharmacol. Ther.* **1993**, *58*, 133–155.

[104] K. J. Garton, P. Yuen, J. Meinwald, K. E. Thummel, E. D. Kharasch, 'Stereoselective metabolism of enflurane by human liver cytochrome P450 2E1', *Drug Metab. Dispos.* **1995**, *23*, 1426–1430.

[105] J. Halpert, 'Covalent modification of lysine during the suicide inactivation of rat liver cytochrome P-450 by chloramphenicol', *Biochem. Pharmacol.* **1981**, *30*, 875–881.

[106] K. Watanabe, S. Narimatsu, I. Yamamoto, H. Yoshimura, 'Hepatic microsomal oxygenation of aldehydes to carboxylic acids', *Biochem. Biophys. Res. Commun.* **1990**, *166*, 1308–1312.

[107] K. Watanabe, S. Narimatsu, I. Yamamoto, H. Yoshimura, 'Oxygenation mechanism of aldehyde to carboxylic acid catalyzed by a cytochrome P450 isozyme', *J. Biol. Chem.* **1991**, *266*, 2709–2711.

[108] R. A. Stearns, P. K. Chakravarty, R. Chen, S. H. Chiu, 'Biotransformation of losartan to its active carboxylic acid metabolite in human liver microsomes', *Drug Metab. Dispos.* **1995**, *23*, 207–215.

[109] M. Bartók, K. L. Láng, 'Oxiranes', in 'Small Ring Heterocycles, Part 3', Ed. A. Hassner, Wiley, New York, 1985, p. 1–196.

[110] C. Chiappe, A. De Rubertis, G. Amato, P. G. Gervasi, 'Stereochemistry of the biotransformation of 1-hexene and 2-methyl-1-hexene with rat liver microsomes and purified P450s of rats and humans', *Chem. Res. Toxicol.* **1998**, *11*, 1487–1493.

[111] C. Chiappe, A. De Rubertis, M. De Carlo, G. Amato, P. G. Gervasi, 'Stereochemial aspects in the 4-vinylcyclohexene biotransformation with rat liver microsomes and purified P450s. Monoepoxides and diols', *Chem. Res. Toxicol.* **2001**, *14*, 492–499.

[112] R. E. Miller, F. P. Guengerich, 'Oxidation of trichloroethylene by liver microsomal cytochrome P-450: evidence for chlorine migration in a transition state not involving trichloroethylene oxide', *Biochemistry* **1982**, *21*, 1090–1097.

[113] K. Lertratanangkoon, M. G. Horning, 'Metabolism of carbamazepine', *Drug Metab. Rev.* **1982**, *10*, 1–10.

[114] B. Rambeck, T. May, U. Juergens, 'Serum concentrations of carbamazepine and its epoxide and diol metabolites in epileptic patients: the influence of dose and comedication', *Ther. Drug Monit.* **1987**, *9*, 298–303.

[115] R. E. Pearce, G. R. Vakkalagadda, J. S. Leeder, 'Pathways of carbamazepine bioactivation in vitro I. Characterization of human cytochromes P450 responsible for the formation of 2- and 3-hydroxylated metabolites', *Drug Metab. Dispos.* **2002**, *30*, 1170–1179.

[116] J. Seidegard, J. W. DePierre, 'Microsomal epoxide hydrolase. Properties, regulation and function', *Biochim. Biophys. Acta* **1983**, *695*, 251–270.

[117] B. Testa, 'Principles of drug metabolism 2: Hydrolysis and conjugation reactions', in 'ADME-Tox Approaches', Eds. B. Testa, H. van de Waterbeemd, Vol. 5 in 'Comprehensive Medicinal Chemistry', 2nd edn., Eds. J. B. Taylor, D. J. Triggle, Elsevier, Oxford, 2007, p. 133–166.

[118] R. A. Halpin, A. G. Porras, L. A. Geer, M. R. Davis, D. Cui, G. A. Doss, E. Woolf, D. Musson, C. Matthews, R. Mazenko, J. I. Schwartz, K. C. Lasseter, K. P. Vyas, T. A. Baillie, 'The disposition and metabolism of rofecoxib, a potent and selective cyclooxygenase-2 inhibitor, in human subjects', *Drug Metab. Dispos.* **2002**, *30*, 684–693; N. Ahuja, A. Singh, B. Singh, 'Rofecoxib: an update on physicochemical, pharmaceutical, pharmacodynamic and pharmacokinetic aspects', *J. Pharm. Pharmacol.* **2003**, *55*, 859–894.

[119] T. S. Dowers, D. A. Rock, D. A. Rock, B. N. S. Perkins, J. P. Jones, 'An analysis of the regioselectivity of aromatic hydroxylation and *N*-oxygenation by cytochrome P450 enzymes', *Drug Metab. Dispos.* **2004**, *32*, 328–332.

[120] D. K. Dalvie, A. S. Katgutkar, S. C. Khojasteh-Bakht, R. S. Obach, J. P. O'Donnell, 'Biotransformation reactions of five-membered aromatic heterocyclic rings', *Chem. Res. Toxicol.* **2002**, *15*, 269–299.

[121] P. Morgan, J. L. Maggs, P. C. B. Page, B. K. Park, 'Oxidative dehalogenation of 2-fluoro-17α-ethynylestradiol in vivo. A distal structure-metabolism relationship of 17α-ethynylation', *Biochem. Pharmacol.* **1992**, *44*, 1717–1724.

[122] T. Ohe, T. Mashino, M. Hirobe, 'Substituent elimination from *p*-substituted phenols by cytochrome P450. *ipso*-substitution by the oxygen atom of the active species', *Drug Metab. Dispos.* **1997**, *25*, 116–122.

[123] S. Safe, D. Jones, O. Hutzinger, 'Metabolism of 4,4'-dihalogenobiphenyls', *J. Chem. Soc., Perkin Trans. 1* **1976**, 357–359.

[124] T. Walle, J. E. Oatis Jr., U. K. Walle, D. R. Knapp, 'New ring-hydroxylated metabolites of propranolol', *Drug Metab. Dispos.* **1982**, *10*, 122–127.

[125] W. L. Nelson, M. J. Bartels, 'Stereoselectivity in the aromatic hydroxylation of propranolol in rats', *Drug Metab. Dispos.* **1984**, *12*, 382–384.

[126] W. L. Nelson, M. J. Bartels, P. J. Bednarski, S. Zhang, K. Messick, J. S. Horng, R. R. Ruffolo Jr., 'The 3,4-catechol derivative of propranolol, a minor dihydroxylated metabolite', *J. Med. Chem.* **1984**, *27*, 857–861.

[127] R. E. Talaat, W. L. Nelson, 'Regioisomeric aromatic dihydroxylation of propranolol', *Drug Metab. Dispos.* **1988**, *16*, 207–211, 212–216.

[128] S. A. Ward, T. Walle, U. K. Walle, G. R. Wilkinson, R. A. Branch, 'Propranolol metabolism is determined by both mephenytoin and debrisoquine hydroxylase activities', *Clin. Pharmacol. Ther.* **1989**, *45*, 72–79.

[129] M. J. Fasco, P. P. Dymerski, J. D. Wos, L. S. Kaminsky, 'A new warfarin metabolite: structure and function', *J. Med. Chem.* **1978**, *21*, 1054–1059.

[130] L. S. Kaminsky, 'Warfarin as a probe of cytochromes P450 function', *Drug Metab. Rev.* **1989**, *20*, 479–487.

[131] A. E. Rettie, K. R. Korzekwa, K. L. Kunze, R. F. Lawrence, A. C. Eddy, T. Aoyama, H. V. Gelboin, F. J. Gonzalez, W. F. Trager, 'Hydroxylation of warfarin by cDNA-expressed cytochromes P450: A role for P4502C9 in the etiology of (*S*)-warfarin-drug interactions', *Chem. Res. Toxicol.* **1992**, *5*, 54–59.

[132] Z. Zhang, M. J. Fasco, Z. Huang, F. P. Guengerich, L. S. Kaminsky, 'Human cytochromes P4501A1 and P4501A2: *R*-Warfarin metabolism as a probe', *Drug Metab. Dispos.* **1995**, *23*, 1339–1345.

[133] J. S. Ngui, Q. Chen, M. Shou, R. W. Wang, R. A. Stearns, T. A. Baillie, W. Tang, 'In vitro stimulation of warfarin metabolism by quinidine: increases in the formation of 4'- and 10-hydroxywarfarin', *Drug Metab. Dispos.* **2001**, *29*, 877–886.

[134] I. N. H. White, 'Suicidal destruction of cytochrome P-450 by ethynyl substituted compounds', *Pharm. Res.* **1984**, *1*, 141–148.

[135] S. E. Schmid, W. Y. W. Au, D. E. Hill, F. F. Kadlubar, W. Slikker Jr., 'Cytochrome P450-dependent oxidation of the 17a-ethynyl group of synthetic steroids', *Drug Metab. Dispos.* **1983**, *11*, 531–536.

[136] E. S. Roberts, N. E. Hopkins, W. L. Alworth, P. F. Hollenberg, 'Mechanism-based inactivation of cytochrome P450 2B1 by 2-ethynylnaphthalene: Identification of an active-site peptide', *Chem. Res. Toxicol.* **1993**, *6*, 470–479.

[137] A. Wade, A. M. Symons, L. Martin, D. V. Parke, 'Metabolic oxidation of the ethynyl group in 4-ethynylbiphenyl', *Biochem. J.* **1979**, *184*, 509–517; A. Wade, A. M. Symons, L. Martin, D. V. Parke, 'The metabolic oxidation of the ethynyl group in 4-ethynylbiphenyl in vitro', *Biochem. J.* **1980**, *188*, 867–872.

[138] J. Ling, K. A. Johnson, Z. Miao, A. Rakhit, M. P. Pantze, M. Hamilton, B. L. Lum, C. Prakash, 'Metabolism and excretion of erlotinib, a small molecule inhibitor of epidermal growth factor receptor tyrosine kinase, in healthy male volunteers', *Drug Metab. Dispos.* **2006**, *34*, 420–426.

[139] I. N. H. White, 'Structure-activity relationships in the destruction of cytochrome P450 mediated by certain ethynyl-substituted compounds in rats', *Biochem. Pharmacol.* **1980**, *29*, 3253–3255.

[140] P. W. Fan, C. Gu, S. A. Marsh, J. C. Stevens, 'Mechanism-based inactivation of cytochrome P450 2B6 by a novel terminal acetylene inhibitor', *Drug Metab. Dispos.* **2003**, *31*, 28–36.

[141] K. K. Khan, Y. Q. He, M. A. Correia, J. R. Halpert, 'Differential oxidation of mifepristone by cytochromes P450 3A4 and 3A5: Selective inactivation of P450 3A4', *Drug Metab. Dispos.* **2002**, *30*, 985–990.

[142] J. W. Gorrod, 'Differentiation of various types of biological oxidation of nitrogen in organic compounds', *Chem.-Biol. Interact.* **1973**, *7*, 289–303.

[143] D. H. Lang, C. K. Yeung, R. M. Peter, C. Ibarra, R. Gasser, K. Itagaki, R. M. Philpot, A. E. Rettie, 'Isoform specificity of trimethylamine *N*-oxygenation by human flavin-containing monooxygenase (FMO) and P450 enzymes', *Biochem. Pharmacol.* **1998**, *56*, 1005–1012.

[144] G. Caron, G. Ermondi, D. Boschi, P. A. Carrupt, R. Fruttero, B. Testa, A. Gasco, 'Structure–property relations in the basicity and lipophilicity of arylalkylamine oxides', *Helv. Chim. Acta* **1999**, *82*, 1630–1639.

[145] E. M. Hawes, T. J. Jawoeski, K. K. Midha, G. McKay, J. W. Hubbard, E. D. Korchinski, 'In vivo metabolism of N-oxides', in 'N-Oxidation of Drugs: Biochemistry, Pharmacology, Toxicology', Eds. P. Hlavida, L. A. Damani, Chapman and Hall, London, 1991, p. 263–286.

[146] U. Breyer-Pfaff, 'The metabolic fate of amitriptyline, nortriptyline and amitryptilinoxide in man', *Drug Metab. Rev.* **2004**, *36*, 723–746.

[147] J. R. Cashman, S. B. Park, C. E. Berkman, L. E. Cashman, 'Role of hepatic flavin-containing monooxygenase 3 in drug and chemical metabolism in adult humans', *Chem.-Biol. Interact.* **1995**, *96*, 33–46.

[148] S. Øie, T. W. Guentert, L. Tolentino, G. Hermodsson, 'Pharmacokinetics of moclobemide in male, virgin female, pregnant and nursing rats', *J. Pharm. Pharmacol.* **1992**, *44*, 413–418.

[149] J. R. Cashman, Y. N. Xiong, L. Xu, A. Janowsky, 'N-Oxygenation of amphetamine and methamphetamine by the human flavin-containing monooxygenase (Form 3): Role in bioactivation and detoxication', *J. Pharmacol. Exp. Ther.* **1999**, *288*, 1251–1260.

[150] J. Lin, C. E. Berkman, J. R. Cashman, 'N-Oxygenation of primary amines and hydroxylamines and retroreduction of hydroxylamines by adult human liver microsomes and adult human flavin-containing monooxygenase 3', *Chem. Res. Toxicol.* **1996**, *9*, 1183–1193.

[151] J. Lin, J. R. Cashman, 'N-Oxygenation of phenylethylamine to the *trans*-oxime by adult human liver flavin-containing monooxygenase and retroreduction of phenylethylamine hydroxylamine by human liver microsomes', *J. Pharmacol. Exp. Ther.* **1997**, *282*, 1269–1279.

[152] K. E. Mc Lane, J. Fisher, K. Ramakrishnan, 'Reductive drug metabolism', *Drug Metab. Rev.* **1983**, *14*, 741–799.

[153] F. P. Guengerich, R. H. Böcker, 'Cytochrome P450-catalyzed dehydrogenation of 1,4-dihydropyridines', *J. Biol. Chem.* **1988**, *263*, 8168–8175.

[154] F. P. Guengerich, W. R. Brian, M. Iwasaki, M. A. Sari, C. Bäärnhielm, P. Berntsson, 'Oxidation of dihydropyridine calcium channel blockers and analogues by human liver cytochrome P450 IIIA4', *J. Med. Chem.* **1991**, *34*, 1838–1844.

[155] F. P. Guengerich, 'N-Hydroxylarylamines', *Drug Metab. Rev.* **2002**, *34*, 607–623; D. Kim, F. P. Guengerich, 'Cytochrome P450 activation of arylamines and heterocyclic amines', *Annu. Rev. Pharmacol. Toxicol.* **2005**, *45*, 27–49.

[156] G. P. Ford, J. W. Thompson, 'Regiochemistry of nucleophilic attack by the guanine 2-amino group at the ring positions of nitrenium ions derived from carcinogenic polycyclic arylamines and nitroarenes: Molecular orbital calculations and simple models', *Chem. Res. Toxicol.* **1999**, *12*, 53–59; G. P. Ford, P. S. Herman, 'Relative stability of nitrenium ions derived from polycyclic aromatic amines. Relationship to mutagenicity', *Chem.-Biol. Interact.* **1992**, *81*, 1–18; G. P. Ford, G. R. Griffin, 'Relative stability of nitrenium ions derived from heterocyclic amine food carcinogens. Relationship to mutagenicity', *Chem.-Biol. Interact.* **1992**, *81*, 19–33; R. S. Kerdar, D. Dehner, D. Wild, 'Reactivity and genotoxicity of arylnitrenium ions in bacterial and mammalian cells', *Toxicol. Lett.* **1993**, *67*, 73–85.

[157] M. D. Tingle, R. Mahmud, J. L. Maggs, M. Pirmohamed, B. K. Park, 'Comparison of the metabolism and toxicity of dapsone in rat, mouse and man', *J. Pharmacol. Exp. Ther.* **1997**, *283*, 817–823.

[158] R. P. Reilly, F. H. Bellevue III, P. M. Woster, C. K. Svensson, 'Comparison of the in vitro cytotoxicity of hydroxylamine metabolites of sulfamethoxazole and dapsone', *Biochem. Pharmacol.* **1998**, *55*, 803–810.

[159] A. E. Cribb, M. Miller, J. S. Leeder, J. Hill, S. P. Spielberg, 'Reactions of the nitroso and hydroxylamine metabolites of sulfamethoxazole with reduced glutathione', *Drug Metab. Dispos.* **1991**, *19*, 900–906.

[160] A. E. Cribb, S. P. Spielberg, 'Sulfamethoxazole is metabolized to the hydroxylamine in humans', *Clin. Pharmacol. Ther.* **1992**, *51*, 522–526.

[161] R. J. Turesky, A. Constable, J. Richoz, N. Varga, J. Markovic, M. V. Martin, F. P. Guengerich, 'Activation of heterocyclic aromatic amines by rat and human microsomes and by purified rat and human cytochrome P450 1A2', *Chem. Res. Toxicol.* **1998**, *11*, 925–936.

[162] L. Koymans, G. M. Donné-Op den Kelder, J. M. te Koppele, N. P. E. Vermeulen, 'Generalized cytochrome P450-mediated oxidation and oxygenation reactions in aromatic substrates with activated N–H, O–H, C–H, or S–H substituents', *Xenobiotica* **1993**, *23*, 633–648.

[163] A. Dipple, C. J. Michejda, E. K. Weisburger, 'Metabolism of chemical carcinogens', *Pharmacol. Ther.* **1985**, *27*, 265–296.

[164] S. D. Nelson, 'Arylamines and arylamides: Oxidation mechanisms', in 'Bioactivation of Foreign Compounds', Ed. M. W. Anders, Academic Press, Orlando, 1985, p. 349–374.

[165] B. Lindeke, 'The non- and postenzymatic chemistry of *N*-oxygenated molecules', *Drug Metab. Rev.* **1982**, *13*, 71–121.

[166] L. Koymans, J. H. Van Lenthe, G. M. Donné-Op den Kelder, N. P. E. Vermeulen, 'Mechanisms of oxidation of phenacetin to reactive metabolites by cytochrome P450: A theoretical study involving radical intermediates', *Mol. Pharmacol.* **1990**, *37*, 452–460.

[167] A. W. Nichols, I. D. Wilson, M. Godejohann, I. K. Nicholson, J. P. Stockcor, 'Identification of phenacetin metabolites in human urine after administration of phenacetin-C^{2}H$_3$: Measurement of futile metabolic deacetylation vis HPLC/MS-SPE-NMR and HPLC-ToF MS', *Xenobiotica* **2006**, *36*, 615–629.

[168] P. P. Fu, 'Metabolism of nitro-polycyclic aromatic hydrocarbons', *Drug Metab. Rev.* **1990**, *22*, 209–268.

[169] S. C. Mitchell, R. H. Waring, 'The early history of xenobiotic sulfoxidation', *Drug Metab. Rev.* **1985**, *16*, 255–284.

[170] S. Oae, A. Mikami, T. Matsuura, K. Ogawa-Asada, Y. Watanabe, K. Fujimori, T. Iyanagi, 'Comparison of sulfide oxygenation mechanism for liver microsomal FAD-containing monooxygenase with that for cytochrome P-450', *Biochem. Biophys. Res. Commun.* **1985**, *131*, 567–573.

[171] K. A. Usmani, E. D. Karoly, E. Hodgson, R. L. Rose, 'In vitro sulfoxidation of thioether compounds by human cytochrome P450 and flavin-containing monooxygenase isoforms with particular reference to the CYP2C subfamily', *Drug Metab. Dispos.* **2004**, *32*, 333–339.

[172] G. Caron, P. Gaillard, P. A. Carrupt, B. Testa, 'Lipophilicity behavior of model and medicinal compounds containing a sulfide, sulfoxide, or sulfone moiety', *Helv. Chim. Acta* **1997**, *80*, 449–462.

[173] D. D. S. Tang-Liu, R. M. Matsumoto, J. I. Usansky, 'Clinical pharmacokinetics and drug metabolism of tazarotene', *Clin. Pharmacokinet.* **1999**, *37*, 273–287.

[174] M. Attar, D. Dong, K. H. J. Ling, D. D. S. Tang-Liu, 'Cytochrome P450 2C8 and flavin-containing monooxygenases are involved in the metabolism of tazarotene acid in humans', *Drug Metab. Dispos.* **2003**, *31*, 476–481.

[175] A. E. Rettie, M. P. Lawton, A. Jafar, M. Sadeque, G. P. Meier, R. M. Philpot, 'Prochiral sulfoxidation as a probe for multiple forms of the microsomal flavin-containing monooxygenase: Studies with rabbit FMO1, FMO2, FMO3 and FMO5 expressed in *Escherichia coli*', *Arch. Biochem. Biophys.* **1994**, *311*, 369–377.

[176] J. R. Cashman, 'Stereoselectivity in S- and N-oxygenation by the mammalian flavin-containing and cytochrome P450 monooxygenases', *Drug Metab. Rev.* **1998**, *30*, 675–707.

[177] H. B. Hucker, S. C. Stauffer, S. D. White, R. E. Rhodes, B. H. Arison, E. R. Umbenhauer, R. J. Bower, F. G. McMahon, 'Physiologic disposition and metabolic fate of a new anti-inflammatory agent, sulindac in the rat, dog, rhesus monkey, and man', *Drug Metab. Dispos.* **1973**, *1*, 721–736.

[178] M. A. Hamman, B. D. Haehner-Daniels, S. A. Wrighton, A. E. Rettie, S. D. Hall, 'Stereoselective sulfoxidation of sulindac sulfide by flavin-containing monooxygenases', *Biochem. Pharmacol.* **2000**, *60*, 7–17.

[179] D. M. Ziegler, 'Recent studies on the structure and function of multisubstrate flavin-containing monooxygenases', *Annu. Rev. Pharmacol. Toxicol.* **1993**, *33*, 179–199.

[180] K. L. Taylor, D. M. Ziegler, 'Studies on substrate specificity of the hog liver flavin-containing monooxygenase. Anionic organic sulfur compounds', *Biochem. Pharmacol.* **1987**, *36*, 141–146.

[181] C. J. Decker, M. S. Rashed, T. A. Baillie, D. Maltby, M. A. Correia, 'Oxidative metabolism of spironolactone: evidence for the involvement of electrophilic thiosteroid species in drug-mediated destruction of rat hepatic cytochrome P450', *Biochemistry* **1989**, *28*, 5128–5136.

[182] C. J. Decker, J. R. Cashman, K. Sugiyama, D. Maltby, M. A. Correia, 'Formation of glutathionyl-spironolactone disulfide by rat liver cytochromes P450 or hog liver flavin-containing monooxygenases: a functional probe of two-electron oxidations of the thiosteroid', *Chem. Res. Toxicol.* **1991**, *4*, 669–677.

[183] C. Teyssier, L. Guenot, M. Suschetet, M. H. Siess, 'Metabolism of diallyl disulfide by human liver microsomal cytochromes P450 and flavin-containing monooxygenases', *Drug Metab. Dispos.* **1999**, *27*, 835–841.

[184] E. Germain, J. Chevalier, M. H. Siess, C. Teyssier, 'Hepatic metabolism of diallyl disulfide in rat and man', *Xenobiotica* **2003**, *33*, 1185–1199.

[185] C. J. Decker, D. R. Doerge, 'Covalent binding of ^{14}C- and ^{35}S-labeled thiocarbamides in rat hepatic microsomes', *Biochem. Pharmacol.* **1992**, *43*, 881–888.

[186] M. C. Dyroff, R. A. Neal, 'Studies of the mechanism of metabolism of thioacetamide S-oxide by rat liver microsomes', *Mol. Pharmacol.* **1983**, *23*, 219–227.

[187] T. A. Vannelli, A. Dykman, P. R. Ortiz de Montellano, 'The antituberculosis drug ethionamide is activated by a flavoprotein monooxygenase', *J. Biol. Chem.* **2002**, *277*, 12824–12829.

[188] J. Halpert, D. Hammond, R. A. Neal, 'Inactivation of purified rat liver cytochrome P450 during the metabolism of parathion (diethyl *p*-nitrophenyl phosphorothionate)', *J. Biol. Chem.* **1980**, *255*, 1080–1089.

[189] N. P. E. Vermeulen, J. G. M. Bessems, R. van de Straat, 'Molecular aspects of paracetamol-induced hepatotoxicity and its mechanism-based prevention', *Drug Metab. Rev.* **1992**, *24*, 367–407.

[190] C. J. Patten, P. E. Thomas, R. L. Guy, M. Lee, F. J. Gonzalez, F. P. Guengerich, C. S. Yang, 'Cytochrome P450 enzymes involved in acetaminophen activation by rat and human liver microsomes and their kinetics', *Chem. Res. Toxicol.* **1993**, *6*, 511–518.

[191] S. S. T Lee, J. T. M: Buters, T. Pineau, P. Fernandez Alguero, F. J. Gonzalez, 'Role of CYP2E1 in the hepatotoxicity of acetaminophen', *J. Biol. Chem.* **1996**, *271*, 12063–12067.

[192] J. G. M. Bessems, M. J. de Groot, E. J. Baede, J. M. te Koppele, N. P. E. Vermeulen, 'Hydrogen atom abstraction of 3,5-disubstituted analogues of paracetamol by horseradish peroxidase and cytochrome P450', *Xenobiotica* **1998**, *28*, 855–875.

[193] D. C. Thompson, J. A. Thompson, M. Sugumaran, P. Moldéus, 'Biological and toxicological consequences of quinone methide formation', *Chem.-Biol. Interact.* **1992**, *86*, 129–162.

[194] J. A. Thompson, A. M. Malkinson, M. D. Wand, S. L. Mastovich, E. W. Mead, K. M. Schullek, W. G. Laudenschlager, 'Oxidative metabolism of butylated hydroxytoluene by hepatic and pulmonary microsomes from rats and mice', *Drug Metab. Dispos.* **1987**, *15*, 833–840.

[195] A. Kamel, J. Davis, M. J. Potchoiba, C. Prakash, 'Metabolism, pharmacokinetic and excretion of a potent tachykinin NK1 receptor antagonist (CP-122,721) in rat: Characterization of a novel oxidative pathway', *Xenobiotica* **2006**, *36*, 235–258.

[196] M. R. Anari, S. Khan, S. D. Jatoe, P. J. O'Brien, 'Cytochrome P450-dependent xenobiotic activation by physiological hydroperoxides in intact hepatocytes', *Eur. J. Drug Metab. Pharmacokinet.* **1997**, *22*, 305–310.

[197] M. Y. Wang, J. G. Liehr, 'Identification of fatty acid hydroperoxide cofactors in the cytochrome P450-mediated oxidation of estrogens to quinone metabolites', *J. Biol. Chem.* **1994**, *269*, 284–291.

[198] M. R. Anari, P. D. Josephy, T. Henry, P. J. O'Brien, 'Hydrogen peroxide supports human and rat cytochrome P450 1A2-catalyzed 2-amino-3-methylimidazo[4,5-*f*]quinoline bioactivation to mutagenic metabolites: Significance of cytochrome P450 peroxidase', *Chem. Res. Toxicol.* **1997**, *10*, 582–588.

[199] R. W. Chadwick, S. E. George, L. D. Claxton, 'Role of the gastrointestinal mucosa and microflora in the bioactivation of dietary and environmental mutagens or carcinogens', *Drug Metab. Rev.* **1992**, *24*, 425–492.

[200] D. R. Koop, 'Oxidative and reductive metabolism by cytochrome P450 2E1', *FASEB J.* **1992**, *6*, 724–730.

[201] A. R. Goeptar, H. Scheerens, N. P. E. Vermeulen, 'Oxygen and xenobiotic reductase activities by cytochrome P450', *Crit. Rev. Toxicol.* **1995**, *25*, 25–65.

[202] D. Perrissoud, B. Testa, 'Inhibiting or potentiating effects of flavonoids on carbon tetrachloride-induced toxicity in isolated rat hepatocytes', *Arzneim.-Forsch. (Drug Res.)* **1986**, *36*, 1249–1253.

[203] W. R. Jondorf, 'Drug metabolism and drug toxicity: Some evolutionary considerations', in 'Concepts in Drug Metabolism, Part B', Eds. P. Jenner, B. Testa, Dekker, New York, 1981, p. 307–376.

[204] W. R. Kelce, C. R. Stone, S. C. Laws, L. E. Gray, J. A. Kemppainen, E. M. Wilson, 'Persistent DDT metabolite *p,p′*-DDE is a potent androgen receptor antagonist', *Nature* **1995**, *375*, 581–585.

[205] M. Manno, S. Cazzaro, M. Rezzadore, 'The mechanism of the suicidal reductive inactivation of microsomal cytochrome P-450 by halothane', *Arch. Toxicol.* **1991**, *65*, 191–198.

[206] D. K. Spracklin, K. E. Thummel, E. D. Kharasch, 'Human reductive halothane metabolism in vitro is catalyzed by cytochrome P450 2A6 and 3A4', *Drug Metab. Dispos.* **1991**, *24*, 976–983.

[207] A. K. Fröhlich, U. Girreser, B. Clement, 'Metabolism of benzamidoxime (N-hydroxyamidine) in human hepatocytes and role of UDP-glucuronosyltransferases', *Xenobiotica* **2005**, *35*, 17–25.

[208] S. Heberling, U. Girreser, S. Wolf, B. Clement, 'Oxygen-insensitive enzymatic reduction of oximes to imines', *Biochem. Pharmacol.* **2006**, *71*, 354–365.

[209] B. Clement, 'Reduction of N-hydroxylated compounds: amidoximes (N-hydroxyamidines) as prodrugs of amidines', *Drug Metab. Rev.* **2002**, *34*, 565–579.

[210] S. Zbaida, C. F. Brewer, W. G. Levine, 'Substrates for microsomal azoreductase. Hammett substituent effects, NMR studies and response to inhibitors', *Drug Metab. Dispos.* **1992**, *20*, 902–908.

[211] W. G. Levine, A. Stoddart, S. Zbaida, 'Multiple mechanisms in hepatic microsomal azoreduction', *Xenobiotica* **1992**, *22*, 1111–1120.

[212] S. Zbaida, 'The mechanism of microsomal azoreduction: predictions based on electronic aspects of structure–activity relationships', *Drug Metab. Rev.* **1995**, *27*, 497–516.

[213] E. M. Cretton, J. P. Sommadossi, 'Reduction of 3′-azido-2′,3′-dideoxynucleosides to their 3′-amino metabolite is mediated by cytochrome P-450 and NADPH-cytochrome P-450 reductase in rat liver microsomes', *Drug Metab. Dispos.* **1993**, *21*, 946–950.

[214] X. R. Pan-Zhou, E. Cretton-Scott, X. J. Zhou, M. X. Yang, J. M. Lasker, J. P. Sommadossi, 'Role of human liver P450s and cytochrome b_5 in the reductive metabolism of 3′-azido-3′-deoxythymidine (AZT) to 3′-amino-3′-deoxythymidine', *Biochem. Pharmacol.* **1998**, *55*, 757–766.

[215] J. E. Biaglow, M. E. Varnes, L. Roizen-Towle, E. P. Clark, E. R. Epp, M. B. Astor, E. J. Hall, 'Biochemistry of reduction of nitro heterocycles', *Biochem. Pharmacol.* **1986**, *35*, 77–90.

[216] V. Purohit, A. K. Basu, 'Mutagenicity of nitroaromatic compounds', *Chem. Res. Toxicol.* **2000**, *13*, 673–692.

[217] J. Butler, B. M. Hoey, 'The one-electron reduction potential of several substrates can be related to their reduction rates by cytochrome P-450 reductase', *Biochim. Biophys. Acta* **1993**, *1161*, 73–78; C. P. Guise, A. T. Wang, A. Theil, D. J. Bridewell, W. R. Wilson, A. V. Patterson, 'Identification of human reductases that activate the dinitrobenzamide mustard prodrug PR-104A: a role for NADPH-cytochrome P450 oxidoreductase under hypoxia', *Biochem. Pharmacol.* **2007**, *74*, 810–820.

[218] J. J. R. Hermans, H. H. W. Thijssen, 'Comparison of the rat liver microsomal metabolism of the enantiomers of warfarin and 4′-nitrowarfarin (acenocoumarol)', *Xenobiotica* **1991**, *21*, 295–307.

[219] K. Ask, N. Décologne, C. Ginies, M. Låg, J. L. Boucher, J. A. Holme, H. Pelczar, P. Camus, 'Metabolism of nilutamide in rat lung', *Biochem. Pharmacol.* **2006**, *71*, 377–395.

[220] W. N. Wu, L. A. McKown, S. Liao, 'Metabolism of the analgesic drug ULTRAM® (tramadol hydrochloride) in humans: API-MS and MS/MS characterization of metabolites', *Xenobiotica* **2002**, *32*, 411–425.

[221] W. N. Wu, L. A. McKown, E. E. Codd, R. B. Raffa, 'Metabolism of two analgesic agents, tramadol N-oxide and tramadol, in specific pathogen-free and axenic mice', *Xenobiotica* **2006**, *36*, 551–565.

[222] S. M. Raleigh, E. Wanogho, M. D. Burke, L. H. Patterson, 'Rat cytochromes P450 (CYP) specifically contribute to the reductive bioactivation of AQ4N, an alkylaminoanthraquinone-di-N-oxide anticancer prodrug', *Xenobiotica* **1999**, *29*, 1115–1122.

[223] P. M. Loadman, D. J. Swaine, M. C. Bibby, K. J. Welham, L. H. Patterson, 'A preclinical pharmacokinetic study of the bioreductive drug AQ4N', *Drug Metab. Dispos.* **2001**, *29*, 422–426.

[224] D. Lang, A. S. Kalgutkar, 'Non-P450 mediated oxidative metabolism of xenobiotics', In 'Drug Metabolizing Enzymes. Cytochrome P450 and Other Enzymes in Drug Discovery and Development', J. Lee, R. S. Obach, M. B. Fisher, Eds. Dekker, New York, 2003, p. 483–540.

[225] M. B. H. Youdim, J. P. M. Finberg, 'New directions in monoamine oxidase A and B selective inhibitors and substrates', *Biochem. Pharmacol.* **1991**, *41*, 155–162.

[226] G. Maret, B. Testa, P. Jenner, N. El Tayar, P. A. Carrupt, 'The MPTP story: MAO activates tetrahydropyridine derivatives to toxins causing parkinsonism', *Drug Metab. Rev.* **1990**, *22*, 291–332.

[227] T. J. Mantle, K. F. Tipton (Eds.), 'Amine oxidases: structure, function and expression', *Biochem. Trans.* **1991**, *19*, 199–233.

[228] M. Strolin Benedetti, P. Dostert, 'Contribution of amine oxidases to the metabolism of xenobiotics', *Drug Metab. Rev.* **1994**, *26*, 507–535.

[229] M. Strolin Benedetti, K. F. Tipton, 'Monoamine oxidases and related amine oxidases as phase I enzymes in the metabolism of xenobiotics', *J. Neural Transm.* **1998**, *52(Suppl.)*, 149–171.

[230] M. Strolin Benedetti, 'Biotransformation of xenobiotics by amine oxidases', *Fundam. Clin. Pharmacol.* **2001**, *15*, 75–84.

[231] P. J. O'Brien, A. G. Siraki, N. Shangari, 'Aldehyde sources, metabolism, molecular toxicity mechanisms, and possible effects on human health', *Crit. Rev. Toxicol.* **2005**, *35*, 609–662.

[232] B. Gong, P. J. Boor, 'The role of amine oxidases in xenobiotic metabolism', *Expert Opin. Drug Metab. Toxicol.* **2006**, *2*, 559–571.

[233] J. P. Klinman, D. Mu, 'Quinoenzymes in biology', *Annu. Rev. Biochem.* **1994**, *63*, 299–344.

[234] R. Medda, A. Padiglia, J. Z. Pedersen, G. Rotilio, A. Finazzi Agrò, G. Floris, 'The reaction mechanism of copper amine oxidase: detection of intermediates by the use of substrates and inhibitors', *Biochemistry* **1995**, *34*, 16375–16381.

[235] A. High, T. Prior, R. A. Bell, P. K. Rangachari, 'Probing the 'active site' of diamine oxidase: structure–activity relations for histamine potentiation by O-alkylhydroxylamines on colonic epithelium', *J. Pharmacol. Exp. Ther.* **1999**, *288*, 490–501.

[236] E. Y. Wang, H. Gao, L. Salter-Cid, J. Zhang, L. Huang, E. M. Podar, A. Miller, J. Zhao, A. O'Rourke, M. D. Linnik, 'Design, synthesis, and biological evaluation of semicarbazide-sensitive amine oxidase (SSAO) inhibitors with anti-inflammatory activity', *J. Med. Chem.* **2006**, *49*, 2166–2173.

[237] R. B. Silverman, 'Radical ideas about monoamine oxidase', *Acc. Chem. Res.* **1995**, *28*, 335–342.

[238] W. Weyler, Y. P. P. Hsu, X. O. Breakefield, 'Biochemistry and genetics of monoamine oxidase', *Pharmacol. Ther.* **1990**, *47*, 391–417.

[239] A. M. Yu, C. P. Granvil, R. L. Haining, K. W. Krausz, J. Corchero, A. Küpfer, J. R. Idle, F. J. Gonzalez, 'The relative contribution of monoamine oxidase and cytochrome P450 isozymes to the metabolic deamination of the trace amine tryptamine', *J. Pharmacol. Exp. Ther.* **2003**, *304*, 539–546; D. S. Theobald, H. H. Maurer, 'Identification of monoamine oxidase and cytochrome P450 isoenzymes involved in the deamination of phenethylamine-derived designer drugs (2C-series)', *Biochem. Pharmacol.* **2007**, *73*, 287–297.

[240] N. Castagnoli Jr., J. M. Rimoldi, J. Bloomquist, K. P. Castagnoli, 'Potential metabolic bioactivation pathways involving cyclic tertiary amines and azaarenes', *Chem. Res. Toxicol.* **1997**, *10*, 924–940.

[241] A. S. Kalgutkar, D. K. Dalvie, N. Castagnoli Jr., T. J. Taylor, 'Interactions of nitrogen-containing xenobiotics with MAO-A and MAO-B: SAR studies on MAO substrates and inhibitors', *Chem. Res. Toxicol.* **2001**, *14*, 1139–1162.

[242] N. Castagnoli Jr., K. P. Castagnoli, G. Magnin, S. Kuttab, J. Shang, 'Studies on the oxidation of 1,4-disubstituted-1,2,3,6-tetrahydropyridines', *Drug Metab. Rev.* **2002**, *34*, 533–547.

[243] B. Rochat, M. Kossel, G. Boss, B. Testa, M. Gillet, P. Baumann, 'Stereoselective biotransformation of the SSRI citalopram and its demethylated metabolites by monoamine oxidases in human liver', *Biochem. Pharmacol.* **1998**, *56*, 15–23.

[244] M. Kossel, C. Gnerre, P. Voirol, M. Amey, B. Rochat, C. Bouras, B. Testa, P. Baumann, 'In vitro biotransformation of the selective serotonin reuptake inhibitor citalopram, its enantiomers and demethylated metabolites by monoamine oxidase in rat and human brain preparations', *Mol. Psychiat.* **2002**, *7*, 181–188.

[245] M. Salva, J. M. Jansat, A. Martinez-Tobed, J. M. Palacios, 'Identification of the human liver enzymes involved in the metabolism of the antimigraine agent almotriptan', *Drug Metab. Dispos.* **2003**, *31*, 404–411.

[246] P. H. Yu, B. A. Davis, A. A. Boulton, 'Aliphatic propargylamines: potent, selective, irreversible monoamine oxidase B inhibitors', *J. Med. Chem.* **1992**, *35*, 3705–3713.

[247] P. H. Yu, B. A. Davis, 'Stereospecific deamination of benzylamine catalyzed by different amine oxidases', *Int. J. Biochem.* **1988**, *20*, 1197–1201.

[248] G. Alton, T. H. Taher, R. J. Beever, M. M. Palcic, 'Stereochemistry of benzylamine oxidation by copper amine oxidases', *Arch. Biochem. Biophys.* **1995**, *316*, 353–361.

[249] F. Yraola, S. Garcia-Vicente, J. Fernandez-Reccio, F. Albericio, A. Zorzano, L. Marti, M. Royo, 'New efficient substrates for SSAO/VAP-1 enzyme: analysis by SARs and computational docking', *J. Med. Chem.* **2006**, *49*, 6197–6208.

[250] A. P. Beresford, P. V. Macrae, D. A. Stopher, 'Metabolism of amlodipine in the rat and dog: a species difference', *Xenobiotica* **1988**, *18*, 169–182.

[251] R. Hille, 'Molybdenum-containing hydroxylases', *Arch. Biochem. Biophys.* **2005**, *433*, 107–116.

[252] E. Garattini, R. Mendel, M. J. Romao, R. Wright, M. Terao, 'Mammalian molybdo-flavoenzymes, an expanding family of proteins: structure, genetics, regulation, function and pathophysiology', *Biochem. J.* **2003**, *372*, 15–32.

[253] K. Okamoto, K. Matsumoto, R. Hille, B. T. Eger, E. F. Pai, T. Nishino, 'The crystal structure of xanthine oxidoreductase during catalysis: Implications for reaction mechanism and enzyme inhibition', *Proc. Natl. Acad. Sci. U.S.A.* **2004**, *101*, 7931–7936.

[254] M. Terao, M. Kurosaki, M. M. Barzago, E. Varasano, A. Boldetti, A. Bastone, M. Fratelli, E. Garattini, 'Avian and canine aldehyde oxidases: Novel insights into the biology and evolution of molybdo-flavoenzymes', *J. Biol. Chem.* **2006**, *281*, 19748–19761.

[255] R. Harrison, 'Physiological roles of xanthine oxidoreductase', *Drug Metab. Rev.* **2004**, *36*, 363–375.

[256] R. Hille, 'The reaction mechanism of oxomolybdenum enzymes', *Biochim. Biophys. Acta* **1994**, *1184*, 143–169.

[257] S. Kitamura, K. Sugihara, S. Ohta, 'Drug-metabolizing ability of molybdenum hydroxylases', *Drug Metab. Pharmacokinet.* **2006**, *21*, 83–96.

[258] F. Lacy, D. A. Gough, G. W. Schmid-Schönbein, 'Role of xanthine oxidase in hydrogen peroxide production', *Free Radical Biol. Med.* **1998**, *25*, 720–727.

[259] C. Galbusera, P. Orth, D. Fedida, T. Spector, 'Superoxide radical production by allopurinol and xanthine oxidase', *Biochem. Pharmacol.* **2006**, *71*, 1747–1752.

[260] C. Beedham, 'Molybdenum hydroxylases as drug-metabolizing enzymes', *Drug Metab. Rev.* **1985**, *16*, 119–156.

[261] C. Beedham, 'The role of non-P450 enzymes in drug oxidation', *Pharm. World Sci.* **1997**, *19*, 255–263.

[262] G. Rastelli, L. Costantino, A. Albasini, 'A model of the interaction of substrates and inhibitors with xanthine oxidase', *J. Am. Chem. Soc.* **1997**, *119*, 3007–3016.

[263] D. O'Connor, P. Jones, M. S. Chambers, R. Maxey, H. J. Szekeres, N. Szeto, P. Scott-Stevens, A. M. Macleod, M. Braun, B. Cato, 'Aldehyde oxidase and its contribution to the metabolism of a structurally novel, functionally selective GABA$_A$ α5-subtype inverse agonist', *Xenobiotica* **2006**, *36*, 315–330.

[264] K. Sugihara, Y. Tayama, K. Shimomiya, D. Yoshimoto, S. Ohta, S. Kitamura, 'Estimation of aldehyde oxidase activity in vivo from conversion ratio of N^1-methylnicotinamide to pyridones, and interspecies variation of the enzyme activity in rats', *Drug Metab. Dispos.* **2006**, *34*, 208–212.

[265] Y. Moriwaki, T. Yamamoto, Y. Nasako, S. Takahashi, M. Suda, K. Hiroishi, T. Hada, K Higashino, 'In vitro oxidation of pyrazinamide and allopurinol by rat liver aldehyde oxidase', *Biochem. Pharmacol.* **1993**, *46*, 975–981.

[266] G. I. Panoutsopoulos, D. Kouretas, C. Beedham, 'Contribution of aldehyde oxidase, xanthine oxidase, and aldehyde dehydrogenase on the oxidation of aromatic aldehydes', *Chem. Res. Toxicol.* **2004**, *17*, 1368–1376.

[267] D. C. Lewis, T. Shibamoto, 'Relative metabolism of quinones to semiquinone radicals in xanthine oxidase system', *J. Appl. Toxicol.* **1989**, *9*, 291–295.

[268] D. Roy, B. Kalyanaraman, J. G. Liehr, 'Xanthine oxidase-catalyzed reduction of estrogen quinones to semiquinones and hydroquinones', *Biochem. Pharmacol.* **1991**, *42*, 1627–1631.

[269] O. Ueda, S. Kitamura, K. Ohashi, K. Sugihara, S. Ohta, 'Xanthine oxidase-catalyzed metabolism of 2-nitrofluorene, a carcinogenic air pollutant, in rat skin', *Drug Metab. Dispos.* **2003**, *31*, 367–372.

[270] R. I. Sanchez, S. Mesia-Vela, F. C. Kauffman, 'Challenges of cancer drug design: a drug metabolism perspective', *Curr. Cancer Drug Targets* **2001**, *1*, 1–32.

[271] P. Reigan, P. N. Edwards, A. Gbaj, C. Cole, S. T. Barry, K. M. Page, S. E. Ashton, R. W. A. Luke, K. T. Douglas, I. J. Stratford, M. Jaffar, R. A. Bryce, S. Freeman, 'Aminoimidazolylmethyluracil analogues as potent inhibitors of thymidine phosphorylase and their bireductive nitroimidazolyl prodrugs', *J. Med. Chem.* **2005**, *48*, 392–402.

[272] C. Beedham, J. Miceli, R. S. Obach, 'Ziprasidone metabolism, aldehyde oxidase, and clinical implications', *J. Clin. Psychopharmacol.* **2003**, *23*, 229–232.

[273] P. J. O'Brien, 'Peroxidases', *Chem.-Biol. Interact.* **2000**, *129*, 113–139.

[274] S. Tafazoli, P. J. O'Brien, 'Peroxidases: a role in the metabolism and side effects of drugs', *Drug Discov. Today* **2005**, *10*, 617–625.

[275] H. B. Dunford, 'One-electron oxidations by peroxidases', *Xenobiotica* **1995**, *25*, 725–733.

[276] J. P. Uetrecht, 'The role of leukocyte-generated reactive metabolites in the pathogenesis of idiosyncratic drug reactions', *Drug Metab. Rev.* **1992**, *24*, 299–366.

[277] J. R. Vane, Y. S. Bakhle, R. M. Botting, 'Cyclooxygenases 1 and 2', *Annu. Rev. Pharmacol. Toxicol.* **1998**, *38*, 97–120.

[278] J. R. Kiefer, J. L. Pawlitz, K. T. Moreland, R. A. Stegeman, W. F. Hood, J. K. Glerse, A. M. Stevens, D. C. Goodwin, S. W. Rowlinson, L. J. Marnett, W. C. Stallings, R. G. Kurumball, 'Structural insights into the stereochemistry of the cyclooxygenase reaction', *Nature* **2000**, *405*, 97–101.

[279] T. E. Eling, J. F. Curtis, 'Xenobiotic metabolism by prostaglandin H synthase', *Pharmacol. Ther.* **1992**, *53*, 261–273.

[280] T. E. Eling, D. C. Thompson, G. L. Foureman, J. F. Curtis, M. F. Hughes, 'Prostaglandin H synthase and xenobiotic oxidation', *Annu. Rev. Pharmacol. Toxicol.* **1990**, *30*, 1–45.

[281] R. Goldman, G. H. Claycamp, M. A. Sweetland, A. V. Sedlov, V. A. Tyurin, E. R. Kisin, Y. Y. Tyurnina, V. B. Ritov, S. L. Wenger, S. G. Grant, V. E. Kagan, 'Myeloperoxidase-catalyzed redox-cycling of phenol promotes lipid peroxidation and thiol oxidation in HL-60 cells', *Free Radical Biol. Med.* **1999**, *27*, 1050–1063.

[282] D. A. Eastmond, M. T. Smith, L. O. Ruzo, D. Ross, 'Metabolic activation of phenol by human myeloperoxidase and horseradish peroxidase', *Mol. Pharmacol.* **1986**, *30*, 674–679.

[283] J. Dai, A. L. Sloat, M. W. Wright, R. A. Manderville, 'Role of phenoxyl radicals in DNA adduction by chlorophenol xenobiotics following peroxidase activation', *Chem. Res. Toxicol.* **2005**, *18*, 771–779.

[284] L. G. Ganousis, D. Goon, T. Zyglewska, K. K. Wu, D. Ross, 'Cell-specific metabolism in mouse bone marrow stroma: studies of activation and detoxification of benzene metabolites', *Mol. Pharmacol.* **1992**, *42*, 1118–1125

[285] R. Snyder, C. C. Hedli, 'An overview of benzene metabolism', *Environ. Health Perspect.* **1996**, *104*, 1165–1171.

[286] R. V. Bhat, V. V. Subrahmanyam, A. Sadler, D. Ross, 'Bioactivation of catechol in rat and human bone marrow cells', *Toxicol. Appl. Pharmacol.* **1988**, *94*, 297–304

[287] R. J. Boatman, J. C. English, L. G. Perry, L. A. Fiorica, 'Covalent protein adducts of hydroquinone in tissues from rats: identification of quantification of sulfhydryl-bound forms', *Chem. Res. Toxicol.* **2000**, *13*, 853–860.

[288] A. S. Kalgutkar, D. K. Dalvie, J. P. O'Donnell, T. J. Taylor, D. C. Sahakian, 'On the diversity of oxidative bioactivation reactions on nitrogen-containing xenobiotics', *Curr. Drug Metab.* **2002**, *3*, 379–424.

[289] J. L. Maggs, D. Williams, M. Pirmohamed, B. K. Park, 'The metabolic formation of reactive intermediates from clozapine, a drug associated with agranulocytosis in man', *J. Pharmacol. Exp. Ther.* **1995**, *275*, 1463–1475.

[290] K. S. Smith, P. L. Smith, T. N. Heady, J. M. Trugman, W. D. Harman, T. L. Macdonald, 'In vitro metabolism of tolcapone to reactive intermediates: relevance to tolcapone liver toxicity', *Chem. Res. Toxicol.* **2003**, *16*, 123–128.

[291] L. J. Marnett, P. Wlodawer, B. Samuelsson, 'Co-oxygenation of organic substrates by the prostaglandin synthetase of sheep vesicular gland', *J. Biol. Chem.* **1975**, *250*, 8510–8517.

[292] P. J. Harvison, R. W. Egan, P. H. Gale, G. D. Christian, B. S. Hill, S. D. Nelson, 'Acetaminophen and analogs as cosubstrates and inhibitors of prostaglandin H synthase', *Chem.-Biol. Interact.* **1988**, *64*, 251–266.

[293] J. F. Curtis, K. Tomer, S. McGown, T. E. Eling, 'Prostaglandin H synthase-catalyzed ring oxygenation of 2-naphthylamine: evidence for two distinct oxidation pathways', *Chem. Res. Toxicol.* **1995**, *8*, 875–883.

[294] L. M. Winn, P. G. Wells, 'Evidence for embryonic prostaglandin H synthase-catalyzed bioactivation and reactive oxygen species-mediated oxidation of cellular macromolecules in phenytoin and benzo[a]pyrene teratogenesis', *Free Radical Biol. Med.* **1997**, *22*, 607–621.

[295] T. Patman, M. J. Wiley, P. G. Wells, 'Free radical-mediated oxidative DNA damage in the mechanism of thalidomide teratogenicity', *Nature Med.* **1999**, *5*, 582–585.

[296] M. J. Cox Rosemond, J. S. Walsh, 'Human carbonyl reduction pathways and a strategy for their study in vitro', *Drug Metab. Rev.* **2004**, *36*, 335–361.

[297] U. C. T. Oppermann, E. Maser, 'Molecular and structural aspects of xenobiotic carbonyl metabolizing enzymes. Role of reductases and dehydrogenases in xenobiotic phase I reactions', *Toxicology* **2000**, *144*, 71–81.

[298] E. Maser, 'Xenobiotic carbonyl reduction and physiological steroid oxidoreduction. The pluripotency of several hydroxysteroid dehydrogenases', *Biochem. Pharmacol.* **1995**, *49*, 421–440.

[299] G. Duester, J. Farrés, M. R. Felder, R. S. Holmes, J. O. Höög, X. Parés, B. V. Plapp, S. J. Yin, H. Jörnvall, 'Recommended nomenclature for the vertebrate alcohol dehydrogenase gene family', *Biochem. Pharmacol.* **1999**, *58*, 389–395.

[300] G. Duester, 'Families of retinoid dehydrogenases regulating vitamin A function', *Eur. J. Biochem.* **2000**, *267*, 4315–4324.

[301] H. Jörnvall, E. Nordling, B. Persson, 'Multiplicity of eukaryotic ADH and other forms', *Chem.-Biol. Interact.* **2003**, *143–144*, 255–261.

[302] B. L. Vallee, D. S. Auld, 'Zinc coordination, function and structure of zinc enzymes and other proteins', *Biochemistry* **1990**, *29*, 5647–5659.

[303] F. L. Gervasio, V. Schettino, S. Mangani, M. Krack, P. Carloni, M. Parrinello, 'Influence of outer-shell metal ligands on the structural and electronic properties of horse liver alcohol dehydrogenase zinc active site', *J. Phys. Chem.* **2003**, *107*, 6886–6892.

[304] M. Frezza, C. di Padova, G. Pozzato, M. Terpin, E. Baraona, C. S. Lieber, 'High blood alcohol levels in women', *N. Engl. J. Med.* **1990**, *322*, 95–99.

[305] M. Radel, D. Goldman, 'Pharmacogenetics of alcohol response and alcoholism: the interplay of genes and environmental factors in thresholds for alcoholism', *Drug Metab. Dispos.* **2001**, *29*, 489–494.

[306] V. Vasiliou, A. Pappa, T. Estey, 'Role of human aldehyde dehydrogenases in endobiotic and xenobiotic metabolism', *Drug Metab. Rev.* **2004**, *36*, 279–299.

[307] V. Vasiliou, A. Bairoch, K. F. Tipton, D. W. Nebert, 'Eukaryotic aldehyde dehydrogenase (*ALDH*) genes: human polymorphism, and recommended nomenclature based on divergent evolution and chromosomal mapping', *Pharmacogenetics* **1999**, *9*, 421–434; www.aldh.org.

[308] V. Vasiliou, A. Pappa, 'Polymorphisms of human aldehyde dehydrogenases', *Pharmacology* **2000**, *61*, 192–198.

[309] J. S. Rodriguez-Zavala, H. Weiner, 'Structural aspects of aldehyde dehydrogenase that influence dimer-tetramer formation', *Biochemistry* **2002**, *41*, 8229–8237.

[310] J. M. Jez, T. G. Flynn, T. M. Penning, 'A new nomenclature for the aldo-keto reductase superfamily', *Biochem. Pharmacol.* **1997**, *54*, 639–647; D. Hyndman, D. R. Bauman, V. V. Heredia, T. M. Penning, 'The aldo-keto reductase superfamily homepage', *Chem.-Biol. Interact.* **2003**, *143–144*, 621–631; www.med.upenn.edu/akr/.

[311] T. M. Penning, Y. Jin, S. Steckelbroeck, T. Lanisnik Rizner, M. Lewis, 'Structure-function of human 3α-hydroxy steroid dehydrogenases: genes and proteins', *Mol. Cell. Endocrinol.* **2004**, *215*, 63–72.

[312] H. K. Lin, C. F. Hung, M. Moore, T. M. Penning, 'Genomic structure of rat 3α-hydroxysteroid/dihydrodiol dehydrogenase (*3α-HSD/DD, AKR1C9*)', *J. Steroid Biochem. Mol. Biol.* **1999**, *71*, 29–39.

[313] T. Ozeki, Y. Takahashi, T. Kume, K. Nakayama, T. Yokoi, K. I. Nunoya, A. Hara, T. Kamataki, 'Co-operative regulation of the transcription of human dihydrodiol dehydrogenase *DD4*/aldo-keto reductase *AKR1C4* gene by hepatocyte nuclear factor (HNF)-4α/γ and HNF-1α', *Biochem. J.* **2001**, *355*, 537–544.

[314] F. P. Guengerich, H. Cai, M. McMahon, J. D. Hayesm T. R. Sutter, J. D. Groopman, Z. Deng, T. M. Harris, 'Reduction of aflatoxin B1 dialdehyde by rat and human aldo-keto reductases', *Chem. Res. Toxicol.* **2001**, *14*, 727–737.

[315] G. L. Forrest, B. Gonzalez, 'Carbonyl reductases', *Chem.-Biol. Interact.* **2000**, *129*, 21–40.

[316] A. Blum, A. Raum, H. J. Martin, E. Maser, ' Human 11β-hydroxysteroid dehydrogenase 1/carbonyl reductase: additional domains for membrane attachment', *Chem.-Biol. Interact.* **2001**, *130–132*, 749–759.

[317] M. E. Baker, 'Rat 3α-hydroxysteroid dehydrogenase: to oxidize or reduce, that is the question', *Endocrinology* **2006**, *147*, 1589–1590.

[318] S. S. Lakhman, D. Ghosh, J. B. Blanco, 'Functional significance of a natural allelic variant of human carbonyl reductase 3 (*CBR3*)', *Drug Metab. Dispos.* **2005**, *33*, 254–257.

[319] D. Ross, 'Quinone reductases multitasking in the metabolic world', *Drug Metab. Rev.* **2004**, *36*, 639–654.

[320] C. E. Foster, M. A. Bianchet, P. Talalay, M. Faig, L. M. Amzel, 'Structures of mammalian cytosolic quinone reductases', *Free Radical Biol. Med.* **2000**, *29*, 241–245.

[321] S. Chen, K. Wu, R. Knox, 'Structure–function studies of DT-diaphorase (NQO1) and NRH:quinone oxidoreductase (NQO2)', *Free Radical Biol. Med.* **2000**, *29*, 276–284.

[322] D. J. Long II, A. K. Jaiswal, 'NRH:quinone oxidoreductase 2 (NQO2)', *Chem.-Biol. Interact.* **2000**, *129*, 99–112.

[323] F. Vella, G. Ferry, P. Delagrange, J. A. Boutin, 'NRH:quinone reductase 2: an enzyme of surprises and mysteries', *Biochem. Pharmacol.* **2005**, *71*, 1–12.

[324] L. P. Olson, J. Luo, Ö. Almarsson, T. C. Bruice, 'Mechanism of aldehyde oxidation catalyzed by horse liver alcohol dehydrogenase', *Biochemistry* **1996**, *35*, 9782–9791.

[325] S. Ramaswamy, H. Eklund, B. V. Plapp, 'Structures of horse live alcohol dehydrogenase complexed with NAD+ and substituted benzyl alcohols', *Biochemistry* **1994**, *33*, 5230–5237.

[326] P. K. Agarwal, S. P. Webb, S. Hammes-Schiffer, 'Computational studies on the mechanism for proton and hydride transfer in liver alcohol dehydrogenase', *J. Am. Chem. Soc.* **2000**, *122*, 4803–4812.

[327] L. A. LeBrun, D. H. Park, S. Ramaswamy, B. V. Plapp, 'Participation of histidine-51 in catalysis by horse liver alcohol dehydrogenase', *Biochemistry* **2004**, *43*, 3014–3026.

[328] A. A. Klyosov, 'Kinetics and specificity of human liver aldehyde dehydrogenases toward aliphatic, aromatic, and fused polycyclic aldehydes', *Biochemistry* **1996**, *35*, 4457–4467.

[329] A. A. Klyosov, L. G. Rashkovetsky, M. K. Tahir, W. M. Keung, 'Possible role of liver cytosolic and mitochondrial aldehyde dehydrogenases in acetaldehyde metabolism', *Biochemistry* **1996**, *35*, 4445–4456.

[330] F. R. Fontaine, R. A. Dunlop, D. R. Petersen, P. C. Burcham, 'Oxidative bioactivation of crotyl alcohol to the toxic endogenous aldehyde crotonaldehyde: association of protein carbonylation with toxicity in mouse hepatocytes', *Chem. Res. Toxicol.* **2002**, *15*, 1051–1058.

[331] R. Lindahl, 'Aldehyde dehydrogenases and their role in carcinogenesis', *Crit. Rev. Biochem. Mol. Biol.* **1992**, *27*, 283–335.

[332] J. E. Patanella, J. S. Walsh, 'Oxidation of carbovir, a carbocyclic nucleoside, by rat liver cytosolic enzymes', *Drug Metab. Dispos.* **1992**, *20*, 912–919.

[333] W. Lenk, D. Löhr, J. Sonnenbichler, 'Pharmacokinetics and biotransformation of diethylene glycol and ethylene glycol in the rat', *Xenobiotica* **1989**, *19*, 961–979.

[334] E. D. Booth, O. Dofferhoff, P. J. Boogaard, W. P. Watson, 'Comparison of the metabolism of ethylene glycol and glycolic acid in vitro by precision-cut tissue slices from female rat, rabbit and human liver', *Xenobiotica* **2004**, *34*, 31–48.

[335] A. K. Sohlenius-Sternbeck, H. von Euler Chelpin, A. Orzechowski, M. M. Halldin, 'Metabolism of sameridine to monocarboxylated products by hepatocytes isolated from the male rat', *Drug Metab. Dispos.* **2000**, *28*, 695–700.

[336] J. J. R. Hermans, H. H. W. Thijssen, 'Stereoselective acetonyl side chain reduction of warfarin and analogs', *Drug Metab. Dispos.* **1992**, *20*, 268–274.

[337] S. J. Porter, A. A. Somogyi, J. M. White, 'Kinetics and inhibition of the formation of 6β-naltrexol from naltrexone in human liver cytosol', *Br. J. Clin. Pharmacol.* **2000**, *50*, 465–471.

[338] U. Breyer-Pfaff, K. Nill, 'Carbonyl reduction of naltrexone and dolasetron by oxidoreductases isolated from human liver cytosol', *J. Pharm. Pharmacol.* **2004**, *56*, 1601–1606.

[339] S. Yamano, F. Ichinose, T. Todaka, S. Toki, 'Purification and characterization of two major forms of naloxone reductase from rabbit liver cytosol, new members of aldo-keto reductase superfamily', *Biol. Pharm. Bull.* **1999**, *22*, 1038–1046.

[340] U. Breyer-Pfaff, H. J. Martin, M. Ernst, E. Maser, 'Enantioselectivity of carbonyl reduction of 4-methylnitrosamino-1-(3-pyridyl)-1-butanone by tissue fractions from human and rat liver and by enzymes isolated from human liver', *Drug Metab. Dispos.* **2004**, *32*, 915–922.

[341] H. J. Martin, U. Breyer-Pfaff, V. Wsol, S. Venz, S. Block, E. Maser, 'Purification and characterization of AKR1B10 from human liver: role in carbonyl reduction of xenobiotics', *Drug Metab. Dispos.* **2006**, *34*, 464–470; J. Dow, C. Berg, 'Stereoselectivity of the carbonyl reduction of dolasetron in rats, dogs and humans', *Chirality* **1995**, *7*, 342–348.

[342] B. Testa, 'Some chemical and stereochemical aspects of diethylpropion metabolism in man', *Acta Pharm. Suec.* **1973**, *10*, 441–454; M. Reist, L. H. Christiansen, P. Christoffersen, P. A. Carrupt, B. Testa, 'Low configurational stability of amfepramone and cathinone: Mechanism and kinetics of chiral inversion', *Chirality* **1995**, *7*, 469–473.

[343] T. M. Penning, 'Dihydrodiol dehydrogenase and its role in polycyclic aromatic hydrocarbon metabolism', *Chem.-Biol. Interact.* **1993**, *89*, 1–34.

[344] T. M. Penning, M. E. Burczynski, C. F. Hung, K. D. McCoull, N. T. Palackal, L. S. Tsuruda, 'Dihydrodiol dehydrogenases and polycyclic aromatic hydrocarbon activation: generation of reactive and redox active o-quinones', *Chem. Res. Toxicol.* **1999**, *12*, 1–18.

[345] N. T. Palackal, S. H. Lee, R. G. Harvey, I. A. Blair, T. M. Penning, 'Activation of polycyclic aromatic hydrocarbon trans-dihydrodiol proximate carcinogens by human aldo-keto reductase (AKR1C) enzymes and their functional overexpression in human lung carcinoma (A549) cells', *J. Biol. Chem.* **2002**, *277*, 24799–24808.

[346] N. T. Palackal, M. E. Burczynski, R. G. Harvey, T. M. Penning, 'The ubiquitous aldehyde reductase (AKR1A1) oxidizes proximate carcinogen trans-dihydrodiols to o-quinones: potential role in polycyclic aromatic hydrocarbon activation', *Biochemistry* **2001**, *40*, 10901–10910.

[347] T. M. Cho, R. L. Rose, E. Hodgson, 'In vitro metabolism of naphthalene by human liver microsomal cytochrome P450 enzymes', *Drug Metab. Dispos.* **2006**, *34*, 176–183.

[348] K. Sugiyama, T. C. Lin Wang, J. T. Simpson, L. Rodriguez, P. F. Kador, S. Sato, 'Aldose reductase catalyzes the oxidation of naphthalene-1,2-dihydrodiol for the formation of ortho-naphthoquinone', *Drug Metab. Dispos.* **1999**, *27*, 60–67.

[349] W. Xue, D. Warshawsky, 'Metabolic activation of polycyclic and heterocyclic aromatic hydrocarbons and DNA damage: a review', *Toxicol. Appl. Pharmacol.* **2005**, *206*, 73–93.

[350] T. M. Penning, S. T. Ohnishi, T. Ohnishi, R. G. Harvey, 'Generation of reactive oxygen species during the enzymatic oxidation of polycyclic aromatic hydrocarbons trans-dihydrodiols catalyzed by dihydrodiol dehydrogenase', *Chem. Res. Toxicol.* **1996**, *9*, 84–92.

[351] T. J. Monks, R. P. Hanzlik, G. M. Cohen, D. Ross, D. G. Graham, 'Quinone chemistry and toxicity', *Toxicol. Appl. Pharmacol.* **1992**, *112*, 2–16; J. L. Bolton, M. A. Trush, T. M. Penning, G. Dryherst, T. J. Monks, 'Role of quinones in toxicology', *Chem. Res. Toxicol.* **2000**, *13*, 135–160.

[352] K. D. McCoull, D. Rindgen, I. A. Blair, T. M. Penning, 'Synthesis and characterization of polycyclic aromatic hydrocarbons *o*-quinone depurinating N7-guanine adducts', *Chem. Res. Toxicol.* **1999**, *12*, 237–246.

[353] K. Seite, M. Murata, K. Hirakawa, Y. Deyashiki, S. Kawanishi, 'Oxidative DNA damage induced by benz[a]anthracene dihydrodiols in the presence of dihydrodiol dehydrogenase', *Chem. Res. Toxicol.* **2004**, *17*, 1445–1451.

[354] J. Jarabak, R. G. Harvey, 'Studies on three reductases which have polycyclic aromatic hydrocarbon quinones as substrates', *Arch. Biochem. Biophys.* **1993**, *303*, 394–401.

[355] G. D. Buffinton, K. Öllinger, A. Brunmark, E. Cadenas, 'DT-Diaphorase-catalyzed reduction of 1,4-naphthoquinone derivatives and glutathionyl-quinone conjugates. Effect of substituents on autoxidation rates', *Biochem. J.* **1989**, *257*, 561–571.

[356] T. J. Monks, S. S. Lau, 'Toxicology of quinone-thioethers', *Crit. Rev. Toxicol.* **1992**, *22*, 243–270.

[357] P. Joseph, D. J. Long II, A. J. P. Klein-Szanto, A. K. Jaiswal, 'Role of NAD(P)H : quinone oxidoreductase I (DT diaphorase) in protection against quinone toxicity', *Biochem. Pharmacol.* **2000**, *60*, 207–214.

[358] R. Munday, 'Activation and detoxification of naphthoquinones by NAD(P)H : quinone oxidoreductase', *Methods Enzymol.* **2004**, *382*, 364–380.

[359] L. J. Chen, E. H. Lebetkin, L. T. Burka, 'Metabolism and disposition of juglone in male F 344 rats', *Xenobiotica* **2005**, *35*, 1019–1034.

[360] R. J. Riley, P. Workman, 'DT-Diaphorase and cancer chemotherapy', *Biochem. Pharmacol.* **1992**, *43*, 1657–1669.

[361] S. M. Bailey, A. D. Lewis, R. J. Knox, L. H. Patterson, G. R. Fisher, P. Workman, 'Reduction of the indoloquinone anticancer drug EO9 by purified DT-diaphorase: a detailed kinetic study and analysis of metabolites', *Biochem. Pharmacol.* **1998**, *56*, 613–621.

[362] G. R. Fisher, P. L. Gutierrez, M. A. Oldcorne, L. H. Patterson, 'NAD(P)H (quinone acceptor) oxidoreductase (DT-diaphorase)-mediated two-electron reduction of anthraquinone-based agents and generation of hydroxyl radicals', *Biochem. Pharmacol.* **1992**, *43*, 575–585.

[363] M. AbuKhader, J. Heap, C. De Matteis, B. Kellam, S. W. Doughty, N. Minton, M. Paoli, 'Binding of the anticancer prodrug CB1954 to the activating enzyme NQO2 revealed by the crystal structure of their complex', *J. Med. Chem.* **2005**, *48*, 7714–7719.

[364] D. Siegel, H. Beall, C. Senekowitsch, M. Kasai, H. Arai, N. W. Gibson, D. Ross, 'Bioreductive activation of mitomycin C by DT-diaphorase', *Biochemistry* **1992**, *31*, 7879–7885.

[365] R. M. Phillips, M. A. Naylor, M. Jaffar, S. W. Doughty, S. A. Everett, A. G. Breen, G. A. Choudry, I. J. Stratford, 'Bioreductive activation of a series of indolquinones by human DT-diaphorase: structure–activity relationships', *J. Med. Chem.* **1999**, *42*, 4071–4080.

[366] P. M. Loadman, R. M. Phillips, L. E. Lim, M. C. Bibby, 'Pharmacological properties of a new aziridinylbenzoquinone, RH1 (2,5-aziridinyl-3-(hydroxymethyl)-6-methyl-1,4-benzoquinone), in mice', *Biochem. Pharmacol.* **2000**, *59*, 831–837.

[367] R. M. Phillips, M. Jaffar, D. J. Maitland, P. M. Loadman, S. D. Shnyder, G. Steabs, P. A. Cooper, A. Race, A. V. Patterson, I. J. Stratford, 'Pharmacological and biological evaluation of a series of substituted 1,4-naphthoquinone bioreductive drugs', *Biochem. Pharmacol.* **2004**, *68*, 2107–2116.

Part 3

Reactions of Hydrolysis and Their Enzymes

This *Part 3* of our biochemical introduction to drug metabolism [1] presents the reactions of hydrolysis and their enzymes. *Parts 1* and *2* have also been published as reviews [2]. As we shall see, reactions of hydrolysis are a major focus of interest in the metabolism of drugs, prodrugs, and other xenobiotics. Yet, even recent monographs on drug metabolism give only partial coverage of metabolic hydrolysis, and its great biochemical diversity and pharmacological significance. The only exception is the 800-page book co-authored by one of us a few years ago, where the diversity of hydrolases and the richness of their substrates are explained and illustrated [3]. Previous writings where reactions of hydrolysis are also presented include two recent chapters in multi-volume works [4][5].

As we have already commented in *Part 1* [1], the metabolism of drugs and other xenobiotics is often a *biphasic process* in which the compound may first undergo a functionalization reaction (phase-I reaction). This introduces or unveils a functional group such as a hydroxy or amino group suitable for coupling with an endogenous molecule or moiety in a second metabolic step known as a conjugation reaction (phase-II reaction). In a number of cases, phase-I metabolites may be excreted prior to conjugation, while many xenobiotics can be directly conjugated. Furthermore, reactions of functionalization may follow some reactions of conjugation, *e.g.*, some conjugates are hydrolyzed and/or oxidized prior to their excretion. Whereas metabolic reactions of oxidation and reduction are universally recognized as being functionalizations, there has been some debate whether reactions of hydrolysis should be classified as conjugations. This is a view we strongly oppose. Indeed, reactions of hydrolysis fulfil none of the criteria that characterize conjugation reactions, since *a*) they are not catalyzed by transferases (EC 2) but by *hydrolases* (EC 3); and *b*) H_2O is not an endogenously synthesized molecule or moiety linked covalently to a cofactor (*Part 4*). On the other hand, metabolic reactions of hydrolysis modify pre-existing functional groups in their substrates and thus meet the definition of functionalization reactions [1][2].

The H_2O molecule, either as a reactant or a product, plays an important role in the metabolism of innumerable endogenous and exogenous compounds. Water is of course a by-product of some metabolic redox reactions, *e.g.*, reactions catalyzed by monooxygenases [2]. However, the focus of this *Part 3* is on non-redox reactions involving H_2O as a reactant or as a product.

As a reactant, the water molecule can be added to a substrate molecule either to cleave it into two molecules, or to yield a single product. Perhaps arbitrarily, we designate cleavage into two molecules as *hydrolysis* (*e.g.*, production of an acid and an alcohol from an ester), and incorporation of H_2O to form a single metabolite as *hydration* (*e.g.*, ring opening of epoxides). However, such a neat nomenclature is not always followed in practice, witness the ring opening of lactones resulting from the addition of a H_2O molecule, which is commonly referred to as hydrolysis rather than hydration in analogy with the same reaction occurring in acyclic carboxylic acid esters.

Non-redox reactions where *water is formed as a product* are reactions of *dehydration*. Such reactions can occur between two substrate molecules, or they can involve two functional groups in a single substrate, either creating a new bond (*e.g.*, lactone formation), or transforming a single into a double bond. In xenobiotic metabolism, dehydration is usually in dynamic equilibrium with hydrolysis or hydration and is of relatively modest significance (see *Chapt. 3.8*).

A complicating characteristic of metabolic reactions of hydrolysis is the fact that they may be partly *nonenzymatic*. Indeed, the nucleophilicity of H_2O makes it an active reagent, especially in synergy with catalysts such as H^+, HO^-, or a base. As a result, the metabolic hydrolysis of some labile esters such as acetates may contain a nonenzymatic component which should not be neglected, especially in prodrug design. And when imines or oximes are hydrolyzed to ketones, there may be no enzyme involved. Some examples will be stressed in this review, but the reader should be aware that nonenzymatic reactions are by no means a rarity in drug metabolism, as illustrated also by the reactivity of glutathione (*Part 4*) [3][6].

Part 3   Reactions of Hydrolysis and Their Enzymes

3.1.   A Survey of Hydrolases

3.2.   The Hydrolysis of Carboxylic Esters

3.3.   Synthetic Reactions of Esterases

3.4.   The Hydrolysis of Amides and Peptides

3.5.   Hydrolytic Ring Opening

3.6.   The Hydrolysis of Esters of Inorganic Acids

3.7.   The Hydration of Epoxides

3.8.   Miscellaneous Reactions

Fig. 3.1. The structure of *Part 3* is as logical as we could have it, with its manifold material organized into eight *Chapters*. First, we shall examine the various hydrolases involved in the hydrolysis of ester and amide groups (*Chapt. 3.1*). There is much in the literature on the hydrolysis of carboxylic esters, especially attempts to design useful prodrugs; *Chapt. 3.2* will be dedicated to a survey of medicinally relevant carboxylic ester groups. The short *Chapt. 3.3* will draw attention to the fact that some carboxylic ester hydrolases are also able to catalyze reactions of xenobiotic esterification or transesterification. The hydrolysis of amides in the broader sense (acyclic amides, lactams, and peptides) is another vast domain (*Chapt. 3.4*). The reversible hydrolysis of lactones, and the hydrolysis of labile rings such as oxazolidines, will form the material of *Chapt. 3.5*. Esters of inorganic acids, particularly phosphates and phosphonates, receive much attention in medicinal chemistry as drugs, prodrugs, or conjugates; their hydrolysis will be presented in *Chapt. 3.6*, while conjugations with phosphoric acid (phosphorylations) will be treated in *Part 4*. This will be followed by another major topic, namely epoxide hydrolases and their reactions (*Chapt. 3.7*). *Part 3* will end with a few unclassifiable reactions of hydration and dehydration, some enzymatic and others not (*Chapt. 3.8*).

3.1. A Survey of Hydrolases

3.1.1. A Selection of Hydrolases (EC 3) with Known or Potential Activity toward Xenobiotic Substrates

EC 3.1 Acting on Ester Bonds	
EC 3.1.1 Carboxylic ester hydrolases	EC 3.1.1.1 Carboxylesterase EC 3.1.1.2 Arylesterase EC 3.1.1.6 Acetylesterase EC 3.1.1.8 Cholinesterase EC 3.1.1.10 Tropinesterase EC 3.1.1.13 Sterol esterase EC 3.1.1.25 1,4-Lactonase EC 3.1.1.55 Acetylsalicylate deacetylase EC 3.1.1.60 Bis(2-ethylhexyl)phthalate esterase EC 3.1.1.67 Fatty-acyl-ethyl-ester synthase
EC 3.1.2 Thiolester hydrolases	EC 3.1.2.3 Succinyl-CoA hydrolase EC 3.1.2.7 Glutathione thiolesterase EC 3.1.2.20 Acyl-CoA hydrolase
EC 3.1.3 Phosphoric monoester hydrolases	EC 3.1.3.1 Alkaline phosphatase EC 3.1.3.2 Acid phosphatase

Figs. 3.2–3.6. We enter the huge domain of hydrolases by way of *Figs. 3.2–3.6* which present a selection of enzymes with *known or potential activity* toward xenobiotic substrates. The classification here is that of the *Nomenclature Committee of the International Union of Biochemistry and Molecular Biology* (*IUBMB*) [7], and a wealth of information will open to the reader who follows the links [8]. The classification of the IUBMB is based mainly on the *nature of the enzymatic reactions*, on the *type of substrates*, and, to a lesser extent, on the *catalytic mechanism* and on the protein sequence. Some of the enzymes in this list are of major significance for us (they are shown in red) and will receive much attention, for example, the *carboxylesterases*, *cholinesterase*, *paraoxonase*, and the *epoxide hydrolases* (which we shall not meet again until *Chapt. 3.7*). Other enzymes are important as a group, namely the *peptidases* (EC 3.4) and the *amidases* (EC 3.5), but too little is known about their specific involvement in xenobiotic metabolism to allow an extensive presentation. However, the main message in *Figs. 3.2–3.6* is the immense variety of hydrolases that do or might act on drugs and other xenobiotics. Clearly, an unlimited territory remains unexplored.

EC 3.1.4 Phosphoric diester hydrolases	EC 3.1.4.1 Phosphodiesterase I
EC 3.1.6 Sulfuric ester hydrolases	EC 3.1.6.1 Arylsulfatase EC 3.1.6.2 Steryl-sulfatase
EC 3.1.7 Diphosphoric monoester hydrolases	EC 3.1.7.1 Prenyl-diphosphatase EC 3.1.7.3 Monoterpenyl-diphosphatase
EC 3.1.8 Phosphoric triester hydrolases	EC 3.1.8.1 Paraoxonase EC 3.1.8.2 Diisopropyl-fluorophosphatase
EC 3.2 Glycosylases	
EC 3.2.1 Glycosidases, *i.e.*, hydrolyzing *O*- and *S*-glycosyl compounds	EC 3.2.1.21 β-Glucosidase EC 3.2.1.31 β-Glucuronidase
EC 3.2.2 Hydrolyzing *N*-glycosyl compounds	EC 3.2.2.1 Purine nucleosidase
EC 3.3 Acting on Ether Bonds	
EC 3.3.2 Ether hydrolases	EC 3.3.2.9 Microsomal epoxide hydrolase EC 3.3.2.10 Soluble epoxide hydrolase
EC 3.4 Acting on Peptide Bonds (Peptidases)	
EC 3.4.11 Aminopeptidases	EC 3.4.11.1 Leucyl aminopeptidase EC 3.4.11.2 Membrane alanyl aminopeptidase

Fig. 3.3.

EC 3.4.11 Aminopeptidases (cont.)	EC 3.4.11.7 Glutamyl aminopeptidase EC 3.4.11.21 Aspartyl aminopeptidase
EC 3.4.13 Dipeptidases	EC 3.4.13.18 Cytosol nonspecific dipeptidase EC 3.4.13.19 Membrane dipeptidase
EC 3.4.14 Dipeptidyl-peptidases and tripeptidyl-peptidases	EC 3.4.14.1 Dipeptidyl-peptidase I EC 3.4.14.2 Dipeptidyl-peptidase II EC 3.4.14.4 Dipeptidyl-peptidase III EC 3.4.14.5 Dipeptidyl-peptidase IV
EC 3.4.16 Serine-type carboxypeptidases	EC 3.4.16.2 Lysosomal Pro-Xaa carboxypeptidase EC 3.4.16.5 Carboxypeptidase C
EC 3.4.17 Metallocarboxypeptidases	EC 3.4.17.1 Carboxypeptidase A EC 3.4.17.2 Carboxypeptidase B EC 3.4.17.3 Lysine carboxypeptidase EC 3.4.17.10 Carboxypeptidase E EC 3.4.17.12 Carboxypeptidase M EC 3.4.17.15 Carboxypeptidase A2 EC 3.4.17.20 Carboxypeptidase U
EC 3.4.18 Cysteine-type carboxypeptidases	EC 3.4.18.1 Cathepsin X
EC 3.4.19 Omega peptidases	EC 3.4.19.1 Acylaminoacyl-peptidase

Fig. 3.4.

EC 3.4.21 Serine endopeptidases	EC 3.4.21.1 Chymotrypsin
	EC 3.4.21.2 Chymotrypsin C
	EC 3.4.21.4 Trypsin
	EC 3.4.21.7 Plasmin
	EC 3.4.21.36 Pancreatic elastase
EC 3.4.22 Cysteine endopeptidases	EC 3.4.22.1 Cathepsin B
	EC 3.4.22.16 Cathepsin H
	EC 3.4.22.27 Cathepsin S
	EC 3.4.22.41 Cathepsin F
	EC 3.4.22.42 Cathepsin O
	EC 3.4.22.52 Calpain-1
EC 3.4.23 Aspartic endopeptidases	EC 3.4.23.1 Pepsin A
	EC 3.4.23.4 Chymosin
	EC 3.4.23.5 Cathepsin D
	EC 3.4.23.34 Cathepsin E
EC 3.4.24 Metalloendopeptidases	EC 3.4.24.11 Neprilysin
	EC 3.4.24.15 Thimet oligopeptidase
	EC 3.4.24.16 Neurolysin
	EC 3.4.24.18 Meprin A
	EC 3.4.24.59 Mitochondrial intermediate peptidase
EC 3.4.25 Threonine endopeptidases	EC 3.4.25.1 Proteasome endopeptidase complex

Fig. 3.5.

EC 3.5 Acting on C–N Bonds, Other Than Peptide Bonds	
EC 3.5.1 In linear amides	EC 3.5.1.4 Amidase
	EC 3.5.1.11 Penicillin amidase
	EC 3.5.1.13 Aryl-acylamidase
	EC 3.5.1.14 Aminoacylase
	EC 3.5.1.19 Nicotinamidase
	EC 3.5.1.32 Hippurate hydrolase
	EC 3.5.1.39 Alkylamidase
	EC 3.5.1.50 Pentanamidase
EC 3.5.2 In cyclic amides	EC 3.5.2.1 Barbiturase
	EC 3.5.2.2 Dihydropyrimidinase
	EC 3.5.2.4 Carboxymethylhydantoinase
	EC 3.5.2.6 β-Lactamase
	EC 3.5.2.16 Maleimide hydrolase
EC 3.5.5 In nitriles	EC 3.5.5.1 Nitrilase
	EC 3.5.5.5 Arylacetonitrilase
	EC 3.5.5.7 Aliphatic nitrilase
EC 3.10 Acting on S–N Bonds	
	EC 3.10.1.2 Cyclamate sulfohydrolase

Fig. 3.6.

3.1.2. Esterases (EC 3.1)

Enzyme ID Card: Carboxylesterases

EC Numbers	EC 3.1.1.1
Enzyme subclass and sub-subclass	*EC 3.1* Hydrolases acting on ester bonds // *EC 3.1.1* Carboxylic ester hydrolases
Systematic name	Carboxylic-ester hydrolase
Synonyms	Ali-Esterases; B-Esterases; *etc.*
Genes families; Human enzymes	*CES1, CES2, CES3, CES4*, and *CES5*; CES1A1 (hCE-1), CES2 (hCE-2), CES3, acyl-CoA hydrolase
Catalytic triad	Ser, Glu, His (belong to serine hydrolases)
Subcellular localization	Endoplasmic reticulum, also cytoplasm and lysosomes
Organs (highest levels)	Liver, brain, lung, small intestine, skin, macrophages
Exogenous substrates	Numerous aliphatic and aromatic esters, also some amides
Endogenous substrates	Vitamin A esters, fatty acid esters
Miscellaneous	Inhibited by organophosphates and bis-nitrophenyl phosphate (BNPP). Occur as monomers, homotrimers, or homohexamers.

Figs. 3.7–3.11. Here, a number of esterases are selected for special attention, criteria of selection being their significance in xenobiotic metabolism and the information available [3][5][7–10]. The first Enzyme ID card (*Fig. 3.7*) presents the *carboxylesterases*, perhaps the most important hydrolases in our context [11–14]. The enzymes have serine as the critical catalytic group (see *Sect. 3.1.4*), and hence are irreversibly inhibited by organophosphates. *Fig. 3.8* summarizes the *arylesterases/paraoxonases*, also grouped under the label of *A-esterases* to indicate that they hydrolyze organophosphorous insecticides and nerve gases, rather than being inhibited by them as are the B-esterases (carboxylesterases). Arylesterases and paraoxonases hydrolyze preferentially aromatic esters and organophosphate triesters, respectively [3][7][8][15–25]. These enzymes are not to be confused with phosphatases (phosphoric monoester hydrolases, see *Fig. 3.10*) and phosphodiesterases [26]. *Fig. 3.9* brings us to the *cholinesterases*, with two enzymes showing a clear preference for basic esters [3][27–32]. While the physiologically all-important acetylcholinesterase has a very narrow specificity, butyrylcholinesterase recognizes many xenobiotic esters. *Fig. 3.10* calls attention to the many *phosphoric monoester hydrolases*, some of which such as acid phosphatase are known to hydrolyze xenobiotic phosphomonoesters [3]. *β-D-Glucuronidase* (*Fig. 3.11*) is another interesting enzyme [3] the role of which will be considered in *Chapt. 3.8*. Other enzymes could also have been highlighted here and will be mentioned when necessary, *e.g.*, *sterol esterase* [33] and the *peroxisomal acyl-coenzyme A thioesterases/hydrolases* [34], which we shall encounter in *Part 4* when discussing the conjugation of xenobiotic acids. A special mention must be made here of a protein that is not an enzyme yet, which cannot be ignored when discussing xenobiotic ester hydrolysis, namely *serum albumin* (see also *Fig. 3.24*) [3][31][35].

Enzyme ID Card: Arylesterases/Paraoxonases	
EC Numbers	EC 3.1.1.2 and EC 3.1.8.1
Enzyme subclass and sub-subclasses	*EC 3.1* Hydrolases acting on ester bonds // *EC 3.1.1* Carboxylic ester hydrolases // *EC 3.1.8* Phosphoric triester hydrolases
Systematic name	Aryl-ester hydrolase; Aryltriphosphate dialkylphosphohydrolase
Synonyms	A-Esterases, serum aryldialkylphosphatases
Gene root and human enzymes	*PON* ⇒ PON1, PON2, PON3 (hPNO3)
Cofactor	Calcium-dependent metalloenzyme
Subcellular localization	Extracellular space (PON1); membrane-bound (PON2)
Organs (highest levels)	Liver, serum; various tissues (PON2)
Exogenous substrates	Aryl esters; aryl dialkyl phosphates; organophosphates; lactones (PON3)
Endogenous substrates	Toxic oxidized lipids
Miscellaneous	Inhibition by heavy metals (*e.g.*, Hg^{2+}). Many polymorphisms for PON1. PON1 and PON3 in HDL are important to prevent atherosclerosis.

Fig. 3.8.

Enzyme ID Card: Cholinesterases	
EC Numbers	EC 3.1.1.7 (Acetylcholinesterase); EC 3.1.1.8 (Cholinesterase)
Enzyme subclass and sub-subclass	*EC 3.1* Hydrolases acting on ester bonds // *EC 3.1.1* Carboxylic ester hydrolases
Systematic names	EC 3.1.1.7 Acetylcholine acetylhydrolase; EC 3.1.1.8 Acylcholine acylhydrolase
Synonyms	EC 3.1.1.7 True cholinesterase; EC 3.1.1.8 Pseudocholinesterase, butyrylcholinesterase
Human genes	EC 3.1.1.7 *ACHE* ; EC 3.1.1.8 *BCHE*
Catalytic triad	Ser, Glu, His (belong to serine hydrolases)
Organs (highest levels)	EC 3.1.1.7 Synapses, erythrocytes; EC 3.1.1.8 Plasma, most cells except erythrocytes
Substrates	EC 3.1.1.7 Narrow specificity for AcChol and analogous acetate esters; EC 3.1.1.8 Broad specificity (mainly basic esters)
Miscellaneous	Homotetramers composed of two dimers. Inhibited by organo-phosphates, physostigmine. EC 3.1.1.7 one known rare variant; EC 3.1.1.8 mutant alleles known.

Fig. 3.9.

Enzyme ID Card: Acid Phosphatase	
EC Numbers	EC 3.1.3.2
Enzyme subclass and sub-subclass	*EC 3.1* Hydrolases acting on ester bonds // *EC 3.1.3* Phosphoric monoester hydrolases
Systematic name	Phosphate-monoester phosphohydrolase (acid optimum)
Synonyms	Acid phosphomonoesterase
Some relevant human genes and enzymes	*ACP1* ⇒ LMW-PTP (low MW cytosolic acid phosphatase), *ACP2* ⇒ LAP (lysosomal acid phosphatase), *ACP6* ⇒ PACPL1 (lysophosphatidic acid phosphatase type 6)
Classification	LMW-PTP: in the low MW phosphotyrosine protein phosphatase family; LAP, PACPL1: in the histidine acid phosphatase family
Subcellular localization	Cytosol (LMW-PTP); lysosomes (LAP); probably secreted (PACPL1)
Organs (highest levels)	LMW-PTP: muscles (adipocytes), blood (red cells); LAP, PACPL1: a variety of organs and tissues (*e.g.*, kidney, heart, small intestine, muscle, liver, prostate, testis, ovary)
Substrates	Broad specificity for phosphoric monoesters

Fig. 3.10.

3.1.3. Glycosylases (EC 3.2)

Enzyme ID Card: β-Glucuronidase

EC Numbers	EC 3.2.1.31
Enzyme subclass and sub-subclass	*EC 3.2* Glycosylases // *EC 3.2.1* Glycosidases, *i.e.*, hydrolyzing *O*- and *S*-glycosyl compounds
Systematic name	β-D-Glucuronoside glucuronosohydrolase
Synonyms	*exo*-β-D-Glucuronidase; ketodase
Human gene	*GUSB*
Catalytic site	Catalytic nucleophile/base = Glutamic acid; catalytic proton donor = Glutamic acid (belongs to the glycosyl hydrolase family 2)
Subcellular localization	Lysosomes, endoplasmic reticulum, blood serum
Organs (highest levels)	Ubiquitous (fibroblasts), colon (also microflora), placenta
Substrates	β-Glucuronides and β-glucosides
Miscellaneous	Defects in *GUSB* are the cause of an autosomal recessive disorder (mucopolysaccharidosis type VII, Sly syndrom). Homotetramer.

Fig. 3.11.

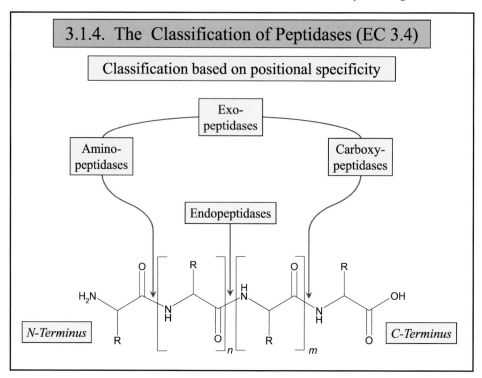

Fig. 3.12. Enzymes known as *peptidases* (= peptide hydrolases = proteases) cleave peptide bonds in peptides *and* proteins [3][7][8]. They represent a field of huge diversity and complexity which many biochemists and molecular biologists are hard at work to explore and clarify [36]. Their involvement in drug metabolism is known in a number of cases, suspected or merely guessed in others. The classification adopted by the *Nomenclature Committee* of the *IUBMB* divides peptidases into classes and sub-classes according to their *positional specificity* in the cleavage of the peptide link in the substrate [7][8]. As explained here, peptidases are divided into *exopeptidases*, which remove one amino acid (or a very few, see *Fig. 3.13*), and *endopeptidases* (previously also known as proteinases), which catalyze the cleavage of peptide bonds away from either end of the polypeptide chain. Exopeptidases are further subdivided into enzymes hydrolyzing at the N-terminus or the C-terminus. Thus, *aminopeptidases* cleave a single amino acid from the N-terminus. *Carboxypeptidases* hydrolyze a single amino acid from the C-terminus of the peptide chain.

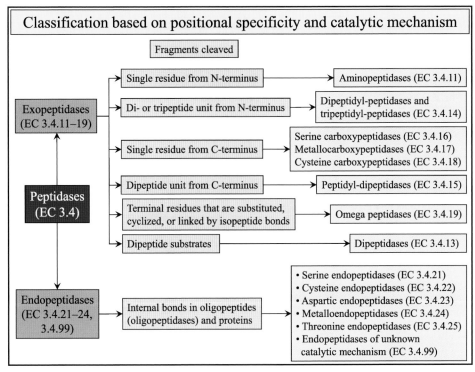

Fig. 3.13. This *Figure* expands the previous one by further subdividing the peptidase classes [3][7][8]. Thus, the peptidases removing a dipeptide or a tripeptide from the N-terminus are the *dipeptidyl-peptidases* and *tripeptidyl-peptidases*, respectively. *Carboxy-peptidases* are further separated into three groups based on their catalytic mechanism, *i.e.*, serine carboxypeptidases, metallocarboxypeptidases, and cysteine carboxypepti-dases. The peptidases splitting off a dipeptide unit from the C-terminus are classified as *peptidyl-dipeptidases*. *Omega peptidases* are enzymes which remove terminal residues that are substituted, cyclized, or linked by isopeptide bonds (peptide linkages other than those of α-carboxy to α-amino groups). Enzymes cleaving dipeptides are simply called *dipeptidases*. *Endopeptidases* are subdivided into six classes based on their catalytic site and mechanism (see caption to *Fig. 3.14*), *i.e.*, serine endopeptidases, cysteine endopeptidases, aspartic endopeptidases, metalloendopeptidases, and the more recently described threonine endopeptidases. The sixth class contains the endopeptidases of yet unknown catalytic mechanism.

Classification based on sequence, with mammalian examples	
Aspartic peptidases (catalytic residues: Asp plus others)	
Clan AA (endopeptidases)	Family A1 (*e.g.*, pepsin, renin and some cathepsins)
Clan AD (endopeptidases)	Family A22 (*e.g.*, impas 1 peptidase)
Cysteine peptidases (catalytic residues: Cys, His, plus others)	
Clan CA (mostly endopeptidases)	Family C1 (*e.g.*, some cathepsins, dipeptidyl-peptidase I) Family C2 (*e.g.*, calpain-2) Family C12 (*e.g.*, ubiquitinyl hydrolase-L1) Family C19 (*e.g.*, ubiquitin-specific peptidase 14)
Clan CD (endopeptidases)	Family C14 (*e.g.*, caspase-1)
Metallopeptidases (catalytic center: Zn^{2+} bound to *His-Glu*-Xaa-Xaa-*His* [HEXXH] or comparable motifs)	
Clan MA (exo- and endopeptidases)	Family M1 (*e.g.*, aminopeptidase N) Family M2 (*e.g.*, angiotensin-converting enzyme) Family M3 (*e.g.*, thimet oligopeptidase) Family M10 (*e.g.*, matrix metallopeptidase-1) Family M13 (*e.g.*, neprilysin)
Clan MC (carboxypeptidases)	Family M14 (*e.g.*, carboxypeptidases A1, A2, A6, B, U)

Figs. 3.14 and 3.15. Another, more recent and more general way to classify peptidases is based on their amino acid sequence, *i.e.*, on evolutionary relationships [36], as illustrated here with mammalian enzymes. Evolutionary relationships are established using algorithms which compare the amino acid sequences and characterize similarities. The peptidases are separated into *catalytic types* according to the chemical nature of the group responsible for catalysis. The major catalytic types are thus *serine* and the related *threonine, cysteine, aspartic, metallo*, and as yet *unclassified peptidases*. The term *family* designates a set of homologous peptidases within a particular type. As explained in the MEROPS Database [36b,c], '*The homology is shown by a significant similarity in amino acid sequence either to the type peptidase of the family, or to another protein that has already been shown to be homologous to the type peptidase, and thus a member of the family. The relationship must exist in the peptidase unit at least. A family can contain a single peptidase if no homologues are known, and a single gene product such as a virus polyprotein can contain more than one peptidase each assigned to a different family*'. Each peptidase family is named with a letter denoting the catalytic type (*e.g.*, A, C, M, S, T, or U) followed by a unique number. Some families are divided into subfamilies when there is evidence of an ancient divergence within the family, *e.g.*, S1A, S1B [36b].

Related families are congregated into clans. As further explained, '*A clan contains all the modern-day peptidases that have arisen from a single evolutionary origin of peptidases. It represents one or more families that show evidence of their evolutionary relationship by their similar tertiary structures, or when structures are not available, by the order of catalytic-site residues in the polypeptide chain and often by common* sequence motifs around the catalytic residues. Each clan is identified with two letters, the first representing the catalytic type of the families included in the clan (with the letter 'P' being used for a clan containing families of more than one of the catalytic types serine, threonine and cysteine)'. Some clans are divided into subclans when there is evidence of an ancient divergence within the clan [36b].

This evolutionary classification has a rational basis, since to date the catalytic mechanism has been established for many peptidases, and the elucidation of their amino acid sequence is progressing rapidly.

The classification has the major advantage of fitting well with the catalytic types, but has no direct connection with the types of reaction listed in *Fig. 3.13*. For example, the families in clan MA include aminopeptidases (in families M1 and M61), carboxy-peptidases (in families M2 and M32), peptidyl-dipeptidases (in family M2), oligopep-tidases (in families M3 and M13), and endopeptidases (in families M4, M10, M12 and others). Nevertheless, the families in clan MA are united by the presence of a *His-Glu*-Xaa-Xaa-*His* (= HEXXH) motif in which the two His residues are zinc ligands and the Glu has a catalytic function. The motif HEXXH occurs in non-peptidase proteins too, but a more specific motif can be defined for clan MA. This larger motif is Xaa-Xbb-Xcc-*His-Glu*-Xbb-Xbb-*His*-Xbb-Xdd in which Xaa is hydrophobic or Thr, Xbb is uncharged, Xcc is any amino acid except Pro, and Xdd is hydrophobic [37].

Classification based on sequence, with mammalian examples (cont.)	
Metallopeptidases (cont.)	
Clan ME	Family M16 (*e.g.*, nardilysin)
Clan MF (aminopeptidases)	Family M17 (*e.g.*, leucyl aminopeptidase)
Clan MH (amino- and carboxypeptidases)	Family M20 (*e.g.*, carnosine dipeptidases I and II)
Clan MJ	Family M19 (*e.g.*, membrane dipeptidase)
Serine peptidases (catalytic residues: His, Asp, Ser, or Ser, Lys)	
Clan SC (endo- and exopeptidases)	Family S9 (*e.g.*, dipeptidyl-peptidase IV, acylaminoacyl-peptidase and prolyl oligopeptidase) Family S28 (*e.g.*, lysosomal Pro-Xaa carboxypeptidase)
Clans of mixed (Cys, Ser, Thr) catalytic type	
Clan PA (endopeptidases)	Family S1 (*e.g.*, chymotrypsin A, trypsins [serine peptidases: His, Asp, Ser]
Clan PB (endopeptidases)	Family T1 (proteasome peptidases)
Clan PC	Family C26 (*e.g.*, gamma-glutamyl hydrolase [a cysteine peptidase: Cys, His])

Fig. 3.15.

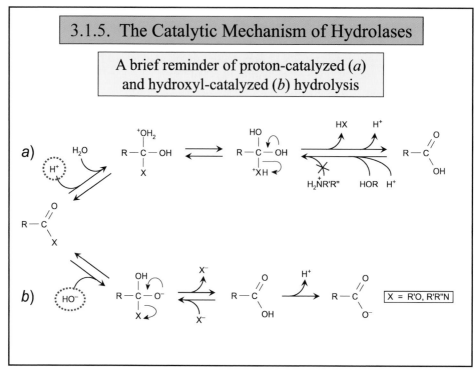

Fig. 3.16. Before discussing the mechanism of cleavage of carboxylic esters and amides by hydrolases, some chemical principles are worth recalling. The *chemical hydrolysis* of carboxylic derivatives can be catalyzed by an acid or a base, the mechanisms being that of addition–elimination *via* a *tetrahedral intermediate*. A general scheme of ester and amide hydrolysis is presented here. In *proton-catalyzed hydrolysis* (specific acid-catalyzed hydrolysis) (*a*), protonation of the carbonyl O-atom leads to a polarization of the carbonyl group, facilitating the addition of the nucleophile, *i.e.*, a H_2O molecule. The acid-catalyzed hydrolysis of esters is reversible because the alcohol or phenol is nucleophilic, whereas that of amides is irreversible because the released amine is protonated in acidic solution and hence has considerably reduced nucleophilicity. In *hydroxyl-catalyzed hydrolysis* (specific base-catalyzed hydrolysis) (*b*), the tetrahedral intermediate is formed by the addition of a nucleophilic HO^- ion. This reaction is irreversible for esters and amides, since the carboxylate ion formed is deprotonated in basic solutions, and hence cannot add the nucleophilic alcohol, phenol or amine. The reactivity of the ester or amide toward a particular nucleophile depends on *1*) the relative electron-donating or withdrawing power of the substituents on the carbonyl group, and *2*) the relative ability of the $-OR'$ or $-NR'R''$ moiety to act as a leaving group. Thus, electronegative substituents accelerate hydrolysis, and esters are more readily hydrolyzed than amides.

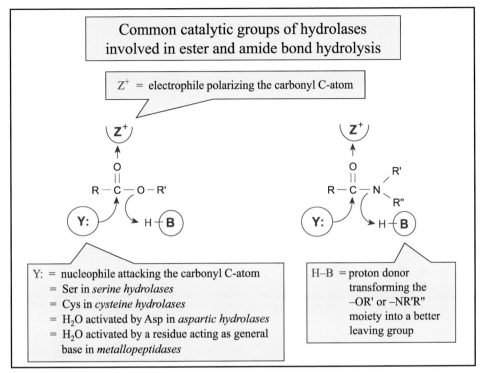

Fig. 3.17. The *enzymatic hydrolysis* of carboxylic derivatives is far more effective than chemical hydrolysis. For example, subtilisin (EC 3.4.21.62) accelerates the hydrolysis of amide bonds at least 10^9- to 10^{10}-fold, due to a large decrease in the free energy of the transition state. All hydrolases include the following three catalytic features in their active site which enormously accelerate rates of hydrolysis. First, they contain an *electrophilic component* (Z^+) which increases the polarization of the carbonyl group in the substrate. Second, they use a *nucleophile* (Y:) to attack the carbonyl C-atom, leading to the formation of a tetrahedral intermediate. And finally, they use a *proton donor* (H−B) to transform the −OR' or −NR'R'' moiety into a better leaving group. These three catalytic functionalities are similar in all hydrolytic enzymes, but the actual functional groups that will perform them differ among hydrolases [3]. Based on the structures of their catalytic sites and as seen in *Figs. 3.14* and *3.15*, hydrolases can be divided into five classes, namely *a*) *serine hydrolases* and *b*) the comparable *threonine hydrolases* where Y: is the OH group of Ser or Thr, respectively; *c*) *cysteine hydrolases* where Y: is the thiol group of Cys; finally *d*) *aspartic hydrolases*, and *e*) *metallohydrolases* (to which the similarly acting calcium-dependent hydrolases can be added), which act by activating (*i.e.*, rendering more nucleophilic) a *H₂O molecule* and allowing it to attack the substrate. In the two last classes, no covalent complex is formed with the enzyme. Hydrolases of yet unknown catalytic mechanism also exist.

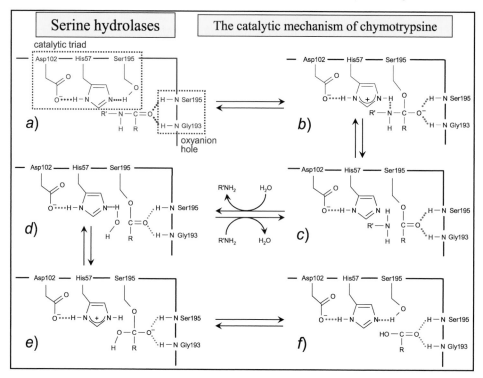

Fig. 3.18. The *catalytic mechanism* of *serine hydrolases* is similar to that of *threonine hydrolases* and *cysteine hydrolases*. All serine hydrolases possess a *catalytic triad* (*Ser-Asp-His* or *Ser-Glu-His*; see *Figs. 3.7* and *3.9*) [38], and a so-called *oxanion hole* (Z$^+$ in *Fig. 3.17*) formed by backbone NH groups. The major catalytic steps (reversible binding, acylation, and deacylation [3][38–40]) can be summarized as shown here using the peptidase chymotrypsin (EC 3.4.21.1) as a prototypical example. This general mechanism is true for all serine hydrolases, be they esterases, amidases, or peptidases. The catalytic cycle begins with the formation of a *non-covalent Michaelis complex* between enzyme and substrate (*Step a*) (non-covalent bonds are in red). *Nucleophilic attack* of the substrate carbonyl C-atom by the OH group of the catalytic serine (here Ser195; Y: in *Fig. 3.17*) forms a covalent tetrahedral intermediate (*Step b*). Transfer of the Ser195 hydroxy H-atom to an imidazole N-atom of His57 is essential. This transfer is facilitated by Asp102 the carboxylate group of which properly orients His57, ensures its appropriate tautomeric form, and stabilizes the positively charged form of His57 in the transition state. The backbone NH groups of Gly193 and Ser195 (*the oxanion hole*) polarize the carbonyl group, further facilitating nucleophilic attack and then stabilizing the resulting oxanion. In *Step c*, the imidazolium H-atom (H−B in *Fig. 3.17*) is transferred to the N-atom of the amide bond which is then cleaved, leaving an acyl–enzyme intermediate. *Deacylation*, the next step in this sequence (*Step d*), occurs when a *molecule of H$_2$O* enters the reaction and substitutes for the amine component. Thus, imidazole activates the H$_2$O molecule by general base catalysis leading to another tetrahedral intermediate (*Step e*). This tetrahedral intermediate decomposes in turn and liberates the carboxylic acid and the free enzyme (*Step f*).

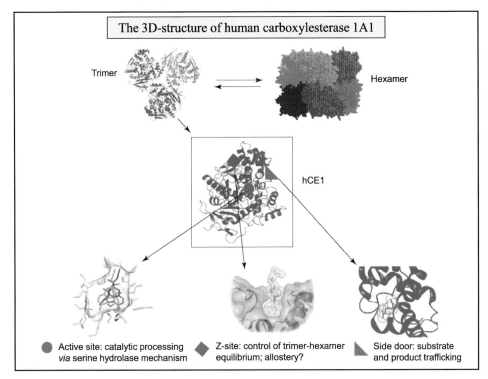

Fig. 3.19. To achieve a better understanding of serine hydrolases, we now look at the *three-dimensional (3D) structure* of a carboxylesterase [40][41]. The ID Card of carboxylesterases (*Fig. 3.7*) mentions that these enzymes occur as monomers, trimers, and hexamers. Rabbit CES and human CES1A1 in their active form have been shown to be glycoproteins. X-Ray crystallographic studies have revealed that they form trimers. In addition, the human enzyme exists in a *trimer ⇌ hexamer equilibrium*, a hexamer consisting of two stacked trimers. Each protein monomer contains three ligand binding sites. The *active site* (*red dot*) contains the catalytic triad and facilitates the docking of substrates. In some cases, substrates dock in more than one orientation simultaneously, as shown here for the opiate antagonist naloxone (the two *green* and *gold* molecules in the lower left corner). The Z-site (*blue lozenge*) is a *ligand-binding groove* which controls the trimer ⇌ hexamer equilibrium of the enzyme, perhaps by playing an allosteric role. It is relatively nonspecific in binding ligands and is shown here with the estrogen receptor modulator tamoxifen, an anticancer drug, bound (*yellow* molecule). The 'side-door' site (*magenta triangle*) appears to be an exit gate to the catalytic site which could facilitate the release of product, as illustrated here for a fatty acid (*cyan* molecule in the lower right corner). It is also postulated that this gate may allow the entrance of substrates. (Reproduced from [39] by permission from *Elsevier*)

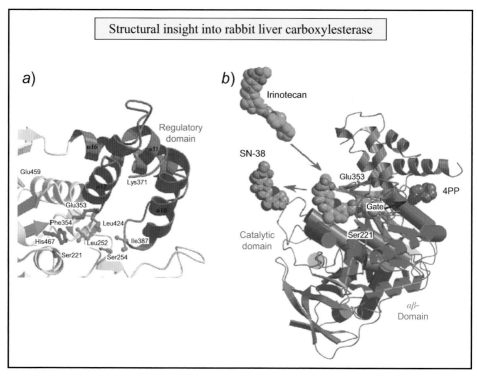

Fig. 3.20. This fascinating *Figure* [41] reveals some details of rabbit carboxylesterase in action. The left side (*a*) shows the *regulatory domain* composed of helices $\alpha9$, $\alpha10$, $\alpha11$, and $\alpha14$ (in *red*), the *catalytic triad* (Ser221, Glu353, and His 467, in *green*), and the gate residues (Leu252, Ser254, Ile387, and Leu424, in *cyan*). Residues that mark the beginning and end of the disordered regions are also labeled (Phe354, Lys371, and Glu 459). The right side (*b*) shows the entire monomeric structure and the proposed motion path of a substrate and its metabolite. The substrate here is *irinotecan* (in *orange*), an antitumor prodrug carbamate whose structure and metabolites we will encounter in *Fig. 3.32*. The substrate enters from the top of the catalytic gorge and fits well into the active site. Note in particular the close proximity between the ester group (the two O-atoms in *red*) and the catalytic Ser221. After cleavage, the active phenol metabolite (SN-38, in *magenta*) leaves *via* the catalytic gorge, while the promoiety product (4-piperidinopiperidine, 4PP, in *purple*) moves past the gate residues and docks temporarily next to the regulatory domain. (Reprinted from [41] by permission from *Macmillan Publishers Ltd.*)

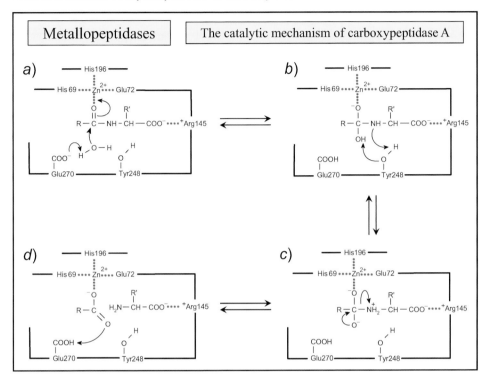

Fig. 3.21. In serine hydrolases (*Fig. 3.18*), an activated H_2O molecule enters the catalytic cycle in a later step to hydrolyze the covalent intermediate. As explained, *metallohydrolases* and aspartic hydrolases do not form a covalent complex with the substrate, but they act by rendering more nucleophilic a *H_2O molecule* and allowing it to attack the substrate. This activation is mediated by a residue acting as general base (*e.g.*, Glu, His, Lys, Arg, or Tyr). The *metal cation* acts as an electrophilic catalyst by orienting and *polarizing the carbonyl (or phosphoryl) O-atom in the substrate*. One of the best known metallopeptidases is pancreatic *carboxypeptidase A* (EC 3.4.17.1) which cleaves the C-terminal peptide bond, or the ester bond of peptides having a free C-terminal carboxy group. The catalytically important Zn^{2+} ion is ligated as shown. This His-Glu-His Zn^{2+}-binding motif indirectly plays the role of the oxyanion hole present in serine and cysteine hydrolases. A number of residues bind the substrate, whose C-terminal carboxylate group interacts with the guanidinium group of Arg145. A simplified representation of the postulated *mechanism* of carboxypeptidase is shown here [3][36a][42]. In *Step a*, the catalytically essential Glu270 initiates a general-base-catalyzed attack of the H_2O molecule on the carbonyl C-atom of the amide bond; this produces a tetrahedral intermediate (*Step b*) whose NH will be protonated, and its OH group deprotonated, by the OH group of Tyr248. The resulting tetrahedral zwitterion (*Step c*) undergoes cleavage of the C−N bond, release of the shortened peptide, and protonation plus release of the C-terminal amino acid (*Step d*).

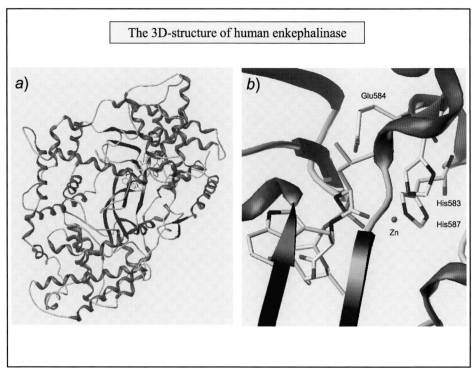

Fig. 3.22. *Neprilysin* (enkephalinase; endopeptidase-24.11; neutral endopeptidase; NEP; EC 3.4.24.11; a member of the peptidase family M13) bears considerable resemblance to other Zn-containing metallopeptidases. It is an oligopeptidase which hydrolyzes enkephalins and a range of other active peptides. Enkephalins are endogenous ligands of opiate receptors, and the prolongation of their action by inhibition of this enzyme has been extensively explored as an approach for pain treatment. The catalytic residues in human enkephalinase are Glu584, Asp650, His711, and Arg717. Binding of the Zn^{2+} cation is contributed mainly by His583, His587, Glu646, and His711, which are part of the His-Glu-Xaa-Xaa-His Zn^{2+}-binding motif. The left side of this 3D image of human enkephalinase obtained by X-ray crystallography shows the structure of the entire protein (*a*). A close-up view (*b*) reveals the Zn^{2+} cation and two of the binding residues (His583 and His587). The catalytic Glu584 is also clearly visible [43].

3.2. The Hydrolysis of Carboxylic Esters

3.2.1. Esters Containing Simple –OR or RCO– Moieties

Esters of medicinal interest containing simple –OR moieties

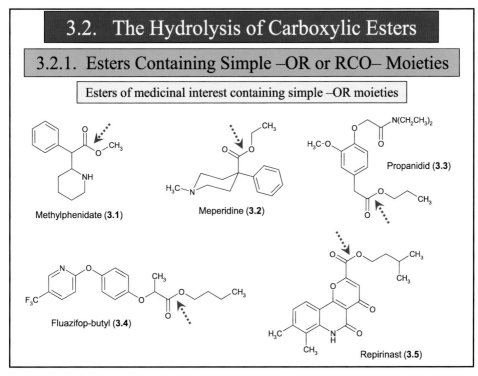

Fig. 3.23. We now leave enzymes in the background, and begin a presentation of the various types of substrates and reactions carried out by hydrolases. *Chapt. 3.2* is dedicated to the hydrolysis of carboxylic esters, where we discuss first the cleavage of simple alkyl and acyl groups, followed by the cleavage of functionalized moieties [3][14]. This *Figure* exemplifies the hydrolysis of medicinally relevant esters featuring a simple – OR moiety. As such, these esters undergo metabolic hydrolysis to a different extent. *Methylphenidate* (**3.1**), a representative *methyl ester*, is a psychoactive drug used as the racemic *threo*-diastereoisomer. Its major metabolic route is by deesterification, but the reaction is relatively slow in human blood at 37° and only moderately enantioselective; both plasma and red blood cells are active [44]. The synthetic opioid *meperidine* (**3.2**; pethidine) is an *ethyl ester* whose metabolism shows analogies and differences with that of methylphenidate. In particular, meperidine is not hydrolyzed in the blood of humans and other animal species. The reaction occurs mainly in the liver, the human enzyme being CES1A1 [45]. Higher alkyl esters are also cleaved. Thus, *propanidid* (**3.3**), a *propyl ester*, is a short-acting anesthetic agent whose duration of action is controlled by its rate of hydrolysis. *Fluazifop-butyl* (**3.4**), a butyl ester, is a herbicide which is rapidly hydrolyzed by human liver carboxylesterases located in the endoplasmic reticulum and cytoplasm. Plasma esterase activity was *ca.* one-hundredth of that in liver microsomes and cytosol, with little activity in the red blood cells [3][10]. *Repirinast* (**3.5**), an *isopentyl ester*, is an antiallergic prodrug whose active metabolite (the acid) reaches peak concentrations in humans *ca.* 1 h after oral administration [46].

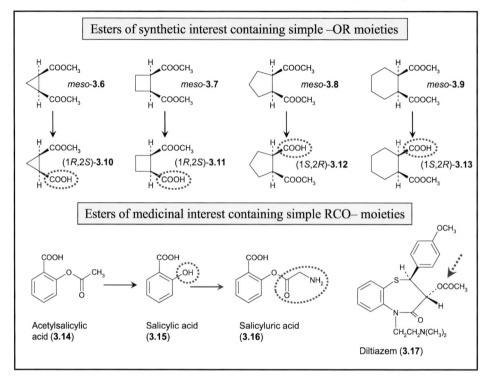

Fig. 3.24. Enzymatic ester hydrolysis is also of interest in synthetic chemistry, allowing, among others, enantiomerically pure chiral synthons to be prepared. The examples shown here are cis-*cycloalkane-1,2-dicarboxylates*, **3.6**, **3.7**, **3.8** and **3.9**. They are *achiral* due to a plane of symmetry (hence their designation as *meso*-stereoisomers [47]), but their monoester metabolites are chiral, allowing *product-enantioselective hydrolysis*. Indeed, substrates **3.6** and **3.7** were converted to the corresponding monoesters **3.10** and **3.11**, respectively, with high enantioselectivity; high but inverse enantioselectivity was seen for the hydrolysis of **3.9**. The cyclopentane homologue **3.8** represented the turning point in the series, its hydrolysis to **3.12** occurring with low enantioselectivity [48]. Moving now to *esters containing simple RCO– moieties*, one cannot escape *acetylsalicylic acid* (**3.14**; aspirin), whose primary metabolite is salicylic acid (**3.15**). Extensive kinetic data have been published on the chemical hydrolysis of aspirin [49a]. Following oral administration, acetylsalicylic acid undergoes a significant first-pass hydrolysis in the intestinal wall and liver, followed by extensive hydrolysis in the blood (serum and red cells), such that no unchanged drug is detectable in the urine of patients whatever the administered dose [49b]. The main human enzymes involved are microsomal and cytosolic carboxylesterases, plasma cholinesterase, and red blood cell arylesterases; serum albumin and nonenzymatic hydrolysis appear to contribute a small percentage of the total salicylic acid formed [3]. The further metabolism of salicylic acid is mainly *via* conjugation with glycine to salicyluric acid (**3.16**; see *Part 4*). *Diltiazem* (**3.17**) is also an acetate, but derived from an alcohol rather than from a phenol like acetylsalicylic acid. The compound is extensively metabolized in humans and animals, with hydrolysis as a major route [3][50].

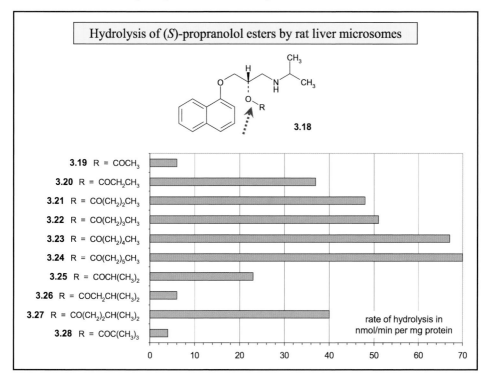

Fig. 3.25. An unexpectedly large number of publications have appeared on the hydrolysis of esters of the β-blocker propranolol (= 1-[(1-methylethyl)amino]-3-(naphthalen-1-yloxy)propan-2-ol). While there is little therapeutic justification for prodrugs of propranolol, these studies make for nice academic exercises and reveal some informative qualitative structure–hydrolysis relationships. For example, a large series of alkanoates of propranolol was prepared and examined for their *in vitro* enantioselective hydrolysis in rat preparations [51]. Our presentation here is limited to the active *(S)-propranolol* (**3.18**; R = H), and its *linear and branched alkanoates, i.e.,* **3.19**–**3.28**, as hydrolyzed by rat liver microsomes. As shown, the hydrolysis of the *linear alkanoates*, **3.19**–**3.24**, increased with increasing chain length. *Branching (i.e., **3.25**–**3.28**) decreased the rate of hydrolysis, a common observation due to steric shielding of the target carbonyl C-atom. This effect was modest when branching was distant from the carbonyl group (*i.e.*, **3.27**), and strong in the case of the highly hindered pivaloyl ester (*i.e.*, **3.28**). The isovaleryl ester, **3.26**, would be expected to be hydrolyzed faster than the isobutanoate ester, **3.25**, and its low rate of hydrolysis is difficult to explain. The hydrolysis of the corresponding esters of (*R*)-propranolol was *ca.* half that of the (*S*)-enantiomers. Hydrolysis in rat plasma was one to two orders of magnitude slower, with the opposite enantioselectivity.

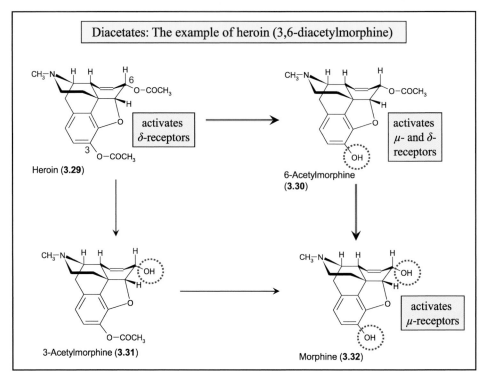

Fig. 3.26. An example of particular importance is *heroin* (**3.29**; 3,6-diacetylmorphine) [3][52][53]. Following *i.v.* administration to human subjects, most of the dose was recovered in the urine as 6-acetylmorphine, morphine, and their glucuronides. Only traces of the parent compound were excreted. Thus, *in vivo* hydrolysis of heroin in humans involves preferentially the 3-Ac group (*i.e.*, the acetylated phenol group), and only then the 6-acetyl group (*i.e.*, the acetylated alcohol group). Studies in human plasma and aqueous buffers confirmed the faster hydrolysis of the 3-Ac moiety. In pH 7.4 buffers at 37°, chemical hydrolysis of the 3-Ac ester group occurs with a half-life of *ca.* 33 h, whereas the hydrolysis of 6-acetylmorphine (**3.30**) to morphine (**3.32**) is slower by one order of magnitude. In human blood, only 6-acetylmorphine was formed from heroin, with no 3-acetylmorphine (**3.31**) or morphine being found. In human plasma at 37°, heroin hydrolysis to 6-acetylmorphine occurs with half-lives of some minutes, cholinesterase being the responsible enzyme. These and other results tend to indicate that the hydrolysis of 6-acetylmorphine to morphine is due to tissue carboxylesterases, in particular cerebral enzymes. The metabolism of heroin is of interest in connection with its *pharmacological activities*. Earlier binding studies to the opiate μ-receptor led to the belief that heroin was a prodrug acting through its metabolites 6-acetylmorphine and morphine. However, heroin is now known to activate δ-*receptors*, whereas morphine activates μ-*receptors* and 6-acetylmorphine acts at both receptor types [54]. Thus, the pharmacodynamic profile of heroin results from both direct and metabolite-mediated effects.

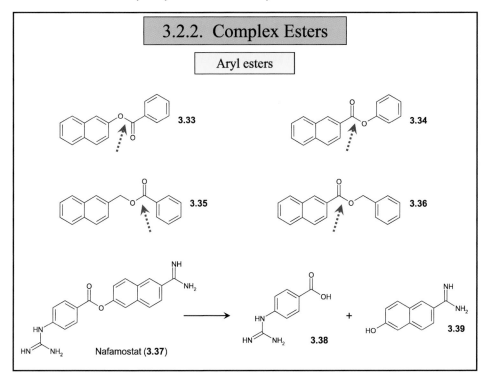

Fig. 3.27. Much information has been gained on the hydrolysis of carboxylic esters with more complex structures than those containing a simple −OR or RCO− moiety. Nevertheless, few useful *structure–metabolism relations* have emerged, excepting some general trends which will come to light in these pages [14]. One such trend is found when comparing the hydrolysis of structurally analogous alkyl and aryl esters. For example, the hydrolysis of *naphthalen-2-yl benzoate* (**3.33**) was two- to threefold faster than that of *phenyl naphthalene-2-carboxylate* (**3.34**) in human and rat liver S9 fraction (*i.e.*, microsomes plus cytosol, see *Part 1*) and in other biological preparations [55]. Furthermore, inserting a CH_2 group between the O-atom and the aromatic ring to yield **3.35** and **3.36** led consistently to a three- to fivefold drop in the rates of hydrolysis. Such results may be explained in part by a direct relation between the rate of enzymatic hydrolysis and the *acidity of the leaving phenol or alcohol*. However, enzymatic factors also play a determining role and may sometimes render impossible any attempt at rationalization. An adequate demonstration of the complexity of enzymatic factors is provided by *nafamostat* (**3.37**), a potent inhibitor of various serine peptidases used in the treatment of acute pancreatitis and disseminated intravascular coagulation. The drug is inactivated by hydrolysis to 4-guanidinobenzoic acid (**3.38**) and 6-amidino-naphthalen-2-ol (**3.39**), a reaction catalyzed in humans by *arylesterase* in erythrocytes and plasma, *carboxylesterase 2* in liver microsomes, and a *long-chain acyl-coenzyme A hydrolase* (presumably palmitoyl-CoA hydrolase, EC 3.1.2.2) in liver cytosol [56].

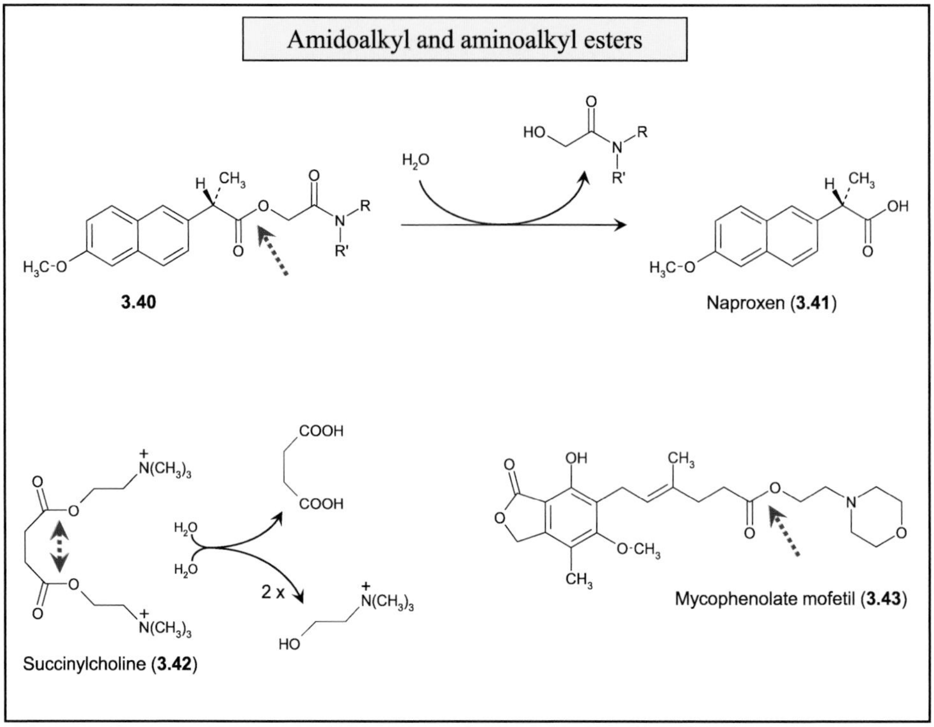

Fig. 3.28. Amidoalkyl and aminoalkyl esters are of noteworthy interest in the design of prodrugs (see *Part 5*). Thus, interesting results have been reported for glycolamide (=2-hydroxyacetamide)-derived esters of *nonsteroidal anti-inflammatory drugs* (NSAIDs) [57], as exemplified here with N,N-*dialkylglycolamide prodrugs*, **3.40**, of naproxen (**3.41**; note that naproxen is the (+)-(*S*)-enantiomer as shown). Whereas the methyl esters of NSAIDs were hydrolyzed very slowly in human plasma (half-lives of 5–150 h), the hydrolysis of the esters derived from glycolamide proceeded rapidly with half-lives in the order of minutes. The nature of the acyl moiety strongly influenced the rate of hydrolysis (500-fold difference between the smallest and the largest acid). And so did the *N,N*-dialkyl groups, a valuable feature in prodrug design. *Aminoalkyl esters* are also known to be readily hydrolyzed in human plasma, most likely by cholinesterase. A typical example is *succinylcholine* (**3.42**), a curarimimetic agent which is rapidly inactivated to succinic acid and choline by plasma cholinesterase, with a half-life of *ca.* 4 min [3][31]. This fast inactivation classifies succinylcholine as a soft drug, although the discovery of this agent predates by decades the concept of *soft drugs* (see *Part 5*). Our last example is that of *mycophenolate mofetil* (**3.43**), an immuno-suppressant prodrug which in humans is rapidly and completely absorbed orally, before being extensively hydrolyzed presystemically to the active mycophenolic acid [58].

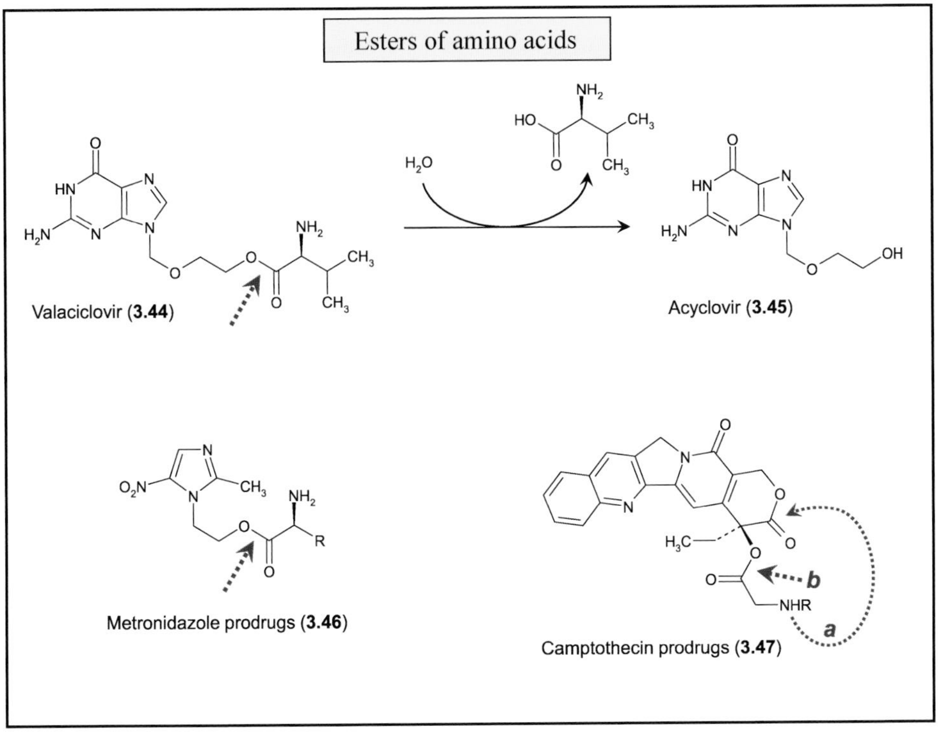

Fig. 3.29. A number of published examples of prodrugs (see *Part 5*) contain an α-*amino-acyl moiety*. This is explained by the lack of toxicity of these natural compounds, an improved solubility of the prodrug, the large range in lipophilicity covered by natural amino acids, and the further diversity allowed by attaching substituents to the $-NH_2$ group. An interesting example is provided by *valaciclovir* (**3.44**), the L-valine ester derived from the antiherpetic drug *acyclovir* (**3.45**) [59]. Valaciclovir showed favorable pharmacokinetic behavior in the rat and monkey. Interestingly, the rat liver enzyme that hydrolyzes valaciclovir has been shown to be a newly described hydrolase of unknown physiological function having a high selectivity for various amino acid esters of acyclovir and differing from typical esterases and peptidases. Similarly, a number of *α-amino-acyl metronidazole prodrugs* (**3.46**; R = side chain of amino acid) were compared for their chemical and serum-catalyzed hydrolysis [60]. The amino acids used for esterification included alanine (Ala), glycine (Gly), isoleucine (Ile), leucine (Leu), lysine (Lys), phenylalanine (Phe), and valine (Val). Under physiological conditions of pH and temperature, half-lives of hydrolysis in human serum ranged from 4.5 min for the Phe ester to 96 h for the Ile ester. Furthermore, the rate of enzymatic hydrolysis was correlated with the rate of HO⁻-catalyzed hydrolysis of the protonated prodrugs, suggesting a marked electronic control in both the chemical and enzymatic reactions. Our last example are glycyl prodrugs of the antitumor agent *camptothecin* (**3.47**; R = H or CH_3) [61], whose objective is to prolong release and improve tumor targeting. Activation occurs nonenzymatically by intramolecular rearrangement followed by cleavage of the promoiety and ultimately effective release of the active lactone.

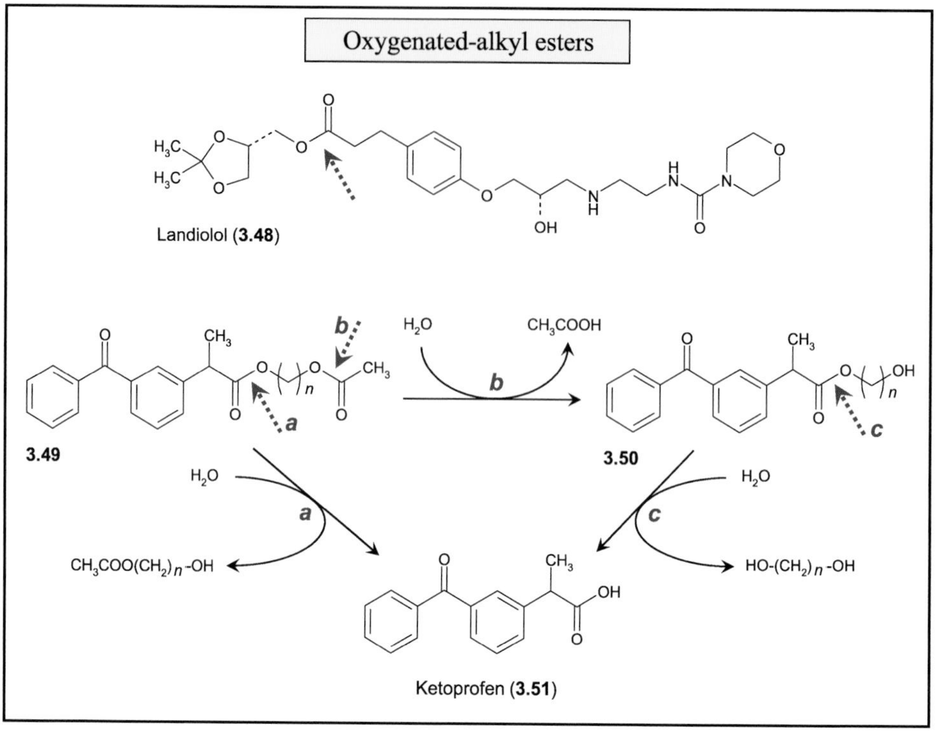

Fig. 3.30. Oxygenated alkyl groups are found in a number of carboxylic esters of medicinal interest. Here, we look at a few examples of *non-acidic alkyl groups*, while esters of diacids are discussed in the next *Figure*. Landiolol (**3.48**) is of interest in this context [62]. Inspection of the central and morpholino-bearing (*right-hand*) side of its chemical structure reveals a β_1-receptor blocking motif, whereas the dioxolanyl-bearing (*left-hand*) side with its ester group is more unusual. And indeed, the compound is a *soft drug*, a useful concept to be developed in *Part 5*. As such, landiolol is a highly active β_1-selective blocker, but very fast hydrolysis is programmed in its metabolically labile ester function. The resulting metabolite is a carboxylic acid whose high polarity is incompatible with any adrenoceptor activity. Low- and high-dose infusion of the drug to healthy human volunteers yielded a *half-life of 3.5 min* due to hydrolysis by plasma cholinesterase and liver carboxylesterases. The lower part of the *Figure* shows *ketoprofen acetoxyalkyl esters* (**3.49**; $n=1–4$). Ketoprofen is a racemic anti-inflammatory drug, and these prodrugs were prepared to investigate the influence of lipophilicity on dermal delivery [63]. The half-life of hydrolysis in human plasma varied from 4 min ($n=1$) to 44 min ($n=3$) when disappearance of the substrate was monitored. Appearance of ketoprofen (**3.51**) was up to three times slower than disappearance of the acetoxyalkyl esters, since its formation was partly direct (*Reaction a*), and partly indirect *via* the intermediate *hydroxyalkyl ester* **3.50** (*Reactions b* and *c*).

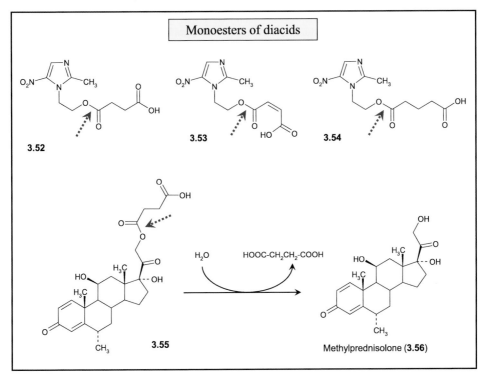

Fig. 3.31. *Monoesters of diacids* represent a special case, as illustrated by a number of potential or marketed prodrugs. One example that attracted marked attention for prodrug design is the antimicrobial *metronidazole* (see also *Fig. 3.29*) [64]. Under physiological conditions, its *hemisuccinate ester*, **3.52**, was hydrolyzed with half-lives of 600–700 h in phosphate buffer and in human plasma, indicating the absence of enzymatic catalysis in this biological medium. Under the same conditions, similar results were obtained with the *hemimaleinate* **3.53**, with half-lives ($t_{1/2}$) of *ca.* 250–350 h. In contrast, the *hemiglutarate* **3.54** was hydrolyzed much faster in human plasma ($t_{1/2}$ *ca.* 16 h) than in phosphate buffer ($t_{1/2}$ *ca.* 800 h). This provides valuable but fragmentary information on the substrate selectivity of human plasma cholinesterase. Another example is provided by *methylprednisolone hemisuccinate* (**3.55**), a clinically useful, soluble prodrug (as the sodium salt) of the corticoid methylprednisolone (**3.56**) [65]. Shelf-lives in commercial solutions at room temperature are high (>2 years), and hydrolysis in human plasma is slow due to the absence of carboxylesterases. In contrast, the prodrug is rapidly activated by hepatic carboxylesterases, for example, rat CES2. In summary, available data indicate that monoesters generally undergo negligible hydrolysis at neutral pH in buffered solutions and in human plasma. In contrast, hydrolysis appears relatively fast in the presence of hepatic hydrolases.

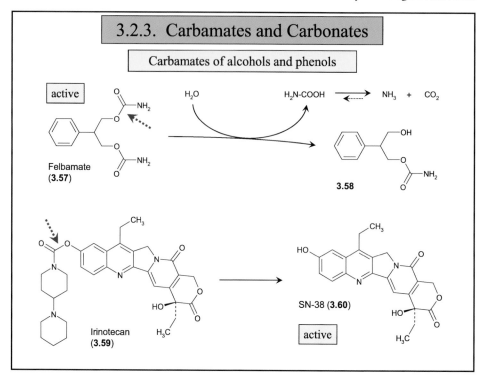

Fig. 3.32. This *Section* is dedicated to carbamates and carbonates, two classes of esters which deserve separate treatment for reasons soon to become apparent [66]. An illustrative example of *carbamates* is the antiepileptic drug *felbamate* (**3.57**). A major urinary metabolite in humans is a carboxylic acid resulting from ester hydrolysis to yield the *monocarbamate* **3.58**, followed by alcohol dehydrogenation [3][67]. In other words, hydrolysis of one ester group in felbamate to form the monocarbamate is a major pathway in humans. This reaction produces not only the alcohol **3.58**, but also *carbamic acid* ($H_2N-COOH$). However, and this is what makes carbamates and carbonates special, the promoiety tends to decarboxylate after hydrolysis. Indeed, carbamic acids ($RR'N-COOH$) are seldom isolated as such but in many cases tend to undergo *spontaneous decarboxylation* as shown. In contrast to felbamate which is inactivated by hydrolysis, *irinotecan* (**3.59**) is a prodrug activated by hydrolytic loss of the carbamate promoiety [68]. Both human CES1 and CES2 hydrolyze irinotecan, with CES2 displaying greater efficiency. The resulting *metabolite SN-38* (**3.60**) is a highly active antitumor agent of the camptothecin class. The reader will remember that we have already encountered irinotecan in *Fig. 3.20* where it is seen entering a carboxylesterase and interacting with its catalytic site, while SN-38 and the decarboxylated promoiety (4-piperidinopiperidine) leave the site.

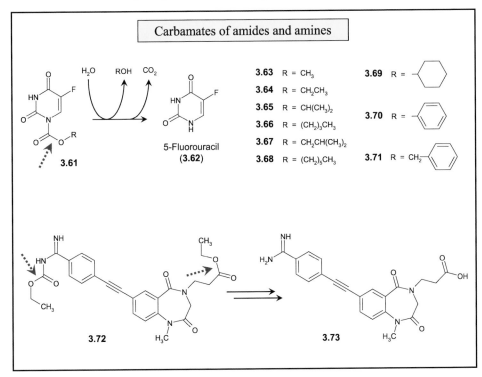

Fig. 3.33. In this *Figure*, we examine *carbamate derivatives of medicinally relevant amides or amines*, a useful strategy in prodrug design for cyclic amides as well as for amines of strong-to-weak basicity. Thus, the literature reports interesting attempts to improve the pharmaceutical and pharmacokinetic properties of *5-fluorouracil* (**3.62**) [3][69]. This antitumor agent, while clinically useful, suffers from poor water solubility, unsatisfactory delivery properties, and low tissue selectivity. A variety of prodrug candidates, **3.61**, were prepared. The lesser lipophilic derivatives showed a somewhat improved water solubility. More importantly, both rectal and oral *bioavailability* in rabbits was markedly improved. Thus, rectal bioavailability was nil for 5-fluorouracil (**3.62**), **3.70**, and **3.71**, low for **3.65**, **3.68**, and **3.69**, close to 50% for **3.63**, **3.64**, and **3.67**, and 100% for **3.66**. *Hydrolytic activation* was investigated in some detail, revealing a relatively rapid chemical hydrolysis, the half-lives under physiological conditions being *ca.* 3–15 h for the alkyl carbamates. The phenyl carbamate proved more labile. Enzymatic hydrolysis in human plasma was extremely rapid, with half-lives between 0.5 and 5 min. The derivatization of a *basic function* is exemplified by the *amidine peptidomimetic* of structure **3.73**, an inhibitor of the platelet membrane glycoprotein GPII$_b$III$_a$ [70]. The compound is a zwitterion at physiological pH and showed limited oral bioavailability. A *double prodrug* approach was examined (see **3.72**). The rates of hydrolysis of the *carbamate function* in buffers increased only slightly from pH 2 to 7, and then sharply in the alkaline range. The rates of hydrolysis were faster with more acidic leaving groups (Et–SH and Ph–OH), suggesting that the nonenzymatic activation of carbamate prodrugs of basic compounds may be tailored to desired values.

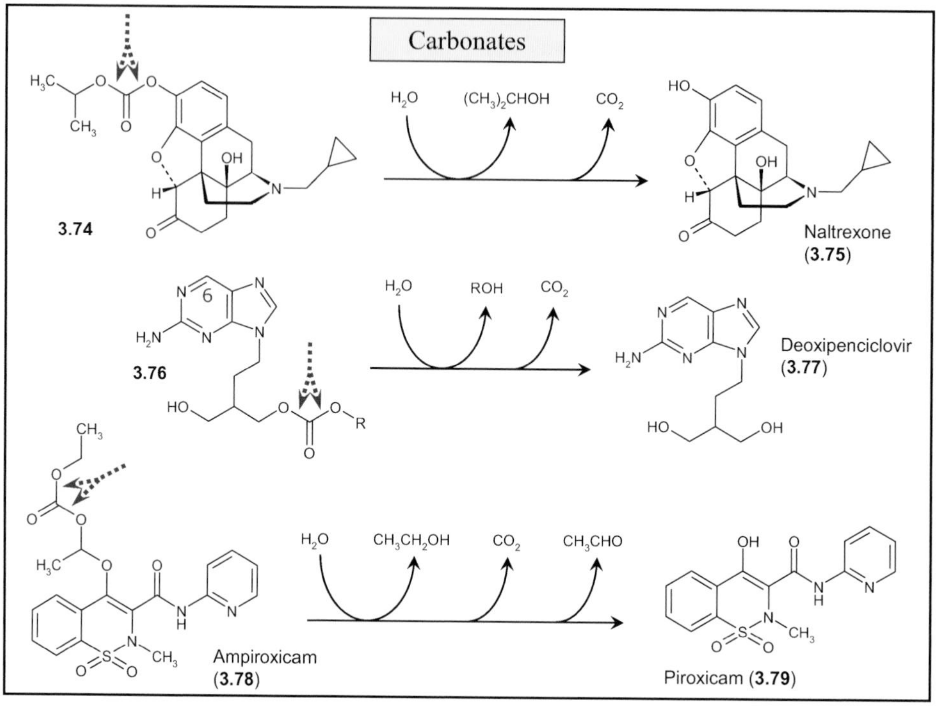

Fig. 3.34. *Carbonates* (alkoxycarbonyl derivatives) are diesters of general formula $R-O-CO-O-R'$. A single *mechanism* operates in the HO^--catalyzed (and presumably also in the enzyme-catalyzed) hydrolysis of carbonates, namely a rate-determining addition of the base to the carbonyl C-atom, followed by breakdown of the intermediate to yield ROH, CO_2, and $R'OH$ [3]. Carbonate prodrugs have been reported for *naltrexone* (**3.75**), a narcotic antagonist used to treat ethanol dependence and opioid addiction. The objective was to develop prodrugs allowing constant drug levels through dermal delivery [71]. Thus, the *(isopropyloxy)carbonyl derivative* **3.74** had a $t_{1/2} < 1$ h in human plasma, in contrast to the stable (*tert*-butoxy)carbonyl derivative. Skin permeability of these esters was markedly lower than that of naltrexone. Our second example is that of *6-deoxypenciclovir* (**3.77**), a bioprecursor (see *Part 5*) of the potent antiviral drug penciclovir [72]. To overcome bioavailability problems, a range of *alkoxycarbonyl derivatives* **3.76** (R = linear and branched alkyl groups) of **3.77** were prepared. Following oral administration, these carbonates led to rats and mice excreting, respectively, 4 and 10 times more penciclovir than after direct administration of the drug, indicating a higher bioavailability of the prodrugs. A more complex case is provided by *ampiroxicam* (**3.78**), which is both a carbonate and an *O*-acyloxymethyl derivative of the anti-inflammatory drug *piroxicam* (**3.79**) [73]. As shown, its breakdown yields EtOH, acetaldehyde, CO_2, and piroxicam. In humans, ampiroxicam was completely and rapidly converted to piroxicam, probably in the intestinal wall during absorption. As a result, most pharmacokinetic parameters of piroxocam (AUC, maximal plasma concentration [C_{max}], and mean $t_{1/2}$) were similar after administration of drug or prodrug. Only the time to reach C_{max} (t_{max}) was notably prolonged after administration of the prodrug, presumably due to its lower solubility and hence slower absorption.

3.3. Synthetic Reactions of Esterases

3.3.1. Reactions of Transesterification

Some examples

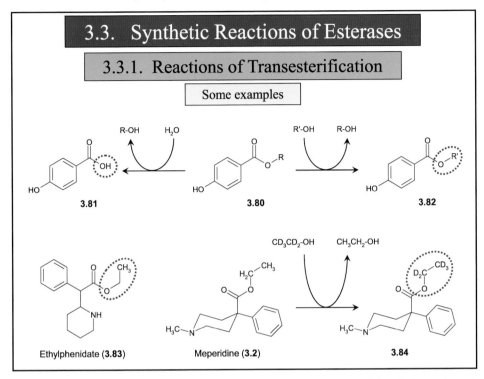

Ethylphenidate (**3.83**)   Meperidine (**3.2**)   **3.84**

Fig. 3.35. This short *Chapter* draws the reader's attention to insufficiently investigated yet toxicologically significant reactions whereby esterases catalyze the transesterification of alkyl esters or the esterification of alcohols. The first cases we present are reactions of *transesterification*, a few examples of which are shown in this *Figure*. Thus, the short-chain *parabens* **3.80** (*p*-hydroxybenzoates; R = Me, Et, or Pr) are widely used as preservatives in food products, cosmetics, and oral pharmaceutical preparations. They are rapidly absorbed in the gastrointestinal tract and hydrolyzed by carboxylesterases to 4-hydroxybenzoic acid (**3.81**). In the presence of EtOH, however, cultures of human intestinal Caco-2 cells catalyzed their transesterification to *ethylparaben* (**3.82**; R' = Et) [74]. The K_m and V_{max} values for transesterification in the presence of EtOH decreased in the series Me > Pr > Bu > heptyl > octyl. The transesterification of methylparaben was *ca.* 20 times faster in the presence of EtOH than with PrOH or BuOH. A medicinal example is that of *methylphenidate* (**3.1** in *Fig. 3.23*) which, in the presence of EtOH, undergoes a carboxylesterase-mediated transesterification to *ethylphenidate* (**3.83**) [75]. A rather intriguing reaction is the transesterification undergone by *meperidine* (**3.2**; see also *Fig. 2.23*) in the presence of carboxylesterase and EtOH [76]. Because meperidine is an ethyl ester, its product of *transesterification* (**3.84**) is identical with the substrate, and its formation could only be demonstrated in the presence of deuterated ethanol.

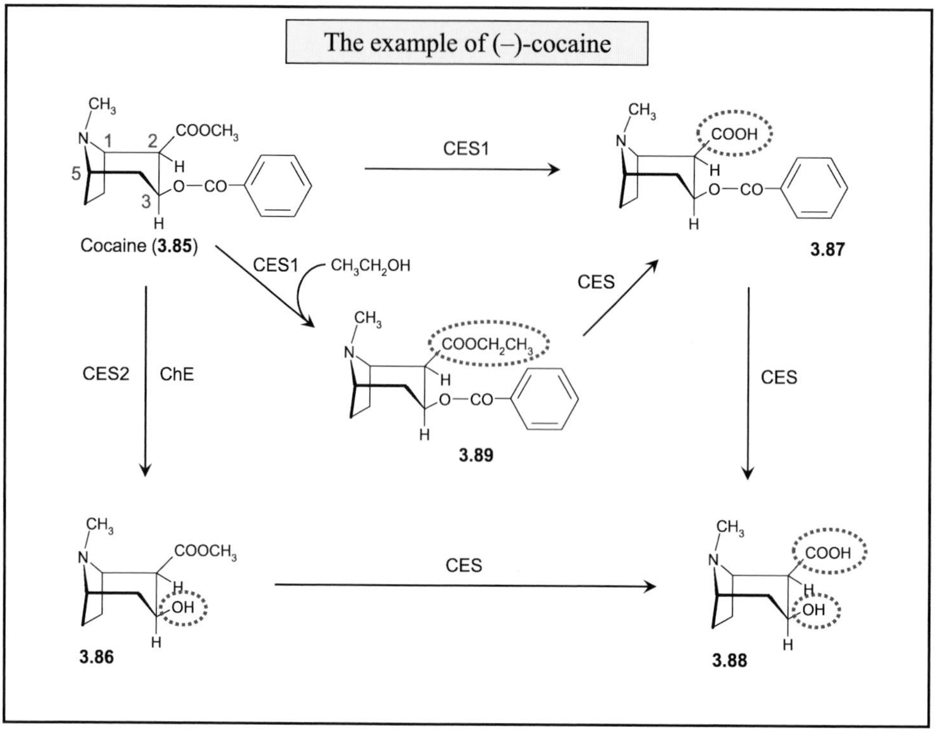

Fig. 3.36. *Natural (–)-cocaine* (**3.85**), which has the (1*R*,2*R*,3*S*,5*S*)-configuration, is a relatively poor substrate of hepatic carboxylesterases and plasma cholinesterase, and a competitive inhibitor of the latter enzyme [77][78]. In contrast, its unnatural enantiomer (+)-(1*S*,2*S*,3*R*,5*R*)-cocaine is a good substrate of carboxylesterases and cholinesterase. Besides a relatively *slow inactivation* by hydrolysis to generate metabolites **3.86**–**3.88**, there is an additional factor which contributes to the toxicity of cocaine, namely its *interaction with EtOH* [3][79–82]. Many cocaine (ab)users simultaneously ingest EtOH probably to experience a potentiation of effects and a decrease in headaches. It is now known that EtOH interferes in two ways with the metabolism of cocaine, first by inhibiting its hydrolysis and second by allowing a *transesterification* to form benzoylecgonine ethyl ester (**3.89**), commonly known as *cocaethylene*. This is a significant fact since cocaethylene retains the pharmacological properties of cocaine and is even more toxic, in particular to the brain and liver. The details of the enzymes involved in the various hydrolase-catalyzed reactions of cocaine is shown in the *Figure*. The *catalytic mechanism* of carboxylesterase-catalyzed transesterification is not fully clarified. Schematically, the nucleophile reacting with the serine-bound acyl group to form the tetrahedral intermediate (*Steps d* and *e* in *Fig. 3.18*) is here a molecule of alcohol instead of one of H_2O.

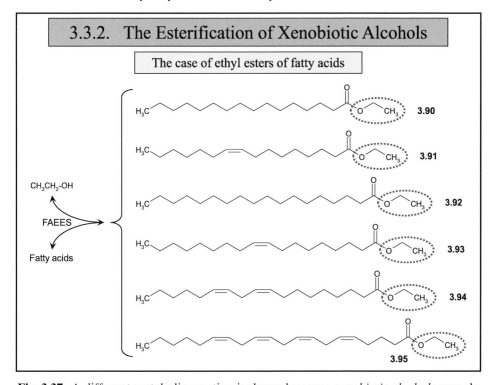

Fig. 3.37. A different metabolic reaction is shown by some *xenobiotic alcohols*, namely their conjugation to *endogenous fatty acids* to form *fatty acid esters* [83–85]. The xenobiotics so metabolized include first and foremost EtOH, as well as a few analogous alcohols of relatively small molecular weight (*e.g.*, MeOH and ClCH₂CH₂OH). A second category of substrates are large and mainly *lipophilic alcohols* such as some cannabinols, codeine, and dipyridamole. The enzymes involved in the fatty acid esterification of these large substrates are acyl-coenzyme A: cholesterol acyltransferase (EC 2.3.1.26; sterol *O*-acyltransferase; ACAT) and other coenzyme A-dependent acyltransferases classified under EC 2.3.1. The central role of coenzyme A in important reactions of conjugation of xenobiotics will be presented in *Part 4*. In the case of *fatty acid ethyl ester* (FAEE) synthesis, the enzyme involved is referred to as fatty-acyl-ethyl-ester synthase (EC 3.1.1.67; FAEES; see *Fig. 3.2*). This enzyme activity is independent of coenzyme A, catalyzes both FAEE synthesis and hydrolysis, is found in liver, adipose tissue and pancreas, and has been shown to be a *carboxylesterase*. Other enzymes believed or postulated to mediate FAEE synthesis are a microsomal acyl-coenzyme A: ethanol acyltransferase, lipoprotein lipase, pancreatic triglyceride lipase, and possibly cholesterol esterase. The FAEE synthesis is marked in human pancreas and liver, and lower in adipose tissue, heart, brain, muscles, and aorta [85]. The *Figure* shows a number of ethyl esters identified in the heart of a human subject acutely intoxicated with EtOH at the time of death. These compounds are *ethyl palmitate* (**3.90**), *ethyl palmitoleate* (**3.91**), *ethyl stearate* (**3.92**), *ethyl oleate* (**3.93**), *ethyl linoleate* (**3.94**), and *ethyl arachidonate* (**3.95**) [85]. These ethyl esters mediate EtOH-induced organ damage and have been proposed as long-lasting markers of EtOH (ab)use.

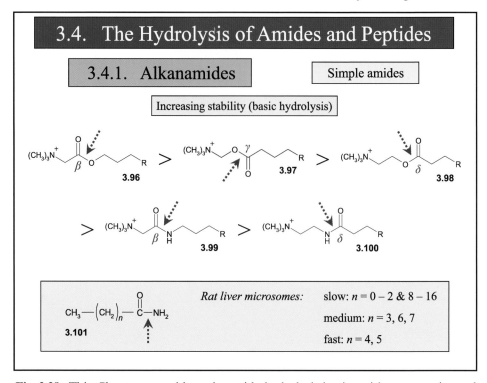

Fig. 3.38. This *Chapter* on amide and peptide hydrolysis begins with a comparison of the relative stability of esters and amides toward specific base-catalyzed (*i.e.*, HO⁻-catalyzed) hydrolysis under neutral or weakly basic conditions. The compounds selected for this presentation are shown here in order of increasing chemical stability [86]. The compounds are *quaternary ammonium antibacterials* of potential interest as *biodegradable disinfectants* and for environmental sanitation. As expected, the three *esters* **3.96**, **3.97**, and **3.98** are less stable than the two *amides* **3.99** and **3.100**. Perhaps less obvious is the stability within each class, which increases with increasing distance between the cationic center and the carbonyl C-atom. This electronic effect highlights the nucleophilic nature of base-catalyzed hydrolysis, and it is enzymatically relevant, since serine hydrolases also act as nucleophilic reagents (see *Fig. 3.18*). The first systematic studies of the metabolic hydrolysis of *primary aliphatic amides* **3.101** ($n = 0$–16) was carried out in the late 1940s [3] by incubating the substrates in rabbit liver preparations. Further investigations using, in particular, chick embryo liver cell cultures confirmed the results [3]. As indicated in the *Figure*, the extent of hydrolysis was very low for the first three homologues, then increased markedly to reach a maximum with hexanamide (**3.101**; $n = 4$) and heptanamide (**3.101**; $n = 5$), and then fell off rapidly. Undecanamide (**3.101**; $n = 9$) and higher homologues were hydrolyzed only to a small extent, like the shortest homologues. *Branching* of the side chain reduced hydrolysis, whereas *ω-phenyl substitution* facilitated it for the shorter amides (four or less aliphatic C-atoms). The hydrolysis of these simple amides involved neither peptidases such as glutaminase or asparaginase, nor proteases such as pepsin, trypsin, or cathepsin.

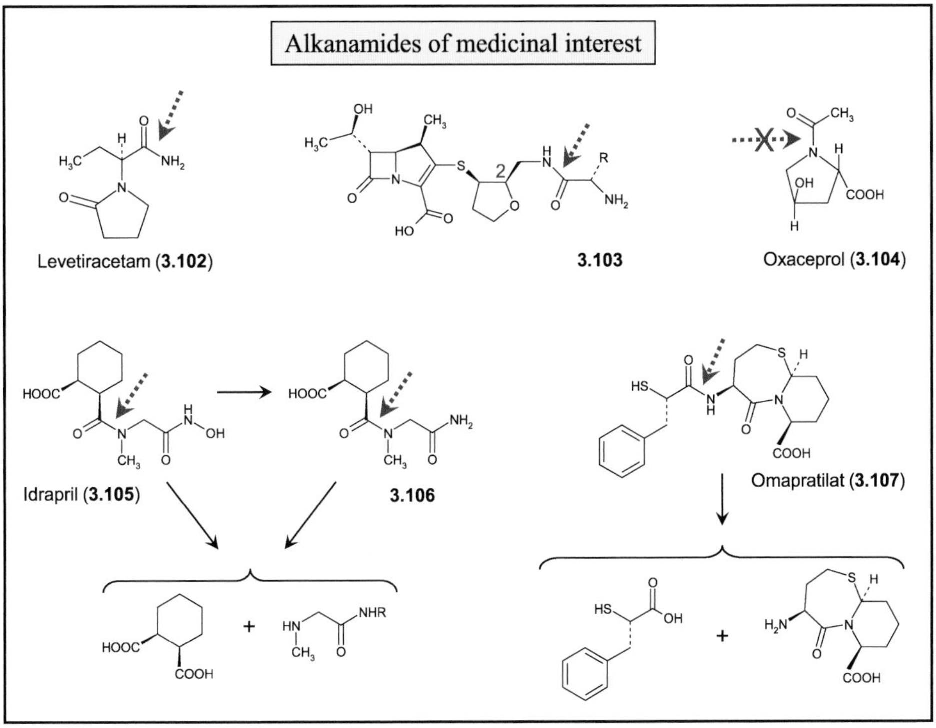

Fig. 3.39. We now examine a few medicinally relevant alkan- or cycloalkanamides, beginning with the antiepileptic agent *levetiracetam* (**3.102**) [87]. This hydrophilic drug is well absorbed orally and is mostly excreted unchanged (*ca.* 2/3 of a dose in humans). Its main biotransformation route is by amide hydrolysis to the corresponding carboxylic acid metabolite. The generic *carbapenem antibiotics* **3.103** are potential prodrugs [88]. The compound with a −CH$_2$NH$_2$ side chain in position (2*R*) showed excellent *in vitro* antibacterial activity yet was poorly active in mice following oral administration. In contrast, the prodrugs containing an L-amino acid, *i.e.*, **3.103**, demonstrated improved efficacy after oral administration, and their absorption and hydrolysis led to high plasmatic levels of the parent drug. Thus, three- to ten-fold increased efficacy was shown by the Ala-, Val-, Ile-, and Phe-substituted prodrugs **3.103** (R = Me, CHMe$_2$, CH(Me)CH$_2$Me, and CH$_2$Ph) against acute lethal infections in mice. In contrast, the D-forms were markedly less active, suggesting an active intestinal absorption process with marked stereoselectivity. The antiphlogistic agent *oxaceprol* (**3.104**) is mentioned here as an example of a highly polar drug which escapes metabolism entirely [89]. As for the ACE inhibitor *idrapril* (**3.105**), metabolic hydrolysis of its amide bond either before (*i.e.*, **3.105**) or after (*i.e.*, **3.106**) *in vivo* reduction led to *cis*-cyclohexane-1,2-dicarboxylic acid as an important urinary metabolite in rats [90]. Our last example is that of the cardiovascular therapeutic agent *omapratilat* (**3.107**) whose metabolism in humans and animals involves a number of reactions, one of which is hydrolytic cleavage of the molecule at its central amide bond [91].

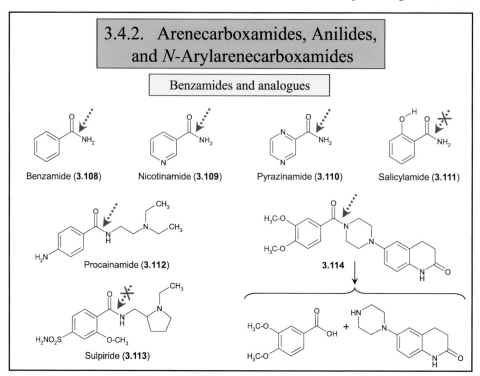

Fig. 3.40. Here, we define arenecarboxamides as having an aromatic ring system attached to the amide carbonyl C-atom (*e.g.*, benzamides). *Benzamide* (**3.108**) itself undergoes hydrolysis to benzoic acid in a variety of species [3]. *Ring substitution* can markedly affect the rate of hydrolysis, depending upon the nature and position of the substituents. Among primary amides of pyridine-carboxylic acids, the hydrolysis of *nicotinamide* (**3.109**) is of physiological importance, since the resulting nicotinic acid serves as a precursor in the synthesis of pyridine nucleotides. The tuberculostatic agent *pyrazinamide* (**3.110**) is a prodrug of the active pyrazinoic acid. To act, it must penetrate intact into *Mycobacterium tuberculosis* where it is hydrolyzed. The resistance of the pathogen to pyrazinamide can in most cases be explained by a loss of hydrolase activity [92]. And since pyrazinoic acid cannot penetrate the bacterium, hydrolysis in the human body is another unfavorable factor. In contrast to pyrazinamide, *salicylamide* (**3.111**) is resistant to hydrolysis in the human body. Indeed, humans administered the drug excreted the totality of the dose as urinary metabolites having the amide moiety intact [93]. Among *secondary and tertiary amides*, the antiarrhythmic agent *procainamide* (**3.112**) exemplifies the difference in metabolic stability between esters and amides. In contrast to its ester analogue (the local anesthetic *procaine*), procainamide is hydrolyzed very slowly in humans, less than 1% of a dose being transformed to *p*-aminobenzoic acid [3]. The antipsychotic drug *sulpiride* (**3.113**) did not undergo hydrolysis in humans and laboratory animals. The hydrolysis of the amide group in the *inotropic agent OPC-8212* (**3.114**) occurred in humans and animals, both products of hydrolysis being identified in rats for example [94].

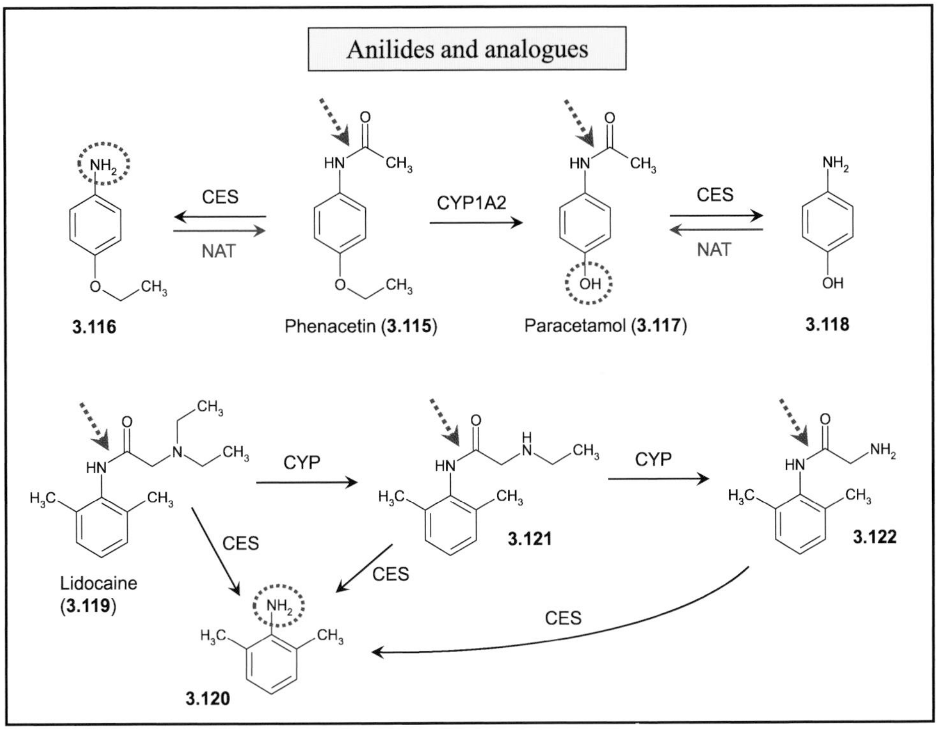

Fig. 3.41. For anilides, hydrolysis may represent a pathway of toxification since it liberates *aromatic amines* which are potentially hematotoxic, nephrotoxic, hepatotoxic, and/or carcinogenic (see *Part 5*). The former drug *phenacetin* (**3.115**) was withdrawn due to its high renal toxicity, but is also believed to cause hemolysis and methemoglobin following its hydrolysis to *phenetidine* (**3.116**) and *N*-hydroxylation of the latter [3]. The hydrolysis of phenacetin in humans occurs mainly in the endoplasmic reticulum of liver cells and is catalyzed by a carboxylesterase [95]. Intriguingly, this reaction is a *futile process* due to the metabolic *N*-acetylation of phenetidine (see *Part 4*). The same is true for *paracetamol* (**3.117**), the major metabolite of phenacetin (see *Part 2*). Thus, phenacetin labeled in its Ac moiety showed futile deacetylation to account an average of *ca.* 30% of the acetylated phenacetin metabolites [96]. *Lidocaine* (**3.119**) is a local anaesthetic and an antiarrhythmic agent which is highly resistant to chemical hydrolysis even in strongly acidic or basic media. Despite the high chemical stability of its amide bond, metabolic hydrolysis represents a major pathway for lidocaine in mammals, with considerable interspecies differences. Thus, rats excreted *ca.* 15% of a dose as products of hydrolysis and their conjugates. In humans, hydrolysis of the amide bond represents the major metabolic pathway, accounting for *ca.* 75% of the amount excreted in urine [3]. The CES-catalyzed routes of formation of *2,6-xylidine* (**3.120**) involve hydrolysis of lidocaine and/or *monoethylglycinexylidine* (**3.121**) and/or *glycinexylidine* (**3.122**) [97]. Interestingly, the *N*-deethylated metabolites were found to be hydrolyzed to a greater extent than the parent compound.

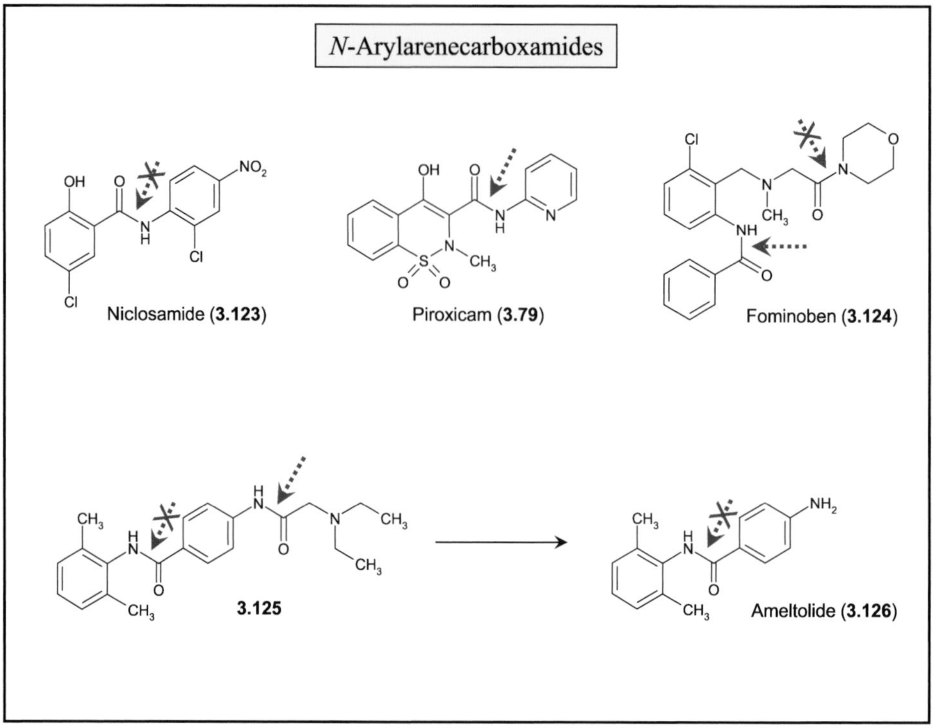

Fig. 3.42. Whereas unsubstituted *N*-phenylbenzamide undergoes fast enzymatic hydrolysis, the introduction of aromatic substituents such as OH, Cl, or NO$_2$ groups markedly reduces the rate of the reaction. The antihelminthic *niclosamide* (**3.123**), which carries the three types of substituents, was not hydrolyzed either by mammalian liver or by helminth tissue preparations. This might be explained by a combination of electronic and steric effects [3]. *Piroxicam* (**3.79**), a well-known anti-inflammatory agent, contains an amide bond between a benzothiazine and a pyridine ring. The acyl product of amide hydrolysis (*i.e.*, 3-carboxy-2-methyl-4-oxobenzothiazine 1,1-dioxide) was isolated from the urine of rhesus monkeys. However, this metabolite was not found in the rat and dog, presumably because it was completely degraded by subsequent breakdown and rearrangement reaction. In humans, the same multistep pathway seems to operate, but the metabolites produced by this route represented less than 5% of a dose. There is no evidence that *other oxicams* undergo amide hydrolysis [98]. Hydrolysis of the amide bond linking the two aromatic rings represents a major metabolic pathway for the antitussive agent *fominoben* (**3.124**) [3]. In humans, *ca.* 30% of the dose were cleaved hydrolytically at the benzamido group. Interestingly, no hydrolysis was observed for the amide bond linking the morpholino moiety to the rest of the molecule. A similar regioselectivity was observed after administration to mice of a prodrug, **3.125**, of the anticonvulsant agent ameltolide [99]. The prodrug and its two *N*-dealkylated metabolites underwent amide hydrolysis at the indicated bond to *ameltolide* (**3.126**), whereas the amide bond linking the two aromatic rings was not hydrolyzed. The same proved true when ameltolide was administered to rats. No convincing explanation can be proposed.

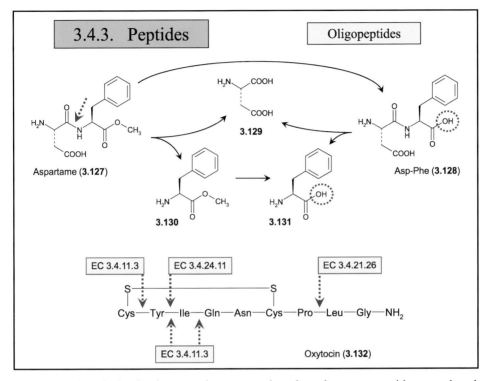

Fig. 3.43. That derivatization may increase rather than decrease peptidase-catalyzed degradation is illustrated with *aspartame* (**3.127**), the C-terminal methyl ester of the dipeptide Asp-Phe. The metabolism of this artificial sweetener in microvillar membranes of human small intestine was compared to that of the underivatized dipeptide **3.128**, a metabolite of aspartame [100]. The activities observed were primarily those of *glutamyl aminopeptidase* (EC 3.4.11.7) as shown by the effects of inhibitors, yielding Asp (**3.129**) and Phe-Me (**3.130**) in the case of aspartame, and Asp (**3.129**) and Phe (**3.131**) in the case of Asp-Phe. The peptide bond was hydrolyzed *ca.* twice faster in aspartame than in Asp-Phe. This is an interesting and favorable situation, given that aspartame is expected to be degraded once it has elicited its effect in the buccal cavity. Our second example is that of *oxytocin* (**3.132**), a potent and specific stimulant of myometrial contractions commonly used to induce labor. This peptide is of interest due to its cyclic structure resulting from an intramolecular disulfide bridge. Here again, degradation by a variety of peptidases is documented [101]. Thus, cleavage of the N-terminal cysteine is catalyzed by an aminopeptidase now known as *cystinyl aminopeptidase* (EC 3.4.11.3; oxytocinase), an enzyme found in the placenta and in the serum of pregnant women. The enzyme acts efficiently to hydrolyze the Cys[1]–Tyr[2] bond, thus opening the ring structure of oxytocin, and then cleaves successive residues from the N-terminal end. At the C-terminus, *prolyl oligopeptidase* (EC 3.4.21.26) cleaves the C-terminal dipeptide. The resulting oxytocin-(1–7) is also a substrate for aminopeptidase activity. Furthermore, *neprilysin* (EC 3.4.24.11) can also play a role in oxytocin degradation, although it seems to act with less efficiency than the two other enzymes.

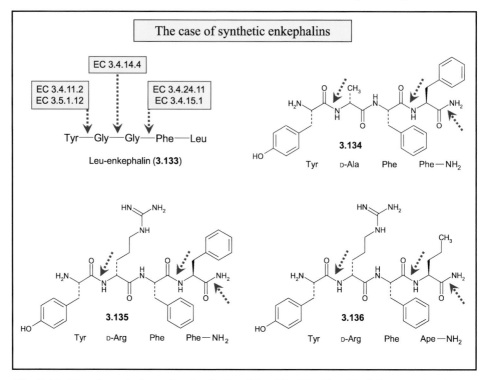

Fig. 3.44. The degradation of *enkephalins* (Tyr-Gly-Gly-Phe-Xaa) has received considerable attention given their biological significance and therapeutic potential. Here, *[Leu⁵]enkephalin* (**3.133**) is taken as an example to illustrate the variety of hydrolytic reactions even a short peptide can be submitted to [3][102]. An important enzyme is obviously *neprilysin* (EC 3.4.24.11; enkephalinase, endopeptidase-24.11) which removes the C-terminal dipeptide. The same site is also cleaved by *peptidyl-dipeptidase A* (EC 3.4.15.1). The N-terminal dipeptide can be cleaved by *dipeptidyl-peptidase III* (EC 3.4.14.4). The N-terminal residue is also quite sensitive to hydrolytic cleavage by various aminopeptidases and particularly *membrane alanyl aminopeptidase* (EC 3.4.11.2; aminopeptidase N). It is interesting to note that the same cleavage is also carried out by *biotinidase* (EC 3.5.1.12), an amidase present in human serum and known to possess aminopeptidase activity. However, the pattern and efficiency of hydrolysis of [Leu⁵]enkephalin, like that of any peptide, will vary considerably as a function of animal species, tissue, and concentration profile. Two tetrapeptides have been isolated from mammalian brain, and found to have high affinity and selectivity for the μ-opioid receptor. These tetrapeptides are endomorphin-1 (Tyr-Pro-Trp-Phe-NH₂) and endomorphin-2 (Tyr-Pro-Phe-Phe-NH₂). A number of active *synthetic analogues of endomorphin* have been prepared to improve their metabolic stability, namely the peptides **3.134**, **3.135**, and **3.136** (Ape = 2-aminopentanoic acid) [103]. The D-amino acid in the 2-position largely but not completely protected the peptides against N-terminal cleavage by aminopeptidases. In contrast, the C-terminal amide did not stabilize them against deamidase and carboxypeptidase activities, although the artificial Ape residue did have a global protective effect.

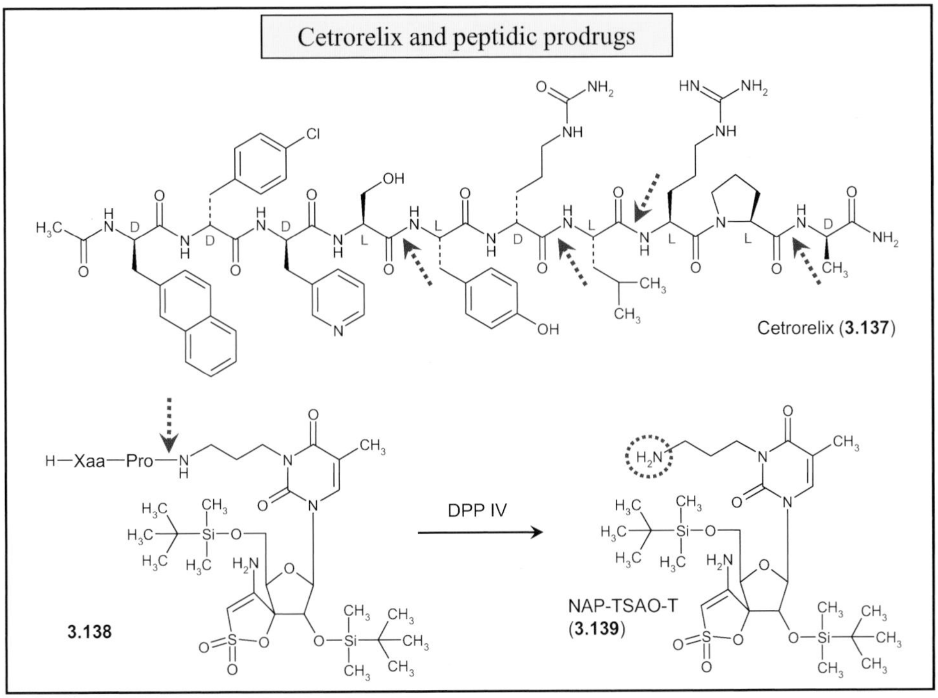

Fig. 3.45. Peptides containing non-proteinogenic amino acids, peptoids, and pseudo-peptides are gaining increasing importance in medicinal chemistry [3][104][105]. The *tetrapeptides* **3.134**, **3.135**, and **3.136** in the previous *Figure* are examples of peptides containing an artificial and/or a D-amino acid. Here, we present *cetrorelix* (**3.137**), a potent antagonist of Luteinizing Hormone-Releasing Hormone (LHRH) receptors, and an example that aptly illustrates the chemical diversity of artificial amino acids that have found their way into promising peptides. Cetrorelix is an N- and C-protected decapeptide containing D-naphthylalanine, D-(*p*-chloro)Phe, D-(pyridin-3-yl)Ala, D-ornithine, and D-Ala as D-/artificial residues. Following subcutaneous administration, the plasma half-life was 35–40 h in rats and 100–130 h in dogs, indicating a remarkable metabolic stability [106]. In both species, only unchanged compound was found in urine, whereas the bile contained up to four metabolites, namely the (1–9)-nonapeptide, the (1–7)-heptapeptide, the (1–6)-hexapeptide, and the (1–4)-tetrapeptide. This indicates that peptidase-related products were the only products identified. Oligopeptides also show promise as *promoieties in prodrugs* targeted to specific peptidases. This is illustrated with dipeptidyl prodrugs of anti HIV compounds, here N^3-*aminopropyl-TSAO-T* (**3.139**; NAT-TSAO-T), a reverse transcriptase inhibitor of the TSAO-T family [107]. HIV mainly infects lymphocytes or macrophages that abundantly express dipeptidyl-peptidase IV (EC 3.4.14.5; DPP IV), an enzyme with high substrate selectivity for peptides with a Pro at the penultimate position of the N-terminus. Several dipeptide prodrugs, *e.g.*, **3.138**, of NAT-TSAO-T were prepared and found to be effectively hydrolyzed by purified DPP IV and to be highly active. Replacing Pro with another residue abolished cleavage by DPP IV but preserved a high activity, a finding that suggests that the dipeptidyl-NAT-TSAO-T (**3.138**) are intrinsically active and cannot be labeled prodrugs.

3.5. Hydrolytic Ring Opening

3.5.1. Cyclic Esters

Lactones of medicinal interest

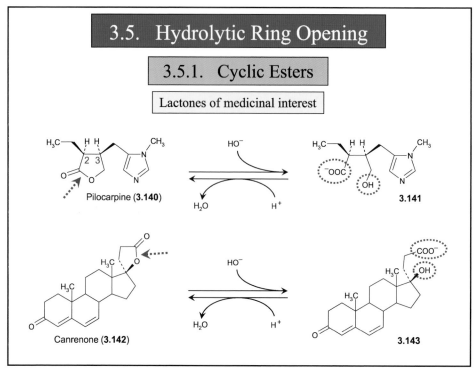

Fig. 3.46. This *Chapter* visits cyclic esters (lactones, cyclic carbamates, and carbonates), cyclic amides (lactams), and cyclic imides. The hydrolysis of such rings is similar to ester or amide hydrolysis in terms of catalytic mechanisms, but differs as far as reaction kinetics and products are concerned. Whereas esters and amides are hydrolyzed to two metabolites/products, lactones and lactams generate a hydroxy acid or an amino acid as the sole metabolite/product of hydrolysis. In fact, the reaction can also be designated as *hydration*. Another characteristic of hydrolytic lactone or lactam opening is its *reversibility*, ring closure with elimination of H_2O occurring at rates and to an extent dependent on substrate and conditions. The hydrolytic ring opening of cyclic esters and amides can be both *enzymatic* and *nonenzymatic*, but it appears that the two components are seldom distinguished in metabolic studies [3]. In this *Figure*, we begin with the *nonenzymatic hydrolysis of medicinally relevant lactones*. This is illustrated with the ophthalmic drug *pilocarpine* (**3.140**) whose absolute configuration is (2*S*,3*R*). Its hydrolytic ring opening is catalyzed by the HO^- anion (activation energy 105 kJ mol^{-1}) and forms the anion of *pilocarpic acid* (**3.141**). The reverse reaction of *lactonization* of pilocarpic acid is H^+-catalyzed and hence favored at low pH values. Thus, the pilocarpine/pilocarpic acid ratio was 1.0 and 6.7 at pH values of 6.0 and 4.0, respectively [3]. The mineralocorticoid antagonist *canrenone* (**3.142**) undergoes a comparable reversible opening to *canrenoate* (**3.143**). Under physiological conditions of pH and temperature, the lactone $\rightleftharpoons$ acid equilibrium was reached after several weeks, whereas it was established in *ca.* 3 h in humans injected with potassium canrenoate. This suggests that the *in vivo* reaction is enzyme-catalyzed.

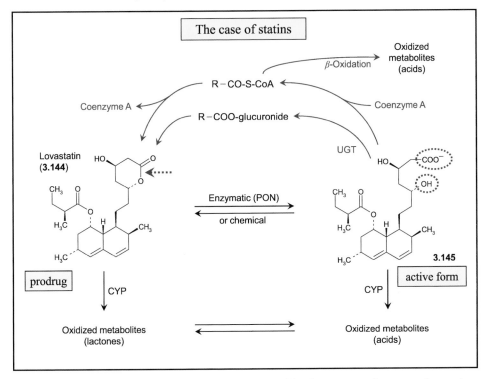

Fig. 3.47. A therapeutic class that uniquely exemplifies lactone prodrugs are the *statins*, *i.e.*, the cholesterol-lowering agents acting by inhibition of 3-hydroxy-3-methylglutaryl-CoA (HMG-CoA) reductase (EC 1.1.1.34). This microsomal enzyme catalyzes the conversion of HMG-CoA to mevalonate, an important rate-limiting step in cholesterol biosynthesis. As cholesterol synthesis occurs mainly in the liver, it is most desirable that *inhibitors of HMG-CoA reductase* exhibit a high selectivity for distribution into their target organ [108]. Two of the marketed statins are used in the lactone, prodrug form (lovastatin and simvastatin), while most others are used as the active hydroxy acids (*e.g.*, atorvastatin, fluvastatin, and pravastatin). The *metabolism* of statins is a complex one [109]. There is a *nonenzymatic* lactone ⇌ acid equilibrium which is comparatively fast under gastric conditions of acidity ($t_{1/2}$ of *ca.* 1 h with an equilibrium constant close to one) but much slower at neutral pH [110]. Enzymatic hydration also occurs, in particular by *serum paraoxonase* [111][112]. As illustrated here with *lovastatin* (**3.144**) [113], the carboxy group in the hydroxy acid form (**3.145**) is an active target of conjugation reactions (see *Part 4*) which play a role in the lactone ⇌ acid equilibrium [113]. Thus, glucuronidation of the carboxy group leads to an acyl-glucuronide which spontaneously undergoes cyclization–elimination to form the lactone [114]. Another pathway is conjugation with Coenzyme A (CoA) to form the thioester, a metabolic intermediate in the β-oxidation of the acid as well as in its lactonization. In summary, many biological factors contribute to the lactone ⇌ acid equilibrium of statins, which is also a major determinant in the passive and active transport of these drugs and in their oxidative metabolism [108a][109c][115].

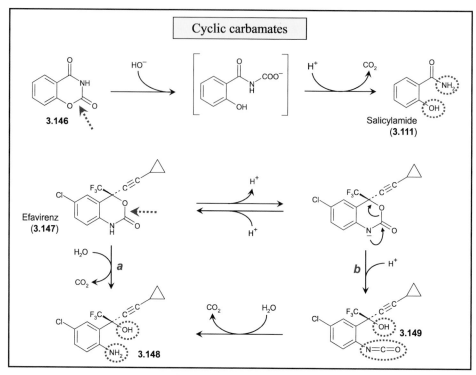

Fig. 3.48. Like lactones, cyclic carbamates and cyclic carbonates undergo ring opening by *hydrolysis of the endocyclic ester bond*. But in contrast to lactones, the reaction is an *irreversible* one due to the breakdown (loss of CO_2) of the primary product. In this *Figure*, we examine two cyclic carbamates of medicinal interest. *2H-1,3-Benzoxazine-2,4(3H)-dione* (**3.146**) is an interesting cyclic carbamate. Hydrolysis of the ester group likely yields the ring-opened carbamic acid as an undetected intermediate, which very rapidly undergoes decarboxylation to the drug *salicylamide* (**3.111**). When the cyclic carbamate was administered to rabbits, extensive hydrolysis to salicylamide was indeed seen [116]. The enzymatic nature of the reaction was also indicated, since the rate of hydrolysis of **3.146** increased strongly from buffer to rabbit plasma to rabbit liver homogenate. *Kinetic and mechanistic insights* into the chemical hydrolysis of cyclic carbamates have been uncovered in the hydrolysis of *efavirenz* (**3.147**), an HIV-1 reverse transcriptase inhibitor used in the treatment of HIV-1 infection [117]. In the acidic and neutral pH range, hydrolysis to **3.148** *via* the intermediate carbamic acid occurred (*Mechanism a*). In the alkaline range, however, deprotonation of the compound favored an elimination–addition (*Mechanism b*) forming the isocyanate intermediate **3.149**, followed by rearrangement and loss of CO_2 to yield **3.148**.

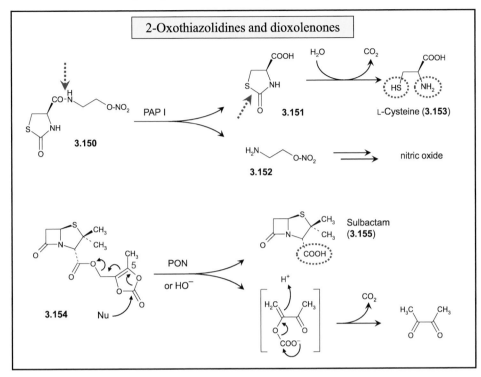

Fig. 3.49. This *Figure* presents two special cases of cyclic esters, namely 2-oxothiazo-lidines (cyclic thiocarbamates) and dioxolenones (a class of cyclic carbonates). *2-Oxothiazolidines* are of interest as *prodrugs of L-cysteine* (**3.153**). Thus, L-*2-oxothiazolidine-4-carboxylic acid* (**3.151**) is a known and active agent against oxidative stress. Its mechanism of action involves fast hydrolysis to L-cysteine, followed by incorporation into the thiol-containing tripeptide *glutathione* (see *Part 4*) [118]. This strategy has been expanded with the prodrug *RS-7897* (**3.150**), whose hydrolysis by pyroglutamyl aminopeptidase I (EC 3.4.19.3; PAP I) in dogs yielded **3.151** and 2-*aminoethyl nitrate* (**3.152**) [119]. The latter is a vasodilating nitrate ester of the same class as nitroglycerine (see *Chapt. 3.6*). *Dioxolenones* (= (5-methyl-2-oxo-1,3-dioxol-4-yl)methyl esters) are exemplified here by a prodrug of *sulbactam* (**3.155**), a β-lactamase inhibitor. The mechanism of the hydrolysis of dioxolenones is summarized in the *Figure*; both *chemical* (base-catalyzed) and *enzymatic* (paraoxonase-catalyzed) hydrolysis have been demonstrated, with the substituent in position 5 influencing the rate of the reaction [3][111][120]. The promoiety breaks down as shown. Following oral administration to mice, the *dioxolenone* **3.154** of *sulbactam* (**3.155**) gave threefold higher serum concentrations of the drug compared to direct administration.

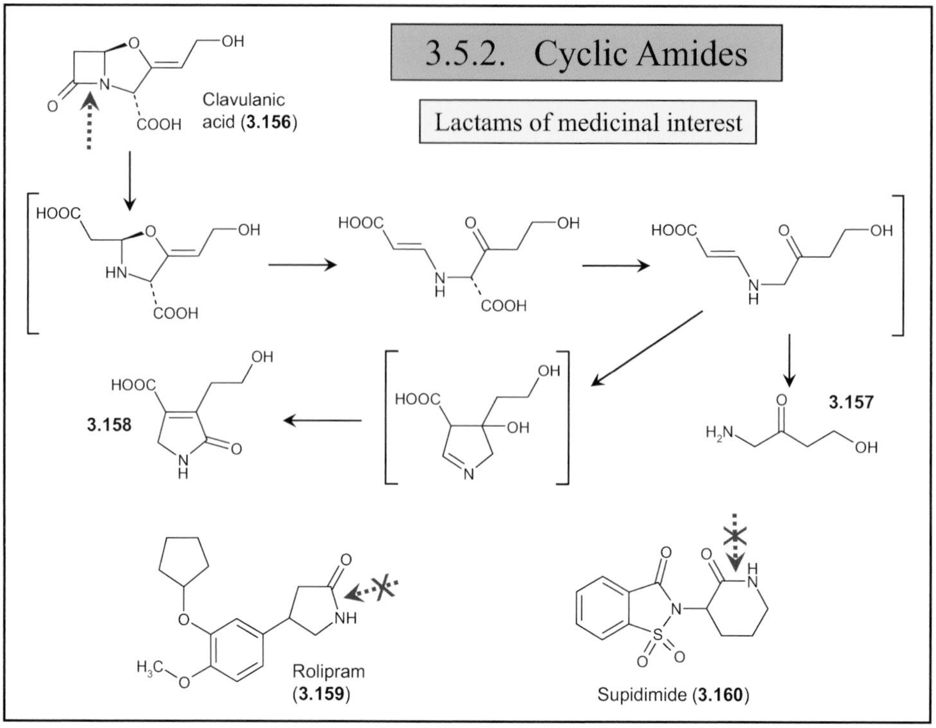

Fig. 3.50. The smallest lactam ring of significance in medicinal chemistry is the four-membered *β-lactam ring*, a well-known structural element of β-lactam antibiotics such as penicillins and cephalosporins. The chemical and biochemical reactivity of the β-lactam ring largely determines the pharmacokinetic and pharmacodynamic behavior of these drugs, which undergo nonenzymatic hydrolysis and rearrangements, and enzymatic hydrolysis in bacteria (*lactamases*; EC 3.5.2.6) and higher organisms. This subject has received a 50-page treatment in [3]. Other important sources of information are [121–123]. To illustrate the metabolic complexity and analytical difficulty of assessing the metabolism of β-lactam antibiotics, we present here the human metabolism of *clavulanic acid* (**3.156**), a mechanism-based inhibitor of β-lactamases and an extensively used potentiator of penicillins [124]. Two major urinary metabolites, **3.157** and **3.158**, were identified, and the *Figure* shows a hypothetical pathway for their formation based on the known hydrolysis and rearrangement products of the drug. *Larger lactam rings* are generally resistant to metabolic hydrolysis. This is seen for example with pyrrolidinones (*γ-lactams*) such as the antidepressant *rolipram* (**3.159**). Metabolic studies in several mammalian species including humans did not reveal any cleavage of the pyrrolidinone ring [125]. Similarly, no metabolite with an opened piperidin-2-one ring was found for *supidimide* (**3.160**). The lactam ring of this potential sedative underwent slow chemical hydrolysis in buffer solutions, but was resistant to metabolic hydrolysis. The other amide bond was stable [126]. Supidimide was primarily metabolized by oxidation of the piperidone ring to yield a glutarimide ring, an easily hydrolyzable system as illustrated in the next *Figure*.

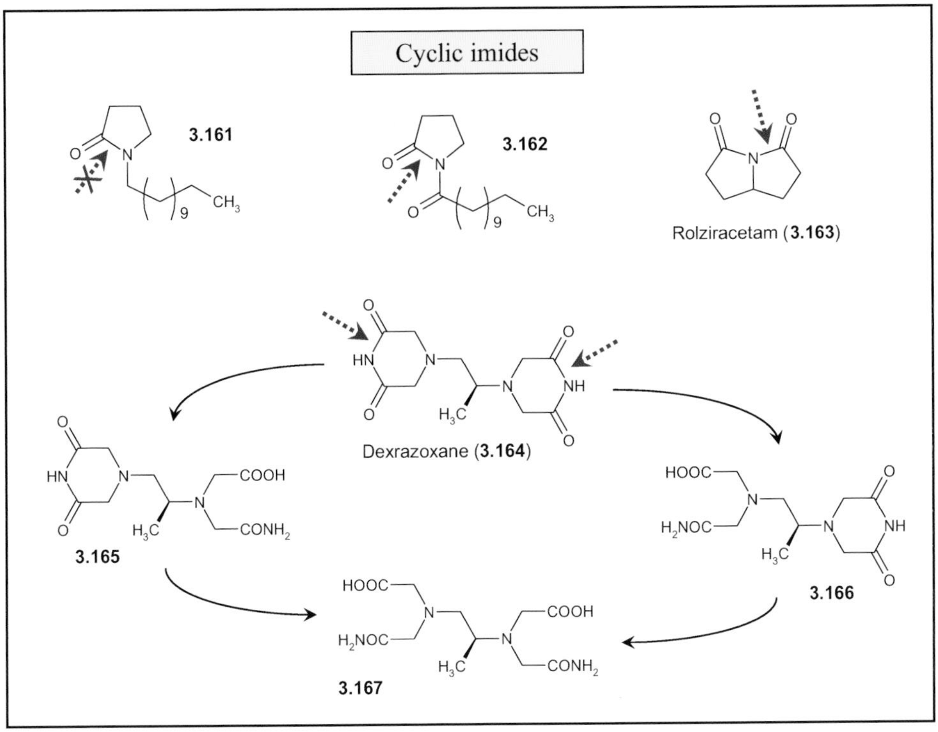

Fig. 3.51. The different susceptibility of lactams and cyclic imides toward enzymatic hydrolysis is nicely illustrated by failed prodrugs of GABA (gamma-aminobutyric acid) based on the pyrrolidin-2-one structure [127]. Indeed, the lactam *1-dodecylpyrrolidin-2-one* (**3.161**) was stable in mouse liver and brain homogenates. In contrast, *1-dodecanoylpyrrolidin-2-one* (**3.162**, which does contain an *imido motif*) was degraded to GABA due to hydrolytic opening of the ring, followed by hydrolysis of the exocyclic amide bond. However, neither derivative increased GABA levels in mouse brain after intraperitoneal administration. A similar conclusion emerges from the metabolism of *rolziracetam* (**3.163**), a nootropic agent whose two fused lactam rings of which create an imide motif. This compound was stable in buffer solutions, but was rapidly metabolized in laboratory animals by exclusive hydrolytic opening of a single ring [128]. The remaining pyrrolidinone ring was resistant to hydrolysis. The reason for this increased lability of cyclic imides compared to lactams appears due to two factors, namely a greater susceptibility to chemical hydrolysis, and the involvement of *dihydropyrimidinase* (EC 3.5.2.2; hydantoinase, see also *Fig. 3.6*) as an enzyme with clear specificity for *cyclic imides* (−CO−NR−CO−) and *cyclic ureides* (−CO−NH−CO−NH−). An example of a *six-membered cyclic imide* is that of *(+)-(S)-dexrazoxane* (**3.164**), a compound shown to protect against doxorubicin-induced cardiotoxicity which acts probably by diffusing into cells and hydrolyzing to its rings-opened, metal-chelating metabolites **3.165**, **3.166**, and **3.167** [129]. Chemical hydrolysis of dexrazoxane under physiological conditions was slow with half-lives of several hours. Dexrazoxane was also hydrolyzed enzymatically in the liver and kidney by dihydropyrimidine aminohydrolase. This enzyme could hydrolyze one but not a second ring in this molecule.

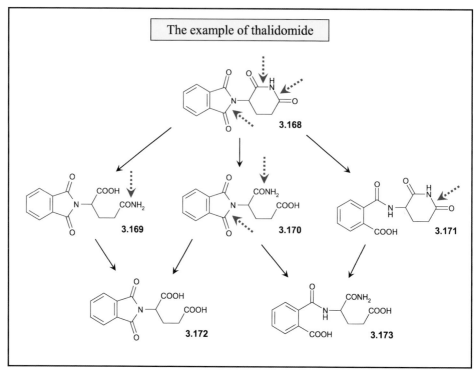

Fig. 3.52. The teratogenicity of *thalidomide* (**3.168**) produced a human tragedy in the late 1950s and very early 1960s. Recently, new clinical uses have been discovered, which have led to thalidomide being authorized again under the strictest conditions of security in the treatment of multiple myeloma and other severe pathologies. The structure of thalidomide shows two cyclic imide moieties, and earlier studies had revealed extensive hydrolysis generating twelve metabolites [3]. The main metabolite in humans was 4-phthalimidoglutaramic acid (**3.170**) and α-(2-carboxybenzamido)-glutaramide (**3.171**). Other metabolites (*e.g.*, **3.169**, **3.172**, and **3.173**) were minor, yet they confirm that all amide bonds are hydrolyzable as illustrated here. These reactions are mainly nonenzymatic, the half-live of disappearance of thalidomide in phosphate buffers under physiological conditions being *ca.* 2 h [130a]. The nonenzymatic nature of thalidomide hydrolysis was confirmed in incubations with mice and human liver microsomes, although metabolite **3.170** was produced enzymatically in rabbit microsomes [130b]. In addition to undergoing hydrolysis, thalidomide is also metabolized by cytochrome P450 to a variety of oxidized products.

3.6. The Hydrolysis of Esters of Inorganic Acids

3.6.1. Sulfates, Sulfamates, and Nitrates

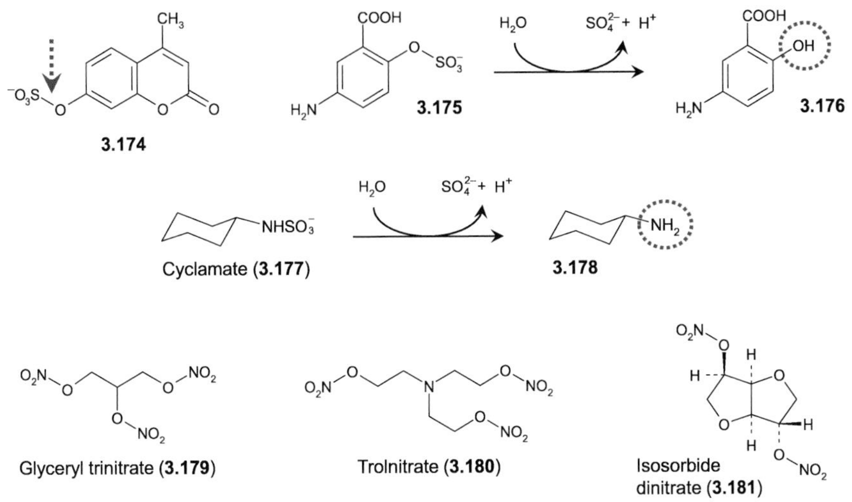

Fig. 3.53. Hydrolyzable derivatives of sulfuric acid include alkyl and aryl sulfates ($R-O-SO_3^-$), alkyl and aryl sulfamates ($R-O-SO_2NH_2$), and sulfamates ($R-NH-SO_3^-$). These compounds have little importance as drugs and prodrugs, but find some industrial applications. The greatest interest of sulfates in the present context is their reversible formation as conjugates of endogenous and exogenous alcohols and phenols (see *Part 4*). A number of enzymes known as *sulfuric ester hydrolases* (EC 3.1.6; see *Fig. 3.3*) are able to hydrolyze sulfate esters, *e.g.*, arylsulfatase (EC 3.1.6.1; sulfatase), steryl-sulfatase (EC 3.1.6.2; steroid sulfatase), and choline-sulfatase (EC 3.1.6.6). Arylsulfatase is of particular interest given its broad substrate specificity and its hydrolysis of sulfate conjugates of phenols, be they drugs or their metabolites [3]. Among *aryl sulfates*, *4-methylumbelliferyl sulfate* (**3.174**) is a convenient substrate sometimes used to investigate some characteristics of sulfate hydrolysis in *in vitro* preparations [3]. Such studies have also served to suggest that a futile cycle regulates sulfate conjugation within hepatocytes. A medicinal example is found with *5-aminosalicylic acid O-sulfate* (**3.175**; 5-ASA sulfate). 5-ASA (**3.176**) is a drug used for the treatment of ulcerative colitis and *Crohn*'s disease of the large intestine, but it can decarboxylate in the gastric juice. 5-ASA Sulfate was, therefore, developed as a prodrug able to reach its site of action (the colon) following oral application [131]. In healthy human subjects, the prodrug was almost completely hydrolyzed in the colon to the active agent. A high fecal and a low urinary excretion of the active metabolite 5-ASA were observed. *Sulfamates* behave differently from sulfates in that they are stable in alkaline conditions but are readily hydrolyzed in acidic

media. Cleavage occurs at the $N-S$ bond, as exemplified by the sweetening agent *cyclamate* (**3.177**). This compound sometimes undergoes metabolic cleavage to yield *cyclohexanamine* (**3.178**), a compound of some toxicological significance. For example, the urine of a group of diabetic patients receiving 1 g of cyclamate per day was examined for cyclamate and cyclohexanamine [132]. There was no significant urinary excretion of cyclohexanamine in the majority of cases (*ca.* 80%), but a small percentage of the subjects (4%) were found to excrete over 20% of the daily dose as cyclohexanamine. The reaction of cleavage, which is mediated by the gut flora, is presumably one of hydrolysis although reduction cannot be excluded.

Organic nitrates ($R-O-NO_2$) and nitrites are coronary vasodilators of great value in the treatment of angina pectoris. The discovery of glyceryl trinitrate and amyl nitrite dates back to the middle of the 19th century, and their introduction into therapy was quick to follow. Besides *glyceryl trinitrate* (**3.179**; trinitroglycerin, GTN), more recent nitrates include *trolnitrate* (**3.180**) and *isosorbide dinitrate* (**3.181**) [133]. These drugs are known collectively as *nitrovasodilators*. Despite the many decades amyl nitrite and glyceryl trinitrate have been used in therapy, it is only in recent years that the molecular mechanism of action of the nitrovasodilators has begun to be understood. The drugs act by releasing *nitric oxide* (NO˙, a neutral radical usually written simply as NO) which produces smooth muscle relaxation in blood vessels and exhibits a range of other biological effects. Thus, bioactivation to yield NO precedes the main therapeutic effect of nitrovasodilators, and would justify their classification as *prodrugs*. Despite the apparent simplicity of their molecular structure, the metabolism of these agents is chemically so complex, and their routes of bioactivation (not discussed here; see [3]) and inactivation so intimately intertwined that a detailed and coherent picture of their behavior is difficult to obtain. *In vivo*, *nitroglycerin* (**3.179**) undergoes fast degradation (duration of action *ca.* 0.5 h), hence its administration transdermally, sublingually, or orally in slow release form. The other agents listed above are given orally and have a duration of action of *ca.* 3–6 h, indicating greater *in vivo* stability. After administration of [^{14}C]nitroglycerin to rats, the urinary metabolites were the two dinitrates (*i.e.*, glycerol-1,3-dinitrate and glycerol-1,2-dinitrate), the two mononitrates (*i.e.*, glycerol-1-nitrate and glycerol-2-nitrate), glycerol, and other unidentified products including acids. These metabolites together represented a small fraction of the dose after oral administration, and no intact drug was detected. In contrast, subcutaneous administration led to the recovery in urine of *ca.* 1% of the dose as nitroglycerin, and *ca.* 40% as nitrate metabolites. A comparable pattern of metabolism was seen in humans. The results indicated a clear regioselective cleavage of the terminal ester group, as also found in dogs.

3.6.2. Phosphates and Analogues

Phosphate prodrugs

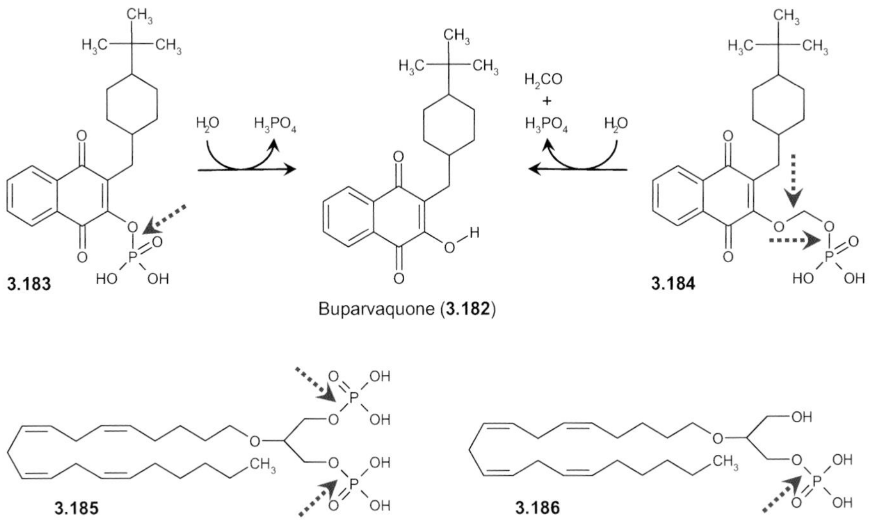

Buparvaquone (**3.182**)

Fig. 3.54. Phosphate esters and analogues such as phosphonates and phosphorami-dates are not an uncommon encounter in medicinal chemistry. In this *Figure*, we begin with phosphate prodrugs, namely compounds that are activated by hydrolytic loss of their phosphate promoiety. The derivatization of phenols or alcohols by phosphate esterification is usually performed to achieve greater solubility, although precipitation or absorption problems may result from premature hydrolysis [134]. Two recent examples illustrate different chemical strategies to achieve better water solubility. Thus, *buparvaquone* (**3.182**) is an effective antileishmania drug belonging to the class of hydroxynaphthoquinones, but its oral and topical availability suffers from poor water solubility. Two phosphate esters were, therefore, prepared, namely the prodrugs **3.183** and **3.184** [135]. Compared to the parent drug, their water solubility was markedly increased in the neutral and acidic pH range. The rates of chemical hydrolysis were rather slow in the acidic pH range, whereas enzymatic hydrolysis was generally fast. Permeation experiments suggested a good potential for topical and oral bioavailability. Note, however, that the hydrolysis of prodrug **3.184** liberates form-aldehyde, a potentially toxic breakdown product. Another example of phosphorylation in prodrug design involves the endocannabinoid *noladin ether*. This cannabinoid CB1 receptor agonist reduces intraocular pressure, but its pharmacological profiling and pharmaceutical development are hindered by a poor aqueous solubility. Its mono-phosphate, **3.186**, and diphosphate, **3.185**, increased the water solubility of noladin ether more than 40,000-fold. They showed high stability against chemical hydrolysis, yet were rapidly hydrolyzed by alkaline phosphatase and liver homogenates to the parent drug [136]. Hydrolysis in 4% cornea homogenates was also fast. When tested *in vivo* in rabbits, the monophosphate ester was very effective in reducing intraocular pressure.

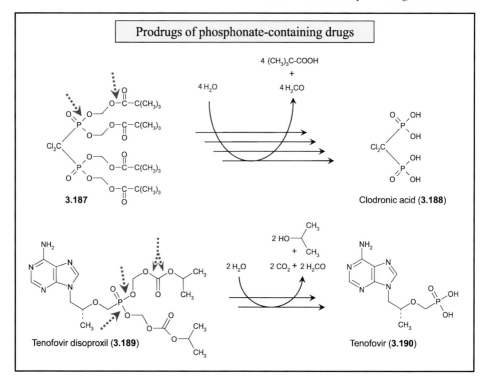

Fig. 3.55. The present and the next two *Figures* cover various cases of drugs whose pharmacophore contains a phosphate ($C-O-PO_3H_2$) or phosphonate ($C-PO_3H_2$) moiety. Their resulting polarity is generally too high to allow good absorption; in addition, biostability problems are encountered for phosphates. We begin here with the simpler case of *phosphonates*, where a prodrug strategy can help overcome bioavailability problems. The highly polar *clodronic acid* (**3.188**) and a number of analogues have demonstrated their clinical value in the treatment of osteoporosis, but they must often be administered by slow intravenous infusion due to their poor oral bioavailability. Esterification to orally available prodrugs is thus an actively investigated strategy. Promising results have for example, been obtained with the *tetrakis[(pivaloyloxy)methyl] clodronate* (**3.187**) [137]. This potential prodrug hydrolyzed rapidly and quantitatively to clodronic acid in rabbit liver homogenates. The tris[(pivaloyloxy)methyl] ester was found to be of particular interest given its adequate lipophilicity and water solubility. Phosphonates are also of interest as *analogues of mononucleotides* active as antiviral and anticancer agents [138][139]. But as exemplified by the anti-HIV and anti-hepatitis B virus agent *tenofovir* (**3.190**; PMPA), such highly polar compounds permeate poorly across epithelial barriers and hence have a poor bioavailability. *Tenofovir disoproxil* (**3.189**) has, therefore, been selected and is marketed as an oral prodrug for tenofovir [140].

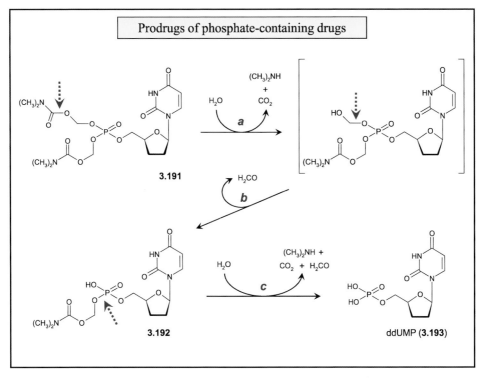

Fig. 3.56. *2′,3′-Dideoxyuridine 5′-monophosphate* (**3.193**; ddUMP) offers an informative example of the difficulties encountered in the design and development of *nucleoside monophosphates* compared to their monophosphonate analogues. Beside a poor cellular penetration common to both classes, nucleoside monophosphates also suffer a fast degradation to the corresponding nucleosides by 5′-nucleotidases and other phosphohydrolases. To be useful, a prodrug strategy must, therefore, ensure extracellular stability of the nucleoside–phosphate bond in order to achieve adequate penetration in target cells. A first promising strategy is illustrated here, and a second one in the next *Figure*. Earlier attempts with a bis(pivaloyloxymethyl) potential prodrug of ddUMP failed due to fast plasmatic hydrolysis. In contrast, *bis[(carbamoyloxy)methyl] derivatives* such as **3.191** were enzymatically stable in human plasma and underwent only slow spontaneous hydrolysis (*Reactions a and b*) which liberated the monoester **3.192** [141]. The latter proved a good substrate of phosphodiesterase I and led to a quantitative liberation of ddUMP (*Reaction c*).

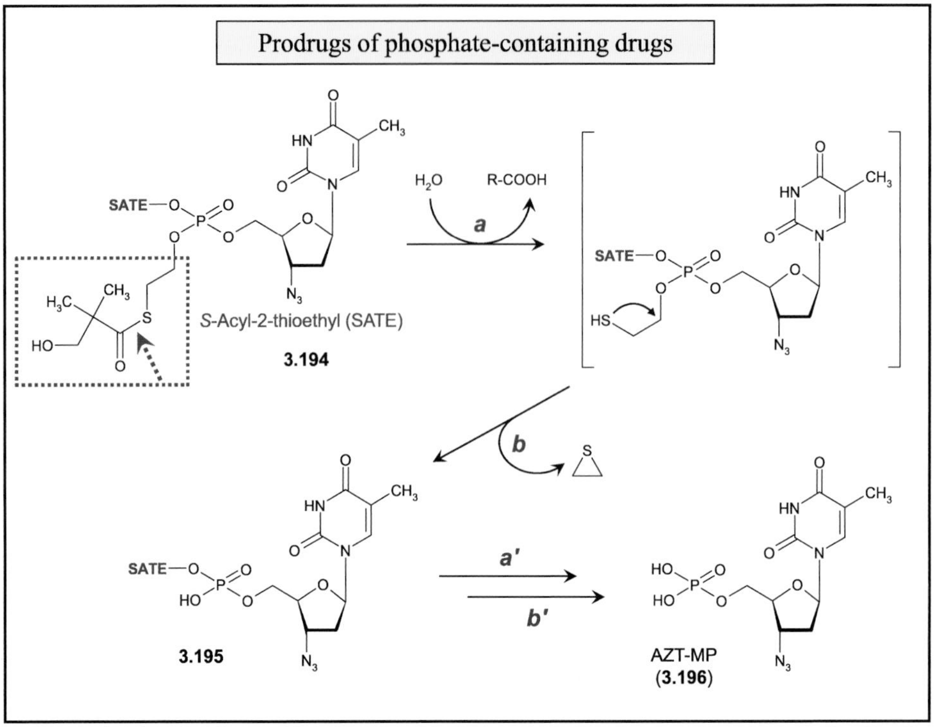

Fig. 3.57. Another promising attempt to achieve cellular delivery of nucleoside monophosphates is the so-called *SATE* approach. Here, two S-*acyl-2-thioethyl promoieties* are used to mask the two acidic O-atoms of a monophosphate moiety, as exemplified here with *bis(SATE)phosphotriester derivatives of zidovudine* (AZT) (**3.194**) [142]. Their mechanism of activation involves an esterase-catalyzed hydrolysis of one thioester bond (*Reaction a*), followed by a spontaneous intramolecular nucleophilic displacement resulting in loss of a thiirane molecule and production of the mono(SATE)phosphodiester **3.195** (*Reaction b*). A similar sequence cleaves the second SATE promoiety and liberates zidovudine monophosphate (**3.196**; *Reactions a'* and *b'*). The rate of activation proved controllable by varying the acyl moiety, with sterically hindered acyl groups (most notably pivaloyl groups) increasing enzymatic stability as expected. Intracellular delivery of AZT 5'-monophosphate and inhibition of HIV replication were indeed achieved with a number of such prodrugs.

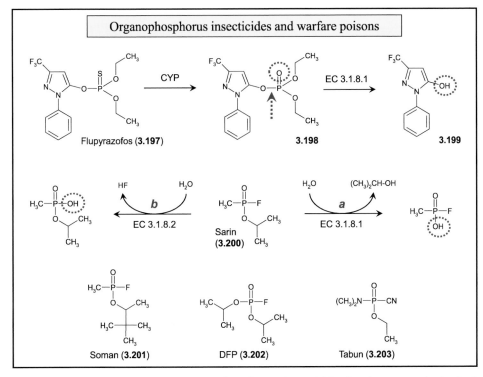

Fig. 3.58. The metabolism of *organophosphorus insecticides* is of great toxicological significance. In *Fig. 2.77* of *Part 2* [2], we saw that the phosphorothioate derivative parathion, a relatively non-toxic insecticide, undergoes CYP-catalyzed oxidative desulfuration to paraoxon. The latter, like its congeners and the P-halide warfare poisons to be discussed below, is highly toxic through its potent inactivation of acetylcholinesterase [143]. The inactivation and detoxification of *paraoxon* and congeneric aryldialkylphosphate esters are catalyzed mostly by various hydrolases classified under EC 3.1.8.1 (aryldialkylphosphatases, paraoxonase, see *Fig. 3.8*), most notably mammalian PON1 and bacterial phosphotriesterase [15–21][144]. *Flupyrazofos* (**3.197**) is a congeneric insecticide whose relatively simple metabolic scheme is quite informative. Indeed, rat liver microsomes formed *flupyrazofos oxon* (**3.198**) as the only detectable primary metabolite [145]. The latter then underwent chemical hydrolysis to the dephosphorylated phenol (**3.199**).

Another important group of organophosphates are the *organophosphorus acid anhydrides of the P–halide type*, namely the highly lethal nerve gases developed (and sometimes used) as warfare poisons. These agents include the phosphono- or phosphorofluoridates *sarin* (**3.200**), *soman* (**3.201**), and *DFP* (**3.202**; diisopropyl phosphorofluoridate), and the phosphoramidocyanidate analogue *tabun* (**3.203**). The P–halide or P–CN bond in these compounds is an anhydride bond. As stated above, their *toxicity* is due to their high efficiency as irreversible inactivators of acetylcholinesterase [146]. As for the *detoxification* of the P–halide anhydrides, it can occur by a number of biochemical mechanisms, namely chemical hydrolysis, enzymatic hydrolysis, and binding to hydrolases such as carboxylesterases, cholinesterases, and albumin [147]. As anhydrides, such compounds are subject to *spontaneous hydrolysis* which liberates a phosphate functionality, and F⁻ or CN⁻ and may contribute to detoxification. Enzymes hydrolyzing phosphorus anhydride bonds are the *organo-phosphorus acid anhydrolases* classified as EC 3.1.8.2 (also known as diisopropyl-fluorophosphatase), an activity related to EC 3.1.8.1 [3]. The two hydrolytic reactions of the P–halide anhydrides are exemplified schematically here with *sarin* (**3.200**), its phosphate ester bond being cleaved preferentially by enzymes classified under EC 3.1.8.1 (*Reaction a*) and its anhydride bond by EC 3.1.8.2 (*Reaction b*).

3.7. The Hydration of Epoxides

3.7.1. Epoxide Hydrolases

Enzyme ID Card: Epoxide Hydrolases (EH)

EC Numbers	EC 3.3.2.9 (microsomal EH) and EC 3.3.2.10 (soluble EH)
Enzyme subclass and sub-subclasses	*EC 3.3* Acting on ether bonds // *EC 3.3.2* Ether hydrolases
Systematic names and synonyms	EC 3.3.2.9 *cis*-stilbene-oxide hydrolase, mEH; EC 3.3.2.10 epoxide hydrolase, cytosolic EH, sEH
Human genes	*EPHX1* ⇒ mEH; *EPHX2* ⇒ sEH
Catalytic triad	Asp (nucleophile), His (general base), Asp/Glu (charge relay acid)
Subcellular localization	mEH: endoplasmic reticulum; sEH: cytoplasm, peroxisome
Organs (highest levels)	mEH: liver; sEH: liver, lung, placenta
Exogenous substrates	A large range of alkene epoxides (oxiranes) and arene epoxides
Endogenous substrates	Epoxides of some unsaturated fatty acids
Miscellaneous	Genetic variation in *EPHX1* may be associated with susceptibility to a pregnancy-induced hypertension known as preeclampsia

Fig. 3.59. Epoxides, also known to chemists as *oxiranes*, result from the monooxygenation of a C=C bond in olefins or aromatic rings. Such reactions of monooxygenation to produce epoxides as metabolites or metabolic intermediates are of utmost importance in drug and xenobiotic metabolism, being catalyzed by cytochromes P450 [2][4][148]. In addition, epoxides are also found as endogenous metabolites (*e.g.*, epoxides of squalene, some steroids, and vitamin K), as natural products (*e.g.*, scopolamine), and as industrial chemicals (*e.g.*, dieldrin). The enzymatic ring opening of oxiranes is a hydrolytic reaction catalyzed by epoxide hydrolases. These enzymes are a group of related enzymes sharing a similar catalytic mechanism but differing in substrate specificity and biochemical characteristics [7][8][149], the most significant of which are summarized in this *Figure*. Epoxide hydrolases are located in many organs and tissues where they play essential physiological roles, *e.g.*, vitamin K₁ oxide reductase [150][151]. They are of utmost significance in molecular toxicology, being involved in the detoxification of reactive arene oxides (see also *Part 5*) [152].

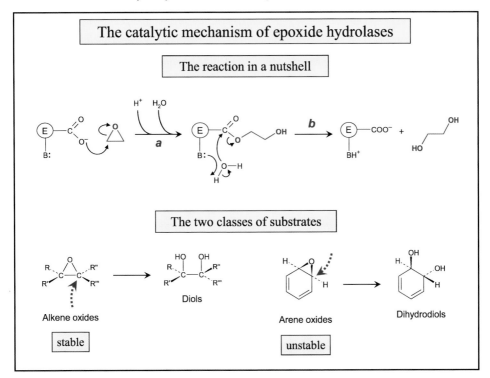

Fig. 3.60. The overall reaction catalyzed by epoxide hydrolases is the addition of a H_2O molecule to an epoxide. Earlier studies had postulated that epoxide hydrolases act by enhancing the nucleophilicity of a H_2O molecule and directing it to attack an epoxide. The correct mechanism is now recognized to be more complex and to involve the formation of an *ester intermediate* [3]. As summarized here, the nucleophilic attack of the substrate is mediated by a carboxylate group in the catalytic site to form the ester intermediate (*Reaction a*). In a second step (*Reaction b*), this intermediate is hydrolyzed by an activated H_2O molecule, leading to enzyme reactivation and product liberation (see *Figs. 3.61 – 3.64* for more details). Turning our attention to *substrates*, we first note that the *chemical reactivity* of epoxides varies widely depending on their chemical structure, and it is often of toxicological significance [3]. From a metabolic and toxicological viewpoint, it is customary to distinguish three classes of epoxides, namely *alkene oxides* (epoxides of C=C bonds, be they isolated or conjugated), *arene oxides* (epoxides of aromatic rings), and the *diol-epoxides*, a very special and highly reactive sub-class of alkene oxides encountered in the metabolism of polycyclic aromatic hydrocarbons (see *Parts 4* and *5*). Alkene oxides thus yield *diols*, whereas arene oxides yield *trans-dihydrodiols*.

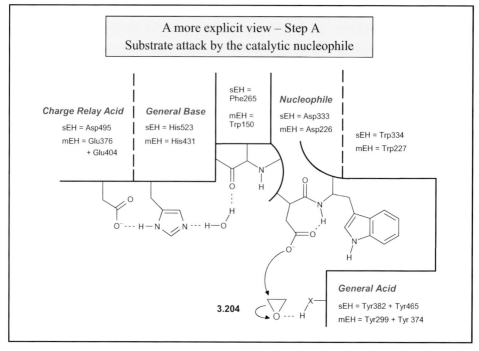

Figs. 3.61–3.64. The human *microsomal epoxide hydrolase* (mEH) contains 455 amino acids (molecular mass of 52.5 kDa) and is the product of the *EPHX1* gene. The human *soluble epoxide hydrolase* (sEH) has 554 amino acids (molecular mass 62.3 kDa) and is the product of the *EPHX2* gene. As schematized in *Figs. 3.61–3.64* with the hydration of oxirane **3.204** to ethylene glycol **3.205**, the reaction mechanism of mEH and sEH involves a *catalytic triad* consisting of a nucleophile, a general base, and a charge relay acid, in close analogy with many other hydrolases [153][154]. The *nucleophile* (Asp333 in human sEH; Asp226 in human mEH) is potentiated by the electrophilic assistance of a number of auxiliary residues (presumably Phe265 plus Trp334 in sEH; Trp150 plus Trp227 in mEH). In addition, activation of the epoxide substrate appears mediated by a general acid (Tyr382 plus Tyr465 in sEH; Tyr299 plus Tyr374 in mEH) (*Step A*, *Fig. 3.61*). Attack of the epoxide by the nucleophile opens the oxirane ring and creates an oxyanion intermediate (*e.g.*, $Asp-CO-O-CH_2CH_2-O^-$), a transition state stabilized by an *oxyanion hole*. It is believed that the terminal amino group of Lys328 may be involved in stabilization or protonation of the oxyanion in mEH. In addition, Phe265 (sEH) or Trp150 (mEH) may also be part of the oxyanion hole. Following protonation of the oxyanion, the former nucleophile now exists as a *β-hydroxyalkyl ester* whose hydrolysis marks the second catalytic step of epoxide hydrolases (*Step B*, *Fig. 3.62*). This hydrolysis involves the activation of a H_2O molecule by the *general base* (His523 in sEH; His431 in mEH), with the assistance of the *charge relay acid* (Asp495 in sEH; Glu376 plus Glu404 in mEH). In the transition state (*Step C, Fig. 3.63*), the tetrahedral intermediate is presumably also stabilized by neighboring residues, whereas the protonated general base will contribute to the final cleavage. Product liberation (*Step D*) is shown in *Fig. 3.64*, with the enzyme poised for a further catalytic cycle.

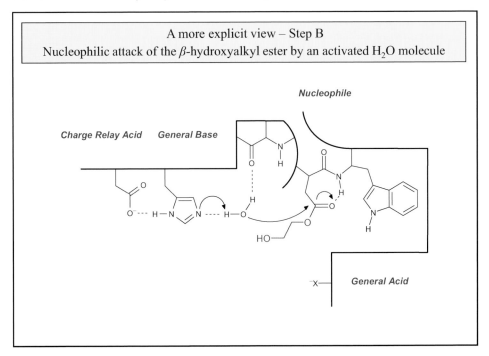

Fig. 3.62.

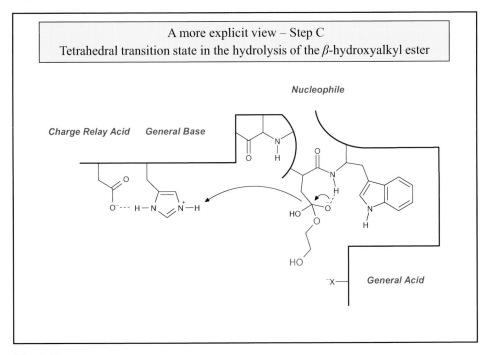

Fig. 3.63.

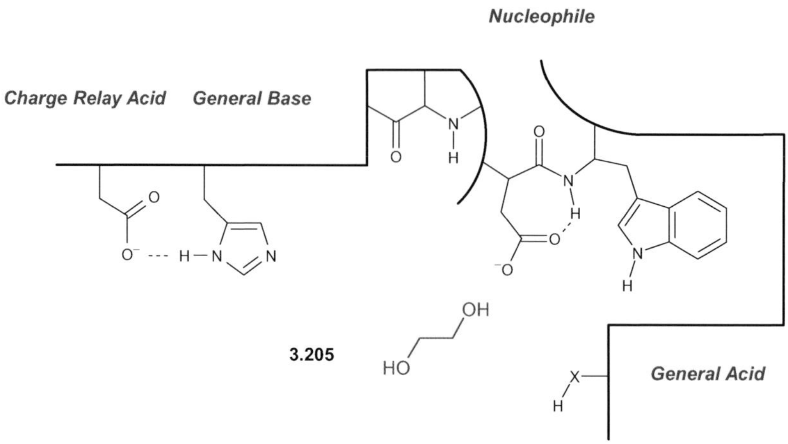

Fig. 3.64.

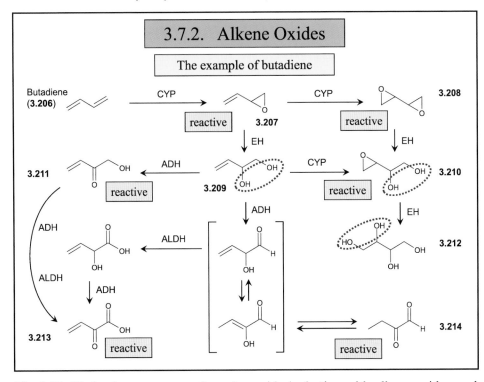

Fig. 3.65. We begin our presentation of epoxide hydration with alkene oxides, and specifically here with the case of a simple conjugated diene. *Buta-1,3-diene* (**3.206**) is a gaseous chemical used heavily in the rubber and plastics industry. Its presence in such industries and in urban air is also a concern. As butadiene is suspected of increasing the risks of hematopoietic cancers, it is classified as probably carcinogenic in humans. Metabolic activation is necessary for butadiene to produce toxicity. Thus, its metabolites *butadiene monoepoxide* (**3.207**; a chiral compound) and *diepoxybutane* (**3.208**, which exists is two enantiomeric and one *meso*-form) reacted with glutathione (see *Part 4*) and nucleic acids (see *Part 5*), as did 3,4-epoxybutane-1,2-diol (**3.210**) [3][155]. In rat liver microsomes, (*R*)- and (*S*)-butadiene monoepoxide (**3.207**) were hydrolyzed by epoxide hydrolase to but-3-ene-1,2-diol (**3.209**) with complete retention of configuration at C(2), indicating attack at C(1). The hydrolysis of diepoxybutane (**3.208**) yielded 3,4-epoxybutane-1,2-diol (**3.210**), which was further hydrated by epoxide hydrolase to erytritol (**3.212**). The metabolite but-3-ene-1,2-diol (**3.209**) is of particular interest, since its further oxidation by alcohol dehydrogenase yielded products such as α,β-unsaturated ketones, **3.211** and **3.213**, which react with nucleophiles such as glutathione. Dehydrogenation of the primary alcoholic group to an α-hydroxy aldehyde, followed by fast rearrangement led to 2-oxobutanal (**3.214**). These postulated intermediates appear to be quite reactive electrophiles trapped by glutathione and other endogenous nucleophiles. In summary, at least part of the chronic toxicity of buta-1,3-diene is due to reactive metabolites bearing an epoxy or α,β-unsaturated carbonyl group. The interplay of cytochromes P450, dehydrogenases, and epoxide hydrolases in generating such metabolites is summarized in this *Figure*.

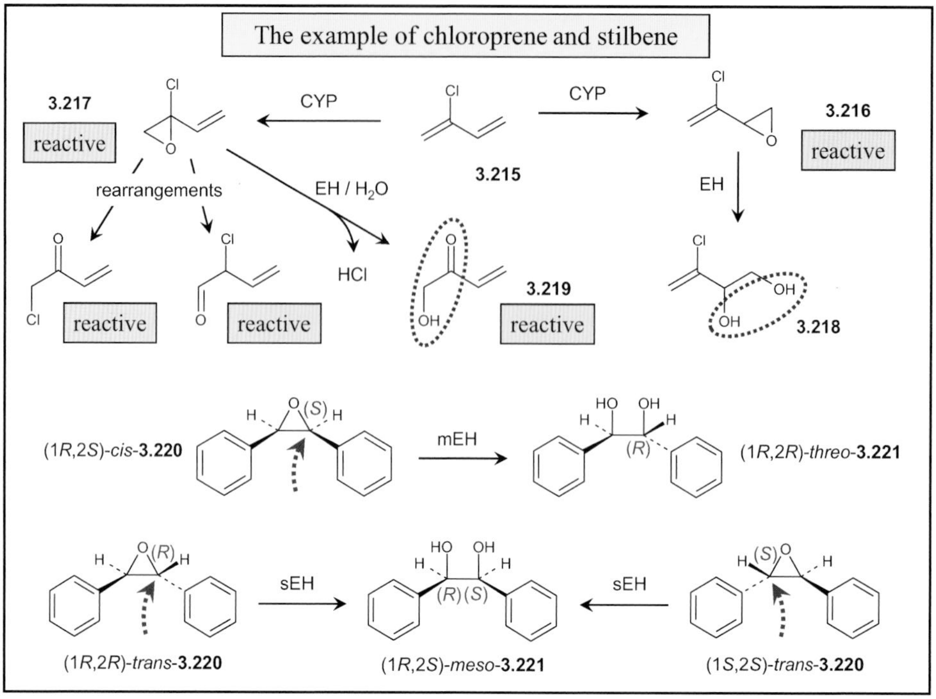

Fig. 3.66. The metabolism of haloalkene oxides such as the epoxides of monochloro-, dichloro-, and trichloroethylene is markedly more complex than that of non-halogenated alkene oxides [3]. Indeed, haloalkene oxides also undergo reactions of rearrangement which often involve halogen migration, yielding more products than simple diols and their own dehydrogenated metabolites. This is illustrated here with *chloroprene* (**3.215**; 2-chlorobuta-1,3-diene) [156]. This industrial compound is used as a monomer in the production of polychloroprene and as an elastomer in rubber goods. Two mono-epoxides are produced by CYPs, namely **3.216** and **3.217**. *(1-Chloroethenyl)oxirane* (**3.216**) reacts with epoxide hydrolase to yield the diol **3.218** and with glutathione to yield conjugates (see *Part 4*), but it appears stable enough not to undergo rearrangement spontaneously. This contrasts with the reactivity of *2-chloro-2-ethenyloxirane* (**3.217**) which *a*) undergoes rearrangement with and without Cl migration, and *b*) reacts with epoxide hydrolase and/or H$_2$O to form the dechlorinated, α,β-unsaturated ketone **3.219**. Another compound of interest is *stilbene oxide* (**3.220**; 2,3-diphenyloxirane) which exists as two diastereoisomers, namely *cis*- and *trans*-stilbene oxide [157]. Both compounds are substrates of epoxide hydrolase to yield *1,2-diphenylethanediol* (**3.221**), with mEH being more active toward *cis*-stilbene oxide, and sEH more active toward *trans*-stilbene oxide [3][149][156]. The hydration of stilbene oxide also demonstrates informative stereochemical features. The hydrolysis of the symmetrical meso-*cis*-stilbene oxide was found to yield exclusively one of the two enantiomeric products, namely (*R,R*)-*threo*-1,2-diphenylethanediol. This implies that enzymatic attack with *inversion of configuration* occurs with high selectivity at the (*S*)-configured C-atom. The *chiral* trans-*stilbene oxide* behaved differently, both enantiomers yielding *meso*-1,2-diphenylethanediol. This means that in both enantiomeric substrates, the enzyme does not discriminate between the two oxirane C-atoms and inverts the configuration of the one it attacks.

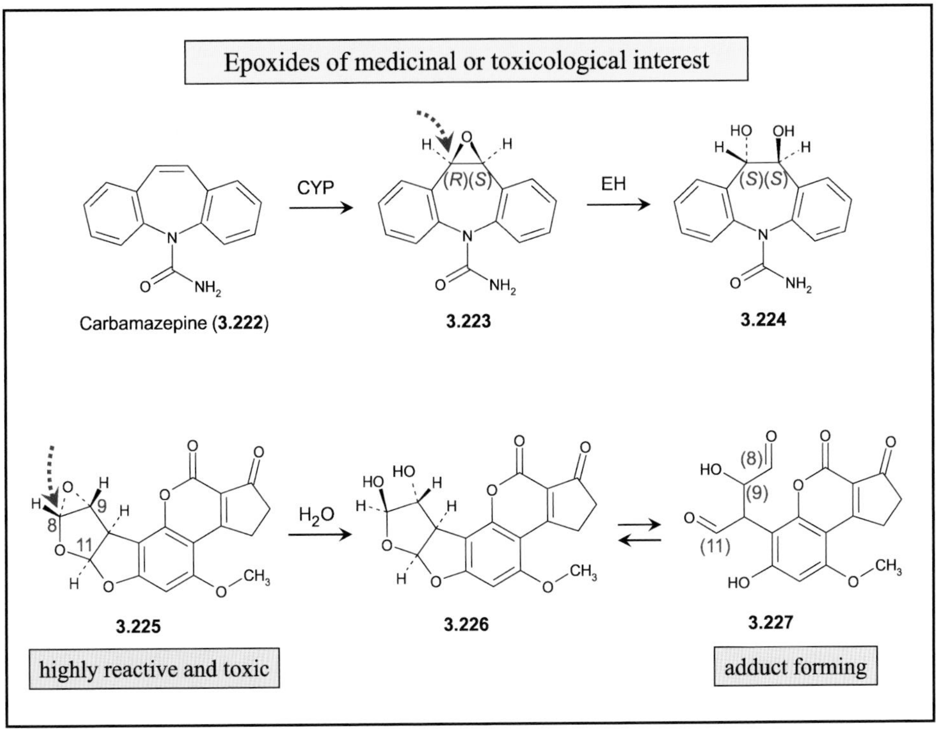

Fig. 3.67. *Carbamazepine* (**3.222**) is a major antiepileptic drug producing well over 30 metabolites [3][158]. Thus, the symmetrical *meso*-10,11-epoxide **3.223** and the 10,11-dihydrodiol **3.224** are urinary metabolites in humans and rats given the drug. The dihydrodiol is mostly the chiral (10*S*,11*S*)-*trans*-enantiomer **3.224**, implying enzymatic attack on the (*R*)-configured C-atom. Since the pharmacologically active 10,11-epoxide is suspected to contribute to clinical toxicity, the EH-catalyzed hydrolysis of the epoxide appears as a reaction of detoxification. Interestingly, EH-catalyzed hydrolysis is much more effective in humans than in laboratory animals. Moving to *toxic compounds*, we encounter the infamous *aflatoxin B1*, a mycotoxin considered to be a major cause of human liver cancer in some parts of the world [159]. Oxidation of aflatoxin B1 at the C(8)=C(9) bond, mainly by CYP3A4, produces the *endo*-8,9-epoxide as a minor metabolite and the exo-8,9-*epoxide* **3.225** as a major one. In contrast to its unreactive and nontoxic *endo*-diastereoisomer, the *exo*-8,9-epoxide is *highly reactive* and *genotoxic*. It reacts extremely rapidly with H_2O by H^+-catalyzed and H_2O-catalyzed (pH 5–10; $t_{1/2}$ *ca.* 1 s) hydrolysis. In this pH range, the predominant product of hydrolysis is the (8*R*,9*R*)-dihydrodiol **3.226**. Thus, aflatoxin B1 exo-8,9-epoxide is possibly the most reactive oxirane of biological relevance, so reactive in fact that EH does not seem to play a role in its metabolism. A further remarkable fact is the relative instability of the dihydrodiol, which under basic conditions exists in equilibrium with a ring-opened α-hydroxy dialdehyde **3.227**. This dialdehyde forms *Schiff* bases with primary NH_2 groups leading to protein adducts. However, its slow rate of formation and its reduction by aldo-keto reductases cast doubts on its toxicological relevance [3][160].

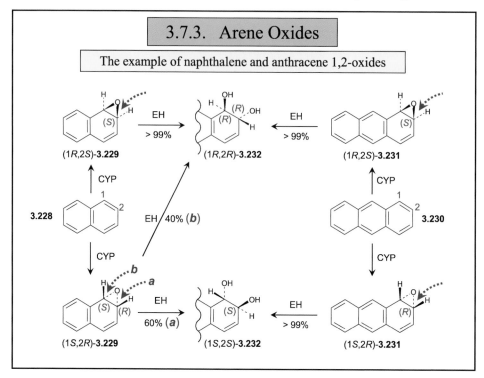

3.7.3. Arene Oxides

The example of naphthalene and anthracene 1,2-oxides

Fig. 3.68. As explained above, arene oxides are hydrated by epoxide hydrolases to the so-called *trans*-dihydrodiols. Like with alkene oxide, enzymatic attack on one of the two oxirane C-atoms occurs with *inversion of configuration*. A limited number of phenyl-containing drugs have been shown to yield a dihydrodiol metabolite in addition to a phenol, as exemplified in *Part 2* with *trans*-dihydro-rofecoxib-3′,4′-diol, a metabolite of the COX-2 inhibitor *rofecoxib* (*Fig. 2.51*; but see also *Fig. 2.49*) [2]. The relative rarity of such metabolites can be explained by the very fast isomerization of benzene oxides to phenols which prevents them from reaching epoxide hydrolase. In contrast, epoxides of polycyclic aromatic hydrocarbons are somewhat less reactive toward H_2O and offer more examples of dihydrodiol metabolites [3]. In this *Figure*, we compare *naphthalene* (**3.228**) and *anthracene* (**3.230**) [161]. Depending on the cytochrome P450 used, the two compounds yielded different ratios of the (+)-(1R,2S)- and (−)-(1S,2R)-enantiomer of their respective epoxides **3.229** and **3.231**. Of relevance here is their subsequent EH-catalyzed hydration, which in three cases proceeded with high stereoselectivity. Only with (−)-(1S,2R)-naphthalene 1,2-oxide was a mixture of the two enantiomeric dihydrodiols formed (**3.232**). The determining factor controlling the absolute configuration of the dihydrodiols was the regioselectivity of nucleophilic hydration. Attack at the *allylic position* (*i.e.*, C(2)) inverted the absolute configuration at this position, whereas attack at the *benzylic position* inverted the configuration at C(1). The mechanistic implication of these findings is that hydration of the two (+)-(1R,2S)-epoxides, **3.229** and **3.231**, occurred at the allylic position, as did hydration of (−)-(1S,2R)-anthracene 1,2-oxide. In contrast, hydration of (−)-(1S,2R)-naphthalene 1,2-oxide occurred at both the benzylic and allylic positions.

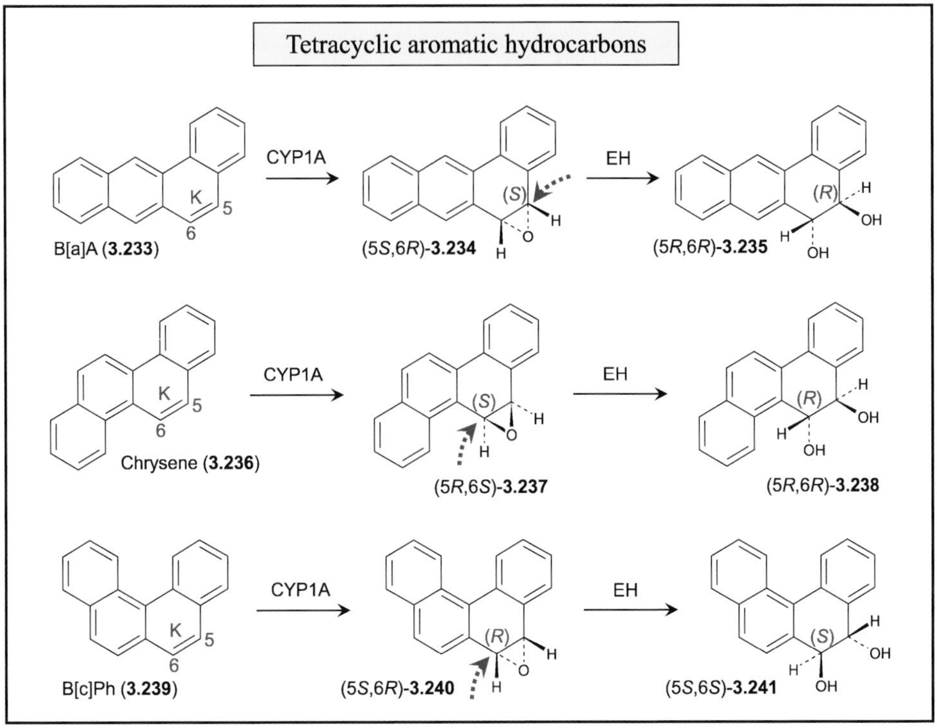

Fig. 3.69. *Polycyclic aromatic hydrocarbons* (PAHs) contain 'regions' which differ in their metabolic behavior and reactivity. *Bay- and fjord-regions* are zones of steric hindrance, *K-regions* are electron-rich ones, and *M-regions* yield dihydrodiols as metabolic precursors of the bay-region diol-epoxides of major toxicological significance (see *Part 5*) [162][163]. Here, we examine three isomeric tetracyclic aromatic hydrocarbons whose metabolism in their K-region reveals further insights into the stereospecificity of epoxide hydrolase. *Benz[a]anthracene* (**3.233**; B[a]A), *chrysene* (**3.236**), and *benzo[c]phenanthrene* (**3.239**; B[c]Ph) are oxidized by CYP1A1 and 1A2 with high stereoselectivity (74–98%) to their 5,6-epoxides, **3.234**, **3.237**, and **3.240**, respectively. The EH-catalyzed hydration of the enantiomers of these *K-region epoxides* to the corresponding *trans*-dihydrodiols, **3.235**, **3.238**, and **3.241**, also occurs with high stereoselectivity (77–98%), allowing informative comparisons to be made [3][164]. With two among the three substrates, *i.e.*, **3.234** and **3.237**, nucleophilic attack is selective for the oxirane C-atom with (*S*)-configuration. And in two cases out of three, nucleophilic attack occurs preferentially at C(6) (*i.e.*, **3.237** and **3.240**). In other words, the *regio- and stereoselectivity* of EH-catalyzed hydration appears to depend not only on local structural factors (*i.e.*, absolute configuration of the site of attack), but also on molecular factors such as the substrate's topology (which influences its positioning in the catalytic site).

3.8. Miscellaneous Reactions

3.8.1. The Hydrolysis of Carbohydrate Conjugates

Natural glycosides

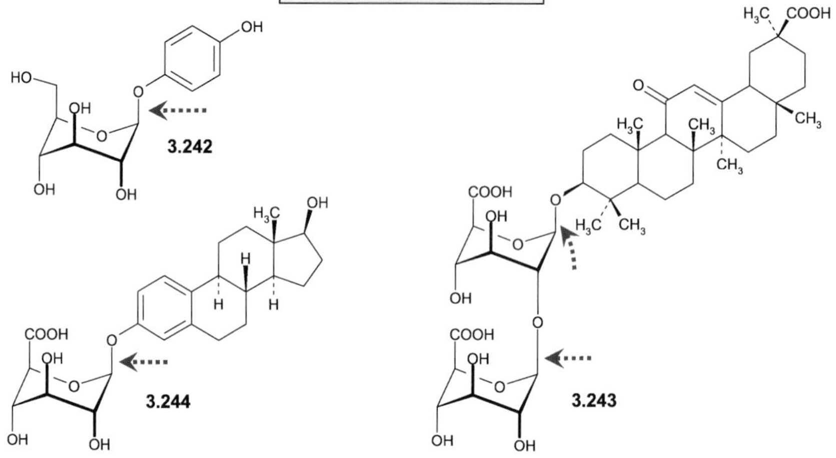

Fig. 3.70. *Chapt. 3.8* concludes this *Part 3* by summarizing a few miscellaneous metabolic reactions which cleave bonds by enzymatic or nonenzymatic hydrolysis [3]. Beginning with *carbohydrate conjugates* (*i.e.*, glycosyl conjugates), we note that their hydrolysis is catalyzed by enzymes classified as *glycosidases* (EC 3.2), the majority of which are glycosidases hydrolyzing *O*-glycosyl compounds (EC 3.2.1) (see *Fig. 3.3*). As far as xenobiotic metabolism is concerned, the most important enzyme is *β-glucuronidase* (EC 3.2.1.31; which removes β-D-glucuronic acid), a ubiquitous enzyme localized in the endoplasmic reticulum, in lysozymes, in blood serum, and also remarkably active in intestinal bacteria (see *Fig. 3.11*) [165]. A few other enzymes such as *β-glucosidase* (EC 3.2.1.21; which removes β-D-glucose) are also of interest. Enzymes cleaving *N*-glycosyl and *S*-glycosyl compounds may also play a role in xenobiotic metabolism. Monomeric carbohydrates in their cyclic form (furanoses and pyranoses) are *hemiacetals*, to become *acetals* when they form *O*-glycosyl conjugates. The C-atom bearing the two O-atoms (C(1)) is the reactive, electrophilic center targeted by glycosidases. Nonenzymatic hydrolysis is also possible, although, as a rule, the reaction is of limited significance under physiological conditions of pH and temperature. O-*Glycosyl compounds* have great significance as natural products, in particular glycosides of anthocyanins, chalcones, cinnamic acids, coumarins, flavones, lignans, xanthones, *etc.* Many of these conjugates are present in foods and enter our body with the diet. Other natural *O*-glycosyl compounds are used as drugs in purified form (*e.g.*, cardiac glycosides) or as active agents in herbal extracts (*e.g.*, *Ginseng* preparations). Whereas metabolic hydrolysis to the aglycone is often documented,

fewer studies seem to have addressed basic enzymological aspects such as the nature and distribution of enzymes, the kinetics of the reactions and structure–metabolism relationships. A relevant example is that of *arbutin* (**3.242**), the *O-glucoside of hydroquinone*. This conjugate is contained in some herbal medicines used as urinary antiseptics; its hydrolysis under the relatively acidic conditions prevailing in urine liberates the active hydroquinone. In a sense, arbutin can be considered as a natural prodrug undergoing site-selective activation [3].

Conjugates of glucuronic acid are also of interest, *e.g.*, *glycyrrhizin* (**3.243**), the sweetener found as a main constituent in liquorice extract, in fact a diglucuronide. Hydrolysis to the monoglucuronide was seen in all examined subcellular fractions of rat liver [166]. The highest activity was localized in lysosomes, but the nuclear, mitochondrial, microsomal, and soluble fractions were also active. The rate of monoglucuronide formation was fastest in human liver lysosomes, and slower in other species. The second hydrolytic reaction, from the monoglucuronide to glycyrrhetic acid, was always markedly slower than the first reaction of hydrolysis, being modest in rat liver lysosomes, slow in mouse, and undetectable in humans and other species. Globally, two metabolic pathways of glycyrrhizin were seen, one a β-D-glucuronidase-dependent direct hydrolysis to glycyrrhetic acid, and the other consisting of two different β-D-glucuronidases hydrolyzing glycyrrhizin first to its monoglucuronide and the latter to glycyrrhetic acid.

As we shall see in *Part 4*, *O-glucuronide formation* is a major reaction of conjugation (*i.e.*, Phase II) of endogenous and exogenous alcohols and phenols. When sufficiently polar and large (having a molecular weight above *ca.* 500 in humans), a number of such glucuronides are transported into the bile and excreted. In such cases, the gut wall and microflora glucuronidases can play a particular role in hydrolyzing glucuronides, rendering possible their subsequent intestinal reabsorption. This sequence of glucuronidation–excretion–deglucuronidation–reabsorption is known as *enterohepatic cycling*. It is sometimes considered as a *futile cycle* despite the fact that it can have clinical or physiological consequences by increasing the apparent half-life of a hormone, a drug or a metabolite. This has been convincingly demonstrated in healthy post-menopausal women dosed orally with the natural hormone *17β-estradiol* [167]. Indeed, the first absorption phase of estradiol was followed after 1–2 h by a second absorption phase which maintained plasma levels practically constant during 24 h. This was due to the formation and enterohepatic cycling of *estradiol-3β-D-glucuronide* (**3.244**) and *estrone-3β-D-glucuronide*. Stated differently, exogenous estradiol and its metabolite estrone followed the circulation route of endogenous estrogen hormones. By maintaining prolonged serum levels of the hormone, the enterohepatic cycling of estrogens is thus far from futile.

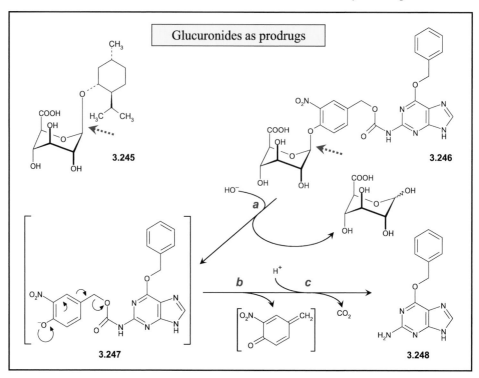

Fig. 3.71. A promising aspect of glucuronide hydrolysis is in *prodrug design* [168], given the potential for tissue-selective hydrolysis and delivery afforded by relatively high glucuronidase activities in tumors and the intestine. An application of this concept is seen with intestine targeting to treat ulcerative colitis and irritable bowel syndrome. Thus, (−)-menthol, the main constituent of peppermint oil, attenuates spasms and motility of the large intestine, but its activity is limited by rapid absorption in the small intestine. *Menthol-β-D-glucuronide* (**3.245**) was, therefore, examined for the colon-specific delivery of menthol [169]. This glucuronide was hydrolyzed by the luminal contents of rat and human colon and caecum, in other words by glucuronidase-rich microflora. A more complex case is illustrated by potential prodrugs of O-*benzylguanine* (**3.248**). This agent inactivates DNA-repair mechanisms, an effect that can improve the effectiveness of chemotherapeutic drugs. However, the lack of tumor specificity of this therapy can lead to undesirable side effects, hence the search for better targeted prodrugs. This has led to the preparation and evaluation of inventive prodrugs whose promoiety is made of a trigger and a self-immolating linker, as exemplified by the *β-D-glucuronide* *prodrugs* **3.246** [170]. Here, the trigger is glucuronic acid, whose cleavage by β-glucuronidase (*Reaction a*) is the initial event in the activation cascade. The linker in the intermediate **3.247** undergoes fast spontaneous 1,6-elimination (*Reaction b*) to a nitro-*p*-quinonemethine (which imme-diately reacts with H_2O to form 4-hydroxy-3-nitrobenzyl alcohol). The carbamic acid liberated during the 1,6-elimination spontaneously decarboxylates (*Reaction c*) to O-benzylguanine **3.248**. This strategy appears of interest in direct prodrug monotherapy as well as in antibody-directed enzyme prodrug therapy (ADEPT, see *Part 5*).

3.8.2. The Hydrolysis of Imines and Oximes

Two examples of medicinal interest

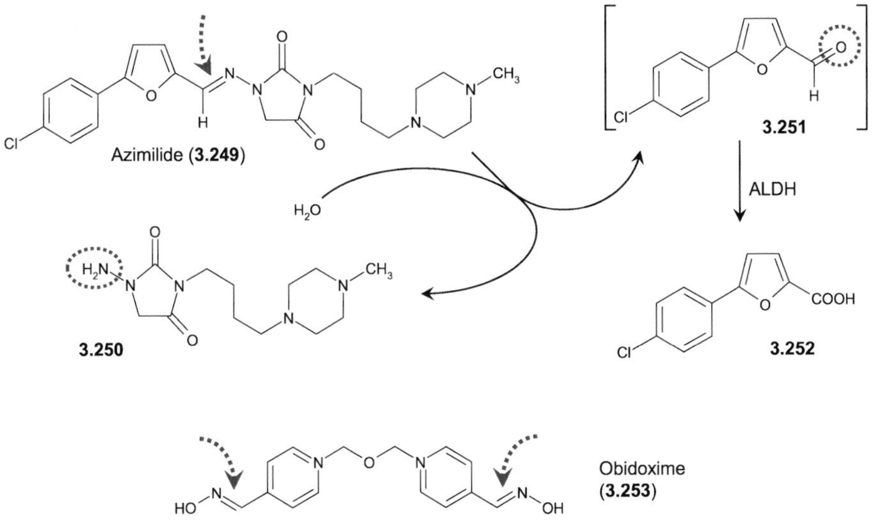

Fig. 3.72. In this *Section*, we summarize the hydrolysis of *imines* ($>C=N-R$, *i.e.*, *Schiff* bases) and *oximes* ($>C=N-OH$). However, the C=N motif is also found in other moieties such as *hydrazones* ($>C=N-NRR'$), *enaminones* ($-C(=O)-CRR'-C(R'')=N-R'''$), *imidates* ($RO-C(R')=N-R''$), *amidines* ($>N-C(R)=N-R'$), *oximines* ($>C=N-OR$), and *isocyanates* ($O=C=N-R$). Such groups occur in drugs, drug metabolites, prodrugs, and other xenobiotics. Their hydrolysis is essentially a *nonenzymatic process*, and the rates will depend not only on the biological context, but also on the structure and properties of the compounds [3]. Two compounds of medicinal interest are presented in this *Figure*. *Azimilide* (**3.249**) is a novel class II antiarrhythmic drug with a unique structure. Its metabolism in humans and in human liver microsomes revealed a number of oxidative pathways catalyzed by CYPs and FMO [171]. In addition, imine cleavage accounted for more than 35% of a dose *in vivo* but was negligible *in vitro*. No evidence was obtained to suggest an enzymatic reaction. The products of this cleavage were identified as the piperazine derivative **3.250** and the acid **3.252**; the primary metabolite **3.251** was not identified due to fast dehydrogenation. Moving to *oximes*, it is known that a number of such agents are used as reactivators of acetylcholinesterase inactivated by organophosphorous poisons (See *Fig. 3.58*). *Obidoxime* (**3.253**), one such agent, undergoes acid-catalyzed hydrolysis to the mono- and dialdehyde plus hydroxylamine [172]. Because the reaction is a reversible one, it can go to completion in very dilute solutions only.

Imines and oximes as prodrugs

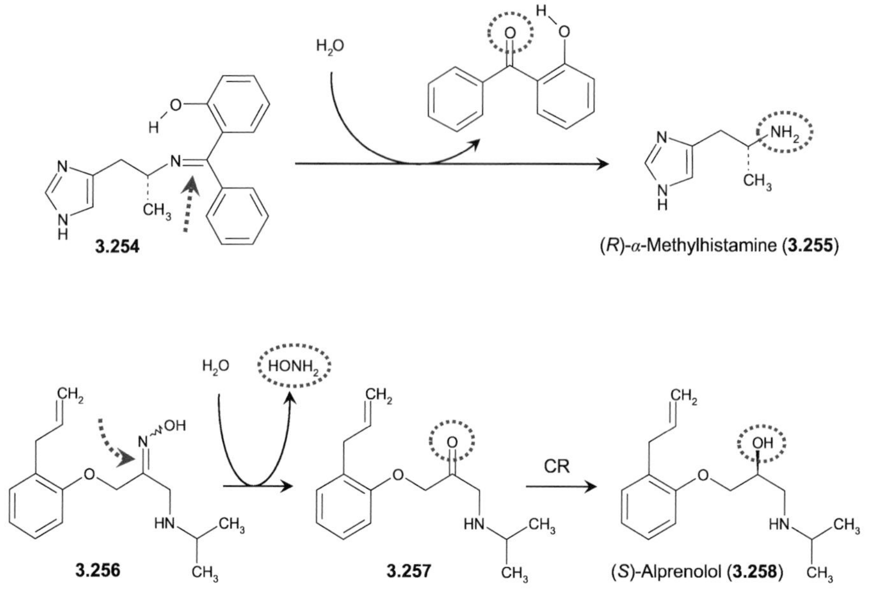

Fig. 3.73. *Azomethine prodrugs of (R)-α-methylhistamine* and in particular compound **3.254** offer an apt illustration of the interest of imines. *(R)-α-Methylhistamine* (**3.255**) is a potent and selective histamine H₃ receptor agonist whose medicinal use is limited by insufficient peroral absorption, poor brain penetration, and rapid metabolism. To circumvent these problems, potential prodrugs were prepared by reacting the drug with 2-hydroxybenzophenone (*i.e.*, **3.254**) and ring-substituted analogues [173]. Most compounds proved readily hydrolyzable in aqueous solutions in the acidic-to-neutral range. Following oral administration to mice, good plasma levels of (*R*)-α-methylhist-amine were seen for a number of derivatives. *In vivo* pharmacological investigations of **3.254** demonstrated anti-inflammatory and antinociceptive properties. These results document the potential of imine prodrugs to improve the pharmacokinetic profile of some primary amines. *Oximes* may also have some potential in prodrug design, as evidenced by *oxime analogues of β-adrenergic blocking agents* [174]. A number of these potential prodrugs, including *alprenoxime* (**3.256**), were readily transformed into the corresponding β-blocker. The metabolic sequence involved first oxime hydrolysis to the ketone **3.257** in a reaction the nonenzymatic nature of which is most probable. Hydrolysis was followed by a stereospecific (and hence enzymatic) ketone reduction to the active enantiomer *(S)-alprenolol* (**3.258**). The stereospecific activation of alprenoxime was *organ-specific* in that it took place in the eye and not systemically, as verified by *in vitro* experiments. When administered locally to rabbits, marked decreases in intraocular pressure were seen, whereas oral administration elicited almost no cardiac effects. Such ketoximes could appear as promising chemical delivery systems in the treatment of glaucoma, particularly when the oxime group was protected by an *O*-Me group.

3.8.3. The Hydrolysis of *Mannich* Bases

Linear *Mannich* bases

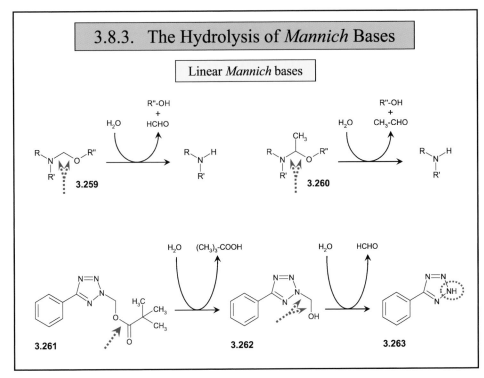

Fig. 3.74. This *Section* presents the hydrolysis of *Mannich* bases, namely compounds containing the $N-CH_2-X$ moiety, where the sp³-C-atom is rendered electrophilic by two flanking heteroatoms. Such compounds comprise among others N-*Mannich* bases ($>N-CH_2-N<$), O-*Mannich* bases (where $X=O$, namely *N*-hydroxymethyl $>N-CH_2-OH$ or *N*-alkoxymethyl $>N-CH_2-OR$ derivatives), and S-*Mannich* bases. *Mannich*-base moieties appear mainly in (potential) prodrugs, where they usually undergo rapid nonenzymatic hydrolysis [175]. This is exemplified here with generic *N*-alkoxymethyl and *N*-alkoxyethyl structures, **3.259** and **3.260**, respectively, whose hydrolysis liberates an alcohol or a phenol, plus formaldehyde or acetaldehyde, respectively. An example of therapeutic potential is found in *N*-acyloxymethyl derivatives of phenyltetrazole. The *tetrazole ring* is of particular interest in drug design due to its remarkable acidity which has led to its use as an isostere of the carboxylic group. For example, 5-phenyltetrazole (**3.263**) with a pK_a of 4.5 is slightly more acidic than benzoic acid. To gain a preliminary insight into the hydrolytic behavior of acyloxymethyl derivatives of 5-phenyltetrazole taken as a model compound, *2-[(pivaloyloxy)methyl]-5-phenyltetrazole* (**3.261**) and its isomer 1-[(pivaloyloxy)-methyl]-5-phenyltetrazole were examined [176]. The compounds were found to be highly sensitive to rat plasma esterases, which hydrolyzed the ester bond. The *N*-hydroxymethyl intermediate **3.262** so produced was short-lived and hydrolyzed nonenzymatically to 5-phenyltetrazole (**3.263**).

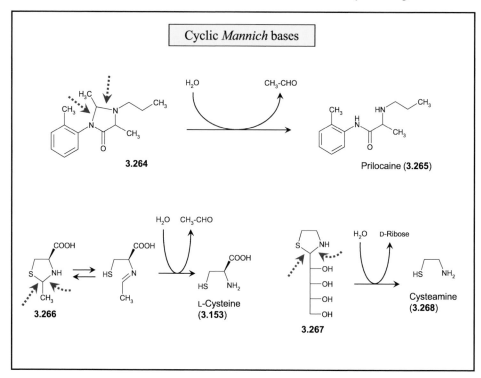

Fig. 3.75. Cyclic *Mannich* bases are not always identified as such, yet their lack of stability is comparable to that of their linear analogues. This is particularly the case for five-membered rings such as *imidazolidines, oxazolidines,* and *thiazolidines,* which contain the $N-CH_2-N$, $N-CH_2-O$, or $N-CH_2-S$ motif, respectively [3]. An example of *cyclic N*-Mannich *bases* is provided by derivatives of *prilocaine* (**3.265**) investigated as potential prodrugs [177]. Prilocaine is a polar local anesthetic agent of relatively short duration of action. To render it more lipophilic and allow its administration in depot oil injectables for post-operative pain control, the drug was reacted with acetaldehyde to form the *imidazolidin-4-one derivative* **3.264**. Its hydrolysis in buffers was fast in the slightly acidic to neutral pH range (half-life *ca.* 0.5–1 h) and increased with decreasing pH. Cyclic *S*-Mannich *bases* are rare in medicinal chemistry, but not completely absent. One example is that of thiazolidines such as *(2RS,4R)-2-methylthiazolidine-4-carboxylic acid* (**3.266**), and analogues as derivatives and chemical delivery systems of L-*cysteine* (**3.153**). These potential produgs underwent direct nonenzymatic hydrolysis to cysteine and the aldehyde originally used in their synthesis. The reaction was fast when the starting aldehyde was acetaldehyde (yielding **3.266**) or a monomeric sugar. This was also seen with the prodrug **3.267**, the product of condensation between *cysteamine* (**3.268**) and ribose. In fact, prodrugs **3.266** and mainly **3.267** showed promising protection against radiation-induced cell death as well as antimutagenic activity [178].

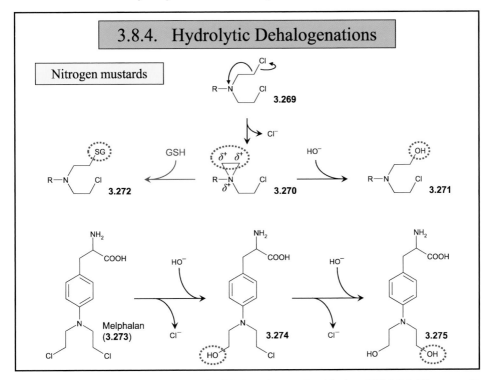

3.8.4. Hydrolytic Dehalogenations

Fig. 3.76. Hydrolases acting on C–halide bonds are classified as EC 3.8.1. The overall reaction of these dehalogenases is a *hydrolytic dehalogenation*, namely the replacement of a halide atom on a C-atom, in most cases an sp^3-C-atom, by a OH group. Most of our knowledge has been obtained from bacterial enzymes. The occurrence of hydrolytic dehalogenation in animals is well-known, but much remains to be discovered regarding the enzymes involved and their mechanisms. Furthermore, *nonenzymatic reactions* remain a distinct possibility when the halogen-bearing C-atom is sufficiently electrophilic [3]. This is seen with (2-chloroethyl)amino derivatives **3.269**, also known as *nitrogen mustards*, which are antitumor agents acting by DNA alkylation. Their mechanism of action is initiated by spontaneous intramolecular nucleophilic substitution to form a highly electrophilic *aziridinium species* **3.270**, which reacts with nucleophiles such as nucleic acids (their target), H_2O (to form the hydroxy analogs **3.271**), glutathione (to form the conjugates **3.272**; see *Part 4*), and others. The drug *melphalan* (**3.273**; phenylalanine mustard) offers a good example of hydrolytic dechlorination. When melphalan was administered to cancer patients, its monohydroxy metabolite, **3.274**, and its dihydroxy metabolite, **3.275**, were detected in the plasma where their combined AUC (area under the plasma-concentration-time curve) amounted to *ca.* 30% of the AUC of the drug [179]. *In vitro* studies have shown that melphalan reacts by the general mechanism discussed above, namely *via* a first and second aziridinium intermediate. Under physiological conditions of temperature and pH, *ca.* 2/3 of the drug had disappeared after 1 h, forming the monohydroxy and the dihydroxy products in comparable amounts.

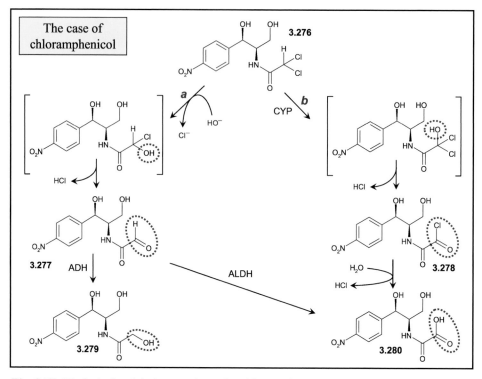

Fig. 3.77. Hydrolytic dehalogenation should not be confused with the *oxidative dehalogenation of haloalkyl groups* (see [2], in particular *Fig. 2.42*). A well-studied example is that of *chloramphenicol* (**3.276**) [180]. Its dichloroacetyl moiety is here of interest and undergoes dechlorination by three established routes: hydrolysis (*Route a*), cytochrome P450-catalyzed oxidation (*Route b*), and glutathione-dependent dechlorination (not shown). The value of this substrate is that the hydrolytic and oxidative routes can be unambiguously distinguished by at least one product. Indeed, *oxidation* at the geminal H-atom produces an unstable *(dichloro)hydroxyacetamido* intermediate which spontaneously eliminates HCl to yield the *oxamoyl chloride derivative* **3.278**. The latter is a highly reactive acyl chloride able to bind covalently to cellular macromolecules and accounts at least in part for the hepatotoxicity of the drug. The oxamoyl chloride also hydrolyzes to yield *chloramphenicol-oxamic acid* **3.280**. Thus, the oxidative dechlorination of chloramphenicol is a toxification pathway to be contrasted with *hydrolytic dechlorination* where replacement of a Cl-atom with a OH group (*Route a*) yields a *(monochloro)hydroxyacetamido* intermediate. The latter, like its dichloro analogue, also eliminates HCl, but the product is an aldehyde, **3.277**, far less reactive than the oxamoyl chloride intermediate **3.278**. *Chloramphenicol-aldehyde* undergoes the expected reduction to the primary alcohol **3.279** and dehydrogenation to the oxamic acid derivative **3.280**. In other words, the oxamic acid derivative is produced by both the oxidative and the hydrolytic dechlorination. In contrast, the *primary alcohol metabolite* **3.279** can be produced only by hydrolytic dechlorination. It is thus an unambiguous marker of this pathway, and it is a known urinary metabolite of chloramphenicol in humans.

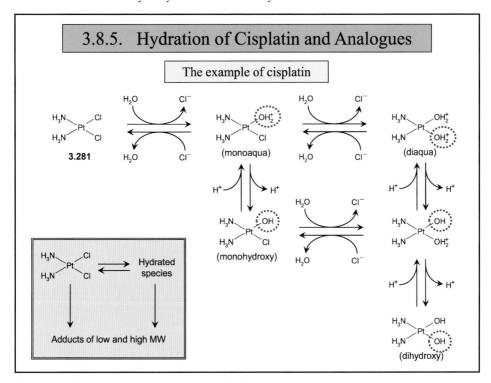

Fig. 3.78. *Cisplatin and analogues* are highly reactive antitumor drugs whose pharma-cokinetic, pharmacodynamic, and toxicological behavior are so much interdependent that they are all but impossible to untangle [181]. These agents act as *electrophiles* which bind covalently to nucleophilic sites on DNA, and particularly N(7) in adenine and guanine. However, their strong electrophilicity is also responsible for reactions with other endogenous nucleophiles of low or high molecular weight (*e.g.*, glutathione and serum albumin). Here, we focus on their *hydration*, a spontaneous reaction which has a strong bearing on their activity and toxicity. The prototypic compound is *cisplatin* (**3.281**; *cis*-diamminodichloroplatinum(II)). In aqueous solution, cisplatin *exchanges Cl for H$_2$O*, a reaction sometimes called *aquation* [3][182]. In a phosphate buffer of pH 7 at 37°, the reaction follows first-order kinetics and proceeds to completion ($t_{1/2}$ *ca.* 2 h). The first product formed is the *monoaqua species*, a positively charged molecule which undergoes deprotonation with a pK_a value of *ca.* 6.6, indicating that the monohydroxy species predominates at physiological pH. The second Cl can also be exchanged, but the equilibrium constant for this displacement is smaller than for the first. This reaction yields the *diaqua species*, a doubly charged molecule whose pK_a values have been reported at *ca.* 5.6–5.9 and 7.3–7.8 to yield the dihydroxy species. Aquation is of significance as an activation reaction, since the monoaqua and diaqua species are recognized to be more reactive toward nucleophiles than cisplatin itself. As shown, the aquation of cisplatin is a *reversible reaction* in the presence of Cl$^-$ ions, and proceeds to an equilibrium which is dependent on pH and Cl$^-$ concentration.

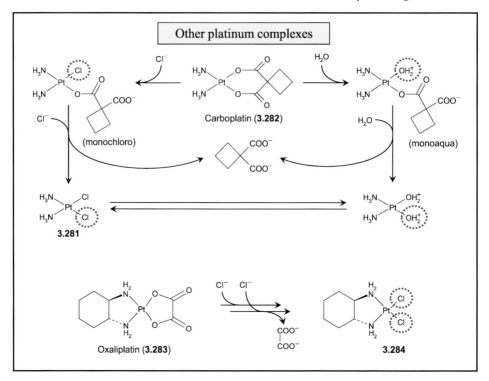

Fig. 3.79. The case of *carboplatin* (**3.282**) is of interest [3][183]. The drug has an activity equivalent to that of cisplatin but is markedly less nephrotoxic, the limiting toxicity now being myelosuppression. Among other nucleophiles, carboplatin reacts with Cl⁻ and H₂O as shown. Stepwise nucleophilic attack replaces one and then the second carboxylate ligand. The end products thus formed are *cisplatin* (**3.281**) and its *diaqua form*. The monoaqua and diaqua species are considered to be the active, DNA-binding forms of carboplatin. In buffered aqueous solutions, the disappearance of carboplatin is again dependent on Cl⁻ concentrations. Another drug is *oxaliplatin* (**3.283**)[184]; its chemical structure is closely related to that of carboplatin, the major difference being the presence of the *trans*-diaminocyclohexane moiety (abbreviated as *dach*). In human plasma at 37°, oxaliplatin rapidly exchanged the first, then the second carboxylate ligand with Cl to yield *dichloro (trans-diaminocyclohexane)platinum(II)* (**3.284**; abbreviated as [PtCl₂(dach)]. The formation of [PtCl₂(dach)] is considered to be an activation pathway, since the metabolite was taken up by tumor cells faster than the parent drug. Another reaction was binding to blood proteins (albumin, globulins, and hemoglobin), as demonstrated in patients. In conclusion, nucleophilic substitutions by H₂O, Cl⁻, low- and high molecular thiols, and other nucleophiles, play a major role in the metabolism of platinum complexes. These reactions condition the activation, deactivation, toxification, detoxification, distribution, and excretion of platinum anticancer drugs. Given their large differences in reactivity and the multiplicity of the factors involved, the pharmacokinetic–pharmacodynamic relations of platinum complexes are particularly difficult to unravel.

REFERENCES

[1] B. Testa, S. D. Krämer, 'The Biochemistry of Drug Metabolism – An Introduction. Part 3: Reactions of Hydrolysis and Their Enzymes', *Chem. Biodiv.* **2007**, *4*, 2031–2122.

[2] B. Testa, S. D. Krämer, 'The Biochemistry of Drug Metabolism – An Introduction. Part 1: Principles and Overview', *Chem. Biodiv.* **2006**, *3*, 1053–1101; B. Testa, S. D. Krämer, 'The Biochemistry of Drug Metabolism – An Introduction. Part 2: Redox Reactions and Their Enzymes', *Chem. Biodiv.* **2007**, *4*, 257–405.

[3] B. Testa, J. M. Mayer, 'Hydrolysis in Drug and Prodrug Metabolism – Chemistry, Biochemistry, and Enzymology', Verlag Helvetica Chimica Acta, Zurich, and Wiley-VCH, Weinheim, 2003.

[4] B. Testa, W. Soine, 'Principles of drug metabolism', in 'Burger's Medicinal Chemistry and Drug Discovery', 6th edn., Ed. D. J. Abraham, Wiley-Interscience, Hoboken, 2003, Vol. 2, p. 431–498.

[5] B. Testa, 'Principles of drug metabolism 2: Hydrolysis and conjugation reactions', in 'ADME-Tox Approaches', Eds. B. Testa, H. van de Waterbeemd, Vol. 5 in 'Comprehensive Medicinal Chemistry', 2nd edn., Eds. J. B. Taylor, D. J. Triggle, Elsevier, Oxford, 2007, p. 133–166.

[6] B. Testa, 'Nonenzymatic contributions to xenobiotic metabolism', *Drug Metab. Rev.* **1982**, *13*, 25–50; B. Ketterer, 'Detoxication reactions of glutathione and glutathione transferases', *Xenobiotica* **1986**, *16*, 957–973; R. N. Armstrong, 'Structure, catalytic mechanism, and evolution of the glutathione transferases', *Chem. Res. Toxicol.* **1997**, *10*, 2–18.

[7] Nomenclature Committee of the International Union of Biochemistry and Molecular Biology (IUBMB), 'Enzyme Nomenclature', www.chem.qmul.ac.uk/iubmb/enzyme.

[8] Brenda: The Comprehensive Enzyme Information System, www.brenda.uni-koeln.de; ExPASy Proteomics Server, www.expasy.org; Enzyme Structure Database, www.ebi.ac.uk/thornton-srv/databases/enzymes; The ESTHER Database, http://bioweb.ensam.inra.fr/ESTHER/definition.

[9] R. A. Totah, A. E. Rettie, 'Principles of drug metabolism 3: Enzymes and tissues', in 'ADME-Tox Approaches', Eds. B. Testa, H. van de Waterbeemd, Vol. 5 in 'Comprehensive Medicinal Chemistry', 2nd edn., Eds. J. B. Taylor, D. J. Triggle, Elsevier, Oxford, 2007, p. 167–191.

[10] N. W. McCracken, P. G. Blain, F. M. Williams, 'Human xenobiotic metabolizing esterases in liver and blood', *Biochem. Pharmacol.* **1993**, *46*, 1125–1129; W. N. Aldridge, 'The esterases: perspectives and problems', *Chem.-Biol. Interact.* **1993**, *87*, 5–13; T. Satoh, P. Taylor, W. F. Bosron, S. P. Sanghani, M. Hosokawa, B. N. La Du, 'Current progress on esterases: from molecular structure to function', *Drug Metab. Dispos.* **2002**, *30*, 488–493.

[11] F. J. Leinweber, 'Possible physiological roles of carboxylic ester hydrolases', *Drug Metab. Rev.* **1987**, *18*, 379–439.

[12] T. Satoh, M. Hosokawa, 'The mammalian carboxylesterases: from molecules to functions', *Annu. Rev. Pharmacol. Toxicol.* **1998**, *38*, 257–288.

[13] T. Imai, M. Imoto, H. Sakamoto, M. Hashimoto, 'Identification of esterases expressed in Caco-2 cells and effects of their hydrolyzing activity in predicting human intestinal absorption', *Drug Metab. Dispos.* **2005**, *33*, 1185–1190; K. Masaki, M. Hashimoto, T. Imai, 'Intestinal first-pass metabolism via carboxylesterase in rat jejunum and ileum', *Drug Metab. Dispos.* **2007**, *35*, 1089–1095.

[14] T. Imai, 'Human carboxylesterase isozymes: catalytic properties and rational drug design', *Drug Metab. Pharmacokinet.* **2006**, *21*, 173–185; M. Hosokawa, T. Furihata, Y. Yaginuma, N. Yamamoto, N. Koyano, A. Fujii, Y. Nagahara, T. Satoh, K. Chiba, 'Genomic structure and transcriptional regulation of the rat, mouse, and human carboxylesterase genes', *Drug Metab. Rev.* **2007**, *39*, 1–15.

[15] M. I. Mackness, H. M. Thompson, A. R. Hardy, C. H. Walker, 'Distinction between 'A'-esterases and arylesterases. Implications for esterase classification', *Biochem. J.* **1987**, *245*, 293–296; B. N. La Du, S. Adkins, C. L. Kuo, D. Lipsig, 'Studies on human serum paraoxonase/arylesterase', *Chem.-Biol. Interact.* **1993**, *87*, 25–34; L. Briseno-Roa, J. Hill, S. Notman, D. Sellers, A. P. Smith, C. M. Timperley, J. Wetherell, N. H. Williams, G. R. Williams, A. R. Fersht, A. D. Griffiths, 'Analogues with fluorescent leaving groups for screening and selection of enzymes that efficiently hydrolyze organophosphorus nerve agents', *J. Med. Chem.* **2006**, *49*, 246–255.

[16] S. L. Primo-Parmo, R. C. Sorenson, J. Teiber, B. N. La Du, 'The human serum paraoxonase/arylesterase gene (*PON1*) is one member of a multigene family', *Genomics* **1996**, *33*, 498–507; D. K.

Sanghera, C. E. Aston, N. Saha, M. I. Kamboh, 'DNA polymorphism in two paraoxonase genes (*PON1* and *PON2*) are associated with the risk of coronary heart disease', *Am. J. Hum. Genet.* **1998**, *62*, 20–24; I. Cascorbi, M. Laule, P. M. Mrozikiewicz, A. Mrozikiewicz, C. Andel, G. Baumann, I. Roots, K. Stangl, 'Mutations in the human paraoxonase 1 gene: frequencies, allelic linkages, and association with coronary artery disease', *Pharmacogenetics* **1999**, *9*, 755–761.

[17] M. M. Benning, J. M. Kuo, F. M. Kaushel, H. M. Holden, 'Three-dimensional structure of phosphotriesterase: an enzyme capable of detoxifying organophosphate nerve agents', *Biochemistry* **1994**, *33*, 15001–15007; J. L. Vanhooke, M. M. Benning, F. M. Raushel, H. M. Holden, 'Three-dimensional structure of the zinc-containing phosphotriesterase with the bound substrate analog diethyl 4-methylbenzylphosphonate', *Biochemistry* **1996**, *35*, 6020–6025.

[18] M. A. Sogorb, I. Sanchez, M. Lopez-Rivadulla, V. Cespedes, E. Vilanova, 'EDTA-resistant and sensitive phosphotriesterase activities associated with albumin and lipoproteins in rabbit serum', *Drug Metab. Dispos.* **1999**, *27*, 53–59.

[19] R. J. Richter, C. E. Furlong, 'Determination of paraoxonase (PON1) status requires more than genotyping', *Pharmacogenetics* **1999**, *9*, 745–753; B. Mackness, M. I. Mackness, S. Arrol, W. Turkie, P. N. Durrington, 'Effect of the molecular polymorphisms of human paraoxonase (PON1) on the rate of hydrolysis of paraoxon', *Br. J. Pharmacol.* **1997**, *122*, 265–168.

[20] L. G. Costa, A. Vitalone, T. B. Cole, C. E. Furlong, 'Modulation of paraoxonase (PON1) activity', *Biochem. Pharmacol.* **2005**, *69*, 541–550; J. F. Teiber, S. S. Billecke, B. N. La Du, D. I. Draganov, 'Estrogen esters as substrates of human paraoxonases', *Arch. Biochem. Biophys.* **2007**, *461*, 24–29.

[21] D. Josse, P. Masson, 'Human plasma paraoxonase (HuPON1): an anti-atherogenic enzyme with organophosphate hydrolase activity', *Ann. Pharm. Fr.* **2001**, *59*, 108–118.

[22] B. N. La Du, S. Billecke, C. Hsu, R. W. Haley, C. A. Broomfield, 'Serum paraoxonase (PON1) isozymes: the quantitative analysis of isozymes affecting individual sensitivity to environmental chemicals', *Drug Metab. Dispos.* **2001**, *29*, 566–569.

[23] H. Lu, J. Zhu, Y. Zang, Y. Ze, J. Qin, 'Cloning, high level expression of paraoxonase-3 in Sf9 cells and pharmacological characterization of its product', *Biochem. Pharmacol.* **2005**, *70*, 1019–1025.

[24] D. M. Shih, L. Gu, Y. R. Xia, M. Navab, W. F. Li, S. Hama, L. W. Castellani, C. E. Furlong, L. G. Costa, A. M. Fogelman, A. J. Lusis, 'Mice lacking serum paraoxonase are susceptible to organophosphate toxicity and atherosclerosis', *Nature* **1998**, *394*, 284–287.

[25] A. F. Hernández, M. C. Gonzalvo, F. Gil, E. Villanueva, A. Pla, 'Divergent effects of classical inducers on rat plasma and microsomal fraction paraoxonase and arylesterase', *Environ. Toxicol. Pharmacol.* **1997**, *3*, 83–86.

[26] R. X. Xu, A. M. Hassell, D. Vanderwall, M. H. Lambert, W. D. Holmes, M. A. Luther, W. J. Roque, M. V. Milbrun, Y. Zhao, H. Ke, R. T. Nolte, 'Atomic structure of PDE4: insights into phosphodiesterase mechanism and specificity', *Science* **2000**, *288*, 1822–1825; Q. Huai, Y. Sun, H. Wang, D. Macdonald, R. Aspiotis, H. Robinson, Z. Huang, H. Ke, 'Enantiomer discrimination illustrated by the high-resolution crystal structures of type 4 phosphodiesterase', *J. Med. Chem.* **2006**, *49*, 1867–1873.

[27] 'Enzymes of the Cholinesterase Family', Eds. D. M. Quinn, A. S. Balasubramanian, B. P. Doctor, P. Taylor, Plenum Press, New York, 1995.

[28] P. Taylor, Z. Radic, 'The cholinesterases: from genes to proteins', *Annu. Rev. Pharmacol. Toxicol.* **1994**, *34*, 281–320; P. Taylor, 'The cholinesterases', *J. Biol. Chem.* **1991**, *266*, 4025–4028; A. Chatonnet, O. Lockridge, 'Comparison of butyrylcholinesterase and acetylcholinesterase', *Biochem. J.* **1989**, *260*, 625–634.

[29] C. F. Bartels, W. Xie, A. K. Miller-Lindholm, L. M. Schopfer, O. Lockridge, 'Determination of the DNA sequences of acetylcholinesterase and butyrylcholinesterase from cat and demonstration of the existence of both in cat plasma', *Biochem. Pharmacol.* **2000**, *60*, 479–487.

[30] N. A. Hosea, H. A. Berman, P. Taylor, 'Specificity and orientation of trigonal carboxylesters and tetrahedral alkylphosphonyl esters in cholinesterases', *Biochemistry* **1995**, *34*, 11528–11536; J. E. Haux, G. B. Quistad, J. E. Casida, 'Phosphobutyrylcholinesterase: phosphorylation of the esteratic site of butyrylcholinesterase by ethephon [(2-chloroethyl)phosphoric acid] dianion', *Chem. Res. Toxicol.* **2000**, *13*, 646–651; W. Luo, Q. Yu, S. S. Kulkarni, D. A. Parrish, H. W. Holloway, D.

Tweedie, A. Shafferman, D. K. Lahiri, A. Brossi, N. H. Greig, 'Inhibition of human acetyl- and butyrylcholinesterase by novel carbamates of (−)- and (+)-tetrahydrofurobenzofuran and methanobenzodioxepine', *J. Med. Chem.* **2006**, *49*, 2174–2185; F. Ekström, Y.-P. Pang, M. Boman, E. Artursson, C. Akfur, S. Börjegren, 'Crystal structures of acetylcholinesterase in complex with HI-6, ortho-7 and obidoxime: structural basis for differences in the ability to reactivate tabun conjugates', *Biochem. Pharmacol.* **2006**, *72*, 597–607.

[31] B. Li, M. Sedlacek, I. Manoharan, R. Boopathy, E. G. Duysen, P. Masson, O. Lockridge, 'Butyrylcholinesterase, paraoxonase, and albumin esterase, but not carboxylesterase, are present in human plasma', *Biochem. Pharmacol.* **2005**, *70*, 1673–1684.

[32] M. Harel, D. M. Quinn, H. K. Nair, I. Silman, J. L. Sussman, 'The X-ray structure of a transition state analog complex reveals the molecular origins of the catalytic power and substrate specificity of acetylcholinesterase', *J. Am. Chem. Soc.* **1996**, *118*, 2340–2346.

[33] S. R. Feaster, D. M. Quinn, B. L. Barnett, 'Molecular modeling of the structures of human and rat pancreatic cholesterol esterases', *Protein Sci.* **1997**, *6*, 73–79.

[34] C. J. Masters, 'On the role of the peroxisome in the metabolism of drugs and xenobiotics', *Biochem. Pharmacol.* **1998**, *56*, 667–673; M. C. Hunt, J. Yamada, L. J. Maltais, M. W. Wright, E. J. Podesta, S. E. H. Alexson, 'A revised nomenclature for mammalian acyl-CoA thioesterases/hydrolases', *J. Lipid Res.* **2005**, *46*, 2029–2032.

[35] T. Peters Jr., 'All about Albumin. Biochemistry, Genetics, and Medical Applications', Academic Press, San Diego, 1996; A. Salvi, P. A. Carrupt, J. M. Mayer, B. Testa, 'Esterase-like activity of human serum albumin toward prodrug esters of nicotinic acid', *Drug Metab. Dispos.* **1997**, *25*, 395–398; Y. Sakurai, S. F. Ma, H. Watanabe, N. Yamaotsu, S. Hirono, Y. Kurono, U. Kragh-Hansen, M. Otagiri, 'Esterase-like activity of serum albumin: characterization of its structural chemistry using *p*-nitrophenyl esters as substrates', *Pharm. Res.* **2004**, *21*, 285–292; F. Yang, C. Bian, L. Zhu, G. Zhao, Z. Huang, M. Huang, 'Effect of human serum albumin on drug metabolism: structural evidence of esterase activity of human serum albumin', *J. Struct. Biol.* **2007**, *157*, 348–355.

[36] a) 'Handbook of Proteolytic Enzymes', 2nd edn., Eds. A. J. Barrett, N. D. Rawlings, J. F. Woessner, Elsevier, Oxford, 2004; b) N. D. Rawlings, F. R. Morton, A. J. Barrett, 'MEROPS: the peptidase database', *Nucleic Acids Res.* **2006**, *34*, D270 – D272; c) MEROPS, the Peptidase Database; http://merops.sanger.ac.uk/.

[37] C. V. Jongeneel, J. Bouvier, A. Bairoch, 'A unique signature identifies a family of zinc-dependent metallopeptidases', *FEBS Lett.* **1989**, *242*, 211–214.

[38] G. Dodson, A. Wlodawer, 'Catalytic triads and their relatives', *Trends Biochem. Sci.* **1998**, *23*, 347–352.

[39] M. R. Redinbo, P. M. Potter, 'Mammalian carboxylesterases: from drug targets to protein therapeutics', *Drug Discov. Today* **2005**, *10*, 313–325.

[40] R. M. Wadkins, J. L. Hyatt, X. Mei, K. J. P. Yoon, M. Wierdl, C. C. Edwards, C. L. Morton, J. C. Obenauer, K. Damodaran, P. Beroza, M. K. Danks, P. M. Potter, 'Identification and character-ization of novel benzil (diphenylethane-1,2-dione) analogues as inhibitors of mammalian carboxylases', *J. Med. Chem.* **2005**, *48*, 2906–2915.

[41] S. Bencharit, C. L. Morton, E. L. Howard-Williams, M. K. Dans, P. M. Potter, M. R. Redinbo, 'Structural insights into CPT-11 activation by mammalian carboxylesterases', *Nat. Struct. Biol.* **2002**, *9*, 337–342.

[42] D. W. Christianson, 'Structural biology of zinc', *Adv. Protein Chem.* **1991**, *42*, 281–355.

[43] C. Oefner, A. D'Arcy, M. Hennig, F. K. Winkler, G. E. Dale, 'Structure of human neutral endopeptidase complexed with phosphoramidon', Protein Data Bank ID: 1dmt, 1999; H. M. Berman, J. Westbrook, Z. Feng, G. Gilliland, T. N. Bhat, H. Weissig, I. N. Shindyalov, P. E. Bourne, 'The Protein Data Bank', *Nucleic Acids Res.* **2000**, *28*, 235–242.

[44] N. R. Srinavas, J. W. Hubbard, G. McKay, E. M. Hawes, K. K. Midha, 'In vitro hydrolysis of *threo*-methylphenidate by blood esterases. Differential and enantioselective interspecies variability', *Chirality* **1991**, *3*, 99–103.

[45] J. Zhang, J. C. Burnell, N. Dumaual, W. F. Bosron, 'Binding and hydrolysis of meperidine by human liver carboxylesterase hCE-1', *J. Pharmacol. Exp. Ther.* **1999**, *290*, 314–318.

[46] H. G. Schaefer, D. Beermann, R. Horstmann, M. Wargenau, B. A. Heibel, J. Kuhlmann, 'Effect of food on the pharmacokinetics of the active metabolite of the prodrug repirinast', *J. Pharm. Sci.* **1993**, *82*, 107–109.

[47] B. Testa, 'Principles of Organic Stereochemistry', Dekker, New York, 1979.

[48] G. Sabbioni, J. B. Jones, 'Enzymes in organic synthesis. 39. Preparations of chiral cyclic acid-esters and bicyclic lactones via stereoselective pig liver esterase catalyzed hydrolyses of cyclic meso diesters', *J. Org. Chem.* **1987**, *52*, 4565–4570.

[49] a) G. Alibrandi, N. Micali, S. Trusso, A. Villari, 'Hydrolysis of aspirin studied by spectrophotometric and fluorometric variable-temperature kinetics', *J. Pharm. Sci.* **1996**, *85*, 1105–1108; b) D. K. Patel, L. J. Notarianni, P. N. Bennett, 'Comparative metabolism of high doses of aspirin in man and rat', *Xenobiotica* **1990**, *20*, 847–854.

[50] L. J. Fraile, J. J. Aramayona, M. A. Bregante, M. A. Garcia, A. R. Abadia, 'Deacetylation of diltiazem by several rabbit tissues', *Pharm. Res.* **1996**, *13*, 1875–1880.

[51] Y. Yoshigae, T. Imai, A. Horita, M. Otagiri, 'Species differences for stereoselective hydrolysis of propranolol prodrugs in plasma and liver', *Chirality* **1997**, *9*, 661–666; Y. Yoshigae, T. Imai, M. Taketani, M. Otagiri, 'Characterization of esterases invoved in the stereoselective hydrolysis of ester-type prodrugs of propranolol in rat liver and plasma', *Chirality* **1999**, *11*, 10–13.

[52] S. Y. Yeh, C. W. Gorodetzky, R. L. McQuinn, 'Urinary excretion of heroin and its metabolites in man', *J. Pharmacol. Exp. Ther.* **1976**, *196*, 249–256; S. Y. Yeh, R. L. McQuinn, C. W. Gorodetzky, 'Identification of diacetylmorphine metabolites in humans', *J. Pharm. Sci.* **1977**, *66*, 201–204; D. A. Barrett, A. L. P. Dyssegaard, P. N. Shaw, 'The effect of temperature and pH on the deacetylation of diamorphine in aqueous solution and in human plasma', *J. Pharm. Pharmacol.* **1992**, *44*, 606–608.

[53] M. R. Brzezinski, B. J. Spink, R. A. Dean, C. E. Berkman, J. R. Cashman, W. F. Bosron, 'Human liver carboxylesterase hCE-1: binding specificity for cocaine, heroin, and their metabolites and analogs', *Drug Metab. Dispos.* **1997**, *25*, 1089–1096.

[54] J. J. Rady, F. Aksu, J. M. Fujimoto, 'The heroin metabolite, 6-monoacetylmorphine, activates *delta* opiod receptors to produce antinociception in Swiss-Webster mice', *J. Pharmacol. Exp. Ther.* **1994**, *268*, 1222–1231.

[55] M. Graffner-Nordberg, K. Sjödin, A. Tunek, A. Hallberg, 'Synthesis and enzymatic hydrolysis of esters, constituting simple models of soft drugs', *Chem. Pharm. Bull.* **1998**, *46*, 591–601.

[56] S. Yamaori, N. Fujiyama, M. Kushihara, T. Funahashi, T. Kimura, I. Yamamoto, T. Sone, M. Isobe, T. Ohshima, K. Matsumura, M. Oda, K. Watanabe, 'Involvement of human blood arylesterases and liver microsomal carboxylesterases in nafamostat hydrolysis', *Drug Metab. Pharmacokinet.* **2006**, *21*, 147–155; S. Yamaori, E. Ukena, N. Fujiyama, T. Funahashi, T. Kimura, I. Yamamoto, T. Ohshima, K. Matsumura, M. Oda, K. Watanabe, 'Nafamostat is hydrolyzed by human liver cytosolic long-chain acyl-CoA hydrolase', *Xenobiotica* **2007**, *37*, 260–270.

[57] H. Bundgaard, N. M. Nielsen, 'Glycolamide esters as novel biolabile prodrug type for non-steroidal anti-inflammatory carboxylic acid drugs', *Int. J. Pharmaceut.* **1988**, *43*, 101–110; L. K. Wadhwa, P. D. Sharma, 'Glycolamide esters of 6-methoxy-2-naphthylacetic acid as potential prodrugs – physicochemical properties, chemical stability and enzymatic hydrolysis', *Int. J. Pharmaceut.* **1995**, *118*, 31–39.

[58] R. E. S. Bullingham, A. J. Nicholls, B. R. Kamm, 'Clinical pharmacokinetics of mycophenolate mofetil', *Clin. Pharmacokinet.* **1998**, *34*, 429–455.

[59] H. Han, R. L. A. de Vrueh, J. K. Rhie, K. M. Y. Covitz, P. L. Smith, C. P. Lee, D. M. Oh, W. Sadée, G. L. Amidon, '5′-Amino acid esters of antiviral nucleosides, acyclovir, and AZT are absorbed by the intestinal PEPT1 peptide transporter', *Pharm. Res.* **1998**, *15*, 1154–1159; T. C. Burnette, J. A. Harrington, J. E. Reardon, B. M. Merrill, P. de Miranda, 'Purification and characterization of a rat liver enzyme that hydrolyzes valaciclovir, the L-valyl ester prodrug of acyclovir', *J. Biol. Chem.* **1995**, *270*, 15827–15831; C. Yang, H. Gao, A. K. Mitra, 'Chemical stability, enzymatic hydrolysis, and nasal uptake of amino acid ester prodrugs of acyclovir', *J. Pharm. Sci.* **2001**, *90*, 617–624.

[60] M. J. Cho, L. C. Haynes, 'Serum-catalyzed hydrolysis of metronidazole amino acid esters', *J. Pharm. Sci.* **1985**, *74*, 883–885; N. M. Mahfouz, M. A. Hassan, 'Synthesis, chemical and enzymatic

hydrolysis, and bioavailability evaluation in rabbits of metronidazole amino acid ester prodrugs with enhanced water solubility', *J. Pharm. Pharmacol.* **2001**, *53*, 841–848.

[61] L. Song, R. Bevins, B. D. Anderson, 'Kinetics and mechanism of activation of α-amino acid ester prodrugs of camptothecins', *J. Med. Chem.* **2006**, *49*, 4344–4355.

[62] M. Murakami, H. Furuie, K. Matsuguma, A. Wanibuchi, S. Kikawa, S. Irie, 'Pharmacokinetics and pharmacodynamics of landiolol hydrochloride, an ultra short-acting β_1-selective blocker, in a dose escalation regimen in healthy male volunteers', *Drug Metab. Pharmacokinet.* **2005**, *20*, 337–344.

[63] J. Rautio, H. Taipale, J. Gynther, J. Vepsalainen, T. Nevalainen, T. Jarvinen, 'In vitro evaluation of acyloxyalkyl esters as dermal prodrugs of ketoprofen and naproxen', *J. Pharm. Sci.* **1998**, *87*, 1622–1628.

[64] C. Larsen, P. Kurtzhals, M. Johansen, 'Kinetics of regeneration of metronidazole from hemiesters of maleic acid, succinic acid and glutaric acid in aqueous buffer, human plasma and pig liver homogenate', *Int. J. Pharmaceut.* **1988**, *41*, 121–129.

[65] T. Furihata, M. Hosokawa, A. Fujii, M. Derbel, T. Satoh, K. Chiba, 'Dexamethasone-induced methylprednisolone hemisuccinate hydrolase: its identification as a member of the rat carboxylesterase 2 family and its unique existence in plasma', *Biochem. Pharmacol.* **2005**, *69*, 1287–1297; M. A. Avery, J. R. Woolfrey, 'Anti-inflammatory steroids', in 'Burger's Medicinal Chemistry and Drug Discovery', 6th edn., Ed. D. J. Abraham, John Wiley & Sons, Hoboken, 2003, Vol. 3, p. 747–853.

[66] T. L. Huang, A. Székács, T. Uematsu, E. Kuwano, A. Parkinson, B. D. Hammock, 'Hydrolysis of carbonates, thiocarbonates, carbamates, and carboxylic esters of α-naphthol, β-naphthol, and *p*-nitrophenol by human, rat, and mouse liver carboxylesterases', *Pharm. Res.* **1993**, *10*, 639–648; R. P. Lee, A. Parkinson, P. G. Forkert, 'Isozyme-selective metabolism of ethyl carbamate by cytochrome P450 (CYP2E1) and carboxylesterase (hydrolase A) enzymes in murine liver microsomes', *Drug Metab. Dispos.* **1998**, *26*, 60–65.

[67] I. M. Kapetanovic, C. D. Torchin, C. D. Thompson, T. A. Miller, P. J. McNeilly, M. L. Macdonald, H. J. Kupferberg, J. L. Perhach, R. D. Sofia, J. M. Strong, 'Potentially reactive cyclic carbamate metabolite of the antiepileptic drug felbamate produced by human liver tissue in vitro', *Drug Metab. Dispos.* **1998**, *26*, 1089–1095; C. M. Dieckhaus, W. L. Santos, R. D. Sofia, T. L. Macdonald, 'The chemistry, toxicology, and identification in rat and human urine of 4-hydroxy-5-phenyl-1,3-oxazaperhydroin-2-one: a reactive metabolite in felbamate bioactivation', *Chem. Res. Toxicol.* **2001**, *14*, 958–964.

[68] M. Xie, D. Yang, M. Wu, B. Xue, B. Yan, 'Mouse liver and kidney carboxylesterase (M-LK) rapidly hydrolyzes antirumor prodrug irinotecan and the N-terminal three quarter sequence determines substrate selectivity', *Drug Metab. Dispos.* **2003**, *31*, 21–27; Y. Ando, Y. Hasegawa, 'Clinical pharmacogentics of irinotecan (CPT-11)', *Drug Metab. Rev.* **2005**, *37*, 565–574; D. J. Burkhart, B. L. Barthel, G. C. Post, B. T. Kalet, J. W. Nafie, R. K. Shoemaker, T. H. Koch, 'Design, synthesis, and preliminary evaluation of doxazolidine carbamates as prodrugs activated by carboxylesterases', *J. Med. Chem.* **2006**, *49*, 7002–7012.

[69] A. Buur, H. Bundgaard, 'Prodrugs of 5-fluorouracil. VIII. Improved rectal and oral delivery of 5-fluorouracil via various prodrugs. Structure-rectal absorption relationships', *Int. J. Pharmaceut.* **1987**, *36*, 41–49.

[70] Z. Shahrokh, E. Lee, A. G. Olivero, R. A. Matamoros, K. D. Robarge, A. Lee, K. J. Weise, B. K. Blackburn, M. F. Powell, 'Stability of alkoxycarbonylamidine prodrugs', *Pharm. Res.* **1998**, *15*, 434–441.

[71] H. K. Vaddi, M. O. Hamad, J. Chen, S. L. Banks, P. A. Cooks, A. L. Stinchcomb, 'Human skin permeation of branched-chain 3-*O*-alkyl ester and carbonate prodrugs of naltrexone', *Pharm. Res.* **2005**, *22*, 758–765.

[72] D. K. Kim, N. Lee, Y. W. Kim, K. Chang, J. S. Kim, G. J. Im, W. S. Choi, I. Jung, T. S. Kim, Y. Y. Hwang, D. S. Min, K. A. Um, Y. B. Cho, K. H. Kim, 'Synthesis and evaluaiton of 2-amino-9-(3-hydroxymethyl-4-alkoxycarbonyloxybut-1-yl)purines as potential prodrugs of penciclovir', *J. Med. Chem.* **1998**, *41*, 3435–3441.

[73] F. C. Falkner, T. M. Twomey, A. P. Borger, D. Garg, D. Weidler, N. Gerber, I. W. Browder, 'Disposition of ampiroxicam, a prodrug of piroxicam, in man', *Xenobiotica* **1990**, *20*, 645–652.

[74] M. Lakeram, A. J. Paine, D. J. Lockley, D. J. Sanders, R. Pendlington, B. Forbes, 'Transesterification of *p*-hydroxybenzoate esters (parabens) by human intestinal (Caco-2) cells', *Xenobiotica* **2006**, *36*, 739–749.

[75] J. S. Markowitz, C. L. Devane, D. W. Boulton, Z. Nahas, S. C. Risch, F. Diamond, K. S. Patrick, 'Ethylphenidate formation in human subjects after the administration of a single dose of methylphenidate and ethanol', *Drug Metab. Dispos.* **2000**, *28*, 620–624; Z. Sun, D. J. Murry, S. P. Sanghani, W. I. Davis, N. Y. Kedishvili, Q. Zou, T. D. Hurley, W. F. Bosron, 'Methylphenidate is stereoselectively hydrolyzed by human carboxylesterase CES1A1', *J. Pharmacol. Exp. Ther.* **2004**, *310*, 469–476; K. S. Patrick, R. L. Williard, A. L. VanWert, J. J. Dowd, J. E. Oatis Jr., L. D. Middaugh, 'Synthesis and pharmacology of ethylphenidate enantiomers: the human transesterification metabolite of methylphenidate and ethanol', *J. Med. Chem.* **2005**, *48*, 2876–2881.

[76] J. A. Bourland, D. K. Martin, M. Mayersohn, 'Carboxylesterase-mediated transesterification of meperidine (Demenol) and methylphenidate (Ritalin) in the presence of [²H₆]ethanol: preliminary in vitro findings using a rat liver preparation', *J. Pharm. Sci.* **1997**, *86*, 1494–1496.

[77] S. P. Jindal, T. Lutz, 'Mass spectrometric studies of cocaine disposition in animals and humans using stable isotope-labeled analogues', *J. Pharm. Sci.* **1989**, *78*, 1009–1014.

[78] S. J. Gatley, 'Activities of the enantiomers of cocaine and some related compounds as substrates and inhibitors of plasma butyrylcholinesterase', *Biochem. Pharmacol.* **1991**, *41*, 1249–1254; R. B. Melchert, C. Göldlin, U. Zweifel, A. A. Welder, U. A. Boelsterli, 'Differential toxicity of cocaine and its enantiomers, (+)-cocaine and (−)-ψ-cocaine, is associated with stereoselective hydrolysis by hepatic carboxylesterases in cultured rat hepatocytes', *Chem.-Biol. Interact.* **1992**, *84*, 243–258.

[79] W. Xie, C. V. Altamirano, C. F. Bartels, R. J. Speirs, J. R. Cashman, O. Lockridge, 'An improved cocaine hydrolase: The A328Y mutant of human butyrylcholinesterase is 4-fold more efficient', *Mol. Pharmacol.* **1999**, *55*, 83–91; H. Sun, M. L. Shen, Y.-P. Pang, O. Lockridge, S. Brimijoin, 'Cocaine metabolism accelerated by a re-engineered human butyrylcholinesterase', *J. Pharmacol. Exp. Ther.* **2002**, *302*, 710–716.

[80] M. R. Brzezinski, T. L. Abraham, C. L. Stone, R. A. Dean, W. F. Bosron, 'Purification and characterization of a human liver cocaine carboxylesterase that catalyzes the production of benzoylecgonine and the formation of cocaethylene from alcohol and cocaine', *Biochem. Pharmacol.* **1994**, *48*, 1747–1755; L. M. Kamendulis, M. R. Brzezinski, E. V. Pindel, W. F. Bosron, R. A. Dean, 'Metabolism of cocaine and heroin is catalyzed by the same human liver carboxylesterase', *J. Pharmacol. Exp. Ther.* **1996**, *279*, 713–717.

[81] S. C. Laizure, T. Mandrell, N. M. Gades, R. B. Parker, 'Cocaethylene metabolism and interaction with cocaine and ethanol: role of carboxylesterases', *Drug Metab. Dispos.* **2003**, *31*, 16–20; R. A. Dean, J. Zhang, M. R. Brzezinski, W. F. Bosron, 'Tissue distribution of cocaine methyl esterase and ethyl transferase activities: Correlation with carboxylesterase protein', *J. Pharmacol. Exp. Ther.* **1995**, *275*, 965–971; J. A. Bourland, D. K. Martin, M. Mayersohn, 'In vitro transesterification of cocaethylene (ethylcocaine) in the presence of ethanol', *Drug Metab. Dispos.* **1998**, *26*, 203–206.

[82] S. M. Roberts, D. L. Phillips, I. R. Tebbett, 'Increased blood and brain cocaine concentrations with ethanol cotreatment in mice', *Drug Metab. Dispos.* **1995**, *23*, 664–666.

[83] P. F. Dodds, 'Xenobiotic lipids: the inclusion of xenobiotic compounds in pathways of lipid synthesis', *Prog. Lipid Res.* **1995**, *34*, 219–247.

[84] M. A. Diczfalusy, I. Björkhem, C. Einarsson, S. E. H. Alexson, 'Formation of fatty acid ethyl esters in rat liver microsomes', *Eur. J. Biochem.* **1999**, *259*, 404–411; B. S. Kaphalia, R. R. Fritz, G. A. S. Ansari, 'Purification and characterization of rat liver microsomal fatty acid ethyl and 2-chloroethyl ester synthase and their relationship with carboxylesterase (pI 6.1)', *Chem. Res. Toxicol.* **1997**, *10*, 211–218; T. Tsujita, M. Sumiyoshi, H. Okuda, 'Fatty acid alcohol ester-synthetizing activity of lipoprotein lipase', *J. Biochem.* **1999**, *126*, 1074–1079; E. Mutch, R. Nave, N. McCracken, K. Zech, F. M. Williams, 'The role of esterases in the metabolism of ciclesonide to desisobutyryl-ciclesonide in human tissue', *Biochem. Pharmacol.* **2007**, *73*, 1657–1664.

[85] M. Laposata, 'Fatty acid ethyl esters: ethanol metabolites which mediate ethanol-induced organ damage and serve as markers of ethanol intake', *Prog. Lipid Res.* **1998**, *37*, 307–316; E. A. Laposata, L. L. Lange, 'Presence of nonoxidative ethanol metabolism in human organs commonly damaged by ethanol abuse', *Science* **1986**, *231*, 497–499.

[86] T. Loftsson, T. Thorsteinsson, M. Másson, 'Hydrolysis kinetics and QSAR investigation of soft antimicrobial agents', *J. Pharm. Pharmacol.* **2005**, *57*, 721–727.

[87] M. Strolin Benedetti, R. Whomsley, J. M. Nicolas, C. Young, E. Baltes, 'Pharmacokinetics and metabolism of ^{14}C-levetiracetam, a new antiepileptic agent, in healthy volunteers', *Eur. J. Clin. Pharmacol.* **2003**, *59*, 621–630; M. Strolin Benedetti, R. Coupez, R. Whomsley, J. M. Nicolas, P. Collart, E. Baltes, 'Comparative pharmacokinetics and metabolism of levetiracetam, a new anti-epileptic agent, in mouse, rat, rabbit and dog', *Xenobiotica* **2004**, *34*, 281–300.

[88] W. J. Weiss, S. M. Mikels, P. J. Petersen, N. V. Jacobus, P. Bitha, Y. I. Lin, R. T. Testa, 'In vivo activities of peptidic prodrugs of novel aminomethyl tetrahydrofuranyl-1β-methylcarbapenems', *Antimicrob. Agents Chemother.* **1999**, *43*, 460–464.

[89] G. Lachmann, B. Siegemund, W. Kusche, 'Pharmacokinetics and metabolism of ^{14}C-oxaceprol in Beagle dogs after intramuscular and oral administration', *Arzneim.-Forsch.* **1990**, *40*, 200–206.

[90] A. Lippi, M. Criscuoli, S. Canali, A. Subissi, 'Reductive metabolism and its role in the disposition of the hydroxamic angiotensin-converting enzyme inhibitor idrapril calcium in rat', *Xenobiotica* **1996**, *26*, 551–558.

[91] R. A. Iyer, J. Mitroka, B. Malhotra, S. Bonacorsi Jr., S. C. Waller, J. K. Rinehart, V. A. Roongta, K. Kripalani, 'Metabolism of [^{14}C]omapatrilat, a sulfhydryl-containing vasopeptidase inhibitor in humans', *Drug Metab. Dispos.* **2001**, *29*, 60–69; R. A. Iyer, B. Malhotra, S. Khan, J. Mitroka, S. Bonacorsi Jr., S. C. Waller, J. K. Rinehart, K. Kripalani, 'Comparative biotransformation of radiolabeled [^{14}C]omapatrilat and stable-labeled [^{13}C$_2$]omapatrilat after oral administration to rats, dogs, and humans', *Drug Metab. Dispos.* **2003**, *31*, 67–75.

[92] M. A. Miller, L. Thibert, F. Desjardins, H. Siddiqi, A. Dascal, 'Testing the susceptibility of *Mycobacterium tuberculosis* to pyrazinamide: comparison of Bactec method with pyrazinamidase assay', *J. Clin. Microbiol.* **1995**, *33*, 2468–2470.

[93] M. E. Morris, G. Levy, 'Determination of salicylamide and five metabolites in biological fluids by HPLC', *J. Pharm. Sci.* **1983**, *72*, 612–617.

[94] G. Miyamoto, H. Sasabe, N. Tominaga, N. Uegaki, M. Tominaga, T. Shimizu, 'Metabolism of a new inotropic agent, 3,4-dihydro-6-[4-(3,4-dimethoxybenzoyl)-1-piperazinyl]-2-(1*H*)-quinolinone (OPC-8212), in the rat, mouse, dog, monkey, and human', *Xenobiotica* **1988**, *18*, 1143–1155.

[95] S. Kudo, K. Umehara, M. Hosokawa, G. Miyamoto, K. Chiba, T. Satoh, 'Phenacetin deacetylase activity in human liver microsomes: distribution, kinetics, and chemical inhibition and stimulation', *J. Pharmacol. Exp. Ther.* **2000**, *294*, 80–88.

[96] A. W. Nicholls, J. C. Lindon, S. Caddick, R. D. Farrant, I. D. Wilson, J. K. Nicholson, 'NMR spectroscopic studies on the metabolism and futile deacetylation of phenacetin in the rat', *Xenobiotica* **1997**, *27*, 1175–1186; A. W. Nicholls, I. D. Wilson, M. Godejohann, J. K. Nicholson, J. P. Shockcor, 'Identification of phenacetin metabolites in human urine after administration of phenacetin-C^{2}H$_3$: measurement of futile metabolic deacetylation via HPLC/MS-SPE-NMR and HPLC-ToF MS', *Xenobiotica* **2006**, *36*, 615–629.

[97] R. J. Parker, J. M. Collins, J. M. Strong, 'Identification of 2,6-xylidine as a major lidocaine metabolite in human liver slices', *Drug Metab. Dispos.* **1996**, *24*, 1167–1173; S. E. H. Axelson, M. Diczfalusy, M. Halldin, S. Swedmark, 'Involvement of liver carboxylesterases in the in vitro metabolism of lidocaine', *Drug Metab. Dispos.* **2002**, *30*, 643–647.

[98] T. F. Woolf, L. L. Radulovic, 'Oxicams: metabolic disposition in man and animals', *Drug Metab. Rev.* **1989**, *21*, 255–276; J. Schmid, U. Busch, G. Trummlitz, A. Prox, S. Kaschke, H. Wachsmuth, 'Meloxicam: metabolic profile and biotransformation products in the rat', *Xenobiotica* **1995**, *25*, 1219–1236.

[99] C. J. Parli, E. Evenson, B. D. Potts, E. Beedle, R. Lawson, D. W. Robertson, J. D. Leander, 'Metabolism of the prodrug DEGA (N-(2,6-dimethylphenyl)-4-[[diethylamino)acetyl]amino]benz-amide) to the potent anticonvulsant LY201116 in mice. Effect of bis-(p-nitrophenyl)phosphate',

Drug Metab. Dispos. **1988**, *16*, 707–711; B. D. Potts, S. Gabriel, C. J. Parli, 'Metabolism, disposition, and pharmacokinetics of a potent anticonvulsant, 4-amino-*N*-(2,6-dimethylphenyl)benzamide (LY201116), in rats', *Drug Metab. Dispos.* **1989**, *17*, 656–661.

[100] N. M. Hooper, R. J. Hesp, S. Tieku, 'Metabolism of aspartame by human and pig intestinal microvillar peptidases', *Biochem. J.* **1994**, *298*, 635–639.

[101] M. Naruki, S. Mizutani, K. Goto, M. Tsujimoto, H. Nakazato, A. Itakura, M. Mizuno, O. Kurauchi, F. Kikkawa, Y. Tomoda, 'Oxytocin is hydrolyzed by an enzyme in human placenta that is identical to the oxytocinase of pregnancy serum', *Peptides* **1996**, *17*, 257–261; B. F. Mitchell, S. Wong, 'Metabolism of oxytocin in human decidua, chorion, and placenta', *J. Clin. Endocrinol. Metab.* **1995**, *80*, 2729–2733.

[102] E. A. Brownson, T. J. Abbruscato, T. J. Gillespie, V. J. Hruby, T. P. Davis, 'Effect of peptidases at the blood brain barrier on the permeability of enkephalin', *J. Pharmacol. Exp. Ther.* **1994**, *270*, 675–680; T. Hiranuma, K. Kitamura, T. Taniguchi, T. Kobasashi, R. Tamaki, M. Kanai, K. Akahori, K. Iwao, T. Oka, 'Effects of three peptidase inhibitors, amastatin, captopril and phosporamidon, on the hydrolysis of [Met[5]]-enkephalin-Arg[6]-Phe[7] and other opioid peptides', *Naunyn-Schmiedebergs Arch. Pharmacol.* **1998**, *357*, 276–282.

[103] E. Krondahl, A. Orzechowski, G. Ekström, H. Lennernäs, 'Rat jejunal permeability and metabolism of μ-selective tetrapeptides in gastrointestinal fluids from humans and rats', *Pharm. Res.* **1997**, *14*, 1780–1785; E. Krondahl, H. von Euler-Chelpin, A. Orzechowski, G. Ekström, H. Lennernäs, 'Investigation of the in-vitro metabolism of three opioid tetrapeptides by pancreatic and intestinal enzymes', *J. Pharm. Pharmacol.* **2000**, *52*, 785–795.

[104] V. J. Hruby, 'Peptide science: exploring the use of chemical principles and interdisciplinary collaboration for understanding life processes', *J. Med. Chem.* **2003**, *46*, 4215–4231.

[105] 'Pseudo-peptides in Drug Discovery', Ed. P. E. Nielsen, Wiley-VCH, Weinheim, 2004.

[106] M. Schwahn, H. Schupke, A. Gasparic, D. Krone, G. Peter, R. Hempel, T. Kronbach, M. Locher, W. Jahn, J. Engel, 'Disposition and metabolism of cetrorelix, a potent luteinizing hormone-releasing hormone antagonist, in rats and dogs', *Drug Metab. Dispos.* **2000**, *28*, 10–20.

[107] C. Garcia-Aparicio, M. C. Bonache, I. De Meester, A. San-Félix, J. Balzarini, M. J. Camarata, S. Velazquez, 'Design and discovery of a novel dipeptidyl-peptidase IV (CD26)-based prodrug approach', *J. Med. Chem.* **2006**, *49*, 5339–5351.

[108] a) B. A. Hamelin, J. Turgeon, 'Hydrophilicity/lipophilicity: relevance for the pharmacology and clinical effects of HMG-CoA reductase inhibitors', *Trends Pharmacol. Sci.* **1998**, *19*, 26–37; b) E. S. Istvan, J. Deisenhofer, 'Structural mechanism for statin inhibition of HMG-CoA reductase', *Science* **2001**, *292*, 1160–1164; c) A. Endo, 'The origin of the statins', *Int. Congr. Ser.* **2004**, *1262*, 3–8.

[109] a) U. Christians, W. Jacobsen, L. C. Floren, 'Metabolism and drug interactions of 3-hydroxy-3-methylglutaryl coenzyme A reductase inhibitors in transplant patients: are the statins mechanistically similar?', *Pharmacol. Ther.* **1998**, *80*, 1–34; b) M. J. Garcia, R. F. Reinoso, A. Sanchez Navarro, J. R. Prous, 'Clinical pharmacokinetics of statins', *Methods Find. Exp. Clin. Pharmacol.* **2003**, *25*, 457–481; c) H. Fujino, T. Saito, Y. Tsunenari, J. Kojima, T. Sakaeda, 'Metabolic properties of the acid and lactone forms of HMG-CoA reductase inhibitors', *Xenobiotica* **2004**, *34*, 961–971; d) G. Caron, G. Ermondi, B. Testa, 'Predicting the oxidative metabolism of statins. An application of the MetaSite algorithm', *Pharm. Res.* **2007**, *24*, 480–501.

[110] M. J. Kaufman, 'Rate and equilibrium constants for acid-catalyzed lactone hydrolysis of HMG-CoA reductase inhibitors', *Int. J. Pharmaceut.* **1990**, *66*, 97–106.

[111] S. Billecke, D. Draganov, R. Councel, P. Stetson, C. Watson, C. Hsu, B. N. La Du, 'Human serum paraoxonase (PON1) isozymes Q and R hydrolyze lactones and cyclic carbonate esters', *Drug Metab. Dispos.* **2000**, *28*, 1335–1342.

[112] J. F. Teiber, D. I. Draganov, B. N. La Du, 'Lactonase and lactonizing activities of human serum paraoxonase (PON1) and rabbit serum PON3', *Biochem. Pharmacol.* **2003**, *66*, 887–896.

[113] D. E. Duggan, I. W. Chen, W. F. Bayne, R. A. Halpin, C. A. Duncan, M. S. Schwartz, R. J. Stubbs, S. Vickers, 'The physiological disposition of lovastatin', *Drug Metab. Dispos.* **1989**, *17*, 166–173; W. Jacobsen, G. Kirchner, K. Hallensleben, L. Mancinelli, M. Deters, I. Hackbarth, L. Z. Benet, K. F. Sewing, U. Christians, 'Comparison of cytochrome P450-dependent metabolism and drug

interactions of the HMG-CoA-reductase inhibitors lovastatin and pravastatin in the liver', *Drug Metab. Dispos.* **1998**, *27*, 173–179.

[114] T. Prueksaritanont, R. Subramanian, X. Fang, B. Ma, Y. Qiu, J. H. Lin, P. G. Pearson, T. A. Baillie, 'Glucuronidation of statins in animals and humans: a novel mechanism of statin lactonization', *Drug Metab. Dispos.* **2002**, *30*, 505–512; H. Fujino, I. Yamada, S. Shimada, M. Yoneda, J. Kojima, 'Metabolic fate of pitavastatin, a new inhibitor of HMG-CoA reductase: human UDP-glucuronosyltransferase enzymes involved in lactonization', *Xenobiotica* **2003**, *33*, 27–41.

[115] T. Sakaeda, H. Fujino, C. Komoto, M. Kakumoto, J. Jin, K. Iwaki, K. Nishiguchi, T. Nakamura, N. Okamura, K. Okumura, 'Effects of acid and lactone forms of eight HMG-CoA reductase inhibitors on CYP-mediated metabolism and MDR1-mediated transport', *Pharm. Res.* **2006**, *23*, 506–512.

[116] A. H. Kahns, J. Moss, H. Bundgaard, 'Improved oral bioavailability of salicylamide in rabbits by a 1,3-benzoxazine-2,4-dione prodrug', *Int. J. Pharmaceut.* **1992**, *78*, 199–202.

[117] M. B. Maurin, S. M. Rowe, K. Blom, M. E. Pierce, 'Kinetics and mechnanism of hydrolysis of efavirenz', *Pharm. Res.* **2002**, *19*, 517–521.

[118] M. M. Corsi, H. H. Maes, K. Wasserman, A. Fulgenzi, G. Gaja, M. E. Ferrero, 'Protection by L-2-oxothiazolidine-4-carboxylic acid of hydrogen peroxide-induced CD3ζ and CD6ζ chain down-regulation in human peripheral blood lymphocytes and lymphokine-activated killer cells', *Biochem. Pharmacol.* **1998**, *56*, 657–662.

[119] K. Abe, M. Yamada, T. Terao, H. Mizuno, Y. Matsuoka, R. Yorikane, T. Tokui, T. Ikeda, 'Novel organic nitrate prodrug (4R)-N-(2-nitroxyethyl)-2-oxothiazolidine-4-carboxamide (RS-7897) serves as a xenobiotic substrate for pyroglutamyl aminopeptidase I in dogs', *Drug Metab. Pharmacokinet.* **2003**, *18*, 373–380.

[120] S. Ikeda, F. Sakamoto, R. Hirayama, Y. Takebe, M. Sotomura, G. Tsukamoto, 'Studies on prodrugs. VIII. Preparation and characterization of (5-methyl-2-oxo-1,3-dioxol-4-yl)methyl esters of sulbactam and its analogs', *Chem. Pharm. Bull.* **1988**, *36*, 218–226; K. Tougou, A. Nakamura, S. Watanabe, Y. Okuyama, A. Morino, 'Paraoxonase has a major role in the hydrolysis of prulifloxacin (NM441), a prodrug of a new antibacterial agent', *Drug Metab. Dispos.* **1998**, *26*, 355–359.

[121] J. M. Ghuysen, 'Serine beta-lactamases and penicillin-binding proteins', *Annu. Rev. Microbiol.* **1991**, *45*, 37–67; J. M. Frère, 'Beta-lactamases and bacterial resistance to antibiotics', *Mol. Microbiol.* **1995**, *16*, 385–395; A. L. Demain, R. P. Elander, 'The beta-lactam antibiotics: past, present, and future', *Antonie van Leeuwenhoek* **1999**, *75*, 5–19.

[122] D. Andreotti, S. Biondi, E. Di Modugno, 'β-Lactam antibiotics', in 'Burger's Medicinal Chemistry and Drug Discovery', 6th edn., Ed. D. J. Abraham, Wiley-Interscience, Hoboken, 2003, Vol. 5, p. 607–735; C. Hubschwerlen, 'β-Lactam antibiotics', in 'Therapeutic Areas II: Cancer, Infectious Diseases, Inflammation & Dermatology', Eds. J. J. Plattner, M. C. Desai, Vol. 7 in 'Comprehensive Medicinal Chemistry', 2nd edn., Eds. J. B. Taylor, D. J. Triggle, Elsevier, Oxford, 2007, p. 479–518.

[123] M. Grover, M. Gulati, B. Singh, S. Singh, 'Correlation of pernicillin structure with rate constant for basic hydrolysis', *Pharm. Pharmacol. Commun.* **2000**, *6*, 355–363; P. Imming, B. Klar, D. Dix, 'Hydrolytic stability versus ring size in lactams: implications for the development of lactam antibiotics and other serine protease inhibitors', *J. Med. Chem.* **2000**, *43*, 4328–4331; M. I. Page, A. P. Laws, 'The chemical reactivity of β-lactams, β-sultams and β-phospholactams', *Tetrahedron Lett.* **2000**, *56*, 5631–5638.

[124] G. C. Bolton, G. D. Allen, B. E. Davies, C. W. Filer, D. J. Jeffery, 'The disposition of clavulanic acid in man', *Xenobiotica* **1986**, *16*, 853–863.

[125] W. Krause, G. Kühne, 'Biotransformation of the antidepressant D,L-rolipram. II. Metabolite patterns in man, rat, rabbit, rhesus and cynomolgus monkey', *Xenobiotica* **1993**, *23*, 1277–1288.

[126] R. Becker, E. Frankus, I. Graudums, W. A. Günzler, F. C. Helm, L. Flohé, 'The metabolic fate of supidimide in the rat', *Arzneim.-Forsch.* **1982**, *32*, 1101–1111.

[127] J. Nakamura, T. Miwa, Y. Mori, H. Saski, 'Comparative studies on the anticonvulsant activity of lipophilic derivatives of γ-aminobutyric acid and 2-pyrrolidinone in mice', *J. Pharmacobiodyn.* **1991**, *14*, 1–8.

[128] A. Black, T. Chang, 'Metabolic disposition of rolziracetam in laboratory animals', *Eur. J. Drug Metab. Pharmacokinet.* **1987**, *12*, 135–143; A. H. Gouliaev, A. Senning, 'Piracetam and other structurally related nootropics', *Brain Res. Rev.* **1994**, *19*, 180–222.

[129] B. B. Hasinoff, R. G. Aoyama, 'Stereoselective metabolism of dexrazoxane (ICRF-187) and levrazoxane (ICRF-186)', *Chirality* **1999**, *11*, 286–290; B. B. Hasinoff, R. G. Aoyama, 'Relative plasma levels of the cardioprotective drug dexrazoxane and its two active ring-opened metabolites in the rat', *Drug Metab. Dispos.* **1999**, *27*, 265–268.

[130] a) M. Reist, P. A. Carrupt, E. Francotte, B. Testa, 'Chiral inversion and hydrolysis of thalidomide: mechanisms and catalysis by bases and serum albumin, and chiral stability of teratogenic metabolites', *Chem. Res. Toxicol.* **1998**, *11*, 1521–1528; b) J. Lu, N. Helsby, B. D. Palmer, M. Tingle, B. C. Baguley, P. Kestell, L. M. Ching. 'Metabolism of thalidomide in liver microsomes of mice, rabbits, and humans', *J. Pharmacol. Exp. Ther.* **2004**, *310*, 571–577.

[131] R. Herzog, J. Leuschner, 'Experimental studies on the pharmacokinetics and toxicity of 5-aminosalicylic acid-*O*-sulfate following local and systemic application', *Arzneim.-Forsch.* **1995**, *45*, 300–303.

[132] N. E. Buss, A. G. Renwick, K. M. Donaldson, C. F. George, 'The metabolism of cyclamate to cyclohexylamine and its cardiovascular consequences in human volunteers', *Toxicol. Appl. Pharmacol.* **1992**, *115*, 199–209.

[133] W. Sneader, 'Organic nitrates', *Drug News Perspect.* **1999**, *12*, 58–63; A. R. Butler, F. W. Flitney, D. L. H. Williams, 'NO, nitrosonium ions, nitroxide ions, nitrosothiols and iron-nitrosyls in biology: a chemist's perspective', *Trends Pharmacol. Sci.* **1995**, *16*, 18–22; H. Schröder, 'Bioactivation of organic nitrates and other nitrovasodilators', in 'Advances in Drug Research', Vol. 28, Eds. B. Testa, U. A. Meyer, Academic Press, London, 1996, p. 253–267.

[134] T. Heimbach, D. M. Oh, L. Y. Li, N. Rodriguez-Hornedo, G. Garcia, D. Fleisher, 'Enzyme-mediated precipitation of parent drug from their phosphate prodrugs', *Int. J. Pharmaceut.* **2003**, *26*, 81–92; T. Heimbach, D. M. Oh, L. Y. Li, M. Forsberg, J. Savolainen, J. Leppänen, Y. Matsunaga, G. Flynn, D. Fleisher, 'Absorption rate limit considerations for oral phosphate prodrugs', *Pharm. Res.* **2003**, *20*, 848–856.

[135] A. Mäntylä, T. Garnier, J. Rautio, T. Nevalainen, J. Vepsäläinen, A. Koskinen, S. L. Croft, T. Järvinen, 'Synthesis, in vitro evaluation, and antileishmanial activity of water-soluble prodrugs of buparvaquone', *J. Med. Chem.* **2004**, *47*, 188–195.

[136] J. Juntunen, J. Vepsäläinen, R. Niemi, K. Laine, T. Järvinen, 'Synthesis, in vitro evaluation, and intraocular pressure effects of water-soluble prodrugs of endocannabinoid noladin ether', *J. Med. Chem.* **2003**, *46*, 5083–5086; J. Juntunen, T. Järvinen, R. Niemi, 'In-vitro corneal permeation of cannabinoids and their water-soluble phosphate ester prodrugs', *J. Pharm. Pharmacol.* **2005**, *57*, 1153–1157.

[137] R. Niemi, J. Vepsäläinen, H. Taipale, T. Järvinen, 'Bisphosphonate prodrugs: synthesis and in vitro evaluation of novel acyloxyalkyl esters of clodronic acid', *J. Med. Chem.* **1999**, *42*, 5053–5058; P. Vachal, J. J. Hale, Z. Lu, E. C. Streckfuss, S. G. Mills, M. MacCoss, D. H. Yin, K. Algayer, K. Manser, F. Kesisoglou, S. Ghosh, L. L. Alani, 'Synthesis and study of alendronate derivatives as potential prodrugs of alendronate sodium for the treatment of low bone density and osteoporosis', *J. Med. Chem.* **2006**, *49*, 3060–3063.

[138] C. R. Wagner, V. V. Iyer, E. J. McIntee, 'Pronucleotides: Toward the in vivo delivery of antiviral and anticancer nucleotides', *Med. Res. Rev.* **2000**, *20*, 417–451.

[139] R. L. Mackman, T. Cihar, 'Prodrug strategies in the design of nucleoside and nucleotide antiviral therapeutics', *Annu. Rep. Med. Chem.* **2004**, *39*, 305–321.

[140] J. Van Gelder, S. Deferme, P. Annaert, L. Naesens, E. de Clercq, G. Van den Mooter, R. Kinget, P. Augustijns, 'Increased absorption of the antiviral ester prodrug tenofovir disoproxil in rat ileum by inhibiting its intestinal metabolism', *Drug Metab. Dispos.* **2000**, *28*, 1394–1396; R. Mallants, K. Van Oosterwyck, L. Van Vaeck, R. Mols, E. de Clercq, P. Augustijns, 'Multidrug resistance-associated protein 2 (MRP2) affects hepatobiliary elimination but not the intestinal disposition of tenofovir disoproxil fumarate and its metabolites', *Xenobiotica* **2005**, *35*, 1055–1066.

[141] S. R. Khan, S. K. Kumar, D. Farquhar, 'Bis(carbamoyloxymethyl) esters of 2',3'-dideoxyuridine 5'-monophosphate (ddUMP) as potential ddUMP prodrugs', *Pharm. Res.* **2005**, *22*, 390–396; S. R. Khan, N. Nowak, W. Plubkett, D. Farquhar, 'Bis(pivaloyloxymethyl) thymidine 5'-phosphate is a cell membrane-permeable precursor of thymidine 5'-phosphate in thymidine kinase deficient CCRF CEM cells', *Biochem. Pharmacol.* **2005**, *69*, 1307–1313.

[142] M. Shafiee, S. Deferme, A. L. Villard, D. Egron, G. Gosselin, J. L. Imbach, T. Lioux, A. Pompon, S. Varray, A. M. Aubertin, G. Van den Mooter, R. Kinget, C. Périgaud, P. Augustijns, 'New bis(SATE) prodrug of AZT 5'-monophosphate: in vitro anti-HIV activity, stability, and potential oral absorption', *J. Pharm. Sci.* **2001**, *90*, 448–463.

[143] F. Worek, H. Thiermann, L. Szinicz, P. Eyer, 'Kinetic analysis of interactions between human acetylcholinesterase, structurally different organophosphorus compounds and oximes', *Biochem. Pharmacol.* **2004**, *68*, 2237–2248.

[144] J. A. Vitarius, L. G. Sultatos, 'Kinetic mechanism of the detoxification of the organophosphate paraoxon by human serum A-esterase', *Drug Metab. Dispos.* **1994**, *22*, 472–478; E. Mutch, A. K. Daly, F. M. Williams, 'The relationship between PON1 phenotype and PON1-192 genotype in detoxification of three oxons by human liver', *Drug Metab. Dispos.* **2007**, *35*, 315–320.

[145] H. S. Lee, S. Jeong, K. Kim, J. H. Kim, S. K. Lee, B. H. Kang, J. K. Roh, 'In vitro metabolism of the new insecticide flupyrazofos by rat liver microsomes', *Xenobiotica* **1997**, *27*, 423–429.

[146] G. B. Quistad, N. Zhang, S. E. Sparks, J. E. Casida, 'Phosphoacetylcholinesterase: Toxicity of phosphorus oxychloride to mammals and insects that can be attributed to selective phosphorylation of acetylcholinesterase by phosphorodichloridic acid', *Chem. Res. Toxicol.* **2000**, *13*, 652–657.

[147] M. Jokanovic, M. Kosanovic, M. Maksimovic, 'Interaction of organophosphorus compounds with carboxylesterases in the rat', *Arch. Toxicol.* **1996**, *70*, 444–450.

[148] W. F. Trager, 'Principles of drug metabolism 1: Redox reactions', in 'ADME-Tox Approaches', Eds. B. Testa, H. van de Waterbeemd, Vol. 5 in 'Comprehensive Medicinal Chemistry', 2nd edn., Eds. J. B. Taylor, D. J. Triggle, Elsevier, Oxford, 2007, p. 87–132.

[149] J. Meijer, J. W. DePierre, 'Cytosolic epoxide hydrolase', *Chem.-Biol. Interact.* **1988**, *64*, 207–249; J. K. Beetham, D. Grant, M. Arand, J. Garbarino, T. Kiyosue, F. Pinot, F. Oesch, W. R. Belknap, K. Shinozaki, B. D. Hammock, 'Gene evolution of epoxide hydrolases and recommended nomenclature', *DNA Cell Biol.* **1995**, *14*, 61–71; M. A. Argiriadi, C. Morisseau, B. D. Hammock, D. W. Christianson, 'Detoxification of environmental mutagens and carcinogens: Structure, mechanism, and evolution of liver epoxide hydrolase', *Proc. Natl. Acad. Sci. U.S.A.* **1999**, *96*, 10637–10642; L. W. Wormhoudt, J. N. Commandeur, N. P. Vermeulen, 'Genetic polymorphisms of human N-acetyltransferase, cytochrome P450, glutathione S-transferase, and epoxide hydrolase enzymes: relevance to xenobiotic metabolism and toxicity', *Crit. Rev. Toxicol.* **1999**, *29*, 59–124; A. J. Fretland, C. J. Omiecinski, 'Epoxide hydrolases: biochemistry and molecular biology', *Chem.-Biol. Interact.* **2000**, *129*, 41–59.

[150] C. J. Omiecinski, L. Aicher, L. Swenson, 'Developmental expression of human microsomal epoxide hydrolase', *J. Pharmacol. Exp. Ther.* **1994**, *269*, 417–423; A. Gaedigk, J. S. Leeder, D. M. Grant, 'Tissue-specific expression and alternative splicing of human microsomal epoxide hydrolase', *DNA Cell Biol.* **1997**, *16*, 1257–1266; E. M. Laurenzana, C. Hassett, C. J. Omiecinski, 'Post-transcriptional regulation of human microsomal epoxide hydrolase', *Pharmacogenetics* **1998**, *8*, 157–167; A. L. Slit, N. J. Cherrington, C. D. Fisher, M. Negishi, C. D. Klaassen, 'Induction of genes for metabolism and transport by *trans*-stilbene oxide in livers of Sprague-Dawley and Wistar-Kyoto rats', *Drug Metab. Dispos.* **2006**, *34*, 1190–1197.

[151] T. M. Guenthner, D. Cai, R. Wallin, 'Co-purification of microsomal epoxide hydrolase with the warfarin-sensitive vitamin K_1 oxide reductase of the vitamin K cycle', *Biochem. Pharmacol.* **1998**, *55*, 169–175; C. Morisseau, B. D. Hammock, 'Epoxide hydrolases: mechanism, inhibitor designs, and biological roles', *Annu. Rev. Pharmacol. Toxicol.* **2005**, *43*, 311–333; J. W. Newman, C. Morisseau, B. D. Hammock, 'Epoxide hydrolases: their roles and interactions with lipid metabolism', *Prog. Lipid Res.* **2005**, *44*, 1–51.

[152] J. Seidegard, G. Ekström, 'The role of human glutathione transferases and epoxide hydrolases in the metabolism of xenobiotics', *Environ. Health Perspect.* **1997**, *105*, 791–799.

[153] F. Pinot, D. F. Grant, J. K. Beetham, A. G. Parker, B. Borhan, S. Landt, A. D. Jones, B. D. Hammock, 'Molecular and biochemical evidence for the involvement of the Asp333-His523 pair in the catalytic mechanism of soluble epoxide hydrolase', *J. Biol. Chem.* **1995**, *270*, 7968–7974; M. Arandt, H. Wagner, F. Oesch, 'Asp[333], Asp[495], and His[523] form the catalytic triad of rat soluble epoxide hydrolase', *J. Biol. Chem.* **1996**, *271*, 4223–4229; R. N. Armstrong, C. S. Cassidy, 'New structural and chemical insight into the catalytic mechanism of epoxide hydrolases', *Drug Metab. Rev.* **2000**, *32*, 327–338; G. A. Gomez, C. Morisseau, B. D. Hammock, D. W. Christianson, 'Structure of human epoxide hydrolase reveals mechanistic inferences on bifunctional catalysis in epoxide and phosphate ester hydrolysis', *Biochemistry* **2004**, *43*, 4716–4723; A. Thomaeus, J. Carlsson, J. Åqvist, M. Widersten, 'Active site of epoxide hydrolases revisited: a noncannonical residue in potato StEH1 promotes both formation and breakdown of the alkylenzyme intermediate', *Biochemistry* **2007**, *46*, 2466–1479.

[154] B. Borhan, A. D. Jones, F. Pinot, D. F. Grant, M. J. Kurth, B. D. Hammock, 'Mechanism of soluble epoxide hydrolase. Formation of an α-hydroxy ester-enzyme intermediate through Asp-333', *J. Biol. Chem.* **1995**, *270*, 26923–26930; R. N. Armstrong, 'Kinetic and chemical mechanism of epoxide hydrolase', *Drug Metab. Rev.* **1999**, *31*, 71–86; E. Y. Lau, Z. E. Newby, T. C. Bruice, 'A theoretical examination of the acid-catalyzed and noncatalyzed ring-opening reaction of an oxirane by nucleophilic addition of acetate. Implications to epoxide hydrolases', *J. Am. Chem. Soc.* **2001**, *123*, 3350–3357; B. Schiøtt, T. C. Bruice, 'Reaction mechanism of soluble epoxide hydrolase: insights from molecular dynamics simulations', *J. Am. Chem. Soc.* **2002**, *124*, 14558–14570; K. H. Hopmann, F. Himo, 'Insights into the reaction mechanism of soluble epoxide hydrolase from theoretical active site mutants', *J. Phys. Chem., B* **2006**, *110*, 21299–21310.

[155] R. A. Kemper, R. J. Krause, A. A. Elfarra, 'Metabolism of butadiene monoxide by freshly isolated hepatocytes from mice and rats: different partitioning between oxidative, hydrolytic, and conjugations pathways', *Drug Metab. Dispos.* **2001**, *29*, 830–836; J. L. Nieusma, D. J. Claffey, C. Maniglier-Poulet, T. Imiolczyk, D. Ross, J. A. Ruth, 'Stereochemical aspects of 1,3-butadiene metabolism and toxicity in rat and mouse liver microsomes and feshly isolated rat hepatocytes', *Chem. Res. Toxicol.* **1997**, *10*, 450–456.

[156] L. Cottrell, B. T. Golding, T. Munter, W. P. Watson, 'In vitro metabolism of chloroprene: species differences, epoxide stereochemistry and a de-chlorination pathway', *Chem. Res. Toxicol.* **2001**, *14*, 1552–1562; T. Munter, L. Cottrell, T. Munter, W. P. Watson, 'Detoxication pathways involving glutathione and epoxide hydrolase in the in vitro metabolism of chloroprene', *Chem. Res. Toxicol.* **2003**, *16*, 1287–1297.

[157] G. Bellucci, C. Chiappe, G. Ingrosso, 'Kinetics and stereochemistry of the microsomal epoxide hydrolase-catalyzed hydrolysis of *cis*-stilbene oxides', *Chirality* **1994**, *6*, 577–582.

[158] G. Bellucci, G. Berti, C. Chiappe, A. Lippi, F. Marioni, 'The metabolism of carbamazepine in humans: steric course of the enzymatic hydrolysis of the 10,11-epoxide', *J. Med. Chem.* **1987**, *30*, 768–773; I. Bernus, R. G. Dickinson, W. D. Hooper, M. J. Eadie, 'Dose-dependent metabolism of carbamazepine in humans', *Epilepsy Res.* **1996**, *24*, 163–172; R. E. Pearce, G. R. Vakkalagadda, J. S. Leeder, 'Pathways of carbamazepine bioactivation in vitro. I. Characterization of human cytochromes P450 responsible for the formation of 2- and 3-hydroxylated metabolites', *Drug Metab. Dispos.* **2002**, *30*, 1170–1179.

[159] J. Marchant, 'Stop cancer before it starts', *New Sci.* **2001**, *170*(2285), 4.

[160] W. W. Johnson, T. M. Harris, F. P. Guengerich, 'Kinetics and mechanism of hydrolysis of aflatoxin B1 *exo*-8,9-epoxide and rearrangement of the dihydrodiol', *J. Am. Chem. Soc.* **1996**, *118*, 8213–8220; W. W. Johnson, H. Yamazaki, T. Shimada, Y. F. Ueng, F. P. Guengerich, 'Aflatoxin B1 8,9-epoxide hydrolysis in the presence of rat and human epoxide hydrolase', *Chem. Res. Toxicol.* **1997**, *10*, 672–676; F. P. Guengerich, W. W. Johnson, 'Kinetics of hydrolysis and reaction of aflatoxin B1 *exo*-8,9-epoxide and relevance to toxicity and detoxication', *Drug Metab. Rev.* **1999**, *31*, 141–158; F. P. Guengerich, H. Cai, M. McMahon, J. D. Hayes, T. R. Sutter, J. D. Groopman, Z. Deng, T. M. Harris, 'Reduction of aflatoxin B_1 dialdehyde by rat and human aldo-keto reductases', *Chem. Res. Toxicol.* **2001**, *14*, 727–737.

[161] P. J. van Bladeren, J. M. Sayer, D. E. Ryan, P. E. Thomas, W. Levin, D. M. Jerina, 'Differential stereoselectivity of cytochrome P450b and P450c in the formation of naphthalene and anthracene 1,2-oxides. The role of epoxide hydrolase in determining the enantiomer composition of the 1,2-dihydrodiols formed', *J. Biol. Chem.* **1985**, *260*, 10226–10235.

[162] B. Oesch-Bartlomowicz, F. Oesch, 'Mechanisms of toxification and detoxification that challenge drug candidates and drugs', in 'ADME-Tox Approaches', Eds. B. Testa, H. van de Waterbeemd, Vol. 5 in 'Comprehensive Medicinal Chemistry', 2nd edn., Eds. J. B. Taylor, D. J. Triggle, Elsevier, Oxford, 2007, p. 193–214.

[163] B. Testa, 'The Metabolism of Drugs and Other Xenobiotics – Biochemistry of Redox Reactions', Academic Press, London, 1995.

[164] M. Shou, F. J. Gonzalez, H. V. Gelboin, 'Stereoselective epoxidation and hydration at the K-region of polycyclic aromatic hydrocarbons by cDNA-expressed cytochromes P450 1A1, 1A2, and epoxide hydrolase', *Biochemistry* **1996**, *35*, 15807–15813.

[165] R. T. Swank, E. K. Novak, L. Zhen, 'Genetic regulation of the subcellular localization and expression of glucuronidase', in 'Conjugation-Deconjugation Reactions in Drug Metabolism and Toxicity', Ed. F. C. Kauffman, Springer, Berlin, 1994, p. 131–160.

[166] T. Akao, T. Akao, M. Hattori, M. Kanaoka, K. Yamamoto, T. Namba, K. Kobashi, 'Hydrolysis of glycyrrhizin in 18β-glycyrrhetyl monoglucuronide by lysosomal β-D-glucuronidase of animal livers', *Biochem. Pharmacol.* **1991**, *41*, 1025–1029; T. Akao, 'Distribution of enzymes involved in the metabolism of glycyrrhizin in various organs of rat', *Biol. Pharm. Bull.* **1998**, *21*, 1036–1044.

[167] T. B. Vree, C. J. Timmer, 'Enterohepatic cycling and pharmacokinetics of oestradiol in postmenopausal women', *J. Pharm. Pharmacol.* **1998**, *50*, 857–864.

[168] E. Palomino, E. H. Walker, S. L. Blumenthal, 'Carbohydrate prodrugs: Potential use for *in situ* activation and drug delivery', *Drugs Future* **1991**, *16*, 1029–1037; V. R. Sinha, R. Kumria, 'Colonic drug delivery: prodrug approach', *Pharm. Res.* **2001**, *18*, 557–564.

[169] H. W. Nolen III, D. R. Friend, 'Menthol-β-D-glucuronide: a potential prodrug for treatment of the irritable bowel syndrome', *Pharm. Res.* **1994**, *11*, 1707–1711.

[170] G. Wei, N. A. Loktionova, A. E. Pegg, E. C. Moschel, 'β-Glucuronidase-cleavable prodrugs of O^6-benzylguanine and O^6-benzylguanine-2′-deoxyguanosine', *J. Med. Chem.* **2005**, *48*, 256–261.

[171] P. Riley, P. C. Figary, J. R. Entwisle, A. L. Roe, G. A. Thompson, R. Ohashi, N. Ohashi, T. J. Moorehead, 'The metabolic profile of azimilide in man: *in vivo* and *in vitro* evaluations', *J. Pharm. Sci.* **2005**, *94*, 2084–2095.

[172] S. Rubnov, I. Shats, D. Levy, S. Amisar, H. Schneider, 'Autocatalytic degradation and stability of obidoxime', *J. Pharm. Pharmacol.* **1999**, *51*, 9–14.

[173] M. Krause, A. Rouleau, H. Stark, P. Luger, R. Lipp, M. Garbarg, J. C. Schwartz, W. Schunack, 'Synthesis, X-ray crystallography, and pharmacokinetics of novel azomethine prodrugs of (R)-α-methylhistamine: highly potent and selective histamine H$_3$ receptor agonists', *J. Med. Chem.* **1995**, *38*, 4070–4079; A. Rouleau, H. Stark, W. Schunack, J. C. Schwartz, 'Anti-inflammatory and antinociceptive properties of BP 2-94, a histamine H$_3$-receptor agonist prodrug', *J. Pharmacol. Exp. Ther.* **2000**, *295*, 219–225.

[174] N. Bodor, A. Elkoussi, 'Improved delivery through biological membranes. LVI. Pharmacological evaluation of alprenoxime – a new potential antiglaucoma agent', *Pharm. Res.* **1991**, *8*, 1389–1395; L. Prokai, W. M. Wu, G. Somogyi, N. Bodor, 'Ocular delivery of the β-adrenergic antagonist alprenolol by sequential bioactivation of its methoxime analogue', *J. Med. Chem.* **1995**, *38*, 2018–2020.

[175] M. Tramontini, L. Angiolini, 'Further advances in the chemistry of Mannich bases', *Tetrahedron* **1990**, *46*, 1791–1837; I. H. Pitman, 'Pro-drugs of amides, imides, and amines', *Med. Res. Rev.* **1981**, *1*, 189–214; J. J. Getz, R. J. Prankerd, K. B. Sloan, 'Mechanism of hydrolysis of benzamidomethyl derivatives of phenols and its implications for prodrug design', *J. Org. Chem.* **1992**, *57*, 1702–1706.

[176] J. Alexander, M. L. Renyer, G. S. Rork, 'Investigation of *N*-[(acyloxy)alkyl] ester as a prodrug model for drugs containing the phenyltetrazole moiety', *J. Pharm. Sci.* **1994**, *83*, 893–897.

[177] S. W. Larsen, M. Sidenius, M. Ankersen, C. Larsen, 'Kinetics of degradation of 4-imidazolinone prodrug types obtained from reacting prilocaine with formaldehyde and acetaldehyde', *Eur. J. Pharm. Sci.* **2003**, *20*, 233–240.

[178] L. Wlodek, H. Rommelspacher, R. Susilo, J. Radomski, G. Höfle, 'Thiazolidine derivatives as source of free L-cysteine in rat tissue', *Biochem. Pharmacol.* **1993**, *46*, 1917–1928; J. C. Roberts, H. L. Phaneuf, J. G. Szakacs, R. T. Zera, J. G. Lamb, M. R. Franklin, 'Differential chemoprotection against acetaminophen-induced hepatotoxicity by latentiated L-cysteines', *Chem. Res. Toxicol.* **1998**, *11*, 1274–1282; B. H. Wilmore, P. B. Cassidy, R. L. Warters, J. C. Roberts, 'Thiazolidine prodrugs as protective agents against γ-radiation-induced toxicity and mutagenesis in V79 cells', *J. Med. Chem.* **2001**, *44*, 2661–2666.

[179] H. K. O. Osterheld, E. Musch, G. E. von Unruh, U. Loos, H. Rauschecker, B. J. Mühlenbruch, 'A sensitive HPLC assay for melphalan and its hydrolysis products in blood and plasma', *Cancer Chemother. Pharmacol.* **1988**, *21*, 156–162; M. G. Bolton, J. Hilton, K. D. Robertson, R. T. Streeper, O. M. Colvin, D. A. Noe, 'Kinetic analysis of the reaction of melphalan with water, phosphate, and glutathione', *Drug Metab. Dispos.* **1993**, *21*, 986–996.

[180] G. F. Bories, J. P. Cravedi, 'Metabolism of chloramphenicol: a story of nearly 50 years', *Drug Metab. Rev.* **1994**, *26*, 767–783.

[181] 'Cisplatin. Chemistry and Biochemistry of a Leading Anticancer Drug', Ed. B. Lippert, Verlag Helvetica Chimica Acta, Zurich, 1999.

[182] D. F. Long, A. J. Repta, 'Cisplatin: Chemistry, distribution and biotransformation', *Biopharm. Drug Dispos.* **1981**, *2*, 1–16; N. Nagai, R. Okuda, M. Kinoshita, H. Ogata, 'Decomposition kinetics of cisplatin in human biological fluids', *J. Pharm. Pharmacol.* **1996**, *48*, 918–924; M. Jennerwein, P. A. Andrews, 'Effect of intracellular chloride on the cellular pharmacodynamics of *cis*-diamminodichloroplatinum(II)', *Drug Metab. Dispos.* **1995**, *23*, 178–184.

[183] M. A. Allsopp, G. J. Sewell, C. G. Rowland, C. M. Rifley, R. L. Schowen, 'The degradation of carboplatin in aqueous solutions containing chloride or other selected nucleophiles', *Int. J. Pharmaceut.* **1991**, *69*, 197–210; S. B. Duffull, B. A. Robinson, 'Clinical pharmacokinetics and dose optimisation of carboplatin', *Clin. Pharmacokinet.* **1997**, *33*, 161–183.

[184] P. Allain, O. Heudi, A. Cailleux, A. Le Bouil, F. Larra, M. Boisdron-Celle, E. Gamelin, 'Early biotransformations of oxaliplatin after its intravenous administration to cancer patients', *Drug Metab. Dispos.* **2000**, *28*, 1379–1384; E. Jerremalm, M. Hedeland, I. Wallin, U. Bondesson, H. Ehrsson, 'Oxaliplatin degradation in the presence of chloride: identification and cytotoxicity of the monochloro monooxalato complex', *Pharm. Res.* **2004**, *21*, 891–894.

Index